ALSO BY JOËL ROBUCHON

L'Atelier of Joël Robuchon

Joël Robuchon Cooking Through the Seasons

La Cuisine de Joël Robuchon: A Seasonal Cookbook

Simply French: The Cuisine of Joël Robuchon

THE COMPLETE ROBUCHON

THE COMPLETE ROBUCHON

Joël Robuchon

TRANSLATED FROM THE FRENCH BY ROBIN H. R. BELLINGER

Alfred A. Knopf   New York   2008

THIS IS A BORZOI BOOK
PUBLISHED BY ALFRED A. KNOPF

Translation copyright © 2008 by Alfred A. Knopf, a division of
Random House, Inc.

All rights reserved. Published in the United States by Alfred A. Knopf,
a division of Random House, Inc., New York, and in Canada
by Random House of Canada Limited, Toronto.

www.aaknopf.com

Knopf, Borzoi Books, and the colophon are registered trademarks of
Random House, Inc.

Originally published in France as *Tout Robuchon* by Perrin, Paris,
in 2006, and subsequently published in a revised edition by Perrin
in 2007.
Copyright © 2006, 2007 by Perrin.

Library of Congress Cataloging-in-Publication Data
Robuchon, Joël, [date]
   [Tout Robuchon. English]
   The complete Robuchon / by Joël Robuchon.—1st ed.
       p.   cm.
   Includes index.
   ISBN 978-0-307-26719-1
   1. Cookery, French.   I. Title.
   TX719.R61313 2008
   641.5941—dc22   2008006521

Manufactured in the United States of America
First American Edition

CONTENTS

ACKNOWLEDGMENTS

This book was written by Joël Robuchon and Vincent Noce.

Georges Pouvel, professor emeritus at the Val de Loire school of fine cuisine, in Blois, provided technical guidance.

In Paris, Eric Bouchenoire, and François Benot, for the desserts, helped to prepare and test the recipes under laboratory conditions. In New York, Gregory Pugin helped with research of American terms and products.

The English translation was done with the invaluable help of Vincent Noce.

THE COMPLETE ROBUCHON

Introduction

BALANCING MEALS

Animals feed themselves; men eat; but only wise men know the art of eating.
—JEAN-ANTHELME BRILLAT-SAVARIN

Proper nourishment calls for a certain balance, within each meal and from one to the next. To be healthy, then, as well as engaged by the singular pleasure of eating, we must all find ways of varying what we eat. We may think of meat or fish as the center of a meal, but fruit, vegetables, dairy products, and grains should find their way to the table whenever we sit down to eat. The proportions may vary according to individual tastes and nutritional requirements, but no single food alone makes a satisfying meal.

A meal at home comprising three or four parts is perhaps not the norm nowadays, but it is eminently civilized and really not so difficult to accomplish: a soup or other starter, a main dish including fish or meat, perhaps a salad, and maybe some cheese before or instead of dessert. Such traditional courses slow the process of eating and extend its pleasure, making contentment with sensible portions more natural.

Health considerations have inspired a sensible restriction of certain foods, but militancy is counterproductive. No one should eat great amounts of fat, but fat carries flavor; just a bit can vastly improve a dish's taste. Like sugar, it should be used sparingly but not eliminated. Vegetable oils are generally healthier than butter, but for certain foods only butter will do. There is likewise no substitute for salt. It should be limited (especially since processed foods contain so much of it), but unless you are on a very special diet, banning it from your kitchen is unnecessary.

These simple ideas apply to feeding ourselves, but how should you plan a meal when you're having friends over?

You must first of all avoid overwhelming them, especially with heavy dishes served from beginning to end. If the main dish is rather rich, your other offerings should bring different qualities and tastes into the mix; for instance, you could have crudités or vegetable soup as a starter, and the dessert could be fruit-based. If you really want to delight your guests, do not plan a meal of foie gras and duck confit, culminating in death by chocolate!

At the same time, try to find something that will tie the whole meal together such as a common flavor note struck in several courses. Wine matters a great deal, but, again, think of balance: If you plan to serve an important wine, you should serve a simple dish that will show it to best advantage—roast lamb for a fine Bordeaux, for example. If you serve a complicated dish, its flavors could interfere with your enjoyment of a memorable bottle.

You must also take into consideration your guests' tastes, inevitable allergies, and religious requirements.

Don't forget that you will want to spend some time with your friends or family, away from the kitchen. It is usually best to prepare as much of the food as possible in advance so that you can enjoy the meal with your guests. This, too, is an important consideration when planning a menu.

The finest meals are planned with the season in mind even if seasonless grocery stores full of produce shipped in from around the world have succeeded in large part at robbing us of this way of thinking about food. In fact, availability is no substitute for flavor. Tasteless strawberries in the middle of winter may be novel, but they are not a treat. They frustrate more than delight us. No cooking trick you can learn trumps quality of ingredients, and respecting the seasons remains the best way of ensuring the most delicious results. Therefore, shop at a farmers' market whenever possible. And whatever you do, be suspicious of appearances. Supermarkets have found they can sell the most tasteless produce as long as it looks good. A market that dares to sell unpretty things may well have something better to offer, and good providers often encourage discerning customers with a taste.

Many people would not care to sit down to a proper meal without wine, especially a holiday feast or dinner with friends.

Drink little but drink well. This is rule number one. You'll be happier and more satisfied if you drink sparingly from a good bottle. The quality of wines made in France and around the world has come a long way, so you have a greater choice than ever.

Unfortunately, wine is not bottled with people who don't want to drink much in mind. It is hard to find good half bottles, in which the wine ages faster and is more liable to become corky tasting. (In large containers, like magnums, wine ages better and lasts longer, because proportionately less of it is exposed to the small amount of air that makes its way into the bottle.)

But with minimal exposure to air, an unfinished bottle can be saved for two to three days. This is better done by transferring the wine to a smaller bottle than with vacuum gadgets. But neither way works at all with Champagne.

Wine should be kept in a cool, dark, humid (80 percent minimum) spot, on its side, in order to keep the cork from drying out. (A dry cork allows extra air into the bottle, resulting in oxidation, which spoils the wine.) If your wine cellar is dry, as is often the case in homes with central heating, you can spray water on the floor periodically or put out a basin of water. Keep the cellar well ventilated so that bad odors cannot collect there. A space for keeping wine certainly should not be used for storing fruit, onions, or even empty crates, which may carry unpleasant odors.

The ideal temperature is 50°F (12°C), but wine keeps very well at higher temperatures (up to 65°F/18°C) as long as it is not subjected to abrupt changes in temperature (such as when the heat is turned on at the beginning of winter) or to vibrations (from a subway, for instance). If you don't have a cellar, cupboards and armoires made for keeping wine work perfectly well.

Wine has a life cycle: After a few years it is good, and then it is even better, but it will eventually decline and even die. Oxidation is the main culprit that will rob it of its savor and leave it tasting bad.

Dry white wine ages faster than red wine. Under proper conditions it generally keeps for a half-dozen years. Sweet white wines, on the other hand, keep for a very long time— thirty years at least; that's when they take on the best flavor. The fine red wines of Burgundy or of the Loire valley can profitably age a dozen years. It is about the same for Bordeaux, Côtes-du-Rhône, and certain wines from the south of France, although the best of these may improve for more than twenty years. All these wines, important or not, will drink very well after just a few years. The ones worth holding longer are relatively few and quite expensive.

How should you go about choosing a wine?

Consider three things: the wine's place of origin, its vintage, and its producer. You should not be blindly drawn to the most talked about makers, whose mystique leads us away from fine alternatives at lower prices, especially with Champagne but also with Burgundies.

Vintage is the year the grapes were harvested. It is important because the quality of wine depends a great deal on how grapes were affected by sunshine, rainfall, and temperature in a given year. Detailed wine guides may be relied upon to distinguish good years from lesser ones, and there is generally clear consensus about these distinctions. In France, vintage is borne in mind, but most drinkers of wine choose according to preferred regions and producers.

Red wine should be served just below room temperature, about 60°F (16°C). This is even more important for today's wines, which tend to have a higher alcohol content and to be sweeter and therefore should be served a bit cooler. If a wine has been cellared, avoid bringing it up to room temperature too abruptly.

White wine should be served a little cooler, at about 55°F (13°C), but definitely not cold. Overchilled, all white wine loses its flavor, even Champagne, which is too routinely left in ice buckets. Sweet white wines can be served colder, even below 50°F (10°C).

A bucket of ice allows you to keep wine at the desired temperature, but you must remove the bottle from time to time to keep it from getting too cold. To chill a wine quickly, throw some coarse salt in with the ice or refrigerate the bottle. Remove it thirty minutes before serving. Don't try to speed-chill wine, especially Champagne, in the freezer; if your mind wanders, the bottle will burst, and you will have an awful mess on your hands.

Good wines, red and white, should in general be decanted—that is, they should be poured into another bottle and swirled an hour or two before a meal. This process oxygenates them, releasing their flavors. The stronger the wine, the longer it should be allowed to breathe before you drink it. Usually the empty bottle is left nearby for presentation. Older wines must be decanted more gently to avoid the transfer of sediment to the receiving vessel. And some wines, those that are fragile, delicate, or very old, do not react well to being opened in advance, since their aromas can dissipate very quickly.

A wine's scents, collectively called the bouquet, are best appreciated in a balloon-shaped glass as large as possible. Champagne is served in a flute, which prolongs bubbling and brings out its fragrance.

If you are serving very different dishes together (for instance, fish and red meat), it is best not to try to find a wine that will suit both of them since it is more likely that it will disappoint in both cases. Approach such combinations carefully, then, aware that they will have a big effect on the way your meal is organized. The greater the number of wines you serve in a single meal, the less you should drink of each one.

If you are serving more than one wine, you must move from light to heavy; a heavy wine, relatively high in alcohol, served first would make it difficult to enjoy a lighter wine served later. Keep this in mind as you compose your menu.

The old rules for pairing are not obsolete even if tastes now encourage breaking them. White wine suits fish, and red wine is appropriate for meat such as lamb and beef. A robust red goes with game. White meats can take a light red just as well as a white. Despite what you often see, cheese, especially goat cheese, goes nicely with white wine. Blue-veined cheeses (Roquefort and blue) call for a fortified wine (port or banyuls) or certain rather rich Champagnes. A sweet wine works equally well with desserts and foie gras.

There is no wine appropriate for salad. Chocolate is also hard to match. A better choice is flat water, or a fortified wine with chocolate accents—or perhaps coffee.

Wine and food must support each other. If a certain dish is powerfully flavored, the wine you serve with it must be powerful, too, if it is to hold up. On the other hand, a powerful wine can obliterate the flavors of a delicate dish. Generally it is a good idea to try to establish a flavor echo between the wine and the dish: a spicy wine for a spicy dish, an acidic wine for fish with lemon sauce, a richer white for chicken.

Champagne is wine, too, and should be chosen as such: keen and alert for an aperitif, stronger and more aromatic for a meal, even stronger for a blue-veined cheese, and sweeter and gentler for dessert.

COOKING METHODS

The composition and nature of the foods to be cooked will determine your method. All these methods develop flavor while altering or even completely transforming a food's appearance, color, and texture; sometimes cooking is the only thing that makes a food edible. You wouldn't want to eat a raw potato, and some foods, such as morels, are dangerous when they are raw.

Your goal should be to come to know and to master all these techniques, for once you have, you can play around with them as you like.

A reminder: You should always wash your hands before cooking. Keep your cooktop, oven, and utensils clean.

GRILLING

Apart from cooking outside over coals (barbecue), this generally refers to quick cooking on a cooktop grill or grill pan. This technique applies heat directly to food from the cooking surface. It is best for small items, and you must monitor cooking time carefully.

The food to be grilled is often coated with a thin film of oil. Food must be seasoned with salt at the beginning of grilling (or just before) and then again when it has been removed from the heat.

Regulate the intensity of the heat according to the type,

volume, and thickness of the food. Red meat, white meat, fish, vegetables, and charcuterie all cook very differently.

Never prick meat while you are grilling it, particularly red meat, or you'll lose juices.

There are four different stages of "doneness" for red meat: rare, which is red throughout but warm in the center; medium rare, which is red in the center but not at the edges; medium, which is barely pink in the middle and brown at the edges; and well done, which is not rosy at all.

The surface of a piece of meat turns brown when grilled on account of the way its amino acids and reducing sugars react to heat. This is called the Maillard reaction, after the scientist who investigated it in the early twentieth century. It resembles, but is not the same as, caramelization, which involves only sugar, no amino acids.

Grilled meat, especially a large piece, must be allowed to rest when it comes off the heat. A cooling rack of some sort (set over a plate to catch juices) is the ideal spot for resting, but a small overturned plate will do the trick, too. While the meat is cooking, its juices withdraw to the center; a resting period gives the juices time to spread throughout the meat again, making it more tender. The ideal resting time is one-half of the cooking time.

BRAISING

This is cooking in a closed vessel, with some liquid and vegetables, spices, or herbs. This method is generally used for pieces of meat that take a long time to cook, and they are usually browned on top of the stove before they are braised.

Certain cuts of meat are especially good for braising even if they can also be cooked other ways:

beef the tip of the rump, chuck, and brisket
veal shoulder (stuffed or not), loin, rib scraps
pork ham, shoulder, loin
lamb stuffed shoulder, leg
offal tongue, heart, sweetbreads
poultry fatted hen, turkey, duck, goose

Some meat, such as game, should be marinated before it is braised; give it a long soak in red or white wine, broth, fumet, stock, or even aromatic oil or water.

Braising can also refer to the cooking of whole, firm-fleshed fish (salmon, turbot, monkfish, carp, etc.) and to the slow cooking of certain vegetables (lettuce, cabbage, endive, celery, artichokes, etc.).

POACHING

This is cooking by total immersion in liquid such as water, stock, court bouillon, milk, or syrup. Any food can be poached.

The poaching liquid can be cold or hot when the food is introduced. In the first case, the liquid and the food exchange more flavor as the liquid comes up to cooking temperature, which is desirable when the poaching liquid is to be made into a sauce, as with a *blanquette,* a white stew.

Very brief poaching, which is usually called blanching, is used to render food more presentable or easier to digest or to eliminate impurities and unpleasantly strong flavors. Cabbage, bacon, and beef are all frequently blanched; afterward, they are rinsed in cold water to finish removing impurities. Some fresh vegetables, too, are blanched, especially green vegetables such as green beans and spinach. Afterward they are chilled in ice water, or "shocked," to preserve their texture and vibrant color.

When food is boiled or simmered, its impurities often make their way to the surface of the liquid, where they form a grayish foam or scum. This substance must be removed with a skimmer, which should be rinsed in cold water after each passage through the hot liquid. Use a ladle or large spoon to remove fat from the surface of the liquid, too.

Some vegetables can be cooked in water at a rolling boil, but for the most part it is better to poach in liquid just below the boiling point, at the point where it is shivering and trembling. Pay close attention, and you will see liquid behaving this way. Such gentle circulation of the liquid will reduce the amount of foam that forms, since foam is the result of bubbles stirring things up in the pot.

EN COCOTTE: COVERED ROASTING

This type of cooking is done in a deep covered vessel such as a Dutch oven or what the French call a *cocotte.* It is suitable for large pieces of meat, poultry, and game that would dry out if they were simply roasted with no cover.

For flavor and sufficient moistness, the meat should be placed on top of vegetables (such as carrots and onions) and aromatic herbs (thyme or bay leaves, for instance). These vegetables and herbs are called the "aromatic dressing."

ROASTING

To roast is to cook by exposure to dry heat, whether in an oven, on a spit, or in a rotisserie.

Large pieces of meat and fish are suitable for roasting, as are some vegetables such as potatoes. Roasting should encourage the formation of a lightly caramelized exterior. Roasted meat must rest at room temperature when it comes out of the oven, preferably on a cooling rack or overturned plate, ideally for half the total cooking time.

IN THE OVEN

In general, the oven should be preheated to 400–475°F (220–250°C). The proper temperature depends on the nature, size, and weight of the food being roasted.

Use a baking dish, sheet pan, or roasting pan not much larger than the roast. If the pan is too large, the drippings are more likely to burn onto it and give the cooking juices an unpleasantly bitter taste.

Whenever you can, it is desirable to roast meat on top of "trimmings"—little bits of meat and fat and chopped-up bones, which your butcher should be able to provide. Salt meat just before or at the very beginning of roasting. As it roasts, a piece of meat should be basted frequently with its own cooking juices and turned with tongs or any other tool that does not pierce it. Do not use a fork, which will puncture the meat and cause it to lose juices.

Red meat should generally be cooked more or less

twenty minutes for the first pound and fifteen minutes for each extra pound.

Chicken should be cooked for a baseline forty-five minutes plus seven minutes per pound total.

When the meat comes out of the oven, season it with salt and pepper at the beginning of its resting time.

ON A SPIT

If you have a chance to spit-roast a piece of meat, season it with salt and coat it with oil, using your fingers or a pastry brush. Impale it firmly on the spit; it should not flop around as the spit turns. Otherwise, follow all the instructions for oven roasting.

PAN FRYING OR SAUTÉING

Thoroughly cooking something in a small amount of fat in a skillet or sauté pan over high heat is called pan frying or sautéing. The high, straight sides of a sauté pan encourage heat to circulate and reduce spattering somewhat.

Often one begins pan frying by heating up a mixture of oil and butter. The oil should always be heated first, before the butter is added to the pan.

This fast cooking method is especially good for small or medium-sized items:

beef and pork   steak, rib eye, tournedos, scallops, chops, medallions
charcuterie   sausages of all kinds
chicken and other poultry   quartered, scallops, breasts
fish   fillets, steaks, breaded fish
crustaceans   shelled langoustines, crayfish
mollusks   sea scallops
game   kid medallions, saddles of rabbit, boar chops
offal   slices of liver, brain, sweatbreads, kidneys
eggs   omelettes, fried eggs
raw vegetables   mushrooms, zucchini, eggplants, potatoes, onions
cooked vegetables   green beans, cauliflower, endives, potatoes

As with roasting, the pan should not be too much larger than the food you are cooking. If there is too much room for cooking juices and fat to spread out, they will burn and turn bitter.

Certain thick pieces that must be cooked all the way through, such as chicken thighs, must be finished in the oven, covered, but they should be removed from the cooking fat (or cooking fat should be removed from the pan) before this final cooking or their texture will be spoiled.

STEWING

This is slow, covered cooking in a good deal of sauce or liquid, used to make stews of all kinds as well as dishes such as coq au vin. Meat, fish, and poultry can be cooked this way, as can vegetables. In the old days, this long, gentle cooking was accomplished by placing a pot next to the hearth fire. Sometimes it is best to marinate meat before it is stewed; this is true of rabbit and goat, for instance.

IN SALT

Food to be cooked in a salt crust is coated with a mixture of coarse salt, flour, water, and perhaps some sort of flavoring and then baked in the oven.

EN PAPILLOTE: IN A PACKET

Here the cooking and serving vessel is a sealed wrapper of parchment paper, aluminum foil, or even a large leaf, such as a banana leaf. The packet is placed in a very hot oven, which cooks the food and makes the wrapping puff up with air. The food can be raw or already cooked, and often a vegetable garnish or sauce of some kind is wrapped up in the packet, too.

Here's how it's done: Cut a circle of parchment paper or aluminum foil large enough to envelop the food comfortably. Grease the circle with butter or oil, being careful not to rip it. Place the food in the center of half the circle and season. If you are using vegetables or anything else, add them. Fold the free side of the circle over the food. At one end, make a small fold to close the packet. Work your way around the half circle, making a series of small, tight folds. Finish with a small fold at each end.

STEAMING

This ancient method of cooking is very common in Asia and is increasingly used in the West. Steaming preserves a food's textural integrity and does not require the addition of fat. The food is placed in a covered basket or is otherwise suspended over the steam of hot water, broth, or *fumet*. Besides the couscoussier, there are steamer baskets, pots fitted with steamers, and even small appliances just for steaming. Some woks have an upper rack that holds vegetables or small crustaceans in such a position that they will be cooked or reheated by the steam of whatever is cooking below.

Food destined for steaming must be perfect, since it will have to stand on its own, without the flavor that comes from fat or browning. This cooking method has the advantage of preserving many of a food's vitamins and minerals.

AU PLAT: IN THE DISH

In this method the food is cooked in a baking dish that will go from oven to table. Most commonly used for fish steaks (salmon, pollock, whiting, sole, turbot, or brill) or fillets (John Dory or cod). When using this method for shellfish, such as sea scallops, cook only the "nut" of meat; the roe or "coral" will explode during cooking.

This is an easy method but requires close attention. Preheat the oven to about 425°F (220°C). The dish (porcelain or Pyrex, capable of sustaining direct exposure to heat) should be generously buttered and given a light sprinkling of salt and freshly ground pepper. Lay the fish in the dish and season it, too. Add enough white wine or fish stock to cover one-third of the fish—about ½ cup (15 cl). (You can buy fish stock, but to make your own, see page 40.) Place the dish on the cooktop and bring the liquid to a boil; then put the dish in the oven to finish cooking, basting the fish frequently with its own buttery juices. When it is finished, the fish should be covered with a thin layer of glossy, syrupy white sauce.

Eggs can also be cooked "in the dish," as you will find in the chapter on egg cookery.

MICROWAVE

The microwave allows for very fast cooking. Thin strips of fish buttered, seasoned with salt and pepper, and sandwiched between two plates can be cooked in just a few seconds. **Never put anything metallic, including aluminum foil and twist ties with a metal wire, into the microwave.** It isn't the best idea to microwave food in plastic containers because there is a possibility that microscopic amounts of plastic will end up in your dinner. Any container placed in the microwave will become very hot very fast, so be extra careful when removing a bowl or plate with your bare hands.

This method cooks food so quickly that it is not easy to control. The microwave is especially useful for reheating foods, but it will dry them out if you leave them too long. It can be used to reheat liquid or even fish, but pastry, pasta, and bread will not fare well. The microwave is superb for softening, melting, or even clarifying butter (page 43). Don't try to use it for large quantities of anything because its heat distribution is very uneven.

SOUS VIDE

Here is a technique that has gotten much attention in the professional kitchens of the United States in recent years. Food is placed in an airless (*sous vide,* or vacuum-packed) container or plastic sack with a vegetable garnish or other seasonings and then heated to the temperature best suited to the food's flavors and nutrients. With no air into which to escape, the flavors of the vegetable garnish or seasonings pass by a kind of osmosis to the main food with which they are sealed.

Done properly, cooking *sous vide* produces healthy food that keeps for a long time in the refrigerator or freezer. A word of caution: Raw meat to be cooked *sous vide* must be kept properly refrigerated at all times before cooking, or else traces of bacteria may bloom into a dangerous culture during the long, low cooking.

One way of cooking *sous vide* is to submerge the sealed packet in simmering water. Be careful when you snip open a finished packet—it will probably squirt very hot water at you.

DEEP FRYING

This refers to cooking or finishing by immersion in very hot fat. Peanut oil is the most commonly used fat for this purpose.

Fat for frying must be able to reach a very high temperature (300–350°F/150–180°C) without smoking. The temperature depends on the size and nature of the food to be fried and on the desired finish (crustiness, color). It is generally desirable for the fat to have a neutral taste so that the food's own flavors are not obscured. Therefore, we fry with peanut or grapeseed oil but not olive oil, which has its own distinctive flavor and smokes at a relatively low temperature.

Before it is fried, food is often coated in something that will form a crust—in some sort of dough or in flour, egg, and bread crumbs. Usually the coating is very thin, like Japanese tempuras.

Deep frying yields food that is crunchy and dry on the outside, soft and tender inside. It must be done at the last minute since fried foods are meant to be eaten immediately.

Proper cooking (as indicated in all recipes in this book that involve frying) ensures minimum absorption of grease. After frying, food should be lifted from the oil in the basket of the fryer, in a skimmer or slotted spoon, or, best of all, in a "spider" or Chinese spoon and then drained on several layers of paper towels. Do not cover or wrap fried food before serving; it will get soggy and sad.

You don't have to use new oil every time you fry, but it must be replaced regularly. It absorbs flavors and bits of cooked food. If you fry fish in oil, that oil will taste like fish, and if you try using it to fry something else, that something else will end up tasting like fish, too. You might keep separate batches of oil for frying separate foods, or you can change the oil every time.

Do not throw (or even drip) water into a pot of hot oil—it will vaporize on contact—and always be careful of spitting oil, which can seriously burn you. Always put the frying pot on a back burner to avoid accidents. Never leave a fryer or pot of hot oil unsupervised: The oil can catch fire. If it does catch fire, again, do not throw water on it. Rather, smother the fire with a lid or towel.

If you do not have a deep fry thermometer, you can check to see whether the oil is hot enough by dropping in a bit of the breading or a small piece of potato. The oil will foam and bubble at once if it is hot enough. If you try to fry food in oil that is not hot enough, it will soak up a good deal of fat and will not get crunchy.

When you have finished, allow the pot of oil to cool. If you plan to keep it for another use, put it through a fine strainer and store it in a cool, dark place, preferably the refrigerator.

TIPS FOR ROASTING, GRILLING, AND PAN FRYING MEAT _____

In France, roasts and certain small pieces of meat are frequently wrapped in something fatty, usually a piece of bacon, meant to add flavor and moisture during cooking. If your butcher does this, ask him not to. The wrapping obscures the meat's flavor, adds unnecessary fat, and is sometimes used to disguise the flavor of meat that is past its prime.

Remove meat from the refrigerator in advance—ten to thirty minutes before you plan to cook it, depending on how large it is and the temperature of your kitchen. (This book assumes a room temperature of about 70°F/20°C.) If your house is much warmer, the meat need not come out of the refrigerator quite as early. Protect meat from flies by covering it with butcher paper, a clean dish towel, or aluminum foil.

Season meat all over with salt and pepper just before cooking. Do not salt red meat, such as beef and lamb, in advance because this will draw the juices. In fact, if possible it is best to salt these meats during cooking, seasoning each surface only after it has been browned. This is not always easy; you must avoid scattering salt all over the skillet, grill, or baking dish.

Either way, the layer of salt and pepper should be fairly even. Instead of dumping on a spoonful of salt or using a salt shaker, take pinches of salt in your fingers and sprinkle them over the meat; this will give you better control and result in more uniform seasoning. The same goes for pepper if you are using preground commercial pepper, though freshly ground pepper is always better. Hold the peppermill almost sideways instead of upright, with a hand beneath it; this will give you a better idea of how much pepper it is releasing.

Meat that will be grilled should be coated thinly, using either a pastry brush or fingers, with neutral oil (sunflower, grapeseed, etc.). Peanut oil can work, too, but be aware of your guests' allergies; peanut allergies can be quite serious. Whether grilling or roasting, avoid olive oil and any intensely flavored oil that can change the way the meat tastes.

GRILLING

The grill or grill pan must be clean. If it isn't, warm it for a minute and then take it off the heat. Do not wet it. Instead, scrub the grooves with a little metal brush and wipe with a paper towel. Drizzle a bit of neutral oil on a dry paper towel and rub it all over the grill.

Heat the grill before placing the meat on it. Over high heat, a grill will take two minutes to heat up. Then lower the heat a bit. The grill should be hot but not so blistering that it will char the meat. When it is hot enough, its grooves should visibly lighten. Hold your hand about 2 inches (5 cm.) from the grill to test its heat or drip a few droplets of water onto it: They should sizzle instantly.

For a pleasing presentation, lay the meat on the grill on a

diagonal. Then, at the appropriate time, give it a quarter turn so that it gets cross-hatch grill marks. Do not press down on a piece of grilling meat with a spatula: You will lose juices.

To turn meat over, it is best to use metal tongs. You could instead use a two-tined fork so large that it can slip all the way under the meat and then turn the meat by using your other hand or a spatula for help. If you use a fork, however, it is important not to puncture the meat, because delicious juices will run out.

PAN FRYING

The skillet or sauté pan must be clean. If it isn't, rinse it under hot water and wipe it out with a paper towel.

Begin by pouring a bit of neutral oil—usually 1 teaspoon—into the skillet. Set it over high heat, turning and tilting the skillet so that the oil spreads all around and the pan is evenly warmed. **It takes about two minutes for oil to get hot.** When you place the meat in the pan, it should sizzle pleasantly right away. Lower the heat a bit.

If you want to add a little flavor, put a small lump of butter (about a teaspoon) into the skillet after the oil but before the meat. If the butter is added before the oil, it is liable to brown very quickly or even burn. Wait and watch the butter melt and foam, turning and twirling the skillet as before. At this point it should not brown. If it does, take the skillet off the heat for a few seconds to keep the butter from burning.

If you do burn fat—you will know when your pan starts to smoke—do not go ahead and use it for cooking. It will ruin what you put into it. Wait a minute for the skillet to cool down so that you don't burn yourself. Then discard the fat. Rinse the skillet with warm water, wipe it out with paper towels, and start over.

When the butter foams (after about one minute), lay the meat in the skillet, preferably with tongs (silicone or wooden if you are using a nonstick skillet; metal utensils can easily ruin nonstick finishes). Lay the meat down gently in a fluid motion away from yourself instead of plopping it into the pan. When it is time to turn the meat over, do so with tongs or a spatula, if necessary helping yourself with your other hand or a spatula. Be especially careful when you are working with a larger piece of meat, such as a rib steak, or one full of blood, such as liver, since these produce more sizzling and splattering.

When the meat begins to cook, the oil or butter will brown. They are not burning; rather, this is the result of a reaction involving the meat juices.

ROASTING

Preheat your oven at least ten minutes in advance. (Your oven may take even longer to heat up. If you want to be absolutely sure the oven is hot enough, buy an oven thermometer.) Red meat is usually cooked in a very hot oven so that the exterior gets seared. Each recipe will indicate when and to what temperature you should preheat your oven. For poultry it is generally recommended that you start with a cool oven so that the meat's exposure to heat will be gradual.

RESTING

Season meat just after cooking with salt (fleur de sel if possible) and pepper. You might also choose to top it with a little lump of cool butter, which will melt slowly as the meat rests.

Do not forget to allow meat to rest on a rack (or small overturned plate) set over a large plate so that the juices have a chance to spread throughout the meat. If you can, lay the side of the meat that was cooked first (or the breast of the chicken) facedown on the rack; these parts are best able to reabsorb the juices.

Small cuts (such as chops and steaks) won't get too cold as they rest, for they retain a lot of interior heat. Large pieces (such as lamb leg and beef rib steak) should be loosely tented with aluminum foil to stay warm. Don't wrap them in aluminum foil; if they are too well enclosed, they will continue to cook and will be overcooked by the time you bring them to the table.

The purpose of the rack or small plate is to keep the meat from sitting in a pool of its own juices, which would ruin its exterior texture. Those juices should be added to any sauce or *jus* before serving because they are flavorful. When you carve the meat, season each slice on both sides with fleur de sel and freshly ground pepper.

KITCHEN EQUIPMENT: *BATTERIE DE CUISINE*

You don't need a vast amount of equipment to make good food. The tools recommended here will suffice both for everyday meals and for dinner parties and holiday feasts at home.

Saucepans in stainless steel or cast iron   1 quart (1 l.), 2 quart (2 l.), 3 quart (3 l.) It is worth splurging on slightly more costly pots that are solid, heavy, and thick-bottomed. Make sure they will work with your burners. Avoid aluminum, to which milk and eggs will stick, in favor of cast iron, enameled cast iron, or stainless steel. Be careful when heating fat in a stainless steel pot: it can stick, darken, and burn rather fast if the heat is a little too high.

If you need a pot larger than 3 quarts (3 l.) use a Dutch oven instead of a saucepan. A Dutch oven's two side handles make it easier to move when it is full and heavy.

Stew pots or Dutch ovens, stainless steel or cast iron   5 quart (5 l.) oval, 5 ½ quart (5.4 l.) round, 6¾ quart (6.75 l.) oval, 13¼ quart (12.8 l.) round. A Dutch oven should be plain, uncoated, but well-seasoned cast iron. Avoid those varnished with colors; they can chip as soon as they get a good knock. An enameled interior that gets chipped can even be dangerous, since particulate matter could make its way into your food.

You can clean cast iron with a sponge but not with steel wool or other metal sponges. For grills, on the other hand, there are small metal sponges that may be used and work well.

A 13¼-quart pot may sound awfully big, but it is useful for poaching a large fowl or making choucroute garni to serve six. Choose a pot with no plastic parts (usually knobs or handles) so that it can safely bake in a hot oven.

Nonstick skillets and other nonstick items   Some people prefer skillets, sauté pans, sheet pans, cake pans, muffin pans, and so on that are coated with nonstick Teflon. Never use metal utensils (spatulas, spoons, or tongs) on Teflon-coated surfaces because they can tear the coating, ruining the pan and encouraging the Teflon to degrade more quickly, perhaps flaking off into your food. Do not scour them with a scouring pad or with steel wool; instead, wash them in hot water with a soft sponge or a plastic brush. If nothing has burned onto the pan, then you probably don't even need to use soap; just rinse with hot water and wipe out with a paper towel until no traces of grease remain. If you have cooked something strong-smelling such as fish or seafood, wipe the skillet out with a paper towel moistened with white vinegar.

If a nonstick skillet is kept in a drawer with other pots and pans that might end up piled on top of it, it should be lined with a piece of paper towel or a dish towel to protect it from damage. Nonstick coating is fragile, and nonstick-coated cookware must be replaced when it is worn with use.

If a skillet is very hot, avoid rinsing it under cold water because it might spit hot matter at you.

Nonstick skillets   10 inches (20–24 cm.) and 12 inches (11–12 cm.) Two should be enough. Small skillets can cook enough food for one or two people, and a large family will need the larger size. A plastic handle is useful if you want to avoid burning your hands, but it can end up burning itself if you aren't careful. If the skillet has a metal handle, it should be at an angle and should have a hole at its base so that it does not conduct heat to your hand.

Sauté pans in cast iron or stainless steel   2 quart (20 cm.), 3 quart (24 cm.), and 4 quart (28 cm.) A sauté pan is a skillet with higher sides, often straight but sometimes flared. The extra height allows you to cook vegetables, for instance, without risking their boiling over and retains a bit of steam. Sauté pans have lids whereas skillets usually do not.

Nonstick wok   12 inches (32 cm.) A large skillet with high sides, Asian in origin and meant for sautéing vegetables over high heat. Try to find one with a small rack along its upper inside edge that allows you to steam small items above as you sauté below.

Cast-iron grill pan for stovetop   rectangular or square, 10¾ inch (30 cm.)

Porcelain baking dishes, preferably with handles   rectangular, 1½ quart (8 inches by 8 inches/24 cm. by 15 cm.) and 3 quart (12 inches by 8 inches/32 cm. by 22 cm.); oval, 2 quart (12½ inch/ 28 cm.)

Porcelain is sturdier than terra cotta and other earthenware and is therefore preferred. An earthenware dish might shatter if you add water to it when it is hot, which you will sometimes want to do to make sauce at the end of cooking. A porcelain dish will not shatter. Rectangular dishes are good for gratins, and the oval dish is for poultry and other roasts.

Porcelain terrine with a lid   3 cups/6½ inches long (600 g./17 cm. long), serving eight to ten

Sheet pans   18 inches by 13 inches (40 cm. by 30 cm.)

Round cake pans   8 inches (20 cm.) and 10 inches (25 cm.) You'll want two of each.

Tart pans   10 inches and 11 inches (26 cm. and 28 cm.)

Square cake pans   8 inches and 9 inches (20 cm. and 22 cm.)

Pie pan   10 or 12 inches (26 cm. or 30 cm.)

Perforated pie pan   12 inches (32 cm.) Useful for cooking a tart crust or pizza very quickly.

Couscoussier or steamer basket   A couscoussier is a two-part pot traditionally used in North Africa to cook couscous: the lower part contains hot stew, stock, or water, and the upper part contains couscous (or anything else you want to steam).

Fryer

Pressure cooker

UTENSILS

If you choose plastic utensils, make sure they can withstand a temperature of at least 425°F (220°C). Avoid utensils with wooden handles, which will fall apart. Wooden utensils must be washed by hand since the dishwasher will ruin them.

Stainless steel ladles, small, medium, and large

Large stainless steel serving spoon

Large stainless steel two-tined fork

Stainless steel skimmer

Chinese spoon, also called a spider—a skimmer with a large basket with large holes

Large wooden spoons and spatulas

Stainless steel whisk

Wooden or silicone paddles

Stainless steel slotted spatula

Large tongs, stainless steel and plastic or silicone (for nonstick cookware)

Scissors

Kitchen shears

Cutting boards

Poultry shears

Vegetable peeler

Pastry brush (do not put it in the dishwasher if it has a wooden handle)

Colander

Small fine strainer

Chinois—a conical fine strainer with very strong mesh, 8 inches (20 cm.), preferably with handles for setting it atop a pot

Peppermill, preferably electric

Grater

Stainless steel mandoline, preferably with a blade that can be changed

Stainless steel skewers for brochettes, 10 inches (25 cm.)

Apple corer

Olive pitter

Nutcracker

Mortar and pestle

Rolling pin

Stainless steel food mill

Herb chopper or small food processor

Garlic press

Electric hand mixer

Food processor

Wand mixer

Oven mitts and potholders

Cooling racks, round and rectangular: Choose large ones (at least 10 inches/25 cm.). Useful for grilled or roasted meat to rest on (place a plate underneath to catch juices) and for pots to rest on after cooking since they cool faster with air underneath them.

MEASURING

Liquid measuring cup

Set of dry ingredient measuring cups

Set of measuring spoons

Scale, preferably electric, that can weigh as little as 1 gram and that can be tared

Meat thermometer, preferably with a probe

Candy or deep fry thermometer

Kitchen timer

_____

French metric measures (grams and kilos, millimeters and centimeters, degrees Celsius) have all been converted for this English-language edition. Most of the time, however, it makes no sense to give an exact conversion. 10 cl. oil is 6.76 tablespoons, which is not very practical. Rounding has therefore been applied wherever it will not affect the recipe: 1 kg., for instance, has been converted as 2 pounds, even though it is really 2.2 pounds; 25 cl. here is 1 cup, even though 1 cup is really 23.5 cl.

Sometimes the conversion has been adapted to the recipe. An example: 100 g. (6.666 tablespoons) butter is usually converted as 6 tablespoons here, which means the recipe calls for slightly less butter than the French original. But in those cases where a little more butter is desirable or necessary, 100 g. is converted as 7 tablespoons.

Despite the fact that spoon and cup measure are widely used in the United States, chefs prefer weight measures, which are more precise. Sugar, salt, flour, and many other ingredients (including butter) can weigh more or less depending on the humidity and their own characteristics. So your cup of butter might weigh 8 ounces when your neighbor's weighs 8½. You will find both cups and weights in these recipes, but if you have a kitchen scale, the weight measures are preferable.

In any case, one thing is certain: cooking is not an exact science. At its best, it is an art, or so we French like to believe. For those who are nevertheless determined to strive for exactitude, here are some of the conversions used in this book.

Liquid	1 teaspoon = ⅙ fl. oz. = 0.5 cl.
	1 tablespoon liquid = ½ fl. oz. = 1.5 cl.
	1 cup = 8 fl. oz. = 23.5 cl.
Fine salt/granulated sugar	1 teaspoon = ⅙ oz. = 5 g.
	1 tablespoon = ½ oz. = 15 g.
	1 cup = 8½ oz. = 240 g.
Coarse salt	1 teaspoon = ⅓ oz. = 10 g.
	1 tablespoon = 1 oz. = 30 g.

Pepper (powdered)	1 teaspoon = $\frac{1}{10}$ oz. = 3 g.
Butter	1 teaspoon = $\frac{1}{6}$ oz. = 5 g.
	1 tablespoon = $\frac{1}{2}$ ounce = 15 g.
	$\frac{1}{2}$ cup = 8 tablespoons = 1 stick = 4.2 oz. = 120 g.
	1 cup = 16 tablespoons = 2 sticks = $8\frac{1}{2}$ oz. = 240 g.
Flour	1 tablespoon = $\frac{1}{3}$ oz. = 10 g.
	1 cup = 5.6 oz. = 160 g.
Cornstarch, yeast, confectioners' sugar	1 teaspoon = 0.09 oz. = 2.7 g.
	1 tablespoon = 0.3 oz. = 8 g.
	1 cup = 4.6 oz. = 130 g.
Crème fraîche, sour cream	1 teaspoon = 0.4 oz. = 12 g.
	1 tablespoon = 1.2 oz. = 35 g.
	$\frac{1}{2}$ cup = 8 oz. = 225 g.
Mustard	1 tablespoon = $\frac{4}{5}$ oz. = 23 g.
Rice	1 tablespoon = $\frac{1}{2}$ oz. = 14 g.
	1 cup = 8 oz. = 220 g.
Grated carrot, celeriac	1 cup = $\frac{1}{4}$ lb. = 120 g.
Sliced beetroot	1 cup = 4.7 oz. = 130 g.
Baby tomatoes (raw, whole)	1 cup = 4.7 oz. = 130 g.
Small potatoes (raw, whole)	1 cup = 5.3 oz. = 150 g.
Diced potatoes (raw)	1 cup = 7 oz. = 200 g.
Button mushrooms (sliced)	1 cup = 1.7 oz. = 50 g.
Lardons	1 cup = $\frac{1}{4}$ lb. = 125 g.
Raisins	1 tablespoon = $\frac{4}{5}$ oz. = 23 g.
Mayonnaise	1 tablespoon = 1 oz. = 30 g.
Capers	1 tablespoon = 0.9 oz. = 25 g.

Dry bread crumbs (best made from dry European-style breakfast rusks if possible)	1 cup = 100 g.

GLOSSARY

This book aims to use the plainest terms possible, but some might require a bit of explanation. The culinary vocabulary is much richer than this glossary, but here is a glimpse, including all the words you will need to understand these recipes.

Aromatics (*aromates*)   Fragrant plants that serve as a base for many dishes: thyme, bay leaf, chervil, savory, rosemary, etc.

Aspic   Cold jelled substance used to coat cold cooked food and frequently to present it in a mold.

Bain-marie   A bowl or pot of boiling or nearly boiling water containing a smaller bowl full of something being gently warmed. Used for delicate foods that should not be put in direct contact with heat.

Beat (*fouetter*)   To mix energetically with an electric mixer, whisk, or fork.

Beurre manié   A mixture of softened butter and flour used to thicken sauces, stews, etc.

Bind (*lier*)   To add something (flour, cornstarch, egg yolk, potato, zucchini) to thicken a sauce.

Blanch (*blanchir*)   To boil briefly. Meat is put into cold water, which is then brought to a boil for a few minutes to eliminate impurities, firm the flesh, or remove excess salt. Green vegetables can be plunged into already-boiling water for a minute or two to remove acidity or unpleasant flavors, fix color, or soften them a bit before further cooking.

Blanquette   A stew of white meat (veal, lamb, or chicken) in a white sauce.

Bouquet garni   A small bundle of herbs and aromatics (such as parsley, thyme, chervil, and bay leaf) dropped into a stew or soup.

Braising (*braiser*)   Long cooking in more or less liquid in a covered container. See page 9.

Bread (*paner*)   To coat with bread crumbs (for frying, for example).

Brown (*dorer*)   To give a food color and flavor, usually without cooking it all the way through. It is generally cooked four to five minutes in some fat over medium heat.

Browned butter (*beurre noisette*)   Butter that has been melted and cooked just long enough to get a light color and nutty taste.

Brunoise   Vegetables cut into very small dice.

Caramelize (*caraméliser*)   To coat with a thin layer of caramel or to cook certain foods until they develop a dark brown color.

Cheesecloth or muslin (*étamine*)   A thin, light fabric used to line strainers for finer straining and sometimes used for sifting. Ingredients that will be simmered are sometimes tied in small muslin sacks to keep them separate during cooking. Can be bought at kitchen supply stores.

Chiffonade   A way of slicing leafy greens (lettuce, sorrel, basil, etc.) into very thin ribbons.

Chinois   A conical strainer with a very fine mesh. The shape is thought to resemble a Chinese hat, hence the name.

Churn (*turbiner*)   To make butter or ice cream.

Clarify (*clarifier*)   To render a broth clear or to remove the water and milk solids from butter, leaving behind a clear yellow fat.

Color (*colorer*)   To make food change color by heating it or by adding vegetable dyes.

Coulis   A juice or light puree of fruits, vegetables, or crustacean's juices.

Court bouillon   An aromatic, quickly made stock usually used to cook fish.

Crepinette   A web of caul fat used to wrap a food and keep it moist during cooking.

Crush (*piler*)   To pulverize a substance (such as peppercorns or spices) in a mortar with a pestle; to whack something such as a piece of garlic with the flat of your knife under the pressure of your fist.

Decant (*décanter*)   To pour a liquid from one container into another in order to remove the deposits at the bottom of the first bottle and to oxygenate the liquid. A necessary step for drinking almost all the great wines, red and white.

Decoction   Flavoring a liquid by means of simmering something in it for a substantial amount of time.

Degerm (*dégermer*)   To slice a clove of garlic in half and lift out its green germ with the tip of a knife.

Deglaze (*déglacer*)   To add a small amount of water, broth, wine, or vinegar to a pan of cooking juices, usually at the end of cooking.

Desalt (*dessaler*)   To remove salt from something (such as salt cod or salt pork) by soaking it in fresh water.

Détrempe   A base dough for rich breads and puff pastry.

Dice (*dés*)   Small cubes; to chop into small cubes.

Drain (*égoutter*)   To put food that has been cooked or cleaned in liquid in a colander so that excess liquid will drip out, perhaps shaking the colander or pressing on the food to get it as dry as possible.

Dress (*habiller*)   To prepare meat, fish, or poultry for cooking.

Duxelles   Minced mushrooms.

Fillet (*lever*)   To remove a fish's fillets by running a knife around their perimeter and lifting them from the skeleton.

Flamber   To pass a plucked chicken (or other bird) through a flame quickly to remove any residual down; to light alcohol on fire by heating it and then touching a match to its surface.

Flour (*fleurer*)   To coat lightly with flour; applies both to items to be fried, which are sometimes floured as part of the breading process, and to cake and tart pans, which are sometimes greased and floured to keep the cake from sticking.

Fluff (*égrainer*)   To separate the grains of cooked rice, bulgur wheat, or couscous by moving a fork through the pot until they are no longer so sticky.

Fricassée   A saucy sauté of small pieces of white meat.

Fritters (*fritots*)   Small fried foods (vegetables, breaded shrimp, zucchini flowers, etc.).

Fromage blanc   A thick, soft, mild, spreadable fresh cheese. Now widely available in the United States, but if you cannot find it, try substituting cream cheese.

Fumet   Fish stock.

Garnish (*garniture*)   Aromatic herbs or vegetables added to a dish just before serving.

Gastrique   A lightly cooked mixture of vinegar and sugar that serves as the base of a sauce.

Giblets (*abats*)   The head, neck, wing tips, feet, gizzard, heart, and liver of poultry or feathered game.

Glaze (*glace*)   Cooked-down, concentrated juices or stock.

Gratin   A dish, often topped with grated cheese, that has been finished under the broiler and therefore has a golden top crust.

Grease (*graisser*)   To rub with butter, oil, or lard.

Ice/frost (*glacer*)   To cover a cake with frosting; to sprinkle with powdered sugar.

Incorporate (*incorporer*)   To mix one ingredient into another until the two are evenly blended.

Infuse (*infuser*)   To soak something in liquid (probably hot) in order to transfer its flavors to the liquid.

Julienne   To chop vegetables into very thin sticks; also, the sticks themselves.

Knead (*pétrir*)   To push and fold a dough to render it homogeneous and pliant.

Loosen (*relâcher*)   To add some liquid to a sauce that is too thick in order to thin it out.

Macédoine   Fruits or vegetables cut into small dice.

Macerate (*macérer*)   To soak food in a liquid (alcohol, vinegar, wine, lemon juice) before consuming it without cooking.

Marbled (*marbré*)   Said of beef with spots and fine lines of white fat.

Marinate (*mariner*)   To soak in a liquid with aromatics to impart flavors before cooking; see page 273 or page 510.

Medallion (*médaillon*)   A thick round slice of fish or meat.

Mince (*hacher*)   To chop into extremely small pieces; also, the small pieces themselves.

Mirepoix   A dice of vegetables sautéed in butter or bacon fat, which serves as a base for stocks and sauces.

Panade   A mixture of flour and butter, or bread crumbs soaked in milk or water, used as the base of a stuffing.

Papillote   A tightly sealed packet (usually of aluminum foil) filled with food and baked in the oven. Also, the small paper frills sometimes placed on the legs of a roast.

Pâte à luter   A raw pastry "snake" wedged between a pot and its lid for a firm seal during cooking.

Peel (*peler*)   To remove the skin, to trim.

Persillade   A garnish of minced parsley and garlic.

Poach (*pocher*)   To cook in barely simmering liquid.

Punch down (*rompre*)   To halt a dough's rising by putting a fist into its blown-up center, after which it will probably be set to rise again.

Quenelle   A small football-shaped dumpling formed with two spoons. Also a shape in which ice cream is served.

Reduction   The action of thickening and strengthening a sauce or liquid by long, slow cooking until a good deal of the water has evaporated; the reduced sauce or liquid itself.

Reserve (*réserver*)   To set an ingredient aside until the recipe calls for it.

Rounds (*rouelles*)   Circular slices of something such as carrots or onions.

Sauté (*sauter*)   To cook uncovered in some fat in a skillet or sauté pan, frequently shaking the pan or moving the food around to prevent sticking.

Save (*rattraper*)   To rebuild a sauce (such as mayonnaise) that has "broken" apart into its component ingredients instead of hanging together as a homogeneous emulsion.

Scallop (*escalope*) A small, thin slice of meat; to carve raw meat into such slices; in English, also a shellfish (*coquille Saint-Jacques*).

Sear (*saisir*) To cook quickly over high heat for color, flavor, and texture.

Season (*assaisonner*) To add salt and pepper (and sometimes spices). The quantities of salt and pepper are usually not specified, for you must taste the dish yourself and add salt and pepper until it pleases you, as in "season to taste."

Seed (*égrainer*) To remove the seeds, such as from a tomato or bell pepper.

Shell (*écosser*) To remove fava beans or other shell beans from their pods.

To shiver, shivering (*frémir, à frémissement*) The stage before boiling, just under a simmer, when the surface of the liquid is trembling but not bubbling.

Shock (*frapper*) To chill quickly, as in a bowl of ice water.

Sieve (*tamiser*) To put through a sieve or strainer in order to eliminate lumps or make into a purée.

Simmer (*mijoter*) A low, slow bubbling, less vigorous than boiling; to cook something slowly over low heat in simmering liquid.

Skim (*écumer*) To use a skimmer to remove foam or scum from the surface of a pot of cooking liquid such as broth.

Sliver (*effiler*) To cut into very thin slices or flakes.

Snip (*ciseler*) To mince (onions and shallots) or actually cut into small pieces with kitchen shears (chives and other herbs).

Stud (*piquer*) To insert tiny bits of fat or garlic into a piece of meat.

Sweat (*suer*) To cook gently in order to remove water and mute flavors that are too strong.

Trim (*éplucher*) To remove the ends and/or outer layers of a vegetable so that what is left is fresh, even, thoroughly edible, and attractive; (*ébarber*): to remove a fish's side fins with scissors; to remove filaments of white from a poached egg; to remove membranes from shellfish meat.

Trimmings (*parures*) Scraps of meat, fat, and chopped-up bones produced by butchering an animal, useful for stocks and stuffings and as a base on which to roast.

Truss (*brider*) To tie up poultry or a game bird with kitchen twine in order to keep its limbs close to the body during cooking, making it easier to handle during cooking and lovelier to look at, at the table.

Trussing needle (*aiguille à brider*) Needle used for trussing poultry before cooking.

Turn (*tourner*) To peel and slice vegetables into an oblong shape for easier and more even cooking and a pleasing presentation.

Unmold (*démouler*)   To remove a cake or tart carefully from its pan.

Well (*fontaine*)   A little hollow at the top of a mound of flour to which liquid is added before mixing.

Whisk (*fouetter*)   To mix energetically with a whisk or electric mixer.

Zest (*zeste*)   The colorful peel of a citrus fruit, not including any of the white pith.

Stocks and Sauces

Stocks

A stock is an enriched and concentrated broth prepared ahead of time to serve as the base that will reinforce a dish's flavors and colors and give it a certain depth and character. You can make a stock of meat, fowl, game, fish (in which case it is called *fumet de poisson*), or even vegetables.

Making a meat stock from scratch takes time. You can find reasonable substitutes at the grocery store, but these bouillon cubes and frozen concoctions will not have the richness of a stock you have made yourself. Below is the recipe for a simple brown stock that starts with a bouillon cube; it takes some time but not nearly as much as a classic brown stock. When you take the trouble to make a stock from scratch, you can save what you don't use and freeze it for future cooking.

Stocks are cooked for a long time and therefore lose a great deal of water. They can then be further concentrated ("reduced") until their texture is thick and their flavor intense, at which point a stock becomes a glaze.

Stocks differ from one another according to whether you use bones, which can be browned with aromatic vegetables or simply added as they are, before they are covered with water (or sometimes wine). Meat bones will give off fat, and stocks made from them must be degreased.

A stock should cook gently, at a bare simmer, really just a shiver. As it bubbles oh-so-quietly, you must skim the grayish foam of impurities rising to its surface. A stock that has bubbled vigorously will yield a cloudy broth, not the clear one desired.

HOW TO SKIM AND DEGREASE A STOCK

To Skim   Half-fill a bowl with cold water. Lift scummy foam from the surface of the stock with a skimmer, rinsing it in the water bowl after each pass. To skim most effectively, carefully move your stockpot or saucepan a little away from the center of the flame, so that the liquid bubbles on one side only. Remove the foam from the tranquil side.

To Degrease Gently pour a ladle of cold water all over the surface of the simmering liquid. The fat will come to the surface; remove it with the ladle or a large spoon. You will take away some of the scum at the same time.

For a completely degreased stock or broth you must let the liquid cool after cooking and then leave it in the refrigerator overnight. The fat will rise to the surface and solidify. The layer of solidified fat will be very easy to remove with a spoon (and, if necessary, more fat can be dabbed off the top of the jelled stock with paper towels). Then you can reheat as needed.

For a broth that is truly pure, or clarified, see the section on consommés (page 78), where you will find recipes that walk you through this long and rather involved process.

JUST A LITTLE SALT

In general, a stock should be minimally salted: It will end up well seasoned without your adding much salt, since you will usually reduce the broth, cooking it down to two-thirds of its original volume or even half for some recipes. As water evaporates, the remaining liquid will become saltier.

WHAT IS A STOCK FOR?

Stock is something in which you can cook certain foods to impart additional flavors; for example, a fish can be poached in a *fumet de poisson,* a chicken in chicken stock, etc. Stock is also used in the making of sauces that accompany meat or fish.

These stocks can be made in advance and kept in the refrigerator or freezer.

VEGETABLE BROTH

Bouillon de légumes

MAKES   about 1 quart (1 l.)
PREPARATION   20 minutes
COOKING   20 minutes

1. Put all the ingredients in a saucepan and cover with about 6 cups (1.5 l.) water. Bring to a boil and carefully skim foam from the surface. Cover and simmer for 20 minutes.
2. Put the broth through a fine strainer lined with cheesecloth (or a clean dish towel), without pressing on the vegetables.
3. The vegetables can be saved and eaten with a vinaigrette (page 59) or sautéed in butter or olive oil.

2 medium leeks, carefully cleaned and roughly chopped
3 medium carrots, peeled and roughly chopped
1 celery stalk, roughly chopped
1 medium tomato, chopped
2 stems parsley
1 tablespoon (20 g.) coarse salt

VEGETABLE STOCK

Fond de légumes

MAKES   about 1 quart (1 l.)
PREPARATION   20 minutes
COOKING   3 hours

This has a more subtle and refined taste than vegetable broth.

1. Pour 6¼ cups (1.5 l.) water into a large saucepan. Add all the ingredients and bring to a boil. Lower the heat and simmer gently for 3 hours, uncovered, skimming foam from the surface every 30 minutes.
2. Pass through a fine strainer lined with cheesecloth (or a clean dish towel); do not press the vegetables to extract liquid.

3 stalks celery, roughly chopped
2 leeks, carefully cleaned and roughly chopped
2 carrots, peeled and roughly chopped
1 onion, peeled and chopped
2 cloves garlic, peeled and chopped
2 cups (500 ml.) dry white wine
2 whole star anise
1 bouquet garni (3 stems parsley, thyme, and ½ bay leaf, wrapped and tied in a leek leaf)
1 scant teaspoon coarse salt
Pepper

WHITE VEAL STOCK

Fond blanc de veau

variation

WHITE CHICKEN STOCK

MAKES about 1 quart (1 l.)
PREPARATION 30 minutes
COOKING 3 hours

This stock is an important ingredient of the light sauces served with white meats and of creamed vegetables and veloutés.

Ask the butcher to chop the bones for you and to give you some veal scraps and trimmings.

1   Clean, trim, and pare the vegetables as necessary. You can cut them into large pieces or leave them whole.
2   Blanch the veal bones and the fatty scraps: Put them in a large saucepan, cover generously with cold water, and bring to a boil. Boil 2 or 3 minutes and then remove the bones with a skimmer. Put them in a colander and rinse well under cold running water.
3   Put the bones in a large saucepan or stockpot with 2 quarts (2 l.) cold water and the coarse salt. Bring to a boil and skim foam from the surface. Add all the vegetables and the bouquet garni and cook gently for about 3 hours.
4   Pass through a fine strainer lined with cheesecloth (or a clean dish towel) before chilling the stock in the refrigerator.

1 carrot
1 onion studded with a whole clove
1 medium leek
$3\frac{1}{2}$ ounces (100 g.) mushrooms
1 stalk celery
1 clove garlic
2 pounds (1 kg.) veal bones, coarsely chopped, plus small bits of veal fat and scraps
$\frac{1}{2}$ teaspoon coarse salt
1 bouquet garni (parsley, thyme, and a bay leaf, wrapped and tied in a green leek leaf)

WHITE CHICKEN STOCK

Fond blanc de volaille

Follow the recipe for white veal stock, replacing the veal bones with the bones and chopped-up carcass of a chicken.

BROWN VEAL STOCK

Fond brun de veau

variations

    BROWN CHICKEN STOCK

    GAME STOCK

    REDUCED BROWN VEAL

      STOCK (MEAT GLAZE)

MAKES   about 1 quart (1 l.)

PREPARATION   15 minutes

OVEN BROWNING   25–40 minutes

COOKING   4 hours

This is indisputably the essential sauce base in classic French cuisine. Cooking veal bones this way produces a meaty juice that can be used in any number of preparations.

    Ask the butcher to chop the bones, a very difficult task without professional instruments.

2 pounds (1 kg.) veal bones, coarsely chopped, plus a few pork bones

1 carrot, peeled and coarsely chopped

1 large onion, peeled and coarsely chopped

One 4-inch (10-cm.) section of celery stalk

¼ pound (100 g.) mushrooms, trimmed and cleaned

1 clove garlic

1 bouquet garni (parsley, thyme, and a bay leaf wrapped and tied in a green leek leaf)

4 sprigs chervil

½ sprig tarragon

2 tomatoes

Salt

1. Preheat the oven to 400°F (200°C) 10 minutes in advance.

2. Put the bones alone in a roasting pan and put the pan in the oven. Let the bones brown for 15 to 30 minutes. Stir them from time to time with a skimmer or a big wooden spoon.

3. Remove the roasting pan from the oven and add the carrot, onion, celery, and mushrooms to the bones, mixing everything well. Put the pan back in the oven for 10 minutes to brown the vegetables. Take the pan out of the oven, remove the bones and vegetables with the skimmer or spoon, leaving the grease in the pan, and put them in a large saucepan or stockpot.

4. Pour 2 quarts (2 l.) cold water into the pot and add the garlic, bouquet garni, herbs, and tomatoes. Bring to the brink of a boil. Add a dash of salt to bring out the flavors. Skim foam from the surface. Simmer gently for 4 hours, never allowing the liquid to roll and boil. It should just shiver. Skim and degrease every 30 minutes.

5. After 4 hours, put the stock through a fine strainer lined with cheesecloth (or a clean dish towel). Allow it to cool and refrigerate it overnight. The next day you can easily remove the solidified fat from the stock's surface.

BROWN CHICKEN STOCK
Fond brun de volaille

Follow the recipe for brown veal stock above, replacing the veal and pork bones with the bones of a chicken.

GAME STOCK
Fond de gibier

This stock is used to make dark, peppery *sauce poivrade* for game and can also be combined with blood, as in a civet.

Follow the recipe for brown veal stock, using instead the bones, carcasses, and fat scraps from your game and adding the additional ingredients.

1 quart (1 l.) chicken broth (page 77 or made from a bouillon cube)
4 cups (1 l.) full-bodied red wine, such as Shiraz
⅓ cup (10 cl.) Cognac
A few coriander seeds
A few juniper berries

REDUCED BROWN VEAL STOCK (MEAT GLAZE)
Fond brun de veau réduit (glace de viande)

REDUCING   2 to 3 hours

If you want a thick jelly to enhance the taste of a sauce, you must make a meat glaze. Let the stock simmer in a saucepan for 2 or 3 hours, skimming foam every 30 minutes, until it is a tenth of its original volume. The taste of this concentrated mixture is so powerful that you will need only a small lump for your sauce. Leftovers can be frozen in an ice cube tray so you can use them as needed.

1 recipe brown veal stock

THICKENED VEAL STOCK

Fond de veau lié

MAKES about 1 quart (1 l.)
PREPARATION 10 minutes
COOKING 10–15 minutes

Veal stock can be thickened to make sauces incorporating port or Madeira, as well as such sauces as bordelaise, Perigueux, and Bercy.

1 Put the veal stock and mushrooms in a saucepan with the chervil and tarragon, and, if you are using it, Madeira or port. Mix the potato starch with 2 tablespoons of water. Add this mixture to the saucepan little by little, constantly stirring the stock without beating it.
2 Bring to a boil and then cook gently for 10 or 15 minutes, skimming 2 or 3 times.

1 quart (1 l.) brown veal stock (not reduced)
¼ pound (100 g.) minced mushrooms
A few sprigs fresh chervil and tarragon
3 tablespoons Madeira or port wine (optional)
1 level tablespoon potato starch or arrowroot powder

SIMPLIFIED BROWN STOCK

Fond brun de viande simplifié

MAKES about 1 quart (1 l.)
PREPARATION 20 minutes
COOKING more than 3 hours

This simple stock can be used in place of any brown stock.

1 Put all the ingredients except the potato starch in a saucepan or stockpot with 8 cups (2 l.) water. Bring to a boil and cook at a low bubble for 2½ hours, skimming every 30 minutes.
2 Remove the solids with a skimmer or slotted spoon. Let the liquid continue to bubble gently, still skimming every 30 minutes, until 1 quart (1 l.) of stock remains.
3 To thicken: Mix 2 tablespoons water with 1 tablespoon potato starch in a small bowl. Stir this mixture into the hot stock with the skimmer.

3 or 4 bouillon cubes
1 carrot, peeled
1 onion, peeled
1 tomato
1 clove garlic
1 bouquet garni (thyme, parsley, and a bay leaf, tied in a bundle)
One 4-inch section of a celery stalk
¼ pound (100 g.) mushrooms, cleaned and with the ends trimmed
4 sprigs chervil
½ sprig tarragon
1 level tablespoon potato starch for thickening (optional)

FISH STOCK

Fumet de poisson

MAKES   1 quart (1 l.)
PREPARATION   20 minutes
COOKING   about 20 minutes

Ask the fishmonger for the bones and heads of lean fish such as turbot, sole, whiting, brill, hake, and John Dory. If possible, make stock from the fish you will use in the dish for which the fumet is destined (for example, use the heads and skeletons of turbot if you plan to use the fumet to prepare turbot). Ask him, too, to remove the gills; their blood will darken the sauce.

1   If the fishmonger has not already done so, remove the brownish red gills from the heads. Carefully wash the bones and heads and let them drain.
2   Melt the butter in a saucepan over low heat. Add the onion, shallot, and mushrooms and cook for 3 minutes without letting them color. Add the dry heads and bones and cook for 3 or 4 minutes.
3   Add the white wine, 6¼ cups (1.5 l.) cold water, and the bouquet garni and bring to a bare simmer, never allowing the stock to reach a constant bubble. Simmer, skimming, for 20 minutes and no longer, or the stock will taste too strong. Allow it to cool for 30 minutes, during which time its impurities will sink to the bottom of the saucepan. Then ladle it out and put it through a fine strainer lined with cheesecloth (or a clean dish towel).

2 pounds (1 kg.) fish heads and bones
2 tablespoons butter
1 large onion, peeled and thinly sliced
1 shallot, peeled and minced
¼ pound (100 g.) mushrooms, cleaned and thinly sliced
⅓ cup (10 cl.) dry white wine
1 bouquet garni (3 branches of parsley, thyme, and a bay leaf, tied together)

SHRIMP BROTH

Bouillon de crevettes

MAKES   about 1 quart (1 l.)
PREPARATION   10 minutes
COOKING   15 minutes
STEEPING   15 minutes

1 pound (500 g.) small gray shrimp
1 bouquet garni (a few stems of parsley, ½ bay leaf,

1. Pour 5 cups (1.25 l.) water into a saucepan or stockpot. Add the shrimp and bouquet garni and bring gently to a simmer. Skim and simmer for 15 minutes and no longer. Remove from the heat, cover, and allow the broth to steep for 15 minutes.
2. Remove the shrimp with a skimmer and discard. Carefully put the broth through a fine strainer lined with cheesecloth (or a clean dish towel). This broth will keep for a few days in the refrigerator.

a few sprigs of thyme, and a small stalk of celery, wrapped and tied in a green leek leaf)

MUSSEL BROTH

Jus de moules

MAKES   about 1½ quarts (1.5 l.)
PREPARATION   25 minutes
COOKING   4 minutes
STEEPING   15 minutes

1. Scrape and scrub the mussels and remove their beards. Wash them in several changes of cold water, but don't leave them to soak.
2. Put the mussels, shallots, bouquet garni, wine, and 1 quart (1 l.) water in a saucepan. Bring to a boil quickly and allow to bubble for 3 minutes. Turn off the heat, cover the pot, and let stand about 15 minutes.
3. Use a skimmer or slotted spoon to remove the mussels to a colander. Allow the broth to rest for a while before putting it very carefully through a fine strainer lined with paper towels. This broth will keep for a few days in the refrigerator.
4. The mussels can be served cold with mayonnaise and fines herbes as a little starter or added to a fennel salad, for instance.

2 pounds (1 kg.) mussels
2 medium shallots, peeled and minced
1 bouquet garni (a few stems of parsley, ½ bay leaf, a few sprigs of thyme, and a small stalk of celery, wrapped and tied in a green leek leaf)
⅓ cup (10 cl.) dry white wine

Sauces

Sauces are indispensable components of many dishes. They can be hot (*beurre blanc,* béchamel) or cold (mayonnaise, vinaigrette). A familiarity with sauce making allows you to turn out complete meals that suit your needs simply by pairing sauces with meat, fish, salad, or almost any food you like.

PORTIONS OF STOCKS AND SAUCES

These recipes may yield more or less sauce than you need for a particular dish. If you need less of a sauce, you can make a smaller quantity by reducing the volume of its ingredients as long as you maintain the original proportions. For example, for mayonnaise the rule is 1 quart (1 l.) of oil to 4 yolks and 1 tablespoon of mustard. If you need less mayonnaise, use 1 cup (25 cl.) of oil, 1 yolk, and 1 level teaspoon of mustard. Another example is béchamel; it consists of 1 quart (1 l.) of milk, 4 tablespoons (60 g.) of butter, and 6 tablespoons (60 g.) of flour. To make half as much, use 2 cups (0.5 l.) of milk, 2 tablespoons of butter, and 3 tablespoons of flour.

BUTTER

Some sauces require diced butter that is very cold, right out of the refrigerator. Other sauces require butter that is soft but not melted. Still others call for butter that has been *clarified,* or purged of its water and impurities.

Sometimes your butter must be soft, with the texture of a pomade. (In fact, this is called a *beurre pommade.*) If your butter is still refrigerator cold, put it in a bowl or ramekin and microwave very briefly until it is softened but not melted.

In general, you should use unsalted butter for cooking. For certain regional dishes that call for salted butter, you should be careful to salt your dish sparingly as you cook.

If you can, use gray shallots; they are harder to find but have a better flavor.

Sauces should not be salted with fleur de sel, for it will dissolve (due to the heat of cooking or the strength of the vinegar or citrus), and its delicate texture will be wasted. Pepper is preferably freshly ground.

Some preparations, such as béarnaise sauce, use mignonette pepper, the crushed black pepper you will recognize from *steak au poivre*. If you don't have any, you can make your own simply by putting peppercorns in a dish towel and crushing them with a rolling pin or the bottom of a heavy saucepan.

CLARIFIED BUTTER
Beurre clarifié

PREPARATION 20 minutes

For some cooking methods and delicate sauces, it is best to use clarified butter, which is butter from which water and impurities have been removed. It isn't hard to make.

IN A BAIN-MARIE Put a kettle of water on to boil. Put the butter in a basin or a small saucepan that you have placed inside a large saucepan. Pour the boiling water into the outer saucepan. There is no need to put this on a lit burner. When the butter has melted, remove its basin from the large saucepan, using a heatproof glove. Set the butter aside to rest for 15 minutes. Don't wait too long, or the butter will solidify again.

A froth, more or less abundant depending on the season and the diet of the cows, will form on top of the butter. Scoop it away with a small skimmer. Now you will see the golden yellow clarified butter; carefully remove it with a little ladle. Dispose of the water and milky-looking impurities left at the bottom of the basin.

IN THE MICROWAVE Put the butter in a microwave-proof basin or ramekin. Microwave it for less than a minute on medium-low. You will need about 1 minute for 1 stick (4 ounces/100 g.) of butter straight out of the refrigerator. Every microwave is different. Carefully adjust the time according to the temperature and amount of butter, erring on the side of caution. It is better to put the butter back into the microwave for 10 more seconds to finish melting than to discover that it has come to a boil.

Remove the froth, which with this method will form immediately. Then remove the clarified butter and dispose of the impurities as described above.

MELTED BUTTER SAUCE

Sauce au beurre fondu

PREPARATION AND COOKING   10 minutes

This melted butter sauce goes well with vegetables and poached or grilled fish and can be accented with minced chervil, parsley, or tarragon.

2 sticks (½ pound/250 g.) butter
Salt
Cayenne pepper
Juice of ½ lemon

1   Cut the cold butter into small cubes and return to the refrigerator.
2   Put ⅓ cup water, a pinch of salt, a dash of cayenne, and the lemon juice into a small saucepan. Bring to a boil and then add one-fourth of the butter, beating briskly with a whisk. As soon as the butter has melted, add half of the remaining butter. Beat it just until the mixture begins to boil again. Add the remaining butter, turn the burner off immediately, and beat the mixture energetically.
3   The melted butter sauce should be milkily opaque and thick enough to coat a spoon. If you aren't going to use it right away, you must keep it warm—between 100° and 120°F/

40° and 50°C. You should be able to touch the side of the saucepan with your bare hand without burning yourself. Whisk the sauce from time to time until you use it.

NANTAIS BUTTER SAUCE

Beurre nantais

PREPARATION   5 minutes
COOKING   10 minutes

This sauce is perfect for poached or grilled freshwater fish.

1   Cut the butter into small cubes and return to the refrigerator.
2   Put the shallots and wine in a small saucepan and bring to a boil. Cook for 5 minutes over low heat. Add the crème fraîche and bring back to a boil. Let the mixture bubble over low heat about 5 minutes; it should reduce until it is thick enough to coat a wooden spoon. (When you lift the spoon from the sauce and draw a finger across the back of the spoon the sauce should be thick enough to hold the pattern you trace.)
3   When the sauce has thickened, vigorously beat in the butter. Once the butter has been incorporated, remove from the heat. Taste and correct seasoning.
4   If a completely smooth sauce is desired, the shallots can be strained out and discarded. You can also add minced chervil, parsley, or tarragon to this sauce.

2 sticks (½ pound/250 g.) unsalted or half-salted butter
2 tablespoons minced shallot
⅓ cup (10 cl.) dry white wine
⅓ cup (10 cl.) crème fraîche
Salt
White pepper
Minced herbs (optional)

WHITE BUTTER SAUCE

Beurre blanc

PREPARATION 5 minutes
COOKING AND REDUCING 25 minutes

A sauce for poached or grilled freshwater fish.

1   Cut the cold butter into small cubes and return to the refrigerator.
2   Put the shallots and wine and/or vinegar in a small saucepan and bring to a boil. Simmer for 20–25 minutes; the size of the saucepan will affect cooking time: The liquid should reduce by about two-thirds. Allow it to cool for 5 minutes in the saucepan off the heat and then briskly beat in the butter. Add salt and pepper to taste.
3   If you like, you can strain the butter sauce to remove the shallots.

2 sticks (½ pound/250 g.) unsalted or half-salted butter just out of the refrigerator
2 tablespoons minced shallot
One of the following according to your taste:
⅓ cup (10 cl.) dry white wine
⅓ cup (10 cl.) white wine vinegar
2½ tablespoons white wine plus 2½ tablespoons white wine vinegar
Salt
White pepper

LEMON AND BUTTER SAUCE

Beurre maître d'hôtel

PREPARATION 5 minutes

This sauce generally accompanies fish.

1   Cut the butter into small cubes 30 minutes in advance and put the cubes in a bowl to soften.
2   Stir with a wooden spatula. Add the lemon juice, parsley, 3 pinches of salt, and 1 pinch of pepper. Taste and adjust salt and pepper if necessary. Hold at room temperature (or freeze) until use.

12 tablespoons (200 g.) butter
Juice of 1 lemon
1 tablespoon minced parsley
Salt
Pepper

RED BUTTER SAUCE

Beurre rouge

PREPARATION   5 minutes
COOKING   20 to 25 minutes

This sauce complements fish that has been grilled, roasted, or cooked in a packet (*en papillote*).

2 sticks (½ pound/250 g.) butter
2 tablespoons minced shallots
1 cup (25 cl.) full-bodied tannic red wine
Salt
Pepper

1   Cut the butter into small cubes and return the cubes to the refrigerator.
2   Put the shallots, wine, a pinch of salt, and a pinch of pepper into a medium saucepan. Bring to a boil and then simmer for 20–25 minutes. Stir frequently, using a wooden spatula to scrape the sides of the pot and loosen the wine deposits that might build up there; they can make the sauce unpleasantly bitter. At the end, lower the heat as much as possible and inspect the bottom of the pot. About 3 tablespoons of syrupy liquid should remain, but it should not stick to the pot.
3   Whisk one-fourth of the cold butter into the reduced liquid. Turn the heat to low. Beat in one-third of the remaining butter. When it has melted, beat in half of the remaining butter. When it has melted, remove from the burner. Add the remaining butter and whisk until it is completely incorporated.
4   Taste for salt and pepper. You can strain the sauce to remove the shallots. Keep it warm, but do not allow it to boil. The best way to keep the sauce warm is in a bain-marie.

BEET SAUCE

Sauce au jus de betterave

PREPARATION   10 minutes

COOKING   35 minutes

Serve this lightly acidic sauce with fish.

1   Use the juicer to obtain ¾ to 1 cup (20 cl.) raw beet juice. If you don't have a juicer, peel the beet and crush it with a food mill. If necessary, put it through a fine strainer to remove the solids. Add 1 tablespoon vinegar to the juice to temper the beet's earthy taste.

2   Heat 2 tablespoons butter in a saucepan, then add the shallots and a pinch of salt. Cook over very low heat for 3 minutes, stirring. When the shallots are translucent, add the beet juice and bring to a boil. Scrape the bottom and sides of the pot with a wooden spoon and leave the mixture to simmer over low heat about 30 minutes. It should reduce by almost two-thirds.

3   Cut the remaining butter, which should be cold, into small cubes. Whisk it in bit by bit over very low heat, beating constantly. Whatever you do, don't let it boil. Once the butter has been incorporated, remove the saucepan from the heat. Add the lemon juice and salt and pepper.

1 medium beet or 2 small ones, raw but washed and scrubbed

1 tablespoon wine vinegar

12 tablespoons (175 g.) butter; (10 tablespoons/150 g. of it well chilled)

2 shallots, peeled and minced

Juice of ½ lemon

Salt

Pepper

special equipment: a juicer (optional)

BÉARNAISE SAUCE

Sauce béarnaise

PREPARATION AND COOKING   45 minutes

This sauce is for meat or grilled fish. Nobody knows for sure how it came to be. People from Béarn (a region in southwest France) maintain that a version of this sauce (using oil instead of butter) has dressed their typical mountain fare since time immemorial. Around 1830, Collinet, then the chef of the Pavillon Henri IV, happened upon the recipe in a culinary tract from the late Renaissance (or, others say, from 1818). Anyway, he created his own version and made it famous.

variation

CHORON SAUCE

2 tablespoons minced tarragon leaves

3 shallots, peeled and minced

⅓ cup (10 cl.) distilled vinegar

Crushed black pepper

4 egg yolks (page 204)

Salt

2 sticks (½ pound/250 g.) butter, clarified (page 43)

1 tablespoon minced chervil

1 Put half of the tarragon and all the shallots and vinegar in a small saucepan with some crushed black pepper. Boil for 25 minutes over low heat to reduce by almost three-fourths. Remove from the heat and leave until lukewarm, 10 minutes or so.

2 While you wait for the reduction to cool, heat some water in a saucepan large enough to hold the small saucepan.

3 Add the yolks to the small pot. Do not add salt. Whisk to combine.

4 Put the small pot in the large one, where the water should be just at the point of simmering. Beat the yolk mixture vigorously. This mixture should foam at the beginning. If it doesn't, add 1 tablespoon water.

5 Cook to a temperature of about 150°F (65°C). The sauce should thicken, taking on the consistency of cream. Scrape the sides of the small pot well with a wooden spatula. The sauce should grow in volume by half. In the end, if you trace a curve in the sauce with a whisk, you should be able to see the bottom of the pot. At this point, stop beating and remove the small pot from the bain-marie. Whisk in salt and pepper.

6 Put a folded dish towel under the pot of sauce to stabilize it. With a small ladle, add the clarified butter little by little, whisking it in as you would incorporate oil into a mayonnaise, until the sauce has taken it all up. Pass the sauce through a fine strainer.

7 Just before serving, add the remaining tarragon and the chervil. Taste and add salt and pepper if necessary.

8 You can cover the béarnaise with a plate to keep it warm. You can leave the shallots in or strain them out as you like.

TO SAVE BROKEN BÉARNAISE Here's what to do if your béarnaise sauce breaks—that is, if its components separate instead of staying together in a uniform emulsion. If the sauce is too cool, put a tablespoon of hot water into a saucepan; if the sauce is too hot, use a tablespoon of cold water. Take a spoonful of the broken sauce and add it drop by drop to the water in the saucepan, beating constantly. Do the same with a second and a third spoonful of broken sauce. You should observe that the sauce is gradually thickening and coming together. Keep adding the broken sauce with a small ladle, never incorporating more than a very small quantity at a time. Once the sauce is nice and thick again, you can increase the doses of broken sauce until all is incorporated. Beat well, until the béarnaise is once more smooth and firm.

CHORON SAUCE

Use a wooden spoon to stir 2 tablespoons crushed tomato into a finished béarnaise. Serve with grilled meat or fish.

1 recipe béarnaise sauce
(page 48)
1 fresh tomato, peeled, seeded, and diced (page 124), or
1 canned tomato, crushed

WHITE ROUX ─────────────────

Roux blanc

PREPARATION AND COOKING   **5 minutes**

This roux is used to thicken soups and to make sauces such as béchamel.

4 tablespoons (60 g.) butter
6 tablespoons (60 g.) flour

1   In a medium saucepan, melt the butter gently, taking care not to let it brown. Dump the flour in all at once and use a whisk to mix it completely with the butter so that there are no lumps. Stir the resulting mixture continuously for 2 or 3 minutes over low heat. It should whiten, foam, and look as if it is boiling, but it should not actually bubble. Remove the saucepan from the heat and allow it to cool.

2   There are also 2 kinds of colored roux, blond and brown, which are obtained when a white roux is left to cook a few minutes more over low heat. They add color to veal stocks, sauces, and soups, but they are hardly ever used.

BÉCHAMEL SAUCE

Sauce béchamel

PREPARATION AND COOKING   10 minutes

For a béchamel sauce to work out, the roux and the milk must be at opposite temperatures: one hot and the other cool.

1 recipe white roux (page 50)
1 quart (1 l.) milk
Salt
Cayenne pepper
Whole nutmeg to grate
   (optional)

1   Make the white roux and allow it to cool. Bring the milk to a boil and pour it over the cooled roux. Whisk the mixture into a sleek, lump-free sauce. Bring to a bubble and cook for 10 minutes at most, stirring and maintaining a very gentle simmer. Season with a pinch of salt, a dash of cayenne, and, if you wish, a few gratings of nutmeg.

2   A cooked béchamel sauce may be passed through a fine strainer to remove any lumps that may have formed.

3   If the sauce will not be used immediately, you must swab its surface with a lump of butter stuck to the end of a fork. This will help prevent the formation of a skin where the sauce meets the air.

MORNAY SAUCE

COOKING   5 minutes

Bring the béchamel to a boil in a saucepan over low heat, stirring with a spatula. Whisk the egg yolks to break them up. On very low heat, stirring constantly, pour the egg yolks slowly into the béchamel. Add the grated cheese and stir until completely melted.

1 recipe béchamel sauce
   (above)
4 egg yolks (page 204)
1 cup (100 g.) grated Gruyère
   cheese

HOLLANDAISE SAUCE

variation
MOUSSELINE SAUCE

PREPARATION AND COOKING   20 minutes

For poached fish and vegetables.

1   Bring a kettle of water to a boil. Put the yolks in a small bowl with 2 tablespoons water. Put this small bowl into a large saucepan and pour the boiling water into the large saucepan so that it comes halfway up the side of the bowl. Whisk the contents of the bowl and turn the heat under the saucepan to high. When the water boils, reduce the heat to low. Don't stop beating the yolks. They should foam and then thicken, taking on the consistency of cream. Use a wooden spatula to scrape the sides of the bowl well to keep the eggs from scrambling.

2   The volume of the sauce should increase by about half. If you can see the bottom of the bowl when you trace a curve with the whisk, it's time to stop cooking. Remove the bowl from the bain-marie but keep whisking until it has cooled appreciably (so you can hold your hand against it without discomfort). Whisk in salt and a dash of cayenne pepper.

3   Put the bowl on top of a folded dish towel on the counter to stabilize it. Pour a thin stream of clarified butter into the yolk mixture with a small ladle, building the sauce by whisking constantly as you would mayonnaise. Keep adding and whisking until all the butter has been incorporated.

4   You can pass the sauce through a fine strainer. If you aren't going to use it right away, keep it warm in the bain-marie, but don't put it on a burner. If the sauce goes over 125°F (60°C), the yolks will coagulate and scramble. Depending on how you will use the sauce, you can add the lemon juice or not.

4 egg yolks (page 204)
Salt
Cayenne pepper
2 sticks (½ pound/250 g.)
    butter, clarified (page 43)
Juice of ½ lemon (optional)

MOUSSELINE SAUCE

Make the hollandaise sauce and add the crème fraîche or heavy cream (lightly whipped if you like) just before serving. This sauce is especially fine with asparagus.

1 recipe hollandaise sauce
    (above)
1 tablespoon crème fraîche or
    heavy cream

MAKES   about 1 quart (1 l.)
PREPARATION   45 minutes
COOKING   3 hours 30 minutes
The marinade must be prepared one or two days in advance.

A fine sauce for game. The same day you plan to make the sauce, ask the butcher for ¾ to 1 cup (20 cl.) blood, preferably from game but pig's blood will do. Keep the blood very cold until you use it.

1   One or 2 days in advance, make the marinade: Wash the bones and let them drain. Bring the wine to a boil in a saucepan. In the meantime, heat the oil in a large saucepan over a high flame. When it is just about to smoke, use a skimmer to add the bones to the hot oil. Brown them well on all sides, turning them with a wooden spoon. When they have acquired good color, remove them with a skimmer and put them in a colander to drain.

2   When the wine boils, set it aflame with a long kitchen match. (Be sure not to do this under your hood or close to an overhead cabinet; the flames can leap very high.) When the flames have died completely, take the saucepan off the heat.

3   In the pot you used for the bones, melt the butter over low heat. Add the carrot, onions, celery, and shallots. Add a pinch of salt and cook over low heat for 10 minutes, stirring, until the vegetables have a nice color. Add the diced leek and cook 5 minutes more over low heat; do not allow them to color.

4   Stir the bones back into the pot with the vegetables. Add the bouquet garni, garlic, and 1 teaspoon juniper berries. Add the wine and turn the heat up to high, using a wooden spatula to scrape any browned bits from the bottom of the pot. As soon as you have scraped up any cooked-on juices, pour everything into a big bowl or terrine and allow to cool. Pour this marinade over the game you plan to cook so the meat is covered, cover with plastic wrap, and refrigerate for 1 or 2 days.

5   One or 2 days later, remove the meat and roast it. The marinade will serve as the base of your sauce. Pour the marinade into a large pot. Add the chicken broth. Bring to a boil and then lower the heat to a simmer. Stir in the tomato and

2 pounds (1 kg.) bones and small bits of fat from game such as boar or deer
2 bottles bold red wine such as Shiraz
⅓ cup (10 cl.) neutral oil, such as peanut or canola
1 teaspoon butter
1 large carrot, peeled and diced
2 large onions, peeled and diced
1 stalk celery, fibrous exterior removed if desired, diced
5 shallots, peeled and diced
Salt
1 leek, white part only, carefully washed and diced
1 bouquet garni (6 sprigs thyme, 4 small stalks celery, and 8 stems parsley, wrapped and tied in 2 white leek leaves)
2 cloves garlic, peeled and degermed (page 122)
1 teaspoon plus 3 juniper berries
1 quart (1 l.) chicken broth (page 77 or made from a bouillon cube)
1 tomato
1 teaspoon tomato paste

(continued)

tomato paste and simmer for 3 hours. Every so often remove grease and foam from the surface with a ladle, rinsing it in a bowl of cold water or under cold running water after each passage through the hot liquid. The bones and vegetables should always be submerged. If necessary, ladle in cold water to cover the solids and degrease.

6   After 3 hours, pass the sauce through a strainer you have placed in a bowl. Return the strained sauce to the pot by putting it through an even finer strainer (if possible, a chinois). Bring the sauce back to a boil and cook until it has reduced by one-third, still degreasing and skimming regularly.

7   As the sauce reduces, crush the 3 juniper berries in a bowl and add 1 teaspoon crushed black pepper. Put the granulated sugar and 2 tablespoons water in a saucepan and melt the sugar over low heat, stirring. Let the mixture simmer until you have a pale caramel, then add the vinegar and crushed juniper berries with crushed black pepper. Ladle 1 quart (1 l.) of the reducing sauce into the caramel and turn off the heat.

8   Put the blood in a bowl. Add a ladleful of the sauce-caramel mixture to the blood, stirring with a wooden spoon. Do the same with 2 more ladles of sauce and then pour the bowl of blood into the pot of sauce, stirring constantly.

9   Put the pot over the lowest possible heat. Heat gently and stir 15 minutes, never allowing the mixture to boil or even to simmer. (The blood will coagulate and the sauce will fall apart if it comes too near a boil.) Put the thickened sauce through a fine strainer. Taste for salt and pepper. You can put the sauce aside and reheat it later, but only over very low heat. You can also freeze it if you must keep it a little longer.

1 teaspoon crushed black
   pepper
2 tablespoons granulated sugar
¾ cup (20 cl.) red wine vinegar
¾ cup (20 cl.) blood (from
   your game if available or
   pig's blood)
Pepper

Cold Sauces

To make these sauces you will rely on a variety of oils and vinegars. There are countless oils, each appropriate for different kinds of salads and vegetables: neutral-tasting oils such as grapeseed, sunflower, corn, and peanut (be aware that some people are acutely allergic to peanuts and therefore peanut oil); and more aromatic oils such as olive, walnut, hazelnut, and rapeseed, which can be very rich.

Aromatic oils (including olive oil) are not appropriate for some sauces such as mayonnaise.

In sauces that must be refrigerated, use oils that won't solidify when chilled such as grapeseed and corn.

There are many vinegars to choose from, too: balsamic, which is very sweet; red or white wine varieties, which can be more or less acidic such as sherry vinegar from Spain; cider vinegar; or distilled.

Most commercially available balsamic vinegars have little to do with the high-quality original, which undergoes long aging in oak barrels in Modena, Italy. Commercial balsamics derive their flavor not from age but from added sugar and caramel. True balsamic can be found in specialty shops and Italian groceries. It is very expensive—the older it is, the heftier the price tag—but its flavor is so powerful that a few drops suffice.

Fleur de sel is not appropriate here, but freshly ground pepper is.

MAYONNAISE

PREPARATION 5 minutes

1 Take the egg and mustard out of the refrigerator at least 30 minutes in advance. This will facilitate emulsification and ensure a firm mayonnaise.

2 Put the yolk and mustard in a big bowl with a pinch of salt, a pinch of pepper, and a few drops of vinegar. You can put a folded dish towel under the bowl to stabilize it.

3 If you can, use an electric mixer. Its speedy beaters will help the mayonnaise come together. Hold the beaters at an angle to the bottom of the bowl; this will also facilitate emulsification. Begin to beat at the highest speed, continuing until the contents of the bowl are completely combined. With the beaters running, begin to add the oil drop by drop and then in a thin stream. Stop adding oil but keep beating. You should soon see the mayonnaise "take," that is, begin to look like thick mayonnaise and not like an oily liquid. When this happens, you can resume adding the oil in a thin stream, still beating, but never add a large amount at once. This could cause the emulsion to liquefy.

4 Taste. If the mayonnaise needs salt, do not add salt directly, for the sauce will not be able to absorb it. Instead, put a

1 egg yolk (page 204)
1 teaspoon Dijon mustard
  (optional)
Salt
White pepper
Drops of vinegar, any kind
1 cup (25 cl.) neutral oil
  (grapeseed, corn, or
  peanut, for example)

*special equipment: whisk or
  handheld electric mixer*

pinch of salt in a bowl and add a bit of vinegar, about half a teaspoon. Dissolve the salt in the vinegar and then stir it into the mayonnaise.

5   The mayonnaise will keep for a few days covered with plastic wrap in the back of the refrigerator.

TO SAVE BROKEN MAYONNAISE   If your mayonnaise falls apart—that is, if its ingredients separate instead of remaining suspended in a homogeneous emulsion—all is not lost. Leave the broken mayonnaise out at room temperature for a half hour. Beat in a half teaspoon of mustard, preferably with an electric mixer. Put a spoonful of warm water in a bowl and beat in a spoonful of the broken mayonnaise, adding it bit by bit and beating at high speed. The mixture should foam. In the same way add a second spoon of the mayonnaise, and then a third. You should see the sauce thickening and "taking." Now using a small ladle, very gradually incorporate the rest of the broken mayonnaise into the new mixture. The finished product will be perfectly smooth and firm.

GARLIC MAYONNAISE

Sauce aïoli

FOR A DISH SERVING   4–6
PREPARATION   10 minutes

For poached cod (page 270) and young spring vegetables.

1   Take the egg out of the refrigerator at least 30 minutes in advance. If you happen to have a potato that has baked at least 50 minutes in its skin, remove 1 tablespoon of its flesh and mash it well with a fork in a large bowl. (This is not required but will help the mayonnaise come together.)

2   Put the crushed garlic, yolk, and lemon juice in the bowl with a pinch of salt, a pinch of white pepper, and a dash of cayenne pepper (and the tablespoon of potato if you are using it). Use a fork to mash everything together until the mixture is homogeneous.

3   Build the sauce as you would mayonnaise. Put the bowl on a

1 egg yolk (page 204)
1 tablespoon baked potato
   (optional)
4–6 garlic cloves (4 large or
   6 small), peeled, degermed
   (page 122), and crushed
1 teaspoon lemon juice
Salt
White pepper
Cayenne pepper
1 cup (25 cl.) olive oil

*special equipment: handheld
   electric mixer*

folded dish towel for stability. Use a handheld electric mixer instead of a whisk if you can. Hold the beaters at an angle to the bottom of the bowl in order to facilitate emulsion. Begin to beat at the highest speed and continue until the contents of the bowl are completely combined. With the beaters running, begin to add the olive oil drop by drop and then in a thin stream. Stop adding oil but keep beating. You should soon see the mixture come together as a thick, consistent sauce. When this happens, you can resume adding the oil in a thin stream, still beating and never adding a large amount at once.

4   If your garlic mayonnaise remains liquid, fails to come together, or falls apart, you can rebuild it as you would mayonnaise (see page 56), adding a spoonful of mashed baked potato if you happen to have it.

MAYONNAISE WITH RED PEPPER, SAFFRON, AND GARLIC FOR BOUILLABAISSE AND FISH SOUP _____

Rouille

FOR A SOUP OR DISH SERVING   4–6
PREPARATION   10 minutes

Rouille means rust in French, and this typically Provençal sauce gets its rusty color from red pepper and saffron.

1   Take the eggs out of the refrigerator at least 30 minutes in advance. Take a potato that has baked at least 50 minutes in its skin and remove 1 tablespoon of its flesh; mash it well with a fork in a large bowl. Add the fish broth, putting it through a fine strainer lined with a paper towel. Mix in the crushed garlic, yolks, and lemon juice. Add the saffron and cayenne pepper. Do not salt; the broth should add enough salt. Thoroughly mix everything in the bowl together.

2   Build the sauce as you would mayonnaise. Put the bowl on a folded dish towel for stability. Use a handheld electric mixer instead of a whisk if you can. Hold the beaters at an angle to the bottom of the bowl in order to facilitate emulsion. Begin to beat at the highest speed, continuing until the contents of the bowl are completely combined. With the beaters run-

2 egg yolks (page 204)
1 tablespoon baked potato
2 tablespoons fish broth
4–6 cloves garlic (4 large or
    6 small), peeled, degermed
    (page 122), and crushed
1 teaspoon lemon juice
Scant ½ teaspoon saffron and
    cayenne pepper
    (½ teaspoon total, with
    slightly more saffron than
    cayenne)
1 cup (25 cl.) olive oil

*special equipment: handheld
    electric mixer*

ning, begin to add the olive oil drop by drop and then in a thin stream. Stop adding oil but keep beating. You should soon see the mixture come together as a thick, consistent sauce. When this happens, you can resume adding the oil in a thin stream, still beating, but never add a large amount at once.

3   *Rouille* comes together more readily than mayonnaise thanks to the inclusion of a bit of baked potato. If your *rouille* does not come together, however, or if it falls apart, you can save it as you would mayonnaise (see page 56) by adding another spoonful of mashed baked potato to the broken sauce at the beginning and using a tablespoon of strained warm fish broth instead of the tablespoon of warm water.

MAYONNAISE WITH TUNA AND ANCHOVIES

Mayonnaise au thon et aux anchois

PREPARATION   5 minutes

In Italy this mayonnaise is served with cold veal in the dish called *vitello tonnato* (see page 127), but it is also good with other cold meats.

1   Remove any bones from the anchovies, with tweezers if necessary. In a blender or food processor, blend the tuna, anchovies, capers, lemon juice, wine, and cooled veal drippings about 1 minute, until completely combined.

2   Add the mayonnaise and mix for 30 seconds.

2 anchovy fillets
One 6-ounce can (125 g.) oil-
     packed tuna, drained
2 tablespoons (25 g.) capers
Juice of 1 lemon
1 tablespoon dry white wine
About 3 tablespoons roast veal
     pan drippings
1 recipe mayonnaise (page 55),
     preferably made with
     grapeseed oil

*special equipment: blender or
food processor*

Vinaigrettes

Here are a few basic recipes that you can use in very simple salads. The recipes for more elaborate dressings (those including additions such as garlic and lardons, and special sauces such as rémoulade and anchoïade) suitable for more elaborate salads can be found in the Salads and Starters chapter.

These recipes make enough vinaigrette to dress salads serving four to six, but you might need more or less depending on your salad ingredients (potato salad, for instance, needs a lot of dressing). To make more or less vinaigrette, simply use more or less of the ingredients, respecting the original proportions (usually one part vinegar to three parts oil).

Salt does not dissolve in oil and therefore must be beaten into the vinegar, lemon juice, or some other ingredient such as mustard before the oil is added.

Mustardy dressings have too strong a flavor for simple green salads. But they can add something really interesting to endive or tomato salads, and the effect can be varied by using different mustards. French mustard is recommended (American mustard is much sweeter), but you can try whole-grain and herbal varieties, too.

Vinaigrettes can be prepared in advance and kept away from the light in a tightly sealed bottle.

A vinaigrette flavored with tarragon, basil, chervil, or other herbs instead of mustard can be served warm with fish that has been steamed, poached, or cooked in a packet.

VINAIGRETTE FOR GREEN SALADS _____

Vinaigrette pour salades vertes

PREPARATION   2 minutes

1   In a bowl, whisk together the vinegar and a pinch of salt. Add 2 twists of pepper from a mill and then the peanut oil. Beat until you have a homogeneous sauce.

2   Vary this dressing by using olive oil or some other flavorful oil, or a combination of neutral and flavorful oils.

1 tablespoon wine vinegar
Salt
White pepper
3 tablespoons peanut oil

SHERRY VINAIGRETTE FOR ROMAINE SALADS _____

Vinaigrette au vinaigre de xérès pour la salade romaine

1 teaspoon tarragon mustard
1 tablespoon sherry vinegar
Pepper
Salt
2 tablespoons olive oil
1 tablespoon peanut oil

PREPARATION   2 minutes

In a bowl, whisk together the mustard, vinegar, and a pinch
of salt. Add a pinch of pepper and then beat in the 2 oils.

MUSTARD VINAIGRETTE FOR TOMATO SALAD _____

Vinaigrette moutardée pour la salade de tomates

PREPARATION   2 minutes

Perfect for a salad of tomatoes, mushrooms, or artichoke
hearts.

In a bowl, whisk the mustard with a pinch of salt and a pinch
of pepper. Beating constantly, pour in the 2 oils very slowly,
little by little. When all the oil has been incorporated, beat in
the vinegar.

1 level tablespoon Dijon
    mustard
Salt
Pepper
2 tablespoons peanut oil
1 tablespoon olive oil
1 tablespoon wine vinegar

WALNUT VINAIGRETTE FOR ENDIVE SALAD _____

Vinaigrette aux noix pour la salade d'endives

PREPARATION   2 minutes

In a bowl, whisk together the vinegar and mustard with a
pinch of salt and a pinch of pepper. Add the oil, whisking
constantly, and then the nuts.

1 tablespoon champagne
    vinegar
1 level teaspoon mustard
Salt
Pepper
3 tablespoons neutral oil
2–3 tablespoons chopped
    walnuts

RASPBERRY VINAIGRETTE FOR MÂCHE

Vinaigrette au vinaigre de framboise pour la salade de mâche

PREPARATION 2 minutes

In a bowl, whisk together the vinegar and a pinch of salt.
Add a pinch of pepper and then beat in the hazelnut oil.

1 tablespoon raspberry vinegar
Salt
Pepper
3 tablespoons hazelnut oil

Lemony Salad Dressings

LEMON DRESSING FOR GRATED CARROT SALAD

Citronnette pour les carottes râpées

PREPARATION 2 minutes

In a bowl, whisk together the lemon juice and a pinch of salt.
Add a pinch of pepper and then beat in the 2 oils.

Juice of 1 lemon, freshly
  squeezed
Salt
Pepper
2 tablespoons olive oil
1 tablespoon peanut oil

CREAMY LEMON DRESSING FOR CUCUMBERS, CELERY, OR GREEN BEANS

Citronnette à la crème ou au yaourt

PREPARATION 2 minutes

In a bowl, whisk together the lemon juice and a pinch of salt.
Add a pinch of pepper and then beat in the 2 oils and mustard, if using. Add the crème fraîche, yogurt, or both and beat
until the dressing is homogeneous.

Juice of 1 lemon, freshly
  squeezed
Salt
Pepper
2 tablespoons olive oil
1 tablespoon peanut oil
1 teaspoon French mustard
  (optional)
Choice of 2 tablespoons crème
  fraîche, 2 tablespoons
  Greek (strained) yogurt, or
  1 tablespoon crème fraîche
  plus 1 tablespoon yogurt

LEMON-WALNUT DRESSING FOR BEET SALAD

Citronnette à l'huile de noix pour la salade de betterave

PREPARATION   2 minutes

In a bowl, whisk together the lemon juice and a pinch of salt. Add a pinch of pepper and then beat in the walnut oil. If you like, add shallot and parsley when you dress beets with this citronnette.

Juice of 1 lemon, freshly
 squeezed
Salt
Pepper
3 tablespoons walnut oil
Minced shallot and parsley
 (optional)

Hotpots, Soups, and Potages

S oup is an ancient food. It can truly be a feast in a bowl, containing not only broth but also meat, game, fowl, or fish, as well as many and varied vegetables. Chicken in a pot and pot roast bear witness to the possibilities. In some cultures, including many in Asia, soup is not just a dish or a course but a complete meal.

In France in the Middle Ages, *soupe* meant bread that had been soaked in broth, as in the present-day *sop*. By extension it came to mean the soaking substance itself, in all its many forms.

At the beginning of the nineteenth century, the current system for classifying soups in France came into use. *Soupe* is the generic term. Although *soupe* and *potage* are often used interchangably, *potage* is most often a vegetable soup in which the vegetables have either been puréed or cut into small pieces. The more refined cream soups and veloutés are potages that have been thickened with cream or egg. Bisques are cream soups prepared with crustaceans.

A hotpot, such as pot-au-feu, is a very basic soup made with a piece of meat, some vegetables, and water. The water becomes broth, and the meat and vegetables become a delicious meal. The broth from a hotpot is often saved and used in other recipes.

Broth (*bouillon*) refers to the liquid element of soup. Consommé is a broth that has been clarified—degreased and left completely clear. It is a complex and outmoded preparation; nevertheless, instructions are given here for those who are really keen to try it.

There are also cold soups made of cooked or raw vegetables.

Certain hearty soups, the kind you can really make a meal of, are the pride of their regions of origin. For these dishes see the chapter on French regional specialties.

Hotpots and Broths

Pot-au-Feu

CHOOSING THE MEAT

You must ask the butcher for a very fresh piece of meat, the opposite of what you would want for roasting, grilling, or frying. Shank, brisket, or bottom round is best. For more flavor you can add some ribs, tail, shoulder, or bottom chuck roast.

BLANCHING THE MEAT

Pot-au-feu must cook slowly and gently to keep the broth relatively clear. It should never boil, achieving instead just a shivery simmer. Some cooks say that the broth "smiles."

One of the secrets to clear broth is to blanch the meat quickly before the long cooking. Put the meat into a large pot or saucepan, cover it with cold water, bring the water to a boil as quickly as possible, and boil for 5 minutes. Use a skimmer to lift the meat out of the broth and into a colander and rinse it under the tap. (Do not just dump the meat and water from the pot into the colander; if you do this, the meat will be coated with coagulant proteins and other impurities at the bottom of the pot.) Dispose of the cooking water and wash the saucepan with hot water before using it again.

Do not salt the water when you begin your pot-au-feu; salt draws out impurities. Add salt only after the water begins to bubble.

SKIMMING AND DEGREASING

Once it is cooking, the pot-au-feu must be regularly skimmed. Lift scummy foam from the surface of the broth with a skimmer, which you should rinse in a bowl of cold water after each pass. To facilitate skimming, carefully move your stockpot or saucepan a little away from the center of the burner so that the liquid bubbles on one side only. The scum gathering on the tranquil side will be easy to remove.

You must also degrease as it cooks. Gently pour a ladleful of cold water all over the surface of the simmering liquid. The fat will come to the surface; remove it with the ladle or a large spoon.

When the meat has finished cooking, what little fat remains should be removed with a large ladle even if it means losing some of the broth. You can use the fatty broth to cook the marrow bone in a separate pot.

COOKING THE MARROW BONE

The marrow bone should be prepared in advance but cooked at the very end. To prepare it, put it in a container and cover with cold salted water (1 tablespoon of salt for every quart/liter of water). Refrigerate overnight or for at least eight hours; this will purge the bone of blood, which lends the dish an unpleasant taste and color.

Just before you sit down to eat, as the pot-au-feu is reheating, cook the bone by putting it in a small saucepan and covering it with fatty broth. Simmer for 15 minutes. Serve the piping hot marrow right away with fleur de sel, freshly ground pepper, and grilled country bread.

CARAMELIZING THE ONIONS

Before putting the onions into the pot-au-feu, cut them in half horizontally and put them cut face down in a nonstick skillet over medium heat. Let them color for 4–5 minutes, until they are golden and caramelized. They will give the broth color and flavor. Stick a whole clove into each caramelized onion.

MAKING THE BOUQUET GARNI

The little bundle of herbs called the bouquet garni is an essential ingredient in many sautées and soups, including pot-au-feu and chicken in a pot. Traditionally, it is made up of a bay leaf, thyme (preferably fresh), flat-leaf parsley, and other aromatic herbs. Rinse the herbs in running water to get rid of any dirt that might otherwise find its way into your broth. Since these herbs will not be eaten, they should be tied into a little bouquet that will be easy to find and remove at the end of cooking. Nevertheless, some little thyme leaves always come loose in the broth. To avoid this, wrap the bouquet in two leek leaves and tie the whole thing with kitchen twine.

VARYING THE VEGETABLES

All kinds of vegetables can mingle happily in the classic pot-au-feu. Just make sure you know how (and for how long) to cook them. Some must be cooked separately, since they would otherwise give the dish an inappropriate taste, color, or consistency. This is true of cabbage, which must be blanched in boiling water and then cooked separately from the pot-au-feu in a bit of its broth. Potatoes must also be cooked separately in a pot of water, for if they are cooked in the pot-au-feu, they will disintegrate slightly and cloud the broth.

If the vegetables you are using will cook at different rates, you can wrap each kind in its own clean, well-knotted dish towel or in large squares of gauze (which can be bought from a drugstore). This way you can remove each vegetable when it has finished cooking without disturbing the others. Keep the vegetables warm in some broth in a covered saucepan until it is time to serve them.

WHAT ABOUT TURNIPS?

It is best to forgo turnips, a taste that puts some people off. They also go bad quickly, making your broth spoil faster than it otherwise would. If you must have them, choose the young small ones, and don't use too many. Parsnips are a good substitute. They are one of those old-fashioned vegetables we've lately rediscovered, which are always good in a pot-au-feu even though they must be cooked separately.

The excellence of pot-au-feu derives in large part from the abundant variety of meats it can offer. In addition to the basic recipe, here you will find a pot-au-feu with five meats, one truly for a special occasion. In a broth, the possible variations in terms of mixing meat and flavors are virtually limitless; you can mix beef and a roasting chicken, pork breast, veal shin, or slices of duck breast. You can even poach a foie gras or cook a leg of lamb.

STORING AND DEGREASING WHILE CHILLED

A pot-au-feu is always better the next day. Overnight it becomes tastier, and once it has been chilled, it can be completely degreased.

Put the broth and meat in a closed container and refrigerate. Put the vegetables in a separate container without broth. (Keeping the meat in the broth will prevent it from drying out; storing the vegetables dry will prevent them from getting soggy.) The next day it will be very easy for you to spoon away all the fat, solidified in a yellow layer on top of the broth. If necessary, you can dab the surface of the broth with paper towels to remove any remaining grease.

DEGREASING A HOT POT-AU-FEU

If you plan to eat the pot-au-feu without letting it sit overnight in the refrigerator, you can degrease it while it is hot, although the result will not be as close to perfect.

Let the pot-au-feu cool as long as possible, perhaps even adding a glass of cold water. Pour the broth through a fine strainer (a chinois if possible) into a tall container with straight sides. The fat should rise to the surface. Use a ladle to remove the layer of fat; after each pass, rinse the ladle under a cold tap or in a bowl of cold water. When the fat seems to be gone, lay a paper towel on the surface of the broth to absorb the remaining surface fat. Throw it away and repeat with several clean paper towels.

CLASSIC POT-AU-FEU

Pot-au-feu classique

SERVES 8
PREPARATION 30 minutes
COOKING 3½ hours

Pot-au-feu is best cooked the day before you plan to eat it. The broth produced by this recipe is a good basic beef broth. You can enjoy some with the meat and vegetables and save some for other uses. Ask the butcher to remove the fat and to tie the meat neatly. If you choose to use a beef roast so that you will have some meat to serve rare, ask for a sirloin tip, prepared and tied like a roast.

1 Put the meat in a large saucepan and cover it with unsalted water. Bring the liquid to a boil. Prepare a skimmer and a small ladle or large spoon and a bowl half full of water. When the pot begins to boil, turn off the heat. Skim the greasy foam from the surface of the liquid, rinsing the skimmer in the bowl after each pass.

2 Lift the meat out of the liquid with the clean skimmer and put it in a colander. Rinse it under running water and leave it to drain. Dispose of the cooking water and clean the saucepan.

3 Wash and peel the vegetables. You can leave them whole or cut them into chunks. Cut the onions in half. Heat a skillet over high heat. Put the onions cut side down in the skillet. Lower the heat to medium and cook for 4 to 5 minutes without allowing them to burn. They should caramelize but not blacken. Place the cloves in 1 onion half.

4 Put the carrots, celery, turnips, bouquet garni, garlic, and meat in the saucepan. Add 4 quarts (4 l.) water but do not salt. Bring to a boil and then lower the heat so that a bare simmer is maintained. Skim the broth. Add 2 tablespoons coarse salt and 8 peppercorns. Cook uncovered over gentle heat for 3 hours, never allowing the broth to bubble vigorously.

5 If you wish to eat the broth vegetables with your pot-au-feu, remove them with a skimmer after 30 or 40 minutes, depending on whether you prefer them more or less tender.

4 pounds (2 kg.) beef for pot-au-feu (shank, rump pot roast, bottom round, brisket, flank, oxtail, chuck pot roast, etc.)

4 medium leeks, white parts only (but save 2 green leaves for the bouquet garni)

2 medium onions

3 whole cloves

8 carrots

2 stalks celery, not too green, or, depending on the season, 5 ounces (150 g.) celery root

4 small turnips (optional; see page 66)

1 bouquet garni (2 sprigs fresh thyme and 10 branches parsley wrapped and tied in a leek leaf)

2 cloves garlic

Coarse salt

Peppercorns

½ ounce (10 g.) peeled gingerroot (optional)

Salt

Fleur de sel

Marrow bones (optional; 1 will serve about 2 people)

2 pounds (1 kg.) sirloin tip (optional), tied like a roast

Cool them in ice water to prevent further cooking and drain. If you are serving a big crowd, you can cook more vegetables separately, perhaps using some of the pot-au-feu broth.

6   Every half hour, add a small ladle or large spoon of cold water to the broth to bring the fat to the surface. Remove the fat with the ladle, rinsing it in the bowl of water after each pass.

7   If you are using the optional ginger, cut it into thin strips and add it to the broth 30 minutes before the end.

8   Remove the pot from the heat and put it on a wire rack to speed its cooling. Taste the broth and add salt if necessary. Remove the meat (and, if they are still there, the vegetables) with a skimmer. When the broth reaches room temperature, put it through a fine strainer.

9   STORING, DEGREASING, AND REHEATING THE POT-AU-FEU Put the broth and meat in a closed container in the refrigerator. Put the vegetables in a separate closed container in the refrigerator. The next day it will be very easy for you to spoon off the solid yellow fat layer on top.

10 When ready to serve, bring the broth containing the meat to a boil and simmer for 5 minutes. Carefully add the vegetables and simmer 5 minutes more. Serve with coarse salt or fleur de sel and the condiments. You can slice the meat and bring it to the table on a platter with the tureen on the side, or you can bring out the meat still in the cooking broth, and carve at the table.

THE MARROW BONE   If you like, add one or more marrow bones.

The night before you plan to eat the pot-au-feu, put the marrow bone in a bowl and cover it with 1 quart (1 l.) cold water, adding 1 tablespoon salt. Refrigerate overnight.

The next day, as the pot-au-feu reheats, put the marrow bone in a small saucepan. Carefully pour a ladle of cold water over the surface of the pot-au-feu. Ladle fatty broth from the surface of the pot-au-feu into the small saucepan until the bone is covered. Simmer for 10 minutes. Serve the marrow very hot, sprinkled with fleur de sel or coarse salt and freshly ground pepper, with toasted country bread on the side.

THE BEEF ROAST   If you are serving a beef roast with your pot-au-feu, begin by reheating the pot-au-feu. When the

Condiments for pot-au-feu: mustard, horseradish, cornichons, pickled onions, etc.

broth begins to bubble, submerge the roast in the hot liquid. Turn up the heat to bring the liquid back to a boil. When it begins to bubble again, lower the heat so that the liquid is simmering. Cook for 10 minutes. Add the vegetables in the pot the last 5 minutes.

OXTAIL POT-AU-FEU

Pot-au-feu de queue de boeuf

SERVES   6

PREPARATION   30 minutes

COOKING   5 hours

Like classic pot-au-feu, this is best made a day in advance.

1   If you are using the marrow bones, the night before you plan to eat the pot-au-feu (or at least 8 hours in advance) put the bones in a container and add 1 quart (1 l.) water or more if necessary to cover completely. Add 1 tablespoon salt, which will draw the blood from the bone. Cover and refrigerate overnight.

2   Put the oxtails in a saucepan and cover them with cold water. Bring the liquid to a boil as quickly as possible and boil for 5 minutes. With a strainer, lift the oxtails from the liquid and put them in a colander. Rinse it in cold water. Dispose of the cooking water and clean the saucepan.

3   Put the oxtails in the saucepan and cover them generously with cold water. Heat until the liquid is almost at the boiling point but do not allow it to bubble; keep it at a bare simmer. Skim the broth as soon as scum appears on its surface.

4   Cut the onions in half horizontally and put them cut side down in a nonstick skillet over medium heat. Allow them to color for 4–5 minutes, until they are golden and caramelized. Press a whole clove into each of 3 of the halves.

5   Add the onions, bouquet garni, and garlic to the broth. Add 1 tablespoon coarse salt and the teaspoon of peppercorns (preferably tied in a small gauze sack). Simmer for 4 hours, skimming every half hour. Pour a small ladle of cold water

4 marrow bones (optional)

Salt

2½ pounds (1.3 kg.) oxtails, chopped into 4-inch pieces and tied up (ask the butcher to do this)

3 onions

3 whole cloves

1 bouquet garni (3 sprigs fresh thyme and 10 branches flat-leaf parsley, wrapped and tied in a green leek leaf)

1 clove garlic

Coarse salt

1 teaspoon peppercorns

6 leeks

6 carrots

2 parsnips

2 stalks celery

½ ounce (10 g.) peeled gingerroot

Pepper

gently over the surface of the simmering broth and use the ladle to remove the liquid fat that rises to the surface. Rinse the skimmer and ladle in cold water after each pass, under the cold tap or in a bowl of water you've prepared for this purpose.

6   While the meat simmers, wash and trim the leeks, carrots, parsnips, and celery. Tie the leeks in a bunch. Cut the ginger-root into small strips.

7   When 4 hours have passed, add the carrots and celery to the broth. Add the leeks, parsnips, and ginger 15 minutes later. Continue to simmer for 45 minutes, skimming and degreasing as before. Taste for salt and pepper.

8   If you are using the marrow bones: 15 minutes before serving the pot-au-feu, gently pour a ladle of cold water over its surface. Spoon some of the fat that rises along with some broth into a small saucepan holding the marrow bones. Keep spooning until the bones are covered with broth and then simmer for 15 minutes.

9   When the pot-au-feu is done, remove and discard the bouquet garni and the little sack of pepper. Arrange the meat on a platter, surrounded by the marrow bones if you are having them. Carefully remove the vegetables from the broth with the skimmer. Remove the twine tying the leeks together and arrange the vegetables on another platter. Fill a tureen with the broth. Serve with pot-au-feu condiments.

Pot-au-feu condiments (coarse salt, cornichons, pickled onions, mustard, etc.)

FIVE-MEAT POT-AU-FEU

Pot-au-feu aux cinq viandes

SERVES   24
PREPARATION   1 hour
COOKING   4½ hours
RESTING   1 hour

This five-meat pot-au-feu is obviously best saved for a celebration, if only on account of the number it serves!

1   The night before you plan to eat the pot-au-feu (or at least 8 hours in advance), put the marrow bones in a container filled with lightly salted cold water, to purge the bones of blood. Refrigerate.

2   To begin cooking the pot-au-feu, put all the meat in a large saucepan and cover it with cold water. (You can do this to all the meat at once, or you can do one meat at a time.) Bring the pot to a boil quickly and boil for 5 minutes. Remove the meat from the liquid with a skimmer, put it in a colander, and rinse under cold water. Put the colander aside so the meat can drain. Dispose of the cooking water and wash the pot. (If you are blanching the meat in batches, use fresh cooking water and a clean pot for each batch.)

3   Put the beef in the Dutch oven and cover it with 2½ gallons (9 l.) cold water. Heat the water until it is just about to boil, then keep it at a bare simmer.

4   Use a skimmer to remove the surface foam and degrease every 30 minutes by carefully pouring a small ladle of cold water over the surface of the broth and removing the fat that rises to the surface. Be sure to skim after the introduction of each new meat.

5   Cut the onions in half horizontally and put them cut side down in a nonstick skillet over medium heat. Let them color for 4–5 minutes, until golden and caramelized; they will infuse the broth with color and flavor. Press the whole cloves into the onion halves.

6   Tie up the garlic and peppercorns in a small gauze sack.

7   When the pot of meat comes to a simmer, add the onions, bouquet garni, and sack of garlic and peppercorns. Add 3 tablespoons coarse salt and half-cover the pot to prevent

12 small marrow bones

MEATS
3 pounds (1.5 kg.) beef, bottom round or brisket
2½ pounds (1.2 kg.) veal shin
2½ pounds (1.2 kg.) leg of lamb, boned
1 duck
1 roasting chicken

AROMATICS
3 medium onions
6 whole cloves
5 cloves garlic, peeled and degermed (page 122)
5 teaspoons peppercorns
1 large bouquet garni (5 sprigs thyme, 2 branches celery, and 20 parsley branches, wrapped and tied in green leek leaves)
Coarse salt

VEGETABLES, WASHED, PEELED, AND TRIMMED
24 small carrots
12 stalks celery, cut into small sticks
24 slender leeks
12 small parsnips

1½ ounces (50 g.) fresh gingerroot, peeled and cut into fine strips
Salt
Pepper

excessive evaporation. Keep the pot simmering gently; do not allow it to boil.

8 When the beef and aromatics have been cooking for 2 hours, add the carrots and celery. Add the leeks and parsnips 15 minutes later. After 45 minutes, remove the vegetables and put them in a saucepan. Cover them with broth from the big pot.

9 Add the veal and lamb and simmer for 45 minutes. Add the duck, chicken, and ginger. Simmer 45 minutes more; the pot should be half-covered.

10 Taste and add salt and pepper if necessary. Off heat, leave the meat in the broth for 30 minutes to an hour. While it rests, remove fat from its surface with a ladle and cold water. Remove as much fat as possible even if it means removing some broth as well. Save this fatty broth for cooking the marrow bones.

11 Put the marrow bones in a saucepan and cover them with the fatty broth. Simmer for 15 minutes.

12 While the marrow bones cook, reheat the meat and vegetables.

13 Arrange everything on platters and serve as soon as possible, covering the meats with a few ladles of broth. Set a tureen of broth and all the condiments on the side.

CONDIMENTS

Fleur de sel
Cornichons
Onions preserved in vinegar
Various mustards
Horseradish

special equipment: very large Dutch oven or stew pot, $12\frac{1}{2}$ quarts or larger

Poule au Pot

STUFFED CHICKEN IN A POT
Poule au pot farcie

SERVES 6
PREPARATION 30 minutes
COOKING 1½ hours

The chicken must be stuffed at least 3 hours in advance of cooking or even, if possible, the night before.

Ask the butcher for a chicken that is ready to cook but includes its giblets (gizzard, liver, heart, neck, and wing tips).

1   Cut the crusts from the bread. Pour the milk in a bowl and crumble the bread into it with your hands. Leave it to soak.

2   Rinse the liver and heart of the chicken (save the gizzard for cooking). Cut them and the ham into small pieces, about ½ inch (1 cm.). Put them in a bowl.

3   Pour the soaking bread into a strainer. Use a big spoon to extract as much milk as possible from it. Add the drained bread to the bowl with the giblets and ham.

4   Rinse the parsley, remove its leaves, and mince them. Peel and mince the garlic. Add the parsley and garlic to the bowl. Break the eggs into a separate bowl, whisk them until they are homogeneous and frothy, and pour them into the big bowl. Add 2 pinches of salt, 2 pinches of grated nutmeg, and 2 pinches of pepper. Mix well with a spoon until you have a homogeneous stuffing.

5   Season the inside of the chicken with salt and pepper. Stuff it with the stuffing, carefully sew up its openings, and truss it (see page 453). Refrigerate the chicken for at least 3 hours, or overnight if possible, so that the stuffing has time to lend it flavor.

6   When you are ready to cook, put the chicken in a big pot. Cover it with 3 quarts (3 l.) cold water or more if necessary to cover the chicken completely. Add the gizzard, neck, and wing tips, and bring to a boil. Simmer over low heat, periodically skimming foam from the surface and rinsing the skimmer after each pass.

4 ounces (100 g.) white sandwich bread
⅓ cup (10 cl.) milk
1 chicken, about 5 pounds (2.5 kg.)
6 ounces (200 g.) cured, uncooked ham
1 bunch flat-leaf parsley
4 cloves garlic
2 eggs
Salt
Grated nutmeg
Pepper
1 bouquet garni (1 bay leaf, 1 sprig fresh thyme, and 6 branches flat-leaf parsley, wrapped and tied in a leek leaf)
2 medium onions
4 whole cloves
Coarse salt
Peppercorns
6 firm-fleshed potatoes— BF 15, if available, or fingerling or Yukon Gold
6 medium carrots
6 medium turnips
2 stalks from the heart of a bunch of celery
6 small leeks
1 green cabbage

7   Rinse the bouquet garni. Peel the onions and press a whole clove into each one. Use the skimmer to place them carefully in the simmering liquid. Add 4 tablespoons coarse salt and 10 peppercorns and simmer for 1 hour.

8   While the chicken simmers, wash and peel the potatoes, carrots, and turnips. Wash the celery and cut it into thirds. Trim the leeks and wash them carefully in warm water. Remove the outer leaves of the cabbage; pull off the rest of the leaves and rinse them.

9   Bring 1 quart (1 l.) water and 1 teaspoon coarse salt to a boil in a pot. Add the cabbage and boil for 5 minutes. Remove the cabbage with a skimmer and leave to drain in a colander after rinsing under cold water to cool.

10   Put the cabbage leaves in a clean dish towel. Mold 6 little cabbage balls, compressing them in the towel to wring out as much water as possible. Arrange the cabbage balls in a small skillet or saucepan, just big enough that they are all pressed against each other.

11   When the chicken has cooked for 1 hour, add to it the carrots, turnips, and celery. Simmer 30 minutes more. As it simmers, use a ladle to pour hot broth into the small pan until the cabbage balls are covered. Cover and cook over low heat for 30 minutes.

12   Put the potatoes in a saucepan and cover them with cold water. Add 1 teaspoon coarse salt, cover, and bring to a boil. Simmer over low heat for 25 minutes.

13   Remove the chicken from the pot and put it in a colander to drain. Carve it (page 454). Carve the stuffing into slices. Arrange the pieces of chicken and slices of stuffing on a big platter, surrounded by the vegetables (or put the vegetables on another plate).

14   Degrease the broth and strain it into a tureen.

Traditionally, the cabbage balls are stuffed with some of the chicken's stuffing. If you choose to do this, cook the stuffed balls in 2 tablespoons butter in a skillet for 5 minutes before you cover them with broth and simmer for 30 minutes.

STEWED CHICKEN

Poule pochée

SERVES 4–6

PREPARATION 25 minutes

COOKING 50 minutes to 1 hour depending on size

Like pot-au-feu, chicken in a pot is best made the night before you want to eat it.

If you get the chicken dressed from a butcher, tell him you need the giblets (neck, liver, heart, gizzard, and wing tips).

1   Wash, trim, and peel the vegetables. Press the cloves in one of the onions. Next to the stovetop place a bowl half filled with water, a skimmer, and a small ladle or large spoon.

2   Put the chicken and giblets in a large pot and cover with unsalted water. Bring the water to a simmer and reduce the heat to low. Skim the foam from the surface, rinsing the skimmer after each passage.

3   With the skimmer, add the vegetables and bouquet garni to the pot, being careful not to splash yourself with boiling water. Add the white peppercorns, bouillon cube, and 4 table-spoons coarse salt.

4   Simmer uncovered over low heat for 40 minutes if the chicken is less than 4 pounds (2 kg.) or 50 minutes if it is larger. Do not allow the broth to boil, or it will turn cloudy and produce lots of foam.

5   Turn off the heat. Put the pot on a rack or open trivet to facilitate cooling. After 5 or 10 minutes, carefully remove the chicken from the broth with the skimmer and a big fork. Once you have a secure grip on the chicken, hold it over the pot for a few seconds to drain off most of the broth. Put it aside on a cutting board. Taste the broth and add salt if necessary.

6   Make sure that the chicken is cooked by inserting the tip of a knife at the thigh joint and pressing the chicken with the back of a fork. The juices that run out should be clear; if you see traces of blood, the chicken is not fully cooked and must be put back in the pot to simmer some more, another 10 minutes or so. If the chicken will not be served immediately, put it back in the broth so that it does not dry out.

2 medium leeks, white parts only (reserve 2 green leaves for bouquet garni)

4 medium carrots

2 stalks celery, not too green; or, depending on the season, ¼ pound (150 g.) celery root

2 medium onions

3 whole cloves

1 chicken, about 3 pounds (1.6 kg.) that serves 4; 5 pounds (2.4 kg.) serves 6, including giblets

1 bouquet garni (3 sprigs thyme and 10 branches parsley, wrapped and tied in 2 green leek leaves)

8 white peppercorns

1 bouillon cube

Coarse salt

Salt

7   If you wish to degrease the broth, see the general instructions for pot-au-feu (page 67). Unlike beef fat, chicken fat does not solidify completely when chilled, but after a night in the refrigerator, the broth from chicken in a pot will develop a yellow layer of liquid fat that will be easy to remove with a ladle or spoon. Use a paper towel to remove the remaining traces of fat from the surface once the yellow layer has been discarded.

CHICKEN BROTH
Bouillon de volaille

SERVES   6
PREPARATION   15 minutes
COOKING   1½ hours

1   Wash, trim, and peel the vegetables. Press the clove into the onion. Next to the stovetop place a bowl half filled with water, a skimmer, and a small ladle or large spoon.

2   Put the chicken parts in the saucepan and cover them with unsalted water. Turn the heat to high. When the water comes to a boil, turn off the heat. Skim the surface foam, rinsing the skimmer after each pass.

3   Remove the chicken parts with the skimmer and put them in a colander. (Do not dump the chicken straight from the pot into the colander, as this will coat the chicken with albumen and other impurities.) Rinse the meat under running water and set it aside to drain. Discard the cooking water and wash the saucepan.

4   Put the chicken back in the pot. Add the vegetables and bouquet garni. Add 2 quarts (2 l.) water, 1 tablespoon coarse salt, and 6 white peppercorns. Bring to a boil, then lower the heat so that the broth simmers gently. Do not allow it to bubble vigorously.

5   After 30 minutes, pour a small ladle or large spoon of cold water over the surface of the broth to bring the fat to the surface. Spoon away the fat and foam, rinsing the ladle or spoon after each pass.

6   If you wish to eat the broth vegetables, remove them with a

2 medium carrots
1 medium leek, white parts only (save 2 green leaves for the bouquet garni)
1 branch celery, not too green, or, depending on the season, 2 ounces (50 g.) celery root
1 medium onion
1 whole clove
1½ pounds (750 g.) chicken parts (wing tips, necks, giblets, and feet, for example)
1 bouquet garni (1 sprig thyme and 6 branches parsley, wrapped and tied in 2 green leek leaves)
Coarse salt
6 white peppercorns
Salt

skimmer after 30–40 minutes, depending on the degree to which you like them cooked. Put them in a colander, rinse under running water, and set them aside to drain. If you do not plan to eat the vegetables (or if you like your vegetables extremely soft), you can leave them in the broth for the entire cooking time.

7   The broth should simmer gently for 1¼ hours total. Degrease with a ladle of cold water and skim the foam every 30 minutes. At the end, taste and add salt if necessary. Put the pot on a rack to encourage it to cool. When the broth has cooled a bit, put it through a fine strainer.

8   To degrease the broth immediately, see the instructions on page 67. Chicken fat does not solidify when chilled the way beef fat does, but if you refrigerate chicken broth overnight, its fat will gather at the surface in a liquid yellow layer and will be very easy to remove with a ladle or spoon. Any fatty deposits left on the surface can be removed with paper towels.

Consommés

Consommés are broths that are completely unclouded because they have been "clarified." Clarification is a rather long and painstaking process. It makes the broth more attractive, but it also robs it of some flavor—and so meat is often added to consommés. In clarification, egg whites draw the impurities out of the broth. The more egg whites you use, the easier it is, but the more flavor is lost as well.

BEEF CONSOMMÉ _____

Consommé de boeuf

SERVES   6–8

PREPARATION   20 minutes

COOKING   35 minutes without ground beef or 1¼ hours
            with ground beef

COOLING AND STRAINING   1¼ to 2 hours

Ask the butcher for his leanest ground beef. This isn't
obligatory but will result in a tastier broth.

1   Wash, peel, and trim the leek, carrot, celery, and tomato. Dice
    them very fine with a knife or in a food processor. Put the
    ground beef, egg whites, and vegetables (but not the chervil)
    in a bowl. Add ⅓ cup cold water and 5 ice cubes to the bowl.
    Blend with an electric wand mixer (or, if you don't have a
    wand mixer, use a whisk or food processor). The mixture
    should foam a bit.

2   Bring the broth to a boil in a saucepan. Ladle one-third of the
    hot broth into the bowl with the meat-egg mixture, stirring
    energetically to keep the egg whites from cooking right
    away. Pour this mixture into the bubbling saucepan of broth.
    Whisk for a few minutes to mix well and bring the broth
    back to a simmer. Scrape the bottom and sides of the pot well
    with a wooden spatula to keep the egg whites from sticking;
    they could accumulate and burn.

3   When it begins to bubble again, you should be able to see that
    the broth is becoming very clear. Stop stirring and lower the
    heat so that the broth simmers only very lightly. Make a little
    hole in the center of the matter gathering and coagulating on
    the broth's surface, a "chimney" for the clarifying liquid.

4   Every 5 minutes, draw some broth through the hole in the
    middle with a ladle and sprinkle it all over the surface.

5   If you are not using ground beef, after 20 minutes add the
    crushed peppercorns and chervil. Cook 10 minutes more.

6   If you are using ground beef, add the crushed peppercorns
    and chervil after 50 minutes. Simmer 10 minutes more, con-
    tinuing to sprinkle the surface with broth every 5 minutes.

7   At the end of cooking, put the saucepan on a rack to encour-
    age cooling. Allow the broth to cool for at least 1 hour or

1 small leek

1 carrot

½ stalk celery

1 peeled tomato

½ pound (250 g.) lean ground
    beef (optional)

2 egg whites (page 204)

Broth from 1 recipe pot-au-feu
    (page 68), degreased
    (about 8 cups)

4 peppercorns, crushed

2 sprigs chervil

even 2 if possible. As it rests it will continue to become clear and recover flavor.

8   Rinse a clean dish towel (not terry cloth and as lint free as possible) for 3 minutes under running water to rid it of any traces of detergent. Use it to line a fine strainer, and place the strainer in a large bowl or saucepan. Remove the coagulated cap from the broth extremely gently so as not to disturb the broth underneath. Ladle the broth through the strainer. Do not dump the broth through the strainer all at once.

9   The resulting consommé should be clear. If traces of fat remain on its surface, you can remove them with a paper towel.

CHICKEN CONSOMMÉ

Consommé de volaille

SERVES   6
PREPARATION   20 minutes
BLANCHING (IF USING CHICKEN PARTS)   10 minutes
COOKING   1 hour with chicken parts or 30 minutes without chicken parts
COOLING AND STRAINING   1¼ to 2¼ hours

1 carrot
1 small leek
½ stalk celery
⅔ pound (300 g.) chicken wing tips, necks, and feet (optional; do not use giblets such as heart and gizzard for this purpose)
Broth from 1 recipe Stewed Chicken (page 76), degreased, or 1 recipe chicken broth made with wings (page 77), degreased; about 8 cups
2 egg whites (page 204) (if you are not using extra chicken parts) or 3 egg whites (page 204) (if you are using extra chicken parts)
2 sprigs chervil
4 peppercorns, crushed

Ask the butcher for some chicken wing tips, necks, and feet, well chopped up. This isn't obligatory but will result in a tastier broth.

1   Wash, peel, and trim the vegetables. Cut them into very fine dice or dice them in a food processor.

2   If you are using extra chicken parts and they have not been chopped up by the butcher, use a large knife or poultry shears to cut them into small pieces. Put the pieces in a saucepan and cover them with unsalted water. Bring the liquid quickly to a boil and then turn off the heat and remove the chicken pieces with a skimmer. Put them in a colander, rinse them under running water, and allow them to drain. (Do not dump the chicken pieces from the pot into the colander; the liquid will coat them with albumen if you do so.)

3   Crush 4 ice cubes in a large bowl. Add the minced vegetables, chicken pieces, ⅓ cup water, and egg whites. Mix well with a whisk until the combination becomes foamy.

4   In a clean saucepan, bring the broth to a boil. Use a ladle to add one-third of the hot broth to the mixture in the bowl, stirring briskly to keep the egg whites from cooking. Pour the chicken-vegetable-broth mixture into the simmering saucepan, whisking for a minute or two to make sure everything is well combined. Bring the broth back to a simmer. Stir with a wooden spatula, scraping the bottom and sides of the pot well to prevent the egg whites from sticking; they could accumulate and burn.

5   When it begins to bubble again, you should be able to see that the broth is becoming very clear. Stop stirring and lower the heat so that the broth simmers only very lightly. Make a little hole in the center of the matter gathering and coagulating on the broth's surface, a "chimney" for the clarifying liquid. Do not allow the chimney to close up, and keep the simmer gentle.

6   Every 5 minutes, with a ladle remove some broth through the hole in the middle and sprinkle it all over the surface.

7   If you are not using extra chicken parts: After 10 minutes, add the chervil and crushed peppercorns. Cook 10 minutes more.

8   If you are using extra chicken parts: After 40 minutes, add the chervil and crushed peppercorns. Simmer 10 minutes more, continuing to sprinkle the surface with broth every 5 minutes.

9   At the end of cooking, put the saucepan on a rack to encourage cooling. Allow the broth to cool for at least 1 hour, or even 2 if possible. As it rests it will continue to become clear and recover flavor.

10 Take a clean dish towel (not terry cloth and as lint free as possible) and rinse it for 3 minutes under running water to rid it of any traces of detergent. Use it to line a fine strainer and place the strainer in a large bowl or saucepan. Remove the coagulated cap from the broth extremely gently so as not to disturb the broth underneath. Ladle the broth through the strainer. Do not dump the broth through the strainer all at once.

11 The resulting consommé should be clear. If traces of fat remain on the surface, you can remove them with a paper towel.

Potage

*P*otage is a French word for vegetable soup. Practically any fresh vegetable or bean can become part of a delicious potage.

The vegetables for soup must be washed very well. This is particularly true of leeks, which often harbor sand and dirt (see page 126).

If you are not going to cook potatoes immediately after peeling or chopping them, keep them in cold water to prevent them from turning brown. The soaking water will become starchy and can be added to some potages for extra body.

You can give a potage more flavor by cooking certain fresh vegetables, such as onions and leeks, in the soup pot in some butter before you add water and other ingredients. These vegetables should be cooked and stirred over low heat for about 3 minutes; neither the vegetables nor the butter should color.

To avoid an unpleasantly strong or even acrid flavor, simmer a potage only until the vegetables are cooked through.

Potage generally tastes best when it includes some butter, which brings out its flavors. According to your diet and your palate, you can increase or reduce the amount of butter used in these recipes. You can even substitute olive oil, although the resulting potage will, of course, taste quite different.

Blended Potages

You can use a food mill to purée vegetables for soup, but today most people use a blender or a handheld wand mixer. Wand mixers are not as common in the United States as they are in France, but they are affordable and extremely useful, especially if you like to make puréed soups. A wand mixer can beat, mix, and purée, and you can put it straight into your soup pot. It is also very easy to wash.

The texture of these potages will, of course, depend on how much you mix them—whether you want to retain small bits of vegetable or reduce everything to a smooth purée. It is hard to overblend with a wand mixer, but a powerful blender used for too long can give soup an unpleasant texture.

Heavy cream and crème fraîche can almost always be substituted for each other.

BLENDED POTATO AND LEEK SOUP _____
Potage Parmentier

SERVES   4–6
PREPARATION   15 minutes
COOKING   40 minutes

The classic blended soup is *potage Parmentier*, named for the man who popularized the potato in France in the eighteenth century. Until then this American import had been thought to be fit only for pigs.

1   Melt 1½ tablespoons butter in a saucepan over very low heat. Add the leeks and cook for 3 minutes, stirring occasionally. They should begin to turn translucent but should not brown. Add 4 cups water and 2 teaspoons coarse salt and bring to a simmer. If scum forms on the surface, remove it with a skimmer. Let the leeks simmer gently for 10 minutes.

2   Use a skimmer to lower the potatoes into the pot, being careful not to splash yourself with the hot water. Bring the pot back to a simmer and cover partially to keep it from boiling over. Simmer gently for 30 minutes.

3   Remove the pot from the heat and blend with a handheld mixer, in a blender, or with a food mill. Bring the puréed potage back to a simmer and then turn off the heat and whisk in the cream. Taste for salt. Just before serving, stir in the rest of the butter and sprinkle with chervil.

2 tablespoons butter
2 medium leeks, white parts only, carefully washed and sliced into 1-inch-thick (2-cm.) rounds
Coarse salt
¾ pound (400 g.) potatoes, peeled and quartered lengthwise and kept in a bowl of cold water
⅓ cup (10 cl.) heavy cream or crème fraîche
Salt
1 teaspoon chervil leaves

VEGETABLE POTAGE

Potage de légumes mixés

SERVES 4
PREPARATION 25 minutes
COOKING 40 minutes

1   Peel the potatoes, cut into quarters lengthwise, and put in a bowl of cold water. Wash and slice the carrots, leek whites, and celery into 1-inch rounds.

2   Melt 1½ tablespoons butter in a saucepan over very low heat. Add the leeks and cook for 3 minutes, stirring occasionally. They should begin to turn translucent but should not brown. Add the broth. Do not add salt.

3   Bring to a simmer and simmer 10 minutes. If the liquid foams, remove the scum with a skimmer. Add the other vegetables, bring back to a boil, and simmer 30 minutes.

4   Remove the pot from the heat and blend. Bring the potage back to a boil and turn off the heat. Whisk in the crème fraîche. Taste and add salt if necessary. Just before serving, add the remaining butter and sprinkle with chervil.

5   Small croutons made of white bread sautéed in butter go well with this soup.

4 medium potatoes
2 medium carrots, peeled
2 medium leeks, whites only
1 stalk celery (or, according to the season, 4 ounces/100 g. celery root)
2 tablespoons butter
1 quart (1 l.) chicken broth (page 77 or made from a bouillon cube)
1 tomato, peeled, seeded, and diced (page 124) (if tomatoes are in season)
⅓ cup (10 cl.) crème fraîche
Salt
1 teaspoon chervil leaves
Croutons (optional)

TOMATO BASIL POTAGE

Potage de tomate au basilic

SERVES 4
PREPARATION 20 minutes
COOKING 20 minutes

1   Peel the onion and chop it coarsely. Dice the 2 peeled and pulped tomatoes into pieces of about ½ inch and put them aside. Wash and quarter the other tomatoes and purée them in a blender or food processor.

2   Put the puréed tomatoes, garlic, bay leaf, cloves, and onion in a saucepan. Bring to a boil, occasionally stirring with a spatula and scraping the bottom and sides of the pot. Lower heat and simmer for 20 minutes.

1 medium onion
1½ pounds (800 g.) tomatoes, 2 of them peeled, seeded, and diced (page 124)
1 clove garlic, peeled and degermed (page 122)
1 bay leaf
2 whole cloves
⅓ cup (10 cl.) heavy cream
Salt
8 basil leaves

3   Pass through a fine strainer (if possible, through a chinois), pressing on the solids with a small ladle to extract as much liquid as possible. Put the strained liquid back in the pot, whisk in the cream, and bring back to a simmer. Taste for salt.

4   Put the diced tomatoes at the bottom of a tureen and pour in the hot soup. Sprinkle the basil leaves on top.

FAST ZUCCHINI POTAGE

Potage de courgettes rapide

SERVES   4
PREPARATION   5 minutes
COOKING   20 minutes

1   Wash the zucchini and cut off their tips. Peel and cut into 4 pieces.

2   Bring to a boil the amount of water recommended on the bouillon cube package and add the bouillon cube. Add the zucchini and simmer for 20 minutes.

3   Blend in a blender or food processor. Add the cheese and blend again. Taste and add salt if necessary.

2 medium zucchini
1 bouillon cube
1 small round cooked cheese, such as Laughing Cow
Salt

CARROT CUMIN POTAGE

Soupe de carottes au cumin

SERVES   4
PREPARATION   10 minutes
COOKING   30 minutes

1   Wash and peel the carrots and potatoes. Cut the carrots into small rounds and dice the potatoes.

2   Warm 2 tablespoons olive oil in a soup pot over medium heat. Add the carrots and potatoes, tossing them in the oil with a wooden spatula. Add the garlic and cumin and stir. Add the broth. Bring to a boil, lower the heat, cover, and simmer for 30 minutes.

¾ pound (400 g.) carrots
¼ pound (150 g.) potatoes
2 tablespoons olive oil
2 cloves garlic, peeled and degermed (see page 122)
Ground cumin
1 quart (1 l.) chicken broth (page 77 or made from a bouillon cube)

(continued)

Juice of 2 oranges
Salt

3 Bring the orange juice to a boil in a small saucepan and then turn the heat to low. Reduce over low heat for 25 minutes. It should be almost syrupy but should not stick or burn.

4 Pour the reduced orange juice into the carrot potage. Cover and simmer 8 minutes more. Blend, taste, and add salt if necessary.

HERB POTAGE

Potage aux herbes

SERVES 4
PREPARATION 25 minutes
COOKING 25 minutes

1 medium onion
5 ounces (150 g.) sorrel leaves
3 ounces (100 g.) spinach
2–3 ounces (75 g.) celery leaves
2–3 ounces (75 g.) watercress
2–3 ounces (75 g.) chervil
2–3 ounces (75 g.) flat-leaf
    parsley leaves
1½ cucumbers
1¼ pounds (600 g.) potatoes
    (preferably bintje,
    eersteling, or Yukon Gold)
2 tablespoons butter
Coarse salt

1 Peel the onion and cut it into thin slices. Trim and wash all the herbs: sorrel, spinach, celery, watercress, chervil, and parsley. Peel the cucumbers, scrape out their seeds, and cut into cubes. Wash, peel, and quarter the potatoes.

2 Put the butter in a saucepan. Add the herbs and cucumbers, cover, and warm gently for 5 minutes. Do not allow the herbs or butter to color. Add 6 cups water and 1 tablespoon coarse salt along with the potatoes. Bring to a boil and simmer for 25 minutes. Blend.

3 Stir in the final butter and crème fraîche. Taste, adding salt if necessary. Sprinkle with basil and chervil.

TO FINISH
1 teaspoon butter
1 level tablespoon crème
    fraîche
Salt
8 small basil leaves
1 tablespoon chervil leaves

BELL PEPPER POTAGE

Soupe de poivrons

SERVES 4
PREPARATION 15 minutes
COOKING 15 minutes

When you have guests, you can serve three different colors of soup simply by making the same recipe with green, yellow, and red peppers. It can be served hot in the winter or cold in the summer.

1 Cut the peppers into ½-inch strips. Peel and quarter the onions.
2 Heat 2 tablespoons olive oil in a saucepan. Add the onions and cook for 3 minutes over low heat, stirring occasionally and without letting them color. When they become translucent, add the pepper strips and thyme. Cook over low heat for 5 minutes, stirring. Add the broth and sugar. Bring to a boil, lower the heat, cover, and simmer no more than 10 minutes.
3 Remove the thyme and blend. Blend in the cold butter. Taste and add salt if necessary.

3 red peppers, peeled and
  seeded (page 130)
2 onions
4 tablespoons olive oil
1 sprig fresh thyme
3 cups (75 cl.) chicken broth
  (page 77 or made from a
  bouillon cube)
1 teaspoon sugar
2 teaspoons butter, chilled
Salt

GREEN PEA POTAGE

Potage Saint-Germain

SERVES 4
PREPARATION 35 minutes
COOKING 10–15 minutes

This potage is named for Saint Germain, Louis XV's minister of war who lends his name to various dishes of peas or split peas. It is even more delicious with croutons made of white bread sautéed in butter.

1   Put 1½ tablespoons butter in a saucepan over low heat. Cook the scallions and lardons 3–4 minutes, stirring occasionally and without allowing them to color. Add the peas and bouquet garni, and cook for 3 minutes. Add the broth. Bring to a simmer and simmer for 15–20 minutes. Remove the peas with a skimmer and put them in a tureen.

2   Blend the potage. Put it through a fine strainer and whisk in the cream. Taste, adding salt and pepper if necessary, and bring back to a simmer. Turn off the heat, stir in the remaining butter, and pour into the tureen with the peas. Sprinkle with chervil.

2 tablespoons butter
3 scallions
¼ pound (100 g.) lardons (page 89)
1¾ pounds (800 g.) shelled green peas, fresh or frozen (if frozen, there is no need to thaw first)
1 bouquet garni (2 sprigs savory and 6 branches parsley, tied in a small bundle)
1 quart (1 l.) broth, chicken or beef (page 77 or page 68 or made from a bouillon cube)
5 tablespoons heavy cream
Salt
Pepper
1 tablespoon chervil leaves

WATERCRESS, SORREL, OR LETTUCE POTAGE

Potage "cressonière," potage à l'oseille, ou potage à la laitue

SERVES 6
PREPARATION 30 minutes
COOKING 30 minutes

To make sorrel potage, replace the watercress with 1 pound (500 g.) sorrel. To make lettuce soup, replace the watercress with 1 pound (500 g.) lettuce.

1   Wash, peel, and quarter the potatoes. Peel the onion and chop it coarsely. Wash the watercress and cut off most of the stems.

1 pound (500 g.) potatoes (bintje or Yukon Gold)
1 small onion
1 pound (500 g.) watercress (about 2 bunches)
1 tablespoon plus 1 teaspoon butter
6 cups (1.5 l.) chicken broth (page 77 or made from bouillon cubes)
Pepper

2   Melt the butter in a saucepan over very low heat. Add the onion and watercress and cook for 5 minutes, stirring and not allowing coloration. Add the broth, potatoes, and some pepper. Bring to a simmer and simmer for 30 minutes.

3   Blend. Add the cream and blend again. Taste and add salt if necessary.

⅓ cup (10 cl.) heavy cream
Salt

Potages with Minced Vegetables

These are soups in which the vegetables have been cut into very regular, very small strips or cubes, usually just ¼ inch (0.5 cm.) across. They are good with lardons, croutons (small cubes of bread sautéed in butter), grated Gruyère, or fresh chervil.

LARDONS

Some of these potages are best served with lardons, small nuggets of bacon that are easy to find in Europe but not very common in the United States. They cannot truly be replaced by strips of bacon, which are drier and saltier. (If you do try using American bacon, reduce the amount of salt you add to the dish.)

It is not difficult, however, to make lardons at home from thick-cut slab bacon (smoked or plain). Remove the rind. Cut the bacon into small pieces (about ¼ to ½ inch/0.5–1 cm.). Lardons cut from unsmoked slab bacon must be blanched to get rid of some of the salt before they are sautéed to finish: Put the lardons in a small saucepan, cover with water, and bring to a boil. After 30 seconds, drain them in a colander and rinse with cold water. Now the lardons can be sautéed as directed in the recipes and scattered atop your soup.

HEARTY POTATO AND LEEK SOUP

Potage parisien

variation

POTATO AND LEEK SOUP
WITH HERBS

SERVES 4
PREPARATION 15 minutes
COOKING 45 minutes

1   Wash the leeks and potatoes, quarter the leeks lengthwise and chop them finely. Peel and cut the potatoes into ½-inch (1 cm.) slices and then cut the slices into ½-inch (1 cm.) sticks. Cut the sticks into slender strips, put them in a bowl, and cover with cold water.

2   Melt 2 tablespoons butter in a saucepan. Add the leeks and cook them over very low heat for 5 minutes. They should become translucent but should not color. Add 1 quart (1 l.) water and 2 teaspoons coarse salt and bring to a simmer. Simmer for 10 minutes. If foam forms on the surface, remove it with a skimmer.

3   Add the potatoes and their soaking water to the pot and bring it back to a simmer. Cover the pot, leaving the lid just slightly ajar to prevent it from boiling over, and simmer for 30 minutes.

4   At the end of cooking, add the 1 teaspoon butter. Taste and add salt if necessary. Sprinkle with chervil just before serving.

2 medium leeks (whites only)
¾ pound (400 g.) potatoes (rattes, fingerling, or Yukon Gold)
2 tablespoons butter plus 1 teaspoon to finish
Coarse salt
Salt
1 teaspoon chervil leaves

POTATO AND LEEK SOUP WITH HERBS

Potage à la maraîchère

SERVES 4
PREPARATION 10 minutes
COOKING 20 minutes

1   Trim the stems from the greens. Cut the leaves into fine strips and sauté them in a skillet with the butter, stirring them with a wooden spoon. Cook for 7–8 minutes, until the water clinging to them from washing has completely evaporated.

2   Twenty minutes before serving, bring the Hearty Potato and Leek Soup to a simmer. Add the vermicelli and simmer until

1 ounce (30 g.) lettuce, sorrel, and spinach leaves, thoroughly washed
1 teaspoon butter
1 recipe Hearty Potato and Leek Soup (above)
½ ounce (15 g.) vermicelli or angel hair pasta, broken

cooked. Add the sautéed greens. Just before serving, sprinkle the soup with chervil.

FARMER'S VEGETABLE SOUP

Potage cultivateur

SERVES   4

PREPARATION   45 minutes

COOKING   55 minutes

1   Wash, peel, and trim the vegetables as necessary.

2   Put 1 quart water and 2 teaspoons coarse salt in a soup pot and turn on the heat. While you wait for the water to boil, cut the green beans into ¼-inch (0.5-cm.) pieces. Boil the green beans and peas for 3 minutes and then put them in a colander and rinse them under cold water until they are cool. Set them aside to drain.

3   Cut the cabbage leaves into thin strips, less than ½ inch (1 cm.) wide, and then mince them as finely as possible.

4   Cut the leeks lengthwise into strips and then cut the strips into small pieces, less than ½ inch (1 cm.) long.

5   Cut the potatoes in half lengthwise and then cut each half into thirds, still lengthwise. Cut these potato sticks into very thin strips, about ⅛ inch (2 or 3 mm.). Put them in a bowl and cover them with cold water. Cut the celery, carrots, and turnips the same way, but do not cover them with cold water.

6   Put 2 tablespoons butter in the soup pot with the leeks, carrots, turnip, and celery. Add 1 teaspoon coarse salt and cook for 3 minutes over low heat, stirring constantly. Add 1½ quarts (1 l.) water and bring to a boil. Add the lardons and cabbage.

7   Simmer for 40 minutes, partially covered with a lid. Add the potatoes and bring back to a boil. Simmer for 15 minutes. Add the green beans and peas and simmer 5 minutes more. Taste and add fine salt if necessary.

8   To serve, whisk in 2 teaspoons butter and sprinkle with chervil. If you like, toast country bread topped with grated Gruyère until the cheese is hot and bubbly. Put a piece of cheese toast in the bottom of each soup bowl and pour the hot soup over.

into small pieces (about 3 tablespoons)

2 tablespoons chervil leaves

20 haricots verts or slender green beans, fresh or frozen

2 tablespoons small peas, fresh or frozen

2 leaves green cabbage

2 leeks, white and tender green parts only

2 medium potatoes (a firm variety such as roseval, belle de Fontenay, ratte, any fingerlings, or Yukon Gold)

1 stalk celery

2 medium carrots

2 small turnips

Coarse salt

2 tablespoons butter, plus 2 teaspoons to finish

2 ounces (50 g.) lardons, blanched (page 89)

Salt

1 teaspoon chervil leaves

4 slices country bread and ½ cup grated Gruyère cheese (optional)

MIXED VEGETABLE POTAGE

Potage julienne Darblay

SERVES 4–6
PREPARATION 30 minutes
COOKING 20 minutes

1. Wash and trim the vegetables. Cut them into small strips (julienne).
2. Warm the butter in a skillet. Add the vegetables, a pinch of sugar, and a pinch of salt. Toss everything together with a wooden spatula. Cover and cook over very low heat for 20 minutes, stirring frequently.
3. To serve, reheat the Blended Potato and Leek Soup. Add the sautéed vegetable garnish when the potage has come to a simmer and turn off the heat. Taste for salt. Sprinkle with chervil and, if you are using them, croutons.

1 leek, white part only
1 medium carrot
1 stalk celery
1 young turnip
2 teaspoons butter
Sugar
Salt
1 recipe Blended Potato and Leek Soup (page 83)
1 teaspoon chervil leaves
Croutons (white bread fried in butter; optional)

OYSTER POTAGE WITH PERIWINKLES

Potage d'huîtres aux bigorneaux

SERVES 4
PREPARATION 5 minutes
COOKING 10 minutes (periwinkles)

1. Wash the periwinkles in several changes of water and leave them in a colander to drain. Pour 2 cups (50 cl.) water into a pot and add the bouquet garni, 1 pinch of pepper, 1 pinch of sea salt, and 1 teaspoon wine vinegar. Bring to a boil and plunge in the periwinkles. Simmer gently for 10 minutes. Let them cool in the cooking water; when they are no longer warm, remove them with a skimmer. Remove the periwinkles from their shells with a pick. Save the periwinkles and discard the shells.
2. Open the oysters and remove them from their shells, saving the liquor (the water inside their shells) in a bowl. Filter the liquor through a fine strainer into another bowl. Put the oysters into that bowl, covered with their own liquor, and keep them in the refrigerator.

½ pound (250 g.) periwinkles (sea snails)
Bouquet garni (1 sprig fresh thyme, ½ bay leaf, and 1 branch flat-leaf parsley, wrapped and tied in a green leek leaf)
Pepper
Sea salt
Wine vinegar
18 oysters
1 leek, white part only
1 medium carrot

3 Wash, trim, and peel the leek, carrot, and shallot. Slice them into very thin rounds, only $\frac{1}{16}$ inch (2 mm.) or so thick.

4 Melt 1 tablespoon butter in the soup pot over low heat. When it foams, add the vegetables and cook for 3 minutes, stirring, over low heat so they do not color. Add 1 cup water and bring to a boil. Simmer for 10 minutes.

5 Take the oysters from the refrigerator and use a skimmer to take them from their liquor. Put them in a tureen or in a deep soup plate. Keep their liquor in the bowl.

6 When the vegetables have simmered 10 minutes, stir in the white wine and crème fraîche with a wooden spoon. Bring the mixture almost back to the boiling point and turn off the heat. Add the oyster liquor and periwinkles. Taste for salt and pepper. Immediately pour the very hot soup over the oysters in their tureen in order to flash-cook them.

1 shallot
1 tablespoon butter
1 cup (25 cl.) dry white wine
1 tablespoon crème fraîche or heavy cream, chilled

Cream Soups and Veloutés

Traditionally, a cream soup is a vegetable broth that has been thickened with cornstarch, potato starch, arrowroot, or other thickener. After cooking, cream is added to make the soup even richer.

A *velouté* is a stock (white chicken or veal stock, or a fumet) thickened with roux (a briefly cooked mixture of flour and butter; see page 50). For this to work, the roux and the stock must be at opposite temperatures when they meet—one hot and the other cold. After cooking, a velouté is, classically, further thickened with cream and egg yolk—more specifically, 4 yolks per quart (or liter) of soup.

Today, few people can tell a cream soup from a velouté—they are that similar in appearance, taste, and preparation. Some vegetables, such as pumpkin, zucchini, beans, and peas, become thick and "creamy" enough without any additions at all. The most important thing is to allow the base flavor to shine through. It isn't unusual today for a "cream soup" to be merely a blended potage with cream added at the end. The cream can be either liquid (heavy cream) or thick (crème fraîche), but crème fraîche is preferred if you are finishing with an egg yolk.

As for bisques, they are cream soups made with crustaceans.

THE BROTHS AND STOCKS YOU START WITH

Cream soups, veloutés, and bisques all begin with broths and stocks. These foundations are best made at home, not least because of the pride you will take in having built a masterpiece of soup from scratch. But now and then when you're pressed for time, you can rely almost as happily on prepared stocks and other grocery store shortcuts. We have chosen to recommend these indispensable substitutes, which are always improving thanks to technological advances and their makers' efforts. Bouillon cubes, which we should not be ashamed to keep in our kitchens, date back to the nineteenth century. But modern techniques such as freezing and vacuum packing (*sous vide*) have considerably improved preprepared stocks. Whatever stock of convenience you choose, be sure to read the label for preparation instructions.

AVOID SALT

Broths and stocks being in general salty enough already, you should not salt cream soups and veloutés. Instead, taste at the end of cooking to determine whether you need to add salt and freshly ground pepper.

CRUSH THE VEGETABLES

A cream soup or velouté should have a rich, very smooth consistency, so the vegetables must be very well blended. You can use a food mill, which will catch fibrous waste in its screen, but an electric mixer will give you the best consistency whether you use a handheld wand mixer or a blender (though if you use an electric mixer with certain fibrous or thick-skinned vegetables, such as asparagus or green beans, you will have to strain the soup after you have blended it). If you can, use a chinois—a large conical strainer against which you crush the soft vegetables with a small ladle or large spoon in order to extract all their juices.

TO LOOSEN A VELOUTÉ

When you make a velouté, put aside a ladle or two of its broth before you blend the rest. If the finished velouté seems too thick when the time comes to serve it, you can dilute it with the reserved broth.

For an even smoother soup, you can add some lightly whipped cream just before serving. Simply put well-chilled cream in a bowl and beat it a little with a handheld electric mixer. Don't go too far. You aren't looking for the kind of thick, peak-holding whipped cream you would use to top a dessert. Put a big spoonful in the soup or serve it on the side so people can add as much as they like.

Cream Soups

CREAM OF PEA AND FAVA BEAN SOUP WITH SAVORY

Crème de petits pois et fèves à la sariette

variation

CREAM OF PEA SOUP
WITH SAVORY

SERVES 4–6
PREPARATION 10 minutes
COOKING 25 minutes

1   Wash the savory. Chop half of it finely and put it aside.
2   Wash the vegetables. Put 1 quart (1 l.) water and 1 level table-spoon coarse salt in a small saucepan and bring to a boil. Boil the peas for 3 minutes; drain and rinse under cold running water.
3   Bring the chicken broth to a boil in a soup pot. Add the fava beans (they should be shelled, but there is no need to peel the beans), peas, unchopped savory, and sugar. Adjust the heat so that the mixture simmers, and simmer for 20 minutes.
4   Blend the soup and put it through a fine strainer. Bring it back to a boil and turn off the heat. As necessary, remove foam from the surface with a skimmer. Add the crème fraîche and taste for salt and pepper. Dice the cold butter and then stir it into the soup. To serve, sprinkle with the reserved chopped savory.

1 bunch savory (or a small amount of thyme if savory is unavailable)
¾ pound (300 g.) shelled peas
¾ pound (300 g.) shelled fava beans
Coarse salt
1 quart (1 l.) chicken broth (page 77 or made from a bouillon cube)
½ teaspoon superfine sugar
⅓ cup (10 cl.) crème fraîche
Salt
Pepper
2 tablespoons butter, well chilled

CREAM OF PEA SOUP WITH SAVORY

Crème de petits pois à la sariette

Follow the recipe above, omitting the fava beans and doubling the quantity of peas.

CREAM OF PEA SOUP WITH MINT _____

Crème de petits pois à la menthe

SERVES 4
PREPARATION AND COOKING 15 minutes

1 Wash and drain the peas.
2 Wash and trim the scallions and slice them into small rounds.
3 Put the olive oil in a soup pot with the scallions and cook for 3 minutes over low heat, stirring. They should begin to turn translucent but should not brown. Add the broth. Do not salt.
4 Add the peas, garlic, mint, and parsley. Add the sugar. Bring quickly to a boil, lower the heat, and simmer for 10 minutes.
5 Take the soup pot off the heat. Blend the soup and put it through a fine strainer.
6 Put the soup back in the pot and bring it back to a boil. If foam forms on the surface, remove it with a skimmer. Stir in the crème fraîche. Taste for salt and pepper.
7 Just before serving, add the butter and sprinkle with the pinch of chopped mint. Top with croutons if you wish.

1 ¾ pounds (800 g.) shelled peas
¼ pound (100 g.) scallions
1 tablespoon olive oil
1 quart (1 l.) chicken broth (page 77 or made from a bouillon cube)
1 clove garlic
1 tablespoon minced mint and 1 tablespoon minced parsley, mixed, plus 1 pinch minced mint
1 teaspoon superfine sugar
⅓ cup (10 cl.) crème fraîche
Salt
Pepper
1 tablespoon plus 1 teaspoon butter
Croutons (optional)

CREAM OF PUMPKIN SOUP

Crème de potiron

SERVES 4–6

PREPARATION AND COOKING   30 minutes

1   Cut the pumpkin flesh into large pieces. Put them in a soup pot with the broth and sugar. Bring to a boil, lower the heat a bit, and cover. Cook over medium heat for 18 minutes; do not cook too long or the pumpkin will turn bitter. When it is cooked, it should be easy to pierce with a table knife.

2   Blend the soup and then bring it back to a simmer, stirring and scraping the bottom and sides with a wooden spatula to keep the pumpkin from sticking and burning. Do this for 6–8 minutes.

3   In a small bowl, thoroughly combine the cornstarch and 2 tablespoons cold water. When the soup has finished simmering, turn off the heat and whisk in the cornstarch solution, adding it in a very thin stream. Stir in the crème fraîche. Taste and add salt if necessary. Dice the chilled butter and stir it into the hot soup.

2 pounds (1 kg.) pumpkin or butternut squash flesh

3¼ cups (80 cl.) chicken broth (page 77 or made from a bouillon cube)

1 teaspoon granulated sugar

2 tablespoons cornstarch

⅓ cup (10 cl.) crème fraîche

Salt

1 tablespoon plus 1 teaspoon butter, well chilled

CREAM OF ZUCCHINI SOUP

Crème de courgettes

SERVES 4

PREPARATION   15 minutes

COOKING   25 minutes

1   Wash the zucchini and cut off their tips. Cut each into 4 pieces (crosswise) and put one piece aside. Peel the rest with a vegetable peeler.

2   With a small knife, slice strips of skin and flesh from the piece of zucchini you set aside, taking about ¼ inch (0.5 cm.) flesh away along with the skin. Add the skinned core to the rest of the peeled zucchini. Cut the plump skin-on strips into ¼-inch (0.5-cm.) cubes. Heat the butter gently in a small skillet and sauté the zucchini cubes for 4 minutes over low heat. Set them aside.

3 medium zucchini

1 teaspoon butter

1 quart (1 l.) chicken broth (page 77 or made from a bouillon cube)

⅓ cup (10 cl.) heavy cream

Salt

Pepper

1 teaspoon chervil leaves

3   Bring the broth to a boil in a soup pot. Plunge in the large uncooked zucchini pieces and simmer for 20 minutes.

4   Blend the soup, add the cream, and blend again. Taste for salt and pepper.

5   Put the sautéed cubes at the bottom of a tureen and pour the hot soup over them. Sprinkle with chervil.

CREAM OF MUSHROOM SOUP

Crème aux pleurotes

SERVES   4
PREPARATION   10 minutes
COOKING   30 minutes

1   Wash the leek in warm water and cut it in half lengthwise and then crosswise into quarters. Carefully clean the mushrooms with paper towels. Peel and mince the shallots.

2   Warm the butter in a soup pot over low heat. Gently sauté the shallots but do not allow them to color. Add the mushrooms and some salt and pepper. Stir well with a wooden spoon or spatula, cover, and cook over very low heat for 2 minutes. Stir again and cook 3 minutes more, still covered.

3   Remove 4 tablespoons mushrooms and set them aside to drain. Leave the soup pot over very low heat. Add the leek and cook for 3 minutes, stirring. Stir in the rice. Add the broth and bring to a boil. Reduce the heat to very low, cover, and simmer for 25 minutes.

4   Turn off the heat. Put a ladleful of broth (but no rice) in a bowl and set it aside. Blend the soup, add the cream, and mix again. If it seems too thick, add some of the extra broth. Taste for salt and pepper.

5   Just before serving, blend again so that the mixture is foamy. Put the reserved sautéed mushrooms at the bottom of a tureen, cover them with soup, and sprinkle with chervil.

1 leek, white part only
1¼ pounds (600 g.) small oyster mushrooms
2 shallots
1 teaspoon butter
Salt
Pepper
¼ cup (50 g.) short-grain rice
1 quart (1 l.) chicken broth (page 77 or made from a bouillon cube)
⅓ cup (10 cl.) heavy cream
1 teaspoon chervil leaves

CREAM OF CELERY SOUP

Crème de céleri

SERVES 4

PREPARATION 20 minutes

COOKING 25 minutes

1 Wash, trim, and peel the vegetables as necessary.

2 Cut the celery root and potatoes into eighths. Cut the leek, zucchini, and carrot in half lengthwise and then crosswise into quarters. Finely dice the carrot and zucchini.

3 Warm the butter in a large soup pot over low heat. Cook the leek for 3 minutes. Add the celery root and potatoes and stir. Add the broth and bring to a boil. Reduce the heat to low, cover, and simmer for 15 minutes.

4 Cook the carrot and zucchini in 2 separate saucepans; in each, bring 1 quart (1 l.) water to a boil with 1 teaspoon coarse salt. Boil each vegetable 2 minutes and then drain in a colander, rinse under cold running water, and set aside to drain.

5 When the soup has simmered for 15 minutes, whisk in the cream, simmer 10 minutes more, and then blend. Add salt and pepper if necessary. Add a dash of grated nutmeg and blend again.

6 Put half of the carrot and zucchini pieces at the bottom of a tureen. Pour the hot soup on top of them and sprinkle with chervil and the remaining carrot and zucchini.

1 pound (500 g.) celery root

2 firm-fleshed potatoes

1 medium leek, white part only

1 medium zucchini

1 carrot

1 teaspoon butter

1 quart (1 l.) chicken broth
    (page 77 or made from a
    bouillon cube)

Coarse salt

⅓ cup (10 cl.) heavy cream

Salt

Pepper

Grated nutmeg

1 teaspoon chervil leaves

CREAM OF CHANTERELLE SOUP

Crème de girolles

SERVES 4
PREPARATION 15 minutes
COOKING 20 minutes

1   Carefully clean the chanterelles with a paper towel. Peel the garlic and onion and slice the onion into rounds. Cut the lardons into pieces about ¼ inch by ½ inch (0.5 cm. by 1 cm.).

2   Put the olive oil and onion in the soup pot and cook over low heat for 2 minutes, not allowing the onion to color. Add the garlic and lardons, stir, and cook 2 minutes more.

3   Add the chanterelles and cook for 2 minutes, still over low heat, stirring. Add the broth and bring to a boil; simmer for 15 minutes.

4   Whisk in the cream. Turn off the heat and blend the soup.

5   Add the lemon juice and mix again. Stir in the cold butter. Taste for salt and pepper. Blend a final time before serving.

1 pound (400 g.) chanterelle mushrooms
1 clove garlic
1 onion
2 ounces (50 g.) lardons (page 89)
1 tablespoon olive oil
1 quart (1 l.) chicken broth (page 77 or made from a bouillon cube)
⅓ cup (10 cl.) heavy cream
Juice of 1 lemon
1 teaspoon butter, well chilled
Salt
Pepper

CREAM OF WHITE BEAN SOUP

Crème de haricots blancs

SERVES   4

PREPARATION   30 minutes

COOKING $2\frac{1}{2}$ hours

1   Peel the carrot. Cut it in half lengthwise and then crosswise into quarters. Peel and quarter the onion, and press the clove into 1 of the quarters.

2   Warm 1 tablespoon butter in a soup pot over low heat. Add the lardons and cook, stirring, for 4 minutes. Remove the lardons with a slotted spoon, set them aside, and add the garlic, beans, carrot, and bouquet garni. Cook for 2 minutes, still over low heat. Cover with water by 1 inch and bring to a boil.

3   Lower the heat and simmer for $2\frac{1}{2}$ hours. Stir every half hour to make sure nothing is sticking to the bottom. After 2 hours, add 1 scant teaspoon coarse salt and stir.

4   Drain the beans and remove the bouquet garni. Blend the beans in a blender or food processor. Taste for salt and pepper, add the cream, and blend again.

5   Heat the broth in the soup pot. When it is about to boil, turn off the heat. Add the bean purée to the broth and blend. Put the mixture through a fine strainer (a chinois if possible), pressing the solids with a spoon to extract as much liquid as possible.

6   Before serving, reheat the lardons in a skillet, stirring and cooking about 2 minutes. Stir a teaspoon of cold butter into the hot soup and sprinkle with lardons or bacon.

1 carrot

1 medium onion

1 whole clove

1 tablespoon plus 1 teaspoon butter, well chilled

$\frac{1}{2}$ pound (200 g.) smoked lardons (page 89)

3 cloves garlic, peeled and degermed (see page 122)

$\frac{3}{4}$ pound (350 g.) dried white beans, such as cannellini

1 bouquet garni (1 branch thyme, 1 small bay leaf, and 3 sprigs parsley, tied in a bundle)

Coarse salt

Pepper

$\frac{3}{4}$ cup (20 cl.) heavy cream

$1\frac{1}{4}$ cups (30 cl.) chicken broth (page 77 or made from a bouillon cube)

CREAM OF BEAN SOUP WITH SMOKED BACON

Crème de haricots au lard

SERVES 4
PREPARATION 30 minutes
COOKING 1 hour

1 onion
1 carrot
2 teaspoons butter
1 pound (400 g.) navy beans
4 thin slices smoked slab bacon
Salt
Pepper
1¼ cups (30 cl.) heavy cream

1. Peel and quarter the onion. Wash and peel the carrot. Cut it in half lengthwise and then cut crosswise into quarters.
2. Warm the butter in a soup pot over low heat. Sauté the onion for 2 minutes, stirring. Add the carrot and beans and stir. Cover generously with water and bring to a boil. If foam forms on the surface, use a skimmer to remove it. Lower the heat and simmer uncovered for 30 minutes. Skim away the foam and simmer 30 minutes more.
3. As the beans cook, preheat the oven to 400°F (200°C). Put the bacon slices on a sheet pan. When the oven has gotten hot, cook the bacon for 10 minutes. Flip the slices and cook 10 minutes more. The bacon should become golden and crispy.
4. When the beans are cooked, remove them from the heat and blend them in a blender or food processor with their cooking liquid. Put the bean purée through a fine strainer (a chinois if possible), pressing the solids with a spoon to extract as much liquid as possible. Put the strained purée back in the soup pot over low heat. Taste for salt and pepper. When it is hot again, gently stir in the cream with a wooden spatula. Turn off the heat and blend again.
5. Pour the hot soup into a tureen and crumble the bacon over the top.

CREAM OF LENTIL SOUP

Crème de lentilles

SERVES   4
PREPARATION   35 minutes
COOKING   1⅔ hours

1   Carefully wash and drain the lentils. Wash the celery and peel away its fibrous outer layer. Cut it into quarters. Wash and peel the carrot. Wash the leek white in warm water. Cut the leek and carrot into half lengthwise and then crosswise into quarters. Rinse the thyme.

2   Melt the butter in a soup pot over low heat and add the lardons. Sauté for 5 minutes over medium heat, stirring with a wooden spoon, until they are golden. Remove them with a slotted spoon to a plate lined with paper towels. Lower the heat and add the vegetables and garlic, stirring well and cooking for 3 minutes. Add the lentils and thyme, and stir for 2 minutes. Add the broth. Bring to a boil, lower the heat, cover, and simmer for 1½ hours.

3   Remove the thyme, blend the soup, and put it through a fine strainer (a chinois if possible), pressing the solids dry with a spoon. Taste and add salt and pepper if necessary.

4   Reheat the soup in its pot. As it reheats, put the lardons in a skillet and sauté, stirring, for 2 minutes. Just before the soup boils, turn off the heat and whisk in the crème fraîche. Pour it into a tureen and sprinkle with the warm lardons (and, if you like, croutons).

¾ pound (300 g.) green lentils
½ small and very green stalk celery
1 carrot
1 leek, white part only
1 sprig thyme
1 tablespoon plus 1 teaspoon butter
¼ pound (100 g.) smoked lardons (page 89)
2 cloves garlic, peeled and degermed (page 122)
1½ quarts (1.5 l.) chicken broth (page 77 or made from a bouillon cube)
Salt
Pepper
⅓ cup (10 cl.) crème fraîche
Croutons (optional)

CREAM OF SPLIT PEA SOUP

Crème de pois cassés

SERVES 4

COOKING   1½ hours

2 tablespoons butter

1 ounce (40 g.) lardons
(page 89)

1 green leek leaf

½ carrot, peeled

½ onion, peeled

¾ pound (300 g.) split peas

1½ quarts (1.5 l.) chicken broth
(page 77 or made from a
bouillon cube)

1 bouquet garni (1 branch
parsley and 1 sprig fresh
thyme, tied together)

1 clove garlic, peeled and
degermed (page 122)

Salt

Pepper

⅓ cup (10 cl.) crème fraîche

1 teaspoon chervil leaves

Croutons (optional)

1   Warm 1 teaspoon butter in a soup pot. Cook the lardons for 3 to 5 minutes over medium heat, stirring with a wooden spatula, until they are golden. Stir in the leek leaf, carrot, onion, and split peas. Set aside a cup of chicken broth and pour the rest into the pot. Add the bouquet garni and garlic. Bring to a boil, lower the heat, cover, and simmer 1½ hours. Every half hour, skim the foam from the surface and make sure all the water has not boiled away. If necessary, add a big glass of water. At the end of cooking, remove the bouquet garni and purée the soup in a blender or food processor. Taste and add salt and pepper if necessary.

2   If the soup seems too thick, add some of the reserved broth. Add the crème fraîche and blend again. To serve, stir the rest of the butter, well chilled, into the piping hot soup. Sprinkle with chervil and, if you wish, croutons.

CREAM OF OYSTER SOUP

Crème d'huîtres

SERVES 4

PREPARATION   25 minutes

COOKING   about 15 minutes

24 small oysters, approximately
1½ ounces (40 g.) each

2 small leeks, white part only

2 shallots

4 teaspoons butter

2 cups (50 cl.) white wine

5 tablespoons crème fraîche

Salt

Pepper

Juice of ½ lemon

1   Open the oysters and remove them from their shells, saving their liquor (the juice in their shells) in a bowl. Put the oysters in another bowl. Filter the liquor through a fine strainer into the bowl with the oysters. Cover with plastic wrap and refrigerate.

2   Trim the leeks and peel the shallots. Cut them in half lengthwise. Cut the leek halves crosswise into 4.

3   Melt 2 teaspoons butter in a soup pot. When it foams, add

the leeks and shallots and cook for 3 minutes over low heat, not allowing the vegetables or the butter to color.

4   Add the wine and 2 cups (50 cl.) water. Bring to a boil and then simmer for 10 minutes. Add 4 tablespoons crème fraîche, mixing well and bringing back to a boil. Add 12 of the oysters and their liquor. Taste for salt and pepper. When the liquid comes back to a boil, turn off the heat.

5   Put everything in the blender with the lemon juice, 2 teaspoons diced cold butter, and 1 tablespoon crème fraîche. Blend until the soup is very smooth and sleek. Put the remaining uncooked oysters in a tureen and cover with the hot soup.

Veloutés _____

ASPARAGUS VELOUTÉ _____

Velouté d'asperges

SERVES   4
PREPARATION   10 minutes
COOKING   20 minutes
REDUCING   30 minutes

1   Wash the asparagus. Cut 2 inches (5 cm.) off the tips and save them for another use. Do not peel the stalks but cut them into 1¼-inch (3-cm.) pieces.

2   Bring the stock or broth to a boil in a soup pot. When it bubbles, add the asparagus pieces and sugar. Turn down the heat, cover, and simmer for 20 minutes.

3   Blend and pass through a fine strainer (a chinois if possible), pressing on the solids with a spoon to extract as much liquid as possible. Put the soup back in the pot, bring back to a boil, and boil about 30 minutes more.

4   Thoroughly mix the cornstarch in a bowl with 1 tablespoon cold water. Beat the yolk and cream together in a bowl large enough to hold all the soup.

5   When the soup in the pot has been reduced by about half, whisk in the cornstarch mixture. Boil for 1 minute, whisking

2 pounds (1 kg.) white
    asparagus
1 quart (1 l.) chicken stock
    (page 36 or store-bought),
    or chicken broth (page 77
    or store-bought or made
    from a bouillon cube)
A bit of sugar (1 cube if you
    have cubes)
¼ cup (30 g.) cornstarch
1 egg yolk (page 204)
1 cup (25 cl.) heavy cream
Salt

constantly, and then gently pour everything into the bowl with the egg-cream mixture, whisking as you pour.

6   Pour the contents of the bowl back into the soup pot and heat very gently in order to thicken. Stir with a spatula and turn off the heat at the first sign of boiling. Blend. Season with salt as necessary.

ARTICHOKE VELOUTÉ

Velouté d'artichaut

SERVES   4
PREPARATION   10 minutes
COOKING   40 minutes

1   Put the artichoke hearts in a bowl half filled with water and lemon juice. Cut them into slices of about ½ inch (1 cm.), putting them back in the water as you go. Carefully wash the leek whites in warm water. Slice them into ½-inch (1-cm.) rounds. Rinse the thyme.

2   Melt the butter in a soup pot. When it foams, add the artichoke hearts and leeks, stirring with a spatula to coat them in butter. Cook 2–3 minutes over low heat, without allowing them to color. Still over low heat add the flour all at once, stirring quickly and well to prevent the formation of lumps. Do not allow the flour to color. As soon as the flour is completely stirred in, add the chicken broth and thyme. Simmer for 35–40 minutes.

3   Remove the thyme. Blend the soup. Add the crème fraîche and blend again. Taste for salt and pepper and sprinkle with chives and chervil.

6 green globe artichoke hearts (page 179)
Lemon juice
2 leeks, white parts only
1 sprig fresh thyme
2 teaspoons butter
1 tablespoon flour
1 quart (1 l.) chicken broth (page 77 or made from a bouillon cube)
¾ cup (20 cl.) crème fraîche
Salt
Pepper
2 tablespoons minced chives
1 teaspoon chervil leaves

CAULIFLOWER VELOUTÉ

Velouté de chou-fleur

SERVES 4
PREPARATION 10 minutes
COOKING 40 minutes

1 Wash the leeks in warm water and slice them into ½-inch (1-cm.) rounds. Remove the stem and core of the cauliflower. Break it into florets and rinse them in 1 quart (1 l.) water mixed with 1 teaspoon white vinegar. Rinse with clean water.

2 Melt the butter in a large pot over low heat and add the leeks; stir them well to coat them with butter. Cook 2–3 minutes, still over low heat, without allowing them to color. Add the flour all at once, stir well, and keep over low heat for 2 minutes, stirring constantly. Turn off the heat and allow the mixture (a "roux") to cool in the pot.

3 In another pot, bring 1 quart (1 l.) water and 1 tablespoon coarse salt to a boil. Add the cauliflower and boil for 1 minute. Remove them from the water with a skimmer, put them in a colander, and rinse them under cold running water. Allow to drain. Set aside 1 small bunch and separate it into tiny florets. Pour the water out of the pot and rinse it with clean water.

4 In the cauliflower-cooking pot, bring the stock to a boil. Have the pot containing the roux nearby. When the stock boils, ladle it into the roux, whisking well the whole time. Ladle all the stock into the roux, whisking constantly. Bring the pot that now contains the roux and the stock almost to a boil. Add the cauliflower, lower the heat, cover, and simmer for 35–40 minutes.

5 In a bowl, beat together the yolks and crème fraîche.

6 Blend the soup. If necessary, use a skimmer to remove foam from its surface. Carefully add the egg-cream mixture to the soup, off the heat, whisking constantly. If you need to reheat it, you must not allow the velouté to boil. Taste and add salt if necessary. Sprinkle with the cauliflower florets and chervil.

2 leeks, white parts only
1 cauliflower (about
    1½ pounds/600–800 g.)
1 teaspoon white vinegar
3 tablespoons butter
¼ cup (40 g.) flour
Coarse salt
1 quart (1 l.) chicken stock
    (page 36)
2 egg yolks (page 204)
⅓ cup (10 cl.) crème fraîche
Salt
1 teaspoon chervil leaves

JERUSALEM ARTICHOKE VELOUTÉ

Velouté de topinambour

SERVES 4
PREPARATION 10 minutes
COOKING 30 minutes

1   Carefully wash the Jerusalem artichokes but do not peel. Dice.
2   Heat 2 tablespoons olive oil in a soup pot over low heat. Add the Jerusalem artichokes and cook for 5 minutes. Add the honey, to caramelize them lightly, and the curry powder. Mix well.
3   Add the broth and bring to a boil. Add the cream and simmer for 30 minutes.
4   Blend. Taste, adding salt and pepper if necessary.

1 pound (500 g.) Jerusalem artichokes (also called sunchokes)
2 tablespoons olive oil
1 teaspoon honey
1 teaspoon curry powder
3 cups (75 cl.) chicken broth (page 77 or made from a bouillon cube)
½ cup (15 cl.) heavy cream
Salt
Pepper

CHESTNUT VELOUTÉ WITH FOIE GRAS, CELERY, AND SMOKED BACON

Velouté de châtaigne au foie gras, céleri, et lard fumé

SERVES 4–6
PREPARATION 15 minutes
COOKING 20 minutes

1   Wash and trim the celery root and cut it into ½-inch (1-cm.) cubes. Cut the foie gras into 1-inch (2-cm.) cubes.
2   Warm 1 tablespoon plus 1 teaspoon butter in a pot over low heat. Add the cooked chestnuts and sauté for 3 minutes, stirring, still over low heat. Add 1 quart (1 l.) water, 2 teaspoons coarse salt, and 2 pinches of pepper. Use a small knife to cut the cardamom pods in half and then remove the seeds with the tip of the knife. Add them to the liquid. Bring to a boil and then simmer for 10 minutes.
3   In another pot bring 1 quart (1 l.) water and 1 tablespoon coarse salt to a boil. Boil the celery root cubes for 2 minutes. Remove them with a skimmer and drain in a colander, first

1 celery root
6 ounces (200 g.) fresh foie gras
4 tablespoons (60 g.) butter
¾ pound (400 g.) vacuum-packed chestnuts, ready to cook
Coarse salt
Pepper
2 cardamom pods
⅓ cup (10 cl.) heavy cream
1 egg yolk (page 204)

rinsing them under cold running water to cool them down. Allow to drain. Wrap the celery root in 3 paper towels and set aside.

4 When the chestnuts have simmered for 10 minutes, blend them with their broth for 2 minutes. Add the heavy cream, the remaining butter, and the egg yolk. Blend again, until the velouté is completely smooth. Taste, adding salt and pepper if necessary. If you wish, you can put this through a fine strainer to be sure of removing the cardamom seeds. Put the soup back in the pot and heat over low heat. It must not boil.

5 Cook the lardons in a skillet over medium heat for 1 minute, stirring with a wooden spoon. Add the cubes of foie gras and cook for 1 minute, stirring them very gently, until they begin to turn golden. Add the celery root cubes, stir, and then turn off the heat. Put the contents of the skillet in a colander and then gently turn the colander out onto a plate lined with paper towels. Add salt and pepper lightly. Put this garnish at the bottom of a tureen and pour the hot soup over it. Sprinkle with the celery leaves.

Salt
3 ounces (100 g.) smoked lardons (page 89)
1 teaspoon minced celery leaves

BISQUES

Bisques bear a strong resemblance to cream soups, but they are distinguished by their use of crustaceans. Crab, lobster, shrimp, and other crustacean broths are reduced by boiling and are thickened with rice starch or cornstarch. They are further enriched by small pieces of the crustacean's flesh and, just before serving, cream and butter.

To serve 4–6 people, you will need 2 pounds (1 kg.) crustaceans. To prepare them for bisque is extremely complicated and requires both fish broth (*fumet de poisson*) and consommé, but you can try it out by following the recipe for the tomato- and white-wine-based sauce called *americaine* (in the recipe Lobster à l'Américaine on page 255).

If this seems daunting, you will be happy to hear that there are also some very fine commercial bisques out there.

Soups

In France, soups are anchored in regional (and even foreign) traditions, which means that there is no one base formula for their preparation. They can include a vast variety of ingredients. Fish and mollusk soups fall into this category.

Fish Soups

CRAB SOUP
Soupe d'étrilles

SERVES 4
PREPARATION 15 minutes
COOKING 40 minutes

1 Rinse the crabs under cold running water. Peel the carrot and onion. Core the fennel. Cut the carrot, onion, and fennel into pieces about ½ inch by 1 inch (1 cm. by 2 cm.).

2 Heat the olive oil in a soup pot over medium heat. Cook the crabs for 5 minutes, stirring.

3 Remove the crabs with a skimmer and put them in a colander to drain. Put them on a cutting board and cut them in half. Put them back in the pot over medium heat. Add the carrot, onion, and fennel; mix well and cook for 3 minutes. Add the pastis, garlic, and tomato paste and mix well. Pour in the white wine. After 2 minutes, add the stock and saffron. Bring almost to a boil and then simmer for 40 minutes over low heat.

4 Remove the crabs and vegetables with a skimmer and then put the broth through a fine strainer (a chinois if possible), pressing on the solids to extract as much liquid as possible. Add the heavy cream and blend the soup broth in a blender or food processor. Taste and add salt and pepper if necessary. If the soup has gotten cold, reheat it gently before serving.

1¼ pounds (600 g.) blue crabs
1 carrot
1 onion
1 small bulb fennel
2 tablespoons olive oil
1 tablespoon pastis
1 clove garlic
2 tablespoons tomato paste
1 cup (25 cl.) dry white wine
1 quart (1 l.) fish stock
    (page 40)
12 stems saffron or 3 good-sized pinches of powdered saffron
⅓ cup (10 cl.) heavy cream, right out of the refrigerator
Salt
Pepper

FISH SOUP

Soupe de poissons

SERVES 4
PREPARATION 35 minutes
COOKING 30 minutes

Ask the fishmonger to scale the fish. You can have them gutted, or, if you prefer a more full-bodied soup, you can leave them whole. This soup does not keep well, quickly turning harsh and sour; it should be eaten as soon as you make it.

1   Peel the onion and slice it into very thin rounds, just less than $\frac{1}{16}$ inch (2 mm.) thick. Wash the tomatoes and cut them into 6 slices each. Peel 2 garlic cloves and quarter them lengthwise. Wash and dry the fennel fronds. Quickly rinse the fish if they seem dirty. Dry them with paper towels.

2   Preheat the broiler. Heat the olive oil in a soup pot over medium heat. Cook the onion, tomatoes, garlic, and bouquet garni for 3 minutes, still over medium heat. Add the fennel fronds and lower the heat. Stir and cook 3 minutes more. Add the fish and tomato paste; cook for 1 minute, stirring gently, and then pour in 1 quart (1 l.) water. It should just cover the fish; if it does not, add enough water to cover. Add the saffron, 2 teaspoons coarse salt, and a pinch of pepper. Bring almost to a boil and then lower the heat and simmer for 30 minutes.

3   Under the broiler, toast the baguette slices on both sides until they are golden. Peel the last clove of garlic, cut it in half, and rub one side of each slice of toast with the cut side of the garlic. Arrange the toasts around the inside circumference of a big, deep platter. Blanket them with grated cheese.

4   When the fish soup has finished cooking, remove the bouquet garni and gently remove the fish with a skimmer. Put them in the middle of the platter. Put the soup through a food mill. Taste and add salt and pepper if necessary. If the soup has gotten too cool, reheat it and pour the hot soup over the platter, being sure to cover the bread. This soup can be served with garlic mayonnaise (page 56) or *rouille* (page 57).

1 medium onion
2 medium tomatoes
3 cloves garlic
1 handful fennel fronds or, if fronds are not available, a morsel of the bulb
1¼ pounds (600 g.) mixed fish, depending on what is available at the market (scorpion fish, gurnard, monkfish, and conger are all inexpensive and good for soup)
3 tablespoons olive oil
1 bouquet garni (1 sprig thyme, ½ bay leaf, and 1 branch flat-leaf parsley, wrapped and tied in a green leek leaf)
2 tablespoons tomato paste
12 saffron stems or 3 generous pinches of powdered saffron
Coarse salt
Pepper
16 slices of baguette
1 cup (3 ounces/100 g.) freshly grated tomme de brebis (a sheep cheese)
Salt

MUSSEL SOUP WITH CILANTRO

Soupe de moules à la coriandre

SERVES 2
PREPARATION 10 minutes
COOKING 14 minutes

1. Scrub the mussels, remove their beards, and wash them in several changes of water. Peel and mince the shallots.
2. Combine the wine and shallots in a soup pot. Bring them to a boil, cover, and cook for 10 minutes over low heat. Turn off the heat.
3. Add the mussels and sprinkle with the coriander seeds and parsley. Stir in the crème fraîche. Turn the heat to high for 2 minutes, then turn it off, cover the pot, and leave it for 2 minutes.
4. Remove the mussels with a skimmer and shell them. Filter the broth through a fine strainer into a bowl. Rinse the pot under hot water and return the strained broth to the pot. Bring to a boil and then remove from the heat. Season with salt and pepper.
5. Place the mussels on a deep platter. Pour the hot soup over them. Sprinkle with cilantro.

2 pounds (1 kg.) mussels
2 shallots
1 cup (25 cl.) dry white wine
1 teaspoon crushed coriander seeds
2 tablespoons flat-leaf parsley leaves
2 tablespoons crème fraîche
Salt
Pepper
1 teaspoon minced cilantro

MUSSEL SOUP WITH CURRY

Soupe de moules au curry

SERVES 4

PREPARATION 25 minutes

COOKING 30 minutes

1   Scrub the mussels, remove their beards, and wash them carefully in several changes of water. Let them drip dry.

2   Wash and mince the leek. Peel the onion and slice it into very thin rounds, less than ⅛ inch (2–3 mm.) thick.

3   Peel the potatoes, wash them, and slice them into rounds.

4   Melt the butter in a soup pot. Add the onion, leek, and potatoes and cook for 2–3 minutes over low heat without allowing them to color. Raise the heat to high and add the mussels, bouquet garni, garlic, and wine. Cover and cook for 2 minutes over high heat. Turn off the burner but leave the covered pot there for 2 minutes. Remove the bouquet garni. Remove the mussels with a skimmer and remove them from their shells.

5   Filter the broth through a fine strainer into a bowl. Rinse the soup pot under hot water.

6   Pour the filtered broth back into the pot and add 1⅔ cups cream. Bring this liquid to a boil and then simmer for 30 minutes. Remove from the heat and add three-fourths of the shelled mussels. Pour everything into a blender and blend until the soup is sleek and voluptuous. Pour the blended soup back into the pot and keep it warm over very low heat.

7   Put the ⅓ cup chilled cream in a bowl with the curry powder and a pinch of salt. Beat until you have a very lightly whipped cream.

8   Give the warm soup a whisk and taste for salt and pepper. Put the remaining mussels in a tureen and cover them with the soup. With a large spoon, carefully drizzle the soup's surface with the curried whipped cream.

2 pounds (1 kg.) mussels

1 leek, white part only

1 medium onion

2 firm-fleshed potatoes (BF 15, fingerling, or Yukon Gold)

1 teaspoon butter

1 bouquet garni (1 sprig fresh thyme, ½ bay leaf, and 1 branch parsley, wrapped and tied in a green leek leaf)

1 clove garlic, peeled and degermed (page 122)

¾ cup (20 cl.) dry white wine

2 cups (50 cl.) heavy cream (⅓ cup should be well chilled to whip)

1 teaspoon curry powder

Salt

Pepper

Cold Soups

Cold soups are generally made with cooked or raw vegetables. They are best when prepared 5–6 hours ahead of time so that the flavors have a chance to marry.

In any event, allow at least 2 hours for a quart (a liter) of soup (serving four people) to chill in the refrigerator after it has cooled to room temperature. You can chill the hot soup immediately by pouring it into a container that has been set in a larger container or bowl filled with ice cubes. You can also put a sealed container of warm soup in the freezer for half an hour to get it fairly cold before you refrigerate it, but this is not a good idea if you are forgetful.

CHILLED TOMATO SOUP

Soupe glacée de tomates

SERVES 4
PREPARATION 5 minutes
COOLING at least 2 hours

1 Blend the tomato flesh into a fine purée. Add the crème fraîche and heavy cream. Blend again and taste for salt and pepper. Cover with plastic wrap and place in the refrigerator to chill.

2 When it's time to eat, toast the bread. Rub it with the clove of garlic and cut it into croutons. Drizzle the soup with the olive oil and sprinkle with croutons and basil.

2 pounds tomatoes, peeled and seeded (page 124)
1 tablespoon crème fraîche
3 tablespoons heavy cream
Salt
Pepper
1 good-sized slice country bread
1 clove garlic, peeled
1 tablespoon olive oil
8 leaves basil

GAZPACHO

Soupe glacée de tomates espagnole

SERVES   4

PREPARATION   30 minutes

Gazpacho should be prepared the night before you plan to eat it.

1   Put 1 of the diced tomatoes in a small bowl. Slice 2 leaves of basil into strips and add them to the tomato. Add 1 tablespoon sherry vinegar and 1 tablespoon olive oil and mix everything together. Cover with plastic wrap and refrigerate.

2   Cut the bell pepper into 6 strips lengthwise. Peel the cucumber and cut it in half lengthwise. Scoop out the seeds with a spoon. Cut each half into 1-inch (2-cm.) sections. Peel the onion and slice it into ⅛-inch (3-mm.) rounds. Thinly slice the clove of garlic. Put all the vegetables in a big bowl with the rest of the diced tomatoes.

3   Cut the crusts off the bread. Cut the bread into ½-inch (1-cm.) cubes and throw the cubes into the big bowl.

4   In a small bowl, whisk together 3 tablespoons sherry vinegar, 3 pinches of salt, and 1 pinch of pepper. Add the tomato paste and juice and whisk again. Whisk in 2 tablespoons olive oil. Pour this mixture over the bread and vegetables, stirring with a big spoon to make sure everything is well combined and the sauce is evenly distributed. Cover with plastic wrap and refrigerate.

5   Keep both bowls in the refrigerator all day or overnight. Just before serving, blend the contents of the large bowl for 45 seconds to 1 minute, until you have a rather thick soup. Taste and add salt and pepper if necessary. Stir in the small bowl of seasoned tomatoes. Sprinkle with the remaining basil and, if you wish, croutons made of white bread fried in olive oil.

2 pounds (1 kg.) tomatoes, peeled, seeded, and diced (page 124)
10 leaves basil
4 tablespoons sherry vinegar
3 tablespoons olive oil
½ red bell pepper, peeled and seeded (page 130)
1 small cucumber or ½ large cucumber
1 medium onion
1 clove garlic, peeled and degermed (page 122)
2 slices white sandwich bread
Salt
Pepper
1 tablespoon tomato paste
1 cup (25 cl.) tomato juice
Croutons (optional)

CHILLED CUCUMBER SOUP

Soupe glacée de concombre

SERVES   4
PREPARATION   20 minutes
COOLING   at least 2 hours

1   Wash and dry the cucumbers. Peel them partially so that evenly sized and spaced strips of skin alternate with peeled strips. Cut them into 1-inch-thick (2-cm.) slices.

2   Cut the crusts off the bread and cut 4 of the slices into 1-inch (2-cm.) cubes. Blend the bread cubes with the cucumbers, garlic, 3 tablespoons olive oil, sherry vinegar, 2 or 3 drops of Tabasco, a pinch of salt, and a pinch of pepper. Taste after tossing and add more salt and pepper if necessary. Cover with plastic wrap and refrigerate.

3   Cut the 4 remaining slices of bread into small dice, about 1/8 inch (2–3 mm.). Heat the peanut oil in a skillet over medium heat. When it is hot, add the diced bread and stir vigorously to coat with hot oil. When the croutons are golden, remove them with a skimmer and put them on a plate lined with paper towels. Sprinkle them with a pinch of salt.

4   To serve, sprinkle the cold soup with the croutons and drizzle with 1 tablespoon olive oil.

2 cucumbers
8 slices white sandwich bread
1 clove garlic, peeled and degermed (page 122)
4 tablespoons olive oil
1 tablespoon sherry vinegar
Tabasco
Salt
Pepper
2 tablespoons peanut oil

CHILLED TOMATO PEPPER SOUP

Soupe glacée de tomate et poivron

SERVES   4
PREPARATION   5 minutes
COOLING   at least 2 hours

1   Peel and quarter the cucumber. Peel the onion and slice it into 1/8-inch (2–3-mm.) rounds.

2   Blend all the vegetables and the garlic. Add the vinegar, olive oil, and a pinch of salt and pepper. Blend again, taste, and adjust the salt and pepper as necessary. Refrigerate at least 2 hours before serving.

1/4 cucumber
1/2 onion
2 large tomatoes, peeled and seeded (page 124)
1 red bell pepper, peeled and seeded (page 130)
1 clove garlic, degermed (page 122)
2 teaspoons red wine vinegar
5 tablespoons olive oil
Salt
Pepper

CHILLED TOMATO SOUP WITH CELERY

Soupe glacée de tomates au céleri

SERVES 4
PREPARATION 10 minutes
COOLING at least 2 hours

1 Preheat the oven to 400–425°F (200–220°C). Arrange the baguette slices on a sheet pan and drizzle each with a small amount of olive oil (about ½ teaspoon per slice). Slip them into the oven for 3–4 minutes, just until they turn pale gold. Set aside with the tapenade.

2 Wash and quarter the tomatoes. Trim the tops from the celery and new onion and cut each into slices about ⅛ inch (2–3 mm.) thick.

3 Blend the tomatoes, celery, and onion for 1 minute, until they are like a thin sauce. Add salt, pepper, and 2–3 drops Tabasco. Blend again. Add 5 tablespoons olive oil and the sherry vinegar. Taste, add salt and pepper if necessary, and put the soup through a fine strainer. To serve, drizzle with 1 tablespoon olive oil, sprinkle with basil leaves, and put out the toast and tapenade.

8 slices baguette
Olive oil
About 4 tablespoons tapenade (page 136 or store-bought)
5 very ripe tomatoes on the vine
1 stalk celery
1 new onion or a scallion
Salt
Pepper
Tabasco
1 tablespoon sherry vinegar
8 leaves basil

Cold Cream Soups

CHILLED CREAM OF CUCUMBER SOUP WITH CURRY

Crème de concombres glacée au curry

SERVES 4
PREPARATION 5 minutes
COOKING 15 minutes
COOLING about 2 hours

1 Wash and peel the cucumbers. Cut them into 6 sections each.

2 Put the cucumbers in a soup pot with the broth. Bring to a near boil and simmer for 15 minutes.

2 medium cucumbers
⅓ cup (10 cl.) chicken broth (page 77 or made from a bouillon cube)
⅓ cup (10 cl.) heavy cream
Salt
Pepper
½ teaspoon curry powder
Tabasco (optional)

3 Blend. Add the cream and blend again. Taste for salt and pepper. Allow to cool and then refrigerate at least 1 hour. Just before serving, sprinkle the soup with curry powder and, if you wish, a few drops of Tabasco.

CHILLED CREAM OF LEEK AND POTATO SOUP ⎯⎯⎯⎯⎯⎯

Crème vichyssoise glacée

SERVES 4
PREPARATION 20 minutes
COOKING 30 minutes
COOLING about 3 hours

This soup takes its name from the spring of Vichy in southeast France. Originally, the vegetables were cooked in a bottle of Vichy water.

1 Slice the whites of the leeks in half. Wash them and slice into ½-inch (1-cm.) half moons. Peel and quarter the potatoes.

2 Melt the butter in a soup pot and add the leeks. Cook over low heat for 3 minutes, stirring and not allowing the leeks or butter to color. Add 1½ quarts (1.5 l.) water and bring to a boil.

3 When the water bubbles, add 1 tablespoon coarse salt, the bouquet garni, and the potatoes. Simmer for 25 minutes.

4 Remove the bouquet garni. Blend the soup well. Add the cream and blend again. Taste for salt and pepper.

5 Allow the soup to cool and then refrigerate it for at least 3 hours. Sprinkle with chives and chervil and serve.

2 leeks, white parts only
¾ pound (300 g.) firm-fleshed potatoes
2 teaspoons butter
Coarse salt
1 bouquet garni (1 sprig fresh thyme and 3 branches parsley, wrapped and tied in a green leek leaf)
1 cup (20 cl.) heavy cream
Salt
Pepper
1 teaspoon minced chives and chervil

CHILLED CREAM OF ZUCCHINI SOUP

Crème de courgettes glacée

SERVES 4
PREPARATION 10 minutes
COOKING 15 minutes

1   Wash the zucchini and quarter them lengthwise. Scoop out the seeds with a spoon but do not peel them. Cut the quarters into 1-inch (2–3-cm.) sections.
2   Peel and quarter the onions.
3   Warm 2 tablespoons olive oil in a soup pot and cook the onions over low heat for 3 minutes, stirring and without allowing them to color. Add the garlic and zucchini pieces. Add salt and then cook over low heat for 10 minutes, stirring. Add the broth and bring to a boil. Add the sugar and simmer for 3 minutes, stirring. Add ⅓ cup (10 cl.) cream and simmer for 2 minutes.
4   Blend the soup. Taste for salt and pepper. Add a pinch of grated nutmeg and ⅓ cup (10 cl.) cream and blend again.
5   Pour the soup into a large bowl and allow it to cool. Cover with plastic wrap and refrigerate at least 1 hour. When it is cold, serve sprinkled with a teaspoon of olive oil.

1½ pounds (650 g.) zucchini
2 medium onions
2 tablespoons plus 1 teaspoon (5 cl.) olive oil
2 cloves garlic, degermed (page 122)
Salt
1 cup (25 cl.) chicken broth (page 77 or made from a bouillon cube)
1 teaspoon superfine sugar
⅔ cup (20 cl.) heavy cream
Pepper
Nutmeg

CHILLED CREAM OF ASPARAGUS SOUP

Crème d'asperges froide

SERVES 4
PREPARATION 10 minutes
COOKING 20 minutes
REDUCING 30 minutes

1   Bring the stock or broth to a boil.
2   Wash the asparagus. Trim off 2 inches (5 cm.) of the tips and put them aside for another use. Do not peel the stalks but cut them into 1-inch (3 cm.) sections.
3   When the broth is boiling, add the asparagus and sugar. Lower the heat, cover the pot, and cook for 20 minutes.

1 quart (1 l.) chicken stock (page 36) or chicken broth (page 77 or made from a bouillon cube)

(continued)

4   Blend the broth and asparagus. Put it through a fine strainer (a chinois if possible), pressing on the solids with a spoon to extract as much liquid as possible. Put the strained liquid back in the pot and boil about 30 minutes more.

5   Combine the cornstarch with a spoonful of cold water in a little bowl. Beat the yolk and ½ cup cream together in a bowl large enough to hold all the soup. Put this bowl near your cooktop.

6   When the asparagus broth has reduced by about half, whisk in the cornstarch mixture. Simmer for 1 minute, whisking the whole time, and then pour the hot broth into the bowl with the yolk-cream mixture, still whisking constantly.

7   Pour the contents of the bowl back into the pot and warm over very low heat in order to thicken the soup. Stir constantly and turn off the heat at the first hint of boiling. Blend the soup and allow it to cool. Taste for salt. Refrigerate for at least 3 hours. Just before serving, add the remaining cream and blend to make the soup frothy.

2 pounds (1 kg.) white asparagus
A bit of sugar (or a sugar cube if you have one)
¼ cup (30 g.) cornstarch
1 egg yolk (page 204)
1 cup (25 cl.) heavy cream
Salt

Crudités and Hors d'Oeuvres

*H*ors means outside. Hors d'oeuvres earned their name in France because they were, once upon a time, thought of as being outside the meal, not part of it. Today, however, hors d'oeuvres, along with soups, are a meal's beginning.

The French tradition is to break the meal into distinct parts that are enjoyed in an orderly progression. The Anglo-Saxon way, on the other hand, is to serve almost everything at once, with meat, vegetable, and starch cozily sharing a plate. The Vietnamese, by contrast, have always tended to snack; instead of sitting down to three discrete meals a day, people eat more frequently in small amounts.

We, too, grab something from the refrigerator or the cupboard as the mood strikes us and as time allows, and for some of us, shared family meals are now the exception. This kind of grazing has more and more supplanted formal, regular eating in contemporary societies throughout the world. The price we pay for the freedom to eat this way is huge. We are losing one of our most intimate social and cultural traditions and the healthy rhythm it gave to family life. And since in the West eating this way tends to mean the repetitive and unthinking consumption of fatty, sugary processed foods, it has led to an alarming spike in obesity.

Eating on the go is now common even in France, especially at lunchtime when many people wolf down the quick store-bought sandwiches that have taken the place of the meals they once would have packed (or, rather, which once would have been prepared by a stay-at-home wife).

Still, despite the enormous changes in the pace and style of everyday life witnessed in the latter twentieth century, France has done a relatively good job of maintaining some semblance of the old family table and meals shared by friends. As with the meal *à la française* that became the standard at the court of Louis XIV, French meals today unfold in courses. But everything is much simpler and lighter. It is no longer necessary to follow the opening soup with a hot or cold first course, fish, and then meat, a salad, some cheese, and a dessert—all preceded by an aperitif and washed down with a digestif. Not to mention the little extras—such as a precursor to dessert, perhaps, crêpes, soufflés, or mousses.

Even if the twenty-first-century meal *à la française* is greatly simplified, it almost always still includes, especially if there is no soup, some sort of hors d'oeuvre—or, better yet, two or three—very often crudités. These are fast and easy dishes that afford a good opportunity to use up leftovers. They can be served with charcuterie, rillettes, or homemade terrines.

FRESHNESS COUNTS

Most of these hors d'oeuvres can be eaten cold or at room temperature. Some nicely complement another dish, such as eggplant caviar, which you might serve with lamb.

Use the freshest, firmest, most beautifully colored ingredients you can. Pay special attention to fish, which spoils quickly, and to any meat or fish you plan to serve uncooked, as is so stylish nowadays.

SEASONING

It is always best to grind fresh pepper. When making a vinaigrette, the salt must be dissolved in the vinegar (or citrus juice) first, as it will not dissolve in oil. See the chapter on sauces for several salad dressings that you can use as you prefer.

REMOVING GARLIC GERM

Especially when raw garlic is to be used as a seasoning, it is important to remove the indigestible germ at the core of the clove. It isn't hard: Peel the clove and cut it in half. With the tip of a knife, pick out the germ that runs the length of the clove.

HAM AND CHEESE MATCHSTICKS

Allumettes de jambon au comté

PREPARATION   10 minutes

Buy enough ham and cheese to make about half a dozen "matchsticks" per diner.

Cut the cheese into ½-by-2-inch (1 cm.-by-5-cm.) sticks. Cut the ham into 2-inch (5-cm.) square pieces. Wrap each piece of cheese in a slice of ham and insert a toothpick to hold it together.

Comté cheese
Ham (boiled ham—the kind you would use for a sandwich) or Swiss air-dried beef (*viande des Grisons*)

FRIED SHRIMP

Crevettes grises poêlées

SERVES   4–6
PREPARATION AND COOKING   5 minutes

1   Melt the butter in a skillet over medium heat. Let it cook for 2–3 minutes, until it begins to brown.
2   Add the shrimp and sauté for 2 minutes, stirring with a wooden spatula. Pepper heavily. Add the brandy and a pinch of salt, and serve immediately with buttered rye bread.

1 tablespoon unsalted butter
About 1 pound (500 g.) cooked tiny, soft-fleshed shrimp
Pepper
Drops of brandy
Salt
Slices of rye bread spread with salted butter for serving

HOW TO PEEL A TOMATO, REMOVE THE SEEDS, AND PREPARE THE TOMATO PULP

A tomato that has been warmed on your cooktop is easy to peel. You can hold it with tongs for just a minute in the burner's flame and then remove its skin. But if that sounds intimidating (or if you do not have a gas cooktop), do the following:

Put a dozen ice cubes in a big bowl half filled with cold water. Put 1 quart (1 l.) water on to boil. Plunge the tomatoes into the boiling water for 10–15 seconds, depending on how large and how ripe they are. If they are small or soft, 10 seconds should be enough. (It isn't a bad idea to set the timer on your microwave to keep precise track of such a short time.) Do not make a little slice in the bottom of the tomatoes before boiling as some people recommend; that will allow unwanted water in.

Remove the tomatoes with a skimmer and submerge them in the bowl of ice water. Remove them immediately and put them in a colander. Then you can peel them easily with a small knife.

Do not leave the tomatoes in the hot water. They will swell up with water and begin to cook.

To seed tomatoes, peeled or not, simply quarter them and scoop out the seeds with a little spoon.

The flesh of peeled, seeded tomatoes can be diced to make tomato pulp, which is also called crushed tomato.

TOMATO SORBET WITH MINT
Sorbet de tomate à la menthe

MAKES   3 cups (75 cl.)
PREPARATION   5 minutes

1   In a blender, purée the tomato pulp. Put the purée through a fine strainer into a bowl and add the sugar, lemon juice, a pinch of salt, and the snipped mint. Mix well.

2   Refrigerate at least 2 hours or overnight. Freeze in an ice-cream maker according to its instructions. If you do not have an ice-cream maker, you can freeze the mixture and then scrape it into a pulp with a spoon to make a granita. Sprinkle with mint leaves to serve.

3 pounds (1½ kg.) plum tomatoes, peeled, seeded, and pulped (see above)
½ cup (130 g.) confectioners' sugar
1 tablespoon lemon juice
Salt
1 tablespoon snipped fresh mint leaves
Leaves from 1 sprig mint for garnish

CELERY AND ROQUEFORT

Céleri-branche au roquefort

SERVES 4–6
PREPARATION 10 minutes

1. Choose celery that is young, green, and tender. Wash it and, if it is very fibrous, peel away the tough outer layer on its convex side. Cut it into fine half moons, about ¼ inch (0.5 cm.) wide.
2. In a bowl, whisk together the vinegars and a pinch of salt. Whisk in the olive oil. Add the cheese and mash it into the vinaigrette with a fork. Toss with the celery and pepper to taste.
3. You can also leave the celery stalks whole and spread their insides with blue cheese or a mixture of Roquefort and butter.

9–10 stalks celery, leaves removed (about 1 pound/500 g.)
1 teaspoon red wine vinegar
2 teaspoons sherry vinegar
Salt
3 tablespoons olive oil
2 ounces (60 g.) crumbled Roquefort or other blue cheese
White pepper

MUSHROOMS AND ARUGULA

Champignons de Paris et roquette

SERVES 4
PREPARATION 10 minutes

1. Cut off the ends of the mushroom stems. Put the mushrooms in a colander and rinse them briefly under cold running water. Drain. Let them dry on paper towels.
2. Whisk the lemon juice with a pinch of salt and a pinch of pepper. Drizzle in the olive oil, whisking the whole time.
3. Wash the arugula and dry it completely. Cut the mushrooms lengthwise into thin slices.
4. With a pastry brush, paint the dressing on the plate you will use to serve the dish. Arrange the mushroom slices in a rosette. Paint the mushrooms and the arugula leaves with dressing. Lay the arugula on top of the mushrooms. (You will have some dressing left over and can use it on a salad.)
5. With a vegetable peeler, shave the Parmesan all over the top. Anoint the dish with the balsamic vinegar.

12 white button mushrooms, cleaned
Juice of ½ lemon
Salt
Pepper
1 tablespoon olive oil
12 leaves arugula
¼ pound (125 g.) Parmesan cheese
4 teaspoons balsamic vinegar

Leeks often contain sand or dirt, which can be very unpleasant if it finds its way into your food. They must therefore be carefully washed several times. Leave them in a bowl filled with warm water for 10 minutes. This will soften them up a bit and make it easier to rid them of sand. Separate the green leaves and scrape out the dirt lodged there. If your recipe requires you to cut the leek in half lengthwise, soak the halves again in warm water, separating even the white leaves of the base a bit. You can also run the slightly separated leek half under cold running water.

Leeks should be cooked in a great deal of boiling salted water. Remove them from their cooking water with a skimmer. (If you just dump them in a colander, you will coat them with any dirt or tiny bugs that fell to the bottom of the pot during cooking.) Then shock and cool them in a bowl of ice water; if you don't, they will get soft and turn grayish. As soon as they are cool, drain them so they don't become engorged with water. Whatever you do, don't leave them in the hot cooking water.

LEEKS VINAIGRETTE

Poireaux vinaigrette

SERVES 4
PREPARATION 5 minutes
COOKING 10 minutes

1 Carefully wash the leeks. Prepare an ice water bath to shock the cooked leeks. Bring 1 quart water and 1 teaspoon coarse salt to a boil. Add the leeks and cook for 10–15 minutes depending on the season. (You can test to see whether they are cooked by pricking the middle of one with the tip of a knife; the flesh of the leek will not resist when it is cooked.) Remove them with a skimmer and plunge them into the ice water bath. Drain.

2 Put a kettle of water on to boil. Put a bowl containing the egg yolks into a larger bowl or a casserole; fill the outer container with almost-boiling water so that it comes halfway up the side of the bowl of yolks. In another bowl, whisk together the vinegar and mustard with a pinch of salt and a pinch of pepper. Whisk in 3 tablespoons oil. Remove the bowl of yolks from its hot water bath (they should be just warm) and add the vinaigrette to the yolks. Add the shallot and chives. Arrange the leeks on a platter and dress with the vinaigrette.

8 medium leeks, whites only
Coarse salt
2 egg yolks (page 204)
1 tablespoon sherry vinegar
1 teaspoon mustard
Salt
Pepper
3 tablespoons neutral oil, such as grapeseed
1 shallot, peeled and minced
1 teaspoon minced chives

VEAL WITH TUNA MAYONNAISE

Vitello tonnato

SERVES 2

PREPARATION AND COOKING 5 minutes

Ask the butcher to slice the veal very thin.

1   Preheat the oven to 400°F (200°C). Oil a sheet pan and arrange the slices of veal on it. Do not let them overlap. Sprinkle the veal slices on both sides with salt and pepper and then use a pastry brush to paint them with olive oil. Cook for 2 minutes.

2   Serve the veal coated with Mayonnaise with Tuna and Anchovies and sprinkled with chives and capers.

¼ pound (100 g.) uncooked veal fillet, thinly sliced
Salt
Pepper
Olive oil
Mayonnaise with Tuna and Anchovies (page 58)
1 tablespoon minced chives
2 teaspoons capers

LEEKS VINAIGRETTE MIMOSA

Poireaux vinaigrette et "oeuf" mimosa

SERVES 4

PREPARATION 10 minutes

COOKING 20–25 minutes

"Mimosa" refers to the garnish of hard-boiled egg.

1   Carefully wash the leek whites in warm water. Tie them into little bundles so the leaves don't separate as they cook.

2   Bring 1½ quarts (1.5 l.) water and 1 tablespoon coarse salt to a boil and add the leeks. Cook for 15–20 minutes, according to their size. (You can test to see whether they are cooked by pricking one in the middle with the tip of a knife. When it is cooked, the flesh of the leek should not resist the knife at all.) Set a rack over a plate. Remove the leeks with a skimmer and set them on the rack.

3   Separate the yolk and the white of the hard-boiled egg. Crumble the yolk with a fork. Crumble the white, either by mincing it or by pressing it through a strainer with not-too-fine a screen.

8 medium leeks, white parts only
Coarse salt
1 hard-boiled egg, shell removed (page 208)
1 tablespoon sherry vinegar
Salt
Pepper
1 teaspoon mustard
3 tablespoons neutral oil, such as grapeseed
1 shallot, peeled and minced
1 tablespoon each minced parsley, chervil, and chives

4 Using a fork, beat the vinegar with 2 pinches of salt. Add a pinch of pepper and the mustard and mix. Beat in the oil.

5 Arrange the still-warm leeks side by side on a plate and dress them with the vinaigrette. Shower them evenly with the crumbled egg, shallot, and herbs.

HUMMUS

Purée de pois chiches (hommos)

variation
HUMMUS WITH TAHINI

PREPARATION 5 minutes
SERVES 6–8

1 Rinse and drain the chickpeas, saving the liquid from the can. Put the chickpeas into a food processor and process for 2 minutes. Add about ½ cup of their canning liquid, the garlic, and the lemon juice. Process for 1 minute. Stir in the olive oil and add salt and pepper to taste.

2 To serve, drizzle with 1 or 2 tablespoons olive oil and sprinkle with parsley. You can also give it a dash of paprika.

One 15-ounce can (300 g.) chickpeas
1 clove garlic, peeled and degermed (page 122)
Juice of 1 lemon
5 tablespoons olive oil plus more for serving
Salt
Pepper
1 teaspoon minced parsley
Paprika (optional)

HUMMUS WITH TAHINI

Purée de pois chiches au sésame

Follow the recipe for hummus, adding ¼ cup plus 2 tablespoons (80 g.) tahin (sesame purée) with the garlic and lemon juice.

THE PREPARATION AND COOKING OF EGGPLANTS (EGGPLANT CAVIAR)

Preheat the oven to 350°F (175°C). Wash the eggplants, dry them completely with paper towels, and then wrap them individually in aluminum foil. Put them on a sheet pan and cook for 1 hour. Cut them in half lengthwise, scoop out the flesh with a spoon, and chop it up coarsely.

TOMATO EGGPLANT CAVIAR

Purée d'aubergines à la tomate

SERVES 4

PREPARATION AND COOKING 20 minutes

This is delicious served cold atop toasted country bread as an hors d'oeuvre or hot alongside meat, especially lamb, or fish.

1   Prepare and cook the eggplants as described on page 128.
2   Peel and chop the onions and garlic. Warm 2 tablespoons olive oil in a skillet over low heat. Add the onions and some salt and pepper and cook for 1 minute, stirring. Add the tomatoes, garlic, and sugar. Add more salt and pepper and sprinkle with the vinegar. Cook for 5 minutes, stirring. Add the eggplant flesh and stir well. Taste for salt and pepper. Cook 5 minutes, still over low heat, stirring.
3   Put the mixture into a blender or food processor and blend well, until it is homogeneous. Add 2 tablespoons olive oil and the fennel fronds and blend again.

6 small eggplants
2 medium onions
6 cloves garlic, degermed
    (page 122)
4 tablespoons olive oil
Salt
Pepper
Pulp of 4 tomatoes (page 124)
1 teaspoon superfine sugar
1 teaspoon wine vinegar
2 tablespoons fennel fronds

CURRY EGGPLANT CAVIAR

Purée d'aubergines au curry

SERVES 4

PREPARATION AND COOKING 1 hour 15 minutes

1   Preheat the oven to 350°F (175°C). Peel the garlic and cut it lengthwise into thin slices. With the tip of a knife, make slits in the eggplants and put garlic slices in the slits. Wrap the eggplants individually in aluminum foil and bake for 1 hour.
2   When you remove the eggplants, cut off their caps. Cut the eggplants into large sections and blend them one at a time in a blender or food processor, adding 2 tablespoons olive oil with each batch of eggplant. Add salt, pepper, and a dash of curry. Blend again. This can be served cold or hot.

1 clove garlic
3 medium eggplants
6 tablespoons olive oil
Salt
Pepper
Dash of curry powder

TO PEEL AND SEED A PEPPER

Choose firm peppers with thick, smooth, shiny skin. Stick a pepper on a fork and hold it over a gas burner, turning it in the flame about 1 minute. Peel it carefully with a small kitchen knife (do not use a vegetable peeler) without removing any flesh. *Or* preheat the oven to 400°F (200°C). Wash the pepper, put it on a sheet pan, and cook for 30 minutes, giving it a turn every 10 minutes. Put it in a bowl, cover the bowl with plastic wrap, and leave for at least 20 minutes. Then it will be easy to remove the skin with your fingers.

To remove its seeds, simply cut off the stem end and slice the pepper in half lengthwise. Scoop out the seeds and white membranes with a small spoon.

RED PEPPER WITH THYME

Poivron rouge au thym

SERVES   4
PREPARATION AND COOKING   20 minutes

1   Quarter the peppers lengthwise. Heat the olive oil in a skillet. Add the peppers and lower the heat to low. Add salt and pepper. Cook for 10–15 minutes, stirring from time to time, until the peppers are very tender. Do not allow them to color. Add the garlic and thyme and cook 2 minutes more, still over low heat. Be careful not to let the garlic color. Turn off the heat, add the vinegar, and mix well.

2   Serve warm or at room temperature. According to your taste, you can add or subtract a clove of garlic. Keep in a closed container in the refrigerator, perhaps adding a little olive oil, but remove 30 minutes before eating.

4 red bell peppers, peeled and seeded (see above)
2 tablespoons olive oil
Salt
Pepper
2 cloves garlic, peeled, degermed (page 122), and minced
1 teaspoon fresh thyme leaves
1½ teaspoons sherry vinegar

PEPPERS AND EGGPLANTS WITH ANCHOVIES

Poivrons et aubergines aux anchois

SERVES 4

PREPARATION AND COOKING 1 hour

1   Preheat the oven to 400°F (200°C). Wash and dry the egg-
    plants and peppers. Line a sheet pan with aluminum foil, put
    the eggplants and peppers on top, and bake for 30 minutes,
    rotating the vegetables every 10 minutes.
2   After removing the eggplants and peppers from the oven,
    put them in a bowl and cover it tightly with plastic wrap.
    Wait for 20 minutes and then peel the vegetables. Cut them
    in half and remove the peppers' seeds with a spoon. Cut the
    peppers and eggplants lengthwise into slices about 1 inch
    (2 cm.) thick and then cut into 2-inch-long (5-cm.) strips.
3   Put the strips into a bowl. Add salt, pepper, and the olive oil.
    Mix well and refrigerate for 15 minutes.
4   To serve, arrange the anchovies on top of the peppers and
    eggplants.

2 eggplants
2 red bell peppers
2 green bell peppers
Salt
Pepper
5 tablespoons olive oil
8 anchovy fillets

RED PEPPER MOUSSE

Mousse de poivron rouge

SERVES 4–6

PREPARATION AND COOKING 1 hour
Prepare 1 day in advance.

1   Preheat the oven to 400°F (200°C). Wash and dry the pep-
    pers. Line a sheet pan with aluminum foil, put the peppers
    on top, bake for 40 minutes, and then put them in a bowl and
    cover it tightly with plastic wrap. Set the bowl aside for
    20 minutes. When the peppers are room temperature, peel
    them, cut them in half, and carefully remove their seeds with
    a small spoon. Blend the pepper flesh in a blender.
2   Whip the cream.
3   Soak the gelatin in a bowl of cold water.
4   Put about one-sixth of the blended pepper flesh in a
    saucepan over low heat. Remove the gelatin from the bowl
    and add it to the saucepan, stirring it in with a spatula (and

4 red bell peppers
1 cup (30 cl.) heavy cream
¼ ounce (6 g.) gelatin leaves
Salt
Pepper
⅓ cup (10 cl.) tomato juice
Celery salt

discarding its soaking water). Take the saucepan off the heat and add the rest of the blended pepper, 1 teaspoon salt, and a twist of pepper. Gently fold in the whipped cream. Refrigerate at least 12 hours or overnight.

5   Prepare a small glass or ramekin for each serving. Put 1 tablespoon tomato juice at the bottom of each, sprinkle with celery salt, and top with the chilled pepper mousse.

CUCUMBERS WITH SALMON ROE

Concombre aux oeufs de saumon

SERVES   4
PREPARATION   15 minutes

1   Wash and dry the cucumber. Chop off its ends but do not peel it. Slice it in half horizontally, then slice these halves in half horizontally on a 45-degree angle. Starting from the beveled end, scoop out the insides of the cucumber, leaving about ¼ inch (0.5 cm.) of flesh all around and at the flat end.

2   Put a dozen ice cubes in a large bowl half filled with water. Bring 1 quart water and 1 teaspoon coarse salt to a boil. Add the cucumbers, boil them for 2 minutes, and then plunge them into the ice water. Leave them there until they are cool, then drain them.

3   Wash the watercress and dry it in a salad spinner. Gently stir the cream into the roe, being careful not to burst the eggs.

4   Fill the cucumbers with the roe. Whisk together the lemon juice and a pinch of salt. Whisk in the olive oil. Top the cucumbers with watercress and sprinkle everything with the lemon-oil dressing.

1 cucumber
Coarse salt
1 bunch watercress
½ cup (15 cl.) heavy cream
½ pound (200 g.) salmon roe
Juice of 1 lemon
Salt
1 tablespoon olive oil

CUCUMBER AND GOAT CHEESE

Concombre au fromage de chèvre

SERVES 4

PREPARATION 15 minutes

1 cucumber
Salt
2 tablespoons distilled vinegar
1 tablespoon wine vinegar
Pepper
3 tablespoons walnut oil
1 tablespoon minced flat-leaf
  parsley
About 6 ounces fresh goat
  cheese
4 radishes

1. Wash and dry the cucumber. Without peeling it, cut it into ½-inch-thick (1-cm.) slices. Put 16 slices on a deep plate and add 2 teaspoons salt and the distilled vinegar. Mix well and refrigerate for 1 hour.

2. Preheat the oven to 350°F (180°C). Whisk together the wine vinegar, a pinch of salt, and a pinch of pepper. Whisk in the walnut oil and then the parsley.

3. Drain the refrigerated cucumber in a colander. Cut the cheese into 8 slices about ½ inch (1 cm.) thick. Line a sheet pan with a silicone baking mat and bake the cheese on top of it for 3 minutes.

4. Cut the leaves off the radishes, wash the radishes, and chop them finely. Arrange 8 cucumber slices in a circle on a platter. Top them with the goat cheese slices and then the 8 remaining slices of cucumber. Put the diced radish in the center, sprinkle with vinaigrette, and serve warm, while the cheese is still soft and oozing.

SMALL ONIONS IN VINEGAR

Petits oignons au vinaigre

MAKES about 1 quart/1 l.

PREPARATION 15 minutes

Prepare 3 weeks in advance.

2 cups (45 cl.) distilled vinegar
3 bunches small cipollini
  onions
2 teaspoons (10 g.) salt
1 clove garlic, peeled and
  degermed (page 122)
2 sprigs tarragon
6 black peppercorns
10 coriander seeds
1 sprig thyme

These onions will keep for four or five months. They are good to eat with ham, salami, cold roast pork, and pot-au-feu.

1. Bring the vinegar to a boil. As soon as it begins to boil, remove it from the heat and allow it to cool. (The brief boil takes the acid edge off the vinegar.) Clean and peel the onions.

2. Put everything in a jar, seal it, and refrigerate for at least 3 weeks.

POT-AU-FEU SALAD

Salade de pot-au-feu

SERVES 2–4
PREPARATION 10 minutes

1   Whisk the mustard and vinegar together with a bit of salt in a bowl big enough to hold the leftovers. Whisk in the peanut oil.

2   Cut the pot-au-feu leftovers into ½-inch (1-cm.) dice. Put them in the bowl with the dressing.

3   Peel and mince the onion. Slice the cornichons into thin rounds. Cut the egg into ½-inch (1-cm.) dice. Add the onion, cornichons, and egg to the bowl and very gently toss everything together. Refrigerate for at least 2 hours or overnight. (If overnight, remove from the refrigerator at least 30 minutes before serving.) Taste for salt and pepper and sprinkle parsley to serve.

1 teaspoon strong mustard
4 tablespoons red wine vinegar
Salt
4 tablespoons peanut oil
Leftovers from a pot-au-feu
    dinner (½ pound/200 g.
    beef, ¼ celery root,
    1 carrot, 1 leek)
1 small new onion
4 cornichons
1 hard-boiled egg (page 208)
Pepper
1 tablespoon minced flat-leaf
    parsley

FRESH SARDINES WITH OLIVES

Sardines fraîches aux olives

SERVES 4
PREPARATION AND COOKING 15 minutes

1   Combine the tomato flesh, olives, and minced chives. Season lightly with salt and pepper.

2   Preheat the oven to 440°F (220°C). Quickly rinse the sardines. Cut the whole chives into 1½-inch (4-cm.) lengths. Season the insides of the sardines with fleur de sel and pepper. Stuff each sardine with 1 teaspoon of the tomato mixture.

3   Sprinkle the sardines with the chives and roll them up, starting with the head and wrapping each one in its own tail.

4   Brush a sheet pan with olive oil and arrange the rolled-up sardines atop it. Bake for 4 minutes. Sprinkle with fleur de sel and serve warm or cold.

2 tomatoes, peeled, seeded,
    and diced (page 124)
2 tablespoons chopped black
    olives, preferably niçoise
1 tablespoon minced chives
Salt
Pepper
8 small fresh sardines
5 whole chives
Fleur de sel
2 tablespoons olive oil

CRAB AND AVOCADO

Avocat au crabe

SERVES   4

PREPARATION   10 minutes

1 Put the crab meat in a bowl with a pinch of fleur de sel, the lime peel, chives, 3 tablespoons olive oil, and all but ½ teaspoon lime juice. (Save the leftover lime juice.) Pepper lightly. Use a fork to combine everything gently.
2 Peel the avocados and remove their pits. Slice.
3 Arrange a ring of avocado slices on each of 4 plates. Put some seasoned crabmeat in the center of each ring. Sprinkle with fleur de sel, the rest of the lime juice, 1 teaspoon olive oil, and the paprika.

½ pound (120 g.) cooked crab meat
Fleur de sel
½ lime (2 strips of peel, minced, plus the juice)
1 teaspoon minced chives
3 tablespoons plus 1 teaspoon olive oil
Pepper
2 avocados
1 pinch of paprika

COLD COCKLES WITH CHORIZO

Coques froides au chorizo

SERVES   4

PREPARATION AND COOKING   15 minutes
Soak cockles 1 day in advance.

1 The day before, put the cockles in salted water (use 1 tablespoon salt per quart/liter) to get rid of the sand they contain.
2 Use your hands to lift the cockles from the salted water. Carefully wash them in several changes of cold water. Put them in a pot with the thyme, chile, and olive oil. Cover and cook over high heat for 2–3 minutes. As soon as the cockles open, they should be taken off the heat or they will overcook. Sprinkle them with the chorizo and toss.
3 Allow the cockles to cool and then remove the empty half of each shell. Serve cold.

1½ pounds (750 g.) cockles
Salt
2 pinches of fresh thyme
1 small chile de arbol
⅓ cup (10 cl.) olive oil
1 tablespoon finely diced chorizo

FRESH ANCHOVY TARTINES

Tartines d'anchois aux aromates

SERVES   4 to 6
PREPARATION   20 minutes

Ask the fishmonger for very fresh anchovies and have him remove the bones.

1   Preheat the broiler. Put the salt-preserved anchovies in a bowl of cold water for 30 minutes to remove some of the salt. Finely chop all the anchovies and put them in a small bowl. Put a trayful of ice cubes into a large bowl and place the bowl of chopped anchovies on top of the ice.
2   Sprinkle the anchovies with the lemon juice and stir to combine.
3   Combine the basil, parsley, half of the Parmesan, and 5 tablespoons olive oil. Put this mixture on top of the anchovies.
4   Toast the bread lightly (do not turn off the broiler when the toast is done). Rub both sides of each slice of toast with the garlic. Sprinkle each with a few drops of the remaining olive oil and arrange on a sheet pan.
5   Top each piece of toast with a tablespoon of the anchovy mixture and some Parmesan. Broil for 3–4 minutes.
6   Serve warm or cold.

4 salt-preserved anchovies
½ pound (240 g.) fresh
   anchovies
Juice of 1 lemon
10 basil leaves
1 tablespoon minced flat-leaf
   parsley
⅓ cup (1 ounce/30 g.) grated
   Parmesan cheese
6 tablespoons olive oil
10–12 baguette slices
1 clove garlic, peeled and
   degermed (page 122)

CLASSIC TAPENADE

Purée d'olives aux anchois (tapenade)

MAKES   8 ounces (250 g.)
PREPARATION   5 minutes

Blend all the ingredients in a blender or food processor. Serve with slices of toasted baguette. If you do not eat the tapenade right away, you can keep it in the refrigerator, but you should top it with a thin protective layer of olive oil before you seal it up and put it away.

10 anchovy fillets
6 ounces (200 g.) small pitted
   black olives
1 clove garlic, peeled and
   degermed (page 122)
1 tablespoon capers
3 tablespoons olive oil

TUNA TAPENADE

Purée d'olives au thon

MAKES   16 ounces (500 g.)
PREPARATION   5 minutes

This tapenade is delicious with grilled country bread but can also be served as a dip with raw vegetables or on top of pasta. To keep it in the refrigerator, top with a thin layer of olive oil before sealing.

Rinse the olives under cold running water and drain them. Blend coarsely in a blender or food processor. Dice the chilled butter and add it to the olives along with the tuna and its oil, lemon juice, mustard, and basil. Add some pepper and pulse a few times. The tuna should end up in small bits but should not be pulverized. Taste for salt and pepper and don't serve too cold.

5 ounces (150 g.) small pitted black olives
4 tablespoons (60 g.) butter, chilled
One 6-ounce (200 g.) can oil-packed tuna
3 tablespoons lemon juice
1 tablespoon mustard
2 tablespoons chopped basil
Pepper
Salt

SARDINE RILLETTES

Rillettes de sardines

SERVES   4
PREPARATION   5 minutes

Crush the sardines into the butter with a fork. Add the other ingredients and mix well. Taste for salt and pepper. Serve with slices of toasted baguette.

One 3.75-ounce can oil-packed sardines
1 teaspoon butter at room temperature
4 ounces (150 g.) cream cheese
1 tablespoon mustard
1 tablespoon minced chives
Salt
Pepper

MACKEREL IN WHITE WINE

Maquereaux au vin blanc

SERVES 6 to 8
PREPARATION 10 minutes
COOKING 2 hours 15 minutes

Ask the fishmonger for small mackerel, called *lisettes* in French, which have a less pronounced taste. Have him remove their heads and gut them.

1   Wash and peel the carrots and peel the onions. Slice the carrots and onions into thin rounds. Bring 1 quart (1 l.) water to a boil and add the carrots, onions, garlic, bouquet garni, tarragon, peppercorns, coriander seeds, cumin seeds, cloves, and 1 teaspoon coarse salt. Cover and simmer for 15 minutes.

2   Rinse the fish under cold water. Drain them and dry with paper towels. Season with salt and pepper on both sides and arrange the fish in a single layer in a deep platter.

3   Add the wine and vinegar to the broth. When it returns to a boil, remove the pot from the heat and pour the broth over the fish. When the liquid and fish have cooled, refrigerate overnight. The next day, serve the fish in their broth.

4 carrots
2 medium onions
4 cloves garlic, peeled and degermed (page 122)
1 bouquet garni (6 branches parsley, 1 small piece of a celery stalk, 1 small bay leaf, and 3 sprigs fresh thyme, bound together)
5 sprigs tarragon, tied together
2 teaspoons peppercorns
2 teaspoons coriander seeds
2 teaspoons cumin seeds
2 whole cloves
Coarse salt
8 small mackerel (about 3–4 pounds total)
Salt
Pepper
¾ cup (20 cl.) white wine
¾ cup (20 cl.) white wine vinegar

MARINATED ANCHOVIES

Anchois marinés

SERVES   4 to 6

PREPARATION   30 minutes

COOKING   6 minutes

This chilled appetizer must be prepared at least 4 hours in advance. If possible, ask the fishmonger to behead the anchovies and remove their bones.

The zest is the outer part of the lemon rind. Cut it lengthwise in long strips with a vegetable peeler (or a zester if you have one). Be sure to take only the yellow part and not the white pith, which is bitter. The lemon must be organic or at least free of pesticides, and washed first.

1   Rinse the anchovies and put them in a deep platter.

2   Wash and trim the fennel. Clean the mushrooms and remove their stems. Wash the zucchini but do not peel it. Cut the fennel, mushrooms, and zucchini into a very small dice, about ⅛ inch (3 mm.) square.

3   Heat 3 tablespoons olive oil in a skillet over medium heat. Add the diced vegetables and a pinch of salt and cook for 2–3 minutes; the vegetables should not soften much. Drain them on a plate lined with paper towels. Put the drained vegetables on top of the anchovies.

4   Peel and mince the onions. Crush the garlic. Bring a big glass of water to a boil and blanch the strips of lemon peel by plunging them into the boiling water for a few seconds. Drain and mince. Wash the thyme and bay leaf.

5   Warm the rest of the olive oil in a sauté pan over low heat. Cook the onions for 3 minutes, stirring with a wooden spatula. Add the vinegar, ⅓ cup (10 cl.) water, the garlic, thyme, bay leaf, crushed black pepper, coriander seeds, and minced lemon zest. Turn the heat up a bit and simmer about 5 minutes. Turn off the heat, remove the garlic, and taste for salt and pepper. Pour the hot marinade over the anchovies. When the fish and marinade have cooled, refrigerate at least 4 hours.

6   Remove the anchovies from the refrigerator 15 minutes before serving. Toast the country bread and eat it with the anchovies.

1 pound (500 g.) very fresh anchovies

1 slice of fennel

4 ounces (150 g.) white button mushrooms

1 small zucchini

⅓ cup (10 cl.) olive oil

Salt

4 small new onions (cipollini or scallions)

1 clove garlic, peeled and degermed (page 122)

Zest of 1 lemon cut in strips

1 sprig fresh thyme

1 bay leaf

⅓ cup (10 cl.) white wine vinegar

½ teaspoon crushed black pepper

¼ teaspoon coriander seeds

Pepper

6 ounces (200 g.) thinly sliced country bread

POTATOES AND SMOKED HERRING

Harengs pommes à l'huile

SERVES   6

DESALTING   2 hours

PREPARATION AND COOKING   45 minutes

Prepare marinade 1 day in advance.

1   Put the herring fillets in a flat-bottomed container. Cover with the milk and leave them for 2 hours to lose some of their salt.

2   Peel the onions. Wash and peel the carrot. Slice them into thin rounds. Wash the thyme and crumble the bay leaves.

3   Drain the herring. Blot them dry with paper towels and put them in a terrine, layering them with the onions, carrot, thyme, and crumbled bay leaves. Sprinkle with the peppercorns and coriander seeds and cover with the oils. Refrigerate for 24 hours.

4   Wash the potatoes but do not peel them. Put them in a saucepan and cover with water. Add 1 teaspoon coarse salt, bring to a boil, and simmer about 30 minutes. (You can determine whether the potatoes are cooked by inserting the tip of a knife; it should slide in easily when the potato is done, but the potato should not be completely mushy.)

5   Drain the potatoes and peel them while they are still warm. Slice them thinly and put them in a bowl with the white wine and shallots. In another bowl, combine the vinegar, a pinch of salt, and a few grindings of pepper. Whisk in ⅓ to ¾ cup (10–15 cl.) of the herring marinade.

6   Dress the warm potatoes with the vinaigrette and toss gently without smashing the potatoes. Sprinkle with parsley and serve with the terrine of marinated herring.

12 fillets smoked herring

1 quart (1 l.) milk

3 small new onions

1 medium carrot

4 sprigs fresh thyme

2 bay leaves

12 black peppercorns

1 teaspoon coriander seeds

¾ cup (20 cl.) peanut oil

1¼ cups (30 cl.) olive oil

2 pounds potatoes (firm salad potatoes—charlottes if you can find them—or new potatoes)

Coarse salt

¾ cup (20 cl.) white wine, preferably muscadet

4 shallots, preferably gray, peeled and minced

5 tablespoons wine vinegar

Salt

Pepper

1 tablespoon minced flat-leaf parsley

special equipment: 10-inch oval terrine with a cover

VEGETABLE CAKE

Cake aux légumes

SERVES   4–6
PREPARATION   30 minutes
COOKING   45 minutes

Make this cake at least 1 hour in advance.

1   Whisk together 6 tablespoons (100 g.) butter and the olive oil. Add 1 teaspoon salt, 3 grindings of pepper, and a dash of grated nutmeg. Whisk in 1 egg and 1 yolk; when they are completely incorporated, whisk in 1 more egg and 1 more yolk. Whisk until the mixture is homogeneous. Sift the flour and baking powder into a bowl. Using a spatula, gently fold the flour into the butter-oil-egg mixture.

2   Put 5 ice cubes in a large bowl half filled with water. Put 1 quart (1 l.) water on to boil with 1 teaspoon coarse salt. Boil the green beans for 10 minutes, then remove them with a skimmer and plunge them into the ice water. Immediately remove them from the ice water and put them in a colander to drain. Do the same with the carrot and the zucchini, but boil the zucchini for only 5 minutes.

3   Cut the vegetables into small dice, along with the tomatoes and Comté. Quarter the olives. Stir everything into the butter-flour mixture until the vegetables are evenly distributed.

4   Butter a cake pan generously with the remaining 2 tablespoons butter. Press the dough into the pan and refrigerate for 1 hour.

5   After it has chilled for an hour, preheat the oven to 350°F (180°C). Bake the cake for 45 minutes. Serve warm or cold.

1 stick (¼ pound/110 g.) butter, softened
4 tablespoons olive oil
Salt
Pepper
Grated nutmeg
2 eggs plus 2 egg yolks (page 204)
2 cups (250 g.) flour
2 teaspoons (10 g.) baking powder
Coarse salt
10 haricots verts or slender green beans
1 small carrot
¼ medium zucchini
3 dried tomatoes (page 588)
4 ounces (150 g.) Comté cheese
1 tablespoon pitted black olives

TUNA CAKE

Cake au thon

PREPARATION AND COOKING   45 minutes

The fish must marinate for at least 24 hours before you prepare the cake.

1   In a bowl, combine the red wine and olive oil. Add the onions, parsley, cilantro, mint, and garlic, and mix well. Add the tuna. Make sure it is completely submerged but do not crumble it up. Cover the bowl with plastic wrap and refrigerate for at least 24 hours.

2   The next day, put the turmeric in a bowl with $1\frac{1}{3}$ cups ($5\frac{3}{4}$ ounces/165 g.) flour, the baking powder, curry powder, 1 teaspoon salt, and 5 grindings of pepper. Whisk to combine.

3   Preheat the oven to 350°F (180°C) and remove a bit of butter from the refrigerator so it will have softened by the time you want to grease the pan. With a whisk or fork, beat together the eggs and yolk, crème fraîche, and cream.

4   Add the flour mixture to the egg-cream mixture. Add the tuna and its marinade and mix gently with a tablespoon, taking care not to break up the tuna too much.

5   Use a pastry brush to butter the loaf pan generously. Coat it with the remaining flour. Fill it two-thirds full of the tuna batter and press the batter down lightly with the back of a spoon. Put the pan on a sheet pan and cook for 45 minutes. (Do not bake the cake directly on an oven rack; it will not cook properly.)

6   After removing the cake from the oven, let it cool in its pan for 10 minutes before unmolding. This cake is best warm but can also be eaten cold or sliced and toasted in a skillet.

6 tablespoons red wine

6 tablespoons olive oil

$\frac{1}{4}$ pound (100 g.) minced onions

1 tablespoon crushed flat-leaf parsley

1 tablespoon chopped cilantro

1 tablespoon chopped fresh mint

1 clove garlic, peeled, degermed (page 122), and minced

One 6-ounce can (160 g.) oil-packed tuna

2 teaspoons turmeric

$1\frac{1}{2}$ cups (185 g.) flour

$1\frac{1}{2}$ teaspoons (6 g.) baking powder

1 tablespoon curry powder

Salt

Pepper

2 eggs plus 1 egg yolk (page 204)

1 tablespoon crème fraîche

3 tablespoons heavy cream

special equipment: loaf pan about 7–8 inches long by 3 inches wide (18 cm. by 7 cm.)

SEA BASS TARTARE

Daurade en mayonnaise

SERVES   4

PREPARATION   30 minutes (15 minutes for eggs;
                    15 minutes for salad)

Fish tartare—uncooked chopped fish—is fashionable at the moment. The name is not quite right, since a tartare is really a dish of chopped uncooked meat (originally it would have been horse meat). It is supposed to have originated in Mongolia, where, according to the legend, the Tartars would ride with meat under their saddles.

    Fatty fish take well to these preparations, which call for strong seasoning. Choose an entire very fresh fish at the fishmonger's and ask him to fillet it for you.

1 egg yolk (page 204)
1 teaspoon mustard
Salt
½ cup (15 cl.) plus
     ½ tablespoon
     grapeseed oil
¼ teaspoon distilled vinegar
2 tablespoons *fromage blanc*
     (or cream cheese)
¾ pound (400 g.) sea bass fillet
3 tablespoons lemon juice
1 shallot, peeled and minced
1 tablespoon chopped flat-leaf
     parsley
1 tablespoon diced cornichons
Pepper
4 quail eggs (optional)
½ carrot
½ leek
1 plain yogurt (about 8 ounces)
1 small bunch chervil

1. Whisk together the egg yolk, mustard, and a pinch of salt. If possible, use a handheld electric mixer and hold it at an angle to the bottom of the bowl. Slowly, in a thin stream, add ½ cup grapeseed oil, whisking constantly. When all the oil has been added, whisk in the vinegar and *fromage blanc*. Cover the mayonnaise with plastic wrap and refrigerate.

2. Mince the sea bass as finely as possible and put it in a bowl. Add 2 tablespoons lemon juice, the shallot, parsley, cornichons, and some salt and pepper, and mix. Incorporate 2 tablespoons mayonnaise. Cover with plastic wrap and refrigerate for at least 1 hour.

3. If you are using the optional quail eggs, remove them from the refrigerator 30 minutes in advance. Put 5 ice cubes in a bowl half filled with water. Bring 1 quart (1 l.) water to a boil and cook the eggs for 3 minutes, moving them around with a skimmer. Carefully remove them and put them in the ice water bath. When they are cool enough to handle, peel the eggs in the cold water and drain them in a colander.

4. Wash and peel the carrot and carefully wash the leek. Chop them up very finely and put them in a bowl. Season with the remaining 1 tablespoon lemon juice, the remaining ½ tablespoon oil, and salt and pepper. Mix well and leave to macerate for 3 minutes. Mix in the yogurt.

5. You can serve this "tartare" stylishly by packing it into small metal cylinders to give it a very regular shape and then

removing the cylinders. Top each serving with a quail egg and a few leaves of chervil. Serve with the carrot-leek salad on the side.

Vegetables *à la Grecque* _____

Coriander, or cilantro, is both an aromatic herb (the leaves) and a spice (the seeds). We usually call the leaves cilantro and the seeds coriander. Coriander seeds, which are often crushed, have a pungent kick and are frequently used in Greek cooking. They can provide the base note for a marinade or a broth, lending the vegetables their special perfume.

Preparations *à la grecque* are usually vegetables cooked in olive oil, white wine, and lemon juice and scented with coriander. The sauce can be thickened with tomato paste.

Many small vegetables are wonderfully well suited to being served *à la grecque.* The recipe for mushrooms can be adapted for small white onions or little florets of cauliflower (or all three at once). Just adjust all quantities according to the volume of vegetables you are using and don't let any of the vegetables lose their firmness in cooking.

Put the raisins to soak in warm water at least 1 hour in advance.

Some people don't like the aggressive flavor and feeling of a coriander seed cracking in their teeth. You can achieve a gentler but even deeper flavor by using powdered coriander seed.

You can serve vegetables *à la grecque* warm, but it is best to make them a day in advance so the flavors have time to mingle. Remove them from the refrigerator at least 30 minutes before eating. If they are cold, much of their taste is lost.

MUSHROOMS À LA GRECQUE
Champignons à la grecque

SERVES   4

This base recipe is a good starting point for many variations. You can, for instance, add diced tomato, curry powder, or saffron at the beginning of cooking.

1   Wash and trim the onions. Cut off the ends of the mushroom stems. Rinse the mushrooms quickly and dry them with paper towels. If they are very small buttons, leave them whole. If not, cut them into ½-inch (1-cm.) pieces.

2   Warm the olive oil in a saucepan. Add the onions and cook them for 10 minutes over low heat, stirring regularly with a wooden spoon. Add the mushrooms, lemon juice, white wine, bouquet garni, coriander seeds, peppercorns, and 3 pinches of salt. Stir, cover, and bring to a boil. Cook for 2 minutes.

3   Pour everything into a bowl. Remove the bouquet garni and the bag of peppercorns if you used a bag. Allow to cool. Serve chilled but not very cold.

1 bunch small new onions or scallions
1 pound (600 g.) white button mushrooms
⅓ cup (10 cl.) olive oil
Juice of 1 lemon
½ cup (15 cl.) dry white wine
1 bouquet garni (5 branches parsley, 1 sprig thyme, ½ bay leaf, 1 sprig cilantro, and 1 small stalk celery, tied together)
1 tablespoon coriander seeds
10 peppercorns, tied in a small cheesecloth bag if possible
Salt

CORIANDER TOMATO MUSHROOMS

Champignons à la coriandre et à la tomate

SERVES 4
PREPARATION 30 minutes
COOKING 9 minutes

Prepare 1 day in advance.

1 At least 1 hour in advance, put the raisins to soak in a bowl of hot water so they plump up. Combine the crushed tomatoes and tomato paste and blend in a blender or food processor until you have a consistent purée.

2 Rinse the mushroom caps and clean them with a paper towel. Quarter them. Peel the onion and slice it into thin rounds.

3 Heat the olive oil in a pot over low heat. Add the onion, coriander seeds, and a pinch of salt and pepper. Cook about 3 minutes over low heat, stirring occasionally; do not let the onions color.

4 Add the wine, powdered coriander, and bouquet garni. Raise the heat to high and bring to a boil. Boil for 5 minutes and then add the mushrooms and lemon juice. Cover and cook for 5 minutes, still over high heat. Remove the mushrooms with a skimmer; put them in a colander to drain. Stir the tomato purée into the pot and boil for 10 minutes, until the sauce has reduced and thickened a bit.

5 Return the mushrooms to the pot along with the drained raisins. Boil for 1 minute. Taste for salt and pepper. Put everything in a bowl to cool. Remove the bouquet garni, cover the bowl with plastic wrap, and refrigerate for 24 hours before eating.

2 ounces (50 g.) raisins
One 15-ounce can crushed tomatoes or 3 medium tomatoes, skinned, seeded, and roughly chopped (page 124)
1 ounce (30 g.) tomato paste
¾ pound (400 g.) button mushroom caps from about 1 pound (500 g.) whole mushrooms; save the stems for soup or stock
1 medium onion
5 tablespoons olive oil
1 tablespoon coriander seeds
Salt
Pepper
1 cup (25 cl.) dry white wine
2 teaspoons powdered coriander
1 bouquet garni (4 branches parsley, 1 very small stalk celery, and 2 sprigs thyme, wrapped and tied in a green leek leaf)
5 tablespoons fresh lemon juice

CORIANDER-MARINATED VEGETABLES

Légumes marinés à la coriandre

SERVES 4

1. Put 2 quarts (2 l.) water in a pot with the garlic, vinegar, sugar, bay leaves, cloves, coriander seeds, and salt. Bring to a rolling boil and then remove the pot from the heat and leave the marinade to infuse.

2. Wash the vegetables. Peel the carrots. Scoop the seeds out of the cucumber. Cut the cucumber, carrots, peppers, zucchini, and celery into little sticks, about 2½ inches long and ¼ inch thick (6 cm. by 0.5 cm.).

3. Put the raisins in a bowl, cover them with some of the hot marinade, and leave them to soak. Put the remaining marinade through a fine strainer into a pot and bring to a boil. Boil the cauliflower for 4 minutes. Remove it with a skimmer and put it in a colander to drain. Put the carrots into the boiling marinade. After 2 minutes, add all the other vegetables and boil 3 minutes more. Put them in a colander to drain and cool; all the vegetables should still be fairly firm.

4. Put the vegetable sticks (but not the cauliflower) in a bowl and pour the raisins and their marinade over. Drizzle with the olive oil and toss. Spread the cauliflower on top and sprinkle with cilantro.

10 cloves garlic, peeled
3 cups (75 cl.) distilled vinegar
½ cup (125 g.) superfine sugar
10 bay leaves
20 whole cloves
3 tablespoons coriander seeds
1 tablespoon salt
6 or 8 cauliflower florets
2 small carrots
1 piece of cucumber, about 6 inches (15 cm.) long
1 red bell pepper, peeled and seeded
1 green bell pepper, peeled and seeded
2 small zucchinis
1 stalk celery
2 ounces (50 g.) raisins
2 tablespoons olive oil
1 teaspoon snipped cilantro leaves

Rillettes and Terrines

Classically, rillettes are bits of pork or goose cooked in their own fat and served in earthen pots, but we have come to call many other spreads by this name. They should be prepared several days in advance.

Terrines should be cooked at least a day in advance. Before cooking they are wrapped in pork caul so that they turn golden and do not dry out. The caul must be soaked for an hour to rid it of impurities and bad tastes. After it has been drained, it is used to line the bottom of the terrine and then folded up over its sides.

There are set proportions of salt and pepper for terrines:

about 1 teaspoon (2–3 g.) ground pepper and about 2 heaping teaspoons (12–14 g.) salt per 2 pounds of meat (1 kg.). A bit of sugar can also be added to aid the terrine's coloration. Combine the salt, pepper, sugar, and spices in a bowl before you add them to the meat so that they will end up evenly distributed.

The earthen vessel traditionally used for cooking terrines is itself called a terrine, and it often lends its name to other foods made in it—for instance, vegetable or fish purées that are not cooked in the oven or wrapped in pork caul. For these dishes the terrine should be lined with plastic wrap to make unmolding easier.

RABBIT TERRINE WITH HAZELNUTS

Terrine de lapin aux noisettes

SERVES 6–8
PREPARATION THE DAY BEFORE COOKING 1 hour
PREPARATION AND COOKING 2 hours

Have the butcher bone the rabbit and cut it into parts. Have the piece of pork throat or belly chopped up, too. Make this terrine three days before you plan to eat it.

1 Check the meat carefully and remove any bits or slivers of bone. Cut it into pieces if this has not already been done.
2 Set aside the rabbit thighs, fillets, and giblets. In a small bowl, combine 2 teaspoons salt, 1 teaspoon white pepper, and a pinch each of coriander, four-spice powder, and grated nutmeg. Sprinkle the rabbit thighs and fillets with some of this mixture.
3 Put the rest of the meat, including the pork, into a food processor or meat grinder and mince. You want to end up with tiny bits of meat, not a purée. Put the ground meat in a bowl and season it with the rest of the spice mixture. Sprinkle with half of the white wine and 3 tablespoons brandy and mix well.
4 Put the thighs and fillets (but not the liver, kidneys, and heart) on top of the ground meat.

1 rabbit, about 3 pounds (1.5 kg.) with its giblets
¾ pound (300 g.) pork throat or belly
Salt
White pepper
Ground coriander
Four-spice powder (a mixture of ginger, nutmeg, cinnamon, and cloves)
Grated nutmeg
1¼ cups (30 cl.) dry white wine
⅓ cup (10 cl.) brandy
1 teaspoon butter
3 shallots, peeled and minced
1 tablespoon (10 g.) flour
1 bay leaf
3 sprigs thyme
1 bunch flat-leaf parsley
1 pork caul
1 egg
⅓ cup (10 cl.) milk
2 heaping teaspoons (10 g.) potato starch
15 shelled hazelnuts

5   Cover with plastic wrap and refrigerate for 24 hours.

6   The next day, warm the butter in a saucepan. Add the shallots and a pinch of salt. Cook over low heat for 3 minutes, stirring, without allowing the shallots to color. Add the kidneys, heart, and 2 tablespoons brandy. Bring to a boil and allow to reduce; this will take only a couple of minutes. Lower the heat, mix in the flour, and add the remaining white wine. Add the bay leaf and simmer for 5 minutes, stirring occasionally. Remove the bay leaf and turn off the heat. Add the thyme and parsley, and allow the mixture to cool.

7   Soak the caul in cold water for 1 hour. Grind the cooked kidneys and heart in a food processor. Add the raw liver, marinated ground meat, and egg, and blend well.

8   Combine the milk and potato starch in a bowl, add it to the ground mixture, and blend. Add the thighs and fillets, and grind coarsely so that morsels of meat can still be seen in the mixture.

9   Preheat the oven to 280°F (140°C). Drain the caul and use it to line the terrine. Put one-third of the meat mixture in the bottom of the terrine. Sprinkle it with about half of the hazelnuts. Add half of the remaining meat mixture and sprinkle with the rest of the hazelnuts. Add the rest of the meat mixture. Fold the caul over the top of the meat.

10   Line the bottom of a deep sheet pan or dish with a piece of parchment paper pricked with holes. Fill it halfway with hot water. Put the terrine in the water and cover it with its lid. Bake for 1½ hours.

11   Take the terrine out of the oven, remove its lid, and allow it to cool for 10 minutes. Cover the terrine with a small board and put a weight on top of the board so that the terrine is pressed. Refrigerate for 3 hours. The terrine will keep for a week in the refrigerator.

CHICKEN LIVER TERRINE

Terrine de foies de volaille

SERVES 10–12
PREPARATION 30 minutes
COOKING 1½ hours

Tell the butcher you are making a terrine and ask him to chop the livers and pork breast. He should also give you the pork caul. Make this terrine two or three days in advance. The terrine should be capable of holding 3 pounds, about 13 inches long.

1 pork caul
4 ounces (100 g.) horn of plenty mushrooms or other small wild mushrooms such as chanterelles
2 tablespoons neutral oil
1½ pounds (750 g.) chicken livers, each chopped into 6 or 8 pieces
1 pound (450 g.) pork breast, chopped up
Salt
Pepper
2 teaspoons confectioners' sugar
½ teaspoon ground coriander
½ teaspoon crushed juniper berries
2 sprigs fresh thyme, leaves separated from the stems

1 One hour in advance, put the caul to soak in a bowl of cold water.

2 Rinse the mushrooms quickly under cold running water and dry them with paper towels. Chop them up. In a skillet, warm the oil over medium heat for 2 minutes. Add the mushrooms and cook for 2 minutes, stirring. Set the mushrooms to drain on a plate lined with a paper towel.

3 Put the pieces of liver and pork in a bowl and mix in the mushrooms.

4 Preheat the oven to 400°F (200°C). Drain the caul. In a small bowl, combine 2 teaspoons salt, 1 teaspoon pepper, the sugar, coriander, juniper berries, and thyme leaves. Thoroughly incorporate this mixture into the meat.

5 Line the terrine with the caul and put the meat mixture into the terrine. Arrange the thyme stems on top and fold the caul over the top of the terrine.

6 Put a kettle on to boil. Line the bottom of a deep sheet pan or dish with a piece of parchment paper pricked with holes. Fill it halfway with hot water. Put the terrine in the water and cover it with its lid. Bake for 1½ hours. Let the terrine cool and then refrigerate for 2 or 3 days before serving.

RABBIT RILLETTES

Rillettes de lapin

SERVES 6–8

COOKING 4 hours

Have the butcher bone the rabbit and pork loin and cut them into cubes. Prepare the rillettes at least three days in advance.

1. One day in advance, combine the rabbit, pork, thyme, bay leaf, juniper berries, peppercorns, and coarse salt. Mix well and refrigerate for 24 hours.

2. The next day, melt 3 tablespoons goose fat in a Dutch oven. Brown the meat over low heat, cooking about 5 minutes. Add to the pot the marinade left in the bowl and the rest of the goose fat. Cover and cook for 4 hours over very low heat. Every half hour, stir the pot with a big spoon to make sure the heat is gentle enough: The meat should not stick to the bottom of the pot.

3. Turn off the heat. Remove the meat from the pot with a skimmer and put it in a colander. Discard the thyme sprigs and bay leaf. Use 2 forks to shred the meat and then stir it back into the hot fat in the pot.

4. Allow the meat to cool in the cooking fat, stirring every 15 minutes to ensure that the meat and fat do not separate.

5. When the rillettes have cooled, put them in a terrine. (Leave any excess grease in the pot.) Refrigerate at least overnight, preferably 2 or 3 days, before eating with grilled bread. The rillettes will keep for 10 days.

1½ pounds (750 g.) rabbit meat, boned and cut into 1 inch (2 cm.) cubes

½ pound (250 g.) pork loin, blade end, boned and cut into 1 inch (2 cm.) cubes

2 sprigs fresh thyme

1 bay leaf

2 juniper berries

1 teaspoon peppercorns

2 teaspoons coarse salt

1½ pounds (750 g.) goose fat

Foie Gras

Foie gras isn't hard to make, but it does require some attention. Because it is so fatty, part of it will inevitably melt away during cooking. It can even melt completely if cooked too long or at too hot a temperature. It is fragile; if you handle it gently, it will be less likely to melt. Don't add truffles, Sauternes, Cognac, or Armagnac; they will obscure the true flavor of the product. The only tricky part of the preparation is the removal of the large veins. Use only the best quality liver.

Foie gras must be carefully seasoned before cooking. Prepare the seasoning in its own bowl so that you will be better able to distribute it evenly. You will need a little less than ½ ounce (14 g.) of salt per 2 pounds (1 kg.) of liver. This is about 3 level teaspoons or 2 heaping teaspoons. Ground pepper need not be measured so exactly. Duck liver needs more pepper than goose. For goose liver, ½ teaspoon of ground pepper (1 g.) per 2 pounds should do; for goose, use 1 teaspoon of ground pepper per 2 pounds. If you like a lot of pepper, you can add a little more but not more than 1½ teaspoons. It is better to pepper lightly so as not to overwhelm the delicate foie gras, and if your guests want more pepper, they can add it at the table. In any event, do not use crushed black pepper, which will not distribute itself evenly and will leave bits in your mouth.

One level teaspoon of sugar per 2 pounds will help the liver develop an attractive color as it cooks.

When you pat on the seasoning, be sure to use a generous amount on the insides of the liver, which will absorb the most flavor.

GENTLE COOKING

Liver must cook at a very low temperature. If it isn't cooked sufficiently, it will develop an unappetizingly grainy texture; if it is overcooked, it will begin to melt.

Do not press it as it cools. Some terrines come with presses that will deform the liver if used to weigh it down. Don't ever use them. Instead, allow it to cool uncovered and then refrigerate the terrine. The cooked foie gras must age for at least a week, two if possible, in the refrigerator. Wrap it well in plastic wrap so it does not absorb odors from other foods in the refrigerator. Do not wrap it in aluminum foil, which will leave behind blackish traces.

Remove the terrine from the refrigerator fifteen minutes before you plan to serve the foie gras, as it should be eaten chilled but not too cold.

Fill a tall glass with hot water. As you slice the foie gras, rinse the knife before each use for clean cuts. Make the slices thin and evenly sized. Serve with thin slices of grilled country bread, fleur de sel, and a pepper mill full of white pepper.

DUCK FOIE GRAS TERRINE

Foies gras de canard en terrine

SERVES   10–12
PREPARATION   30 minutes
COOKING   50 minutes

Foie gras must be prepared several days in advance. Use a porcelain or enameled cast-iron terrine.

2 duck livers weighing
  2 pounds (1 kg.) total
Salt
Ground white pepper
1 level teaspoon (6 g.)
  granulated sugar
½ teaspoon four-spice powder
  (a powdered mixture of
  nutmeg, cinnamon, ginger,
  and cloves)
Pinch of grated nutmeg

1   Separate the lobes of the livers, using your hands to pull them apart delicately. With a small, sharp knife, gently scrape away any traces of bile (greenish patches) or blood (which is red).

2   Cut a small piece (about 1 inch/2.5 cm. wide) from the narrowest end of each lobe. This will allow the salt to permeate the liver and to drain it of blood. Put 3 quarts (3 l.) very cold water in a large terrine with 3 tablespoons salt. Put the lobes in the water and seal the terrine tightly with plastic wrap. Refrigerate for 6 hours as the salt purges the blood.

3   Remove the lobes from the salted water. Drain and dry them carefully with paper towels. Put them on a large, clean dish towel. With a small, very sharp knife, scrape away the thin skin at the end of each lobe. Take one of the large lobes and make a 1½-inch-deep (3-cm.) incision along its length. Pull the 2 sides apart and use the knife carefully to pull out the 2 veins, one after the other. Do the same with the other large lobe and for the 2 small lobes, each of which contains only 1 vein to remove. The operation is more delicate on the small lobes; avoid piercing or tearing the flesh. If the vein will not come out, don't force it. Scrape away any green or red traces you see.

4   Make the seasoning: In a bowl, combine 2 heaping teaspoons salt (14 g.), 1 level teaspoon ground white pepper (about 1.5 to 2 g.), the sugar, four-spice powder, and nutmeg. With a brush, season the lobes evenly with this mixture, but

don't handle them too much or too roughly; they are fragile. Put the seasoned lobes in a big bowl and cover with plastic wrap. Refrigerate 8–12 hours, turning the lobes 2 or 3 times as they rest.

5 The next day, line a baking dish a little larger than the terrine with a piece of parchment paper pierced with a fork. This will prevent the bain-marie liquid from splattering the foie gras. Cut another piece of parchment paper to line the terrine, bottom and sides.

6 Put a large lobe in the terrine, silky side down, pressing on it gently to eliminate air pockets. After pressing air pockets from the other lobes, put the 2 small ones into the terrine and put the remaining large lobe on top, with its silky side facing up. Carefully wipe the sides of the terrine with paper towels. Cover the terrine with parchment paper and press down on it gently to achieve a relatively flat surface. Refrigerate for at least 1 hour.

7 Preheat the oven to 250°F (120°C). Bring a large pot of water to a boil. Put the terrine in the lined baking dish and place in the oven. Fill the baking dish with the boiling water so that the water is 1 inch (2 cm.) from the top of the terrine. The temperature of the water will fall to 155–160°F (70°C), which is the temperature it should be throughout the cooking time. (If you have a thermometer, you can check and adjust the heat as necessary.) Bake the terrine in the oven for 50–55 minutes.

8 Remove the terrine from the oven. Carefully pour all the liquid from the terrine into a measuring cup and let it rest for a few minutes. The juices should fall to the bottom, leaving a clear layer of fat on top. Pour this fat back into the terrine so that it covers the lobes. Dispose of the juices.

9 The terrine should rest uncovered for 3 hours. Do not weigh it down. When it is completely cool, cover the terrine and refrigerate about 12 hours, at which point the fat should be solid and the liver firm. Remove the cover and wrap the terrine well in plastic wrap. Refrigerate at least 3 or 4 days. If you have wrapped it well, the foie gras will keep for up to 10 days.

GOOSE FOIE GRAS TERRINE

Foie gras d'oie

SERVES 6–8
PREPARATION 30 minutes
COOKING 1 hour

1 Follow the recipe for duck foie gras terrine, but use a smaller terrine and the amount of seasoning indicated here. Cut the large lobe in 2 and put half of it on the bottom of the terrine, rounded side down, and the other half on top. Pack everything down well to remove air pockets and then put the entire small lobe on top, smooth side up. Press down again.

2 Cook for 1 hour at 200–210°F (100°C). Turn off the oven but leave the terrine inside 15 minutes more without opening the door.

1 raw goose foie gras weighing 1½ pounds (700 g.)
2 level teaspoons (10 g.) salt
Scant ½ teaspoon (about 8 g.) ground pepper
½ teaspoon (3 g.) granulated sugar
¼ teaspoon four-spice powder

Salads and Starters

Salads _____

For the simplest salads use the vinaigrettes in the Stocks and Sauces chapter.

Choose the freshest salad greens and vegetables you can, ones that are vibrant and healthy looking. Always wash them carefully. Even prewashed greens in a bag should be rinsed at home before consumption. They are very convenient, of course, but their packagers generally use preservatives that change the way they taste.

To wash the greens (such as lettuce, escarole, and frisée) for a salad, remove the outermost leaves and cut out the stem. Pluck off all the leaves and soak them in a sinkful of cold water to which you have added ¾ cup of distilled white vinegar, which will get rid of any little bugs that may have stowed away. Lift the leaves from the water into a colander, rinse them, let them drain in the colander, and dry them—in a salad spinner if possible or else by wringing them extremely gently in a clean dish towel. If you have used a basin or a large salad bowl to wash your greens, do not dump the bowl of soaking leaves into the colander; if you do, you will dump the dirt right back onto them.

Some greens, such as whole branches of mâche (lamb's lettuce), watercress, and dandelion, tend to be full of dirt and sand and must be soaked in several changes of water. However, they are often sold already separated into leaves and cleaned. Industrially farmed produce (such as some white button or cup mushrooms, endive, and leeks) is often practically dirt-free; it is therefore easier to clean but not necessarily better in any other regard.

TO STORE WASHED SALAD GREENS OR RAW VEGETABLES _____

If you are not going to use washed greens immediately, wrap them in a clean, dry dish towel and put them in a bin at the bottom of the refrigerator that is not too cold. Do not store salad greens or raw vegetables in plastic bags; moisture will bead up inside, and the greens will spoil quickly.

If greens have lost a little freshness, pick off any yellowed or spoiled parts and revive the salvageable greens in a very cold water bath. Drain and dry as usual.

TO SHRED GREENS OR VEGETABLES

If you have time, shredding or grating by hand usually produces the best results, but some vegetables (such as cabbage and celery root) are far easier to shred in the food processor.

Once they have been chopped or grated, some vegetables will turn very quickly if they are not protected from the air in a bath of water (potatoes) or water and lemon juice (artichoke hearts, white button mushrooms, celery root, and apples). But this precaution isn't necessary if you are going to eat or cook the vegetable right away, or if you can immediately toss it with the salad dressing—the best solution, since the dressing will protect the cut vegetable from the air and infuse it with flavor.

Other vegetables should be briefly boiled (or *blanched*) to soften them a bit, rid them of impurities, or make them easier to peel. Blanching is always quick and should always be followed with a rapid cooling (under the tap if they are small or if they are larger in a bowl of ice water) so that the vegetables do not continue to cook. Blanched vegetables should certainly not be left in the blanching water or the cooling water, or they will soak it up.

TO COOK A VEGETABLE FOR SALAD

By the same token, when a vegetable destined for a salad is cooked in boiling water, it should be cooled immediately, either under cold running water or in a bowl of ice water. Otherwise it will continue to cook, become too soft, and lose its color. This rapid cooling is especially important if you are making a salad that depends on vibrant colors and a fine crunch—green beans, tomatoes, and celery root.

A vinaigrette is made in two steps: Since salt does not dissolve in oil, you must dissolve it first in your acid element (vinegar or lemon juice) or in some other ingredient (such as mustard). Then the oil is whisked in to produce a homogeneous blend. Some salad ingredients, such as potatoes, need more vinaigrette than others. Here you will find a recommended amount of vinaigrette for each salad, but you may find that you want to add more. Some people have a problem with some flavorings—such as shallots, onion, garlic, croutons, or chervil. If you or your guests do not favor these ingredients, you can generally use less than indicated in the recipe or forgo them entirely. If you are lacking some of the aromatic herbs called for, just use the ones you have on hand. Experiment.

MAKE SALAD IN ADVANCE

It is best to prepare a vegetable-based (as opposed to lettuce-based) salad several hours in advance so that the vegetables have time to take on the flavor of the dressing. But salad should be eaten the day it is made; the next day its acidic ingredients will have robbed it of its texture, color, and beauty. Once you have prepared your salad, keep it in the refrigerator in a closed container or in a salad bowl sealed with plastic wrap. Remove it from the refrigerator at least a half hour before you plan to eat it; eaten too cold, salad loses much of its flavor.

LITTLE ADDITIONS

Here are some nice ways to embellish a salad.

shallots (finely sliced)   the gray ones are best.
aromatic herbs   chervil, chives, tarragon, basil, etc., all chopped very
    finely. As for parsley, use flat-leaf parsley (also called Italian parsley) instead of curly. Rinse the herbs under cold running water and let them drain in a colander. Dry them well with a clean dish towel

or paper towels. Mince the herbs (preferably in a mini food processor or herb chopper) or snip them finely with sharp kitchen shears.

raisins   Soak them for at least an hour in warm water to soften.

garlic (finely chopped or crushed)   Peel each clove, cut it in half, and remove the indigestible germ with the tip of your knife.

pine nuts, sliced almonds, coriander seeds, hazelnuts, etc.   Toasting these additions in a nonstick skillet or on a sheet pan will make them crunchier and more flavorful. You don't have to add oil; they are already full of it. Keep the heat low, stir frequently, and observe closely, for they can blacken and burn very quickly.

fresh almonds or walnuts   Fresh nuts lend a fine color, inimitable crunch, and splendid flavor to salads. Remove their shells but do not toast them.

lardons   Heat 1–2 teaspoons neutral oil (grapeseed, sunflower, or peanut) in a skillet over medium heat. Add the lardons and cook for 3 minutes, stirring with a wooden spatula, until they are golden. Don't cook them too long or they will become too salty.

Carrots

Choose medium-sized carrots for salad. Large carrots are better for soup. Young carrots are crunchy but are sometimes lacking in sugar. Scraping them with the dull edge of a knife is enough to peel them; for very young carrots, nothing more than a good scrub with a brush reserved for cleaning vegetables is needed.

GRATED CARROTS WITH ORANGE JUICE

Carottes râpées au jus d'orange

SERVES   4
PREPARATION   30 minutes plus 5 minutes

Combine the carrots, orange juice, sugar, and cinnamon in a bowl with a dash of salt. Allow 30 minutes for the flavors to marry. Add the orange flower water, toss again, and serve.

4–6 medium carrots (about 10 ounces/300 g. total), washed, peeled, and finely grated to make 2½ cups
Juice of 1 orange
2 teaspoons confectioners' sugar
1 teaspoon cinnamon
Salt
2 teaspoons orange flower water

GRATED CARROTS WITH LEMON AND GARLIC _____

Carottes râpées au citron et à l'ail

SERVES 4
PREPARATION 5 minutes

Toss the carrots, garlic, and lemony vinaigrette together in a bowl. Season lightly with pepper, stir, and sprinkle with parsley.

4–6 medium carrots (about 10 ounces/300 g. total), washed, peeled, and grated to make 2½ cups
1 clove garlic, peeled, degermed (page 122), and minced
1 recipe lemon vinaigrette (page 61, same quantity)
Freshly ground pepper
2 teaspoons minced flat-leaf parsley

GRATED CARROTS WITH RAISINS AND CILANTRO _____

Carottes râpées aux raisins et à la coriandre

SERVES 4
PREPARATION 1 hour plus 10 minutes
RESTING 3–4 hours

1 Put the raisins in a bowl and cover them with hot water. Leave at least 1 hour to soften.
2 Whisk the vinegar with a pinch of salt and a pinch of pepper. Whisk in the oil.
3 Toast the coriander seeds in a skillet over very low heat. Do not add any oil and do not allow the seeds to color.
4 Drain the raisins. Combine the carrots, raisins, coriander seeds, and snipped cilantro in a bowl. Toss with the vinaigrette. Refrigerate for 3–4 hours before serving.

2 tablespoons raisins
2 teaspoons red wine vinegar
Salt
Pepper
1½ tablespoons peanut oil
1 teaspoon coriander seeds
4–6 medium carrots (about 10 ounces/300 g. total), washed, peeled, and grated to make 2½ cups
1 small bunch cilantro, washed and snipped

Cucumbers

Cucumbers are naturally chock-full of water. Traditionally, to make them crunchier, they are "drained" by means of copious salting, which draws out water. But this can leave a cucumber pulpy, rather like a watermelon. Here is a better way.

Peel the cucumber. Cut it in half lengthwise and scoop out the seeds with a spoon. Thinly slice the cucumber, sprinkle lightly with salt, and mix well in a bowl. Top with a few ice cubes and refrigerate for 1 hour; the flesh of the cucumber will firm up as it releases water. When you remove the cucumber from the refrigerator, taste it. If it is too salty, rinse it well and put it aside to drain.

This draining must be done just before the meal, or the cucumber will continue to lose water. Do not salt the dressing that you will use with cucumbers drained in this fashion.

CUCUMBER CURRY SALAD

Salade de concombre au curry

SERVES 4
PREPARATION 5 minutes

Stir together the crème fraîche, yogurt, and curry powder. Toss with the drained cucumber. Add pepper and taste for salt.

1½ tablespoons crème fraîche
1½ tablespoons plain whole-milk yogurt
1 teaspoon curry powder
1 cucumber, thinly sliced and drained as above
Pepper
Salt

Beets

Choose small or even baby beets. The larger ones are less sweet, more fibrous, and earthier tasting. There are small, long beets that are delicious. Beets are usually cooked, although they can be shaved and eaten raw. Cooking them takes some time. Here's how to do it.

Wash the beets well, scrubbing off all traces of dirt.

TO STEAM Put the beets in a steamer over a good amount of boiling water. Cover and steam over medium heat about 45 minutes, until they are tender all the way through. You can check for doneness by piercing one beet with a small, sharp knife; it should meet no resistance if the beet is cooked.

TO BAKE Preheat the oven to 250°F/120°C. Bake the beets in a dish for 1 hour and 40 minutes to 2 hours, depending on their size.

IN A PRESSURE COOKER Cook about 20 minutes on low heat.

TO MICROWAVE Put the beets in a microwave-safe container with ¼ cup water. Cover the container and cook for 10 minutes on high.

When the beets have cooled off a bit, peel them (you should be able to slip off their skins with your fingers) and cut them into small sticks or ½-inch (1.5-cm.) dice. Be careful. The inside of the cooked beet can be very, very hot. Season. Dress the beets with vinaigrette while they are still warm, and they will absorb it nicely.

BEET AND WALNUT SALAD

Salade de betterave aux noix

SERVES 4–6
PREPARATION 5 minutes

Toss the still-warm beets with the vinaigrette. Just before serving, stir in the nuts. Pepper generously.

3–4 medium-sized beets, cooked (store-bought or as above), peeled, and diced
1 recipe lemon vinaigrette made with walnut oil (page 62)
2 tablespoons chopped fresh walnuts
Pepper

HORSERADISH BEETS

Betterave au raifort

SERVES 4–6

PREPARATION 5 minutes

1 teaspoon red wine vinegar

1 teaspoon sherry vinegar

Salt

1 tablespoon olive oil

1 tablespoon peanut oil

1 tablespoon crème fraîche

2 tablespoons grated hot
    horseradish

Pepper

3–4 medium beets, cooked,
    peeled, and diced

Whisk the 2 vinegars together with a pinch of salt. Slowly whisk in the oils, continuing until you have a homogeneous sauce. Stir in the crème fraîche and horseradish. Add pepper according to taste and toss the beets with the vinaigrette.

Celery

Celery comes in two forms: the familiar green bunch of celery stalks and the knobby white celery root. Celery stalks are excellent in salads. Choose small, tender green stalks; the smallest ones are the best. The larger ones can be quite fibrous. Remove the fibers by peeling the convex side. Wash the stalk well, perhaps scraping even the concave side with a knife.

Celery root should be grated. Extremely crunchy, it is better raw than cooked in a salad.

CELERY ROOT RÉMOULADE

Céleri rémoulade

SERVES 4–6

PREPARATION 10 minutes

½ cup (15 cl.) mayonnaise
    (page 55 or store-bought)

2 teaspoons capers

2 medium cornichons, chopped
    into small dice

1 teaspoon minced flat-leaf
    parsley

½ teaspoon minced chervil

½ teaspoon minced fresh
    tarragon

¾ to 1 pound (400 g.) celery
    root, to make about 3 cups
    grated

Juice of 1 lemon

Salt

Pepper

1. Make the rémoulade sauce: Stir together the mayonnaise, capers, cornichons, parsley, chervil, and tarragon.
2. Trim, wash, and peel the celery root. Quarter it and grate the quarters in a food processor or by hand. Immediately toss the grated celery root with lemon juice to prevent it from browning.
3. Stir the rémoulade sauce into the grated celery root and taste for salt and pepper. Serve chilled but not too cold.

CELERY ROOT SALAD WITH A CREAMY SAUCE

Salade de céleri à la crème

SERVES 6

PREPARATION 5 minutes

Trim, wash, and peel the celery root. Quarter it and grate finely. Immediately toss the grated celery root with the dressing. Peel, core, and grate the apple; stir the grated apple into the salad. Taste for salt and pepper.

1 pound (500 g.) celery root (4 cups grated)
1 creamy lemon dressing (page 61, same quantity)
1 Granny Smith apple
Salt
Pepper

CELERY ROOT WITH ENDIVE AND WALNUTS

Salade de céleri et endives aux noix

SERVES 4

PREPARATION 10 minutes

1   Whisk the vinegar and mustard together with a pinch of salt and a pinch of pepper. Whisk in the oil.
2   Bring 1 quart (1 l.) water to a boil with 1 tablespoon coarse salt and the lemon juice. Boil the grated celery root for 30 seconds and then remove it to a colander and rinse under cold running water. Drain.
3   Toss everything together in a salad bowl. Sprinkle with chives.

2 teaspoons wine vinegar
2 teaspoons strong mustard
Salt
Pepper
2 tablespoons hazelnut oil
Coarse salt
Juice of 1 lemon
10 ounces (300 g.) celery root, trimmed, peeled, and grated to make 2½ cups
12 small bunches mâche, carefully washed and dried
1 endive, washed, dried, and separated into leaves
1 Granny Smith apple, peeled, cored, and cut into fat sticks
1 teaspoon minced chives

CELERY ROOT MAYONNAISE

Salade de céleri à la mayonnaise

SERVES 4–6
PREPARATION 15 minutes

This is a different take on Celery Root Rémoulade (page 163).

1 Whisk the mayonnaise with the horseradish and cream. Grate the apple finely, preferably in a food processor. Stir it into the mayonnaise mixture.

2 Bring 1 quart (1 l.) water to a boil with 1 tablespoon coarse salt and the lemon juice. Boil the grated celery root for 30 seconds; remove it to a colander and rinse under cold running water. Drain.

3 Stir the celery root into the apple mixture. Taste for salt and pepper and sprinkle with chervil.

1½ tablespoons mayonnaise (page 55 or store-bought)
1 tablespoon grated horseradish
1 tablespoon heavy cream
1 Granny Smith apple, cored but not peeled
Coarse salt
Juice of 1 lemon
1 pound (500 g.) celery root, trimmed, peeled, and grated to make 4 cups
Salt
Pepper
1 teaspoon chervil leaves

CELERY SALAD WITH SHRIMP

Salade de céleri-branche aux crevettes

SERVES 4
PREPARATION 15 minutes

1 Toss the celery and apple pieces with the lemon juice.

2 Peel 12 of the shrimp and remove their heads. Cut them into 6 pieces each. The pieces should be slightly larger than the apple and celery pieces. Toss with the apples and celery, and 1½ tablespoons mayonnaise. Add the chives and toss again.

3 Whisk together 1 tablespoon mayonnaise and 2 teaspoons water. Pour this mixture over the salad. Decorate with the 4 whole shrimp. Sprinkle with celery leaves and serve cold (but not chilled).

8 stalks celery, cleaned, trimmed, and cut into ¼-inch (½-cm.) sections
2 Granny Smith apples, washed and cut into small dice
Juice of 1 lemon
16 large cooked shrimp
2½ tablespoons mayonnaise (page 55 or store-bought)
1 tablespoon minced chives
1 teaspoon celery leaves

ROQUEFORT CELERY SALAD

Salade de céleri-branche au roquefort

SERVES 4–6
PREPARATION 5 minutes

Whisk the 2 vinegars together with a bit of salt. Whisk in the olive oil. Crush the cheese into the vinaigrette with a fork. Toss with the celery. Add pepper to taste.

1 teaspoon red wine vinegar
2 teaspoons sherry vinegar
Salt
2 tablespoons olive oil
2 ounces (60 g.) Roquefort or blue cheese
10 tender celery stalks (about 1 pound/500 g. total), washed, trimmed, and sliced into ⅛-inch (3-mm.) strips
Pepper

Button or Cup Mushrooms

To prepare these mushrooms for use, cut off the base of the stem. If they are fairly clean, as they often are when bought from a supermarket, simply wipe them with paper towels. If they have a lot of dirt on them, rinse them quickly under cold running water. Do not leave them to soak in water. Drain them well in a colander and dry them carefully with a clean dish towel or paper towels.

The stems are not as tender as the caps and can be saved to be cooked for another dish such as stock or soup.

PARMESAN MUSHROOM SALAD

Salade de champignons de Paris au parmesan

SERVES 4

PREPARATION 10 minutes

1   Combine the lemon juice and garlic in a bowl. Add the herbs, salt, and pepper and mix with a fork. Stir in the olive oil.

2   Stir the mushroom slices into the dressing, coating them well. Use a vegetable peeler to shave Parmesan over the top.

Juice of one lemon

1 clove garlic, peeled, degermed (page 122), and minced

1 tablespoon minced flat-leaf parsley

1 tablespoon minced fresh basil

1 tablespoon minced fresh tarragon

½ teaspoon fresh thyme leaves

Salt

Pepper

2 tablespoons olive oil

1 pound (500 g.) white button or cup mushrooms, cleaned and cut into thin slices

2 ounces (60 g.) Parmesan cheese

CREAMY MUSHROOM AND GREEN BEAN SALAD

Salade de haricots verts et champignons à la crème

SERVES 4

PREPARATION 10 minutes

COOKING 10 minutes

1   Bring 1½ quarts (1.5 l.) water to a boil with 1 tablespoon coarse salt. Prepare a large bowl half filled with water and a tray of ice cubes. Boil the haricots verts or green beans for 10 minutes, drain them, and then plunge them into the ice water bath. When they have cooled, remove them and put them in a colander to drain.

2   Whisk the lemon juice with a pinch of salt and a pinch of pepper. Whisk in the crème fraîche and then stir in the parsley and shallot.

3   In a bowl, combine the mushrooms and haricots. Toss with the dressing to coat.

Coarse salt

1 pound (500 g.) haricots verts (or green beans), washed and with ends trimmed off

Juice of 1 lemon

Salt

Pepper

6 tablespoons (10 cl.) crème fraîche

1 tablespoon minced flat-leaf parsley

1 shallot, peeled and minced

4 white button or cup mushrooms, cleaned and sliced thinly from top to bottom

Fava Beans

The skin of fava beans is unpleasantly thick and indigestible. Once you have removed the beans from their pods, they must be peeled. It is possible to peel raw beans, but it is much easier to peel beans you have blanched. Put 5 or 6 ice cubes in a bowl of cold water. Put 1 quart (1 l.) water on to boil with 1 tablespoon coarse salt. Remove the beans from their pods and boil for 1 minute. Drain them in a colander and then plunge them into the ice water. Remove after 1 minute. It should now be easy to slip the beans out of their skins.

MESCLUN WITH FAVA BEANS AND FRESH ALMONDS

Mesclun, fèves, et amandes fraîches

SERVES 4

PREPARATION 5 minutes

Whisk the vinegar with salt and pepper in the salad bowl. Whisk in the olive oil. Toss with the mesclun, fava beans, and all but 6 of the almonds until the greens are well coated with dressing. Sprinkle with the herbs and the remaining almonds. Finish with a very few drops of vinegar and a bit of fleur de sel.

$1\frac{1}{2}$ tablespoons sherry vinegar
Salt
Pepper
3 tablespoons olive oil
$\frac{3}{4}$ pound (14 ounces/400 g.) mesclun salad greens (if possible, frisée, treviso radicchio, watercress, mâche, and arugula), carefully washed and dried
$\frac{1}{2}$ pound (2 cups/250 g.) shelled and peeled fava beans (from about 2 pounds/1 kg. whole bean pods)
$\frac{1}{2}$ pound (250 g.) fresh almonds, peeled
3 tablespoons minced mixed herbs (if possible, chervil, sage, tarragon, dill, basil, marjoram, flat-leaf parsley, and mint)
Fleur de sel

Dandelions

The word *dandelion* comes from the French *dents de lion,* (lion's teeth), as the plant was once called on account of its jagged-edged leaves. (Today the French word for dandelion is *pissenlit,* which finds its counterpart in the plant's English folk name, *pissabed.*) Choose young, tender, light green dandelion greens for salad. Wash them well in at least two changes of water without pulling the leaves apart. Cut off the root end.

Raw dandelions can be tough, which is why many preparations call for them to be heated and thereby softened a bit; they can be doused with vinegar that has been heated in the skillet with lardons, for instance, or, if they are especially stiff, tossed in the still-hot skillet itself. If you want to avoid fatty, bacony dressing, you can choose a mustardy vinaigrette instead; but in this case the dandelion greens must be very young and tender.

DANDELION SALAD

Salade de pissenlits au lard

SERVES   4

PREPARATION   10 minutes

1 teaspoon neutral oil (such as peanut, sunflower, or grapeseed)

1½ cups (200 g.) smoked lardons, cut from smoked slab bacon (page 89)

¾ pound (400 g.) dandelion greens, carefully trimmed, washed, and dried

2 tablespoons sherry vinegar

Salt

Pepper

4 hard- or soft-boiled eggs (optional; page 208 or 205), cut in half

Croutons rubbed with garlic (optional)

1   Heat the oil in a skillet over low heat. Add the lardons and cook for 3 minutes, stirring with a wooden spatula. Remove the lardons with a slotted spoon and put them on top of the greens.

2   Reheat the skillet and add the vinegar, a pinch of salt, and a pinch of pepper. When this sauce bubbles, pour it over the greens and toss well. Serve immediately, topped with the eggs and croutons if you are using them.

Anchovy Salads

ANCHOÏADE

PREPARATION 10 minutes

Anchoïade is a garlic and anchovy dressing beloved by people who favor strong flavors. If you have some left over after making a salad, spread it on a ham or chicken sandwich.

Put a colander on top of a deep plate or shallow bowl. Drain the anchovies in the colander, collecting their packing oil in the plate under the colander. Mince the drained anchovies. Spread the garlic and parsley on top of the anchovies and chop everything to combine. Put the minced mixture in a bowl and stir in the anchovy packing oil.

One 2-ounce (50–60 g.) container anchovy fillets packed in olive oil
3 cloves garlic, peeled, degermed (page 122), and minced
2 tablespoons minced flat-leaf parsley

RED CABBAGE AND GREEN PEPPER SALAD WITH ANCHOÏADE

Salade de chou rouge et de poivron à l'anchois

SERVES 4–6
PREPARATION 15 minutes
MARINATE at least 6 hours

Green cabbage and red pepper can be used for a nice variation. Marinate the cabbage in lemon juice or white wine vinegar instead of red wine vinegar, which will stain green cabbage. You can also replace the cabbage with minced fennel (which should also be marinated in lemon juice or white wine vinegar instead of red), using a red or green pepper—or both.

1   Put the vinegar in a saucepan large enough to hold all the shredded cabbage and bring to a boil over medium heat. Turn off the heat, add the cabbage, and mix well with a spoon. Cover

2 tablespoons red wine vinegar
½ red cabbage (about 1½ pounds/750 g.), washed and finely shredded
1 green bell pepper, peeled and cut into small dice (½ inch by 1 inch/1 cm. by 2 cm.)
1 recipe anchoïade (see above or store-bought)

and leave to marinate for at least 6 hours. (If you complete this step the day before, refrigerate the steeping cabbage.)

2 Put the cabbage on a platter and add the diced green pepper. Prepare the anchoïade at the last minute and toss with the cabbage. Taste for salt and pepper.

Salt
Pepper

RIVIERA SALAD

Salade Riviera

SERVES 4

PREPARATION 5 minutes

1 In the salad bowl, whisk the mustard and vinegar with a pinch of salt and a pinch of pepper until well combined. Whisk in the oil.

2 Add the frisée, red pepper, artichoke hearts, anchovies, and olives to the salad bowl. Toss to combine.

3 Arrange the tomato slices on top of the salad. Sprinkle with fleur de sel and slices of onion.

1 tablespoon mustard
1 tablespoon red wine vinegar
Salt
Pepper
3 tablespoons olive oil infused
   with tarragon
1 head frisée, washed and
   dried
1 small red bell pepper, seeded
   and cut into strips
2 baby artichoke hearts (see
   page 179)
8 anchovy fillets
8 green olives, pitted
2 firm tomatoes, sliced into
   rounds
Fleur de sel
2 small cipollini onions sliced
   into thin rounds

NIÇOISE SALAD

Salade niçoise

SERVES 8

PREPARATION 30 minutes

Besides the egg, anchovy, and tuna, nothing in a true Niçoise salad is cooked. Traditionally, the tomatoes would be salted three times, and adding cooked potatoes would be sacrilegious.

1 tablespoon lemon juice
6 tablespoons olive oil
4 baby artichoke hearts (page
   179) in a bowl of water
   with lemon juice
½ pound (250 g.) small fava
   beans, shelled and peeled
   (page 168)

(continued)

NIÇOISE SALAD (cont.)

1 Combine the lemon juice and 2 tablespoons olive oil in a bowl. Cut the artichoke hearts vertically into very thin slices, adding the slices to the bowl of lemon juice and olive oil as you go.

2 Put the fava beans into a bowl with 1 tablespoon olive oil and toss.

3 Put the cucumber slices on a deep plate, salt lightly, top with about 10 ice cubes, and refrigerate.

4 Put 10 olives in a blender or food processor with half of the garlic clove (reserving the other half), 4 anchovy fillets, 1 tablespoon vinegar, 1 tablespoon olive oil, a pinch of salt (careful: the anchovies are already salted) and a pinch of pepper. Blend to combine. Add the bell pepper slices to this sauce.

5 Put the tomatoes on a plate and salt lightly.

6 Whisk together 1 tablespoon vinegar and a pinch of salt. Whisk in 3 tablespoons olive oil and pepper to taste.

7 Drain and crumble the tuna.

8 Rub the inside of a salad bowl or serving platter with the other half of the garlic clove. Arrange all the ingredients, including the onions and eggs, in the bowl and drizzle with the vinaigrette. Sprinkle with basil, a little pinch of fleur de sel, and additional pepper if you wish.

1 small cucumber, peeled and sliced into thin rounds
30 small black olives, pitted
1 clove garlic, peeled and degermed (page 122)
8 anchovy fillets packed in oil
2 tablespoons wine vinegar
Salt
Pepper
1 bell pepper (about 6 ounces/185 g.), washed, seeded, and cut into thin strips
3 medium tomatoes, washed and quartered or sliced into rounds
3 ounces (100 g.) tuna packed in oil
3 small cipollini onions, peeled and minced
2 hard-boiled eggs, shelled and quartered or sliced into rounds (page 208)
8 small basil leaves, coarsely chopped
Fleur de sel

Potatoes

For salad, choose firm-fleshed potatoes: charlottes, rattes, Russian bananas, new potatoes, and fingerlings such as rose finn apple (also known as rose fir). Try to find potatoes that are all about the same size, preferably small and oblong. Wash and scrub them well. Put the clean potatoes in a saucepan and cover them with cold water. Add some coarse salt (1½ teaspoons for 1 quart/1 l. water). Bring the water to a boil and cook for 20–30 minutes, depending on the size and type of potatoes. They are done when the tip of a knife meets no resistance, but do not cook them too long. They will disintegrate instead of remaining firm when the time comes to slice or dice them for a salad. If you are preparing them in advance, put them in the refrigerator, uncovered, after peeling them and cutting them up; this will firm them up a bit.

Potatoes easily soak up acidic ingredients such as lemon juice, wine, and vinegar, especially if they are still warm. (If you like, you can warm cold potatoes with a very brief turn in the microwave.) Serve potato salads warm if you can. Do not just pull them from the refrigerator and put them on the table.

Small potatoes will taste best if they are steamed instead of boiled. Steam them over 1 quart (1 l.) boiling water about 45 minutes. Steaming water does not need to be salted.

Potato salad accompanies all kinds of dishes: smoked salmon, herring, pot-au-feu leftovers, cold chicken, some cold fish, and sausages. It is easiest to slice the potatoes into rounds, but they can also be cubed or cut into small sticks. Play with seasonings, oils, and vinegars to vary your potato salads. Try adding mustard, olives, capers, anchovies, hard- or soft-boiled eggs, and minced aromatic herbs, all of which suit potatoes marvelously well.

MÂCHE WITH POTATOES AND TRUFFLES _____

Salade de mâche, pommes de terre, et truffes

SERVES 4

PREPARATION 15 minutes

The truffle vinaigrette must be prepared at least four hours in advance.

1 Brush the truffle with a clean, never used toothbrush. Peel the truffle with a vegetable peeler or very sharp knife. Do not throw the peelings away. Put the truffle in a sealed container and refrigerate. Put the peelings in the bowl of vinaigrette.

2 If the potatoes are no longer warm, warm them briefly in the microwave. Put the warm potatoes in a salad bowl and coat with the vinaigrette. Cover with plastic wrap and set aside for 4 hours; do not refrigerate.

1 big or 2 small whole black truffles

12 small potatoes (rattes, charlottes, rose finn apples, or Russian bananas), steamed for about 45 minutes, peeled, and sliced into rounds

1 vinaigrette made with peanut oil (page 59, same quantity)

(continued)

3   Thirty minutes before serving, remove the potatoes from the bowl with a skimmer. Put them in a colander set over a plate to catch the dressing that drips off them. Save the bowl of vinaigrette.

4   Remove the truffle from the refrigerator. With a sharp knife or mandoline, slice it as thinly as possible. Toss the slices quickly in the vinaigrette remaining in the potato bowl but remove them immediately to a plate; do not allow them to soak.

5   Add the mâche to the bowl of vinaigrette. Add the vinaigrette that has collected in the plate under the potatoes and toss well. Arrange the potato and truffle slices in a rosette atop the greens, overlapping each other. Sprinkle with fleur de sel and chives.

6 ounces (5 cups/185 g.) mâche, carefully washed in several changes of water and dried in a salad spinner or with paper towels
Fleur de sel
1 tablespoon snipped chives

SHRIMP AND POTATO SALAD

Salade de pommes de terre et crevettes

SERVES   4–6
PREPARATION   10 minutes

Slice the warm potatoes thickly into a bowl. Sprinkle with a tablespoon of vinegar. Add the mayonnaise and toss to coat. Arrange the shrimp and mussels on top and sprinkle with onions and herbs.

1 pound (500 g.) small potatoes (such as rattes, charlottes, rose finn apples, or Russian bananas), cooked and peeled
1 tablespoon cider vinegar or white wine vinegar
Mayonnaise (page 55, with 2 yolks and 1 cup oil)
¼–½ pound (150 g.) cooked tiny soft-fleshed shrimp, tails only
¼–½ pound (150 g.) small cooked mussels
2 small cipollini onions, peeled and minced
2 tablespoons mixed minced parsley, chervil, tarragon, and chives

POTATO AND CELERY SALAD WITH HAM

Salade de pommes de terre et céleri-branche au jambon

SERVES   4–6

PREPARATION   15 minutes

1   Put the still-warm potatoes in a bowl and sprinkle with the vinegar. Mix well.

2   Peel the celery well, retaining only the tender white center. Chop it very fine and add it to the bowl of potatoes.

3   Combine the lemon juice with a pinch of salt and a pinch of pepper. Sprinkle it over the bowl of celery and potatoes.

4   Whisk together the cream, 1 tablespoon herbs, a pinch of salt, and a pinch of pepper. Pour it into the bowl of vegetables and mix everything well. Scatter the ham over the top and garnish with the remaining spoonful of herbs.

2 pounds (1 kg.) potatoes (such as rattes), cooked, peeled, and sliced into rounds

1 tablespoon cider vinegar

2 stalks celery, washed

Juice of 1 lemon

Salt

Pepper

1 cup (25 cl.) heavy cream

2 tablespoons mixed minced herbs (parsley, chervil, and chives)

¼ pound (100 g.) cured ham, cut into ½-inch (1-cm.) long sticks

POTATO SALAD WITH CELERY ROOT

Salade de pommes de terre au céleri

SERVES   6–8

PREPARATION   20 minutes

COOKING   15 minutes

If you like, you can add hard-boiled egg (page 208), tuna fish, or cold fish or chicken to this salad.

1   Sprinkle the warm cubed potatoes with the white wine and stir.

2   Trim and peel the celery root and cut it into ½-inch (1-cm.) cubes. Put the celery root in a saucepan, cover it with cold water, and add salt and vinegar. Bring to a boil and simmer for 10 minutes, until the celery root has softened. Drain in a colander and rinse under cold running water. Line a bowl with a clean dish towel or paper towels and use to dry the cooked drained celery root.

3   Whisk together the mustard, lemon juice, sugar, and a pinch of salt. Whisk in the cream and horseradish.

2 pounds (1 kg.) potatoes (such as rattes, charlottes, rose finn apples, or Russian bananas), cooked (see page 172), peeled, and cut into ½-inch (1-cm.) cubes

1 cup (25 cl.) white wine

1 pound (500 g.) celery root

Salt

1 tablespoon distilled white vinegar

2 tablespoons mustard

Juice of ½ lemon

2 teaspoons sugar

1 cup (25 cl.) heavy cream

1 tablespoon grated horseradish

(continued)

4   Add the celery root to the potatoes and toss with the dressing; toss very gently, being careful not to crush the celery root cubes. Top with minced onions, parsley, fleur de sel, and pepper.

2 tablespoons minced new onions
1 tablespoon minced parsley
Fleur de sel
Pepper

HERBED POTATO SALAD

Salade de pommes de terre aux herbes

SERVES   4–6
PREPARATION   20 minutes
COOKING   30 minutes

1   Put the potatoes and dill sprig in a saucepan with 1 teaspoon coarse salt. Cover with cold water, bring to a boil, and simmer for 20–25 minutes. Drain the potatoes. Peel them and cut them into thick slices. Put the slices, still warm, in a bowl and sprinkle with 1 tablespoon sherry vinegar. Toss.

2   Put a blanket of spinach and sorrel leaves down on a platter. Top with a layer of lettuce leaves, setting aside 12 leaves from the heart of the bunch. Sprinkle with the mixed herbs and a bit of salt; drizzle with 1 teaspoon sherry vinegar.

3   Whisk together the mustard, $1\frac{1}{2}$ tablespoons sherry vinegar, a pinch of salt, and a pinch of pepper. Whisk in the olive oil. Toss this vinaigrette with the potatoes.

4   Arrange the potatoes in the center of the platter of greens. Place the hard-boiled egg quarters around the edge. Sprinkle the onions, radishes, and chives over the whole and serve.

2 pounds (1 kg.) small potatoes (such as rattes, charlottes, rose finn apples, or Russian bananas)
1 sprig dill
Coarse salt
$2\frac{1}{2}$ tablespoons plus 1 teaspoon sherry vinegar
Salt
1 handful spinach leaves, washed and with the stems removed
1 handful sorrel leaves, washed and with the stems removed
1 head lettuce, washed and dried
2 tablespoons mixed minced chervil, dill, and mint
1 tablespoon mustard
Pepper
2 tablespoons olive oil
2 hard-boiled eggs (page 208), quartered
1 or 2 small cipollini onions, peeled and minced
5 radishes, washed and cut into small sticks
1 tablespoon minced chives

POTATO SALAD À LA PARISIENNE

Salade de pommes de terre à la parisienne

SERVES 6–8

PREPARATION   10 minutes

1   Slice the still-warm potatoes ⅛ inch (3–4 mm.) thick. Put them in a bowl and toss with the white wine. Cover with plastic wrap and set aside in a warm place.

2   Just before serving, while the potatoes are still warm, mix them with the vinaigrette. Sprinkle with the shallots, onions, and herbs. Taste for salt and pepper; you might need to add a bit of vinegar, too. Serve warm, reheating in the microwave if necessary, about 15 seconds.

2 pounds (1 kg.) potatoes (such as rattes, charlottes, rose finn apples, or Russian bananas), cooked (page 172) and peeled

1 cup (25 cl.) white wine

1 vinaigrette made with neutral oil (page 59, same quantity)

2 shallots, peeled and minced

2 small cipollini onions or 1 medium, minced

2 tablespoons mixed minced parsley, chervil, chives, and tarragon

Salt

Pepper

Endives

Look for endives that are firm and medium-sized. Remove the outer leaves, then use the tip of a knife to cut out the bitter heart and core. If the knife is small, you can remove this cone by slicing in a circle on the bias. Rinse the leaves and drain them; dry with a paper towel. Do not put the leaves to soak in a basin of water, which will make them more bitter.

ENDIVE AND WATERCRESS SALAD

Salade d'endives et de cresson

SERVES 4

COOKING   (optional quail eggs) 10 minutes

PREPARATION   5 minutes

1   If you are using the quail eggs, prepare a bowl filled with cold water and 5 or 6 ice cubes. Bring 2 cups (50 cl.) water to a boil in a saucepan. Boil the eggs for 5 minutes; remove them with a slotted spoon and plunge them into the ice water. Remove their shells and cut them in half.

8 quail eggs (optional)

(continued)

2   Spread the watercress on a platter and dress with a little more than half of the dressing. Toss well. Spread the endive leaves on top and dress with the rest of the sauce.

3   Sprinkle with chervil. Decorate with the quail eggs and olives.

1 bunch watercress, washed and dried

1 mustardy, creamy, lemon dressing (page 61)

16 leaves from the hearts of 2 endives, washed and dried

1 teaspoon chervil leaves

6 black olives, pitted and quartered (optional)

BEETS AND ENDIVES WITH SMOKED DUCK

Betterave et endives au magret fumé

SERVES   4

PREPARATION   20 minutes

1   Whisk 1 tablespoon tarragon vinegar with a pinch of salt and a pinch of pepper. Whisk in the hazelnut oil. Put 1 tablespoon vinaigrette aside.

2   Toss the beets, endives, apple, and chives with the vinaigrette. Spread the salad on a platter and arrange the duck on top. Sprinkle with the reserved spoon of vinaigrette.

1 tablespoon tarragon vinegar

Salt

Pepper

$2\frac{1}{2}$ tablespoons hazelnut oil

2 small, round beets, cooked (page 162), peeled, and cut into $\frac{1}{2}$-inch (1-cm.) dice

2 small endives, washed and cut lengthwise into $\frac{1}{4}$-inch ($\frac{1}{2}$-cm.) slices and then into sections $1\frac{1}{2}$ to 2 inches (3–4 cm.) long

1 Granny Smith apple, cored and cut into sticks

1 tablespoon chive pieces 1 inch long (2.5 cm.)

16 slices smoked duck

Artichokes

There are two kinds of artichokes. The baby artichoke, which in France is called *de Provence* (from Provence) or *artichaut violet* because of its purple coloring, can be eaten raw or cooked. Only the heart is eaten. The larger variety, the green globe artichoke, called *de Bretagne* in France (from Brittany), must be cooked. Its heart is delicious, but its petals also have a good edible portion.

The "Jerusalem artichoke" is actually not an artichoke at all.

TO PREPARE BABY ARTICHOKES

Only the hearts of baby artichokes are eaten. You can nibble on them raw—simply washed, quartered, and sprinkled with fleur de sel and perhaps spritzed with lemon juice and olive oil.

For other preparations you will have to remove the heart. Here's how to do it: Have a lemon handy. Do not slice the stem off with a knife; twist it off with your hand, drawing with it the fibers of the heart. This will make it softer. Now use a small knife, preferably stainless steel. Put the artichoke on its side on your work counter and cut out the fibrous part in the center of the heart. Then peel off the fine outer layer of the heart at the bottom, just the way you would peel an orange. If you see dark spots on the heart, remove them with the tip of the knife. Cut out the base of the leaves around, but not too much, keeping the heart intact. Cut off the leaves two-thirds of the way up, about 1 inch (2.5 cm.). Cut off the bottom leaves entirely, revealing the choke. Use a tablespoon to scrape out the choke; if necessary, use a paper towel to remove any trace of the inedible choke.

Artichoke hearts darken very quickly due to oxidation. If you are not using the artichoke heart immediately—even if you are just preparing the other hearts—rub them all over with half a lemon and plunge them into a bowl of lemon water.

Now the hearts are ready to be cut into thin, crunchy slices for a salad or for cooking.

TO COOK A LARGE GREEN ARTICHOKE

If you have a large green artichoke, you can boil it whole for 45 minutes in salty water (1 teaspoon coarse salt for 1 quart/1 l. water) or cook it for 20 minutes in a pressure cooker (with the same amount of salt). You can then remove the petals and eat the edible part (cold or warm) with a sauce (a vinaigrette—see page 59—or a mixture of 1 teaspoon melted butter and 1 tablespoon crème fraîche warmed over low heat and seasoned with a pinch of salt and pepper).

Take each leaf with your fingers, dip the fleshy part in the sauce, and eat it. At the end there will remain a sort of pointed hat of small pale leaves. Pull it out as a whole; most of it is edible. Then remove the fuzzy choke with a spoon and cut the heart to eat it with that same sauce.

TO SHAPE AND COOK A GREEN GLOBE ARTICHOKE HEART

Some preparations require cooked artichoke hearts. If it is a green globe, you can first cook it as explained above. Then allow it to cool and remove the petals and fuzzy choke. This is the easiest way, but it results in a very cooked heart, and when you pull out the petals, you also pull out the tastiest part of the heart.

Here is another way:

Add the juice of a lemon to a bowl of cold water; save one of the juiced lemon halves.

Do not cut off the artichoke's stem. In order to remove as much inedible fiber as possible, tear it out with your hand, wrapping it in a towel and twisting it away from the body of the artichoke.

Put the artichoke on its side on a cutting board. With a paring knife, slice thin strips off the bottom of the heart, as you would peel an orange, always keeping the artichoke pressed against the work surface. Be thorough about cutting fibers away from the center and cutting off the toughest petals surrounding the base, but don't cut off too much—you don't want to cut away the entire heart. If you see any blackened flesh, cut it away.

Turn the artichoke and cut off the petals up to the circular bulge of its cap. Then cut off its cap entirely. Slice away any remaining petals. Use a tablespoon to scrape out the choke. Once you have done this, rub the heart with the lemon half, especially the inside. Put it in the bowl of lemon water; do not delay because oxidation will cause the heart to begin to darken immediately. Keep it in the lemon water while you prepare the other artichokes and until it is time for boiling.

COOKING AN ARTICHOKE HEART

In a small saucepan, bring to a boil just enough water to cover the artichokes (which will, in any case, float). Add 1 tablespoon olive oil, the juice of half a lemon, and a pinch of salt. When the water bubbles, boil the artichoke hearts uncovered for 8 minutes (for baby artichokes) to 10 minutes (for larger green ones) so that they will remain crunchy. If you want the hearts soft instead of crisp, cook 15–20 minutes total; verify that they are cooked with the tip of a knife, which will slide easily into a cooked vegetable. Drain the artichoke hearts in a colander or on a rack. Toss them with sauce or olive oil while they are still warm so that they take on as much flavor as possible.

BABY ARTICHOKES AND MÂCHE WITH CHICKEN LIVERS ____
Salade d'artichauts et de mâche aux foies de volaille

SERVES 4
PREPARATION   10 minutes
COOKING   4 minutes

1   Separate the 2 lobes of each chicken liver. Remove any traces of green bile. Season with salt and pepper. Heat the oil and butter in a skillet over medium heat. When the butter begins to foam, add the livers to the skillet and cook for 4 minutes, stirring. Remove them to a plate but leave their juices in the skillet.

2   Toss the mâche with 1 tablespoon vinaigrette. Arrange the artichoke slices on top in a rosette. Drizzle evenly with the rest of the vinaigrette.

3   Slice the chicken livers and arrange them on top of the salad.

4   If you are avoiding fat, you can skip the following instructions and finish the salad. If you wish to use the pan juices,

4 chicken livers
Salt
Pepper
1 teaspoon neutral oil
½ teaspoon butter
6 ounces (6 cups/200 g.) mâche, carefully washed in several changes of water and dried
Vinaigrette made with olive oil (page 59, same quantity)

heat the skillet over medium heat. Add the vinegar and use a wooden spatula to scrape up the hardened juices in the pan. When the vinegar is boiling and the drippings are all scraped up, pour the juices over the livers on the salad.

5   Season with fleur de sel and pepper and sprinkle with minced chives.

4 baby artichoke hearts, cooked for 8 minutes (page 179) and sliced into rounds

2 teaspoons red wine vinegar (optional)

Fleur de sel

1 teaspoon minced chives

BABY ARTICHOKES AND MÂCHE WITH SAUTÉED FOIE GRAS

Salade d'artichauts et de mâche au foie gras poêlé

SERVES   4
PREPARATION   10 minutes
COOKING   4 minutes

1   Check the foie gras for veins; if any remain, remove them gently. Remove any traces of green bile. Season well with salt and pepper.

2   Heat the skillet over medium heat. Cook the slices of foie gras for 2 minutes on each side, still over medium heat. Remove them to a plate, saving the juices in the skillet. Use a tablespoon to remove the fat from the pan. (You might want to save it for another dish, such as fried potatoes.)

3   Toss the mâche with 1 tablespoon vinaigrette. Arrange the artichoke slices on top in a rosette. Drizzle evenly with the remaining vinaigrette.

4   Arrange the foie gras slices on top of the salad.

5   If you are avoiding fat, you can skip the following instructions and finish the salad. If you wish to use the pan juices, heat the skillet over medium heat. Add the vinegar and use a wooden spatula to scrape up the hardened juices in the pan. When the vinegar is boiling and the drippings are all scraped up, pour the juices over the foie gras on the salad.

6   Season with fleur de sel and pepper and sprinkle with minced chives.

4 slices raw foie gras (about 2 ounces/60 g. each)

Salt

Pepper

6 ounces (6 cups/200 g.) mâche, carefully washed in several changes of water and dried

Vinaigrette made with olive oil (page 59, same quantity)

4 baby artichoke hearts, cooked for 8 minutes and sliced into rounds (page 179)

2 teaspoons red wine vinegar

Fleur de sel

1 teaspoon minced chives

VEGETABLE HODGEPODGE

Méli-mélo de légumes

Make this salad with the freshest seasonal vegetables you can find. Carrots, radishes, celery stalks, fennel, green asparagus, baby artichoke hearts, and cauliflower are all good candidates (about 1 pound to serve 6).

3 tablespoons olive oil
1 sprig thyme, rinsed
1 clove garlic, peeled and
    degermed (page 122)
1 small hot pepper
Vegetables
Juice of ½ lemon
Salt
Pepper
1 tablespoon chervil leaves
Fleur de sel

1   The night before, prepare an aromatic oil: Combine the olive oil, thyme, garlic, and hot pepper. Cover.

2   The next day, wash and trim the vegetables. With a knife or a mandoline, slice them very fine. Whisk 2 tablespoons lemon juice with a dash of salt and a grinding of pepper. Whisk in 2 tablespoons aromatic oil, filtered through a fine strainer. Add the vegetables and toss well.

3   Just before serving, sprinkle the salad with the remaining oil, the chervil leaves, fleur de sel, and pepper.

Composed Salads

ARUGULA AND PARMESAN SALAD

Salade de roquette au parmesan

SERVES   4
PREPARATION   10 minutes

1   Put an oven rack in the top position and preheat the broiler to the highest heat.

2   Whisk the lemon juice with a pinch of salt and a pinch of pepper. Whisk in the olive oil.

3   Arrange the pancetta on a sheet pan. When the broiler is hot, cook the pancetta for 2–3 minutes on the top rack. Remove the pancetta and set 2 slices aside. Chop the others into small bits.

4   Put the chopped pancetta, arugula, Parmesan shavings, and olives in a salad bowl and toss well with the dressing. Cut the 2 whole slices of pancetta in half and put them on top of the salad.

2 teaspoons lemon juice
Salt
Pepper
2 tablespoons olive oil
6 thin slices pancetta or bacon
½ pound (220 g.) arugula,
    washed and dried
2 ounces (60 g.) Parmesan
    cheese, shaved with a
    vegetable peeler
24 black olives, pitted

PASTA SALAD

Spaghettis en salade

SERVES 4
PREPARATION 10 minutes
COOKING 10 minutes
RESTING at least 30 minutes

1 Bring 2 quarts (2 l.) water to a boil with 1 tablespoon olive oil and 1 tablespoon coarse salt. Cook the pasta according to package instructions, stirring 3 or 4 times during the course of cooking. Turn off the heat but leave the pasta in the cooking water 1 minute more. Pasta for salad should be cooked slightly more than al dente. Drain and rinse under cold water.

2 Purée the basil with 5 tablespoons olive oil, the lemon juice, garlic if using, and some salt and pepper. Toss this mixture with the pasta and refrigerate for at least 30 minutes before serving as a first course.

6 tablespoons (10 cl.) olive oil
Coarse salt
½ pound (200 g.) spaghetti
3 ounces (100 g.) basil leaves
Juice of ½ lemon
½ clove garlic, peeled and
    degermed (page 122;
    optional)
Salt
Pepper

FRISÉE WITH LARDONS

Frisée aux lardons

SERVES 4
PREPARATION 10 minutes

1 Gently heat 2 teaspoons peanut oil and the garlic in a skillet for 3 minutes, stirring. Add the lardons and brown for 3 minutes, stirring. Remove the lardons with a slotted spoon and leave the fat in the pan. Discard the garlic.

2 Whisk the mustard with a pinch of salt and a pinch of pepper. Whisk together 1 tablespoon vinegar and 2 tablespoons peanut oil. Toss with the frisée. Scatter the lardons on top.

3 Reheat the skillet. Add 1 teaspoon vinegar. When it bubbles, pour it over the salad. (You can skip this step if you do not want to consume the fat left in the pan, but the lardons should still be warm when the salad is served.)

4 Top the salad with poached eggs and croutons.

2 tablespoons plus 2 teaspoons
    peanut oil
1 clove garlic, peeled
½ pound (200 g.) lardons
    (page 89)
1 teaspoon mustard
Salt
Pepper
1 tablespoon plus 1 teaspoon
    wine vinegar
½–¾ pound (300 g.) frisée,
    washed and dried
4 poached eggs (page 210)
8 small croutons

SCANDINAVIAN-STYLE POTATO AND SMOKED FISH SALAD

Salade de pommes de terre et poisson fumé

SERVES   6–8
PREPARATION   15 minutes
RESTING   (for the cucumber) 20 minutes

1   Cook the potatoes with the dill sprigs following the instructions on page 172. Peel the potatoes and cut into ½-inch (1-cm.) cubes.

2   Peel the cucumber, cut it in half, and scoop out the seeds with a spoon. Grate it on the large holes of a grater over a deep plate. Salt lightly, top with 5 ice cubes, and refrigerate for 20 minutes.

3   Remove the cucumber and put it to drain in a colander on top of a bowl that will catch its liquids. Taste. If the cucumber is too salty, rinse it quickly under cold running water and put it back over the bowl to drain. Add the vodka to the bowl under the cucumber.

4   If the potato cubes are no longer warm, warm them quickly in the microwave (about 15 seconds). Toss them with the liquid in the bowl beneath the cucumber.

5   Whisk together the mustard, lemon juice, and sugar with a pinch of salt and a pinch of pepper. Whisk in the crème fraîche little by little. Stir in the horseradish.

6   Add the cucumber to the potatoes and toss with the dressing. Sprinkle with the minced dill and, if you are using them, the salmon eggs. Serve the smoked fish on a separate plate, with more horseradish on the side.

2 pounds (1 kg.) potatoes (such as charlottes, rose finn apples, or Russian bananas)
2 sprigs dill
1 cucumber
Salt
1 teaspoon vodka
2 tablespoons mustard
Juice of ½ lemon
1 teaspoon confectioners' sugar
Pepper
8 ounces (250 g.) crème fraîche
Horseradish
1 tablespoon minced dill
Salmon eggs (optional), at least 1 tablespoon
Smoked fish such as salmon or trout, 1 slice per person

BRUSSELS SPROUTS AND CHICKEN LIVERS _____

Salade aux choux de Bruxelles et foies de volaille

SERVES 4–6
PREPARATION 20 minutes
COOKING 15 minutes

1 Pick over the Brussels sprouts, discarding any leaves (or entire sprouts) that have spoiled. Wash them carefully.
2 Bring 1½ quarts (1.5 l.) water to a boil with 1 teaspoon coarse salt. Boil the Brussels sprouts for 2 minutes; drain in a colander and rinse under cold water.
3 Remove any traces of green bile from the livers with a small knife; cut out a bit of the surrounding flesh.
4 Heat the oil and butter in a skillet over medium heat; tilt the skillet back and forth to spread the fats around evenly. When the butter foams, add the livers. Stir for 1 minute and then season with salt and pepper. Cook 2–3 minutes more, stirring. You want them to remain pink at the center. Remove them with a slotted spoon but do not discard the fat in the pan.
5 Stir the shallot and garlic into the vinaigrette.
6 Bring 1½ quarts (1.5 l.) water to a boil with 1 teaspoon coarse salt. When it starts to boil, add the Brussels sprouts. Cook for 20 minutes over very low heat. (You can also cook them for 10 minutes in a pressure cooker.) Drain in a colander and rinse under cold water. Put them in a bowl with the chestnuts and toss with the vinaigrette. Top with the livers.
7 Reheat the skillet over medium heat. Add the vinegar and scrape the bottom of the skillet with a wooden spatula. When the juices bubble, pour them over the livers. Add pepper to the salad and sprinkle with chervil and chives. Serve warm.

2 pounds (1 kg.) Brussels sprouts
Coarse salt
½ pound (200 g.) chicken livers
1 teaspoon oil
1 teaspoon butter
Salt
Pepper
1 shallot, peeled and minced
1 clove garlic, peeled, degermed (page 122), and minced
Vinaigrette made with neutral oil (page 59)
6 ounces (185 g.) cooked chestnuts
1 teaspoon vinegar
1 teaspoon chervil leaves
2 teaspoons snipped chives

SCALLOPS AND CHANTERELLES

Salade de saint-jacques aux girolles

SERVES   4
PREPARATION   15 minutes
COOKING   about 5 minutes

1   Rinse the scallops under cold running water and dry them with paper towels. With a thin, sharp knife, slice each one horizontally into 4 rounds, beginning at the base and steadying the scallop with your hand. Lay the rounds side by side on a large tray.

2   Mix 2 tablespoons olive oil and a pinch each of saffron, salt, and white pepper. Use a pastry brush to coat the scallops completely with this mixture. Cover the tray of scallops with plastic wrap and refrigerate.

3   Whisk the cider vinegar with a pinch of salt. Whisk in the peanut oil. Add white pepper to taste.

4   Stack the endive leaves on top of one another and slice them lengthwise into ¼-inch (0.5-cm.) strips. Put them in a bowl and toss with half of the vinaigrette. Add the treviso radicchio or mâche and the remaining vinaigrette and toss well.

5   If any of the chanterelles are large, quarter them lengthwise. If you are using button mushrooms, chop them coarsely.

6   Put 2 tablespoons olive oil in a skillet with the onion and fennel slices. Cook over medium heat for 2–3 minutes, stirring, until the onion has softened and is transparent. Raise the heat to medium high and add the mushrooms. Cook for 3–4 minutes, until the vegetable liquids have evaporated. Taste for salt and pepper.

7   Remove the scallops from the refrigerator and arrange them in a ring around the salad. Put the mushrooms in the center and sprinkle with a bit of fleur de sel.

8 large scallops
4 tablespoons olive oil
Saffron
Salt
White pepper
1 tablespoon cider vinegar
3 tablespoons peanut oil
1 endive, washed and drained
1 small head treviso radicchio, washed and dried (or the same quantity of mâche, carefully washed in several changes of water and dried)
½ pound (120 g.) chanterelles or white button mushrooms, wiped clean with paper towels
1 cipollini onion, thinly sliced
1 small bulb fennel, thinly sliced
Fleur de sel

MUSSEL SALAD

Salade de moules

variation

HERBED MUSSEL SALAD

SERVES   4

PREPARATION   15 minutes

COOKING   4 minutes

RESTING   2–3 hours

1 Scrape and scrub the mussels and remove their beards. Wash them in several changes of water. Put them in a saucepan with the garlic, white wine, and some pepper. Cover and cook over high heat. When you hear the liquid begin to bubble, set a timer for 2 minutes and then check the pot. When the first mussels have opened, remove the pot from the heat but leave it covered 2 minutes more.

2 Remove the mussels with a skimmer and put them in a colander set over a bowl to catch their juice. Put the juice through a fine strainer.

3 When the mussels have cooled a bit, remove their top shells, leaving the flesh in the bottom half shell.

4 Stir a dash of Tabasco into the mayonnaise. Little by little, whisk in the strained mussel juice until you have a smooth sauce. Put the mussels on a platter and coat with the mayonnaise. Sprinkle with chives. Cover with plastic wrap and refrigerate for 2 or 3 hours before serving. Serve chilled but not very cold.

$1\frac{1}{2}$ pounds (750 g.) mussels

1 clove garlic, peeled and
   minced

6 tablespoons (10 cl.) dry white
   wine

Pepper

Tabasco

$1\frac{1}{2}$ tablespoons mayonnaise
   made with neutral oil,
   preferably grapeseed oil
   (page 55 or store-bought)

2 teaspoons minced chives

HERBED MUSSEL SALAD

Salade de moules aux herbes

Use 2 pounds (1 kg.) mussels. Instead of garlic, use 2 shallots, peeled and minced. Instead of leaving the mussels in their shells, remove them. Instead of sprinkling the finished salad with chives, stir in 1 teaspoon each minced chives, chervil, and tarragon.

Starters

For the most part, these first courses can be enjoyed cold, warm, or hot.

CHICKEN AND LEEK SKEWERS

Petites brochettes de poulet et poireaux

SERVES   4
PREPARATION   15 minutes
COOKING   2 minutes

1   Slice the leeks lengthwise into 8 pieces each and then cut these slices into sections 1½ inches (3 cm.) long. Bring 1 quart (1 l.) water to a boil and add 1 teaspoon coarse salt and the leeks. Cook for 2 minutes and then drain and rinse under cold running water. Leave in a colander to drain.

2   Chop the chicken into chunks 1½ inches by ½ inch (3 cm. by 1 cm.). You should get about 12. Thigh meat is juicier, but breasts are easier to cut up.

3   Stick the chicken and leeks on the skewers, alternating chicken and leek. Dust each skewer lightly with curry powder and sprinkle with a few drops of soy sauce. Leave for 5 minutes, turning once or twice. Don't leave them too long, or the soy sauce will make the chicken too salty.

4   Heat the butter in a skillet over low heat. When it foams, cook the skewers over medium heat for 5 minutes, turning them so that all sides are exposed to the direct heat until they are quite golden. Add pepper and serve.

4 small leeks, carefully washed in warm water

Coarse salt

2 boneless chicken thighs or breasts

Curry powder

Soy sauce

1 teaspoon butter

Pepper

special equipment: 4 wooden skewers

BAY SCALLOP SKEWERS

Petites brochettes de pétoncles

SERVES 4
PREPARATION 5 minutes
COOKING 5 minutes

Though you may be able to find frozen bay scallops, they are much better fresh and are harvested in the winter months. A bay scallop is smaller than a sea scallop. In France, sea scallops are the greater delicacy, but bay scallops in the United States are often better than the small ones found in France.

½ pound (250 g.) shelled bay scallops (about 3 dozen)
1 tablespoon olive oil
2 tablespoons butter
1 teaspoon soy sauce
2 teaspoons red wine vinegar
Fleur de sel
Crushed pepper, preferably white, otherwise black
1 teaspoon thyme leaves

special equipment: 8 wooden skewers

1   Rinse the scallop meat quickly under cold water. Drain and dry with paper towels. Put 4 or 5 scallops on each of 8 skewers.
2   Heat the olive oil in a skillet over medium heat. Add 1 tablespoon butter and heat 2 minutes more. When the butter foams, add the skewers in a single layer. Cook on the first side for 1 minute, then flip and cook 1 minute more.
3   Add the soy sauce, vinegar, and the remaining butter to the skillet. Shake the pan gently to roll the skewers in the sauce. When they are nicely coated, set the skewers aside so that excess sauce drips off; they should not carry much excess sauce. Taste, add a pinch of fleur de sel if necessary, and sprinkle with crushed pepper and thyme leaves.

STUFFED VEGETABLES

Légumes farcis

SERVES 4
PREPARATION 45 minutes
COOKING 20 minutes

Stuffed vegetables can be served hot or cold. These *petits farcis,* which we might call "little stuffers," are a typical dish from Nice on the Riviera. This recipe does not need to be followed to the letter; it can accommodate whatever cooked meat you happen to have on hand—chicken, lamb, roast pork, veal, anything at all. Pot-au-feu leftovers make especially nice stuffing. Depending on your taste, you might add sausage meat, cooked rice, or bread soaked in milk. You can just as easily change the vegetable to be stuffed: tomatoes, onions, peppers, artichoke hearts, large mushrooms, and potatoes are all good candidates. Cooking time will change, however, when you change the vegetable.

If you serve the vegetables cold, also serve a mesclun salad (see Mesclun with Fava Beans and Fresh Almonds, page 168).

1   Bring 1½ quarts (1.5 l.) water to a boil with 2 teaspoons coarse salt. Prepare a large bowl half filled with water and a dozen ice cubes. When the water is bubbling, boil the zucchini for 1 minute. Remove them with a skimmer and plunge them into the ice water. After 30 seconds, remove them to a colander to drain. Dry them with paper towels. Cut them in half lengthwise and scoop out their flesh, leaving a bare ¼ inch (0.5 cm.) of flesh attached to the skin all around. Chop the flesh up.

2   Heat 1 tablespoon olive oil in a skillet over medium heat. Put the eggplants in the skillet and cook for 5 minutes, turning them so that all sides are exposed to the heat. Allow the eggplants to cool before cutting them in half lengthwise. Remove and chop the flesh as with the zucchinis. Put 1 tablespoon olive oil into the same skillet over low heat; cook the eggplant flesh for 5 minutes, stirring.

3   Preheat the oven to 400°F/200°C.

4   Cut off the tops and bottoms of the 4 small tomatoes. Set the tops aside to use as caps, and cut off only enough of the bot-

Coarse salt

2 zucchini, 3 ounces (100 g.) each

6 tablespoons (10 cl.) olive oil

2 eggplants, 3 ounces (100 g.) each

4 small tomatoes, whole, and 1 medium tomato (about 3 ounces/100 g.), peeled, seeded, and diced (page 124)

6 ounces (200 g.) ham, finely chopped

¾ pound (400 g.) roast chicken (meat only, no bones), finely chopped

1 cup (3 ounces/100 g.) freshly grated Parmesan cheese

2 shallots, peeled and minced

2 cloves garlic, peeled and minced

3 ounces (2 cups chopped/ 100 g.) button mushrooms, end of the stem removed, cleaned, and chopped

5 branches flat-leaf parsley, leaves only, minced

Pepper

Salt

4 teaspoons butter

6 tablespoons (10 cl.) chicken broth (page 77 or made from a bouillon cube)

toms to allow the tomatoes to stand steadily. Scoop out their cores and seeds with a small spoon and discard.

5   In a bowl, combine the ham, chicken, Parmesan, shallots, garlic, mushrooms, and parsley. Mix until you have a homogeneous stuffing. Sprinkle with a pinch of pepper.

6   Divide the stuffing into 3 equal parts. Into one stir the chopped zucchini flesh, into another the eggplants, and into the last the peeled, seeded, and diced tomatoes.

7   Sprinkle salt and pepper on the insides of the hollowed vegetables. Use a pastry brush to paint them lightly with oil.

8   Fill each vegetable with its corresponding stuffing. Cover the tomatoes with their caps. Brush a sheet pan or baking dish large enough to hold all the vegetables with 1 tablespoon olive oil. Arrange them on the pan in a single layer and drizzle with the remaining oil. Put ½ teaspoon butter on top of each stuffed vegetable (a little more on the zucchini and eggplants, a little less on the tomatoes) and pour the broth into the sheet pan. Bake in the preheated oven for 20 minutes. If the broth seems to be evaporating too quickly, you can add a bit of water to the pan.

9   When the vegetables are cooked, arrange them on a platter and coat them with the juices collected in the sheet pan. Serve hot, warm, or cold.

Savory Tarts

Tart crust can be bought ready-made, of course, but *pâte brisée,* or short crust, is best made at home. Here is a recipe. Be aware that recipes involving phyllo dough (which you will probably want to buy premade, perhaps frozen) should be prepared several hours in advance and kept at room temperature.

PÂTE BRISÉE

About 14 ounces (400 g.) dough, for a tart serving 8 people
PREPARATION   15 minutes
CHILLING   1 hour

1   Put the flour in a large bowl (or, if you are very confident, on your work surface). Shape it into a mountain with a crater at its peak (this is called a well). Into the well, and in this order, put the salt, egg yolk, and butter. Use the tips of your fingers to mix these wet ingredients into the flour until all is intimately incorporated into a dough that holds together. Add 5 tablespoons water and keep mixing to form a smooth ball of dough. Work as quickly as possible so that the dough does not become tough.

2   Divide the dough into 4 small balls. Flatten each one with a single push with the palm of your hand and then the 4 together without kneading. Wrap the dough in plastic wrap and refrigerate for at least 1 hour.

3   When the time comes to roll out the dough, be sure to flour the rolling pin and work surface well to avoid sticky bits of dough collecting on the pin and spoiling your smooth crust.

1½ cups (250 g.) sifted flour
1 scant teaspoon salt (5 g.)
1 egg yolk (see page 204)
1 stick (¼ pound/115 g.) butter, diced and at room temperature (or softened 10 seconds in the microwave if necessary)

PUFF PASTRY TART BASE

Fond de pâte feuilletée

For a tart serving 4–6 people
PREPARATION   5 minutes
CHILLING   20 minutes
PRE-BAKING   15–20 minutes

This base can be topped with vegetables, tomatoes, ratatouille, sautéed onions, or any number of things and then cooked again.

1   Sprinkle the work surface with flour. With a rolling pin, roll the puff pastry out to a thickness of ⅛ inch (3 mm.) or even

Flour for dusting
1½ cups (250 g.) store-bought puff pastry
1 egg

less. Its shape should correspond to the shape of the tart mold you plan to use.

2   Wet a paper towel and use it to moisten the tart mold. Drape the rolled dough, smooth side up, over the mold and refrigerate for 20 minutes. Preheat the oven to 440°F/220°C.

3   Remove the mold from the refrigerator. Whisk the egg and use a pastry brush to paint the tart base with egg. Bake for 15–20 minutes; the tart should not color too much.

PHYLLO TART BASE

Fond de tarte au phyllo

For a tart serving 6 people
PREPARATION   5 minutes
CHILLING   10 minutes
PRE-BAKING   10 minutes

This base can be topped with ratatouille, vegetables, and other toppings before being baked again. This kind of tart should be prepared a few hours in advance and kept at room temperature until serving.

1 tablespoon butter at room temperature or softened in the microwave
4 sheets phyllo dough

special equipment: 2 sheet pans

1   Preheat the oven to 400°F/200°C. Place a phyllo layer on a sheet pan. With a pastry brush, paint it with the softened butter. Put a layer on top and paint it, too, with softened butter. Top with another layer and paint with butter. Continue with all the dough, but do not butter the top of the top layer. Refrigerate for at least 10 minutes.

2   When the oven is hot and the dough has been refrigerated for at least 10 minutes, remove the sheet pan from the refrigerator. Top with a piece of parchment paper and place the other sheet pan on top. Lower the oven temperature to 350°F/180°C and put the 2 pans in the oven for 10 minutes, until the pastry looks barely golden or blond. Remove the top baking sheet and parchment paper to finish the tart with the topping of your choice and baking again.

You can make a tart base any size and shape you like by cutting the raw pastry layers as you please and stacking them as described above.

QUICHE

Quiche aux oeufs et lardons

SERVES 8
PREPARATION 10 minutes
COOKING 30 minutes

The French took the word *quiche* from the German word for cake, *kuchen*. Quiche has long been a specialty in Lorraine, an eastern region close to Germany. It had a place on the holiday tables of the dukes of Lorraine in their capital, Nancy, as early as the sixteenth century. At that time, however, the crust was made of bread, not pastry. Today some add Gruyère, especially in Paris, but it is not traditional.

1   Generously butter the tart mold. Flour the work surface and rolling pin. Roll out the pâte brisée to a thickness of about ⅛ inch (3 mm.). Drape the dough over the mold, fit it in, and cut off any dough that hangs over the edges. Refrigerate.

2   Preheat the oven to 440°F/220°C. Whisk together the eggs and yolks. Add the milk, cream, a dash of cayenne pepper, and a bit of salt. Add 1 or 2 gratings of nutmeg and whisk everything together. Put the mixture through a fine strainer.

3   Heat 1 teaspoon butter in a skillet over low heat; when it foams, add the lardons. Stir for 3 minutes, always over low heat. Drain the lardons on a dish lined with paper towels.

4   Remove the dough-lined tart pan from the refrigerator. Put the lardons in the dish and pour in the egg mixture. Bake for 5 minutes, then lower the heat to 350°F/180°C and bake about 25 minutes more, until the quiche has become golden.

Butter
Flour for dusting
14 ounces (400 g.) pâte brisée (store-bought or page 192)
3 eggs plus 2 yolks (page 204)
1 cup (25 cl.) milk
1 cup (25 cl.) heavy cream
Cayenne pepper (or a red hot pepper)
Salt
Nutmeg
1 cup (200 g.) smoked lardons (page 89)

special equipment: 10-inch tart mold (either a pie plate or a tart mold with a removable bottom)

ONION TART

Tarte à l'oignon

SERVES 4
PREPARATION 30 minutes
COOKING 40 minutes (onions) plus 50–55 minutes (tart)

1 Preheat the oven to 350°F/180°C. Flour the work surface and rolling pin and roll the dough out to about ⅛ inch (3 mm.) thick. Generously butter the tart mold. Drape the dough over the mold, fit it in, and trim off any dough that hangs over the edges. Cover the dough with aluminum foil and top the foil with dried beans or pie weights. Bake for 20 minutes.

2 Warm 1 teaspoon butter in a skillet for 2 minutes over low heat. Add the lardons and cook for 2 minutes, stirring. Add the onions and stir for 5 minutes. Cover and cook for 30 minutes, still over low heat, stirring every 5 minutes.

3 Whisk the eggs until they are homogeneous and foamy. Whisk in the milk, cream, a grating or two of nutmeg, and a bit of salt and pepper.

4 Remove the aluminum foil and beans from the tart pan. Bake the naked tart crust 2 minutes more. Arrange the lardons and onions evenly in the tart crust, pour in the egg mixture, and bake for 30–35 minutes.

Flour for dusting
14 ounces (400 g.) pâte brisée, salted (store-bought or page 192)
Butter
1 ounce (30 g.) smoked lardons (page 89)
1 cup (200 g.) cipollini onions, peeled and sliced into thin rounds
2 eggs
10 tablespoons (15 cl.) milk
10 tablespoons (15 cl.) heavy cream
Nutmeg
Salt
Pepper

special equipment: 8-inch tart mold
1 handful dried beans or pie weights

BABY MACKEREL TART

Tarte fine de lisette

SERVES   4–6

PREPARATION AND COOKING   about 45 minutes

Ask the fishmonger to fillet the mackerel.

1   Preheat the oven to 400°F/200°C and put an oven rack in the second slot from the top. Heat 2 tablespoons olive oil in a saucepan over low heat. Add the minced onion and cook for 3 minutes, stirring. Add the garlic, thyme, and bay leaf, and cook 3 minutes more. Add 4 of the diced tomatoes, a little salt, the sugar, and stir. Cook for 7 minutes over low heat.

2   Put in a blender or food processor the 2 remaining tomatoes, half of the lemon juice, the olives, basil, 6 tablespoons (10 cl.) olive oil, and a little salt and pepper. Blend coarsely and pour the saucy mixture into a bowl.

3   Spread the tapenade on the precooked tart base, leaving a border of 1 inch (2 cm.) all around. Spread the tomatoes from the skillet on top, leaving a border of ½ inch (1 cm.) all around.

4   Season the mackerel fillets with salt and pepper on both sides. Sprinkle with the remaining lemon juice. Arrange them on top of the tart, skin sides up. Bake on a high rack in the oven for 2–3 minutes. Remove as soon as the fish begin to turn white. While they bake, microwave the blender sauce for 1 minute. Spoon the warm sauce around the fish and sprinkle with fleur de sel, Espelette pepper, and Parmesan shavings.

8 tablespoons (11 cl.) olive oil

1 medium onion, peeled and minced

1 clove garlic, peeled and degermed (page 122)

1 small sprig fresh thyme

1 small bay leaf

6 large tomatoes, peeled, seeded, and diced (page 124)

Salt

2 pinches superfine sugar

Juice of 1 lemon

16 pitted black olives

1 tablespoon basil leaves, cut into chiffonade (thin strips)

Pepper

1 tablespoon tapenade (store-bought or page 136)

Puff pastry or phyllo tart base, already cooked (pages 192–93)

Fillets of 12 small mackerel, each whole fish weighing 3 ounces (80–100 g.)

Fleur de sel

Ground Espelette pepper (substitute chili powder or hot paprika if necessary)

⅔ ounce (20 g.) Parmesan cheese, cut into shavings with a vegetable peeler

TOMATO AND PEPPER TART

Tarte aux tomates et poivrons

SERVES 6

PREPARATION   15 minutes

COOKING   10 minutes (tomato mixture) plus 8 minutes
(tart)

1. Preheat the oven to 400°F/200°C. Slice 4 of the tomatoes into rounds 1 inch (2.5 cm.) thick. Cut the other tomatoes into small dice.

2. Add the bell pepper slices to the bowl of tomato slices.

3. Melt 2 tablespoons butter, pour it over the peppers and tomatoes, and stir.

4. Put 2 tablespoons butter and 4 tablespoons olive oil in a saucepan with the onion. Add a little salt and cook over medium heat for 3–4 minutes, stirring and without allowing the onions or butter to color. Add the garlic, bouquet garni, chopped tomatoes, tomato paste, sugar, salt, and pepper. Allow to cook over medium heat until all the water has evaporated. Remove the garlic and bouquet garni. Taste for salt and pepper. Stir in the basil.

5. Spread the hot tomato mixture evenly over the precooked tart base. Arrange the tomato and pepper rounds on top and bake in the oven for 8 minutes. Sprinkle with fleur de sel, white pepper, and crumbled thyme. Drizzle with 2 tablespoons olive oil.

6 large tomatoes, peeled and
    seeded (page 124)

3 green bell peppers, peeled,
    seeded (page 130), and
    sliced into uniform rounds

4 tablespoons (50 g.) butter

6 tablespoons (10 cl.) olive oil

1 large onion, peeled and
    minced

Salt

4 cloves garlic, peeled

1 bouquet garni (5 stems
    parsley, 1 small stalk celery,
    and 3 sprigs fresh thyme,
    wrapped and tied in a
    green leek leaf)

2 tablespoons tomato paste

1 tablespoon (20 g.) granulated
    sugar

Pepper

2 tablespoons chopped fresh
    basil

Phyllo Tart Base, already
    cooked (page 193)

Fleur de sel

White pepper

4 sprigs fresh thyme, crumbled

POTATO-HERB TART

Tourte de pommes de terre aux herbes

SERVES 4
PREPARATION 20 minutes
COOKING 20 minutes

¾ pound (200 g.) potatoes (belles de Fontenay, rattes, charlottes, rose finn apples, or Russian bananas)
½ head of garlic
1 sprig thyme
Coarse salt
1 tablespoon minced flat-leaf parsley
1 tablespoon minced chives
Pepper
1 egg plus 1 yolk (page 204)
Eight 5-inch (12-cm.) circles puff pastry (page 192), already cooked
6 tablespoons (10 cl.) heavy cream
Salt

1 Wash the potatoes and put them unpeeled in a saucepan. Cover with cold water and add the garlic, thyme, and 1 teaspoon coarse salt. Bring to a boil and simmer for 15–20 minutes. Drain and allow to cool.

2 Peel the potatoes and slice them into ¼-inch (0.5-cm.) rounds. Toss the potato slices gently with the parsley and chives and a grinding of pepper.

3 Preheat the oven to 350°F/180°C. Beat 1 egg with a dash of salt. Use a pastry brush and cold water to paint a border ½ inch (1–2 cm.) thick around the circumference of each puff pastry circle. Build a rosette of potato slices on each of 4 circles, leaving the ½-inch border uncovered. You should use about 12 potato slices per tart. Cover the 4 potato-topped circles with the 4 remaining circles and pinch the edges together all around so that the 2 pieces of dough stick together. Lightly paint the tops of the tarts with egg; do not allow the egg wash to drip onto the bottom half of the tart. (If it does run over, gently wipe it away with paper towels.) Line a sheet pan with a piece of parchment paper. Put the tarts on the paper, being careful not to drip egg onto their bottoms.

4 With a small knife, cut a small round opening (about ½ inch/ 1 cm.) in the center of each tart. Do not discard the circles of dough you remove; put them on the sheet pan with the tarts. Slide into this opening a small tube of aluminum foil just large enough to allow the handle of a tablespoon to enter; this is the "chimney."

5 You can also use the tip of a knife to impress a decorative pattern on top of the tarts or to crimp their edges.

6 Refrigerate the tarts and small circles of dough on the sheet pan for 10 minutes and then put them straight into the preheated oven. Remove the sheet from the oven after 15 minutes and then remove the small circles of pastry and set them aside. Beat the cream and yolk with salt and pepper. Pour 2 tablespoons of this cream mixture into each tart through its chim-

ney. Put the tarts back in the oven for 5 minutes. When they are out of the oven, remove their chimneys and put the small circles of pastry back in the chimney holes.

SAUSAGE IN BRIOCHE

Saucisson en brioche

SERVES 4–6
PREPARATION 15 minutes
COOKING about 1 hour

1 Put the sausage in a small saucepan, cover with cold water, and warm over medium-high heat until the water begins to shiver. Lower the heat and cook for 30 minutes. Do not allow the water to boil. Remove the sausage and take off its casing while it is still hot. Refrigerate the sausage.

2 Preheat the oven to 440°F/220°C. Flatten the dough into a rectangle about 2–3 inches (6 cm.) longer than the sausage and 6 inches (15 cm.) wide.

3 Put the flour in a dish. Beat the egg in a cup. Use a pastry brush to paint the sausage with egg and then roll it in the flour, coating it evenly. Paint another coat of egg onto the floury sausage.

4 Lay the sausage on the brioche dough. Delicately wrap it in dough, taking care to make the dough stick to the sausage. Line a sheet pan with parchment paper and put the sausage in brioche on top. Bake about 20 minutes.

1 raw sausage (Italian, German, bratwurst, smoked or unsmoked), about 1 pound (500 g.)
14 ounces (400 g.) savory brioche dough, store-bought
2 tablespoons flour
1 egg

Fritters and Small Fry

Breading and batters used for deep frying are thinner today because of changes in diet and thanks to the influence of Japanese cuisine, with its delicious tempuras that use only a very light coating of batter. In northern Africa, tuna or meat is also fried in a thin layer of a dough called *brik*. Ready-made, store-bought brik is great for wrapping up a shrimp.

Peanut oil is good for frying. Frying oil should always be neutral; do not use aromatic oils such as olive. For these small quantities, 1 quart (1 l.) oil should be enough. If you have a fryer, by all means use it, but if you do not, a deep skillet will do. Always put the cooking vessel on a back burner to avoid accidents; a splash of hot oil can burn skin very badly.

Never leave oil to heat unwatched. Hot oil can catch fire, even without being exposed to another flame. If you forget a covered pot of hot oil on a hot stove (even over very low heat), *do not* just remove the cover. The inrush of air can cause an explosion. Turn off the heat and leave the pot to cool, covered.

If you do find yourself with a grease fire on your hands, don't panic. Smother the fire with a large lid. *Do not* throw water on a grease fire.

CONTROLLING THE TEMPERATURE

Fritters should be crispy but not burned. Heat the oil to 350°F/180°C to obtain best results. Oil heats rapidly; 1 quart (1 l.) takes less than 5 minutes to reach this temperature, and it can reach the target temperature much faster on an induction cooktop. Lower the heat when the target temperature is reached even if this means you have to turn it up a bit later. The oil should not start to smoke; if it does, it is too hot. If this happens, lower the heat to a minimum (or turn it off) until the temperature drops. If you don't have a thermometer, you can check whether it is hot enough by dropping in a bit of dough or a very small piece of potato: The oil should bubble up immediately and turn the dough golden without burning it. Remove the test dough to prevent it from burning. Don't try to cook too many fritters at once, as this will lower the temperature of the oil and they will take longer to cook, soaking up more fat and losing some crunchiness. Work in batches if necessary.

DRAINING FRITTERS

The best utensil for removing fritters from hot oil is a large Chinese spoon; it looks like a large-holed metal net on the end of a stick of bamboo. But you can also use a skimmer. Put the fritters on a plate lined with paper towels to wick away the excess fat, and turn them once to drain the other side as well.

Do not cover hot fritters with paper towels, aluminum foil, or anything else. They will become soggy. Fritters should really be eaten right away, hot but not burning, sprinkled with a bit of fleur de sel and two or three grindings of pepper. A dash of hot pepper sauce, such as Tabasco, can also be good.

Allow the cooking vessel to cool for a long time. If you want to save the oil and use it again, pour it through a fine strainer and funnel it into an empty bottle. Seal the bottle and keep it in a cool, dark place; heat and light will make it degrade faster.

Don't fry different things in the same oil (for instance, don't fry fish in oil that has been used to fry meat, and vice versa). The oil picks up flavors and will transmit them to other foods if you cross-fry. After a couple of uses or several months (or if it begins to smoke and burn too easily), throw the oil away.

SHRIMP ENVELOPES WITH BASIL

Papillotes de crevettes au basilic

SERVES   4

PREPARATION AND COOKING   20 minutes

1   At least 30 minutes in advance, put the olive oil in the refrigerator.

2   Put 24 basil leaves in a blender or food processor. Add the garlic, olive oil, and some salt and pepper. Blend.

3   Put the shrimp on a plate on top of some paper towels. Dry them and season with pepper on both sides. Top each shrimp with a basil leaf.

4   Quarter the brik leaves. Roll each shrimp in a piece of brik, pressing the dough so you can seal the package. Fasten the package with a toothpick, which should go straight through the shrimp.

6 tablespoons (10 cl.) olive oil
1 bunch basil, leaves only,
    washed (you need
    36 leaves; if you want to
    fry some leaves as well,
    you need about 50)
2 cloves garlic, peeled
Salt
Pepper
12 large shrimp tails, shelled

(continued)

5   Heat the peanut oil. Line a plate with 4 pieces of paper towel. When the oil reaches 350°F/180°C (after 4 or 5 minutes), fry the shrimp packages for 40 seconds, turning them once with a Chinese spoon or skimmer. Do this in 2 or 3 batches. Do not crowd the shrimp packages in the pot; the temperature of the oil will drop rapidly, and they will take too long to cook. Remove the cooked packages with a skimmer. Drain them in a colander for a brief minute and then put them on the plate lined with paper towels.

6   If you wish, you can fry 12 more basil leaves in cooler oil, 270°F/130°C. If you do not have a thermometer, test the temperature by dropping in a leaf: It should not burn. When the temperature is correct, drop in the leaves and remove them immediately. Drain them on paper towels and add a little salt. Fried basil leaves make a lovely and delicious decoration for serving these shrimp packages.

3 leaves of brik dough (page 199)
1 quart (1 l.) peanut oil for frying

special equipment: 12 wooden toothpicks

Eggs

 uy the freshest eggs you can find. If you are going to eat
 eggs raw, soft-boiled, or poached, they must not be more
than a week old. It is really best to buy fresh local eggs at a
farmers' market if possible.

The color of the egg's shell does not indicate anything
about the way it tastes.

STORING EGGS

Keep eggs in the refrigerator, either in their carton or in a
closed compartment. Egg shells are porous, allowing eggs to
absorb the flavors and odors of other foods. You don't want
to keep eggs with onions, garlic, smoked fish, or melon. On
the other hand, you can make truffled scrambled eggs simply
by storing the eggs you plan to use in a sealed container with
a truffle for 24 hours. The eggs will taste of truffle, and you
can keep the truffle for another use.

Contrary to usual practice, eggs should be stored pointy-
end down to prevent the yolk from rising to the air chamber
within the egg. The older an egg is, the more air it has inside.
This is why old eggs float in water while fresh ones sink to
the bottom. Eggs can be cooked three or even four weeks
after having been laid, but only the freshest should be eaten
soft-boiled or poached.

CRACKING EGGS

If your eggs are a little dirty, wash them carefully in water
just before using.

Crack eggs with a single sharp little tap, not too strong,
on a cutting board or work surface. Industrially farmed eggs
have a more fragile shell. Eggs should not be broken on the
side of a bowl, as this encourages bits of shell to fall in. If you
do see shell pieces in the egg, simply remove them with your
fingers.

Set two cups on a plate. Break an egg in half over one of the cups, allowing as much of the white as possible to fall into the cup. Gently, so as not to break it, pass the yolk back and forth between the two halves of the shell, dropping more white into the cup with each transfer. When nothing but a bit of filament remains on the yolk, remove it with one of the egg shells (if you are confident you can do so without breaking the yolk) and add it to the whites. Then drop the yolk into the other cup.

COOKING EGGS

There are two main categories of egg cookery: eggs cooked in the shell (such as soft-cooked, simmered, and hard-boiled) and eggs cooked without their shells (whole: fried, poached, or in a ramekin; or mixed: scrambled or in an omelette).

You can generally count on people eating two eggs each; you might need to add a few eggs if you are scrambling them or making an omelette, unless you are feeding children.

When cooking eggs in a pot of water, do not salt the water. If the egg is in its shell, the salt will not make any difference, and if it is unshelled, the salt will liquefy the albumen in the white.

Before cooking soft- or hard-boiled eggs, check to see whether they are cracked. A crack looks like a little pencil scribble and might show a glossy bit of leaking white. If you aren't sure whether an egg is cracked, gently tap it against another; if they are without cracks, they should give off a little thud, whereas a cracked egg sounds hollow. Avoid boiling a cracked egg.

Eggs should be removed from the refrigerator at least a half hour before being cooked in boiling water. If this precaution is not taken, they will crack on contact and leak some white into the water. If you forget to remove them early or don't have time to wait, pass cold eggs under warm running water or leave them in a bowl of warm water for as long as it takes your cooking pot to come to a boil.

When the water boils, carefully lower the eggs into the pot with a skimmer or spoon, depositing them gently at the bottom. Don't tumble them in, or they might break. After cooking, rinse them in cold running water. This stops the cooking and makes the shell easier to remove. If you plan to eat the egg immediately, rinsing it under cold water will also keep the shell from burning you.

When frying eggs, crack them into a bowl instead of directly into the skillet. Cracking the egg directly into the skillet makes it cook unevenly, and if you happen to break the yolk, you will have quite a mess in the skillet.

For aesthetic reasons it is best to avoid salting the top of a frying egg. The salt will leave white traces on the yolk and little pits in the white. Salt after cooking, and salt the white only.

Never use silver or silverplate to scramble or whisk eggs.

SOFT-BOILED EGGS WITH TOAST SOLDIERS ——————
Oeufs à la coque

SERVES   1
COOKING   3–4 minutes

This is also fine topped with mushroom purée, diced sautéed chicken liver or foie gras, truffles, or caviar. (If you use caviar, you will not need to salt the egg.) The toast "soldiers" should be cut thin enough to dunk into the egg.

2 very fresh eggs, no more than
    a few days old
1 piece buttered toast, cut into
    6 thin slices
Fleur de sel
Pepper

1   Take the eggs out of the refrigerator at least 30 minutes in advance and pass them under warm running water. Make sure they are not cracked.
2   Bring to a boil 3 cups (75 cl.) water (or enough water to cover the eggs). Do not salt. When it bubbles, lower the eggs in all the way to the bottom with a skimmer or spoon. The water should quickly come back to a boil; once it does, count 3 minutes and then remove the eggs with a skimmer. If the eggs were not removed from the refrigerator 30 minutes in advance and are still chilled, boil 4 minutes instead of 3.
3   Put the warm eggs in a colander and rinse them under cold running water for 30 seconds. At this point the white should be semi-solid and the yolk should still be liquid.
4   Put the egg in an egg cup, the round end at the bottom. Cut

off the upper end with an egg cutter, if you have one, or with a small kitchen knife, giving the shell a short sharp tap. (You can also open the 2 eggs into a bowl and season with a pinch of fleur de sel, pepper, and a pinch of grated or powdered nutmeg. Eat them with a spoon and serve the buttered toast on the side.)

5   Dunk the toast soldiers into the soft egg, seasoned with a bit of fleur de sel and pepper.

CODDLED EGGS

Oeufs mollets

SERVES   1

COOKING   5 minutes

These eggs are slightly more cooked than soft-boiled eggs. The whites are no longer the least bit runny, but the yolk is still liquid and creamy.

2 very fresh eggs, no more than a few days old

1   Take the eggs out of the refrigerator at least 30 minutes in advance and pass them under warm running water. Make sure they are not cracked. Prepare a bowl of cold water, perhaps adding a few ice cubes.

2   Bring to a boil 3 cups (75 cl.) water or enough water to cover the eggs. Do not salt. When it bubbles, lower the eggs in all the way to the bottom with a skimmer or spoon. The water should quickly come back to a boil; once it does, boil for 5 minutes and then remove the eggs with a skimmer to the bowl of cold water.

3   If you do not plan to eat the eggs immediately, allow them to cool in the water for at least 5 minutes. It will be easier to peel the eggs in the bowl of cold water than out of it.

4   You can keep the peeled eggs in the cold water or in a stainless steel container in the refrigerator. Serve them cold or hot. Reheat by simmering the peeled egg for 1 minute in water with 1 teaspoon coarse salt.

CODDLED EGGS WITH SPINACH

Oeufs mollets aux épinards

SERVES 4

PREPARATION AND COOKING 40 minutes

1 Bring 2 quarts (2 l.) water to a boil with 1½ tablespoons coarse salt. Prepare a bowl of cold water with a tray of ice cubes. Plunge the clean spinach into the bubbling water. If the spinach is young and tender, remove it as soon as the water comes back to a boil. If it is older and larger, cook 2 minutes more after the resumption of boiling. Immediately plunge the cooked spinach into the ice water and then drain in a colander.

2 If you are using frozen spinach, follow the package instructions to cook.

3 Use your hands to squeeze as much water as possible from the drained spinach. Spread the spinach on a cutting board. Take a handful, form it into a ball, and chop it 3 or 4 times. Do the same with the rest of the spinach.

4 Preheat the broiler. Use a pastry brush to grease a sheet pan with butter. Bring 2 cups (50 cl.) water to a boil with 1 teaspoon coarse salt.

5 While you are waiting for the broiler to heat up and the water to boil, heat the butter in a saucepan over low heat. When it foams, add the spinach and stir well with a wooden spoon. Cook for 1–2 minutes and then sprinkle with salt, pepper, and a pinch of grated nutmeg. Spread the spinach on the sheet pan.

6 When the water comes to a boil, turn off the heat. Slip the eggs into the water one by one with a skimmer and then remove them immediately, beginning with the first one you put in. Arrange them on top of the spinach.

7 Coat each egg with Mornay sauce. Cover the eggs with spinach and top the whole with grated Gruyère. Broil for 2 minutes to brown. Do not leave under the broiler too long or the eggs will get tough.

Coarse salt

2 pounds (1 kg.) fresh spinach, washed in several changes of water and tough stems removed, or 14 ounces (400 g.) frozen spinach

3 tablespoons butter, plus extra for greasing the sheet pan

Salt

Pepper

Nutmeg

8 coddled eggs, already cooked (page 206)

2 cups (50 cl.) Mornay sauce (page 51)

¾ cup (75 g.) grated Gruyère cheese

HARD-BOILED EGGS

Oeufs durs

SERVES 1

COOKING 10 minutes

The white of a hard-boiled egg should be completely solid, and the yolk should be cooked through as well. Do not cook for too long, however, or the yolk will turn an unpleasant grayish green. If you do not plan to eat hard-boiled eggs right away, keep them in the refrigerator in a sealed container to prevent the sharing of odors.

2 fresh eggs

1   Take the eggs out of the refrigerator at least 30 minutes in advance and pass them under warm running water. Make sure they are not cracked. Prepare a bowl of cold water, perhaps adding a few ice cubes.

2   Bring to a boil 3 cups (75 cl.) water or enough water to cover the eggs. Do not salt. When it bubbles, lower the eggs in all the way to the bottom with a skimmer or spoon. The water should quickly come back to a boil; once it does, boil for 10 minutes and then remove the eggs with a skimmer to the bowl of cold water.

3   If you do not plan to eat the eggs immediately, allow them to cool in the water for at least 5 minutes. *Do not* leave them in their cooking water; this will make the white stick to the shell, and they will be very difficult to peel.

HARD-BOILED EGGS WITH MAYONNAISE

Oeufs durs mayonnaise

1 small head lettuce, washed, dried, and cut into thick strips
8 hard-boiled eggs (see above), shelled and cut in half lengthwise
1 cup (25 cl.) mayonnaise (page 55 or store-bought)

SERVES 4

PREPARATION 5 minutes

Spread a blanket of lettuce on a serving platter. Arrange the halved eggs on top. If the mayonnaise is homemade, whisk in a tablespoon of water. Dollop each egg with a large spoonful of mayonnaise.

HERBED DEVILED EGGS

Oeufs durs mimosa

SERVES 4

PREPARATION 10 minutes

1   Spread a blanket of lettuce on a platter.
2   Remove the yolks from the eggs. Arrange the whites on top of the lettuce and put the yolks on a cutting board. Chop them up finely or crush them with a fork; either way, leave little bits—do not mash them into a paste. In a bowl, combine the yolks and mayonnaise well. Mix in the herbs.
3   Spoon a bit of the yolk mixture into each egg white on the platter and serve.

1 small head lettuce, washed, dried, and cut into thick strips
8 hard-boiled eggs (page 208), shelled and sliced in half lengthwise
1 cup (25 cl.) mayonnaise (page 55 or store-bought)
1 tablespoon minced parsley
1 tablespoon minced tarragon
1 tablespoon minced chervil

ONION-SMOTHERED EGGS

Oeufs "à la tripe"

SERVES 4

PREPARATION AND COOKING 40 minutes

1   Warm the butter in a saucepan over low heat. Add the onion and cook over very low heat for 15–20 minutes, stirring every 5 minutes. Keep an eye on the heat. The onion should not color but should seem to melt into a kind of purée. Stir in the béchamel and cook 10 minutes more, stirring from time to time. Season to taste with salt, pepper, and nutmeg.
2   While the sauce cooks, slice the eggs into rounds $\frac{1}{2}$ inch (1 cm.) thick. Arrange the slices on a buttered platter.
3   Coat the egg slices with the very hot sauce.

2 tablespoons butter
1 large onion, trimmed, peeled, and minced
2 cups (50 cl.) béchamel sauce (page 51)
Salt
Pepper
Grated nutmeg
8 hard-boiled eggs (page 208), shelled

POACHED EGGS
Oeufs pochés

SERVES 1

COOKING 3 minutes

2 very fresh eggs

3 tablespoons (5 cl.) distilled white vinegar

1   Poach only the freshest eggs; the whites of older eggs tend to spread through the cooking water. To make uniformly shaped poached eggs, you can use egg rings and other implements that will keep the egg round. In this case the eggs must be just barely covered with water. You may find them quite useful if you frequently poach small eggs. Poached eggs make a fine addition to salads, mushrooms, ratatouille, and spinach. Try them hot with a spoonful of crème fraîche.

2   Prepare a bowl filled with cold water and a few ice cubes. Bring 1½ quarts (1.5 l.) unsalted water to a boil. Boil the eggs, still in their shells, for exactly 30 seconds. (This will firm up the surface edge of the white a bit, making the poaching easier.) Remove the eggs with a skimmer and put them into the cold water or simply rinse them under cold running water. Do not discard the hot water or take it off the heat.

3   Pour the vinegar into the pot of water. Bring it back to a boil over low heat. One at a time, break each egg into a small bowl and then slip it into the water. (Do not try to cook too many eggs at the same time; cook no more than 3 or 4 at once.) Use a skimmer to gather the white back in to envelop the yolk. Keep an eye on the heat: The vinegar may encourage the water to boil over. Cook about 3 minutes.

4   If you are going to eat the eggs immediately, remove them with the skimmer and put them on a plate. Wipe away any water that collects on the plate. The presentation will be more pleasing if you remove any strands of white that form on the surface.

5   If you are not going to eat the eggs right away and are concerned about presentation, slip them into the ice water after removing them from the simmering pot. When they have cooled, remove them and cut away the strands of white with scissors or a sharp knife.

6   These eggs can be served cold. To serve them hot, reheat them for 1 minute in simmering water to which you have added a teaspoon of coarse salt.

POACHED EGGS IN RED WINE SAUCE

Oeufs en meurette

SERVES 4

PREPARATION 15 minutes

COOKING 50 minutes or 70 minutes depending on the
method

Here are two ways of making *oeufs en meurette:* with the traditional flour-thickened sauce of Burgundy and with a flour-free reduced wine sauce. If you like, add 5 ounces (150 g.) small onions (cipollini, if possible), boiled for 1 minute and then cooked gently with butter for 20 minutes in a covered skillet. You can also add 5 ounces (150 g.) cup or button mushrooms, sautéed with butter for 5 minutes.

1   Put the lardons in a saucepan, cover them with cold water, and bring to a boil. As soon as the water boils, remove the lardons to a colander, rinse with cold water, and leave them to drain.

2   Rinse the bouquet garni. Preheat the broiler. Mince 2 of the garlic cloves. In a stockpot or large saucepan, melt 3 tablespoons butter over low heat. Add the onion and shallots, stirring well with a wooden spatula or spoon. Add the wine, bouquet garni, minced garlic, a pinch of crushed pepper, and the whole clove. Do not salt. Simmer for 20 minutes; the wine should reduce by about a third.

3   When the broiler is hot, toast the bread for 2 minutes on each side. Rub the toast with the remaining garlic clove and place side by side on a platter, or put 2 slices each on 4 individual plates.

4   Put the wine through a fine strainer into another stockpot or saucepan, one with tall, straight sides if possible. Bring to a boil and then reduce the heat to low. Taste for salt and pepper.

5   Half-fill a large bowl with warm water. Break each egg into its own small bowl. Slip half of the eggs into the simmering reduced wine. Cook for 3–4 minutes at a low simmer, depending on the size of the eggs. Remove them with a skimmer and slip them into the bowl of warm water. Do the same with the remaining eggs. When you have finished, do not turn off the heat under the pot.

4 ounces (150 g.) lardons
   (page 89)
1 bouquet garni (2 stems flat-
   leaf parsley, 1 sprig fresh
   thyme, and 1 small bay
   leaf, tied together)
3 cloves garlic, peeled
6 or 11 tablespoons (100 g. or
   170 g.) butter, depending
   on the method you choose
1 medium onion, peeled and
   minced
2 shallots, peeled and minced
1 bottle Pinot Noir
Crushed black pepper
1 whole clove
8 small slices country bread
8 very fresh eggs
1 cup (25 cl.) chicken broth
   (page 77 or made from a
   bouillon cube)
Salt
Pepper

6   For a more elegant presentation, use scissors or a sharp knife to snip the strands of white on the eggs' surfaces. Drain the eggs. Preheat the oven to 460°F (240°C).

7   Add the broth to the wine. Add a pinch of salt and return to a boil.

8   In the meantime, gently cook the lardons for 5 minutes in a skillet, stirring constantly with a wooden spatula. Drain the browned lardons in a colander.

9   There are 2 ways to finish the sauce: the traditional Burgundy style, with flour, or a simple reduction, without flour.

TRADITIONAL METHOD

1   With a fork, combine well ¼ cup (30 g.) sifted flour and 2 tablespoons softened butter. (If the butter is still cold, put it in a bowl and soften it in the microwave.) Add this mixture to the simmering wine, whisking it in completely. Turn off the heat.

2   Taste for salt and pepper and whisk in 1 tablespoon cold butter.

REDUCTION METHOD

1   Allow the wine to cook at a quiet bubble for 20 minutes. Turn the heat to very low. Dice 1 stick (120 g.) chilled butter and stir it into the no-longer-boiling wine with a wooden spoon.

2   Put your sauce through a fine strainer. Put it back in the pot along with the lardons. Taste for salt and pepper. Reheat without allowing the mixture to boil.

3   Lay each egg on a piece of toast. Put the plates back in the oven for 1–2 minutes to reheat the eggs. Coat the eggs with sauce.

FRIED EGGS

Oeufs poêlés

SERVES 1
COOKING 2 minutes

This method produces an egg with a perfectly solidified white and a yolk that stays creamy but hot. It is easiest to fry eggs in a small nonstick skillet.

Break the eggs with a sharp tap on a flat surface and empty them into a bowl. (If you break eggs directly into the skillet, you will be in trouble if the yolk gets broken.) Gently heat the oil in the skillet and then add the butter. Turn the skillet to spread the fats around. When the butter foams, add a pinch of salt. Turn the skillet again. Gently slide the eggs into the skillet. Cook for 2 minutes over low heat, shaking the pan a bit to keep the eggs from sticking. Slide the eggs onto a plate.

2 eggs
Scant ½ teaspoon neutral oil
Scant ½ teaspoon butter
Salt

FRIED EGGS WITH CABBAGE AND LARDONS

Oeufs poêlés au chou et lardons

SERVES 4
PREPARATION 10 minutes
COOKING 7 minutes

1   Remove the large outer leaves of the cabbage and cut away the core. Wash the leaves in water with distilled vinegar— 1 tablespoon for 1 quart (1 l.). Rub the leaves well. Drain the cabbage and slice it into strips ½ inch by ¼ inch (1 cm. by 0.5 cm.).

2   Melt the butter in a pot over low heat and add the lardons. Add the cabbage and a pinch of salt and stir. Cover and cook over low heat for 5 minutes.

3   Follow the recipe for fried eggs above. Serve the fried eggs on top of the cabbage and lardons, sprinkled with minced chives.

¼ green cabbage
1 tablespoon distilled white
   vinegar
1 tablespoon butter
2 ounces (60 g.) lardons,
   blanched (page 89)
Salt
4 fried eggs (see above)
1 bunch chives, minced

EGGS IN THE DISH

Oeufs au plat

SERVES 1

COOKING 2 minutes

Here is another way to "fry" eggs. The texture and taste are just slightly different: Here the white is almost completely solid and milky-colored, and the yolk becomes thick and creamy.

2 eggs
1 teaspoon butter
Salt
Pepper

special equipment: a small heat-resistant plate made of porcelain, glass, or stainless steel (the kind of shallow dish in which one makes crème brûlée)

Break the eggs into a bowl. Heat the butter in the heat-resistant plate over low heat. Turn the plate to spread the butter around. Be sure to wear oven mitts if the plate does not have a handle; they tend to heat up very quickly. When the butter foams, add a pinch of salt and a pinch of pepper and turn the plate around again. Gently slide the eggs onto the plate. Cook for 2 minutes over low heat. The white should coagulate in this time, and it should look smooth and uncratered. Serve on the cooking plate.

EGGS IN THE OVEN

Oeufs au plat au four

SERVES   1

COOKING   2 minutes

In this recipe the eggs start on the cooktop and finish in the oven. To serve two, use two small plates to cook and four cups for separating the eggs.

2 eggs
1 teaspoon butter
Salt
Pepper
Balsamic vinegar (optional)
4 buttered toast fingers
Fleur de sel

1   Ten minutes in advance, preheat the oven to 475°F/250°C. Break each egg and separate the whites and yolks into 2 small bowls.

2   Melt the butter in the egg plate over low heat. Add a pinch of salt and a pinch of pepper and twirl the plate to spread everything around. Be sure to use oven mitts if necessary; these plates get very hot very quickly. Pour the whites onto the

plate and cook over low heat for 30 seconds; they should become semi-coagulated. Turn off the heat, pour the yolks over the whites, and put the plate in the oven for 1½ minutes.

3   The yolks should be creamy. If you like, sprinkle 3 drops balsamic vinegar on the whites. Serve on the cooking plate with buttered toast fingers, sprinkled with fleur de sel and pepper to taste.

special equipment: a small heat-resistant plate made of porcelain, glass, or stainless steel (the kind of shallow dish in which one makes crème brûlée)

BAKED EGGS

Oeufs cocotte

SERVES   1

COOKING   5–10 minutes (depending on the cooking method and size of the eggs)

This method of cooking eggs produces a very smooth white and a creamy yolk. Garnish with tomato sauce, crème fraîche, or Madeira sauce, or try putting some mushroom purée into the ramekin before adding and cooking the eggs.

Butter
Salt
2 fresh eggs

special equipment: 2 ovenproof porcelain or glass ramekins

1   Bring 1 quart (1 l.) water to a boil in a kettle or saucepan. Butter the insides of the ramekins and deposit a small pinch of salt in each one. Crack the eggs carefully into the ramekins. If you are cooking the eggs in the oven instead of on the cooktop, preheat the oven to 400°F/200°C and put a rack in the upper-middle position.

2   Take a small saucepan (just large enough to hold both ramekins) and line the bottom with parchment paper pricked with a fork; this will keep the water from boiling over and cannot be skipped if you are baking the eggs in the oven.

3   Put the ramekins in the saucepan. Pour in the boiling water, enough to reach halfway up the ramekins. Be very careful not to splash it into the ramekins. Now the eggs can be cooked either on the cooktop or in the oven:

ON THE COOKTOP   Put the saucepan over low heat so that the water bath bubbles gently. Cook 5 minutes for small eggs, 6–7 minutes for medium-sized eggs, and 8–9 minutes for large ones. You should be able to see the white coagulating and the liquid yolk. Do not wait for the white to solidify completely, or the yolk will solidify, too. A thin film of liquid white will solidify after the eggs have been removed from the heat.

IN THE OVEN   Put the saucepan in the preheated oven on the rack just above the middle. Be careful not to splash water into the ramekins. Cook 6 minutes for small eggs, 8–9 minutes for medium-sized eggs, and 10 minutes for very large ones. You should be able to see the white coagulating and the liquid yolk. Do not wait for the white to solidify completely, or the yolk will solidify, too. A thin film of liquid white will solidify after the eggs have been removed from the oven.

For a slightly more cooked yolk, cover the pot for the last bit of cooking.

BAKED EGGS WITH MUSHROOM CREAM
Oeufs cocotte à la crème de champignons

SERVES   4
PREPARATION   10 minutes
COOKING   12 minutes

1   Melt the butter in a saucepan over low heat. Add the shallots and cook for 2 minutes, stirring with a wooden spatula. Add the mushrooms and stir. Add 2 tablespoons cream and stir. Add 2 pinches of salt and 2 pinches of pepper. Cook over very low heat for 10 minutes. Blend the mixture in a blender or food processor. Add the remaining cream and taste for salt and pepper. Pour back into the saucepan and cover.
2   Prepare the baked eggs according to the previous recipe.
3   When the eggs are ready, reheat the mushroom cream for 1 minute over low heat. Pour the mushroom cream over the eggs, sprinkle with chives, and serve in the ramekins with grilled bread or toast fingers on the side.

2 tablespoons butter
2 shallots, peeled and minced
½ pound (220 g.) cup mushrooms, cleaned and sliced into thin strips
3 tablespoons heavy cream
Salt
Pepper
2 recipes Baked Eggs (page 215) using 4 eggs total
1 teaspoon minced chives
4 slices grilled bread or 16 toast fingers (optional)

BAKED EGGS WITH TOMATO

Oeufs cocotte à la tomate

SERVES 4
PREPARATION 5 minutes
COOKING 20 minutes

1 Heat the olive oil in a skillet over medium heat. Cook the tomatoes for 5 minutes and then add the garlic, parsley, sugar, a pinch of salt, and a pinch of pepper.
2 Butter 4 ramekins and distribute the tomato sauce evenly among them. Crack an egg into each ramekin and cook for 15 minutes, following the instructions for Baked Eggs (page 215).
3 Garnish each ramekin with a basil leaf and serve with toast fingers.

$1\frac{1}{2}$ tablespoons olive oil
4 tomatoes, peeled, seeded (page 124), and chopped into $\frac{1}{2}$-inch (1-cm.) dice
1 clove garlic, peeled and minced
1 tablespoon minced flat-leaf parsley
1 pinch of superfine sugar
Salt
Pepper
Butter
4 large eggs
4 small basil leaves
16 toast fingers

OMELETTE

SERVES 2–4
COOKING 6–8 minutes for a moist and juicy omelette; 10 minutes for a slightly more cooked omelette

Making an omelette with more than 12 eggs requires a very large pan and is much more difficult to do well. You are better off making two separate omelettes if you plan to use more than 12 eggs. Omelettes can, of course, take any number of garnishes before or after cooking: mixed herbs, ham, lardons, potatoes, and so forth.

6–12 eggs (3 per person)
Salt
Pepper
1 teaspoon neutral oil
1 tablespoon butter

1 Break the eggs into a large bowl. Season with a pinch of salt and a pinch of pepper. Beat firmly with a fork or, preferably, a whisk to obtain a foamy mixture.
2 Heat the oil in a skillet over low heat. Add 2 teaspoons butter and cook for 2 minutes over medium heat. Twirl the skillet to distribute the fats evenly over its bottom and sides. When

the butter foams, pour in the beaten eggs. They should immediately begin to solidify. Reduce the heat to low.

3   With a wooden spatula, quickly scrape up the eggs cooked on the bottom and sides of the pan, pulling them to the center. Use a corner of the spatula to prick small holes in the cooking eggs. Spin the skillet regularly for an even distribution of heat. Pull the cooked parts from the bottom and the sides to the center several times. After 5 minutes, simply shake the skillet so that the omelette gets "polished." Cook over low heat 1 to 2 minutes more (3 minutes more if you are using 12 eggs) for a moist omelette. If you like a firmer omelette, cook 3 minutes more.

4   Turn off the heat and add the remaining teaspoon butter to the pan. Allow it to melt all around the omelette; this will take care of any potential sticking.

5   For a lovely presentation, serve the omelette flipped or rolled:

FLIPPED OMELETTE   Take your plate in one hand and the skillet in the other. Hold the plate on top of the skillet and then quickly flip the skillet over, holding the plate against it the whole time so that the omelette ends up on the plate, smooth side up.

ROLLED OMELETTE   Tilt the skillet so that the omelette slides a little to one side, up against the edge. Use a spatula to lift the side opposite the handle and fold the omelette in half. Use a fork to make the folded edge more round. Shake the pan with short, sharp movements to make the omelette roll over itself. Use the fork to make it rounder if necessary. Tilt the skillet over the serving plate and slip the rolled omelette out.

ROLLED OMELETTE WITH MUSHROOMS

Omelette roulée aux champignons

SERVES   4
PREPARATION   10 minutes
COOKING   25–30 minutes (including mushroom-cooking time)

2 tablespoons butter
½ pound (200 g.) button

1   Heat 1 tablespoon butter in a skillet over medium heat. Add the mushrooms and cook for 5 minutes, stirring with a wooden spoon.

2   Crack the eggs into a large bowl. Beat with 1½ teaspoons salt and 4 grindings of pepper. Mix well but not to the point of foaminess. Add the mushrooms.

3   Rinse the skillet with hot water and wipe it dry with a paper towel. Add the oil and warm over medium heat. Add 1 tablespoon butter and heat for 2 minutes. When the butter is quite foamy, pour in the egg-mushroom mixture. Stir immediately.

4   Follow the Omelette recipe on page 217, finishing with the rolled version.

mushrooms, cleaned (page 598) and sliced vertically into thin strips
12 eggs
Salt
Pepper
1 teaspoon neutral oil

FLAT SPANISH OMELETTE

Omelette plate à l'espagnole

SERVES   4

PREPARATION   20 minutes

COOKING   40 minutes for the garnishes plus 15 minutes for the omelette

This recipe makes four individual omelettes.

1   To make the tomato sauce, heat the olive oil in a saucepan over medium heat. Add the onion and cook for 20 minutes, stirring with a wooden spoon. Add the peppers, tomatoes, garlic, and bouquet garni with a pinch of salt and a pinch of pepper. Lower the heat and cook gently for 20 minutes.

2   Crack 3 eggs into each of 4 bowls. Put a pinch of salt and a pinch of pepper in each bowl and beat with a fork.

3   Warm the neutral oil in a skillet over medium heat. Add the butter. When the butter foams, pour in one of the bowls of eggs and stir with a wooden spatula. Stir for 3 minutes or until the eggs begin to coagulate into clumps. Lower the heat and flip the omelette over. Leave for 1 minute and then slide onto a plate.

4   Cook the other 3 omelettes the same way and serve with the tomato sauce on top.

1 tablespoon olive oil
1 medium onion, peeled, cut in half vertically, and sliced into half moons ⅛ inch (3 mm.) thick
2 medium green bell peppers, peeled, seeded (page 130), and sliced into strips 1½ inches by ⅛ inch (3 cm. by 3 mm.)
4 medium tomatoes, peeled, seeded (page 124), and diced
2 cloves garlic, peeled and degermed (page 122)
1 bouquet garni (1 piece of bay leaf, 6 stems parsley, and 3 sprigs thyme, tied together)
Salt
Pepper
12 eggs
½ teaspoon neutral oil
½ teaspoon butter

HERBED OMELETTE

Omelette aux fines herbes

SERVES   4
PREPARATION   10 minutes

Follow the instructions for a 12-egg omelette, beating ½ tea-spoon salt, 4 grindings of pepper, and all the herbs into the eggs before whisking and cooking. At the end, present the omelette rolled.

A 12-egg omelette (page 217)
1 teaspoon each minced fresh
    parsley, chervil, chives, and
    tarragon

POTATO AND LARDON OMELETTE

Omelette aux pommes de terre et lardons

SERVES   4
PREPARATION   15 minutes
COOKING   10 minutes for the potatoes plus 8 minutes for
              the omelette

1   Rinse the diced potatoes in cold water and dry them with a clean dish towel or paper towels. This will remove some of their starch.

2   Heat the oil in a skillet over low heat. Add the butter and heat 3 minutes more. Add the potatoes, lardons, and parsley. Raise the heat to medium and sauté for 10 minutes. Drain on a plate lined with paper towels.

3   Follow the instructions for a moist, juicy omelette (page 217), beating the crème fraîche into the eggs before cooking. Because bacon is included, use less salt than you usually would, and add pepper to taste. When the omelette is ready, pour the potatoes and lardons into its center and fold it in half to serve.

1 pound (500 g.) potatoes
    (preferably rattes), peeled
    and cut into ½-inch (1-cm.)
    dice
1 teaspoon neutral oil
2 tablespoons (30 g.) butter
5 ounces (150 g.) lardons
    (page 89)
2 tablespoons minced parsley
3 tablespoons crème fraîche
12 eggs
Salt
Pepper

EGGS SCRAMBLED IN A BAIN-MARIE

Oeufs brouillés au bain-marie

SERVES 1

COOKING 18 minutes

Scrambled eggs demand the cook's attention and patience. Only careful cooking will result in uniformly soft, creamy eggs. You may garnish scrambled eggs with ham, cheese, mushrooms, tomato, asparagus tips, shrimp, crayfish, or any number of other delicious foods.

    Scrambled eggs cooked in a bain-marie are lighter and fluffier than those cooked in a skillet and have a better texture. This method takes more time but gives the cook greater control over the consistency of the eggs since they will not coagulate or dry out nearly as quickly. If you are worried about overcooking eggs, give this method a try. Some people like to add a half cup of whole milk to the eggs when they are beaten, but this will slow the cooking down even more.

3 eggs
Salt
Pepper
1 teaspoon butter
1 teaspoon crème fraîche

1 Bring a kettle full of water to a boil. Choose a bowl and a pot for cooking. The bowl should be able to hold the eggs, and the pot should be able to hold the bowl with some room to spare. The bowl must be safe for a bain-marie (that is, it will be surrounded by boiling water and sitting inside the pot on top of the lit burner; a porcelain bowl is best).

2 Crack the eggs into a different bowl. Add a pinch of salt and a pinch of pepper and whisk energetically until the mixture is completely homogeneous. You should not be able to see streaks of yolk and white.

3 Smear the interior of your bowl with butter, paying as much attention to the sides as the bottom (eggs tend to stick to the sides). Put the eggs in the bowl and the bowl in the pot. Pour the boiling water into the pot so that it comes halfway up the side of the bowl; be careful not to splash any water into the eggs. If you don't have enough boiling water, add some hot water so it comes halfway up the side of the egg bowl.

4 Put the pot over a flame hot enough to bring the water to a simmer. Lower the heat so that the water bubbles very gently. Stir the eggs with a wooden spoon or spatula regu-

larly but not constantly, scraping the bottom and sides well. After 15 minutes, begin to stir constantly, since the eggs will be coagulating more readily at this point. Cook about 3 minutes more. When the eggs begin to become a thick custardy cream, turn off the heat. Wearing heat-proof mitts, remove the bowl from the bain-marie and stir it a little more off the heat. Taste for salt and pepper and stir in the crème fraîche.

SCRAMBLED EGGS IN A PAN

Oeufs brouillés

SERVES 2

COOKING 3–4 minutes

1 For scrambled eggs it is best to use a normal skillet or a skillet with sloping sides instead of a straight-sided sauté pan. Smear the interior of the skillet with the butter.

2 Crack the eggs into a large bowl. Season with a pinch of salt and a pinch of pepper and then whisk energetically until the mixture is homogeneous. You should not be able to see unmixed traces of white or yolk.

3 Pour the eggs into the cold buttered skillet and put it over very low heat. Once the heat is on, stir constantly with a wooden spatula, carefully scraping the bottom and sides of the skillet to prevent the eggs from sticking. Make sure the heat stays as low as possible.

4 If the eggs clump up too much and seem to be at risk of drying out, you can take them off the heat, beat another egg in a bowl, and stir it into the skillet. Mix it in well to restore creamy richness to the whole.

5 Cook for 3–4 minutes, always stirring and always over gentle heat. When the eggs begin to become a thick custardy cream, remove the skillet from the heat. It's okay if they still look a little liquidy: They will continue to cook in the skillet off the heat.

6 Keep stirring off the heat, detaching any clumps that form on the pan. Taste for salt and pepper. Stir in the crème fraîche, if you like.

1 teaspoon butter

6 eggs

Salt

Pepper

1 teaspoon crème fraîche (optional)

7   Serve the eggs immediately. Do not leave them in the skillet, for they will continue to cook and dry out.

ASPARAGUS FOR SCRAMBLED EGGS _____

Oeufs brouillés aux asperges

SERVES   4
PREPARATION   10 minutes
COOKING   10 minutes

1   Peel the asparagus, cut off the tough end of the stems, wash them, and tie them into 2 bundles. Bring to a boil 3 quarts (3 l.) water (or enough to cover both bunches of asparagus) with 2 tablespoons coarse salt. Prepare a large bowl half filled with water and a dozen ice cubes.

2   Plunge the asparagus into the boiling water and cook for 5 minutes after the water comes back to a boil. Remove with a skimmer and plunge into the ice water. Allow the asparagus to cool a bit and then untie and drain in a colander.

3   Prepare the scrambled eggs.

4   Melt the butter in a skillet over low heat. Leave for 2 minutes; when the butter foams, add the asparagus and cook for 3 minutes, rolling them around in the butter. Add a little salt and pepper. Serve the asparagus on top of the scrambled eggs.

1½ pounds (0.75 kg.) (4 small bunches) green asparagus
Coarse salt
4 recipes Eggs Scrambled in a Bain-marie, page 221 (12 eggs total)
2 teaspoons butter
Salt
Pepper

SCRAMBLED EGGS WITH CHEESE _____

Oeufs brouillés au fromage

SERVES   4
PREPARATION   5 minutes

Prepare the 12 scrambled eggs. Off the heat, gently mix in the Gruyère and crème fraîche. Taste for salt and pepper, and serve sprinkled with croutons if you like.

12 scrambled eggs (page 221 or 222)
1 cup (100 g.) grated Gruyère cheese
1 tablespoon crème fraîche
Salt
Pepper
Croutons (optional)

SCRAMBLED EGGS WITH BASQUE PEPPERS (PIPERADE) ____
Oeufs brouillés en piperade

SERVES 4
PREPARATION 10 minutes
COOKING 45 minutes

This Basque specialty normally uses local dried ham (from the city of Bayonne) and a local pepper (produced in a place named Espelette). Despite the near universal preference for red bell peppers, this dish should be prepared with green ones.

1   Put the onions and olive oil in a skillet or sauté pan. Add a little salt and cook over low heat for 5 minutes, stirring constantly with a wooden spatula. Add the bell peppers, garlic, and bouquet garni, and stir and cook 5 minutes more. Add the diced tomatoes, salt, pepper, and Espelette pepper. Stir well, cover, and simmer for 30 minutes over low heat, stirring from time to time.

2   Break the eggs into a large bowl. Add a little salt and pepper and then beat well. Remove the bouquet garni from the piperade sauce and pour in the eggs. Stir with a spatula for a few minutes over low heat, until the mixture takes on the appearance and consistency of scrambled eggs.

3   Heat a skillet over medium heat. Lay the slices of ham in it, flip them after a few seconds, and remove them after a few more seconds.

4   Spread the eggs and piperade on a serving dish and arrange the ham slices all around them.

2 medium onions, peeled and sliced into thin rounds
3 tablespoons olive oil
Salt
2 green bell peppers, seeded and cut into 1-inch (2-cm.) strips
2 cloves garlic, peeled and minced
1 bouquet garni (1 sprig fresh thyme, ½ bay leaf, and 2 stems flat-leaf parsley, tied together)
1½ pounds (750 g.) tomatoes, peeled, seeded (page 124), and cut into ½-inch (1-cm.) dice
Pepper
1 not-too-hot pepper, preferably Espelette, seeded and cut into 1-inch (2-cm.) strips, or 1 teaspoon ground Espelette pepper (which can be replaced by New Mexico chili powder or hot paprika)
12 eggs
4 slices dry-cured ham

Fish and Seafood

Shellfish

S hellfish are small sea mollusks that live in shells. They are divided into two groups based on type of shell: bivalves have a two-piece shell joined by a hinge (oysters, mussels, clams, cockles, scallops, bay scallops, razor clams, and so forth), and univalves or gastropods live in a one-piece shell (periwinkles, abalones, sea snails, and so forth). Bivalves can be eaten raw or cooked.

Clams

Clams are very sandy and must be washed gently in several changes of water just before cooking or eating. Do not leave them to soak. When you buy a clam, it should be shut tight and should smell clearly and strongly of the sea, a fine blend of sand and seaweed.

Especially fleshy clams are usually eaten raw. They can also be stuffed with garlic and parsley or perhaps mushrooms, pumpkin and other winter squashes, thyme, or chives. But they should be just barely cooked; they take only a few seconds.

Clams produce the best cooking juices, the most subtle and the tastiest.

CLAMS IN GREEN SAUCE

Palourdes en sauce verte

SERVES 4
PREPARATION AND COOKING 15 minutes

1 Wash the clams carefully under running water. Do not do this in advance.

4 pounds (2 kg.) clams

(continued)

2   Bring some water (just enough to cover the clams) to a boil in a large pot. Boil the clams for 10 seconds. As soon as they begin to open, remove them with a skimmer; clams should be just barely open. Keep the cooking water in the pot.

3   Remove the clams from their shells over a bowl, catching their juices in the bowl. Leave the bowl to settle for a few minutes so that any impurities fall to the bottom. Being careful not to stir up any settled debris, ladle the cooking juice and shell juice through a fine strainer into a big bowl.

4   Arrange the clams on a deep platter. Preheat the oven to 250°F/120°C.

5   Heat the olive oil in a small saucepan over a low flame. When it is hot, add the garlic and cook for 1 minute, stirring. The garlic should not color, so adjust the heat accordingly. Still over very low heat, stir in the parsley and cook for 20 seconds. Stir in the flour and cook for 1 minute. Add the clams' cooking and shell juices. Mix well and turn off the heat. Coat the clams with sauce and bake for 1 minute, just to warm them up, and serve.

2 tablespoons olive oil
4 cloves garlic, peeled, degermed (page 122), and minced
3 tablespoons minced parsley
1½ teaspoons flour

STUFFED CLAMS

Palourdes farcies

SERVES 4
PREPARATION AND COOKING   40 minutes

1   Carefully wash the clams in several changes of water just before cooking them.

2   Put the wine in a large pot with half of the minced shallots and a few grindings of pepper. Raise the heat to high. When the wine is simmering, add the clams and leave them over high heat for 10 seconds. As soon as they begin to open, remove them from the pot with a skimmer. Then remove each clam from its shell, keeping half of the shell. Spread a bed of coarse salt on a sheet pan or ovenproof dish and nestle the half shells in the salt.

3   Mince the mushrooms finely, preferably in a food processor or chopper. Sprinkle them with lemon juice and toss.

48 clams
1⅔ cups (40 cl.) white wine, preferably Chardonnay
4 shallots, peeled and minced
Pepper
1 pound (500 g.) coarse salt
¾ pound (400 g.) white button or cup mushrooms, stems removed, rinsed, and cleaned (you can save the stems for a soup)
1 lemon

4   Heat 1 tablespoon butter in a small saucepan over medium heat. When it foams, lower the heat and cook the remaining shallots for 3 minutes without allowing them to color. Season with 2 pinches of salt and add the minced mushrooms; stir and cook for 3 minutes. Taste for salt and pepper. Spread the mushroom-shallot stuffing on a plate and put it in the refrigerator to cool.

5   Preheat the broiler.

6   When the stuffing is completely cool, stir in the remaining softened butter. Add the parsley and garlic and taste for salt and pepper.

7   Put a clam in each half shell. With a spatula or spoon, dollop each one with the stuffing, making sure to cover the clam well. Broil for 2 minutes to brown.

2 sticks ($\frac{1}{2}$ pound/220 g.) butter at room temperature
Salt
$1\frac{1}{2}$ tablespoons minced flat-leaf parsley
1 clove garlic, peeled and crushed

Cockles

Cockles are a small, mild shellfish. They are very common in France and are relatively cheap all year round; in the United States they are rare but not impossible to find. They do contain a great deal of sand, however, and must be washed in several changes of water and then put in a container large enough that they do not overlap one another too much. Cover them with cold water, adding $1\frac{1}{2}$ tablespoons (20 g.) salt per quart (1 l.). Put the container in the refrigerator and leave it for 8–10 hours without moving or stirring while the cockles discharge their sand. Remove them carefully with a skimmer or by hand and avoid stirring up the sand at the bottom. Then wash them again.

COCKLES WITH SAFFRON AND THYME

Coques au safran et au thym

SERVES 4

PREPARATION AND COOKING 20 minutes

1 Put the cockles and 1 tablespoon butter in a large pot. Season with pepper. Cover and put over high heat for 1–2 minutes, shaking the pot every once in a while. When the cockles have opened, turn off the heat. Remove the cockles with a skimmer, leaving their juices behind. Remove the flesh from the shells and put it in a large bowl. Cover with plastic wrap.

2 Heat the remaining butter in a small saucepan over low heat. When it foams, add the onion and fennel. Add a little salt and cook for 2 minutes over low heat, stirring with a wooden spoon. Pour in the cooking juice from the cockle pot and bring to a boil. Simmer for 3 minutes. Add the saffron and cream and simmer, stirring, until the sauce has reduced by half. Taste for salt and pepper. Pass the sauce through a fine strainer into the bowl of cockles. Sprinkle with the chives and thyme.

2 pounds (1 kg.) cockles, carefully washed (page 227)
2 tablespoons butter
Pepper
¼ medium onion, sliced into thin strips
¼ fennel bulb, sliced into thin strips
Salt
4–5 stems saffron
½ cup (10 cl.) heavy cream
1 teaspoon minced chives
Leaves from 1 sprig fresh thyme (do not use dried thyme)

Mussels

Mussels are raised on posts made of oak from which the bark has not been stripped—mussel beds. They are half-immersed in the water and covered with young mussels.

CHOOSING MUSSELS

Mussels should be alive when you buy them. A mussel that has opened and will not close when you give it a little pinch is dead and must be rejected.

If you do not plan to cook the mussels immediately, remove them from the packaging and put them in a large bowl; cover it with a very damp dish towel and put it in the vegetable drawer of your refrigerator.

To clean the mussels, rinse them under running water.

Cultivated mussels ought to be clean, and usually they are not sandy inside; nevertheless, they must be scrubbed well in order to remove grit and dirt from the shell. Strip away the mussels' grasping filaments (their "beards") and then wash them in several changes of water, scrubbing them energetically each time. Do not leave them to soak in the water, however, or they will open and lose their internal seawater, which contributes much to their flavor.

Mussels can be eaten raw, if you like, with lemon juice and rye bread slathered with salted butter. Open by holding the shell between the thumb and index finger of one hand and sliding the top and bottom parts apart just enough to slip in a dull knife or letter opener between them. Slip it in $\frac{1}{2}$ inch (1 cm.) deep and cut the foot, which should be about two-thirds of the way up the side of the shell. Gently scrape the inside of the top shell to detach the outer membrane. Open the mussel, cut the cords at the hinge, and remove the top shell.

Mussels are, however, usually eaten cooked. It is imperative that they not be overcooked. As soon as a mussel opens, it is cooked. Three minutes over high heat should be enough. You will want to add minced shallot and parsley and a bit of white wine before cooking. A good way to find the right cooking time is to cook in two stages: First, cook covered over high heat for 2 minutes; the first mussels should open. Then turn off the heat but leave the pot covered 2 or 3 minutes more, giving all the mussels time to open. Discard those that stay closed. Once it is filtered the cooking juice makes a wonderful base for a sauce or a soup.

MARINER'S MUSSELS

Moules à la marinière

SERVES 4
PREPARATION 10 minutes
COOKING 5 minutes

2 shallots, peeled and minced
1 cup (20 cl.) dry white wine, preferably Chardonnay
1 bouquet garni (2 sprigs thyme, 6 stems parsley, and $\frac{1}{2}$ bay leaf, tied together)
4 tablespoons (65 g.) butter
(continued)

1 Put the shallots, wine, bouquet garni, and 1 tablespoon butter in a large saucepan or Dutch oven. Bring to a boil over high heat and simmer for 5 minutes. Add the mussels and a

few grindings of pepper and stir. Cover the pot and cook for 2 minutes over high heat. Shake the pot, turn off the heat, and leave the pot covered 3 minutes more.

2   With a skimmer remove the mussels to a deep dish. Keep them warm by tenting them loosely with aluminum foil.

3   Put the cooking juices through a fine strainer into a saucepan and bring to a boil. Reduce 2 minutes, then briskly whisk in the remaining butter until completely incorporated. Stir in the chopped parsley, taste for salt and pepper, and pour the sauce over the mussels.

4 pounds (2 kg.) cultivated mussels, beards removed, scrubbed, and carefully washed in several changes of water (page 228)
Pepper
2 tablespoons chopped flat-leaf parsley
Salt

CREAMY MUSSELS

Mouclade

SERVES   4
PREPARATION   10 minutes
COOKING   about 25 minutes

You can add a spoonful of curry powder as the mussels cook if you like.

4 pounds (2 kg.) Mariner's Mussels (page 229)
3 tablespoons crème fraîche
Powdered thyme
Salt
Pepper

1   Preheat the oven to 260°F/130°C. Use a skimmer to remove the cooked mussels to a colander, leaving their cooking juices in the pot. Remove each mussel's upper shell and arrange the half mussels more or less side by side in a deep baking dish. Put the baking dish in the oven.

2   Put the cooking juices through a fine strainer into a small saucepan. Bring to a boil and leave over high heat until the juices have reduced by half. This should take 15–20 minutes. Add the crème fraîche and a dash of powdered thyme and bring back to a boil, stirring with a wooden spoon. Taste for salt and pepper. Remove the mussels from the oven, slather them with sauce, and slip them back into the oven for a few minutes. Serve piping hot.

CURRIED MUSSELS AND COCKLES

Moules et coques au curry

SERVES   4

PREPARATION   5 minutes

COOKING   5 minutes

1   The night before cooking, soak the cockles (page 227).
2   The next day, drain the cockles and carefully wash them in several changes of water. Put ¼ cup water in a large pot or Dutch oven with the onion and shallots. Cook over medium heat for 5 minutes. Add the curry powder, bouquet garni, and white wine. Bring to a boil and boil for 1 minute.
3   Add the mussels and cockles to the pot along with several grindings of pepper. Cover and cook for 2 minutes over high heat, shaking the pot occasionally. Turn off the heat but leave the pot covered 3 minutes more. Check the mussels; they should all be open now. Discard any mussels that remain closed.
4   Remove the shellfish with a skimmer and put them in a deep platter. Remove the bouquet garni. Off the heat, whisk the *fromage blanc* or crème fraîche into the cooking juices. Taste for salt and pepper. Pour the sauce over the shellfish and sprinkle with chervil.

2 pounds (1 kg.) cockles

1 small onion, peeled and minced

3 shallots, peeled and minced

1 teaspoon curry powder

1 bouquet garni (2 sprigs thyme and 2 small stalks celery, wrapped and tied in a green leek leaf)

½ cup (10 cl.) white wine

2 pounds (1 kg.) mussels, beards removed, scrubbed, and carefully cleaned (page 228)

Pepper

2 tablespoons *fromage blanc* or crème fraîche

Salt

1 tablespoon minced chervil

Oysters

People have loved to eat oysters for ages. Our earliest ancestors consumed them in Neolithic grottos, and they were popular in ancient China, Rome, and Greece as well.

CHOOSING OYSTERS

When you buy oysters, they should be alive. They should be tightly closed or should at least close up as soon as they are touched. The shell should be moist. If it is dry, then you know the oyster has been out of the water for a long time. Each one should be quite heavy, since it should be full of water. If they are being sold in a container, check the packaging to see when they were harvested and packed.

If you must wait a few days to eat oysters, pile them on a flat surface, making sure each one is right side up. Wrap the whole in a damp cloth and keep it at the bottom of the refrigerator. Put a cover and a weight on top to keep them from opening up and leaking their water. They should not be stored at temperatures higher than 45°F/8°C, but neither should they be kept too cold. Once they are frozen, they will be no good.

Rinse oysters under running water before opening. Discard any oyster that is open. It could be dead and therefore toxic.

It is best to open oysters at the very last minute. Use an oyster knife, preferably with a round metal piece between the handle and the blade that can stop the knife if it slips. If the knife does not have this device, protect your hand, or even both hands, with a dish towel, a thick rubber glove, or a potholder.

Most of the oysters we eat are deeply cupped Eastern or Atlantic oysters (*Crassostrea virginica*). To open one, hold it in your palm, flat shell on top and the hinge (the pointed side) toward you. Put the point of your knife on the curved side, on a darker crevice that is about two-thirds of the way down from the hinge. Insert the knife between the two shells, pushing hard and rocking the blade from left to right, keeping it horizontal. Insert the knife about 1 inch (1.5 cm.) to cut the upper muscle (the abductor muscle) from the lid. Gently scrape the inside of the upper shell to remove the thin outer membrane without piercing the oyster. Remove the top shell. Do not cut the foot; leave the oyster attached to the shell.

Discard the liquid inside the oyster (its "liquor"); it will produce more, cleaner liquid as it rests. Never wash or rinse an oyster. It will lose all taste and freshness. Put the open oysters side by side on a large platter or plate, perhaps blanketed with seaweed or even just a piece of crumpled aluminum foil to hold the shells stable. Oysters should not be eaten too cold, so nestling them into a bed of ice, although it might keep them a little longer, is not recommended.

Flat oysters (*Ostrea edulis,* also called European or Belons) have become rare. To open a flat oyster, put the oyster on your palm, the flat shell on top and the hinge toward your fingers. Put the point of the knife against the hinge between the two shells. Push hard and rock the blade from left to right, keeping it horizontal. Slide the knife under the top shell without breaking it. From the side, cut the upper muscle and then proceed as for rounded cup oysters (page 232).

It is best to eat oysters as soon as they have been opened, but if you must wait a little while, replace their top shells and keep them in a cool place, preferably the refrigerator. This is really not recommended but will work in a pinch.

Purists prefer their oysters plain or perhaps with a pinch of white pepper. Some people like a squeeze of lemon juice, minced shallots macerated in wine vinegar, or other condiments, but these additions interfere with the subtle flavors of the oyster. Eat them with slices of rye bread spread with salted butter.

COOKED OYSTERS

Oysters can also be cooked, of course. Once upon a time they were even served browned. If you want them to keep their delicate flavor, it is better to sear them quickly. You can poach them as part of a fish platter or to accompany shellfish soup. In any case, oysters destined to be cooked should be fleshy and milky-looking. Cook them very briefly, or they will toughen.

HOT OYSTERS WITH FENNEL AND CURRY

Huîtres chaudes au fenouil et au curry

SERVES 4
PREPARATION   10 minutes
COOKING   1 minute plus 5 minutes for the sauce

1 Remove the oysters from their shells (page 232), collecting their juices in a bowl as you go. Filter the juices through a fine strainer lined with a paper towel and set aside.

24 Eastern/Atlantic oysters

(continued)

2 Put the shallots in a saucepan with the wine and 1 teaspoon butter. Bring to a boil and simmer for 10 minutes.

3 In the meantime, smear butter all over the inside of a pot large enough to hold all the oysters. Put the oysters inside; you want them to be crowded. Add the filtered oyster juices to the saucepan with the shallot-wine mixture and bring to a boil. As soon as it bubbles, turn the heat under the oysters to medium and pour the bubbling shallot-wine mixture over them. After 30 seconds, quickly flip all the oysters over. Wait 30 seconds more and immediately turn off the heat.

4 Quickly remove the oysters from the pot with a skimmer and spread them over a platter. Do not discard their cooking liquid. Allow them to cool a little and then cut away their viscous membranes with scissors.

5 Melt 1 teaspoon butter in a saucepan over medium heat. When it foams, add the onion and fennel and cook for 3 minutes, stirring occasionally. Add the oysters' cooking liquid, crème fraîche, and curry powder. Bring to a boil and simmer for 5 minutes. Taste for salt and add only if necessary and very lightly. Add pepper to taste.

6 Dice 1½ teaspoons very cold butter. Pass the sauce through a fine strainer into another saucepan. Stir in the cold diced butter with a wooden spoon. Add the oysters very briefly, just to heat them up a little bit.

7 Remove the oysters with a skimmer. Stir the chives and roe into the sauce. Pour the sauce over the oysters to serve.

2 shallots, peeled and minced
1 cup (20 cl.) white wine
3½ teaspoons butter plus more for coating the pot
1 onion, peeled and minced
½ bulb fennel, trimmed and minced
2 tablespoons crème fraîche
1 pinch of curry powder
Salt
Pepper
1 tablespoon minced chives
2 tablespoons salmon roe

Periwinkles and Sea Snails

Periwinkles and sea snails must be carefully washed in several changes of water and then cooked in vigorously simmering water with fresh thyme, a bay leaf, parsley, and 1½ tablespoons salt per quart (1 l.) of water. (Or, even better, you can cook them in seawater that you have filtered through a fine strainer.)

Periwinkles will take 5 minutes to cook. Drop them into already boiling water. If you put them in cold water and bring it to a boil, they will retract into their shells and will be very difficult to remove. Leave them in the cooking water as it cools. Eat them plain, using a pick.

Sea snails should be cooked for 10–12 minutes if they are on the small side and 15 minutes maximum if they are large. Do not overcook them, or they will toughen. Eat them with mayonnaise (store-bought or see page 55), perhaps mustardy. Use a pick and have bread and salted butter on the side.

Sea Scallops

This large bivalve from the seabed, with its shell of remarkably colored stripes, is the king of mollusks when it comes to eating.

The French name for scallops is *coquilles Saint-Jacques*. French pilgrims used to make their way on foot to Santiago (Saint Jacques) de Compostela in Spain, and on the way they would recognize one another by the pearly shells from the Galician coast they carried, which eventually took on the name of their destination.

If you can, buy live sea scallops still in their tightly sealed shells. They should be quite heavy (5 or 6 shells per 2 pounds/1 kg.) and shut tight, and the perfectly white, translucent flesh should be firm.

If the scallops contain "coral" or roe (as they might, depending on the season and their place of origin), it will be a vivid orange. Common wisdom holds that scallops containing roe are the best, but this is not so. The slightly bitter roe alters the elegance of the scallops' taste and texture.

Scallops are a true delight. They have an extremely fine taste, just barely sweet, and lend themselves to many preparations that respect their subtle perfume. Don't mask it with overwhelming ingredients. By the same token, sea scallops should not be breaded or coated with flour. Scallops can be cooked by almost any method except steaming, which will make them shrink and toughen. For maximum succulence, cook scallops at the very last minute and for the briefest time possible.

It is possible to eat scallops raw: Slice the meat horizontally into two or three strips and toss in an instant marinade of lemon juice, olive oil, a pinch of saffron, and perhaps a bit of cider vinegar, too.

It is also possible to cook opened scallops in the shell,

with the flesh still attached on the inside. Cook them for 4 or 5 minutes under a very hot broiler with a pinch of white pepper or perhaps butter and fresh thyme leaves. Scallops can be grilled on the barbecue or on a skewer, or sautéed in a bit of butter. Depending on your preference, add some minced shallots and parsley, as they do in Bordeaux, or garlic and parsley, which is the Mediterranean way.

You should serve three or four scallops per person.

OPENING SEA SCALLOPS

If you plan to cook the scallops as soon as you get home, you can ask the fishmonger to open them for you. But it is best to enjoy scallops as fresh as possible and therefore to open them at the last minute. To do this yourself, put on a thick potholder or rubber glove, or wrap your hand in a dish towel, and hold the rounded part of the shell in this protected hand, the hinge side of the shell farthest away from you. Slip a firm knife blade between the two shells at the spot where the foot should be. Cut the foot, slicing along the length of the top shell. The top shell should open, and it will then be easy to remove.

Rinse the bottom shell under a gentle stream of running water to eliminate any sand. Use a soup spoon to detach the nugget of flesh from the shell and then use your fingers to push the foot so that it detaches from the shell (unless you are going to cook the scallops attached to the shell). Remove the beard (the viscous parts) and the frilly membrane (the pouch and the blackish thread around the meat) using your fingers. If the scallop contains "coral" (roe), cut it out; it is edible. Rinse the meat again in cold water, but do not let it soak. If you are not using the scallops immediately, cover the meat with a lightly dampened dish towel and put it in the refrigerator. (Covering the scallops with aluminum foil or plastic wrap will cause them to become mushy.) In any case, don't wait too long to eat the scallops; don't forget them, even in the refrigerator, and avoid buying shucked scallops wrapped in plastic at the store.

SEA SCALLOPS WITH SHREDDED ENDIVES _____

Saint-jacques à l'effilochée d'endives

SERVES 4

PREPARATION 20 minutes

COOKING 8 minutes for the endives plus 1–2 minutes for the scallops

Duck fat gives a special taste to this dish and can attain very high heat without burning, allowing the scallops to be cooked very quickly. If you do not have duck fat, use 1½ tablespoons butter and 1 teaspoon neutral oil.

1 Melt ½ tablespoon duck fat (or butter) in a small saucepan over low heat. When it is hot, cook the shallot for 3 minutes over low heat, stirring; do not allow the shallot to color. Add the wine, bring to a boil, and boil for 10 minutes. Stir in the cream and bring back to a quiet bubble. Season with the saffron, a pinch of salt, and a dash of pepper. Take off the heat and leave to infuse.

2 In a larger saucepan, melt 1 tablespoon duck fat (or butter) over low heat. When it is hot, add the endive strips and toss them well to coat with fat. Season with ⅓ teaspoon salt and a good-sized pinch of pepper, and then cook for 7–8 minutes over low heat, stirring with a wooden spatula. The endives should stay white and slightly crunchy. Taste. If they seem too bitter, sprinkle them with a pinch of sugar at the end of cooking.

3 Line a plate with 4 pieces of paper towel, stacked on top of each other. Rinse and dry the scallops. Season each one with a small pinch of pepper.

4 Melt 1 teaspoon duck fat (or oil) in a skillet over high heat. When it is hot, add the scallops and cook for 30 seconds to 1 minute on each side. Remove to the towel-lined plate.

5 Gently reheat the endives and the wine-cream sauce, stirring the sauce well.

6 Spread a bed of coarse salt on a serving platter. Nestle the shells in the salt and put 3 scallops in each shell. Divide the endives among the shells and top each with 1 teaspoon sauce. Sprinkle with chervil and serve with the rest of the sauce on the side.

1½ tablespoons plus 1 teaspoon duck fat

1 shallot, peeled and minced

½ cup (10 cl.) white wine

1 cup (25 cl.) heavy cream

12 saffron pistils

Salt

Pepper

4 endives, washed and sliced into strips ½ inch by 1 inch (1 cm. by 2 cm.)

1 pinch of sugar

12 shucked sea scallops

1 pound (500 g.) coarse salt (for presentation)

4 sea scallop shells, rounded half, washed and dried (for presentation)

1 teaspoon chervil leaves

BROILED SEA SCALLOPS

Saint-jacques grillées

SERVES 4
PREPARATION 10 minutes
COOKING 3 minutes

1   Preheat the broiler. Rinse the scallops and dry with paper towels. Place them on your work surface. Press each scallop with the palm of your hand and cut it in 2 horizontally. Brush the scallops all over with butter and distribute them among the shells, overlapping one another as little as possible. Sprinkle with white pepper and thyme leaves.
2   Spread a bed of coarse salt in a sheet pan and nestle the shells in the salt. When the broiler is hot, broil the scallops in the shells for 3 minutes. The meat should turn golden and should be just barely cooked. Sprinkle a bit of parsley over the meat and serve in the shell.

12 shucked sea scallops
1 tablespoon butter, melted
4 scallop shells, rounded part only, washed and dried
White pepper
3 sprigs fresh thyme, leaves only
1 pound (500 g.) coarse salt
1 teaspoon minced flat-leaf parsley

SEA SCALLOPS IN THE SHELL, WITH LEEKS

Saint-jacques en coquille aux poireaux

SERVES 4
SOAKING THE BEARDS 1 hour
PREPARATION 30 minutes
COOKING 4–6 minutes

1   Wash and open the scallops. Leave the meat attached to the shell but remove the beards (the viscous membranes). Wash the beards and the meat. Soak the beards in water to cover for 1 hour before proceeding.
2   Peel the carrot, celery root, and 1 leek. Wash the carrot, leek, and celery. Cut them all into pieces about ½ inch (1 cm.). Chop the shallot.
3   Heat 1 tablespoon olive oil in a saucepan over medium heat. Add ½ tablespoon butter, the carrot, celery, shallot, and drained beards. Lower the heat. Cook for 3 minutes over low heat, stirring with a wooden spatula and not allowing them to color.

8 sea scallops, attached to the round shell and cleaned (page 235)
1 carrot
2 ounces (⅓ cup sliced/50 g.) celery root
3 small leeks, white part only, washed well in warm water
1 shallot
Olive oil

4　Over high heat, add the bouquet garni and wine. When the wine comes to a boil, add about ½ cup (10 cl.) water, or enough to cover the beards. Season with a pinch of salt and a dash of pepper. Cook for 10 minutes at a simmer, skimming foam from the surface every once in a while and rinsing the skimmer in a bowl of cold water after every pass.

5　Preheat the oven to 475°F/250°C.

6　Slice 2 of the leek whites into 2-inch (5–6-cm.) sticks. Bring a pot of water to a boil and cook the leeks for 1 minute. Immediately rinse them under cold water to stop the cooking. Drain them and set aside.

7　On a sheet pan, make 8 little nests of coarse salt to hold the shells steadily. Arrange the shells on the sheet, sprinkling each one with a pinch of pepper and a few drops of olive oil. Bake for 5–6 minutes, depending on their size. You want the scallops to be just barely cooked.

8　While the scallops bake, begin to prepare the sauce. Strain the beard cooking liquid through a fine colander or a chinois into a small saucepan. Bring to a boil and allow it to bubble away for 10 minutes. Dice 1 tablespoon very cold butter. Off the heat, whisk the diced butter in bit by bit. Stir in the blanched leeks.

9　Arrange the shells on a platter. Use a slotted spoon or skimmer to distribute the saucy leeks among the shells and around the meat in each one. Drizzle them with a little more of their sauce.

½ tablespoon butter plus 1 tablespoon very cold butter

1 bouquet garni (2 sprigs thyme, ½ bay leaf, and 5 stems parsley, tied together)

½ cup (10 cl.) white wine

Salt

Pepper

1 pound (500 g.) coarse salt (for stabilizing shells)

SEA SCALLOPS WITH FRESH GINGER

Saint-jacques au gingembre frais

SERVES 4

PREPARATION AND COOKING 40 minutes

This dish is supposed to be a first course. If you serve it as a main dish, count 12 to 16 scallops and 3 or 4 leeks for 4 people.

1   Melt ½ tablespoon butter in a small saucepan over low heat. Add the leek whites and cook for 3 minutes, stirring with a wooden spoon; do not allow them to color. Season with 2 pinches of salt and 1 pinch of pepper and set aside.

2   Cut away one-fourth of the ginger. Peel this small piece and slice it into filaments ⅛ inch (3 mm.) thick. Bring 2 cups (50 cl.) water to a boil in a small saucepan. Boil the shredded ginger for 1 minute and then rinse under cold running water for 30 seconds. Drain and set aside. Rinse the saucepan.

3   Melt ½ tablespoon butter in a small saucepan over low heat. When it foams, cook the shallots for 3 minutes over low heat, stirring; do not allow them to color. Add the leek greens and cook 2 minutes more. Add the vermouth, bouquet garni, and the remaining chunk of ginger. Cook 3 minutes more. Add the crème fraîche, bring to a boil, and then lower the heat and simmer them for 10 minutes. Pass through a fine strainer into the other small saucepan and stir in ½ tablespoon butter. Season with a pinch of salt and a dash of pepper and stir in the blanched ginger strips.

4   Spread the leeks on a platter and cover with ginger sauce.

5   Rinse and dry the scallop meat. Place the scallops on a work surface. Cut each scallop in 2 horizontally. Heat the oil in a large skillet. Sear the scallops for 1 minute on each side. Season with a pinch of salt and a dash of pepper and arrange on top of the leeks.

1½ tablespoons butter

2 leeks, whites washed well in warm water and cut into sticks 2 inches (5 cm.) long, 2 green leek leaves washed and sliced into strips

Salt

White pepper

1½ ounces (40 g.) peeled fresh gingerroot

5 shallots, peeled and minced

½ cup (10 cl.) dry vermouth

1 bouquet garni (2 sprigs thyme, 5 stems parsley, and 5 celery leaves, wrapped and tied in a green leek leaf)

2 cups (50 cl.) crème fraîche

8 large shucked sea scallops

1 teaspoon neutral oil

Squid

BASQUE CALAMARI

Blancs de calmar basquaise

SERVES 4
PREPARATION 10 minutes
COOKING 40 minutes

1 Wash the squid and dry with paper towels. Cut into strips ⅛ inch (3–4 mm.) thick and refrigerate.

2 Warm the olive oil in a medium saucepan over low heat. Cook the peppers for 2 minutes, stirring with a wooden spatula. Add the onions and cook 2 minutes more.

3 Add the squid and cook for 2 minutes over low heat. Add the garlic, some pepper, and the Espelette pepper (or substitute). Cover and cook gently for 15 minutes. Stir in the tomatoes, add the bouquet garni, and let the pot simmer uncovered for 20 minutes. Taste for salt and pepper. Sprinkle with parsley and serve.

1 pound (500 g.) squid
1½ tablespoons olive oil
1 green bell pepper and 1 red bell pepper, peeled and seeded (page 130)
2 medium onions, sliced into rounds ⅛ inch (2–3 mm.) thick
2 cloves garlic, degermed (page 122) and crushed
Pepper
1 dash Espelette pepper (substitute hot paprika or chili powder if necessary)
4 large tomatoes, peeled, seeded, and diced (page 124)
1 bouquet garni (1 sprig thyme, 4 branches parsley, and ½ bay leaf, tied in a bundle)
Salt
½ tablespoon minced flat-leaf parsley

Crustaceans

Edible crustaceans are sorted into two categories according to their shape: those that are mostly tail or have an elongated abdomen (lobster, rock lobster, shrimp, and crayfish) and those whose bodies are mostly rounded abdomen (crab, hermit crab, and spider crab).

All crustaceans live in sandy or rocky seabeds close to the shore (except for crayfish, which live only in running fresh water). Almost all crustaceans have the peculiar habit of turning red when cooked; this is because their shells contain both violet and red pigments, and the violet pigments are eradicated by heat.

Our thoughts tend to turn to lobsters, rock lobsters, and langoustines at festive moments such as Christmas and New Year's Eve. They are, however, at their best (and sold at the best prices) during the summer.

Avoid buying crustaceans that have already been cooked (except perhaps for certain shrimp that are found fresh only very rarely and then only from fishmongers who are rather close to the sea). Precooked crustaceans are generally animals that were cooked just before spoiling, to avoid losing them altogether, and are therefore not top quality. It is better to buy live crustaceans.

They should be alive and active; tails and other appendages should not seem droopy; eyes should be bright; joints should be full, light-colored, and transparent. (They are covered by a cartilaginous membrane that blackens when the animal is no longer fresh.) They should smell pleasant; as soon as it dies, a crustacean begins to decompose, and its flavor goes off very quickly. When presented with two crustaceans of the same size, take the one that weighs more.

Females are preferable to males; their flesh is more tender and flavorful. To sex the animal, turn it on its back: Females have a hollow in their belly, which is where they keep their eggs, while the male stomach is convex.

Wash live crustaceans under cold water; you might even need to scrub them to get rid of dirt and other impurities that will give off an unpleasant taste when they are cooked. Cook crustaceans as soon as possible: Flavor depends on freshness here. If you must, keep them covered with a damp cloth in a bin in the refrigerator. Whatever you do, do not keep them in a plastic bag, as they will quickly suffocate and die.

Here are some guidelines for how much you will need to buy:

very small soft-fleshed shrimp that turn gray
  when cooked: almost 2 ounces (50 g.) per person as an appetizer

small firm-fleshed shrimp that turn pink when
   cooked: 2 ounces (60 g.) per person
langoustines that weigh 2 ounces (60 g.) each:
   8 per person
1 lobster or rock lobster, 1¼–2½ pounds
   (600–800 g.) for two people

Crabs

Crab is a generic term for crustaceans with a small, round abdomen under a large, rigid shell. There are three main types that we eat:

spider crab (page 261)   The large crab, such as the Dungeness, also called Pacific edible crab, rock crab, red rock crab, or the European edible *Cancer pagurus* (very common in France, where it is called *tourteau* or *dormeur,* which means sleeper.) It is wider than it is long and has a smooth, red-brown shell and large pincers. It lives in rocky coastal bottoms. Choose lively crabs of equal size, taking the heaviest ones. Females are preferable to males, and May, June, and July are the best months.
green crabs   are much smaller but otherwise like large crabs. They are usually eaten stuffed.
Atlantic blue crabs   are rather small and are mostly used to prepare soups and sauces.

All of them (except the blue crabs) are usually prepared in the same way: poached in court bouillon. If you are close to the sea, you can cook them in well-filtered seawater instead.

TO COOK A LARGE CRAB

Wash and scrub the crabs (one crab will serve one or two), holding them from the back. Keep their pincers bound and avoid placing your hand flat against their bellies, since they might be able to grab you with their feet. After cleaning, use scissors to cut the rubber bands on the claws. The simplest way to cook them is to boil them in 1½ quarts (1.5 l.) water and 1 tablespoon coarse salt. It is better, however, to boil them in court bouillon. You can use store-bought vegetable court bouillon or bouillon powder, adding ½ teaspoon coarse salt. Or you can make your own with 1½ quarts (1.5 l.) water, 1 tablespoon coarse salt, a bouquet garni (1 small bay leaf, 3 sprigs fresh thyme, 5 stems parsley, and 1 small celery stalk tied together), 1 chopped carrot, 1 chopped onion, and ½ cup (10 cl.) distilled white vinegar.

Put the crab in a large pot and cover with court bouillon, adding water to cover if necessary. Bring to a boil and then simmer for 20–25 minutes for a crab that weighs 2 pounds (1 kg.). Allow to cool in the broth off the heat about 20 minutes. Serve with a mayonnaise, perhaps a mustardy one (store-bought or see page 55). Avoid putting the cooked crabmeat in the refrigerator if possible.

STUFFED CRABS

Crabes farcis

SERVES   4
COOKING THE CRABS   15 minutes
PREPARING AND COOKING THE STUFFING   30 minutes
The baguette must soak overnight.

You can also make this with lump crabmeat and get some crab shells from the fishmonger.

¼ stale baguette plus ¼ cup dry bread crumbs
4 small crabs (¾ pound/350 g. each)
1 pound (500 g.) coarse salt
1 tablespoon neutral oil
1 medium onion, peeled and minced
1 clove garlic, peeled and degermed (page 122)
1 tablespoon minced chives
½ teaspoon fresh thyme leaves
1 tablespoon chopped parsley

1   The night before, crumble or tear the baguette into pieces and put them to soak in a bowl filled with water.
2   The next day, clean the crabs. Bring 2 quarts (2 l.) water and 1½ tablespoons coarse salt to a boil in a large pot. Simmer the crabs for 15 minutes. Allow them to cool in the pot off the heat for 20 minutes and then remove all the meat. Wash the shells carefully and set them aside.
3   Drain the soaked baguette, squeezing it to remove as much water as possible. Blend it in a blender or food processor and set aside.

4   Preheat the broiler. Heat the oil in a saucepan (large enough to hold all the crabmeat) over low heat. Add the onion and garlic and cook for 3 minutes, stirring with a wooden spatula. Do not allow them to color. Add the chives, thyme, and parsley and stir. Add the drained bread. Turn the heat up to medium and stir in the crabmeat. Mix well to incorporate all the ingredients evenly. Take the pan off the heat.

5   Cut a $\frac{1}{16}$-inch (1.5-mm.) section of the hot pepper. Pulp this bit in a garlic press over a saucer or chop it as finely as possible. Pour the mashed hot pepper into the pot of stuffing and stir it in well. (Wash your hands carefully now; you will burn your eyes if you accidentally touch them after touching the hot pepper, and even after washing you should still not put your hands anywhere near your eyes.) Add a dash of cumin, $\frac{1}{2}$ teaspoon salt, and a pinch of pepper to the stuffing. Taste and add more salt, pepper, or hot pepper if necessary.

6   Fill the shells generously with the stuffing. Make 4 little beds of coarse salt on a sheet pan and lay a stuffed crab on each one. Top with a scattering of bread crumbs and broil for 5 minutes. Arrange the crabs on a platter and serve.

1 small red or green hot pepper
     such as serrano
Powdered cumin
Salt
Pepper

Crayfish

Crayfish are the only edible freshwater crustaceans. They once filled France's rivers and streams but were dwindling for many years. Although the trend seems to be reversing itself now, fishing for them is still strictly regulated.

Certain varieties are now being farmed with success. Crayfish with red legs are the largest and the best. They are really something, with their fine flesh and elaborate markings, and in France they are found principally in the central region called Auvergne. Most crayfish in France are, however, imported. Most crayfish in the United States come from Louisiana.

Fished or bought live, crayfish should be soaked for two or three hours in a container of water fed by a stream of running water. Then the intestine, which is full of sand, waste, and residue, must be removed, for it will lend the crustacean a bitter taste. In France this is called *castration,* but in English it is called *deveining,* as with shrimp. Either way, the operation must be performed just before cooking or the animal will collapse, or perhaps after cooking if the intestine is visible. Either way—live or cooked—you can remove the crayfish intestine by taking the central fin at the end of the tail and pulling it off by gently twisting it left and right.

The most common way to cook crayfish is this: Put the deveined crayfish in a large pot. Pour in dry white wine up to one-third of their depth. Add 3 grindings of pepper, 1 clove degermed garlic (page 122), a bouquet garni (3 sprigs thyme, preferably fresh, 5 stems flat-leaf parsley, and 1 small celery stalk), and 2 pinches of coarse salt. Cover and cook for 10–12 minutes over high heat, shaking the pot frequently to toss the crayfish about. Eat the crayfish hot, warm, or cool (but not cold).

Langoustine

Despite its name, the langoustine is not a small *langouste.* Its body more closely resembles that of a lobster, and its light pink shell does not change color dramatically when cooked. Summer is the time to eat langoustines, which are also called Dublin Bay prawns and Norway lobster.

Buy a glossy langoustine with gleaming black eyes; they cannot live long out of water and must be cooked very soon after they are caught.

They take well to other cooking methods, but poaching in court bouillon is still the simplest and most practical way. These langoustines are cooked whole, right in their shells. To poach about 24 of them, prepare a court bouillon with 1 quart (1 l.) water, 1 finely chopped carrot and medium onion, 1 bouquet garni (a few branches of parsley, a sprig of thyme, ½ bay leaf, and a leek leaf), 1 teaspoon coarse salt, and a pinch of pepper. You can also add a little star anise and 2 or 3 gratings of orange zest. Simmer for 20 minutes and then add 1 cup (25 cl.) white wine (a Chardonnay, for instance) and 1 teaspoon distilled white vinegar. Bring back to a simmer for a few minutes before adding the cleaned langoustines. Bring back to a boil as quickly as possible and cook for 4–6 minutes depending on their size. Drain but do not rinse them, and never put them in the refrigerator, where they will lose their taste.

They can be eaten hot, warm, or cold.

Hot, they can be served with a melted butter sauce

(page 44) brightened with chopped chervil or with a bit of the cooking broth that has been reduced and simmered with ½ teaspoon butter and ½ to 1 tablespoon crème fraîche for about 10 minutes.

Warm, they can be eaten with a warm vinaigrette.

Cold, they must not be overwhelmed with sauces or condiments that will mask their surpassingly delicate flavor. Mayonnaise made without too much mustard (page 55) is one of the best choices here.

To prepare shelled langoustine tails (whether the animal is cooked or not), remove the head from the tail. Slide one blade of a pair of kitchen shears underneath the first two or three rings of the tail and snip. Remove these rings and then pull the end of the tail while holding on to the shelled portion. The shell should come off in one piece. Shelled langoustine tails are sometimes called scampi, but not everything called scampi in the United States is a shelled langoustine tail.

Langoustines also make superb fritters, which the Italians call *scampi fritti.* In this case, the tails are separated from the bodies and removed from their shells before cooking. They are then dipped in batter and fried at 325–350°F/160–175°C before being served hot and crisp, accompanied by mayonnaise mixed with minced fines herbes, capers, and cornichons (rather like a tartar sauce) or perhaps tomato sauce flavored with basil.

POACHED LANGOUSTINES

Langoustines à la nage

SERVES 4
PREPARATION AND COOKING 50 minutes

1 Preheat the oven to 400°F/200°C. Put 1 gallon (4 l.) water in a large pot with the carrot, onion, celery, orange zest, bouquet garni, fennel seeds, star anise, peppercorns, and 2 tablespoons coarse salt. Simmer gently for 20 minutes.

2 In the meantime, make the sauce. Line a sheet pan with parchment paper, put the tomatoes and garlic on it, and roast in the preheated oven for 20 minutes. Allow them to cool and then skin the tomatoes. Cut the garlic cloves in half and degerm (page 122).

1 medium carrot, peeled and
   diced
1 large onion, peeled and diced
1 cup (50 g.) celery stalks,
   washed and diced
4 strips orange zest from an
   organic orange

(continued)

3 In a blender or food processor, blend the tomatoes, garlic, nuts, yogurt, vinegar, and parsley. Pass the sauce through a fine strainer into a sauceboat. Taste for salt and pepper.

4 Plunge the live langoustines into the bubbling court bouillon and cook them for 2 minutes. Drain and serve with the sauce on the side.

1 bouquet garni (2 sprigs thyme, 1 bay leaf, and 5 branches parsley, wrapped and tied in a green leek leaf if possible)
1 pinch of fennel seeds
$\frac{1}{4}$ star anise pod
3 teaspoons peppercorns
Coarse salt
3 very ripe tomatoes
4 cloves garlic
$\frac{1}{3}$ cup (50 g.) mixed hazelnuts, almonds, and pine nuts
4 ounces (100 g.) plain yogurt
1 tablespoon sherry vinegar
1 tablespoon chopped flat-leaf parsley
Salt
Pepper
16–20 live langoustines (depending on their size)

LANGOUSTINE FRICASSÉE WITH ZUCCHINI AND MUSHROOMS

Fricassée de langoustines aux courgettes et aux champignons

SERVES 4
PREPARATION AND COOKING 30 minutes

1 Using a vegetable peeler, slice 8 thin strips of skin from each zucchini.

2 Rinse the langoustine tails and dry them with paper towels. Roll each one in a strip of zucchini so that the zucchini spirals around the tail. Secure with toothpicks and set aside.

3 Heat the peanut oil in a large sauté pan or skillet. When it is quite hot, add the chanterelles and season them with 2 pinches of salt and a pinch of pepper. Add the shallots and cook for 5 minutes over medium heat. Remove the chanterelles with a slotted spoon and set them aside, keeping them warm.

2 small, firm zucchini
16 fresh shelled langoustine tails (page 247)
2 tablespoons peanut oil
$\frac{1}{2}$ pound (250 g.) chanterelle mushrooms, cleaned
Salt
Pepper
2 shallots, peeled and minced
1 tablespoon butter

4   In the same pan, still containing the shallots, melt the butter over high heat. When it is hot, add the oyster mushrooms, 2 pinches of salt, and a pinch of pepper. Cook for 3 minutes over medium-low heat, stirring occasionally. Add the chanterelles, garlic, and parsley, and stir. Taste for salt and pepper and remove everything with a slotted spoon.

5   In the same pan, melt the goose fat over high heat. When it is quite hot, sauté the langoustine rolls for 2 minutes per side (4 minutes total). Season with 1 teaspoon salt and 2 pinches of pepper. Sprinkle with the thyme leaves.

6   Remove the toothpicks, arrange the langoustines in the center of a platter, and surround them with the sautéed mushrooms.

½ pound (250 g.) oyster mushrooms, cleaned
2 cloves garlic, peeled, degermed (page 122), and minced
1 tablespoon minced flat-leaf parsley
1½ tablespoons goose fat
1 pinch of fresh thyme leaves

special equipment: wooden toothpicks

STEAMED LANGOUSTINES WITH CREAM

Langoustines vapeur à la crème

SERVES   4
PREPARATION AND COOKING   1 hour

1   Remove the langoustines' heads. Snip the first 2 rings of their tails with kitchen shears and pull their bodies from the shells. Carefully remove their tails. Set aside the heads and claws.

2   Heat 1 tablespoon olive oil in a large saucepan or Dutch oven over low heat. Add the onion, shallot, celery, and fennel and cook for 3 minutes, stirring with a wooden spoon. Season with 2 pinches of salt, add the bouquet garni, and leave the vegetables over very low heat.

3   Heat 1 tablespoon olive oil in a skillet over medium heat. Add the langoustine heads and claws. Stir with a wooden spoon for 2 minutes, and then add them to the saucepan of vegetables. Add the cream to the saucepan along with a pinch of salt and a pinch of crushed black pepper. Bring to a simmer and simmer for 15 minutes. Turn off the heat and allow to rest for 10 minutes.

4   Bring 1 quart (1 l.) water to a boil in a pot fitted with a steamer basket (or bring 3 quarts/3 l. water to boil in a cous-coussier if you happen to have one).

20 live langoustines
2 tablespoons olive oil
1 medium onion, peeled and sliced into strips no thicker than ¼ inch (0.5 cm.)
1 shallot, peeled and sliced into strips no thicker than ¼ inch (0.5 cm.)
¼ celery heart, tender parts only, cut into ½-inch (1-cm.) sections
¼ fennel bulb, tender parts only, sliced into strips ½ inch (1 cm.) thick
Salt
1 bouquet garni (1 sprig fresh thyme, 4 sprigs parsley, and 1 small celery stalk, tied together)

(continued)

5   When the cream sauce has rested for 10 minutes, put it through a fine strainer into a small bowl. Pour it back into the saucepan and stir the simmering cream sauce over low heat until it takes on a rich, smooth consistency. Stir in the butter and lemon juice and turn off the heat. Taste for salt and pepper.

6   When the water for steaming boils, put the langoustine tails in the steamer basket and cover. Steam for 2 minutes. Arrange the langoustines on a platter or on individual plates, sprinkle lightly with fleur de sel, and pour the sauce over.

2 cups (50 cl.) heavy cream
Crushed black pepper
1 teaspoon butter
½ teaspoon lemon juice
Fleur de sel

LANGOUSTINES IN BRIK PACKETS WITH BASIL

Papillotes de langoustine au basilic

SERVES   4
PREPARATION AND COOKING   30 minutes

1   Put the olive oil in the refrigerator. Wash the langoustines and remove the shell from their tails. Remove their entrails with the tip of a knife. Pepper lightly on both sides.

2   Set aside 36 of the prettiest basil leaves and gently fold a paper towel around them so that they will be completely dried. Put the rest of the basil in the bowl of a blender or food processor with the chilled olive oil, garlic, 3 pinches of salt, and 1 pinch of pepper. Blend thoroughly and set aside.

3   Put 1 of the basil leaves on top of each langoustine tail. Quarter each brik leaf and wrap each tail and its basil leaf in a piece of dough. Fold and pinch the piece of brik together along the edges and fasten with a toothpick through the prawn tail to form a little packet.

4   Heat the frying oil. Prepare a plate lined with 4 paper towels. After 4 or 5 minutes, the oil should be hot enough (350°F/180°C) to fry the packets. (Work in batches to avoid crowding them.) Fry for 30 seconds and then turn them with a skimmer or Chinese spoon and fry for 10 seconds on the other side. (You might use the timer on your microwave to count the time precisely.) Turn off the heat and remove the langoustine packets to the plate lined with paper towels.

½ cup (10 cl.) olive oil
12 live langoustines
Pepper
1 bunch basil, washed and stemmed
1 clove garlic, peeled, degermed (page 122), and chopped
Salt
3 leaves brik dough (page 199)
3 quarts (3 l.) neutral oil for frying
Fleur de sel

special equipment: toothpicks

5   Reheat the oil over low heat until it reaches 260°F/130°C. If you are not sure of the temperature and do not have a thermometer, drop in a test leaf of basil: At the proper temperature it will sizzle lightly but will not burn. Lower the remaining basil leaves into the oil quickly. Remove immediately with the skimmer and drain on paper towels.

6   Arrange the packets in the middle of a platter (you can use the draining plate if you remove the paper towels). Nestle the fried basil leaves among the packets and pour a ring of sauce around the whole. Serve the rest of the sauce on the side along with the fleur de sel. These treats must be eaten right away while they are still piping hot.

LANGOUSTINES WITH ANGEL HAIR AND SPICED OIL

Langoustines aux cheveux d'ange à l'huile épicée

SERVES   4

PREPARATION AND COOKING   50 minutes

To remove the seeds from the vanilla beans, slice the beans in two and scoop or scrape out the seeds with a small spoon. You can keep the emptied pods in a canister with sugar.

1   Put all the ingredients for the spiced oil in a blender or food processor. Blend for 1 minute and set aside.

2   Bring 1 quart (1 l.) water to a boil in a large pot with 1 tablespoon coarse salt. Cook the pasta al dente and drain in a colander.

3   In a bowl, beat together the eggs, 6 pinches of salt, 2 pinches of pepper, and 1 tablespoon olive oil.

4   Put a platter and 3 deep plates side by side. Put the flour into the first plate, the beaten eggs into the second, and the cooked pasta into the third. Coat each langoustine tail well in flour, then in egg, and then cover it with pasta, patting it to make the pasta stick all around. As you go, set the tails on the platter.

5   Heat the frying oil. Prepare a platter lined with 4 layers of paper towel. After 4 or 5 minutes, when the oil is hot (350°F/180°C), fry the langoustine tails. If your pot is large

FOR THE SPICED OIL

¾ cup plus 1 tablespoon (20 cl.) olive oil

3 tablespoons pink peppercorns

Seeds of 4 vanilla beans

2 tablespoons sesame seeds

Seeds of 6 pods star anise (slice off the points of the star to remove the seeds)

2 tablespoons mustard seed

FOR THE REST

Coarse salt

¼ pound (3 ounces/100 g.) capellini (angel hair pasta)

3 eggs

Pepper

1 tablespoon olive oil

(continued)

enough, you can do them all at once, but if you must, work in 2 batches. Fry for 30 seconds, then flip them over with a skimmer or Chinese spoon and fry 10 seconds more. (You might use the timer on your microwave to measure the time precisely.) Turn off the heat and remove the langoustines with a skimmer or slotted spoon, letting them drain a minute on the paper towel–lined platter.

6   Arrange the drained langoustines on a serving platter and drizzle a ring of the spiced oil around them. Serve immediately while they are still quite hot. Serve the rest of the spiced oil on the side.

⅓ cup (50 g.) flour
12 large live langoustines (shelled tails only; see page 247)
3 quarts (3 l.) peanut oil for frying

CREAMED TRUFFLED LANGOUSTINES

Crème de langoustines à la truffe

SERVES   4
PREPARATION   20 minutes
COOKING   30 minutes

1   Rinse the langoustines and remove their shells. Use scissors to snip the first few rings on the belly and then pull the bodies from the shells. Remove the heads from the bodies. Remove the guts with a knife and dry the langoustines with a paper towel. Keep the langoustines in the refrigerator until you are ready to use them. Do not discard their heads.

2   Heat 1 tablespoon olive oil in a skillet or sauté pan over medium heat. Add the chopped vegetables and bouquet garni. Sprinkle with 2 pinches of salt and stir with a wooden spoon. Cook over low heat for 4 minutes, stirring. Turn off the heat and set the sautéed vegetables aside.

3   Heat 1 tablespoon olive oil in a large saucepan or pot over a high flame. Add the langoustine heads and cook, stirring, for 4 minutes over high heat. Add the vegetables to the pot and then the cream, 2 pinches of salt, and 2 pinches of white pepper. Bring to a boil, then lower the heat and simmer for 10 minutes. Turn off the heat, stir, cover with plastic wrap, and allow to steep for 10 minutes.

4   Put the cream through a fine strainer (or, even better, a chi-

12 live langoustines
2½ tablespoons olive oil
1 small fennel bulb, washed, trimmed, and sliced into thin strips
1 small stalk celery, washed, fibrous parts peeled away, and sliced into thin strips
1 small onion, peeled and minced
1 shallot, peeled and minced
1 bouquet garni (2 stalks celery, 6 branches parsley, and 2 sprigs thyme, wrapped and tied in a white leek leaf)
Salt
2 cups (50 cl.) heavy cream
White pepper

nois) into a saucepan, pressing on the langoustine heads with a ladle or large spoon. Dice the cold butter. Bring the strained cream to a simmer and stir in the diced butter with a wooden spoon. Add the lemon juice, Cognac, and a pinch of cayenne pepper. Taste, adding more salt or more hot pepper as you like. Leave the saucepan over the lowest possible heat.

5 Line a platter with 2 layers of paper towels. Take the langoustine tails from the refrigerator and season with salt and a pinch of white pepper. Heat ½ tablespoon olive oil in the skillet over high heat for 1 minute. Put the tails in the skillet in a single layer; do not crowd them. Cook for 3 minutes, still over high heat, and then turn them and cook 2 minutes more. Remove them to a tureen and cover with the hot cream. Sprinkle with minced truffle.

3 tablespoons cold butter
1 teaspoon lemon juice
½ teaspoon Cognac
Cayenne pepper (or any
    powdered hot pepper)
1 tablespoon minced truffle

Lobster

This cold-water crustacean makes a luxurious meal and is especially appropriate for festive occasions. A lobster can live for half a century and grow to an astonishing size, as much as 3 feet (1 m.) long and 40 pounds (20 kg.).

In France, European lobsters are said to be the best in the world. They inhabit European waters from the north of Norway to the Mediterranean, making their homes in rocky areas up to 360 feet (120 m.) deep. They are a murky blue. Brittany lobsters, from the coast of Finistère in that region, are beloved for their fine aromatic flesh. They are similar to the lobsters caught in the seas of the United Kingdom and Ireland.

Their American cousins are reddish brown and have more of a pot belly. They are found off the eastern coast of Canada and the northeastern coast of the United States. They are generally half as expensive as European lobsters.

Lobsters should be bought alive, of course, and should be vigorous, bright-eyed, and fresh smelling. If they have spent too much time in a crate or a tank, they will not smell or taste as nice. Choose lobsters that seem heavy for their size; choose females, if possible, for their more delectable flesh. Turn the lobster over on its back: a female will have a hollow in its belly, which is where it carries eggs, while a male's belly is rounded. Reject any crustacean carrying eggs under its tail; it will be worn-out and therefore not so tasty.

Avoid buying precooked lobster. It's usually the crustaceans that are about to spoil that end up being cooked. The flesh of a dead crustacean liquefies and runs off as viscous matter, not an appetizing business.

When you buy a lobster, be sure not to keep it in a closed plastic bag. It will suffocate, die, and decompose very quickly. Put it in a bin at the bottom of the refrigerator on top of a damp dish towel (or, if possible, on a bed of seaweed).

When you prepare to cook the lobster, the first step is to wash it under running water to eliminate any impurities that might introduce bad flavors during cooking.

One can serve lobster simmered in court bouillon (see page 246; omit the zest), steamed (but this will toughen the flesh a bit), broiled, or roasted. Before a lobster is broiled or roasted, it should be cooked for 2 minutes in boiling salted water in order to kill it as quickly as possible.

To broil, cleave the lobster in half lengthwise. Crack the pincers slightly with a nutcracker, small hammer, or lobster cracker. Season the flesh with salt and pepper, and sprinkle it with a bit of olive oil that you have infused with a dash of curry, a morsel of star anise, a clove of garlic, and a few leaves of basil. Broil it in the oven with the flesh facing the broiler but not so close that it will dry out. Do not turn the lobster halves during cooking. You want to keep all their juices in their shells if possible. Cook for 5–10 minutes, according to the size.

A whole lobster can also be roasted in a very hot oven (460°F/240°C) for 10–15 minutes (for one that is 1 to 1½ pounds [500–800 g.] and has been poached for 2 minutes). Baste well with olive oil as it cooks. When the shell has turned red, you can cover the lobster with a handful of seaweed, if you have some, to finish the cooking. In days past, the fishermen of Brittany would cook their lobsters this way in wooden lobster pots.

Lobster can be chopped and pan fried in butter. After boiling the lobster for 2 minutes, chop it into sections without removing the shell. Cook the sections very quickly (a few minutes only) in a bit of butter over medium-high heat, stirring with a wooden spoon. Season with a pinch of curry or paprika and a pinch of salt.

One of the nicest ways to cook lobster is to simmer it in just enough court bouillon to cover. (Use the court bouillon on page 244 or 246, omitting the zest.) Let it cook about 15 minutes after the water has started simmering, on very low heat (do not boil), or even in a pressure cooker, which allows you to use a very small amount of liquid.

LOBSTER À L'AMÉRICAINE _____

SERVES   4
PREPARATION   20 minutes
COOKING   about 15 minutes

A l'armoricaine ("in the Amorican way") or *à l'américaine* ("in the American way")? The father of this dish is said to be Pierre Fraysse, who ran the Parisian restaurant Peter's in the 1860s. He had worked in the United States and named this dish to honor his transatlantic clients. Fraysse was a native of Sète, not far from Montpellier in the south of France, and it seems that this dish had long been known as *homard à la provençale*, or Provençal lobster. Nevertheless, certain historians of gastronomy claim that this dish was created in Brittany (one of whose ancient names is Armorica), without offering the slightest proof. Consequently, you will sometimes see this dish called *homard à l'armoricaine*, especially in Brittany.

1   Clean the lobsters by rinsing them under running water. In a large pot, bring to a boil enough water to cover the lobsters: about 2 quarts (2 l.), plus 1 tablespoon coarse salt. When the water is bubbling, immerse the lobsters and cook for 2 minutes. Drain them and remove their claws. Remove the head from the body. Cleave the head and chest in half lengthwise, eliminating any pockets of debris. Scoop the roe and creamy substances into a bowl. Chop each tail into 4 chunks. Crack the claw shell to facilitate removal of flesh after cooking.

2   Heat ½ tablespoon butter over low heat in a saucepan. Add the onion, shallots, garlic, and a pinch of salt. Cook for 3 minutes without allowing the vegetables or butter to color. Stir frequently with a wooden spatula. Set aside.

2 live lobsters, 1¼–1½ pounds (600–700 g.) each
Coarse salt
2 sticks (½ pound/230 g.) butter
1 onion, peeled and minced
4 shallots, peeled and minced
2 cloves garlic, unpeeled and lightly crushed with the palm of your hand on the chopping board
Salt

(continued)

3   Heat the olive oil in a large pot for 2 minutes. Season each chunk of lobster tail with a small pinch of salt and a dash of pepper. When the oil is very hot, put the lobster tail chunks, body pieces, and claws in the pot. Cook about 3 minutes over medium-high heat, stirring and tossing constantly until the shells have turned quite red.

4   Add the tomatoes, the onion-shallot-garlic mixture, bouquet garni, 2 teaspoons of tarragon, and a dash of cayenne pepper. Sprinkle the Cognac over and allow it to cook away as the mixture comes to a boil, then add the wine. Mix well and add the fish stock and tomato paste. Bring to a boil quickly over high heat. Cover the pot, lower the heat, and cook at a gentle simmer about 8 minutes, stirring once or twice.

5   Remove the lobster pieces to a platter and keep them warm, tenting them with a piece of aluminum foil. Do not turn off the heat under the large pot.

6   Mash the roe and creamy bits together with a fork and then mash in the remaining butter. Remove the bouquet garni and whisk in the roe-butter to thicken the sauce. As soon as the sauce begins to bubble, turn off the heat and taste for salt and pepper. Pour the sauce over the lobster and sprinkle with the remaining teaspoon of minced tarragon.

4 tablespoons olive oil
Pepper
3 tomatoes, peeled, seeded, and diced (page 124)
1 bouquet garni (1 sprig fresh thyme and 3 sprigs flat-leaf parsley, tied together)
3 teaspoons minced tarragon
Cayenne pepper (or any powdered hot pepper)
$1\frac{1}{2}$ tablespoons Cognac
2 cups (50 cl.) dry white wine (such as Muscadet)
2 cups (50 cl.) fish stock (page 40 or store-bought)
$1\frac{1}{2}$ tablespoons tomato paste

LOBSTER WITH TRUFFLES AND CHESTNUTS

Homard à la truffe et aux marrons

SERVES   4
PREPARATION AND COOKING   20 minutes
COOKING THE CHESTNUTS   25 minutes
PREPARING THE STOCK   25 minutes

1   Preheat the oven to 400°F/200°C.

2   Rinse and clean the lobsters. In a large pot, bring to a boil about 2 quarts (2 l.) water (or enough to cover the lobsters) with 1 tablespoon coarse salt. When it bubbles, cook the lobsters for 2 minutes. Drain them and then separate the heads from the tails. Cleave the head/chests in half lengthwise, scooping away any traces of debris. Chop each tail into 4 equal chunks without removing the shell. Chop the head

2 live lobsters, 1 pound (500 g.) each
Coarse salt
$1\frac{1}{2}$ tablespoons butter
20 fresh chestnuts, peeled

into pieces. Remove the roe and set it aside. Save any bits of the shell for the stock. Remove the shell from the claws.

3   COOK THE CHESTNUTS   Melt ½ tablespoon butter in a large ovenproof saucepan or Dutch oven with a lid, preferably something pretty enough to bring to the table since you will serve from this pot. Add the peeled chestnuts and cook over medium-low heat until just beginning to turn gold, about 3 minutes. Add the bouquet garni, chicken broth, a pinch of pepper and bring to a boil. Cut a piece of parchment paper the size of the saucepan's lid. Prick a few holes in the paper with a fork and put it over the pot of chestnuts. Bake in the preheated oven for 20 minutes, covered only by the paper, not the lid.

4   PREPARE THE PASTRY   Put the flour, 3 of the eggs, and 3 egg whites, and rosemary in the bowl of a food processor (using the plastic dough blade) with a pinch of sugar and a pinch of salt. Pulse until you have obtained homogeneous dough. Pull it into a ball, cover with plastic wrap, and refrigerate.

5   PREPARE THE STOCK   Heat 1 tablespoon olive oil in a saucepan large enough to hold all the vegetables. When it is hot, cook the shallot, onion, carrot, celery, fennel, and garlic over low heat about 3 minutes, stirring regularly with a wooden spoon. Do not allow the vegetables to color. Season with ½ teaspoon salt and a pinch of pepper while cooking. Taste for salt and pepper at the end and then set aside.

6   Heat 2 tablespoons olive oil in a large pot. When it is quite hot, cook over medium-high heat the reserved pieces of shell until they are nice and red (about 3 minutes), stirring well with a wooden spoon. Add the cooked vegetables to the pot of shells, cover everything with water, and add the bouquet garni, star anise, saffron, fennel seeds, peppercorns, dried tomatoes, and tomato paste. Stir well and bring to a simmer. Cover and simmer for 15 minutes. Taste, correcting salt and pepper if necessary. Put the stock through a fine strainer or chinois, pressing the solid matter to extract as much juice as possible.

7   FINISH THE DISH   After removing the chestnuts from the oven, raise the temperature to 475°F/250°C. Prepare the roe butter: Use a fork to mash the roe into 1 tablespoon softened butter until you have a homogeneous pomade. Put it in the refrigerator.

8   Season each piece of lobster with a pinch of salt and a dash

1 bouquet garni (2 sprigs thyme, 1 bay leaf, and 5 stems parsley, wrapped and tied in a green leek leaf)

1 cup (25 cl.) chicken broth (page 77, or made with a bouillon cube)

Pepper

2 tablespoons olive oil

Salt

2 cloves garlic

2 sprigs rosemary

2 star anise pods

8 dried tomatoes (page 588 or store-bought)

3 ounces (80 g.) diced truffles

½ bunch basil

4 pinches of curry powder

FOR THE PASTRY (OR USE THE RECIPE FOR *PÂTE À LUTER*, SEALING PASTRY, ON PAGE 383)

3 cups (360 g.) flour

4 eggs plus 3 egg whites (page 204)

Leaves from 1 sprig fresh rosemary

Sugar

Salt

FOR THE STOCK (OR USE THE RECIPE FOR FISH STOCK ON PAGE 40 OR STORE-BOUGHT)

5 tablespoons olive oil

1 shallot, peeled and sliced into ¼-inch (0.5-cm.) rounds

½ onion, peeled and sliced into ¼-inch (0.5-cm.) rounds

½ carrot, peeled and sliced into ¼-inch (0.5-cm.) rounds

(continued)

Lobster with Truffles and Chestnuts   257

of pepper. Give them a very light dusting of curry powder. Heat 2 tablespoons olive oil in a skillet or sauté pan. When it is quite hot, cook the pieces of lobster over medium-high heat until their shells have turned red (about 3 minutes). Remove them to a platter. Cook the claws the same way, giving them about 1 minute per side.

9   Having removed the chestnuts to a bowl, rinse their saucepan with hot water and wipe it out with a paper towel but do not wash. Pour in the stock. Add the pieces of lobster, chestnuts, garlic, rosemary, star anise, tomatoes, and truffles. Spread the roe butter over the pieces of lobster. Everything should be snugly nestled in the pot. Sprinkle with basil leaves and cover.

10 In a bowl, beat the last egg with a few drops of cold water. Take the dough out of the refrigerator. Roll it for sealing into a long tube as long as the circumference of the pot's top edge. Press the dough all around the top edge of the pot and press the lid down on it so that the dough seals the lid and the top of the pot. For a pleasing presentation you can cut the shapes with a small knife. Using a pastry brush, paint the dough with the beaten egg. Bake for 8 minutes.

11 Serve straight from the pot, removing the sealing pastry in front of your guests. The pastry is not meant to be eaten, but when you break it open, the sudden release of aromas will delight everyone at the table.

½ celery stalk, cleaned and sliced into ¼-inch (0.5-cm.) rounds

½ bulb fennel, trimmed, cleaned, and sliced into ¼-inch (0.5-cm.) rounds

1 clove garlic, peeled and degermed (see page 122)

Salt

Pepper

1 bouquet garni (1 sprig fresh thyme and 3 stems flat-leaf parsley, tied together)

1 star anise

1 pinch of saffron

1 pinch of fennel seeds

10 black peppercorns

8 dried tomatoes (page 588)

1 tablespoon tomato paste

LOBSTER WITH SAUTERNES

Homard au sauternes

SERVES   4

PREPARATION   15 minutes

COOKING THE LOBSTER   4 minutes

Here is a dish that uses a pressure cooker to prepare lobster. Sauternes is a sweet white wine from Bordeaux.

1   Rinse the lobsters under cold running water. Bring to a boil 3 quarts (3 l.) water (or enough to cover the lobsters com-

2 live lobsters, 1¾–2 pounds (800–900 g.) each

Coarse salt

1½ tablespoons butter

2 carrots, peeled and sliced into rounds ⅛ inch (3 mm.) thick

pletely) with 1 tablespoon coarse salt. Boil the lobsters for 2 minutes and then drain them.

2   Heat ½ tablespoon butter in a saucepan. When it foams, add the carrots and onions and cook for 3 minutes over low heat. Stir them regularly with a wooden spoon and do not allow them to color. Drain the cooked carrots and onions.

3   Into the pressure cooker put the lobsters, carrots, onions, Sauternes, orange juice, ginger, saffron, and 1 tablespoon butter. Add ½ teaspoon coarse salt and a pinch of pepper. Cover and cook over high heat, counting 4 minutes after the rotation of the valve. Shake the pressure cooker regularly to keep everything from sticking together. Leave covered for 3 minutes after the cooking is complete.

4   Remove the lobsters and cut them in half lengthwise. Remove the dark guts from the tail and the sandy debris from the head. Put the 4 half tails on a hot platter.

5   Bring the cooking juices to a boil. Taste for salt and pepper and sprinkle with parsley. Pour the sauce over the lobster so that it is studded with the bits of carrot and onion.

6 small new onions, peeled and sliced into rounds ⅛ inch (3 mm.) thick
2½ cups (60 cl.) Sauternes
1 cup (20 cl.) orange juice
1 teaspoon shredded fresh ginger
10 stems saffron
Pepper
Salt
1 tablespoon minced flat-leaf parsley

Rock Lobster (*Langouste*)

Rock lobster is called *langouste* in French and is known by several other names in English: spiny lobster, thorny lobster, and crawfish. (Its name is sometimes confused with that of the freshwater crayfish, a mistake easy enough to understand but a mistake nonetheless, like the American habit of making the opposite mistake and calling crayfish crawfish.)

This luxurious product is distinguished by its large antennae and lack of pincers. There are several varieties. The most commonly sold are from the south of France, the Caribbean Sea, Portugal, and Mauritania, but the finest, most scrumptious rock lobster is the red langouste or langouste royale. It lives in the rocky bottoms of the English Channel, the Atlantic, and the Mediterranean. Its shell is reddish brown and dappled with violet, and its flesh is tastiest between April and the end of September.

Fresh rock lobsters must be bought live, with all their limbs intact and no holes in their shells. Only their antennae, which are very long and fragile, can have suffered any harm. Here again the females are to be preferred; you will know them by the little flippers on their bellies.

It is best not to buy a rock lobster larger than 4 pounds (2 kg.); its texture and taste will not be the best.

Rock lobsters can be eaten hot, warm, or cold. Poaching in court bouillon is one of the best ways to cook them, but they can just as well be broiled or roasted.

To make the court bouillon, follow the recipe for court bouillon for langoustines (page 246), omitting the orange zest. Simmer the rock lobsters in this broth for 12–15 minutes (for lobsters of 1 pound/500–600 g. or so) or 20 minutes (for a lobster weighing 1½ to 2 pounds/800 g. to 1 kg.). Drain after cooking.

If you plan to eat the rock lobster hot, let it rest for 10 minutes or so at room temperature before bringing it to the table. This will give the flesh time to relax.

If you plan to eat the langouste cold, do not put it in the refrigerator or it will lose its savor.

To roast or broil a rock lobster weighing about 1½ pounds (600–800 g.), first boil it for 2 or 3 minutes to kill it as quickly as possible so that the flesh will be more tender. Then use a large, sturdy knife to cleave the lobster in half lengthwise. Remove the pocket of sandy debris in the head as well as the intestine, which runs the length of the tail. Place the halves on a sheet pan or other ovenproof dish, flesh side up, and season with salt, pepper, and a few lumps of salted butter. Bake in a preheated 440°F/220°C oven or under the broiler for 10–12 minutes. Do not flip them while cooking; you don't want to lose the juices in the shell. When you remove them from the oven, brush them with a little melted butter.

When cooking a rock lobster on a grill or a barbecue, never expose the flesh side directly to the heat. It will dry out, losing its juices and with them much of its flavor. All that will be left is a burnt taste.

Avoid using too many aromatic herbs, for the rock lobster's flesh is so delicious that it should be able to stand on its own.

Shrimp

The shrimp is one of the most popular crustaceans among diners, but it is also certainly the most fragile. For this reason, shrimp in France are often cooked right on the boat as soon as they are caught. Small, sweet gray-fleshed shrimp are an ideal *amuse-bouche* (literally, "mouth amuser"—a bite-sized morsel); medium-sized shrimp, such as the pink-fleshed shrimp of the Mediterranean and the tropics, are frequently frozen; and the rather large shrimp called *gambas*, which can also be frozen, are often cooked *à la plancha*, on a hot metal plate, or in a cast-iron skillet as they are in Spain.

A good shrimp smells delectably of the sea. Its shell should be very glossy. Once shrimp have been cooked, do not leave them in the refrigerator for long.

If you find the small, soft variety of shrimp (*crevettes grises*) available for purchase live, prepare a court bouillon: Bring 1 quart (1 l.) water to a boil with 1 tablespoon coarse salt, 1 sprig thyme, 1 bay leaf, and some pepper. Plunge the live shrimp into the simmering broth and cook for 2 minutes at most. Drain the shrimp, allow them to cool, and eat them with country bread spread with salted butter. If you like, you can also cook them in seawater carefully filtered through a fine colander. Or melt 1 teaspoon butter in a skillet and sauté the shrimp for 2–3 minutes over medium-high heat. Grind some pepper over the shrimp and serve immediately.

If you are lucky enough to come across uncooked rock-pool prawns (*Paelaemon elegans*), called "bouquets" in France, put just a bit of salted water in a large pot: The prawns should be not quite covered rather than swimming in water. Bring the water to a boil and then add the prawns and cook for 3 minutes, shaking the pot vigorously every once in a while to toss the prawns around and ensure even cooking. If necessary, cook them in batches rather than layering them deep in the pot; you can use the same cooking water for all the batches. Drain and allow the prawns to cool before serving them with bread and butter. Do not serve them chilled, though.

Spider Crabs

Spider crabs (*Maja squinado*) are some of the tastiest members of the crustacean family. These spiny-shelled creatures abound along the French coast, to the delight of the gourmets who love their fine, fragrant flesh.

They are reddish and not bigger than about 10 inches (25 cm.), with small claws.

Unlike many crabs, spider crabs never leave the water.

A spider crab must be bought live and should be heavy in the hand. If you can, buy females for their delicate flesh. Look for the tongue under the shell; in a female it should be large, and in a male, smaller.

Before cooking the spider crab, you must wash it in running water. If it looks crusty and dirty, scrub it well so that these impurities do not spoil the flavor during cooking. Then make sure the claws and legs are intact and free of mutilations. If there is a gap or gash of some kind, use your fingers to knead some soft white sandwich bread into a little plug and stop up the hole. This will keep the crab from leaking during cooking.

Cook the crabs as soon as possible; freshness is all when it comes to their flavor. The simplest cooking method is to boil the crab in salted water (1 tablespoon coarse salt per 2 quarts/2 l. water) for 20–25 minutes. A bit more complicated but even better is to boil the crab in court bouillon (a poaching liquid to which you have added some simple seasoning: ½ cup/10 cl. distilled white vinegar; 1 tablespoon coarse salt; 1 or 2 carrots; an onion cut in 6 or 8 pieces; a bouquet garni made of 2 or 3 sprigs thyme, preferably fresh, 5 stems parsley, and 1 small celery stalk, tied together. You might buy ready-made court bouillon, too). Take the pot off the heat and allow it to cool before you remove the crab. If you can, avoid keeping cooked spider crabs in the refrigerator; it changes the way they taste. They really should be enjoyed as soon as possible after cooking.

You can eat spider crabs whole or shelled. To extract the flesh from the shell, remove the claws and legs and then crush them with a nutcracker to make an opening through which you can remove the flesh. Open the body by sliding the tip of a big knife in between the shell and breastplate and pulling them apart. Remove all flesh from the body: First use a spoon to scoop out the creamy substance and put it in a bowl, and then use tweezers to remove the flesh. Whisk a bit of mustard and some salt and pepper into the creamy substance and then whisk in oil drop by drop. It's as if you're making a mayonnaise but with the crab-cream replacing the egg yolk. Finish with 1 teaspoon mayonnaise (store-bought or see page 55) and strain the sauce. Add some minced herbs and toss this sea-scented sauce with the crab meat.

SPIDER CRAB WITH AROMATICS

Araignée de mer aux aromates

SERVES 4

COOKING 20 minutes plus 20 minutes cooling time

PREPARATION OF THE VEGETABLES AND ROLLS 35 minutes

1 Wash and scrub the crabs. In a pot large enough to hold the crabs, bring to a very gentle boil just enough court bouillon to cover the crabs. Add the crabs and cook for about 20 minutes at a simmer. Take the pot from the heat, allow it to cool for 20 minutes without removing the crabs, and then remove the crabs and pick their meat as described on page 262.

2 Peel the zucchini, discarding all but 2 strips of its skin. Cut the skin into pieces ½ inch by ¼ inch (1 cm. by 0.5 cm.). Chop the rest of ½ zucchini into small dice about ¼ inch (0.5 cm.).

3 Bring 1 quart (1 l.) water and 1 teaspoon coarse salt to a boil in a saucepan. Boil the diced bell pepper for 1 minute. Remove it with a skimmer, cool it under cold water, and drain. Boil the zucchini skin for 2 minutes, cool under cold water, and drain. Mix the bell pepper, zucchini skin, zucchini, and mushrooms together in a dish. Season with a pinch of salt and a dash of pepper and mix well.

4 Measure 14 ounces (400 g.) crab flesh and use a fork to mix it with the egg whites and 3 tablespoons crème fraîche. Season with a pinch of pepper and mix again.

5 Cut 12 squares of aluminum foil that measure 6 inches by 6 inches (15 cm. by 15 cm.). Butter them and deposit about 1 heaping tablespoon (35 g.) of the crab mixture on each one. Roll them into cylinders and fold and pinch the edges shut to ensure that they are sealed tight.

6 Melt 2 teaspoons butter in a dish in the microwave. Set it beside the dish of vegetables.

7 Bring 2 quarts (2 l.) water to a near boil in a large pot over high heat; the water should just be shivering. Put in half of the crab packets and cook about 3 minutes; then do the same

4 pounds (2 kg.) large, heavy spider crabs (enough to make about 14 ounces meat)

2 quarts (2 l.) court bouillon (store-bought or homemade, page 262)

1 zucchini

Coarse salt

1 red bell pepper, peeled (page 130), seeded, and cut into ¼ inch (0.5 cm.) dice

5 button or cup mushrooms, cleaned, dried, and cut into ¼ inch (0.5 cm.) dice

Salt

Pepper

2 egg whites (page 204)

2 cups (50 cl.) crème fraîche

1½ tablespoons butter

Curry or saffron (optional)

for the other half. Drain the packets and remove the crab from the foil. Season with a pinch of salt and a pinch of curry or saffron (optional). Roll the crab in the melted butter and then in the vegetables so that the crab rolls are covered in a thin layer of vegetables.

8   Heat 2 teaspoons butter in a skillet. When it foams, cook the crab rolls for 2 minutes over low heat, gently moving them about with a wooden spatula so they cook evenly. They should color only just barely.

Saltwater Fish

Of the many food products that underwent substantial changes in the second half of the twentieth century, fish was one of the most dramatically altered. Increased consumption caused several species to be endangered, and other even rarer fish virtually disappeared. The current boom in aquaculture would seem to augur well for the future of fish, but too often farming conditions are geared to maximize profit instead of quality. Salmon is the poster fish for this phenomenon: Once rare, it is now abundantly available year-round but is usually too fatty.

Fish are incredibly rich in protein and vitamins as well as phosphorus and magnesium. They also contain iodine, which is particularly useful to the human organism. The fat content of most fish, on the other hand, is low.

Whether it is saltwater or fresh, whole or filleted or carved into steaks, the fish is a candidate for every cooking method. But it is a delicate product, and its flesh can change quite rapidly. Its quality fluctuates as the seasons change. During its spawning season, a fish becomes leaner and will not be as tasty.

CHOOSING FISH

Whole fish must have a very firm, glistening body, and its scales should be well attached. Its eyes should be bright, clear, and convex; they should not be cloudily veiled. The odor should be light and pleasing, and the belly should not be pierced or split open. The gills, which you will find beneath the flaps at the base of the head, should be damp, lustrous, and colored a fine vivid red (except for those fish, such as turbot and brill, whose gills are properly grayish).

Fish fillets and steaks should have a pleasing smell. They should be satiny, with a slightly pearly gleam, and the flesh should remain firm but elastic.

EATING FRESH FISH

Eat fresh fish as soon as possible after buying it. If you can't eat it right away, wrap it with plastic wrap or a clean towel and put it in the coldest part of the refrigerator.

It is best not to try to freeze fresh fish yourself. Its extremely delicate flesh is best frozen by superfast methods that you cannot replicate at home. Poorly frozen fish will be dry and stringy.

For maximum taste, cook fish whole. During cooking, the bones will give the flesh flavor as will the skin. The thin layer of fat beneath the skin develops flavor and protects the flesh from the intense heat of cooking. Certain flat fish (sole, lemon sole or sand dab, and turbot) have black skin that is inedible, but their white skin may be eaten if it is scaled.

CARVED FISH

Not all fish can be cooked whole. There are different ways to carve a fish for cooking.

FILLETS All flat or round fish can be cut into fillets. The fish is cut in half, and the bones and skin are removed.

SECTIONS This preparation is for flat fish (such as turbot, brill, sole, and lemon sole). The fish is chopped into sections right through the skeleton.

STEAKS When a round fish (such as salmon, cod, monkfish, hake, and tuna) is sectioned as described above, the sections are called steaks.

If you are not sure whether your fish is sufficiently cooked, use a sharp knife to make an incision about ½ inch or ¾ inch (1 cm. or 2 cm.) long with a sharp knife at the thickest part of the fish, near its spine. Gently pull the 2 sides of the incision apart. The flesh around the spine should no longer be translucent; it should be opaque and white, and it should be easy to pull away from the spine. If you like a less cooked fish, the spine should still show pinkish traces. You might not like the way the incision looks when you present your fish, but you will know that it is perfectly cooked.

A fillet is cooked when the flesh is opaque white (rather than translucent) at its thickest point.

Some fish, such as salmon, tuna, and swordfish, are cooked just like steak: rare (barely warm at the center), medium (a warm, opaque center), or well done. Even if you enjoy these fish rare, don't try cooking them at extremely low temperatures (less than 150°F/65°C); this could disseminate toxins instead of eliminating them. Instead, cook the fish at a high temperature for a shorter amount of time.

Cod

Cod is a popular fish. Because it keeps so well, it was for centuries an indispensable food, especially in Christian societies where it could be enjoyed even on certain fast days. Cod can be fished in many waters and has at times been an issue in the conflicts of great powers. Like so many other species, cod has fallen victim to overfishing.

Today, cod is fished as it was in the past, by trailing multiple lines behind a small boat. Once caught, it is gutted on the boat, but the liver is set aside. The head is cut off, but the tongue and cheeks are saved. It is salted on the boat, if it is to be salted. Cod dried without the addition of salt is called "stockfish"—a very strong-tasting food indeed. These are ancient traditions. Once upon a time the fishermen of Newfoundland in Canada would preserve the fish by burying it in the dunes, where it would freeze for the winter. They would come back for it a season later when it was defrosted.

Fine cod specimens have thick fillets with visible scales,

brown skin on their backs, and silver on their bellies. Salt cod should be white and should not smell unpleasant.

Dried cod must be thoroughly washed, chopped into 4-ounce (125-g.) pieces, and then soaked in cold water, skin side up, to rid it of some of its salt. Change the water four times a day. Dried salt cod must soak for two days, bone-in salt cod should soak for one day, and a boneless fillet of salt cod should soak for twelve hours.

You can prepare your own "instant" salt cod by scrubbing a piece of fresh cod with coarse salt. Leave it in the refrigerator for about one hour and then rinse it well. Proceed with your recipe without soaking.

To poach salt cod, put it in a large saucepan (don't crowd the pieces) with cold water to cover and a bouquet garni (thyme, parsley, and a bay leaf). Bring to a boil. As soon as the water bubbles, cover the pot, and leave the fish in the hot water for 15 to 20 minutes. (You could also poach it at a very low simmer for 8 minutes.) Drain, let it cool for 3 minutes, remove the skin, and flake the fish with your fingers. The warm fish makes a good salad with warm potatoes, onions, minced shallots, minced parsley, red wine vinegar, and olive oil.

FRIED COD WITH CABBAGE

Cabillaud poêlé au chou

SERVES   4

PREPARATION   10 minutes

COOKING   5 minutes for the fish plus 10 minutes for the cabbage

Ask the fishmonger to slice the fillet into 4 fat pieces and to leave the skin on.

1   Bring 2 quarts (2 l.) water to a boil in a large pot with 1 tablespoon coarse salt. Simmer the cabbage leaves for 10 minutes and then remove them to a colander. Rinse them under cold running water to cool and then leave to drain.

2   Season each side of the cod fillet pieces with a good pinch of salt and a dash of pepper. Heat 2 tablespoons olive oil in a

Coarse salt

Leaves of 1 green cabbage

1 skin-on cod fillet (about 1½ pounds/800 g. total), sliced into 4 equal pieces

Salt

Pepper

2½ tablespoons olive oil

(continued)

skillet. When it is quite hot, place the fillets in the pan, skin side down, and cook for 3 minutes over medium-high heat. Turn and cook for 2 minutes on the skinless side. The cod is cooked when it is opaque white all the way through.

3   Chop the drained cabbage leaves into 1-inch (2-cm.) strips. Heat ½ tablespoon olive oil in a sauté pan over low heat, add the cabbage, and stir to coat with the hot oil. Add the smoked salmon and stir for a minute or two. When everything is heated through, taste for salt and pepper.

4   Serve the cod on a bed of cabbage sprinkled with fleur de sel, freshly ground pepper, and chervil.

1 slice smoked salmon, approximately 3 ounces (80 g.), trimmed into ¼-inch (0.5-cm.) morsels

Fleur de sel

1 teaspoon chervil leaves

PAN FRIED COD FILLETS WITH ZUCCHINI

Filets de cabillaud poêlés aux courgettes

SERVES   4
PREPARATION   15 minutes
COOKING   about 5 minutes

1   Heat 1 tablespoon oil and 1 teaspoon butter in a skillet over medium heat. When the butter foams, add the zucchini pieces and cook for 1–2 minutes per side over medium heat, stirring with a wooden spatula. Season with salt and pepper. Cover the skillet with aluminum foil to keep warm.

2   Wash the fish and dry with paper towels. Season both sides of each fillet with salt and pepper. Spread the flour in a dish (or right on your work surface) and coat the fish with it, shaking each piece gently to get rid of any excess.

3   Heat the remaining oil over rather high heat in a skillet large enough to hold all 4 fillets comfortably. Add 1 teaspoon butter. When the butter foams, place the fillets in the skillet. Brown for 3 minutes over medium-high heat and then turn them with a spatula and cook the second side for 2–3 minutes, depending on their thickness.

4   Arrange the fillets on a serving platter with the zucchini slices all around them.

5   Melt the remaining butter in the skillet over low heat. Add the lemon juice, stir to combine, and pour it over the cod. Scatter chopped parsley over the top.

3 tablespoons (20 cl.) neutral oil

5 tablespoons (80 g.) butter

4 small zucchini, washed and cut on the diagonal into slices ¼ inch (0.5 cm.) thick

Salt

Pepper

4 cod fillets, skinless or with skin on, about 4 ounces (160 g.) each

½ cup (50 g.) flour

Juice of 1 lemon

1 tablespoon chopped flat-leaf parsley

FRIED COD WITH AROMATIC HERBS

Cabillaud poêlé aux aromates

SERVES 4
PREPARATION 25 minutes
COOKING 5 minutes

1. Wash the zucchini and slice their skin off in strips, taking ¼ inch (0.5 cm.) of flesh with the skin. (You will not need the core of the zucchini for this dish.) Slice these strips into thin strips horizontally.

2. Bring 1 quart (1 l.) water to a boil with 1 tablespoon coarse salt. Boil the zucchini for 2 minutes. Remove with a skimmer to a colander and rinse under cold running water. Add the pepper strips to the colander.

3. Bring the water back to a boil and cook the fava beans for 3 minutes. With a skimmer, remove them to another colander and rinse under cold water until they have cooled. Drain.

4. Wash the fish and dry with paper towels. Sprinkle the fish all over with salt and pepper. Heat 2 tablespoons olive oil in a skillet over high heat and fry the fish for 3 minutes. Turn with a spatula or with tongs and cook for 2 minutes on the other side. The fish should become golden during cooking.

5. Set aside 2 teaspoons cold butter and dice the rest. Bring the soy sauce to a boil in a small saucepan. Turn off the heat and whisk in the diced butter.

6. Bring the salted water back to a boil. In the meantime, heat the 2 teaspoons butter in a skillet over medium heat. When it foams, add the mushroom slices and cook for 1–2 minutes. Season with salt and pepper.

7. Plunge the zucchini and peppers into the boiling water. After 10 seconds, add the fava beans and boil 30 seconds more.

8. Coat the cod with the soy-butter sauce, blanket it with hot vegetables, and sprinkle with parsley.

4 small or 2 medium zucchini
Coarse salt
8 bell peppers, 4 red and 4 green, peeled (page 130), seeded, and sliced into thin strips
2 ounces (50 g.) shucked and peeled fava beans (page 168)
4 cod fillets, skinless or with skin on, approximately 6 ounces (180 g.) each
Salt
Pepper
2 tablespoons olive oil
5 tablespoons (75 g.) butter, well chilled
½ cup (10 cl.) soy sauce
4 white mushrooms, trimmed, rinsed, and sliced into thin strips
1 tablespoon minced flat-leaf parsley

SALT COD PURÉE

Brandade de morue

SERVES 4
SOAKING 12–18 hours
COOKING 8 minutes
FINISHING 20 minutes

Brandade de morue has become something of a trendy dish in the United States in recent years. In France it is associated with the city of Nîmes; it is also made in Marseille, Toulon, and Nice, although in these cities garlic is used (which would never happen in Nîmes). The French writer Alphonse Daudet, a son of Nîmes who hosted "brandade dinners" in Paris in the nineteenth century, did not tolerate the addition of mashed potatoes, something that today is common practice.

2 pounds (1 kg.) salt cod fillets
1⅓ cups (30 cl.) heavy cream
1–2 cups (20–40 cl.) olive oil
White pepper

1   Choose salt cod fillets that are thick and very white. Rinse them under cold running water and then immerse them, skin side up, in a large bowl or pot filled with cold water. Leave them for 12 to 18 hours, depending on their thickness, to soak out the salt, changing the water two or three times during soaking.

2   Drain the fillets in a colander. Chop them into pieces the size of your palm. Put them in a pot, skin side up, with 3 quarts (3 l.) cold water. Put the pot over low heat and bring it almost to a boil. Lower the heat to cook the fish for 8 minutes without allowing the water to boil. Regularly remove foam from the surface with a skimmer that you rinse in a bowl of cold water after each passage.

3   Carefully drain the cod pieces by using a skimmer to lift them out of the hot water and into a colander. Allow them to cool a bit and then carefully remove the skin and bones while flaking the fish with the tips of your fingers.

4   Bring the cream to a boil in a small saucepan over high heat. Turn off the heat. In a large pot heat 4 tablespoons olive oil. Add the flaked fish and stir energetically with a wooden spatula over low heat until you have a fine, doughlike substance.

5   Still over low heat, add 2 tablespoons cream and stir well to combine. Add 1 tablespoon olive oil and stir to combine. Keep doing this, alternating cream and olive oil, until the mixture is saturated and incapable of absorbing more. This

should take about 15 minutes. Give it a few grinds of pepper and taste for salt. Add more salt and pepper if necessary.

6 The finished *brandade* should be a uniform purée, airy and very white. Heap it into a smooth dome on a deep dish and serve.

Smoked Haddock

Haddock is excellent smoked. Choose a plush-feeling salted haddock that is neither too dry nor too salty. If it is too salty (as is often the case now), it must be desalinated by soaking—in milk if possible—which will render it tender.

Commercial producers tend to oversalt haddock so that it will keep longer. Once upon a time one would keep the soaking milk and use it for cooking, but today, unless you are dealing with a particularly fine specimen, it is better to change the milk so that the finished dish is not too salty.

POACHED SMOKED HADDOCK WITH MELTED BUTTER
Haddock poché au beurre fondu

SERVES 4
SOAKING 30 minutes
COOKING 15 minutes

Serve this dish with creamed spinach and steamed potatoes.

1 Put the haddock skin side up in a dish as deep as the fish is thick and cover it with milk; leave to soak for 30 minutes.

2 Pour 2 cups (50 cl.) milk into a saucepan large enough to hold the fish. Add 1 quart (1 l.) water and the bay leaf; there should be just enough liquid to cover the fish when the haddock is eventually added to the pot. Bring the pot almost to a boil and add the fish, skin side up. Cover and leave to poach extremely gently for 15 minutes; do not allow the liquid to boil.

3 Serve with melted butter sauce or crème fraîche on the side. If you like, top the fish with a soft-boiled or poached egg. Garnish with minced parsley.

1½ pounds (750 g.) smoked haddock
2 cups (50 cl.) whole milk, plus more for soaking
1 bay leaf
1 teaspoon Melted Butter Sauce (page 44) or 1 tablespoon crème fraîche
4 eggs, poached (page 210) or soft-boiled (page 205) (optional)
1 teaspoon minced flat-leaf parsley

Herring

Although it is somewhat neglected today, herring was in the not so distant past a highly desirable delicacy. During the autumn months when it is carrying soft roe or eggs, it is at its gastronomic peak. After January—after it reproduces—its flesh is drier.

Fresh herring should exhibit firm flesh, gleaming scales, and red eyes and gills. It is extremely fragile; the loss of scales is one sign that it has gone bad. Herring at the most delicious point of its reproductive cycle will have thick sides where it is usually quite trim. Herring is sold without being gutted. A fishmonger should gut it without damaging the roe or eggs.

If you want to try to scale and gut fresh herring yourself, all you have to do is wipe it down one or two times. Remove its guts through the gills, wash it quickly, and wipe it dry. If you want to cook it whole, you can score it with small incisions every half inch or inch (1 or 2 cm.) down the backbone on each side. This will aid the cooking and allow fat to run off the fish. It is also possible to remove the fillets, but you might want to leave this (and the scaling and gutting) to the fishmonger.

GRILLED HERRING WITH MUSTARD

Harengs grillés à la moutarde

SERVES 4
PREPARATION 15 minutes
COOKING 10 minutes

1 Preheat the oven to 350°F/180°C. Rinse the herrings quickly and dry with paper towels. Make a series of shallow incisions along the back on each side. Season each herring with 2 pinches of salt and 1 pinch of pepper and brush with oil.

2 Heat a heavy grill pan on the cooktop. Put the fish on the hot grill for 3 minutes. Turn them and cook on the second side for 2 minutes. Remove them from the grill to a sheet pan and use a pastry brush to coat each herring with a film of mustard. Bake the herrings in the oven for 4 minutes.

4–8 small fresh herrings (depending on size; about 1 pound total), scaled, gutted, and fins removed
Salt
Pepper
Neutral oil
Mustard

MARINATED HERRING "DIEPPE STYLE"

Harengs marinés dieppoise

SERVES 4

PREPARATION 50 minutes

This dish must be prepared the day before you plan to serve it so the herrings have time to marinate.

Ask the fishmonger to remove the herrings' heads, guts, and scales.

1. Put the carrots, 1 teaspoon coarse salt, bouquet garni, and garlic in a pot with 1 quart (1 l.) water. Bring to a boil, cover, and simmer for 15 minutes. Add the onions, wine, and vinegar, and boil for 15 minutes. Turn off the heat, stir in the peppercorns and star anise, and leave to infuse and cool.

2. Put the herrings in a saucepan and cover them with the cooled marinade. Gradually bring the broth to a near boil and poach the fish for 10 minutes. Do not allow the liquid to bubble.

3. Let the herrings cool in their marinade and then refrigerate overnight, still in the marinade.

2 medium carrots, peeled and sliced into rather thin rounds, less than ¼ inch (0.5 cm.) thick

Coarse salt

1 bouquet garni (1 bay leaf, 1 small stalk celery, 3 stems parsley, 1 sprig thyme, and 1 bay leaf, wrapped and tied in a leek leaf)

1 clove garlic

2 medium onions, peeled and cut into strips ⅛ inch (3 mm.) thick

1 cup (25 cl.) white wine

2 tablespoons distilled white vinegar

10 peppercorns

1 star anise

4–8 small herrings (depending on size; about 1 pound total), heads, guts, and scales removed

ROAST HERRING IN MUSTARD SAUCE

Harengs rôtis sauce moutarde

SERVES 4
PREPARATION 15 minutes
COOKING 12 minutes

1 Preheat the oven to 440°F/220°C. Remove the scales from the herrings by rubbing them with paper towels. Cut off their fins and remove their guts through the gills without removing the roe or eggs. Rinse them quickly and dry with paper towels. Make shallow incisions along the backbone on each side.

2 Spread a thin layer of coarse salt on a sheet pan. Lay the herrings on top of it and brush them with softened butter.

3 Put the shallot and wine in a small saucepan. Bring to a gentle bubble and allow to simmer; turn off the heat when only 1 tablespoon of liquid remains. Prepare the béchamel sauce and add it to the shalloty wine. Bring to a boil for just a few moments and then stir in the mustard off the heat with a wooden spatula. Taste for salt and pepper.

4 Bake the herrings for 6 minutes. Flip them over and cook for 6 minutes on the other side.

5 Remove the herrings from the sheet pan and use a pastry brush to sweep away any coarse salt that has stuck to them. Serve with the sauce on the side.

4–8 small herrings (depending on size; about 1 pound total)
Coarse salt
2 teaspoons butter, softened
1 shallot, minced
1 cup (25 cl.) dry white wine
1⅔ cups (40 cl.) béchamel sauce (page 51)
2 tablespoons mustard
Salt
Pepper

John Dory

An oval-shaped coastal rockfish, bronze with silvery flecks, the John Dory is notable for its large head and the black markings on each side of its body. In France the fish is called *Saint-pierre* (Saint Peter). Legend sees in these black marks the fingerprints of Saint Peter, who grabbed the fish to throw it back into the water. The story also maintains that the apostle removed a piece of money from the fish's mouth on instructions from Jesus.

The firm white flesh of this fish is easy to remove from the bone and therefore lends itself to any number of culinary applications. John Dory is one of the finest fish in the sea.

JOHN DORY WITH TOMATOES AND OLIVES _____

Saint-pierre aux tomates et olives

SERVES 4

PREPARATION 30 minutes

COOKING 25–30 minutes

Ask the fishmonger to remove the fish's head, guts, and skin.

1 Preheat the oven to 350°F/180°C.

2 Rinse the fish under cold running water and dry with paper towels. Season with salt and pepper on both sides. Make small incisions in the fish at regular intervals. Insert about two-thirds of the olive slivers and 16 half leaves of basil. Paint the fish on both sides with 1 tablespoon olive oil.

3 Peel the lemon completely by slicing away its rind and all of its white pith, exposing the juicy yellow flesh. Slice the flesh thinly and remove the seeds.

4 Bring the chicken stock to a boil in a small saucepan.

5 Lay 6 of the fennel stalks in a baking dish. Lay the John Dory on top of them and top it with the tomatoes, fennel bulb, lemon slices, garlic, and the remaining olive slivers and basil. Season with salt and pepper and lay the rest of the wild fennel on top. Pour 4 tablespoons olive oil over everything and then pour the hot chicken stock over as well.

5 Bake for 15 minutes. Use a large spoon to baste the top of the fish with the juices collected in the dish. Bake 10–15 minutes more. The fish is ready when the flesh is white and opaque and the fillet is easily detached from the bone.

1 John Dory, about 3 pounds (1.5 kg.), head, guts, and skin removed

Salt

Pepper

30 small black olives, preferably Niçoise, pits removed and quartered lengthwise

1 bunch basil

Olive oil

1 lemon

2 cups (50 cl.) chicken stock (page 36 or store-bought)

12 stalks wild fennel

6 medium tomatoes, peeled, seeded (page 124), and quartered

1 fennel bulb, thick outer layers discarded and remaining heart quartered

6 cloves garlic, peeled and degermed (page 122)

JOHN DORY WITH ALMONDS AND CONFIT TOMATOES

Saint-pierre aux amandes et tomates confits

SERVES   4
PREPARATION   1½ hours
COOKING   10–15 minutes

Ask the fishmonger to remove the John Dory's head, guts, and skin. Have him remove the gills and ask him to give you the head to take home.

1   Preheat the oven to 175°F/80°C.
2   Brush a small baking dish with 1 tablespoon olive oil. Set the tomatoes on it side by side and dust them lightly with salt, confectioners' sugar, and pepper. Add to the dish 4 sprigs thyme and 4 cloves garlic. Pour 1 tablespoon olive oil over the whole and bake for 1½ hours.
3   When the tomatoes have finished baking, allow them to cool. Remove the thyme. Raise the oven temperature to 350°F/180°C.
4   Season the fish with salt and pepper, evenly coating both sides. Pour ½ cup plus 2 tablespoons (12 cl.) olive oil into a large baking dish and lay the fish in its center. Scatter around it the onion halves, the remaining garlic halves, lemon quarters, and almonds. Roll each baked tomato quarter up and arrange them around the fish. Add the parsley and remaining sprigs of thyme. Sprinkle with a pinch of crushed black pepper.
5   Dice the butter and dot it on the fish. Bake for 15 minutes and then pour the stock over. Bake 10–15 minutes more, until the flesh is opaque and white and easy to pull from the bone. Serve in the baking dish.

¾ cup (15 cl.) olive oil
4 tomatoes, peeled, seeded (page 124), and quartered
Salt
Confectioners' sugar
Pepper
8 sprigs fresh thyme
8 cloves garlic, peeled and sliced in half lengthwise
1 John Dory, 3 pounds (1.5 kg.), head, guts, and skin removed
8 small new or cipollini onions, sliced in half
2 lemons, quartered
3 ounces (90 g.) fresh almonds, skinned
1 tablespoon chopped parsley
Crushed black pepper
2 tablespoons butter
1⅓ cups (30 cl.) fish stock (page 40 or store-bought)

JOHN DORY À LA PROVENÇALE

Saint-pierre aux arômes de Provence

SERVES 4

PREPARATION 1½ hours

COOKING 15 minutes

Ask the fishmonger to remove the John Dory's head, guts, and fins.

1   Preheat the oven to 175°F/80°C.

2   Brush a small baking dish with 1 tablespoon olive oil. Lay the tomato quarters in the dish and dust lightly with salt, confectioners' sugar, and pepper. Add the thyme and 2 cloves garlic, split in half. Pour another tablespoon of olive oil over the top and bake for 1½ hours.

3   Bring 1 quart (1 l.) water to a boil with 2 teaspoons coarse salt. Prepare a large bowl half-filled with water and a tray of ice cubes. When the pot is bubbling, boil the fennel for 5 minutes. Remove it to the ice water with a skimmer. Leave for 2 minutes to cool and then drain in a colander. Do the same with the remaining garlic cloves, then the onions, then the shallots, leaving them in the boiling salted water for 3 minutes each and using new water every time. Shock each vegetable in the ice water after cooking and put them all aside in the same colander.

4   When the tomatoes have finished cooking, remove from the oven and raise the oven temperature to 350°F/180°C.

5   Melt 1 tablespoon butter in a sauté pan or skillet. When it foams, add the fennel, shallots, onions, and garlic, and cook for 5 minutes over low heat, stirring with a wooden spoon.

6   In the meantime, peel the lemon completely by cutting away its skin and white pith, exposing the juicy yellow flesh. Chop it into small dice, remove the seeds, and set it aside.

7   Rinse the fish under cold running water. Season it with salt and pepper on both sides. Butter a baking dish and lay the fish in it. Put the fennel, shallots, onions, and garlic all around the fish. Sprinkle with a good-sized pinch of crushed black pepper and add salt lightly if you think it necessary. Add the star anise and drizzle with 3 tablespoons olive oil. Bake for 7 minutes.

5 tablespoons olive oil

4 medium tomatoes, peeled, seeded (page 124), and quartered

Salt

Confectioners' sugar

Pepper

4 sprigs thyme

8 cloves garlic, peeled and degermed (page 122)

Coarse salt

12 baby fennel bulbs

6 small white onions, peeled and sliced in half

12 shallots, peeled and sliced in half

1 tablespoon plus 1 teaspoon butter for greasing the dish

1 lemon

1 John Dory, about 3 pounds (1.5 kg.) or 2 fish weighing about 1¼ to 1½ pounds (600–800 g.) each, heads, guts, and fins removed

Crushed black pepper

2 star anise pods

(continued)

8 Bring the broth or consommé to a boil in a small saucepan and keep it at a simmer. When the fish has baked for 7 minutes, baste it with its cooking juices and then pour the hot consommé or broth over the whole dish. Bake 8 minutes more.

9 Heat the baked tomatoes, diced lemon, and olives in a small saucepan over low heat, stirring with a wooden spoon. When you remove the fish from the oven, baste it and the vegetables with its cooking juices and then top it with the tomato mixture. Garnish with basil leaves and serve.

2 cups (40 cl.) chicken broth or consommé (pages 77 and 80 or store-bought)

3 tablespoons Niçoise olives, pitted and chopped into small dice

1 bunch basil, leaves only

Mackerel and Baby Mackerel

The mackerel (like its little sister, which in French is called *lisette*) is a fragile fish and must be eaten very fresh. Never buy mackerel with an open or pierced belly, and cook them as soon as possible after buying.

BABY MACKEREL WITH WHITE WINE

Lisettes au vin blanc

SERVES 4
PREPARATION 25 minutes
COOKING 2 hours
The mackerel must be prepared the night before you plan to eat it.

1 The night before: Wash the fish and dry with paper towels. Bring 2 quarts (2 l.) water to a boil in a pot. Add the carrots, onions, garlic, bouquet garni, tarragon, peppercorns, coriander seeds, cumin seeds, cloves, and 3 pinches of salt. Bring to a simmer and allow to bubble gently 15 minutes, covered, over low heat.

2 In the meantime, season each mackerel on both sides with 1 good-sized pinch of salt and a dash of pepper.

3 When the broth has simmered for 15 minutes, add the white wine and vinegar. Bring back to the beginning of a boil and

8 baby mackerel (about 1½ pounds/0.75 kg. total), heads removed and gutted (ask the fishmonger to do this)

4 carrots, peeled and sliced on the diagonal into rounds ⅛ inch (3 mm.) thick

2 medium onions, peeled and sliced into thin rounds

turn off the heat. Slip the fish into the broth and allow to rest for 2 hours.

4   Refrigerate the pot overnight. The next day, discard the bouquet garni and serve the mackerel with the vegetables and broth on the side.

4 cloves garlic, degermed (page 122) and coarsely chopped

1 bouquet garni (2 sprigs thyme, 1 bay leaf, and 5 stems parsley, wrapped and tied in a green leek leaf)

5 sprigs tarragon

$\frac{1}{2}$ tablespoon black peppercorns

$\frac{1}{2}$ tablespoon coriander seeds

$\frac{1}{2}$ tablespoon cumin seeds

2 whole cloves

Salt

Pepper

1 cup (20 cl.) dry white wine

1 cup (20 cl.) distilled white vinegar

GRILLED MACKEREL WITH MUSTARD SAUCE _____

Maquereaux grillés sauce moutarde

SERVES   4
PREPARATION   15 minutes
COOKING   12 minutes

1   Preheat the oven to 350°F/180°C. Prepare the béchamel sauce.

2   Put the shallot and wine in a small saucepan. Bring gently to a boil, then lower the heat and hold at a simmer. Keep an eye on it as the fish cooks, turning off the heat when the liquid has bubbled down to about 1 tablespoon of thick sauce.

3   Rinse the fish and dry them with paper towels. Season with salt and pepper, and roll them in the peanut oil. Get a cast-iron grill pan good and hot and then lower the heat. Grill the mackerel for 4 minutes on one side and then 4 minutes on the other. Remove them to a sheet pan and bake for 4 minutes.

4   When the shalloty wine has cooked down to 1 tablespoon,

$1\frac{2}{3}$ cups (40 cl.) béchamel sauce (page 51)

1 shallot, peeled and minced

$\frac{2}{3}$ cup (10 cl.) dry white wine

8–12 small mackerel (depending on size; about $1\frac{1}{2}$ pounds/0.75 kg. total), gutted

Salt

Pepper

$1\frac{1}{2}$ tablespoons peanut oil

1 tablespoon mustard

add the béchamel. Bring it to a boil and then turn off the heat and incorporate the mustard, stirring with a spatula. Taste for salt and pepper.

5   Arrange the mackerel on a serving plate and serve the sauce on the side.

Monkfish

Because its head is so unsightly, monkfish is usually sold headless, sometimes as "monkfish tail." In France it is also called *gigot de mer* after a leg of lamb, or *gigot,* because of its shape and its especially firm flesh. A piece of cartilage runs through a monkfish tail, but it is otherwise without bones.

To make sure monkfish is fresh, check to see that its fillets are rounded, dense, and glossy, not shrinking away. The flesh should be very white but showing a delicate network of small blood vessels, and the skin should be glistening.

BAKED MONKFISH

Lotte au four

SERVES   4
PREPARATION   15 minutes
COOKING   8 minutes

1   Bring a small saucepan of water to a boil. Slice 2 of the garlic cloves into shards ⅛ inch (2 mm.) thick. Boil the garlic pieces for 10 seconds and drain.

2   Preheat the oven to 450°F/230°C. Wash and dry the monkfish. Stud the monkfish with garlic by fitting the slivers into small incisions made with the point of a knife all over the fish. Season the fish with 1 teaspoon salt and 2 pinches of pepper.

3   Melt 3 tablespoons butter in an oven-safe pot or saucepan. Add the fish and the 3 remaining cloves garlic to the pot and brown lightly on all sides over low heat, about 30 seconds per side. Add the thyme to the pot and put it in the oven and

5 cloves garlic, peeled and degermed (page 122)
2 monkfish fillets, about 10 ounces (300 g.) each
Salt
Pepper
3 tablespoons butter
5 sprigs thyme
1 tablespoon wine vinegar

bake for 5 minutes. Add the vinegar to the pot and bake 3 minutes more. The monkfish is cooked when it is opaque throughout—no longer translucent at the center—and can easily be pulled away from its central piece of cartilage.

4   When the fish is cooked, remove the fillets from the cartilaginous dorsal spine, chop them into pieces, and serve with the cooking juices.

MONKFISH WITH GARLIC AND FENNEL CREAM   _____

Lotte à l'ail, crème de fenouil

SERVES   4

PREPARATION   40 minutes

COOKING   9 minutes

Ask the fishmonger to fillet the fish and to chop its dorsal spine into 4 pieces.

1   Prepare Baked Monkfish without adding vinegar or garlic cloves to the pot in the third step. (The fish itself should still be studded with garlic slivers.)

2   Wash the fish's cartilaginous dorsal spine. Melt ½ tablespoon butter in a saucepan over medium heat and add the onion and fennel. Season with a heaping ¼ teaspoon salt and 1 pinch of pepper. Cook for 5 minutes, stirring with a wooden spoon. Add the pieces of the dorsal spine and cook 3 minutes more. Add the wine and let it bubble away for 3 minutes. Add the crème fraîche and simmer for 5 minutes. Remove the bones and blend the sauce in a blender or food processor until it is smooth. Put it through a fine strainer into a saucepan. Cover and keep the sauce warm over very low heat.

3   Dice 2 teaspoons chilled butter. Add it to the sauce bit by bit, stirring constantly, until all the butter has melted and the sauce is rich and creamy. Taste for salt and pepper.

4   Coat the fish with the sauce and serve the rest on the side in a sauceboat.

1 recipe Baked Monkfish (page 280) but without the addition of garlic and vinegar as it cooks

½ tablespoon plus 2 teaspoons butter, chilled

1 large onion, peeled and sliced into thin rounds (less than ¼ inch/0.5 cm. thick)

1 large fennel bulb, trimmed and sliced into thin rounds (less than ¼ inch/0.5 cm. thick)

Salt

Pepper

1 cup (25 cl.) dry white wine (preferably Chardonnay)

⅔ cup (15 cl.) crème fraîche

MONKFISH WITH TOMATOES, ZUCCHINI, AND THYME _____

Lotte aux tomates, courgettes, et thym

SERVES   4
PREPARATION   15 minutes
COOKING   25 minutes

Instead of monkfish, you could use other white fish fillets, such as porgy or halibut.

1   Wash the fish and dry it with paper towels. Preheat the oven to 350°F/180°C.
2   Spread the onions and shallots in a sheet pan and toss them with 1 tablespoon olive oil. Add the bay leaves, 5 sprigs thyme, 2 pinches of salt and 1 pinch of pepper. Lay the fish on top of the vegetables. Spread the tomatoes, zucchini, and lemon over and around the fish. Pour the wine over all and drizzle with 2 tablespoons olive oil and add 5 sprigs thyme. Season evenly with ½ teaspoon salt and a scant ½ teaspoon pepper.
3   Bake for 25 minutes. The fish is cooked when it is opaque all the way through, even at the center, and the flesh is easy to pull away from the central cartilage spine.

1¼ pounds (600 g.) monkfish, skinned and chopped into 4 pieces
2 medium onions, peeled and sliced into rounds ⅛ inch (3 mm.) thick
6 shallots, peeled and chopped in half
Olive oil
2 bay leaves, crumbled
1 small bunch fresh thyme
Salt
Pepper
4 medium tomatoes, sliced into thin rounds
4 small zucchini, peeled in strips lengthwise, so that stripes of peel and flesh alternate, and sliced into thin rounds (less than ¼ inch/0.5 cm.)
1 organic lemon, washed and sliced into rounds ⅛ inch (3 mm.) thick
2 cups (50 cl.) dry white wine, preferably Chardonnay

MONKFISH IN A SALT CRUST _____

Lotte en croûte de sel

SERVES   4
PREPARATION   10 minutes
COOKING   45 minutes

1   Preheat the oven to 460°F/240°C. Carefully wash the monkfish and pat it dry with paper towels.
2   Spread a bed of coarse salt about 1 inch (2 or 3 cm.) thick in a sheet pan. Lay the fish on top of it and cover it with more

1¼ pounds (600 g.) monkfish
2 pounds (1 kg.) coarse salt
Pepper
Olive oil

salt; it should be completely buried in salt. Sprinkle it with a few drops of water. Bake for 45 minutes.

3 Bring the fish to the table and shatter the salt crust. Be careful not to let salt fall all over the fish. If necessary, brush away any salt that does fall. When the fish is quite revealed, remove the skin and slice away the fillets. Sprinkle the fillets with pepper, drizzle with a little olive oil, and serve.

PURSLANE SALAD WITH ROAST MONKFISH CHEEKS _____

Joues de lotte rôties en salade

SERVES 4
PREPARATION 25 minutes
COOKING 2–3 minutes

Purslane is a hardy garden green cultivated in the north of France, in Belgium, and in the United States. Its leaves and young stems have a slightly tangy flavor.

2 tablespoons shrimp broth (page 40)
1 tablespoon wine vinegar
Salt
Pepper
4 tablespoons olive oil
8 monkfish cheeks
$\frac{1}{2}$ pound (200 g.) purslane, washed and dried
4 medium tomatoes, peeled, seeded, and diced (page 124)
2 ounces (60 g.) green olives (preferably picholine), pits removed and sliced lengthwise into $\frac{1}{8}$-inch (3-mm.) slivers

1 In a blender or food processor, blend the shrimp broth and vinegar with 2 pinches of salt and 1 pinch of pepper. Add 2 tablespoons olive oil bit by bit, running the machine the whole time. Refrigerate the mixture.

2 Season the monkfish cheeks with salt and pepper on both sides. Heat 2 tablespoons olive oil in a skillet. When it is hot, brown the monkfish cheeks lightly on both sides over low heat; they should stay soft and toothsome, so do not overcook into toughness. Put them aside on a rack, covered with aluminum foil to keep them warm.

3 Toss the purslane with the shrimp vinaigrette. Add the tomatoes and olives and mix well.

4 Heap the salad on a platter and scatter the still-warm monkfish cheeks all over.

MONKFISH WITH BELL PEPPERS AND TAPENADE SAUCE ___

Lotte aux poivrons, sauce tapenade

SERVES   4
PREPARATION   20 minutes
COOKING   2–3 minutes

1   Bring the cream to a simmer in a small saucepan. Add the tapenade and continue to cook, stirring well with a wooden spoon. Just before the mixture boils, add a pinch of pepper and turn off the heat. Set the saucepan aside off the heat.

2   Heat 1 tablespoon olive oil in a saucepan over low heat. Add the bell peppers, season with ½ teaspoon salt and a pinch of pepper, and cook for 5 minutes, still over low heat, stirring. The peppers should not lose all their crunch. Taste for salt and pepper.

3   Heat 2 tablespoons olive oil in a skillet. When it is very hot, cook the monkfish slices over medium-high heat until they are opaque throughout (about 2–3 minutes total), turning once during cooking.

4   Lay the cooked monkfish slices on a plate and season them on both sides with a pinch of salt and a dash of pepper. Reheat the sauce over very low heat for 2 minutes.

5   Stack the peppers in the middle of a heated platter, arrange the monkfish pieces in a ring around them, and pour the sauce all around.

¼ cup (5 cl.) heavy cream
2 tablespoons (30 g.) tapenade
    (page 136 or store-bought)
Pepper
3 tablespoons olive oil
2 green bell peppers and 2 red
    bell peppers, seeded and
    chopped into strips 1 inch
    by ½ in. (2 cm. by 1 cm.)
Salt
8 pieces monkfish, about
    3 ounces (90 g.) each,
    sliced into slabs ½–1 inch
    (1–2 cm.) thick

MONKFISH FRICASSÉE WITH MUSHROOMS ———————

Fricassée de lotte aux champignons

SERVES 4
PREPARATION 20 minutes
COOKING 15 minutes

1 Rinse the fish under cold running water and dry with paper towels. Preheat the oven to 400°F/200°C.

2 Heat 1 tablespoon olive oil in an ovenproof saucepan or pot. Add the butter and when it melts, cook the onions over low heat for 2 minutes, stirring with a wooden spoon. Do not allow the onions to color. Add the mushrooms, stirring well to coat them in fat. Cook for 5 minutes, still over low heat, and then stir in salt and pepper to taste. Turn off the heat.

3 Heat 2 tablespoons olive oil in a skillet large enough to hold all the fish slices. Lay them in the skillet without overlapping and cook for 2 minutes over low heat. Flip and cook the other side for 2 minutes.

4 Remove the fish to the saucepan of onions and mushrooms, but keep the heat on under the skillet. Stir the cooking juices in the skillet, scraping the bottom, and simmer for 3 minutes. Add the wine, turn the heat to high, and boil briskly for 3 minutes.

5 Put the saucepan with the fish into the oven. Meanwhile, lower the heat under the skillet and stir in the cream; simmer for 2 minutes. Taste for salt and pepper and sprinkle with parsley. Remove the pot from the oven and serve the fish with the cream sauce.

¾ pound (400 g.) monkfish fillet cut in 8 slices (ask the fishmonger to slice the fish)
3 tablespoons olive oil
1 tablespoon butter
4 small new or cipollini onions, peeled and minced
½ pound (200 g.) very small white button mushrooms, trimmed, cleaned, and sliced lengthwise into halves or thirds
Salt
Pepper
½ cup (10 cl.) dry white wine
¾ cup (20 cl.) heavy cream
1 tablespoon minced flat-leaf parsley

Pollack ———————

Two large, round Atlantic fish similar in shape to whiting are called pollack. Yellow pollack (which is also called colin) is smaller and firmer-fleshed than black pollack (which is also called black cod). Black pollack is a dark coppery color, and yellow pollack has a gray belly with a gray-green sheen. This lean fish is usually found in steaks or fillets; it can be poached, baked, or cooked in a sauce.

YELLOW POLLACK WITH CABBAGE

Lieu jaune au chou

SERVES 4

PREPARATION 20 minutes

COOKING 10 minutes

1   Put 1 quart (1 l.) water on to boil in a large pot fitted with a steamer basket.

2   Season each side of each piece of fish with a large pinch of salt and a pinch of pepper. Put each piece on a square of plastic wrap; sprinkle with thyme and drizzle 1 scant tablespoon olive oil total over all 4 pieces. Fold the plastic wrap over the fish to seal the packets tightly. Set aside.

3   Dice the cold butter. Bring the vinegar to a boil in a small saucepan and boil for 2 minutes. Add the stock and bring to a boil. Little by little, stirring with a spatula, add the diced butter. Taste for salt and pepper and turn off the heat.

4   Put the fish packets in the steamer basket and pack the cabbage all around them. Season with 3 pinches of salt and 1 pinch of pepper. Cover and cook for 10 minutes.

5   Reheat the vinegar-butter sauce over gentle heat. Remove the fish from their wrapping and lay them on a bed of cabbage. Coat with the warmed sauce and garnish with onions and chives.

4 pieces yellow pollack, about 5 ounces (150 g.) each, bone in, skin on, and scales removed

Salt

Pepper

1 small bunch thyme

1 tablespoon olive oil

1 tablespoon very cold butter

¼ cup sherry vinegar

¼ cup fish stock (page 40 or store-bought)

16 cabbage leaves, blanched (page 556) and cut into strips 1 inch by ½ inch (2 cm. by 1 cm.)

8 new or cipollini onions, peeled and sliced into rounds ⅛ inch (3 mm.) thick

2 small bunches chives, snipped into ⅛-inch (3-mm.) sections

Red Mullet

Red mullet is an especially prized fish thanks to its delicate flesh and refined taste. Unfortunately, it is seldom available in the United States. Red mullet from the Mediterranean is much better than the variety found off the West African coast. Striped red mullet is a rockfish and should not be confused with sea robin, which is much more common and has a completely unrelated, undistinguished flavor.

A fresh red mullet is a lovely shade of pink, more or less intense, with taut skin, firm flesh, a solid belly, and clear, bulging eyes.

Red mullet is not always gutted before it is cooked. For this reason it is sometimes called in France *la bécasse de la mer*, "the woodcock of the sea," after the bird traditionally cooked with its insides intact.

Although it is full of bones, you can cook red mullet whole. Just fry it in a skillet, making a few shallow incisions in the fish's skin and putting some aromatics (thyme, fennel, rosemary) in the pan. The fish's flesh will take on the flavors of the aromatics.

RED MULLET FILLETS WITH SAFFRON CREAM _____
Filets de rougets à la crème de safran

SERVES   4

PREPARATION AND COOKING   20 minutes

Ask the fishmonger to fillet and scale the fish for you. Have him cut the backbone into pieces and take the heads and bones home to use in this recipe.

1   Bring the stock to a boil over high heat and let it bubble away for 15 minutes. Add the saffron, stir well, and then add the cream. Lower the heat to medium, bring back to a boil, and cook 10 minutes more. Taste for salt and pepper.

2   Rinse and dry the fish fillets. Prepare a plate lined with paper towels. Heat the olive oil in a skillet. When it is quite hot, add the fillets to the pan, skin side down, and sear for approximately 30 seconds over high heat. As soon as their edges begin to turn white, turn the fillets over and cook 30 seconds more on the other side. The fish is cooked when it is opaque white throughout. Remove it to the paper towel–lined plate to get rid of some of the excess fat.

3   Put the fillets on a platter. Pour a ring of saffron-cream sauce around them and put the rest in a sauceboat to serve on the side. Sprinkle with fleur de sel, a grinding of pepper, and the chervil leaves.

1½ cups (35 cl.) fish stock (page 40 or store-bought)
Dash of powdered saffron
½ cup (10 cl.) heavy cream
Salt
Pepper
Fillets of 6 red mullets (each whole fish weighing 2–2½ pounds/1 kg.), scaled
2 tablespoons olive oil
Fleur de sel
1 teaspoon chervil leaves

RED MULLET FILLETS WITH OLIVE OIL EMULSION

Filets de rouget à l'émulsion d'huile d'olive

SERVES 4
PREPARATION about 40 minutes
COOKING 1 minute

1. Rinse the fillets under cold running water and dry with paper towels. Carefully rinse the heads and bones.

2. Heat 2 tablespoons olive oil in a saucepan. Add the onion and shallot and cook for 3 minutes over low heat, stirring with a wooden spoon. Add the fish heads and bones, stir, and cook for 3 minutes. Add the bouquet garni and enough water to cover everything in the pot. Add a pinch of coarse salt and bring to a boil, then simmer over low heat for 5 minutes. Put this stock through a fine strainer into a small saucepan. Bring to a boil and allow the stock to bubble away until only about 5 tablespoons of it remain. Turn off the heat.

3. Squeeze the basil leaves hard to bruise them and then add them to the small saucepan of stock. Cover and leave to infuse for 5 minutes. Put it through a fine strainer again, into a bowl, and then pour the strained contents of the bowl back into the saucepan.

4. Reheat this infused stock over low heat. Begin to add ¼ cup plus 2 tablespoons (10 cl.) olive oil in a very thin stream, whisking energetically and constantly. Then whisk in the butter. Taste for salt and pepper. Add the tomato, minced basil, and lemon juice. Leave the saucepan over very low heat while you cook the fish.

5. Heat two skillets, 1 tablespoon of olive oil in each one, over a rather high flame for 1 minute. Place the red mullet fillets gently in the hot skillets, skin side down. Season the exposed sides with salt and pepper and cook for 30 seconds. Flip the fish with a spatula or tongs and cook 30 seconds more, seasoning the now-exposed skin side with salt and pepper.

6. Coat a platter or 4 plates with the basil sauce, top with the hot fillets, and serve immediately.

Fillets of 4 red mullets (each whole fish weighing 2–2½ pounds/1 kg.), scaled, plus the heads and backbones of the fish
½ cup plus 2 tablespoons (15 cl.) olive oil
½ medium onion, peeled and sliced into thin rounds
1 shallot, peeled and sliced into thin rounds
1 bouquet garni (½ bay leaf, 4 sprigs thyme, and 5 stems parsley, tied together)
Coarse salt
1 handful basil leaves
1 teaspoon butter
Salt
Pepper
1 tomato, peeled, seeded, and diced (page 124)
1 tablespoon minced basil
Juice of ½ lemon

RED MULLET ON THE BONE WITH CROUTONS

Rougets barbets à l'arête

SERVES 4
PREPARATION 10 minutes
COOKING 15 minutes

1   Preheat the oven to 400°F/200°C. Wash the fish by wiping them with paper towels. Set the livers aside. Season the inside of each fish with 2 good pinches of salt and 1 pinch of pepper. Put 2 sprigs rosemary, 2 sprigs thyme, and 4 fronds fennel inside each fish.

2   Finely chop the remaining thyme, rosemary, and fennel. Mix the coarse salt with 1 tablespoon of each chopped herb and spread a little bed of this herbed salt on a sheet pan. Lay the fish atop the salt and drizzle it with ½ tablespoon olive oil. Bake for 15 minutes. The fish is cooked when the flesh along the backbone is white and opaque and easy to pull from the bone.

3   While the fish bakes, use a fork to mash its liver with the chopped basil, ½ tablespoon olive oil, a pinch of salt, and a pinch of pepper. Toast or grill the baguette slices, spread them with the liver mixture, and set them on a sheet pan. When the fish come out of the oven, bake these croutons for 1 minute. Serve the fish with the croutons.

2 fat red mullets, about
    ½ pound (250 g.) each,
    gutted but not scaled, with
    their livers
Salt
Pepper
1 small bunch rosemary
1 small bunch thyme
1 small bunch fennel fronds
1 pound (500 g.) coarse salt
1 tablespoon olive oil
1 teaspoon chopped basil
8 slices baguette

NIÇOISE RED MULLET WITH OLIVES

Rougets aux olives, à la niçoise

SERVES 4
PREPARATION 20 minutes
COOKING 15 minutes

Ask the fishmonger to scale and gut the fish but leave their livers inside.

1 Bring 1 quart (1 l.) water to a boil. When it bubbles, plunge in 1 of the lemons and boil for 10 seconds before removing with a skimmer. When it has cooled a little, slice 4 thin rounds, removing the seeds, and set aside.

2 Heat 4 tablespoons olive oil in a large sauté pan or saucepan. Add the onions and a pinch of salt. Cook over low heat for 3 minutes, stirring with a wooden spoon. Add the tomatoes, garlic, and thyme. Raise the heat to high and cook for 10 minutes, stirring.

3 Preheat the oven to 350°F/160°C.

4 Spread the flour over a cutting board or work surface. Rinse the fish under cold running water and dry them completely with paper towels. Roll them in the flour and leave them side by side.

5 Heat 3 tablespoons olive oil in a large skillet over a high flame for 1 minute. Lay 4 of the fish gently in the skillet, head first and tail away from you to avoid splattering yourself with oil. Cook over high heat for 30 seconds and then turn them with a wooden spatula and sear the second side for 30 seconds. Remove them carefully to a baking dish. Cook the other 4 fish the same way. Lay all the fish side by side on the baking dish. Sprinkle pepper and salt lightly on both sides of each fish.

6 Cover the fish with the tomato sauce and arrange the anchovy fillets and lemon slices on top. Scatter the capers and olives over the whole and bake for about 10 minutes. The fish is cooked when it is no longer translucent and is easy to flake from the bone.

7 Remove the dish from the oven and pour the juice of the remaining lemon over the fish. Wipe clean the sides of the dish. Sprinkle the fish with basil leaves and serve right away.

2 small organic lemons, washed
½ cup (10 cl.) olive oil
2 small white new onions, peeled and minced
Salt
4 medium tomatoes, very ripe, peeled, seeded, and diced (page 124)
1 clove garlic, peeled and minced
1 teaspoon fresh thyme leaves
1 cup (140 g.) flour
8 red mullets, about 3–5 ounces (100–150 g.) each, scaled and gutted
Pepper
8 oil-packed anchovy fillets
3 ounces (80 g.) capers
3 ounces (80 g.) pitted Niçoise olives
1 bunch basil, leaves only

Salmon

This fish is, of course, extremely popular, but the ubiquitous farm-raised variety lacks much of the appeal of wild salmon, which is still hard to come by. Choose a lean fish; the white stripes or parts on its sides should be thin.

It is traditional to poach salmon—the whole fish if it is small, or steaks if it is large—and to serve it with mousseline sauce (page 52) or *beurre blanc* (page 46) on the side. Cold salmon can be accompanied by mayonnaise (page 55). You might also braise salmon in Champagne or red wine.

But it is more common today to sauté salmon fillets or to roast them in the oven or in packets. It is imperative that salmon be cooked gently—almost undercooked, even, and never dry—if it is to keep its appealing, yielding texture.

PAN FRIED SALMON WITH CABBAGE

Saumon poêlé au chou

SERVES 4
PREPARATION 15 minutes
COOKING 4 minutes

1 Melt 1½ tablespoons butter in a saucepan or pot large enough to hold all the cabbage. When it is hot, add the cabbage and cook for 3 minutes over low heat, stirring with a wooden spoon. Cover and cook for 5 minutes; the cabbage should soften but should still have some crunch. Stir in 4 tablespoons crème fraîche and cook for 1 minute. Taste for salt and pepper. Remove the pot from the heat but keep it warm.

2 Melt ½ tablespoon butter in a small saucepan with a pinch of salt. When it is hot, sauté the shallot for 3 minutes over medium heat, stirring. Add the wine and vinegar, bring to a boil, and then lower the heat and simmer for 5 minutes. Remove the saucepan from the heat and gradually whisk in the remaining cream. Stir in the 6 tablespoons chilled, diced butter. The sauce should be glossy and smooth. Taste and add salt and pepper if necessary. Cover the sauce and keep it over very low heat.

1 stick (¼ pound/120 g.) butter, 6 tablespoons of it diced and chilled

1 green cabbage, about 1½ pounds (750 g.), leaves separated and blanched (page 556)

1⅓ cups (15 cl.) crème fraîche

Salt

Pepper

1 shallot, peeled and minced

¼ cup (5 cl.) dry white wine, preferably Chardonnay

¼ cup (5 cl.) sherry vinegar

(continued)

3   Rinse the salmon and dry it with paper towels. With a sharp knife, score a crosshatch pattern on each piece; you should cut through the skin and just barely into the flesh. Season both sides of each fillet with a generous pinch of salt and a pinch of pepper.

4   Heat the oil in a large skillet over a high flame. When it is hot, put the salmon in the pan, skin side down, and cook for 3 minutes, until the skin is crispy. Flip the fillets and cook for 1 minute on the other side. If you like your salmon rare, the heart of the fillet should be barely warm and vividly red, not opaque at all. If you like your fish well done, leave it 1 or 2 minutes more, but do not overcook it: It will dry out. Leave the salmon in the skillet but turn off the heat.

5   Divide the cabbage among 4 plates that you have warmed in the oven or microwave. Lay the salmon skin side down on the cabbage and pour the hot sauce around the cabbage. Sprinkle with chervil or chives.

20 ounces (600 g.) salmon fillet in 4 pieces, skin on but scaled

1 tablespoon neutral oil

1 tablespoon chervil leaves or chopped chives

GRILLED SALMON WITH *BEURRE BLANC*

Saumon grillé au beurre blanc

SERVES   4

PREPARATION   20 minutes

COOKING THE SALMON   6 minutes

1   Put the shallots and onions in a saucepan with the vinegar over very low heat and stir with a wooden spoon. Cook for 10 minutes, stirring, always over very low heat. Add the chopped garlic. Whisk in the butter bit by bit and season with salt.

2   Bring 1 quart (1 l.) water to a boil in a pot large enough to hold both the water and a bowlful of the melted butter sauce. Turn the heat to very low, pour the melted butter sauce into a small bowl, and place the bowl in the pot of water. You just want to keep the sauce warm.

3   In the meantime, saturate the thyme with peanut oil and then use it like a paintbrush to spread oil on the salmon steaks. This will give the salmon a pleasant scent.

2 ounces (50 g.) minced shallots

1 heaping tablespoon (15 g.) minced onion

½ cup (10 cl.) white wine vinegar

1 big pinch chopped garlic

1½ sticks (6 ounces/200 g.) butter, diced

Salt

1 small bunch fresh thyme

2 tablespoons peanut oil

4 salmon steaks, ½ pound (120 g.) each

Fleur de sel

Pepper

4   Heat a cast-iron grill pan. When it is quite hot, lay the fish on it and cook for 2–3 minutes per side, depending on their thickness.

5   Remove the steaks to a platter and season with a dash of fleur de sel and a dash of pepper. Serve the sauce on the side, perhaps seasoned with a grinding of pepper.

SALMON WITH SORREL
Saumon à l'oseille

SERVES   4
PREPARATION   15 minutes
COOKING   5 minutes

1   Rinse and dry the fish. Heat a sauté pan or skillet over medium heat. When it is hot, put the salmon scallops in it, skin side down. Let the fish brown for 4 minutes and then turn it with a spatula to cook for 2 minutes on the other side. It should be seared on the outside and almost raw inside.

2   Remove the salmon from the skillet and salt it lightly on the skinless side. Place on a plate lined with paper towels and tent with aluminum foil to keep warm.

3   Pour the fish stock into the skillet with the cream and butter. Turn the heat to low, mix with a spatula, and simmer for 5 minutes. Add the sorrel, cover the skillet, and wilt for 1 minute. Taste for salt and pepper.

4   Make a bed of sorrel cream on a platter and arrange the salmon scallops on top of it. Grind some pepper over and serve immediately.

4 skin-on salmon scallops (thin slices), about ¼ pound (120 g.) each
Salt
½ cup (10 cl.) fish stock (page 40 or store-bought)
2 cups (50 cl.) heavy cream
2 tablespoons butter
5 ounces (200 g.) sorrel, leaves plucked, washed carefully, and drained
Pepper

SALMON IN A PACKET

Saumon en papillote

SERVES 4
PREPARATION 20 minutes
COOKING 7 minutes

1 Rinse and dry the fish. Melt 2 tablespoons butter in a saucepan; add all the vegetables and a dash of salt. Turn the heat to low and stir with a wooden spoon. Cover and cook over low heat for 7 minutes.

2 Preheat the oven to 475°F/250°C.

3 Season the scallops with salt and pepper on both sides. Cut 4 pieces of parchment paper that measure 15 inches by 25 inches (40 cm. by 60 cm.). Paint 1 side of each piece of paper with the remaining butter, softened. Lay a piece of salmon on each paper, top each one with one-fourth of the vegetables, and sprinkle with 1 tablespoon stock. Fold up the packets several times on each side to seal them well. For a pretty golden color, brush the outsides of the packets with the vegetables' cooking butter.

4 Put the packets on a sheet pan and bake for 7 minutes. If you like well-done fish, bake 2–3 minutes more.

5 Use scissors to snip a hole in the top of each packet and serve.

4 salmon scallops, about ¼ pound (120 g.) each, skinless or skin on
4 tablespoons (70 g.) butter
20 ounces (600 g.) small vegetables, varied according to the season (perhaps 2 carrots, 2 stalks celery, 6 small onions, 10 green asparagus tips, 2 heaping tablespoons baby peas, 2 shallots), washed, trimmed, and cut into pieces ¼ inch by ⅛ inch (5 mm. by 3 mm.)
Salt
Pepper
4 tablespoons fish stock (page 40 or store-bought)

SALMON *AU CHAMPAGNE*

SERVES   4

PREPARATION   20 minutes

COOKING   30 minutes plus 30 minutes for the vegetables

1   Preheat the oven to 400°F/200°C. Put 2 tablespoons butter in a saucepan with the carrots, onions, and celery root. Season with a dash of salt. Stir over very low heat for 5 to 10 minutes. The vegetables will cook more or less quickly depending on their thickness.

2   Heat 1 teaspoon butter in a sauté pan. Cook the shallots over very low heat for 3 minutes, stirring with a wooden spoon. Add the mushrooms and cook for 5 minutes, stirring. Add all the other vegetables and stir and cook for 5 minutes. Turn off the heat and stir in the parsley.

3   Rinse the salmon under cold running water and dry with paper towels. Season the flesh well with salt and pepper and sprinkle the skin with 4 dashes of salt.

4   Spread the vegetables in a baking dish. Add half of the Champagne or Chardonnay, cover with a sheet of aluminum foil, and place the salmon steak on top of the foil. Coat the salmon with the remaining butter. Bake for 15 minutes. Baste the salmon steak by spooning the melted butter and cooking juices over it and then bake 15 minutes more.

5   Remove the salmon to a plate and tent it with aluminum foil to keep warm.

6   Remove the aluminum foil from the dish of vegetables, allowing the collected juices to trickle into the vegetables. Put the vegetables and juices into a saucepan with the rest of the Champagne. Stir and bring to a boil, then lower the heat and simmer for 5 minutes. Stir in the crème fraîche and then just bring to a bubble again. Taste for salt and pepper.

7   Remove the salmon's skin. Serve the fish with the sauce on the side.

3 tablespoons butter

2 carrots, peeled and chopped into strips ¼ inch (0.5 cm.) thick

4 new onions, peeled and chopped into strips ¼ inch (0.5 cm.) thick

4 ounces (100 g.) celery root, cut into 8 pieces and then into strips ¼ inch (0.5 cm.) thick

Salt

2 shallots, peeled and minced

4 ounces (100 g.) white mushrooms, trimmed, rinsed, and cut into halves or quarters if they are big

1 tablespoon chopped flat-leaf parsley

1 large salmon steak, about 2 pounds (1 kg.); ask the fishmonger to remove the scales

Pepper

1 cup (20 cl.) Champagne (or Chardonnay)

3 tablespoons crème fraîche

GRILLED SALMON WITH BÉARNAISE SAUCE

Saumon grillé sauce béarnaise

SERVES 4
PREPARATION 5 minutes
COOKING 6–7 minutes

1   Put a rack in the upper third of the oven and preheat to 370°F/190°C. Rinse and dry the fish. Brush the fish with a small amount of oil and then season with salt and pepper.

2   Heat a cast-iron grill pan. When it is hot, lay the salmon steaks on the grill on a diagonal. Cook for 2 minutes and then rotate them a quarter turn without flipping them over so that the grill sears hatch marks into the steaks. Cook for 2 minutes in this new position. Flip the steaks and cook the other side the same way, 4 minutes more.

3   Remove the steaks to a sheet pan and slip them into the oven on the rack. Finish the cooking with 2 or 3 minutes in the oven.

4   Remove the skin from each steak. Serve with a quartered lemon and béarnaise sauce on the side.

4 salmon steaks, 6–7 ounces (180–200 g.) each
Neutral oil
Salt
Pepper
1 lemon, quartered
½ recipe béarnaise sauce (page 48; use half the quantity indicated for each ingredient)

DILLED SALMON

Saumon mariné à l'aneth

variation
FENNEL-MARINATED
SALMON

SERVES 4
PREPARATION 15 minutes
The marinade must be prepared two days in advance.

A very popular dish in Sweden.

1   Two days before you plan to eat the salmon, check it for tiny bones and remove them with tweezers. With a large needle or a fork, prick the skin all over to make about 20 shallow holes. Rinse and dry the fish.

2   Mix the chopped dill with the salt, sugar, and white pepper.

3   Lay the salmon in a nonmetallic dish in which it fits as snugly as possible without squeezing. Rub it all over with the

1 salmon fillet, 1¼ pounds (600 g.), skin on and scales removed, preferably from the middle of the fish
1 tablespoon coarsely chopped dill
1 tablespoon salt
2 teaspoons sugar
1 teaspoon crushed white pepper

dill mixture and leave at room temperature until you can see that the salt and sugar have melted. Cover with plastic wrap and refrigerate for 48 hours, flipping it 3 or 4 times over the course of the marination.

4   When it's time to eat the salmon, remove it from the refrigerator, wipe it off, and cut it into very thin slices, as you would smoked fish.

FENNEL-MARINATED SALMON
Saumon mariné au fenouil

This dish is prepared just like Dilled Salmon. The dill is replaced with 1 tablespoon fennel seeds.

GRILLED SALMON WITH RED BUTTER _____
Saumon grillé au beurre rouge

SERVES   4
PREPARATION   30 minutes
COOKING   30 minutes

1   Put the shallots in a saucepan with the Shiraz, a pinch of salt, and a dash of pepper. Bring to a boil over high heat and boil for 25 minutes.

2   Reduce the heat to low so that the mixture no longer boils and stir in the cold diced butter bit by bit with a wooden spoon. When you have incorporated two-thirds of the butter, season with 2 pinches of salt and a pinch of pepper. Stir in the rest of the butter off the heat. If you like, you can pass the sauce through a strainer to remove the shallots. Cover to keep warm.

3   Preheat the oven to 400°F/200°C and heat a grill pan. Brush the salmon steak with a bit of oil. Season each side with ½ teaspoon salt and 2 pinches of pepper. Grill gently for 5 minutes on each side. Remove the steak to a sheet pan and bake for 9 minutes. Turn it over and bake 9 minutes more. If

2 shallots, peeled and minced
2 cups (50 cl.) Shiraz
Salt
Pepper
1 stick (¼ pound/115 g.) cold
    butter, diced
Neutral oil
1 salmon steak, about 2 pounds
    (1 kg.), scales removed

you like rare salmon, at its center it should be barely warm and still a vivid ruby color. If you like it a bit more cooked, leave it 5 minutes more, but do not overcook it.

4   Warm the red butter sauce over low heat for 2 minutes. Remove the skin from the steaks and lay them on a hot platter. Slice into thin slabs at the table and serve the red butter in a sauceboat on the side.

Sardines

The sardine is an excellent small fish that must be eaten very fresh. We usually eat sardines that have been preserved in olive oil. They do give off a very strong odor when cooked, and for this reason many people save them for summertime barbecues and other out-of-doors occasions.

GRILLED FRESH SARDINES

Sardines grillées

SERVES   4
PREPARATION   5 minutes
COOKING   7 minutes

1   Season the sardines with salt and pepper and brush them lightly with the neutral oil. Cook them on the hot grill of a barbecue for 4 minutes and then turn and cook them over medium heat 3 minutes more. At this stage the skin of the sardines will be beginning to crackle.

2   Remove the sardines to a serving platter. Anoint each one with a few drops of olive oil and sprinkle with fleur de sel. Serve the lemon quarters, butter, and bread on the side.

16 small fresh sardines, scaled, gutted, and carefully washed
Salt
Pepper
Neutral oil
Olive oil
Fleur de sel
1 lemon, quartered
Lightly salted butter
Country bread

SARDINE *ESCABÈCHE*

Escabèche de sardines à la provençale

SERVES   4

PREPARATION AND COOKING   25 minutes

Escabèche is a traditional Provençal preparation in which fish is marinated and served cold. You must make this dish a day or two before you plan to eat it. Ask the fishmonger to fillet the sardines for you.

1   Rinse the sardines and dry them with paper towels. Remove all the bones with tweezers.

2   Heat 5 tablespoons olive oil in a saucepan. Add the garlic, fennel, and carrot and cook for 2 minutes over very low heat, stirring with a wooden spoon. Season with 2 pinches of salt and pour in the wine. Bring to a boil. Put the lemon and orange juices through a fine strainer into the saucepan. Add the bay leaf and bring back to a boil. Season with 2 pinches of crushed black pepper and simmer for 2 minutes. Turn off the heat, add the mint, and leave to infuse.

3   Heat 2 tablespoons olive oil in a skillet for 2 minutes. Lay the sardines in the pan, skin side down. Cook for 20 seconds, quickly sprinkling each with a pinch of salt, and then turn and cook for 10 seconds on the other side. The fillets are cooked when they have turned white around the edges.

4   Lay the fillets side by side in a deep dish and top them with the tomatoes. Pour the mint-infused vegetables over. Cover with plastic wrap and refrigerate for 1 or 2 days.

5   Remove from the refrigerator 30 minutes before serving. The *escabèche* should be well chilled but not straight from the refrigerator.

8 sardines, fillets only

7 tablespoons olive oil

1 clove garlic, peeled

3 tablespoons fennel bulb diced very small ($\frac{1}{8}$ inch/ 2–3 mm.)

1 carrot, peeled and diced very small ($\frac{1}{8}$ inch/2–3 mm.)

Salt

1 cup (20 cl.) dry white wine, such as Chardonnay

Juice of 1 lemon

Juice of $\frac{1}{2}$ orange

$\frac{1}{2}$ bay leaf

Crushed black pepper

8 small mint leaves

2 medium tomatoes, peeled, seeded, and diced (page 124)

Sea Bass

In the French Mediterranean, sea bass is called *loup* (wolf) because it is a carnivore. (The *loubine* is a smaller specimen.) On France's Atlantic coast, sea bass is called *bar*. Each region claims that its species is the better, but they are actually the very same one.

Rock sea bass, on the other hand, is a superior fish, but it is also unfortunately rare. Along the Atlantic coast of the United States, you will find it under the name black sea bass.

SEA BASS WITH CRISPY SKIN AND A LIGHT SAUCE

Bar à la peau croustillante, sauce allégée

SERVES 4
PREPARATION 30 minutes
COOKING 10 minutes

1   Preheat the broiler.
2   Put the shallot, crushed white pepper, sprig of tarragon, and vinegar in a small saucepan. Bring to a boil and reduce the liquid until the pan is practically dry. Only a tablespoon of liquid should remain when you finish. Remove the sprig of tarragon.
3   Bring 1 quart (1 l.) water to a boil in a kettle or pot. Use a fork to beat the egg yolks with 1½ tablespoons cold water and a small pinch of salt in a heat-proof bowl or small Dutch oven. Put the bowl in a large pot and pour the almost boiling water into the pot until it reaches halfway up the side of the bowl. Be careful not to splash hot water into the bowl of yolks. Put the pot over very low heat and whisk the yolks energetically and continuously for about 5 minutes, until the mixture begins to thicken. At the end, when you trace an *s* with your whisk, you should be able to see the bottom of the bowl. (This mixture is a sabayon.) Remove the bowl from the water bath and whisk 1 minute more. Whisk in 1 tablespoon vinegar-shallot mixture and the *fromage blanc*. Add the chopped tarragon and taste for salt and pepper.
4   Arrange the pieces of fish on a sheet pan, skin side up. Season

1 tablespoon minced shallot
½ teaspoon crushed white pepper
1 sprig fresh tarragon plus 1 tablespoon chopped fresh tarragon
6 tablespoons (10 cl.) distilled white vinegar
2 egg yolks (page 204)
Salt
6 ounces (150 g.) *fromage blanc*
Pepper
4 fillets sea bass, 5 ounces (150 g.) each, skin on and bone in
Coarse salt

the skin with coarse salt, using 2 teaspoons total. Broil for 8 minutes under the preheated broiler, until the skin is golden.

5   In the meantime, reheat the bowl of sauce in the water bath over low heat, whisking frequently.

6   When the fish is out of the oven, delicately remove the salt-encrusted skin from each piece, being careful not to tear the skin or pull apart the flesh. If salt falls on the fish flesh, use a pastry brush to sweep it off.

7   Arrange the fish on a platter. Top each piece with a table-spoon of sauce. Set the salty, crispy skins beside the fish and serve the rest of the sauce in a sauceboat.

SEA BASS WITH FLEUR DE SEL AND AROMATICS _____
Blanc de bar à la fleur de sel et aux aromates

SERVES   4

PREPARATION   20 minutes

COOKING   7 minutes for the fish plus 15 minutes for the vegetables

1   Bring 1 quart (1 l.) water to a boil with 1 tablespoon coarse salt. Prepare a large bowl half filled with water and a tray of ice cubes. When the water bubbles, cook the fennel and leeks for 5 minutes. With a skimmer, remove them to the ice water and leave them just long enough to cool down. Drain in a colander.

2   Rinse the sea bass fillets and dry them with a paper towel. Season both sides of each piece of fish with salt and pepper.

3   Cut 6 tablespoons (75 g.) butter into small pieces and put them in a microwave-safe bowl. (Keep the rest of the butter in the refrigerator.) Microwave the pieces of butter for 30 seconds on low or just long enough to soften. Add 4 pieces of dried tomato, the sweet red pepper or paprika, 2 tablespoons olive oil, and the crustless bread. Add salt and pepper and mix well, until you have a homogeneous, doughy substance.

4   Lay a rectangle of parchment paper on a cutting board or work surface. Roll the dough mixture out on the paper until

Coarse salt

4 small bulbs fennel, washed and trimmed

12 small leeks, washed and trimmed

4 skinless sea bass fillets, 5–6 ounces (155–185 g.) each

Salt

Pepper

2 sticks (½ pound/220 g.) butter

3 large tomatoes, quartered and dried (store-bought or see page 588 for dried)

⅓ teaspoon sweet red niora pepper or sweet paprika

3 tablespoons olive oil

3 ounces (100 g.) good-quality white sandwich bread, crusts removed

(continued)

it is 1/8 inch (3 mm.) thick. Cover with another piece of parchment paper and refrigerate.

5   Preheat the oven to 475°F/250°C and put one of the oven racks in the top third of the oven.

6   Melt almost 7 tablespoons (100 g.) butter in a sauté pan or skillet over low heat. When it foams, add the grape juice and 3 tablespoons vinegar. Raise the heat to medium and stir with a wooden spatula. Add the lemon peel and stir for 2 minutes. Turn off the heat.

7   Melt 1½ tablespoons butter in a saucepan big enough to hold the fennel and leeks. When it foams, add the fennel and leeks and stir with a wooden spoon over low heat. Add the star anise and the rest of the dried tomatoes. Stir and leave over low heat.

8   Remove the remaining butter from the refrigerator. Cut it into 8 thin slices and arrange them on a sheet pan at regular intervals. Put a piece of fish on top of each piece of butter. Drizzle 1 tablespoon olive oil over all the fish and bake for 4 minutes.

9   When the fish is out of the oven, heat the broiler at the highest possible temperature. Remove the sheet of dough from the refrigerator and remove the top piece of parchment paper from it. Invert the dough onto the fish and remove the other piece of parchment paper. Put the fish back in the oven to broil for 3 minutes.

10 In the meantime, add 1 tablespoon vinegar to the saucepan with the vegetables. Raise the heat to medium for 1 minute.

11 Arrange the vegetables on one side of a platter and the fish on the other. Surround the whole with a ring of sauce and the basil leaves. Sprinkle with fleur de sel and serve the rest of the sauce on the side.

3 tablespoons grape juice
4 tablespoons wine vinegar
½ teaspoon preserved lemon peel
8 star anise
12 small basil leaves
Fleur de sel

BROILED SEA BASS WITH EGGPLANT AND HERBS _____

Blanc de bar grillé à l'aubergine et aux herbes

SERVES   4

PREPARATION   50 minutes

COOKING   10 minutes

The eggplant marinade must be made at least 1 hour in advance.

1   Slice the eggplants in half lengthwise and then into slabs ½ inch (1 cm.) thick. Spread them over a deep platter or sheet pan and season with salt, pepper, and 1 teaspoon fresh thyme leaves. Sprinkle with ½ cup (10 cl.) olive oil, toss, and allow to rest for 1 hour.

2   Rinse the fish fillets and dry them with paper towels. Season each piece with salt and pepper on both sides. Arrange them on a sheet pan skin side up, side by side, and sprinkle them with ½ cup (10 cl.) olive oil.

3   Cook the eggplant slices in a dry skillet over low heat for 10 minutes. Flip them with a wooden spatula and cook the second side for 10 minutes as well.

4   Preheat the broiler.

5   Line a plate with 3 layers of paper towels. Bring the frying oil to 280°F/140°C in a fryer or a large pot. The oil should be hot enough to turn the onions blond but not darken them. If you don't have a thermometer, test a small piece of onion before adding all of them; if the test piece blackens, turn off the heat before trying again. When the oil is the correct temperature, add the onions and allow them to turn golden, turning them with a skimmer. Remove the fried onions with a skimmer or slotted spoon and drain them on the paper towel–lined plate. Taste and add salt as necessary.

6   Scatter the thyme sprigs and garlic around the fish on the sheet pan. Broil for 10 minutes.

7   Melt 1 teaspoon butter in a skillet and cook the bell pepper for 2 minutes over medium heat. Add a little salt, season with pepper, and add the diced olives. Stir and then remove the peppers and olives to drain in a colander.

8   Melt 1 teaspoon butter in the skillet over low heat. When it foams and begins to color, add the vinegar and soy sauce. Keep warm over the lowest possible heat.

2 medium eggplants
Salt
Pepper
1 teaspoon fresh thyme leaves
    and 5 sprigs thyme
1 cup (20 cl.) olive oil
4 skin-on sea bass fillets,
    6 ounces (180 g.) each
2 cups (50 cl.) neutral oil for
    frying
4 new white onions, trimmed
    and sliced into thin rounds
2 cloves garlic, crushed
2 teaspoons butter
1 red bell pepper, peeled,
    seeded, and diced (page
    130)
20 black olives, pitted and
    diced
1 tablespoon red wine vinegar
½ teaspoon soy sauce
1 small handful arugula and
    watercress, washed
1 teaspoon each minced
    tarragon, basil, dill, chervil,
    and flat-leaf parsley
¼ cup (6 cl.) vinaigrette
    (page 59)
3 scallions, minced
Crushed black pepper
Fleur de sel

9   Toss the arugula, watercress, and minced herbs with the
    vinaigrette. Divide the salad among 4 plates (or make 4 piles
    on a serving platter) and top each one with 2 slices of egg-
    plant and a sea bass fillet. Spoon peppers and olives over
    each fillet and sprinkle with minced scallions and fried
    onions. Sprinkle a few drops of the warm butter, vinegar, and
    soy sauce mixture over the whole and season with crushed
    black pepper and fleur de sel.

GRILLED SEA BASS WITH FENNEL

Loups grillés au fenouil

SERVES   4
PREPARING THE GRILL   about 1 hour
PREPARATION   15 minutes
COOKING   about 40 minutes (fish and zucchini)

1   Prepare a wood fire. You want it to get to the point where the
    flames have died down completely but the embers are still
    glowing hot. Heat the grill over the embers.
2   Rinse the fish under cold running water and dry well with a
    paper towel. Season with 2 pinches of salt and a pinch of pep-
    per on each side. Season the cavity with the same amount of
    salt and pepper. (If you are using 2 small fish, use 3 pinches of
    salt and 2 of pepper total.) Stuff the cavity with 10 fennel
    fronds.
3   Spread the zucchini ribbons on a platter. Sprinkle with
    6 tablespoons (10 cl.) olive oil and the thyme leaves.
4   Throw the rest of the fennel fronds on the embers and allow
    them to burn away. Then lay the fish on the grill. The cook-
    ing time is entirely dependent on the heat of the embers and
    the position of the grill. The smaller fish are cooked when
    their skin is visibly grilled (6–8 minutes per side), and the
    large fish is cooked when its skin is nearly blackened (about
    10 minutes per side).
5   Remove the fish with a flat spatula and put it on a plate cov-
    ered with aluminum foil. With a small knife, slice around the

2 line-caught sea bass, about
    1½ pounds (750 g.) each,
    or 1 line-caught sea bass,
    3 pounds (1.5 kg.), gutted
    but not scaled
Salt
Pepper
30 fennel fronds
4 medium zucchini, washed
    and sliced lengthwise into
    strips ¼ inch (0.5 cm.)
    thick
¾ cup (15 cl.) olive oil
4 sprigs fresh thyme, leaves
    only
Juice of 1 lemon
Fleur de sel

circumference of the fish, just below the head, in order to peel away the skin carefully. Slip the skinned fish onto a platter and tent with aluminum foil to keep warm.

6 Season both sides of the zucchini strips with salt and pepper and grill them for 2 minutes per side. You can do this in batches if necessary.

7 Roll the grilled zucchini strips into little cylinders and lay them all around the fish. Pour the rest of the olive oil and a few drops of lemon juice over the fish and sprinkle with a pinch of fleur de sel. Serve right away, very hot.

8 If you can't grill over wood, preheat your oven's broiler at its maximum temperature for 15 minutes. Lay a piece of aluminum foil on one of the oven racks and cook the fish on top of it, 6 minutes per side for the small fish and 10 minutes per side for the large one. Cook the zucchini strips in a very hot skillet in 2 tablespoons olive oil for 2 minutes per side.

Sea Bream

Dozens of varieties of this fish, easily identified by its rounded silvery flanks and oval shape, live near the Atlantic and Mediterranean coasts of France. The best is the gilt-head (*Sparus aurata*), which owes its names to a golden stripe on its forehead. In French it is called *daurade royale.* In the United States there are the gray sea bream from Florida, the red-drum fished from Massachusetts to Florida, and a pinkish sea bream called the blackspot.

In France, the main species are the highly prized *royale,* the *rose* (blackspot sea bream), and the *gris* (gray or black sea bream). The latter two are spelled, as in English, *dorade.* Only the *royale* earns the precious spelling *daurade,* although the pronunciation is exactly the same. You can see that the French take food seriously indeed.

SEA BREAM IN A SALT CRUST

Daurade en croûte de sel

SERVES   4
PREPARATION   15 minutes
COOKING   45 minutes

Ask the fishmonger to trim the fish (that is, cut off its fins), gut it, and remove the gills but not the scales.

1 whole sea bream, about
    3 pounds (1.5 kg.)
Pepper
Salt
2 sprigs fresh thyme
1 teaspoon cilantro leaves
4 pounds (2 kg.) coarse salt
1 tablespoon olive oil
Juice of ½ lemon (optional)

1   Preheat the oven to 460°F/240°C. Quickly rinse the fish under cold running water and dry with paper towels. Season its cavity with 2 pinches of pepper, salt, thyme, and cilantro.

2   Spread a bed of coarse salt 1 inch (2 cm.) thick on a baking dish (preferably ceramic, large enough to hold the fish, and pretty enough to bring to the table). Lay the fish on the salt and flip it over so that it is entirely covered with salt. Sprinkle its surface with a few drops of water.

3   Bake for 45 minutes on the bed of salt. Take the baking dish from the oven straight to the table. In front of your guests, gently shatter the salt crust so you have access to the fish and then remove its skin. Cut out the fillets by running a thin, sharp knife around the base of the fish's head and down its backbone on each side. If necessary, use a pastry brush to sweep any traces of salt off the fillets. Pepper each fillet lightly before drizzling it with the olive oil and, if you like, a teaspoon of lemon juice.

SEA BREAM WRAPPED IN SEAWEED AND SALT _____

Daurade en croûte de sel et d'algues

SERVES 4
PREPARATION 15 minutes
COOKING 45 minutes

This recipe is the same as Sea Bream in a Salt Crust (page 306) except that it includes seaweed, which will imbue the fish with its marine perfume. If you can't find seaweed, try an aromatic variation by mixing thyme, bay leaf, star anise, or cilantro into the salt. As before, ask the fishmonger to remove the fish's fins, guts, and gills but leave its scales in place.

1 sea bream, about 3 pounds (1.5 kg.)
¾ pound (300 g.) fresh green seaweed, carefully washed (do not use dried seaweed for this dish)
6 pounds (3 kg.) coarse salt
Pepper
1 tablespoon olive oil
Juice of ½ lemon (optional)

1   Preheat the oven to 460°F/240°C.
2   Quickly rinse the fish under cold running water. Dry it with paper towels.
3   Bring 2 quarts (2 l.) water to a boil in a large pot. Prepare a large bowl half filled with cold water and a tray of ice cubes. When the pot of water bubbles, plunge in the seaweed. As soon as the water comes back to a boil, remove the seaweed to the ice water bath. When it has chilled, put it to drain in a colander.
4   Mix the seaweed with the coarse salt and spread one-third of the mixture on a sheet pan or baking dish (preferably ceramic, large enough to hold the fish, and pretty enough to bring to the table). Season the inside of the fish with 2 pinches of pepper and lay it on top of the salt bed and sea-weed. Cover it entirely with the remaining salt and seaweed mixture.
5   Bake for 45 minutes. Take the sheet pan from the oven straight to the table. In front of your guests, gently shatter the salt crust so you have access to the fish and then remove its skin. Cut out the fillets by running a thin, sharp knife around the base of the fish's head and down its backbone on each side. With a pastry brush, carefully sweep any traces of salt off the fish. Drizzle with the olive oil and, if you like, a teaspoon of lemon juice.

BAKED SEA BREAM

Daurade au four

SERVES 4
PREPARATION 1 minute
COOKING 30–40 minutes

1   Preheat the oven to 400°F/200°C.
2   Quickly rinse the fish under cold running water and dry it with paper towels. Spread the onions and shallot over a sheet pan or baking dish and toss them with 1 tablespoon olive oil. Add the bay leaves, half of the thyme, ½ teaspoon salt, and 2 pinches of pepper.
3   Season the outside of the fish with 2 generous pinches of salt and 1 pinch of pepper. Season the cavity the same way. Lay the fish on top of the vegetables on the sheet pan. Lay the tomato, zucchini, and lemon slices on top of the fish. Pour the wine and 3 tablespoons olive oil over and add the rest of the thyme. Sprinkle with 1 teaspoon salt and 2 pinches of pepper.
4   Bake for 30–40 minutes, depending on the thickness of the fish. It is cooked when the flesh is opaque white and can be easily pulled from the backbone. Serve immediately after removing from the oven.

1 sea bream, 2–2½ pounds (1–1.2 kg.), gutted and scaled
3 medium onions, peeled and sliced into rounds ⅛ inch (3 mm.) thick
1 shallot, peeled and quartered
¼ cup olive oil
2 bay leaves
8 sprigs thyme
Salt
Pepper
1 tomato, sliced into thin rounds
1 small zucchini, sliced into thin rounds
1 lemon, sliced into thin rounds
2 cups (50 cl.) dry white wine

SEA BREAM STUFFED WITH SHELLFISH

Daurade farcie aux coquillages

SERVES 3 or 4
PREPARATION 20 minutes
COOKING 20 minutes
The cockles must be soaked the night before (see page 227).

This stuffing can also be used in other fish.

1   Soak the cockles the night before.
2   The next day, preheat the oven to 400°F/200°C. Lift the cockles from their soaking water with your hands and rinse them several times.

1 pound (500 g.) cockles
1 pound (500 g.) mussels
1 sea bream, 1½ pounds (750 g.), gutted and scaled
4 pitted black olives
Zest of 1 orange

3   Wash the mussels in several changes of water, scrubbing them and removing their beards.

4   Rinse the fish quickly under cold running water. Dry it with paper towels.

5   Put ½ cup (10 cl.) water in a large pot with the mussels and cockles and bring to a boil. Cover and cook over high heat for 4 minutes, shaking the pot once or twice. Remove the mussels and cockles with a skimmer and take them out of their shells.

6   In a blender or food processor, purée the olives and orange zest. Add the dill, cumin seeds, almonds (if you are using them), shelled mussels and cockles, a good pinch of pepper, and a generous tablespoon of olive oil. Blend again until well combined.

7   Season the inside of the fish with 1 generous pinch of pepper and stuff with the blended mixture. Lay the fish on a sheet pan, brush it with olive oil, and bake about 20 minutes. The fish is cooked when the flesh around its backbone is white and opaque and can be easily pulled from the bone.

2 tablespoons dill fronds
1 teaspoon cumin seeds
⅔ cup (100 g.) fresh almonds, peeled (optional but desirable if fresh almonds are available)
Pepper
2 tablespoons olive oil

SEA BREAM À LA PROVENÇALE I

Daurade à la provençale

SERVES   4

PREPARATION   20 minutes

COOKING   25 minutes for the fish plus 20 minutes for the tomatoes

1   Quickly rinse the fish under cold running water. Dry with paper towels.

2   Preheat the oven to 460°F/240°C.

3   Heat 2 tablespoons olive oil in a saucepan over low heat. Cook the chopped onion for 3 minutes, stirring with a wooden spoon; do not allow the onion to color. Add the tomato and

1 sea bream, about 3 pounds (1.5 kg.), gutted, fins removed, and scaled
¼ cup olive oil
1 onion, peeled and finely chopped
1 pound (500 g.) tomatoes, peeled, seeded, and diced (page 124)

(continued)

bell pepper pieces, 2 thyme sprigs, and the crushed garlic. Cover and cook for 15 minutes over low heat, stirring every 5 minutes. The mixture should eventually thicken, taking on the consistency of a compote. Season with salt and pepper.

4 Put the chopped star anise and 1 sprig thyme inside the fish along with 2 generous pinches of salt and 1 pinch of pepper. Season each outside flank of the fish with 2 generous pinches of salt and 1 pinch of pepper.

5 Lay the fish on a sheet pan or baking dish, preferably ceramic. Cover it with 2 tablespoons olive oil and the tomato–bell pepper mixture. If you were able to find new garlic, rinse it. If it is regular garlic, crush the unpeeled cloves and add them to the baking dish. Lay the lemon slices over the fish and bake for 25 minutes, rotating the dish halfway through for uniform cooking. The fish is cooked when its flesh is white and opaque and easily pulled from the backbone.

6 Garnish with celery leaves and serve.

1 red bell pepper, peeled, seeded (page 130), and sliced into strips ½ inch by 1 inch (1 cm. by 2 cm.)

4 sprigs fresh thyme

2 cloves garlic, peeled, degermed (page 122), and crushed, plus 8 whole cloves garlic, new if possible

Salt

Pepper

2 star anise pods, roughly chopped

1 organic lemon, washed, sliced into rounds less than ¼ inch (0.5 cm.) thick, and seeds removed

2 tablespoons small celery leaves

SEA BREAM *À LA PROVENÇALE* II

Daurade aux arômes de Provence

SERVES 4
PREPARATION 45 minutes
COOKING 40 minutes

1 Preheat the oven to 400°F/200°C. Rinse the fish quickly and dry with paper towels.

2 Bring 1 quart (1 l.) water to a boil in a large pot with 1 teaspoon coarse salt. Separately and for 3 minutes each, plunge the shallots, onions, and fennel into the boiling water. Remove each vegetable to a colander, cool under cold running water, and drain. Halve each vegetable lengthwise.

3 Heat 1 tablespoon olive oil in a large saucepan and cook the shallots, onions, and fennel over low heat for 5 minutes, stirring with a wooden spoon. Taste for salt and pepper.

1 sea bream, about 3 pounds (1.5 kg.), gutted and with the gills removed

Coarse salt

12 shallots, peeled

6 new white or cipollini onions, peeled

12 baby fennel bulbs, washed and trimmed of the thick outer layer if necessary

6 tablespoons (10 cl.) olive oil

Salt

Pepper

4   Season the inside and outside of the fish with salt and pepper. Lay the fish on a sheet pan or baking dish and scatter the olives, shallots, onions, fennel, tomatoes, star anise, and garlic around it. Sprinkle with thyme and basil and lay the lemon slices on top of the fish. Pour the remaining olive oil and the white wine over the whole. Bake for 40 minutes and serve right away in the baking dish.

12 black olives, with or without pits
12 cherry tomatoes, peeled and seeded
1 star anise pod
1 clove garlic, unpeeled
1 tablespoon fresh thyme leaves
1 tablespoon chopped basil
1 organic lemon, washed and sliced into thin rounds
2 cups (50 cl.) dry white wine

SEA BREAM IN A PACKET WITH SAFFRON

Daurade en papillote au safran

SERVES   4
PREPARATION   40 minutes
COOKING   10 minutes

1   Quickly rinse the fish under cold running water and dry with paper towels.
2   Heat 2 tablespoons olive oil in a skillet over low heat. Add the onions and 1 scant teaspoon salt. Cook for 3 minutes, stirring with a wooden spoon; do not allow the onions to color. Add the tomatoes and stir. Add the saffron threads and cook for 15 minutes over low heat, stirring every 5 minutes. Stir in the olives and taste for salt and pepper.
3   Preheat the broiler. Cut 4 pieces of aluminum foil measuring about 1½ feet square (45 cm. by 45 cm.). Leave a clean 1-inch (2-cm.) border all around the edge, and in the middle of each piece layer one-fourth of the tomato mixture, a fillet, 1 tablespoon white wine, and 1 sprig rosemary. Fold the foil over itself and fold up the edges 2 or 3 times to make sure the packet is completely sealed. Lay the 4 packets on a sheet pan and broil for 10 minutes. If you prefer fish well done, you might cook the packets 2 or 3 minutes more.
4   Remove the packets and set each one on a heated plate. Present the plates to your guests and cut a hole in the top of each packet to open carefully. The juices inside are very hot.

Fillets of 2 gray sea bream, each whole fish weighing about 1½ pounds (750 g.), skin on and scaled
2 tablespoons olive oil
2 medium onions, peeled and sliced into rounds ⅛ inch (3 mm.) thick
Salt
4 medium tomatoes, peeled, seeded, and diced (page 124)
Pinch of saffron threads
20 black olives, pits removed
Pepper
4 tablespoons dry white wine
4 sprigs rosemary

Sea Trout

The spotted sea trout, also called salmon trout (its flesh resembles salmon's), lives in estuarine and coastal waters. It migrates along the coasts and rivers according to the season. In the United States, most of it is fished in the Gulf of Mexico. When its diet is especially rich in small crustaceans, as is the case in most aquaculture farms, its flesh turns pinker.

SEA TROUT WITH CURRIED CARROT "TAGLIATELLE"

Truite de mer aux "tagliatelles" de carotte au curry

SERVES 4
PREPARATION TIME 15 minutes
COOKING TIME 5 minutes

1 Rinse the fish under cold running water and dry with paper towels.

2 Using a mandoline, cut the carrots into very thin ribbons. Using a knife, slice the ribbons so thin that they resemble pasta.

3 Bring 2 cups (50 cl.) water to a boil with 1 teaspoon coarse salt. Cook the carrot for 1–2 minutes; remove with a skimmer to a colander and rinse with cold water for 1 minute. Drain.

4 Heat 1 tablespoon olive oil in a saucepan. Add the carrot, curry powder, vinegar, garlic, and basil. Season with salt and pepper, stir with a wooden spoon, and leave over low heat, stirring occasionally.

5 Season the fish with salt and pepper on both sides. Heat 1 tablespoon olive oil in a large skillet over medium heat for 1 minute. Carefully lay the fish in the hot skillet, setting the end near you in the skillet first and laying the fish away from you so as to avoid splashing yourself with hot oil. Cook for 2 minutes and then flip and cook for 30 seconds on the other side. (You might set the timer on your microwave to keep track exactly.)

6 Heap the carrot "tagliatelle" on a platter and lay the fish atop it.

4 sea trout scallops (thin slices), about 6 ounces (180 g.) each

¾ pound (400 g.) carrots, washed, peeled, and ends trimmed

Coarse salt

2 tablespoons olive oil

Pinch of curry powder

1 teaspoon sherry vinegar

1 clove garlic, peeled, degermed (page 122), and minced

8 basil leaves, minced

Salt

Pepper

Skate

The skate's pale pink flesh has a very delicate taste and a unique texture. It is a lean, cartilaginous fish, completely boneless and without scales. It is large and flat and shaped like a wing with a long, skinny tail. There are many types of skate, but the most delicious is the one called *thornback*.

Skates are usually skinned. To figure out whether a skate is fresh, see if it is enrobed in a viscous substance; the flesh continues to secrete this substance for about ten hours after the fish is caught. Eliminate the viscous matter by washing the skate well in several changes of water.

Skate is poached or fried and can also be cooked in packets.

SKATE WING WITH CAPERS

Aile de raie aux câpres

SERVES 4
PREPARATION 2 minutes
COOKING 13 minutes

1 Put the peppercorns, vinegar, and bouquet garni into a large pot with 6 cups (1.5 l.) water and 1 tablespoon coarse salt. Clean and rinse the skate well and lower it into the pot; do your best not to crowd the pieces of skate or make them overlap. Bring almost to a boil and adjust the heat so the water shivers for 3 minutes. Remove any foam from the surface with a skimmer. Turn off the heat, cover the pot, and allow it to rest for 10 minutes.

2 Drain the skate and arrange it on a platter. Scatter the capers all over. Melt the butter in a skillet for 1 minute over high heat. When it foams, pour it all over the skate. Sprinkle with croutons, if you like, and parsley.

4 peppercorns
1 cup (20 cl.) distilled vinegar
1 bouquet garni (1 leek leaf,
    1 small stalk celery, 4 stems
    parsley, 1 small sprig
    thyme, and ½ bay leaf, tied
    together)
Coarse salt
4 pieces skin-on skate wing,
    ½ pound (250 g.) each
3 tablespoons capers
5 tablespoons (80 g.) butter
1 cup croutons made from
    white bread (optional)
1 teaspoon minced parsley

FRIED SKATE WING WITH CABBAGE

Ailerons de raie poêlée au chou

SERVES 4
PREPARATION 40 minutes
COOKING 4 minutes

1 Carefully wash the skate in a good deal of water, until its viscous coating is gone. Dry it with paper towels. Thoroughly scrub the mussels, removing their beards, and wash in several changes of water.

2 Bring 1 quart (1 l.) water to a boil in a pot with 1 teaspoon coarse salt. Prepare a bowl filled with cold water and a tray of ice cubes. When the pot is bubbling, add the cabbage and boil for 5 minutes. With a skimmer, remove the cabbage to the ice water. Allow it to cool for 2–3 minutes and then drain in a colander. Pull the leaves apart.

3 Put the mussels in a large pot. Add pepper and stir. Cover the pot and cook for 4 minutes over high heat, shaking the pot often. Remove the mussels with a skimmer and then take them out of their shells. Set the mussel meat aside and reserve the cooking juices in the pot.

4 Whisk the vinegar with 2 pinches of salt. Add 1 tablespoon mussel cooking juice from the pot, pouring it through a strainer. Add the peanut and hazelnut oils and capers and whisk again.

5 Season the skate on both sides with salt, pepper, and a pinch of curry powder. Heat the olive oil in a large skillet. Add the skate without overlapping the pieces and cook for 2 minutes over high heat. Flip with a spatula to cook the other side for 2 minutes. Remove from the skillet and tent with aluminum foil to keep warm.

6 Melt the butter in a saucepan. Add the cabbage, mussel meat, hazelnuts, tomatoes, and shallot. Cook for 5 minutes over rather high heat, stirring. Taste for salt and pepper and then layer the bottom of a serving platter with this mixture. Place the skate atop the sauce and coat with the vinaigrette. Serve right away.

4 pieces skate, about 6 ounces (220 g.) each
1 pound (500 g.) mussels
Coarse salt
1 small, tender green cabbage, outer leaves removed, quartered, and cored
Pepper
1 tablespoon balsamic vinegar
Salt
1 tablespoon peanut oil
1 tablespoon hazelnut oil
1 teaspoon chopped capers
Curry powder
3 tablespoons olive oil
½ stick (50 g.) butter
12 hazelnuts, peeled and chopped
2 tomatoes, peeled, seeded, and diced (page 124)
1 shallot, peeled and minced

ROASTED BABY THORNBACK SKATE

Raiteau au plat

SERVES   4
PREPARATION   15 minutes
COOKING   4 minutes

1   Preheat the oven to 440°F/220°C.

2   Using a pastry brush, coat the egg plates with butter.

3   Wash the skate several times, rinsing until its viscous coating is completely gone. Season the skate on both sides with salt and pepper. Set each fillet on a buttered oven-safe plate and top each with 1 teaspoon butter.

4   Peel the lemons by slicing away their rinds completely so that no pith is left and the juicy flesh is completely exposed. Cut them into small dice.

5   Put the plates of fish in the oven for 4 minutes. In the meantime, heat 1 tablespoon butter in a frying pan. When it foams and begins to color, add 4 tablespoons diced tomatoes, 4 tablespoons diced lemon, the capers, and the parsley. Season with 2 pinches of salt and 1 pinch of pepper and stir.

6   When the fish is cooked—when its flesh is white and opaque—remove it from the oven. Divide the contents of the skillet among the plates and serve immediately.

4 baby thornback skate fillets,
    about 4 ounces (125 g.)
    each
Salt
Pepper
3 tablespoons butter
3 or 4 lemons
3 or 4 medium tomatoes,
    peeled (page 124) and
    chopped into very small
    dice
2 tablespoons capers, chopped
1 tablespoon minced flat-leaf
    parsley

*special equipment: 4 oven-safe
    glass or ceramic plates*

SKATE WITH CABBAGE

Raie au chou

SERVES   4
PREPARATION   10 minutes
COOKING   15–20 minutes

1   Wash the skate well in a good deal of water to eliminate its viscous coating. Put it into a large pot with 2 quarts (2 l.) water, 1 tablespoon coarse salt, the vinegar, and the bouquet garni. If the skate is not submerged, add water to cover. Bring to a boil, reduce the heat immediately, and simmer for 3–4 minutes. Turn off the heat, cover the pot, and let it sit for 5–10 minutes, until its flesh is white and opaque and easy to separate from the bone.

2   Warm the diced tomatoes in a small saucepan over low heat. Add 2 tablespoons vinaigrette and stir.

3   Dunk the blanched cabbage leaves into the fish's cooking broth long enough to heat them up. Remove them with a skimmer, drain, squeeze out the excess liquid, and arrange them in the center of a serving platter. Drizzle with 2 table-spoons vinaigrette. Remove the skin from the skate and remove the flesh from the bone. Flake it and put it on top of the cabbage. Top with the warmed tomatoes and then the minced onions. Sprinkle with chives, chervil, fleur de sel, and black pepper. Whisk the vinaigrette and pour it over the whole.

1 piece skate, about 2 pounds (1 kg.)
Coarse salt
1⅔ cups (40 cl.) malt vinegar
1 bouquet garni (1 small stalk celery, 6 stems parsley, and 2 sprigs thyme, tied together)
4 medium tomatoes, peeled, seeded, and diced (page 124)
1 recipe vinaigrette (page 59)
½ small green cabbage, leaves plucked and blanched (page 556)
4 small white onions, peeled and minced
1 teaspoon minced chives
1 teaspoon minced chervil
Fleur de sel
Crushed black pepper

Sole

Sole has an advantage over other fish in that it cannot be farmed. You may be certain, therefore, that the sole you buy is wild.

The majestic sole is our flat fish par excellence. The ancient Romans respectfully called it "Jupiter's sandal." (The word *sole* comes from the Latin word for sandal, *solea.*) It became fashionable in seventeenth-century France and enjoyed another vogue in the 1800s. In the United States sole is often confused with other flat fish, such as lemon sole, which are not as fine as the real Pacific or Atlantic sole.

Dover sole is the finest variety, with its firm, white flesh and delicate taste. A sole's eyes are on the right side of its head. Its skin should be viscous, its scales firm and firmly attached, its gills wine-red, and its eye bulging and brilliant. The blind side should be bright white.

Avoid buying precut fillets, for fishmongers often carve them from fish that are about to go bad.

TO PREPARE SOLE

Use kitchen shears to snip away the side fins and the long fin running all around the fish, beginning at the tail. Lay the fish on a work surface or cutting board, white side down and tail toward you. With a knife, make an incision in the skin just above the tail fin.

Hold the end of the tail with the tips of your fingers and use the blade of a knife to scrape the fish from tail to head in order to loosen the skin a bit by detaching it from the flesh. Grab the skin with a paper towel and pull it toward the head to remove the black skin entirely. Turn the fish over and scrape the other side the same way, tail to head. Turn the fish over again and make a 2- to 3-inch (4- to 6-cm.) incision ½ inch (1 cm.) from the edge of the fish, beginning near the base of the head and running along the right side. Lift the blackish parts and the egg sac, if there is one, out of the fish with the tip of a knife and remove the gills.

Carefully rinse the fish under cold running water and keep chilled until cooking time.

SOLE MEUNIÈRE

SERVES   4
PREPARATION   5 minutes
COOKING   8 minutes

Ask the fishmonger to remove the black skin and scale the white skin.

1   Carefully wash the fish and dry them with paper towels. Season with salt and pepper.

2   Just before cooking, dust the fish with flour; tap them gently against one another to knock off any excess flour.

3   If you can, cook the sole 2 at a time. Heat 1 tablespoon oil and 1 teaspoon butter in a skillet. When the butter foams, lay 2 soles in the pan, white skin side down, and let them cook over medium-low heat for 4 minutes. Swirl the skillet for uniform coloring. Use a spatula to turn the fish and cook 4 minutes on the other side, spooning the cooking fat over them from time to time.

4   Remove the first 2 fish and cook the other 2 the same way, adding 1 tablespoon oil if necessary. Arrange all the fish on a serving plate.

5   Melt the rest of the butter in the skillet. When it is almost nut brown, add the juice of 1 lemon, swirl the skillet, and pour the hot lemony butter over the fish. Garnish each fish with a lemon quarter and serve.

4 soles, ½ pound (250 g.) each
Salt
Pepper
4 tablespoons flour
1 or 2 tablespoons neutral oil
3 tablespoons butter
2 lemons, 1 juiced and
    1 quartered

NORMANDY SOLE

Filets de sole normande

SERVES   4

PREPARATION AND COOKING   1 hour

Sole was famously prepared this way—poached and covered in an ivory reduction sauce—at the Parisian restaurant Le Rocher de Cancale, where Balzac was a devoted diner. Some people, persuaded that they have discovered the "true" recipe, maintain that the sole must be baked, not poached with an aromatic garnish.

Have the fishmonger remove the fillets and chop up the heads and bones.

1   MAKE THE STOCK   Heat the butter in a saucepan or soup pot. When it foams, add the onion and cook for 3 minutes over low heat without allowing it to color. Add the chopped fish heads and bones, and cook 3 minutes more over low heat, stirring regularly with a wooden spoon. Add the bouquet garni and pour in the Chardonnay and the same amount (1 cup/ 20 cl.) of water. Add ½ teaspoon coarse salt and a pinch of pepper. Bring to a boil and simmer for 15 minutes. Remove the pot from the heat. Allow the stock to rest for 10 minutes before putting it through a fine strainer into another pot.

2   PREPARE THE GARNISH   Melt ½ tablespoon butter in a large saucepan or pot. When it foams, add the shallot and cook for 2 minutes over very low heat. Pour the Chardonnay into the pot along with the mussels and 2 pinches of pepper. Stir, cover, and cook over high heat for 4 minutes, shaking the pot frequently during cooking. Remove the pot from the heat, drain the mussels, and remove them from their shells. Do not discard the cooking juices. Put them through a fine strainer into a bowl and set aside. This part of the garnish will be stirred into the sauce.

3   Heat ½ tablespoon butter, 1 tablespoon water, 1 teaspoon lemon juice, and the mushrooms in a small saucepan. Cook for 5 minutes over high heat, stirring often. Taste for salt and pepper. Remove from the heat and set aside. This part of the garnish will be reheated with the fish.

4   Put the oyster liquor in a saucepan with 1 teaspoon butter

FISH STOCK (OR USE THE RECIPE FOR FISH STOCK ON PAGE 40 OR STORE-BOUGHT)

1 teaspoon butter

1 medium onion, peeled and minced

Chopped-up heads and bones of the fish

1 small bouquet garni (1 sprig thyme, 1 stalk celery, 3 stems parsley, and 2 leek leaves, tied together)

1 cup (20 cl.) Chardonnay

Coarse salt

Pepper

GARNISH

1 tablespoon plus 1 teaspoon butter

1 shallot, peeled and chopped

½ cup (10 cl.) Chardonnay

1 pound (500 g.) mussels, scrubbed and rinsed (see page 228)

Pepper

1 teaspoon lemon juice

4 large white mushrooms, trimmed and cleaned, stems separated from caps

4 medium-sized oysters, removed from their shells (page 232), their liquid reserved and strained

(continued)

and a pinch of pepper. Add the shelled oysters and cook over high heat. Just before the liquid boils, turn off the heat. Now that the oysters are poached, remove their viscous membrane with kitchen shears. Set the trimmed oysters aside. This part of the garnish will be stirred into the sauce.

5   COOK THE FISH   Preheat the oven to 350°F/180°C.

6   Rinse and dry the sole fillets and fold them in half. Use ½ teaspoon butter to grease a baking dish large enough to hold the folded fillets and spread the chopped shallot over its bottom. Season with 2 pinches of salt and 1 pinch of pepper and lay the folded fillets on top. Add to the dish 3 tablespoons Chardonnay, the stock, the mussels' cooking liquid, and the mushrooms. Cut a piece of parchment paper the size of the top of the dish and butter it. Lay it on top of the dish, buttered side down. Bake for 5 minutes.

7   Take the dish out of the oven, remove the fish from the dish with a skimmer or a slotted spoon, and set them aside. Do not turn off the oven.

8   MAKE THE SAUCE   Pour the cooking juices into a saucepan, bring to a boil, and boil for 10 minutes. Pour in half of the cream and boil 5 minutes more over medium heat. Whip the remaining well-chilled cream until it is quite firm. Put the contents of the saucepan through a fine strainer into a bowl and fold in the whipped cream. Gently stir in the garnish of mussels, oysters, and shrimp.

9   FINISH THE DISH   Lay the sole in a baking dish and arrange the sautéed mushrooms around it. Slip the dish into the oven for 3–4 minutes, still at 350°F/180°C, to reheat.

10 Add a few drops of lemon juice to the sauce and season to taste with salt and pepper. Cover the fillets and mushrooms with the garnish-filled sauce and sprinkle with chopped parsley to serve.

¼ pound (100 g.) large pink shrimp, cooked and peeled
Salt

FISH
2 soles, 1¼ pounds (600 g.) each
1 teaspoon butter
½ shallot, peeled and chopped
Salt
Pepper
3 tablespoons Chardonnay

SAUCE
1 cup (20 cl.) heavy cream, well chilled

TO FINISH
Drops lemon juice
Salt
Pepper
2 tablespoons chopped parsley

FILLET OF SOLE WITH ARTICHOKES AND MUSHROOMS

Filets de sole aux artichauts et champignons

SERVES 4

PREPARATION 30 minutes

COOKING 1 hour and 20 minutes for the stock and basil
sauce, 40 minutes for the vermouth sauce, plus
3 minutes for the fish

Ask the fishmonger to fillet the fish and give you the
chopped-up heads and bones.

1 PREPARE THE STOCK Heat the butter in a saucepan over
medium heat. Add the onion and cook for 2 minutes, stirring
with a wooden spoon. Add the fish heads and bones and
cook 3 minutes more. Add the bouquet garni, Chardonnay,
and 1 cup (20 cl.) water. Bring to a simmer and simmer for
20 minutes. Turn off the heat and let the stock rest for
10 minutes before putting it through a fine strainer into
another saucepan.

2 PREPARE THE GARNISH Cut the artichoke heart into ¼-inch
(0.5-cm.) dice. Toss the artichoke heart dice in the lemon juice.

3 Heat 1 teaspoon oil and 1 tablespoon butter in a skillet. Add
the artichoke and mushroom dice and sauté for 1 minute
over rather high heat, stirring. Remove them from the pan
and set them aside, but do not clean the pan.

4 BEGIN TO MAKE THE BASIL SAUCE Put the strained stock
back on the stovetop and boil for 30 minutes to reduce. Stir
in 1 cup heavy cream and cook over low heat until the sauce
is syrupy. Remove from the heat.

5 BEGIN TO MAKE THE VERMOUTH SAUCE Put the shallots in
a small saucepan with the vermouth and simmer for 20 minutes. Add the soy sauce, bring back to a boil, and then
remove from the heat and set aside.

6 PREPARE THE FISH FOR COOKING Rinse the fish and pat
dry. Use a small, sharp knife to make a few incisions in the
skin, on the bias, to prevent the skin from shrinking and
curling up during cooking. Beat the egg yolks with ½ teaspoon water and a pinch of salt.

7 Finish the garnish. Reheat the artichoke and mushroom dice
in their still-buttery skillet. Season with salt and pepper.

FISH STOCK

1 tablespoon butter

1 onion, peeled and cut into
slivers

Chopped-up heads and bones
of the fish

1 bouquet garni (1 sprig thyme,
1 stalk celery, and 5 stems
parsley, wrapped and tied
in a white leek leaf)

1 cup (20 cl.) Chardonnay

GARNISH

1 large green globe artichoke
heart (page 179)

Juice of ¼ lemon

1 teaspoon olive oil

1 teaspoon butter

3 ounces (80 g.) white button
mushrooms, trimmed,
cleaned, and cut into
¼-inch (0.5-cm.) dice

Salt

Pepper

BASIL SAUCE

1 cup (20 cl.) heavy cream

1 tablespoon butter

Salt

Pepper

(continued)

8   Finish the basil sauce. Reheat the stock and cream reduction. Stir in 1 tablespoon butter with a wooden spoon. Taste for salt and pepper and stir in the diced tomato and minced basil.

9   Finish the vermouth sauce. Reheat, stir in 1 tablespoon butter, and taste for salt and pepper.

10 Cook the fish. Use a pastry brush to paint the fish with the beaten egg yolks and cover with chopped parsley on both sides. Heat 1 teaspoon oil and 1 tablespoon butter in a skillet over medium heat. Add the fish and cook for 1½ minutes, seasoning the exposed sides with salt and pepper. Turn them over, season, and cook 1 minute on the second side.

11 Finish the dish. Cover the fillets with the mushroom and artichoke garnish. Sprinkle with chervil and drizzle with vermouth sauce. Serve the rest of the vermouth sauce on the side, along with the basil sauce.

1 large tomato, peeled, seeded (page 124), and cut into ¼-inch (0.5-cm.) dice

4 basil leaves, minced

VERMOUTH SAUCE

2 shallots, peeled and minced

½ cup (15 cl.) dry vermouth (preferably Noilly Prat)

3 tablespoons (5 cl.) soy sauce

1 tablespoon well-chilled butter

Salt

Pepper

FISH

2 soles, about 1 pound (500–600 g.) each

2 egg yolks (page 204)

Salt

2 tablespoons chopped parsley

1 teaspoon neutral oil

1 tablespoon butter

Salt

Pepper

TO FINISH

1 tablespoon chervil leaves

DEEP-FRIED SOLE GOUJONNETTES

Goujonnettes de filets de sole frites

SERVES   4

PREPARATION AND COOKING   15 minutes

A goujonnette is a small piece of fish, usually deep-fried.

1   Rinse and dry the fish. Slice it on the diagonal into small strips about 1 inch by 2–3 inches (2 cm. by 5–7 cm.).

2   Beat the eggs in a bowl with the milk, olive oil, 1 teaspoon

Fillets of 2 (1 pound/500–600 g.) soles

4 eggs

2 tablespoons milk

2 tablespoons olive oil

salt, and a pinch of pepper. Spread the flour in one large flat dish and the bread crumbs in another.

3   Begin to heat the oil for frying to 350°F/180°C. Prepare a plate lined with paper towels.

4   Roll the fish strips in the flour, dip them in the beaten egg, and then coat them in bread crumbs. Pat the coating on with your hands and lay the fish on a plate.

5   When the oil is hot enough, fry the goujonnettes. (Oil that is hot enough will fizz up with small bubbles when the fish hit it.) Remove when they have turned a light gold and set them to drain on the paper towel–lined plate. Season lightly with salt.

6   Fry the parsley for a few seconds and salt it, too.

7   Serve goujonnettes with the fried parsley and quartered lemons, with the sauce on the side.

Salt
Pepper
1 tablespoon flour
1 cup dry bread crumbs
Neutral oil for frying
1 cup curly parsley leaves, washed and very well dried
2 lemons, quartered
Béarnaise sauce (page 48) or tartar sauce

SOLE BENOÎT

Soles au plat à la façon de Benoît

SERVES   4

PREPARATION   20 minutes

COOKING   8 minutes for the fish plus 4 minutes for the mussels

Ask the fishmonger to remove the fins, gills, and guts from the fish; to remove the black skin but leave the white; and to scale the fish.

1   Preheat the oven to 440°F/220°C.

2   Rinse and dry the fish. Lay the fish next to one another on a work surface, skin side down. Make an incision on the skinless side of each fish at the level of the central bone. Lift the fillets gently by slipping a knife from the center toward the edges. Tuck ½ teaspoon butter into this pocket.

3   Butter a very large ovenproof baking dish (large enough to hold all the fish in a single layer, or use 2 dishes if necessary). Spread the shallots over the bottom of the dish and lay the fish on top, white skin side down. Season each fish with 2 generous pinches of salt and a dash of pepper. Spritz the lemon juice and cider all over and bake for 8 minutes.

4 soles, ½ pound (250 g.) each
2 teaspoons butter plus extra for greasing the baking dish
4 shallots, peeled and chopped
Salt
Pepper
Juice of 1 lemon
1 cup (20 cl.) hard cider
(continued)

4   In the meantime, put the cleaned mussels in a large pot with 2 pinches of pepper. Cover and cook over high heat for 4 minutes, shaking the pot frequently until they open. Take them out of the pot immediately with a slotted spoon and remove them from their shells. Save and carefully strain their cooking juices.

5   After 8 minutes, check to see whether the sole is cooked: With the tip of a knife, lift the bone from the flesh. If this is easy to do, the fish is cooked.

6   Add the cream to the baking dish along with the mussels' cooking juices and the mussels themselves. Sprinkle with chervil, 1 scant teaspoon salt, and a pinch of pepper. Bake 3 minutes more, just long enough to reheat the whole.

1½ pounds (700 g.) mussels, well scrubbed and washed in several changes of water
1 cup (20 cl.) heavy cream
1 tablespoon chervil leaves

PAN FRIED SOLE WITH ZUCCHINI

Soles poêlées aux courgettes

SERVES   4

PREPARATION AND COOKING   30 minutes

Ask the fishmonger to remove the guts, head, fins, and black skin from the fish and remove the scales from the white skin.

1   Preheat the oven to 250°F/120°C and set an ovenproof plate or platter in it to warm.

2   Rinse and dry the fish. Put the milk in a deep dish and the flour on a plate. One by one, dip the fish in the milk, allow to drip-dry a few seconds, and then coat with flour. Gently tap them together to knock off any excess flour. Set them aside, white skin side up, until the pan is ready for cooking.

3   Heat 2 tablespoons peanut oil in a large skillet over low heat. When it is hot, add 1 tablespoon butter. When the butter foams, lay 2 of the fish in the skillet, white skin side down, and cook over low heat until they have taken on some color, about 4 minutes per side. Regularly spoon the cooking fat over them, especially over their thick centers, which take the longest to cook. Check to see whether the fish is cooked by using a knife to lift the bone from the skinless side. If this is

4 soles, ½ pound (250 g.) each
½ cup milk
⅔ cup (100 g.) flour
4 tablespoons peanut oil
1 tablespoon butter
4 small zucchini, washed and sliced on the bias into rounds ¼ inch (0.5 cm.) thick
Salt
Pepper
Juice of 1 lemon
1 tablespoon snipped chives

easy to do, the fish is finished. Remove them to the warmed plate or platter and put them in the oven with the door ajar. Cook the remaining fish the same way in the same skillet. Add more oil and butter only if necessary (it should not be).

4   Heat the remaining peanut oil in a skillet. When it is hot, cook the zucchini slices for 3–4 minutes over medium heat, stirring, until they begin to soften. Season with 1 scant teaspoon salt and a pinch of pepper and stir.

5   Scatter the zucchini around the fish on a serving platter. Anoint each fish with a few drops of lemon juice and sprinkle with chives.

Tuna

There are fifty different species of tuna or tuna-like fish living in tropical and subtropical waters all over the world, but only a few of these species (for instance, yellowfin, albacore, skipjack, and big-eye tuna) are commercialized. The bluefin is highly prized, to the point that it is now threatened by overfishing.

Tuna must be very fresh. The best part is the belly, called *ventrèche* in French. Its deep red color calls to mind beef, and indeed it is cooked like beef: very fast, over high heat. Once cooked, it should be warm inside but stay raw, or almost raw. Overcooking will toughen it.

Tuna travels huge distances in search of food. Some can reach 360 pounds (180 kg.). This carnivore generally enjoys a long life and therefore ingests more heavy metals over time than many other fish. Heavy metals such as mercury, dumped in the ocean by human activity, accumulate at every step of the food chain; animals at the top ingest all the heavy metals consumed by their prey and their prey's prey and so on. For this reason, no one should eat huge amounts of tuna or eat it too frequently. Pregnant women and young children should take special care.

Never cook tuna at a low temperature (under 150°F/65°C) as this can spread any toxins the fish might contain, leading to serious health problems.

MARINATED TUNA WITH TOMATO

Thon mariné

SERVES 4
PREPARATION 15 minutes

The tomatoes need to marinate overnight.

1   Cut the tomatoes into very small cubes (about ⅛ inch/ 2 mm.). Put them in a bowl with the olive oil, stir, cover, and marinate for 24 hours.

2   One hour before serving, rinse the fish and dry it with paper towels. Cut it into slices about ⅛ inch (2 mm.) thick. Put the slices side by side on a serving dish or on individual plates. Cover with plastic wrap and refrigerate.

3   Just before serving, remove the tuna from the refrigerator and discard the plastic wrap. Scatter the marinated tomato cubes over the fish and add a few drops of the marinating oil. Season evenly with Espelette pepper, the crushed peppercorns, and fleur de sel. If you like, sprinkle with chives.

8 dried tomatoes, (page 588 or store-bought)
3 tablespoons olive oil
1 pound very fresh tuna fillet, preferably bluefin
1 dash powdered Espelette pepper or New Mexico chili powder
4 peppercorns (Sarawak or Malabar, if possible), crushed
Fleur de sel
1 teaspoon minced chives (optional)

TUNA WITH A SOY SAUCE

Thon à la sauce soja

SERVES 4
PREPARATION 45 minutes
COOKING 5 minutes

1   Warm the soy sauce, vinegar, ¼ cup olive oil, and garlic in a small saucepan over high heat. When the mixture comes to a boil, lower the heat and simmer for about 25 minutes, until it is reduced to about a third of its original volume. Remove the saucepan from the heat and cover it with a plate.

2   While the sauce simmers, spread the flour on a plate. Toss the onion slices in the flour and tap them to remove the excess. Warm the neutral oil in a frying pan over high heat. Prepare a plate lined with 4 or 5 sheets of paper towel. When the oil is hot (320°F/160°C), lower the floured onion slices

2 tablespoons soy sauce
¼ cup wine vinegar
¼ cup plus 1 tablespoon olive oil
1 clove garlic, peeled and quartered
⅔ cup (80 g.) flour
5 small onions, peeled and thinly sliced
1 cup (25 cl.) neutral oil

into it. Flip them with a skimmer. As soon as they are blond—they should not darken—remove them with the skimmer to a colander. When most of the oil has dripped off, drain them further on the plate of paper towels. Sprinkle with fleur de sel.

3   Rinse the fish and dry with paper towels. Season on both sides with the crushed black pepper and a pinch of salt.

4   Remove the garlic from the saucepan of reduced sauce and warm the sauce over low heat, stirring in the capers, green pepper, both kinds of olives, piquillo strips, and thyme leaves.

5   Warm the remaining olive oil in a skillet over high heat. When it is very hot, sear the tuna 2 minutes per side, flipping carefully with plastic tongs or a wooden spatula. It should still be raw inside; if you prefer tuna slightly more cooked, leave it a minute or two extra per side, but be careful not to overcook it. Remove the cooked tuna to a plate.

6   Slice the tuna ½ inch (1.5 cm.) thick. Arrange the slices on a serving dish or individual dishes, top with the warm sauce, surround with dried tomato quarters, and sprinkle with the fried onions.

Fleur de sel
1½ pounds tuna belly
Generous ½ teaspoon crushed
    black pepper
Salt
1 tablespoon capers
1 teaspoon green pepper
1 tablespoon small black olives,
    pitted and cut into ⅛-inch
    (2.5-mm.) cubes
1 tablespoon green olives,
    pitted and cut into ⅛-inch
    (2.5-mm.) cubes
Twenty ½-inch (1.5-cm.) wide
    strips jarred piquillo
    peppers
Pinch fresh thyme leaves
4 dried tomatoes (page 588 or
    store-bought), quartered

Turbot

Turbot is one of the finest fish. Its white, firm, flaky flesh has earned it the title of "King of Lent."

This flat fish lives in the sandy bottoms of the Atlantic and Mediterranean coasts. Like sole, its eyes are on one side of its head. It is scaleless, white on one side and brownish on the other. Only the white skin is edible.

Turbot can be poached, grilled, fried, cooked in a packet, or cooked in sauce. A large specimen is usually carved into fillets or steaks. A small turbot is often grilled whole.

It is crucial not to overcook turbot, for its delicate flesh will lose its delightful taste and texture.

TURBOT STEAKS DUGLÉRÉ

Tronçons de turbot Dugléré

SERVES 4
PREPARATION 5 minutes
COOKING 25 minutes

1 Heat the olive oil in a skillet. Cook the tomatoes for 5 minutes over low heat, stirring with a wooden spoon. Add the garlic, a pinch of salt, and a pinch of pepper. Turn off the heat.

2 Heat 2 teaspoons butter in a large saucepan or pot. Add the onion and shallots and cook for 3 minutes over low heat, stirring with a wooden spoon. Add the tomato mixture, mix well to combine, and remove from the burner.

3 Rinse the fish for 2 minutes under cold running water. Dry with paper towels, season with salt and pepper, and then slip the fish into the pot of vegetables. Add the fish stock and bring to a simmer. Cover and cook gently for 15 minutes. Check to see that the fish is cooked by trying to lift a bone from the flesh; if it comes apart easily, the turbot is cooked.

4 Take the fish out of the pot and remove its black skin. Arrange the fish on a serving platter and tent with aluminum foil.

5 Bring the sauce in the pot to a boil and boil for 4 minutes, stirring with a wooden spoon. Turn the heat to very low and stir in the remaining 4 teaspoons butter, which should be well chilled. Turn off the heat. Taste for salt and pepper, and stir in the chervil.

6 Dress the turbot with the sauce and serve.

2 tablespoons olive oil

4 medium tomatoes, peeled, seeded, and chopped into ½-inch (1-cm.) dice (page 124)

1 clove garlic, peeled and minced

Salt

Pepper

2 tablespoons butter, well chilled

1 medium onion, peeled and minced

4 medium shallots, peeled and minced

4 turbot steaks, 9–10 ounces (280–300 g.) each

2 cups (40 cl.) fish stock (page 40 or store-bought)

1 tablespoon chervil leaves

GRILLED TURBOT WITH CHORON SAUCE

Turbot grillé, sauce Choron

SERVES 4
PREPARATION 20 minutes
COOKING 15 minutes

1 Preheat the oven to 410°F/210°C. Rinse the turbot slices and let them sit under running water for a couple of minutes. Drain.

2 Put the olive oil in a dish with the crumbled thyme and bay leaf. Dry the fish with paper towels, season all over with salt and pepper, and then lay it in the seasoned oil. Turn the fish in the oil to coat well.

3 Heat a cast-iron grill pan. When it is very hot, lay the fish on it on a diagonal. After 2 minutes, give each piece a quarter turn to make crosshatch grill marks and cook 2 minutes more. Flip the fish over and cook the other side the same way.

4 Remove the fish to a baking dish in a single layer. Paint them with the seasoned olive oil and finish by cooking in the oven for 10 minutes.

5 Lay the fish slices on a serving platter and surround them with the halved lemons and parsley stems. Serve the hot Choron sauce on the side in a sauceboat.

4 turbot steaks, 9–10 ounces (280–300 g.) each
1 tablespoon olive oil
1 sprig thyme, crumbled
½ bay leaf, crumbled
Salt
Pepper
2 lemons, halved
4 stems parsley
Choron sauce (page 50); use half the quantity indicated for each ingredient

ROASTED BABY TURBOT WITH THYME BLOSSOMS ————

Turbotin rôti à la fleur de thym

SERVES 4
PREPARATION 10 minutes
COOKING 15–20 minutes

Ask the fishmonger to gut the fish and trim their fins.

1   Preheat the oven as hot as possible (530°F/270°C.).
2   Put the potatoes in a large pot and cover them with cold water. Add 2 teaspoons coarse salt, bring to boil, and simmer for 15–20 minutes, until the potatoes are just cooked but not overcooked. (A fork will slide easily into the flesh.)
3   In the meantime, rinse the fish under cold running water and dry them with paper towels. Pour 3 tablespoons olive oil into a baking dish large enough to hold both fish but not too much bigger than that. Lay the fish in the oil side by side and season on both sides with the thyme blossoms and some salt and pepper. Pour the remaining 3 tablespoons olive oil over the fish and bake for 15 minutes.
4   Peel the cooked potatoes and slice them into thin rounds. Lay them around the rim of a serving platter and sprinkle with fleur de sel, crushed black pepper, and chives.
5   The fish is cooked when its flesh is white and opaque and easy to remove from the bone. At this point, take it from the oven to a cutting board. Remove the skin and carve out the fillets. Lay the fillets in the center of the serving platter and season with salt and pepper. Sprinkle with parsley. Drizzle a thin stream of best-quality olive oil over the fish and potatoes and serve.

4 medium firm-fleshed potatoes, such as roseval or waxy red boiling potatoes, scrubbed clean
Coarse salt
2 small turbot, about 2 pounds (1 kg.) each
6 tablespoons olive oil
1 teaspoon fresh thyme blossoms
Salt
Pepper
Fleur de sel
Crushed black pepper
1 tablespoon snipped chives
1 teaspoon minced flat-leaf parsley
Best-quality olive oil to finish

STEAMED TURBOT WITH AROMATIC OIL

Turbot à la vapeur à l'huile aromatise

SERVES 4

PREPARATION 40 minutes

COOKING 5 minutes

The oil must be prepared the night before.

Ask the fishmonger to fillet the fish and skin the fillets.

1   The night before, use a vegetable peeler to slice strips of skin and flesh ⅓ inch (8 mm.) thick from the zucchini; cut strips into small dice.

2   Bring 1 quart (1 l.) water to a boil with 2 teaspoons coarse salt. When the water bubbles, cook the zucchini, celery, and fennel for 2 minutes. Remove them with a skimmer to a colander and rinse under cold water until they have cooled a bit. Allow them to drain in the colander.

3   Put the red and green bell peppers, mushroom, basil, bouquet garni, olive oil, olives, tomatoes, hot chili pepper, and garlic in a small bowl with the zucchini, celery, and fennel. Add ½ teaspoon salt and cover with plastic wrap. Refrigerate or leave out at room temperature.

4   The next day, slice the peel and pith from the orange and lemon so that their juicy flesh is completely exposed. Cut into small dice, removing the pits.

5   Bring water to a boil in a saucepan fitted with a steamer basket. Rinse the turbot fillets under cold running water and dry them with paper towels. Season with salt and pepper on both sides. Prepare 4 pieces of plastic wrap, each one large enough to wrap up a fillet. Lay a fillet on each piece, add 1 teaspoon butter and a sprig of thyme, and then seal the packets well. Place the packets in the steamer basket, cover the pot, and cook for 5 minutes.

6   In the meantime, remove the hot pepper, garlic, and bouquet garni from the oil. Pour the oil into a small saucepan set over low heat. Add the orange and lemon, and stir with a wooden spoon.

7   Snip the packets open with scissors; they are very hot inside, so be careful. Remove the fish to a platter and coat with the warm aromatic oil.

1 zucchini

Coarse salt

1 stalk celery (fibrous parts removed if necessary), cut into small dice

¼ fennel bulb (thick outer layer removed), cut into small dice

1 red bell pepper, peeled, seeded (page 130), and cut into small dice

1 green bell pepper, peeled, seeded (page 130), and cut into small dice

1 large white mushroom, trimmed, cleaned, and cut into small dice

1 bunch basil, leaves only, washed and dried

1 small bouquet garni (1 small celery stalk, 3 sprigs thyme, and 5 sprigs flat-leaf parsley, tied together)

1 cup (25 cl.) olive oil

4 green olives, pitted and cut into small dice

2 small tomatoes, peeled, seeded, and cut into small dice (page 124)

½ small hot chili pepper

1 clove garlic, peeled and degermed (page 122)

Salt

½ orange

½ lemon

4 turbot fillets, about 6 ounces (200 g.) each

Pepper

4 teaspoons butter

4 sprigs thyme

POACHED TURBOT WITH BASIL

Blanc de turbot au basilic

SERVES   4
PREPARATION   10 minutes
COOKING   10–12 minutes

You can also prepare this recipe with slices of turbot instead of fillets. If you use slices, cook them with the skin on but remove the skin before serving. Bake slightly longer—12 to 14 minutes total.

1   Preheat the oven to 300°F/150°C.

2   Rinse the turbot fillets under cold running water and dry with paper towels. Season with salt and pepper on both sides.

3   If you have a long, narrow fish pan, heat 1 tablespoon butter in it. (If you do not have a fish pan, use a large ovenproof saucepan that can hold the fish in a single layer.) Add the minced onions and some salt, stir with a wooden spoon, and cook over low heat for 3 minutes, stirring frequently. Turn off the heat.

4   Lay the fish in the fish pan or saucepan and add the fish stock and white wine. Cut out a piece of parchment paper the size and shape of the pan and prick it a few times with a fork or the tip of a knife. Lay the paper atop the fish. Bake the fish for 10–12 minutes. Two minutes before removing the fish from the oven, slip a serving platter into the oven to warm. When the fish is finished cooking, remove it to the warm platter and cover with the parchment paper.

5   Put the fish pan with the liquid over high heat. Bring to a boil and cook until the liquid has been reduced by two-thirds. Turn off the heat, add the remaining 2 tablespoons butter, and stir with a wooden spatula. Stir in the diced tomatoes and basil. Taste for salt and pepper. Remove the parchment paper from the fish and pour the sauce over.

4 skinless turbot fillets, about
  6 ounces (200 g.) each
Salt
Pepper
3 tablespoons butter
4 small new white onions,
  peeled and minced
1 cup (20 cl.) fish stock (page
  40 or store-bought) or
  water if necessary
1 cup (20 cl.) white wine,
  preferably Chardonnay
2 medium tomatoes, peeled,
  seeded, and cut into small
  dice (page 124)
1 bunch basil, washed, leaves
  only

POACHED TURBOT WITH HOLLANDAISE SAUCE _____

Turbot poché, sauce hollandaise

SERVES 4
PREPARATION 5 minutes
COOKING 15 minutes

1 Rinse the fish slices and let them sit under cold running water for a few minutes. Put them in a large pot in a single layer; they should not crowd one another. Cover them with cold water and then add the milk and some coarse salt.

2 Gently bring the liquid in the pot almost but not quite to a boil. Keep the liquid at this shuddering temperature over very low heat for 15 minutes to poach the fish.

3 Take the fish out of the pot with a skimmer or slotted spoon and remove their skin. Serve with the halved lemons and with the hollandaise sauce on the side.

4 turbot steaks, about ½ pound (280–300 g.) each
1 cup (25 cl.) milk
Coarse salt
2 lemons, halved
Hollandaise sauce (page 52, using half of the quantity indicated for each ingredient)

Whiting _____

Whiting is a fish that does not frequently find its way to our tables. Its flesh, however, is quite tasty, it's easy to digest, and it's inexpensive to boot.

Choose a whiting that isn't too big—no larger than ¾ pound (400 g.). The back should be quite round, the body silvery and shining, and the eye bulging, lively, clear, and unclouded. The best whitings are line-caught and gutted immediately. You will know them by their open bellies.

Eat whiting very fresh, for its taste degrades rapidly. Like most fish, whiting must not be kept in the refrigerator at home for more than twenty-four hours. Whiting is usually eaten in fillets to avoid the bones, but it can also be eaten whole. However it is prepared, it will not do to cook it too long, for its fragile flesh will disintegrate.

COLBERT FRIED WHITING

Merlans frits Colbert

SERVES   4
PREPARATION   20 minutes
COOKING   about 5 minutes

Fish preparations that call for fillets to be dipped into egg and bread crumbs and then fried are called *Colbert,* after the prime minister of Louis XIV. Ask the fishmonger to clip off the whitings' fins, to gut them through the gills, and to remove their bones.

4 whiting, ⅓–½ pound (150–225 g.) each
3 quarts (3 l.) neutral oil for frying
4 eggs
2 tablespoons olive oil
2½ cups dry bread crumbs
⅔ cup (100 g.) flour
Salt
Pepper
1 tablespoon minced parsley
1 lemon, sliced
1 recipe *beurre maître d'hôtel* (page 46)

1   Wash and dry the whiting. If the fishmonger did not remove the bones, make an incision along each side of the backbone of each fish, cutting with a sharp knife right next to the bone to detach the flesh. Snip the backbone with kitchen shears at each end (head and tail), remove it, and discard it. Open the fish a bit, gently, to form a sort of pocket. Rinse this cavity under cold running water and dry with paper towels.

2   Heat the frying oil in a fryer or heavy pot.

3   Beat the eggs in a deep dish with the olive oil. Put the bread crumbs in a second dish and the flour in a third. Set the dishes next to one another in a row: flour, egg, and crumbs.

4   Prepare a plate lined with 4 layers of paper towels. When the frying oil reaches 350°F/180°C, dip the skin side of a whiting in the flour and then in the eggs. Coat the skin side generously with bread crumbs and slip the fish into the hot oil. Repeat for the other fish. Fry until the fish is a lovely light gold, about 5 minutes. Flip with a skimmer after 3 minutes. Do not crowd the fish during frying. Remove with the skimmer to the paper towel–lined plate.

5   Season each fish with 2 pinches of salt and a pinch of pepper. Sprinkle with parsley and serve with lemon slices and *beurre maître d'hôtel* on the side.

WHITING FILLETS BERCY

Filets de merlan au plat Bercy

SERVES 4
PREPARATION 10 minutes
COOKING 6–8 minutes

The food stands of Bercy—the part of Paris that was long home to the largest wine merchants in Europe—were once known for preparing many of their dishes with wine and shallots, whether the star of the meal was fried or grilled meat, eggs, or a fish stew.

8 whiting fillets
Salt
Pepper
3 tablespoons butter
    (2 teaspoons melted)
2 shallots, peeled and minced
1 cup (20 cl.) dry white wine
1 sprig thyme
Juice of 1 lemon
1 tablespoon chopped flat-leaf
    parsley

1 Preheat the oven to 450°F/220°C. Gently rinse the whiting fillets and dry with paper towels. Season each fillet with 2 pinches of salt and a dash of pepper.
2 Grease a large baking dish with the melted butter; you can spread it on with a pastry brush. Sprinkle it with the minced shallots. Season with a pinch of salt and a dash of pepper.
3 Lay the fillets on the baking dish. Dot them with a scant 2 tablespoons butter chopped into small pieces. Pour the wine into the baking dish without dousing the whiting. Toss in the thyme and bake for 6–8 minutes, basting frequently with pan juices. Put an empty ovenproof serving plate into the oven to warm. The fish is cooked when the flesh is white and opaque all the way through.
4 Remove the fish to the hot serving plate.
5 Pour the cooking juices from the baking dish into a small saucepan with the lemon juice. Turn the heat to low and gradually stir in 1 teaspoon diced butter. Off the heat, stir in the parsley.
6 Pour the sauce over the whiting and serve immediately.

FRIED WHITING MEUNIÈRE

Merlans poêlés meunière

SERVES 4
PREPARATION 5 minutes
COOKING 6–8 minutes

Preparations *"à la meunière"* call for fish to be fried after being dipped in flour, for the meunière was the miller's wife.
Ask the fishmonger to remove the fins and guts.

1   Rinse the fish and dry them with paper towels. Season each one inside and out with 2 pinches of salt and a pinch of pepper. Sprinkle them all over with flour and then tap them gently to knock off any excess flour.

2   Heat the oil in a skillet and add 1 teaspoon butter. When the butter foams, cook the whiting for 3–4 minutes over low heat until they are prettily and evenly colored. Turn them with a spatula and cook for 3–4 minutes on the other side.

3   Remove the fish to a platter and arrange them diagonally. Add the rest of the butter to the skillet, still over low heat. When it is foamy and beginning to color, add the lemon juice. Pour the lemony butter over the whiting.

4 whiting, 6 ounces (180 g.) each
Salt
Pepper
3 tablespoons flour
3 tablespoons neutral oil
2 tablespoons butter
Juice of 1 lemon

WHITING WITH FENNEL, ANISE, AND TOMATO

Dos de merlan poêlé aux aromates

SERVES 4
PREPARATION 15 minutes
COOKING 8 minutes

Ask the fishmonger to gut the whiting and remove their fins, heads, and lateral bones.

1   Rinse the fish and dry with paper towels. Put them on a plate and season with salt and pepper inside and out.

2   Bring 1 quart (1 l.) water to a boil with 1 teaspoon coarse salt. Boil the fennel, asparagus, and leeks for 2 minutes. Remove them to a colander.

4 whiting, 6 ounces (180 g.) each
Salt
Pepper
Coarse salt
4 baby fennel bulbs, cleaned and trimmed

3   Melt 1 tablespoon butter in a skillet. When it foams, add the vegetables and tomatoes and stir well over low heat. Leave the skillet over low heat, remembering to stir the vegetables every 5 minutes.

4   Melt 1 tablespoon butter in a large skillet over medium heat. When it foams, carefully add the fish to the pan and cook for 3–4 minutes. Turn them gently with a spatula to cook 3–4 minutes on the other side, still over medium heat. The fish are cooked when their flesh is white and opaque throughout and can be easily pulled from the bone.

5   Stir 2 tablespoons vinegar into the skillet of vegetables and taste for salt and pepper. Remove the vegetables and lay them on a platter or on individual plates in this order: fennel, leek, tomato, and asparagus, topped by a leaf of basil. Set the fish on top of the vegetables.

6   Turn the heat under the fish-cooking skillet to high and add the rest of the vinegar, the star anise, and the chicken consommé or broth. Cook, stirring, for 2 or 3 minutes and then taste for salt and pepper. Pour the sauce over the fish.

4 small asparagus stalks, cleaned and tough ends removed
4 small leeks, carefully cleaned
2 tablespoons butter
4 dried tomatoes, (page 588 or store-bought)
3 tablespoons plus 1 teaspoon (5 cl.) wine vinegar
4 small basil leaves
1 star anise pod
2 tablespoons chicken consommé or broth (see page 80 and 77 or ready-made)

BREADED WHITING FILLETS WITH *BEURRE MAÎTRE D'HÔTEL*

Filets de merlan panés, beurre maître d'hôtel

SERVES   4
PREPARATION   15 minutes
COOKING   5–7 minutes

Ask the fishmonger to fillet and skin the fish.

1   Rinse the fish under cold running water and dry with paper towels. Put 3 deep dishes side by side: put the flour in the first, the eggs in the second, and the bread crumbs in the third. Season the eggs with salt and pepper and beat with a fork or a whisk. Dip both sides of each fillet in the flour, then the eggs, and then the crumbs. Pat the fillets all over on both sides with the broad side of a knife to make the breading stick and to even it out. For a more elegant presentation, you might use the back edge of the knife to score a crosshatch pattern in the breading.

8 skinless whiting fillets, cut from whole fish weighing about ½ pound (220–250 g.) each
1 tablespoon flour
2 eggs
1½ cups dry bread crumbs
Salt
Pepper

(continued)

2 Prepare the *beurre maître d'hôtel*.

3 Heat the oil and then the butter in a large skillet over fairly high heat. When the butter foams, lay the fillets side by side in the pan and brown for 3–4 minutes, depending on thickness. Flip with a spatula and cook for 2–3 minutes on the second side.

4 Arrange the fried fillets on a serving platter with a slice of *beurre maître d'hôtel* on top of each one.

1 recipe *beurre maître d'hôtel* (page 46)

2 tablespoons neutral oil

2 tablespoons butter

Freshwater Fish

Freshwater fish, once a common ingredient in the regional cuisines of France, have become rather rare as pollution has increased. Trout, which can be farmed, are an exception. Recipes for freshwater fish often have deep roots in local traditions. This is the case with *matelote,* a freshwater fish stew; you will find the recipe, called Eel Stew, on page 691, in the chapter on regional dishes.

TROUT MEUNIÈRE

Truites meunières

SERVES 4

PREPARATION 10 minutes

COOKING 10 minutes

1 Carefully rinse the trout under a thin stream of cold running water. You want to wash away the last bits of blood that gather along the backbone. Leave the fish in a bowl filled with ice water for a few minutes and then dry them with paper towels and put them in the refrigerator.

2 When you are ready to cook the fish, season them with salt and pepper inside and out. Dust them with flour and tap them gently against one another to knock off any excess.

3 Heat the oil and 1 tablespoon butter in a skillet. When the

4 trout, about ½ pound (220–250 g.) each, gutted and fins trimmed

Salt

Pepper

8 tablespoons flour

1 tablespoon neutral oil

3 tablespoons butter

Juice of 1 lemon

butter foams, lay the trout in the pan with their heads to the left and their backs toward you; this will make them easier to flip. Brown over medium heat for 5–6 minutes. Shake the skillet gently to achieve uniform coloring. Flip all the trout and brown for 4–5 minutes on the other side. Occasionally spoon the cooking fat over the fish. Remove the cooked fish to a serving platter.

4   Melt the remaining butter in the skillet. Add the lemon juice, stir, and pour the lemony butter over the trout.

TROUT POACHED IN COURT BOUILLON WITH TWO SAUCES

Truite pochée au court-bouillon aux deux sauces

SERVES   4

PREPARATION   10 minutes plus 30 minutes for the court bouillon

COOKING   10 minutes

The court bouillon must be prepared at least 1 hour in advance.

1   Carefully rinse the trout under cold running water to get rid of any spots of blood gathered along the backbone. Put the trout in a bowl of ice water and leave to soak for a few minutes. Dry with paper towels and refrigerate.

2   Prepare the court bouillon: In a large pot, bring 1 quart (1 l.) water to a boil with the bouquet garni, garlic, carrots, and 1 tablespoon coarse salt. Cover and boil for 10 minutes. Add the onion slices and Chardonnay, and boil 8–10 minutes more, uncovered. Add the peppercorns, star anise, and lemon juice. Remove from the heat and allow to cool completely. (If you choose to use store-bought powdered court bouillon instead, add it to 1 quart/1 l. water, according to the proportions recommended on the packet, and add ½ cup/10 cl. Chardonnay and the lemon juice.)

3   Prepare the Melted Butter Sauce and Nantais Butter Sauce while the court bouillon cools.

4   To cook the trout, lay them in a large pot. Pour the court bouillon over them and bring it almost to a boil over high

4 trout, ½ pound (250 g.) each
1 bouquet garni (3 stems
  parsley, 1 sprig thyme, and
  ½ bay leaf, wrapped and
  tied in a leek leaf)
1 clove garlic, peeled
2 medium carrots, peeled and
  sliced into rounds ¼ inch
  (0.5 cm.) thick
Coarse salt
1 large onion, trimmed, peeled,
  and sliced into rounds
  ¼ inch (0.5 cm.) thick
½ cup (10 cl.) Chardonnay
6 peppercorns
1 star anise
Juice of ½ lemon
(continued)

heat. Lower the heat and cook at a very gentle simmer for 8 minutes. Remove the fish with a skimmer or slotted spoon to a deep serving dish. Remove some of the vegetables from the cooking liquid and spread them evenly around the fish. Pour a little of the court bouillon over the fish and sprinkle with chopped parsley. Serve the 2 sauces hot on the side so that each diner can choose his favorite.

Melted Butter Sauce (page 44; use half the quantity indicated for each ingredient)

Nantais Butter Sauce (page 45; use half the quantity indicated for each ingredient)

1 tablespoon chopped parsley

SHAD POACHED IN COURT BOUILLON WITH HERBS ———

Alose pochée au court-bouillon, beurre aux herbes

SERVES 4
PREPARATION 45 minutes
COOKING 25 minutes

1 Carefully rinse the shad under cold running water. Leave it for 30 minutes in a bowl filled with cold water and a trayful of ice cubes.

2 Put the onions, carrots, and bouquet garni in a pot with the coarse salt and 2½ quarts (2.5 l.) water. Bring to a boil and simmer for 25–30 minutes. Add the vinegar and peppercorns and allow this court bouillon to cool.

3 Place the shad on top of a shallow rack placed in the bottom of a large pot or on the rack of a fish poacher if you have one. Cover it with the cooled court bouillon; if necessary, you can add cold water to cover the fish. Bring the liquid just to a bare simmer and leave to poach without boiling for 15 minutes. Turn off the heat and leave for 10 minutes. Lift the rack from the pot, allowing the fish to drip dry. Carefully remove its skin.

4 Brush the skinned fish with 1 teaspoon herbed Nantais Butter Sauce and serve the rest on the side in a sauceboat.

1 shad, about 2½ pounds (1.2 kg.), scales, guts, and gills removed

2 large onions, peeled and thinly sliced

2 medium carrots, peeled and thinly sliced

1 bouquet garni (1 small celery stalk, 5 stems parsley, 1 sprig thyme, and ½ bay leaf, wrapped and tied in a leek leaf)

2 tablespoons coarse salt

½ cup (10 cl.) distilled vinegar

10 peppercorns

Nantais Butter Sauce (page 45; use half the quantity indicated for each ingredient and mix in half a small bundle of chervil chopped at the end)

FRESHWATER EEL IN HERB SAUCE _____

Anguilles au vert

SERVES   4

PREPARATION   25 minutes

COOKING   20 minutes plus 25 minutes for the potatoes

1   Gently scrape the eels with a sharp knife to remove their protective grease. Rinse them under running water and dry with paper towels. Season all over with salt and pepper and refrigerate.

2   Put the potatoes in a large pot with 2 quarts (2 l.) cold water and 2 tablespoons coarse salt. Bring to a boil, lower the heat, and simmer for 25 minutes. Don't overcook them: They are done when a fork or knife slides into their flesh without meeting any resistance, and they should certainly not be so cooked that they are crumbling away.

3   Preheat the oven to 300°F/150°C while the potatoes become cool enough to handle. Peel the cooked potatoes and slice them into thin rounds. Paint a large baking dish with butter and line it with potato slices (they can overlap a bit). Season the crème fraîche and egg yolks lightly with salt and pepper and beat together with a fork. Pour this mixture over the potatoes. Put the dish in the oven and leave it there as you finish cooking.

4   Remove the eels from the refrigerator. Heat the olive oil in a large pot over high flame. Add 5 tablespoons (75 g.) butter. When it foams, add the pieces of eel and stir with a wooden spoon. Brown for 5 minutes, stirring. Remove the eel pieces with a skimmer or slotted spoon and put them in a colander to drain.

5   Melt the remaining butter in another pot over low heat. Add the greens and minced herbs. Add 2 pinches of salt, stir with a wooden spoon, and cook for 3 minutes over low heat, stirring. Add the pieces of eel and the wine. Raise the heat to high and then bring to a simmer and simmer for 5 minutes, stirring. Add the fish stock and capers, lower the heat, and cook 5 minutes more. Remove from the heat and allow to cool for a minute.

6   To serve, remove the dish from the oven and pour the eel pieces and herb and caper sauce over the potatoes. Taste for salt and pepper.

2 pounds (1 kg.) freshwater eels, skinned and chopped into sections about 2 inches (5 cm.) long

Salt

Pepper

2 pounds (500 g.) potatoes, preferably fingerlings or another firm-fleshed variety

Coarse salt

1 stick (¼ pound/120 g.) butter

¾ cup (20 cl.) crème fraîche

3 egg yolks (page 204)

3 ounces (100 g.) sorrel, well washed, dried, trimmed, and finely chopped

2 ounces (60 g.) nettles, well washed, dried, trimmed, and finely chopped

3 ounces (100 g.) spinach, well washed, dried, trimmed, and finely chopped

1 tarragon leaf, washed, dried, and minced

3 sage leaves, washed, dried, and minced

1 blade savory, washed, dried, and minced

10 stems flat-leaf parsley, washed, dried, and minced

1⅔ cups (40 cl.) dry white wine

½ cup (10 cl.) fish stock (page 40 or store-bought)

2 tablespoons capers

PIKE DUMPLINGS

Quenelles de brochet

SERVES   4

PREPARATION   35 minutes

COOKING   1 hour

The quenelles must be prepared at least 2 hours in advance.

The pike, a great carnivore that inhabits lakes and rivers, has very fine flesh. It can be served simply poached, with salted butter, but its many bones make this preparation somewhat inconvenient for the diner. For this reason it is often enjoyed mashed and made into a quenelle—a sort of football-shaped dumpling—one of the specialties of Lyon.

1   Check the pike flesh carefully and discard any small bones you find. Put it back in the refrigerator.

2   PREPARE THE QUENELLES   Combine the milk and butter in a saucepan. Season with 2 pinches of salt and a dash of pepper and bring to a boil. Turn the heat to low and vigorously stir in the flour with a wooden spatula until the mixture pulls away from the sides of the pot. Whisk in 1 egg and finish stirring it in with the spatula. Remove the pot from the heat and allow it to cool to room temperature.

3   In a blender or food processor, blend this mixture and the chilled pike flesh. Blend in the clarified butter. Season with 2 pinches of salt, a dash of pepper, 5 pinches of grated nutmeg, and blend again. While running the blender or processor, add the remaining 2 eggs and egg whites. Refrigerate this mixture for 2 hours along with 2 tablespoons that you will use to form the quenelles.

4   PREPARE THE VELOUTÉ SAUCE   Melt the butter in a saucepan and then stir in the flour. Cook gently for 3 minutes, stirring constantly without allowing the mixture to brown. Briskly and bit by bit stir in the fish stock and then the cream. Bring to a gentle boil and cook for 4 minutes. Taste for salt and pepper.

5   FORM AND COOK THE QUENELLES   Preheat the oven to 400°F/200°C. Bring 3 quarts (3 l.) water to a boil in a large pot. Lower the heat so the liquid just simmers and then add 1½ tablespoons coarse salt, the thyme, and the garlic.

FOR THE QUENELLES

10 ounces (300 g.) raw, boneless pike flesh, very cold

1 cup (20 cl.) milk

2 tablespoons butter

Salt

Pepper

⅔ cup (75 g.) flour

3 large eggs plus 2 egg whites (page 204), very cold

2 tablespoons butter, clarified (page 43)

Freshly grated nutmeg

Coarse salt

1 sprig thyme

2 cloves garlic, peeled

FOR THE VELOUTÉ SAUCE

2 teaspoons butter

1 heaping tablespoon flour

½ cup (25 cl.) fish stock (page 40 or store-bought)

½ cup (25 cl.) heavy cream, very cold

Salt

Pepper

6   Take a tablespoon of the chilled mixture from the refrigerator and use the other chilled tablespoon to roll it into a roundish tapered shape, like a football. When all the quenelles are shaped, gently lower them into the simmering water and cook for 7 minutes, until they are quite puffed up. Remove them with a skimmer or slotted spoon.

7   Butter a porcelain baking dish and lay the quenelles in it in a single layer, leaving some space in between. Cover them with the velouté sauce and bake in the oven for 20 minutes.

PIKE OR PICKEREL ROASTED WITH WILD MUSHROOMS ____
Brochet (ou sandre) rôti aux mousserons

SERVES   4
PREPARATION   30 minutes
COOKING   20 minutes

This pike dish comes from Vesoul in the east of France. If you like, use pickerel or perch instead of pike.

1   Preheat the oven to 410°F/210°C.

2   Rinse the fish, washing the interior well. Dry the fish with paper towels, taking special care with the cavity. Season with salt and pepper inside and out.

3   Remove and discard the stems of the mushrooms. Rinse the caps quickly under gentle running water. Dry them in a salad spinner. Chop the larger caps into halves or even into quarters. Pat the caps completely dry with paper towels.

4   Use a pastry brush to paint 5 tablespoons (75 g.) butter all over the bottom of a baking dish large enough to hold the fish. Spread one-third of the minced shallots and garlic over the butter and lay the fish on top. Bake for 8 minutes, basting twice by using a large spoon to pour cooking juices over the fish. After 8 minutes, remove the dish and turn the fish over with a large spatula. Spoon juices over the newly exposed side and bake 7 minutes more.

5   In the meantime, melt the remaining butter in a large pot or sauté pan over low heat. Add the rest of the minced shallots and garlic and season with 2 pinches of salt. Stir with a

1 pike, pickerel, or perch, about 3 pounds (1.5 kg.), guts, scales, and gills removed

Salt

Pepper

½ pound (300 g.) small wild forest mushrooms, preferably St. George's mushrooms or small porcini

1 stick (¼ pound/115 g.) butter

6 shallots and 2 cloves garlic, peeled and minced together

2 tablespoons olive oil

Juice of 1 lemon

1 tablespoon minced flat-leaf parsley

wooden spoon, cover, and cook over the lowest heat possible for 4 minutes, shaking the pot every now and then.

6   Heat the olive oil in a skillet for 1 minute over a high flame. Add the mushrooms and cook, still over high heat, for 2 minutes, stirring with a wooden spoon. Season with 2 pinches of salt and 1 pinch of pepper. Add the sautéed shallots and garlic, stir, and turn off the heat.

7   When the fish has baked for 15 minutes total, remove it from the oven. Baste it again with its juices. Pour the mushrooms all around it and bake 5 minutes more.

8   When the fish comes out of the oven, remove its skin and carve out the fillets. Put the fillets in the center of a serving platter. Season with salt and pepper on both sides and spritz with lemon juice. Cover with mushrooms, sprinkle with parsley, and serve.

PICKEREL (OR PERCH) WITH *BEURRE BLANC* _____

Sandre au beurre blanc

SERVES   6

PREPARATION   40 minutes

COOKING   25 minutes

1   Bring 4 quarts (4 l.) water to a boil in a large pot with the first 8 ingredients listed. Adjust the heat so the pot simmers, and simmer for 20 minutes. Add the vinegar and white wine and pour this court bouillon into a fish cooker (poissonière) to cool.

2   Wash the fish, paying special attention to the central cavity. Put it in the fish cooker and bring the court bouillon almost to a bubble over high heat. Then reduce the heat to low and simmer very gently for 20 minutes. Do not allow the liquid to boil.

3   In the meantime, prepare the *beurre blanc.*

4   When the fish has cooked for 20 minutes, turn off the heat but leave the fish in the hot court bouillon for 5 minutes. Then remove the fish to a large serving dish. Carefully remove its skin and season with salt and pepper on both sides. Pour a little of the hot court bouillon over and serve the *beurre blanc* on the side.

1 medium carrot, peeled and chopped into small pieces

1 medium onion, peeled and chopped into small pieces

2 stalks celery, trimmed and chopped into small pieces

Zest of 1 organic lemon

1 bouquet garni (2 sprigs thyme, ½ bay leaf, and 6 stems parsley, wrapped and tied in 2 leek leaves)

¼ star anise

2 teaspoons peppercorns

1 tablespoon coarse salt

½ cup (10 cl.) white wine vinegar

½ cup (10 cl.) dry white wine, preferably Muscadet

1 pickerel or perch, about 3 pounds (1.5 kg.), gutted and scaled

White Butter Sauce (*beurre blanc*), page 46, using half white wine and half white vinegar

Salt

Pepper

ROASTED PICKEREL (OR PERCH) WITH CREAMED CELERY ROOT

Sandre rôti au céleri à la crème

SERVES 4
PREPARATION 50 minutes
COOKING 5 minutes

Ingredients:

2 cups (50 cl.) heavy cream
1 cup (25 cl.) dry white wine, preferably Muscadet
2 shallots, peeled and minced
4 pieces of pickerel or perch with skin on, about ¼ pound (120 g.) each
1 celery root
½ lemon
Coarse salt
2 sticks (½ pound/215 g.) butter, well chilled
Pinch of superfine sugar
Salt
Pepper
1 tablespoon olive oil
2 tablespoons cilantro leaves

1   Bring the cream to a boil in a small saucepan. Let it simmer over low heat until it has been reduced by three-fourths; this will take 20–25 minutes. Let it cool off the heat.

2   Put the white wine in another small saucepan with the shallots. Bring to a boil and then simmer until 2–3 tablespoons of liquid remain. This should take 25–30 minutes. Near the end, be careful not to let the reduced wine burn.

3   In the meantime, rinse the fish under cold running water. Dry it with paper towels and set it aside.

4   Trim and wash the celery root. Rub it with the lemon half and chop it into ¼-inch (0.5-cm.) dice. Bring 1 quart (1 l.) water to a boil in a pot with 1 teaspoon coarse salt. Prepare a bowl half filled with water and a tray of ice cubes. Prepare a plate lined with 3 layers of paper towels. When the pot is bubbling, cook the celery root dice for 3 minutes. Remove with a skimmer and shock in the ice water for 1 minute. Remove to a colander to drain and then spread on the paper towel–lined plate to dry.

5   When the wine has been reduced, set aside 2 tablespoons chilled butter and dice the rest. Over very low heat gradually stir in the diced butter with a whisk. Add the superfine sugar and some salt and pepper. Pour the sauce into a heat-proof bowl, put the bowl in a large pot, and pour hot water into the large pot so that it reaches halfway up the side of the bowl of sauce. Turn the heat on under the pot so that the water simmers very gently.

6   Add the celery root to the saucepan of cooled, reduced cream. Season with salt and pepper, stir with a wooden spoon, and reheat over a low flame.

7   Season the fish with salt and pepper on both sides. With a sharp knife, make 3 or 4 incisions on the diagonal in the skin of each piece of fish.

8   Heat the olive oil and the remaining butter in a skillet over

low heat. When the butter foams, place the fish gently in the skillet, skin side up, and cook over low heat for 5 minutes, regularly spooning the cooking fat over the fish. Flip the fish with tongs or a spatula and brown the skin side for 30 seconds.

9   Make 4 little heaps of the celery root cream on a serving platter. Lay a piece of fish atop each pile, skin side up. Stir 1 tablespoon cilantro leaves into the sauce and pour some sauce on the fish. Sprinkle the platter with the rest of the cilantro leaves and serve the rest of the sauce on the side.

Offal and Stuffing

Offal

The organs and nonskeletal muscles of the animals we eat are not the most prominent of meats. For a long time they were thought of as less "noble" than more traditional cuts, despite the fact that their taste can be even more delectable, depending on the piece. They are liable to degrade quite quickly, however, and so are hard to keep. In recent years their popularity has been dealt a blow by worries about mad cow disease, and some can no longer be sold legally in France.

This is a shame, for the unusual flavors offered by offal can enrich a menu and broaden its range. The most commonly eaten are liver, kidneys, sweetbreads, and brains. Throughout France you will find many different regional preparations of tripe.

It is imperative that you trust the quality and freshness of organ meats. Once home, keep them in sealed containers in the coldest part of the refrigerator (38°F/3°C) and don't keep them around for too long before cooking.

CHOOSING LIVER AND KIDNEYS

There are two categories of offal: red and white. The quality of red offal, like liver and kidneys, can be judged by its color: The brighter it is, the better.

Veal liver and kidneys should be pink instead of dark red. The nerves should be removed from the liver, as should the thin, clear membrane that surrounds it. Usually it is pan fried, but it should not be floured first. Once cooked, it should be rosy; do not overcook it for it will dry out.

Veal and lamb kidneys should be a pinkish color tending toward gray, and they should be small, for they develop an unpleasantly strong taste as the animal ages and they grow larger. Pork kidneys and livers are more vibrantly colored. Pork liver is usually used in terrines or pâtés.

White offal includes brains and sweetbreads, which are usually taken from calves or lambs.

PREPARING BRAINS

Before brains are cooked, they must be rinsed under cold running water. Then the surface membrane and veins are removed. Afterward, the brain should be soaked for 1 hour in vinegar water (add 1 tablespoon distilled white vinegar per 1 quart/1 l. water) to be purged of blood, and then it should be rinsed again. Now it is ready to be cooked—whether by poaching a few minutes at a light simmer in salted water or, even better, court bouillon, or sliced finely and pan fried in a bit of oil and butter.

PREPARING SWEETBREADS

Sweetbreads are actually the thymus glands, very delicately flavored morsels that go nicely with mushrooms. This is a slightly mysterious part of a calf, lamb, or kid that disappears when the young animal matures. It comprises an elongated part and a round part, which is called the nut. Take the nut if you can; the other, firmer section is not as delicious or as toothsome and more firm. Before sweetbreads are cooked, they must be soaked in salted water (1 tablespoon salt per 1 quart/1 l. water) for 6–8 hours in the refrigerator; this will purge them of blood. After soaking, put the sweetbreads to drain in a colander. Then put them in a large pot and cover well with cold water. Add salt to the water and bring it to a boil. Boil the sweetbreads gently for 2 minutes, then remove them to a colander and rinse under cold running water for 10 minutes. Gently remove the transparent membrane, cartilaginous bits, and nerves or veins, being careful not to damage the sweetbreads. Wrap them in a clean dish towel and place this package between two plates with a weight on top. Leave it weighted for an hour, during which time it will expel excess water and take on a more regular shape.

STEWED SWEETBREADS WITH PORCINIS

Ris de veau en cocotte aux cèpes

SERVES 4
PREPARATION   5 minutes
COOKING   35 minutes

1   Preheat the oven to 400°F/200°C.

2   Season the blanched and pressed sweetbreads (see page 349) with 2 pinches of salt and 1 pinch of pepper. Melt the butter in a pot pretty enough to take to the table. When it foams, add the sweetbreads and cook for 5 minutes over low heat, until their bottoms are golden. Turn the sweetbreads with tongs or a spatula and brown the other side for 5 minutes. Remove them to a plate, season again lightly with salt and pepper, and tent with aluminum foil to keep warm.

3   In the same pot, melt the goose fat over medium-high heat. Add the mushrooms, lower the heat to a gentle flame, and brown for 4 minutes. Turn the mushrooms and cook 4 minutes on the second side. Season with a pinch of salt and put the browned sweetbreads back in the pot. Put the pot in the oven and cook for 7 minutes. Add the juices left over from a chicken or veal roast and bake 3 minutes more, just long enough to caramelize the sweetbreads. Serve directly from the cooking pot.

4 sweetbread "nuts," prepared as described on page 349
Salt
Pepper
1½ tablespoons butter
2 teaspoons goose fat
¾ pound (400 g.) small porcini mushrooms, brushed, wiped clean, and sliced in half lengthwise
Juices of roast chicken or veal

PAN-GRILLED LAMB KIDNEYS

Rognons d'agneau grillés

SERVES   1
PREPARATION   2–5 minutes
COOKING   2 minutes
RESTING   1 minutes

Ask the butcher to open the kidneys and remove the hard white hollow at the center.

1   Remove the kidneys from the refrigerator 10 minutes in advance. Look at them closely and remove any scraps of skin

3 lamb kidneys, opened and prepared
Neutral oil
Salt
Pepper

or hard bits with a sharp knife. Prepare a cooling rack over a large plate or platter. (If you don't have a rack, you can use a small overturned plate.)

2   To prevent the kidneys from curling up as they cook, skewer the inside convex face with two toothpicks or wooden skewers: Pierce one side and push vertically from the inside face to the outside face. Do the same with the other toothpick or skewer on the other side of the kidney. If you would prefer not to do this, slice each kidney in 2 to separate the bean-shaped halves.

3   Preheat a grill pan over high heat. Brush the kidneys with a bit of oil and season lightly with salt and pepper.

4   When the grill is hot, place the kidneys on it, internal side down. Cook for 1 minute and then turn with tongs or a fork, taking care not to puncture the flesh. Grill the other side for 1 minute.

5   Remove the kidneys to the cooling rack, internal side down. Season with fleur de sel and pepper, and allow to rest for 1 minute. Put ¼ teaspoon butter in the hollow of each kidney and eat.

Fleur de sel
1 teaspoon butter

special equipment: toothpicks

PAN FRIED LAMB KIDNEYS

Rognons d'agneau poêlés

SERVES   1
PREPARATION   2–5 minutes
COOKING   4 minutes
RESTING   2 minutes

Ask the butcher to open the kidneys and remove the hard white hollow at the center.

3 lamb kidneys, opened and prepared
Salt
Pepper
1 teaspoon neutral oil
2 teaspoons butter
Fleur de sel

1   Remove the kidneys from the refrigerator 10 minutes ahead of time. Look at them closely: Remove any scraps of skin or hard bits with a sharp knife. If it has not been done already, slice them in 2 to separate the bean-shaped halves. Season lightly with salt and pepper.

2   Prepare a cooling rack over a large plate or platter. (If you don't have a rack, you can use a small overturned plate.)

3   Heat the oil in a skillet over medium heat. Add 1 teaspoon of the butter. When it foams, carefully put the kidneys in the pan, internal side down. Lower the heat a bit and cook for 2 minutes, tilting and swirling the skillet to make sure the fat spreads under the kidneys.

4   Flip the kidneys with tongs or a spatula. Cook for 2 minutes on the other side, still tilting and swirling the skillet.

5   Remove the kidneys to the cooling rack. If you like, you can put ¼ teaspoon butter in the hollow of each kidney. Season with fleur de sel and pepper and allow to rest for 2 minutes.

LITTLE LAMB KIDNEY SKEWERS

Petites brochettes de rognons d'agneau

SERVES   4
PREPARATION   2 minutes
COOKING   4–6 minutes

Ask the butcher to open the kidneys and remove the hard white hollow at the center.

8 lamb kidneys, opened and prepared
Salt
Pepper
1 teaspoon neutral oil
1 teaspoon butter
1 tablespoon strong mustard
1 tablespoon chopped flat-leaf parsley

special equipment: 4 wooden skewers

1   Remove the kidneys from the refrigerator 10 minutes ahead of time. Look at them closely: Remove any scraps of skin or hard bits with a sharp knife. If it has not been done already, cut them in 2 to separate the bean-shaped halves. Season lightly with salt and pepper.

2   Preheat the broiler. Heat the oil in a skillet over medium heat. Add the butter; when it foams, carefully lay the kidneys in the skillet, internal side down. Lower the heat a bit and cook for 1 minute, tilting and swirling the skillet to make sure the fat spreads under the kidneys. Flip the kidneys with tongs or a spatula and cook for 1 minute on the other side.

3   Remove the kidneys to a plate. Season lightly with salt and pepper and thread 2 kidneys onto each of 4 wooden skewers. Brush them with mustard and sprinkle with chopped parsley. Place them on a sheet pan and put them in the oven on a rack two-thirds of the way up for 2 minutes. Turn and cook 2 minutes more. You can also finish the skewers on a very

hot grill or in a barbecue pit instead of the oven, cooking them for 1 minute on each side instead of 2.

VEAL KIDNEYS IN THEIR OWN FAT

Rognons de veau à la Baugé

SERVES   4

PREPARATION AND COOKING   30 minutes

The village of Baugé, in the northern Saumurois region in the Loire valley, made its reputation with a recipe for veal liver stuffed with chicken livers and a veal kidney prepared this way. Ask the butcher to leave a thin layer of fat around the kidneys—about $\frac{1}{16}$–$\frac{1}{8}$ inch (2–3 mm.) thick. He should also cut each one into 4 slices and trim and prepare them. See if he can give you some bits of the kidneys' fatty envelopes.

- 3 small veal kidneys, prepared as described in the headnote
- 1 teaspoon neutral oil
- 1 teaspoon butter
- 3 shallots, peeled and minced
- Salt
- Pepper
- 6 ounces (200 g.) cup mushrooms, trimmed, washed, and dried, and cut vertically into $\frac{1}{4}$-inch (0.5-cm.) slices
- $\frac{1}{2}$ cup (10 cl.) white wine
- $\frac{1}{2}$ cup (10 cl.) heavy cream
- 1 tablespoon mustard
- 1 tablespoon minced flat-leaf parsley

1   Remove the kidneys from the refrigerator 15 minutes in advance.

2   In a large saucepan or pot over very low heat, melt the little bits of kidney fat. This should take at least 5 minutes.

3   In the meantime, heat the oil and the butter in a skillet. Cook the shallots for 3 minutes over very low heat, stirring with a wooden spatula. Sprinkle with a pinch of salt and a pinch of pepper and set the shallots aside.

4   Season both sides of each slice of kidney with salt and pepper. Remove from the pot any fat that has not melted. Turn the heat to high and sauté the kidneys for 2 minutes. Flip them with tongs or a spatula and brown the other side for 2 minutes. Lower the heat under the pot. Remove the kidneys to a plate, season lightly with salt and pepper again, and tent with aluminum foil to keep them warm.

5   Add the mushrooms to the pot and turn the heat to medium. Cook for 5 minutes, stirring to coat them well with the cooking fat. Remove the mushrooms to the plate of kidneys.

6   Do not turn off the heat under the pot in which you cooked the kidneys and mushrooms. Add the wine and bring to a boil; simmer until it has been reduced by half (about

15–20 minutes). Turn off the heat and stir in the cream. Whisk in the mustard. Taste for salt and pepper.

7   Remove the remaining fatty filaments from the kidneys. Put the kidneys and mushrooms back into the pot of sauce. Reheat for 1 minute over very low heat and then turn the kidneys and cook 1 minute more, just long enough for them to warm up. The sauce should not boil. Sprinkle with parsley and serve.

VEAL KIDNEYS WITH PORCINIS

Rognons de veau aux cèpes

SERVES   4

PREPARATION   20 minutes

COOKING   20 minutes plus 8 minutes for the mushrooms

1   Remove the kidneys from the refrigerator 20 minutes in advance.

2   Chop one-fifth of the mushrooms into small dice (about 1 cup/100 g. diced) and then put them in the bowl of a blender or food processor with ½ cup (10 cl.) water. Blend. Add the mayonnaise and mix. Add the vinegar and season with salt and pepper. Blend again. Add the chives and blend again. Put this sauce aside.

3   Cut the caps of the remaining mushrooms in half. Heat 1 tablespoon peanut oil in a skillet or sauté pan over medium heat for 2 minutes. Add the mushrooms and cook for 10 minutes, stirring with a wooden spoon. Season with salt and pepper and drain.

4   Season each kidney with 2 pinches of salt and 1 pinch of pepper. Heat 1 teaspoon peanut oil in a large pot, then add 1 tablespoon butter. When the butter foams, add the kidneys and cook for 2 minutes over medium heat. Turn the kidneys with tongs or a spatula and brown the other side for 2 minutes. Lower the heat a bit and cook for 8 minutes, swirling the skillet and basting the kidneys with the cooking juices. Turn the kidneys and cook 8 minutes more over medium heat, continuing to baste. Remove the kidneys to a plate, season lightly with salt and pepper, and tent with aluminum

2 whole veal kidneys, trimmed and prepared by the butcher but not sliced open

1 pound (500 g.) porcini mushrooms, carefully brushed and wiped clean with a paper towel

4 tablespoons (100 g.) mayonnaise (page 55 or store-bought)

1 tablespoon wine vinegar

Salt

Pepper

1 tablespoon chopped chives

1 tablespoon plus 1 teaspoon peanut oil

2 tablespoons butter

1 shallot, peeled and minced

2 cloves garlic, peeled and degermed (page 122)

1 tablespoon mustard

1 teaspoon chopped flat-leaf parsley

foil. (They should not be sealed in aluminum foil—just covered.)

5 Melt 1 tablespoon butter in a saucepan over low heat. When it foams, add the shallot and cook for 3 minutes, stirring with a wooden spoon. Season with a pinch of salt. Add the mushrooms and garlic and cook for 4 minutes, stirring, still over low heat. Add the kidneys and cook 2 minutes per side, just long enough to warm them up. Turn off the heat, stir in the mustard, and sprinkle with parsley. Serve the mushroom-mayonnaise on the side.

SLICED AND GRILLED VEAL LIVER

Tranche de foie de veau grillée

SERVES 1
PREPARATION 2 minutes
COOKING 4 minutes (for a medium-rare finish)
RESTING 2 minutes

In France the custom is to cook liver medium rare (pink in the middle). You can grill or pan fry it a little longer, but do not overcook or it will toughen.

1 slice veal liver, ¼ pound (120 g.)
Salt
Pepper
Neutral oil
Fleur de sel
½ teaspoon butter (optional)

1 Remove the liver from the refrigerator 10 minutes in advance. Heat a grill pan over a medium flame.

2 Season the liver with salt and pepper on both sides and brush it lightly with oil. When the grill is ready, lay the liver on it on a diagonal. Cook for 1 minute, lowering the heat a bit. Flip with tongs or use a large fork and your hand, being careful not to pierce the liver. Cook for 1 minute. Flip the liver back to the first side, rotating it a quarter so that the grill marks will make a crosshatch pattern. Cook for 1 minute and then flip back to the second side, rotating a quarter to achieve a crosshatch pattern. Cook for 1 minute.

3 Remove the liver to a plate. Season with fleur de sel and pepper on both sides. If you like, add the butter. Allow to rest for 2 minutes before serving.

SLICED AND PAN FRIED VEAL LIVER

Tranche de foie de veau poêlée

variation

SLICED AND PAN FRIED
VEAL LIVER WITH
SMOKED BACON

SERVES 1
PREPARATION 2 minutes
COOKING 4 minutes (for a rare finish)
RESTING 2 minutes

1 Remove the liver from the refrigerator 10 minutes in advance.

2 Just before cooking, season the liver with salt and pepper on both sides. Heat the oil in a skillet over medium heat. Add the butter and tilt the skillet to melt it all over the bottom. When the butter is foaming but not yet browning, lower the heat and lay the liver in the skillet. Lay it in a motion away from you to avoid spitting fat. Cook for 2 minutes, turning the skillet and basting the liver with cooking fat. Flip the liver with plastic tongs or 2 spatulas, careful not to splatter yourself with hot fat. Cook for 2 minutes on the second side, continuing to baste and turn.

3 Remove the liver to a plate and season with fleur de sel and pepper on both sides. Let it rest for 2 minutes before serving.

1 slice veal liver, ¼ pound (120 g.)
Salt
Pepper
1 teaspoon neutral oil
½ teaspoon butter
Fleur de sel

SLICED AND PAN FRIED VEAL LIVER WITH SMOKED BACON

Tranche de foie de veau poêlée au lard fumé

SERVES 4
COOKING 5 minutes

1 Heat the oil in a skillet over low heat. When it is hot, add the bacon slices and cook for 2 minutes per side over low heat or to desired crispness. Remove them to a plate.

2 Fry the liver in the same skillet, following the instructions in the recipe above but without adding any extra oil or butter. Serve the bacon with the liver.

1 teaspoon neutral oil
8 slices smoked bacon
4 slices veal liver, ¼ pound (120 g.) each

LAMB'S LIVER WITH TENDER CARROTS

Foie d'agneau aux carottes fondantes

SERVES 4
PREPARATION 10 minutes
COOKING 15 minutes
Begin cooking the carrots 10 minutes before frying the liver.

1 Heat 1 tablespoon oil in a large saucepan or pot. Add 1 tea-spoon butter. When it melts, add the onions and cook for 5 minutes over low heat, stirring with a wooden spoon. Do not allow the onions to color. Add the carrots, cumin, a pinch of salt, and a pinch of pepper. Add enough cold water just to cover the vegetables. Add the bouquet garni and bring to a boil. Lower the heat, cover with a piece of parchment paper pricked with a fork, and simmer for 15 minutes. The water should practically disappear. Near the end of cooking, keep an eye on the saucepan to make sure the carrots are not stick-ing to the bottom.

2 Fry the liver according to the recipe for veal liver on page 356. Remove the liver to a plate.

3 Cook the minced garlic in the skillet you used to cook the liver over very low heat for 3 minutes, stirring to prevent it from coloring. Add the vinegar and orange juice. Bring to a boil and then lower the heat so the liquid simmers. Simmer gently for 5 minutes. Turn off the heat and stir in the remain-ing butter. Taste both this sauce and the carrots for salt and pepper.

4 Coat the slices of liver with the garlic–orange juice sauce and serve with the carrots. Garnish with chervil leaves.

1 tablespoon neutral oil
2 tablespoons butter
12 cipollini onions, peeled and sliced into thin rounds $\frac{1}{16}$–$\frac{1}{8}$ inch (2–3 mm.) thick
16 small new carrots, peeled and sliced into thin rounds $\frac{1}{16}$–$\frac{1}{8}$ inch (2–3 mm.) thick
2 pinches of cumin powder
Salt
Pepper
Bouquet garni (1 sprig fresh thyme and 4 stems parsley, tied together)
4 slices lamb liver, $\frac{1}{4}$ pound (120 g.) each
1 clove garlic, peeled, degermed (page 122), and minced
1 tablespoon wine vinegar
Juice of 1 orange
1 teaspoon chervil leaves

Stuffing

Stuffing is a mixture of chopped ingredients that can be raw or cooked and cut large or small. There are all kinds of stuffing—for fowl, for meat, for game, for fish, for crusta-ceans, and even for vegetables. Stuffings can also be used to make pâtés, terrines, and *ballotines* (a piece of meat, usually fowl, that has been boned, stuffed, rolled up, and cooked).

They enrich, flavor, and improve their edible vessels even as they keep them from drying out during cooking.

There are three main types of stuffing, grouped by their base ingredient: meat and offal, fish and other seafood, and vegetables. It is important to pay close attention to seasoning and to the choice of aromatics, spices, stocks, and alcohol, for these flavors will be intensified in the finished dish.

TRUFFLED STUFFING FOR CHRISTMAS

Farce truffée de Noël

FOR A CAPON, FAT CHICKEN, OR TURKEY OF $5\frac{1}{2}$ TO $6\frac{1}{2}$ POUNDS (2.8–3.4 KG.)

PREPARATION AND COOKING   20 minutes

Stuffing must be prepared before you plan to roast the fowl.

1   Heat the lard in a skillet for 3 minutes over very low heat, stirring with a wooden spatula to encourage it to melt. When it has melted, add the diced gizzard and liver and cook over low heat, stirring, for 1 minute. Turn the heat to high add the chicken livers. Cook for 1 minute, stirring. Season with 1 pinch of salt and 2 pinches of pepper and stir. Pour the whole into a bowl, cover with plastic wrap, and refrigerate.

2   Just before stuffing the fowl, cut the scraps of foie gras into $\frac{1}{2}$-inch (1-cm.) dice. Chop the truffle very finely. Stir the foie gras and truffle into the bowl of gizzard and livers. Taste and, if necessary, season lightly with salt and pepper. Stuff the fowl. (For roasting the fowl, see the Poultry and Rabbit chapter.)

3 ounces (100 g.) lard, rind removed, cut into very small dice

Gizzard and liver of fowl to be stuffed, cut into very small dice

$\frac{1}{4}$ pound (100 g.) chicken livers, cut into very small dice

Salt

Pepper

$\frac{1}{4}$ pound (150 g.) foie gras scraps, raw or cooked

1 medium truffle

Butcher's Meats

Lamb

Lamb is one of the most refined of meats. Roasted, it is without question the best match for the great red wines.

The younger the lamb, the better its meat. The flesh of a nursing lamb (or "milk lamb") should be completely white, and that of a weaned lamb will be pale pink. As the lamb becomes a sheep, its flesh, becoming mutton, turns redder and redder. The look of the fat is another key indicator of lamb's quality: It should be white, firm, and abundant, especially around the kidneys.

LAMB: BONE IN

It is always best to cook lamb with its bones intact if possible. Carving might be more difficult this way, but the meat will taste much better. If you plan to make a sauce from the roasting juices, you might even add some extra bones to the roasting pan.

GARLIC AND THYME

It is not a good idea to stud a lamb with garlic by slipping slivered cloves into slits in its flesh (the allium is too pungent for such a delicate meat), but you might want to toss a head or two of garlic, still in its skin, into the roasting pan or add a bit of crushed garlic to flavor a stew. You can also add any herb you like—wild thyme, rosemary, basil, or even cumin, which is commonly used to season lamb in northern Africa—but the delicate fragrance of fresh thyme is thought to go best with lamb.

The best time to eat lamb is January to May; it is at its peak in March and April.

VARIETIES AND NAMES

Good lamb is raised not for its wool but for the quality of its meat.

The stable of sheep raised in France includes more than thirty varieties. The most famous are from the Alpilles, a range of small mountains in Provence, where their flesh becomes very fragrant. Pauillac, in Bordeaux, has made milk lamb its specialty; it is excellent, but its underdeveloped flesh can remain firm even after cooking. Limousin, Poitou, and Berry all furnish deliciously fatty lambs. Several regions near the sea (Mont-Saint-Michel, Avranches, the Cotentin Peninsula) raise "presalted" lambs, so called because they graze in pastures that are sometimes covered by the tide. This gives their flesh a rather special taste. These lambs are very few, though, and therefore hard to come by.

A fine lamb is well rounded and even voluptuous. Its age, feed, and place of origin are the principal criteria that determine its taste and quality.

LAMB AT EVERY AGE

Baby lamb, or *agnelet,* is an animal whose only sustenance has been its mother's milk. They are very hard to find in the United States and the United Kingdom. They are slaughtered between twenty-eight and thirty-five days of age and do not weigh more than 12 pounds (6 kg.).

A milk lamb has not yet been weaned from mother's milk and formula and has not yet begun to graze. They are slaughtered between thirty and forty days of age and weigh about 16 to 18 pounds (8 or 9 kg.).

Most of the lamb we eat is slaughtered between 70 and 150 days of age. The best is without question the "100-day lamb," which is traditionally eaten at Easter. This lamb is weaned, but most of its nourishment has come from milk plus a little tender spring grass. For this reason it is also called "white lamb" or, in French, *laiton*. At the butcher it will weigh 36 to 40 pounds (18–20 kg.).

Slaughtered between 180 and 270 days (6 and 9 months), a lamb has had time to graze in its native pastures. Then it is called a *broutard* in French and a "grass-fed lamb" in English. Its meat has more color, and its fat is not as brightly white; for this reason it is also called "gray lamb." Its taste is somewhat stronger than young lamb. This lamb is found at the butcher most frequently between September and January.

LAMB BROCHETTE

Brochette d'agneau

SERVES 1

PREPARATION 10 minutes (includes cubing the meat and chopping the vegetables)

COOKING 14 minutes

RESTING 2 minutes

1. Remove the meat from the refrigerator 10 minutes in advance. Prepare a cooling rack set over a large plate or platter. (If you do not have a rack, use a small overturned plate.) Put the lamb cubes in one bowl and the vegetables in another. Season the vegetables lightly with salt and pepper.

2. Heat 1 tablespoon oil in a skillet over medium heat. Brown the meat for 3 minutes, still over medium heat, turning the cubes to brown on all sides. Remove them to the cooling rack and season with salt and pepper.

3. Wipe the skillet clean with a paper towel. Heat another tablespoon of oil in it over medium heat. Cook the vegetables for 4 minutes, stirring constantly. Remove the vegetables to a bowl.

4. Wipe the skillet clean with a paper towel. Make the brochette: Thread the meat and vegetables onto the skewer, alternating vegetables and meat and beginning and ending with the onion slices. Heat the remaining tablespoon oil in the skillet over high heat. Lay the brochette in the skillet and

4 cubes cut from a lamb leg steak, about ¼ pound (100 g.) total, each cube about 1½ inches (3 cm.) square

1 medium onion, cut into rounds 1½ inches (3 cm.) thick

3 slices red and green bell peppers, chopped into squares of a uniform size

Salt

Pepper

3 tablespoons neutral oil

Fleur de sel

special equipment: 1 wooden skewer

lower the heat a bit. Cook for 7 minutes, turning regularly so it browns evenly.

5   Remove the brochette to the cooling rack and let it rest for 2 minutes before eating. Season lightly with fleur de sel and pepper and serve.

BUTCHER'S BROCHETTE

Brochette du boucher

SERVES   1
COOKING   10 minutes
RESTING   4 minutes

Using store-bought skewers of cubed meat is fast and easy, but the bits of meat and vegetable won't be quite cooked through.

1   Remove the brochette from the refrigerator 10 minutes in advance. Prepare a cooling rack over a large plate or platter. (If you don't have a rack, use a small overturned plate.)

2   Heat the oil in a skillet over high heat. Season the brochette evenly with salt and pepper and then place it in the skillet and lower the heat to medium. Cook for 8 minutes, turning the brochette so all sides are browned evenly.

3   Remove the cooked brochette to the cooling rack. Season with fleur de sel and pepper. Let rest for 4 minutes before eating.

1 store-bought lamb brochette (chunks of lamb on a wooden skewer), ¼ pound (150–160 g.)
1 tablespoon neutral oil
Salt
Pepper
Fleur de sel

PAN FRIED LAMB LEG STEAK

Tranche de gigot poêlée

variation

LAMB LEG STEAKS WITH
TOMATO SAUCE

SERVES   1
PREPARATION   2 minutes
COOKING   8 minutes
RESTING   4 minutes

1   Remove the meat from the refrigerator 10 minutes in advance and put it on a cutting board. Make 6 evenly spaced cuts in the white part of the steak's edge; this is to prevent the slice from curling up during cooking. Prepare a cooling rack over a large plate. (If you do not have a rack, place a small overturned plate on top of a larger plate.)

2   Heat the oil in a skillet over medium heat. Lightly season the steak with salt and pepper on both sides. When the skillet is hot, use tongs or a spatula to lay the steak in the skillet, using a motion away from you to prevent splattering. Lower the heat a bit and cook for 4 minutes. From time to time, tilt and roll the skillet to spread the cooking fat under the meat. Turn the steak with the tongs, 2 spatulas, or a spatula and your hand. Cook for 4 minutes on the other side.

3   Remove the steak to the cooling rack. Season with fleur de sel and pepper on both sides. Allow it to rest for 2 minutes on one side and then turn and allow it to rest for 2 minutes on the other side.

1 lamb leg steak, about
   4 ounces (150 g.)
1 teaspoon neutral oil
Salt
Pepper
Fleur de sel

LAMB LEG STEAKS WITH TOMATO SAUCE

Tranches de gigot à la tomate

SERVES 2

PREPARATION AND COOKING THE SAUCE 15 minutes

1 Remove the steaks from the refrigerator.

2 Heat 1 tablespoon olive oil in a saucepan over low heat. Add the garlic and some salt and pepper and cook over very low heat about 3 minutes, stirring from time to time; the garlic should not color. Add the tomatoes, thyme, and rosemary and stir. Season with salt and pepper and cook over low heat for 5 minutes. Remove the thyme and rosemary.

3 Fry the lamb leg steaks as in the previous recipe but begin with 1 tablespoon olive oil in the skillet instead of 1 teaspoon neutral oil.

4 Serve the steaks surrounded by the tomato sauce.

2 lamb leg steaks, about
    4 ounces (150 g.) each
2 tablespoons olive oil
4 cloves garlic, peeled,
    degermed (page 122), and
    sliced lengthwise into
    thin slivers
Salt
Pepper
2 medium tomatoes, peeled,
    seeded, and diced
    (page 124)
2 sprigs fresh thyme
2 sprigs fresh rosemary

MUTTON CHOPS CHAMPVALLON

Côtes de mouton Champvallon

SERVES   4

PREPARATION   20 minutes

COOKING   1 hour and 5 minutes

This dish is traditionally prepared with mutton steaks, which have a stronger taste than lamb and take longer to cook. You might prefer to make it with lamb chops. Champvallon is a village in Burgundy.

Ask the butcher for chops from the first five ribs (shoulder chops), well trimmed and with the nerve removed from the backbone.

1   Remove the meat from the refrigerator before you prepare all the vegetables.

2   Melt 3 tablespoons butter in a saucepan over very low heat. Add the onions and cook for 5 minutes over very low heat. Stir and do not allow the onion to color.

3   Put the potato slices in a bowl with the onions, ¾ of the parsley, and a pinch of salt. Mix well.

4   Preheat the oven to 440°F/220°C. Heat the oil in a skillet over medium heat. Sear the meat for 1–2 minutes per side. You want each side to be nicely browned. Remove the meat to a plate.

5   Rub the garlic all over the inside of a baking dish large enough to hold the potatoes and meat. Butter the bottom and sides of the dish generously. Spread half of the potato-onion mixture in the dish and season with pepper. Lay the meat on top and cover with the rest of the potato-onion mixture. Sprinkle with the remaining parsley.

6   Pour the broth into the baking dish, along with any juices that collected under the resting meat. Slip a bouquet garni into the potatoes on either side of the dish. Bake for 1 hour.

7   As the dish bakes, pack its contents down with a wooden spatula every once in a while. If the potatoes take on too much color, cover the dish with aluminum foil until it comes out of the oven.

8 mutton steaks or lamb chops

3 tablespoons butter, plus extra for greasing the dish

5 medium onions, sliced into rounds ⅛ inch (3 mm.) thick

2 pounds (1 kg.) firm-fleshed potatoes (such as charlottes), peeled and sliced into rounds ⅛ inch (3 mm.) thick

1 bunch parsley, leaves only

Salt

1 teaspoon neutral oil

1 clove garlic, peeled and chopped in half

Pepper

2 cups (50 cl.) chicken broth (page 77 or made from a bouillon cube)

2 bouquets garnis (in each one 3 sprigs thyme, ½ bay leaf, and 6 stems parsley, tied together)

PAN-GRILLED LAMB CHOPS _____

Côtes d'agneau grillées

SERVES 1
PREPARATION 2 minutes
COOKING 5 minutes
RESTING 1 minute

1 Remove the chops from the refrigerator 10 minutes in advance. Prepare a cooling rack or a small overturned plate over a large plate.

2 Preheat the grill over high heat. Season the chops lightly on both sides with salt and pepper. Brush them lightly with oil. When the grill is hot, lay the chops on it, bones to the right. To lay the chops on the grill use tongs or a large fork underneath, being careful not to puncture the meat, and your other hand on top. Right away you will hear a delicious sizzling, but this should not be accompanied by a lot of smoke. If the meat or oil is smoking, lower the heat.

3 Cook for 1 minute, then flip and cook 1 minute more. Flip again, rotating the chops a quarter turn so that the grill marks make a crisscross pattern. Cook for 1 minute, flip again, and cook 1 minute more.

4 To finish cooking and make the fat at the edge of the chops turn golden, arrange them so they are standing vertically on their edges, leaning against one another and perhaps against the edge of the pan. Alternately, you can halve a potato lengthwise and prop each chop between the 2 potato pieces. Cook in this vertical position for 1 minute.

5 Remove the chops to the cooling rack. Season with salt (fleur de sel if possible) and pepper. Allow them to rest for 1 minute, preferably with the side that was seared first facing down. This browned side is the prettiest to present on the plate. To serve, arrange the chops so their bones cross one another and, if you like, garnish with watercress.

2 or 3 lamb chops, about ½ pound (220 g.) total, trimmed, with more or less fat according to your taste
Salt
Pepper
Neutral oil
Fleur de sel (optional)
1 bunch watercress, washed and dried (optional)

PAN FRIED LAMB CHOPS
WITH TOMATOES AND ZUCCHINI _____

Côtes d'agneau poêlées aux tomates et aux courgettes

SERVES 4

PREPARATION 20 minutes

COOKING 20 minutes for the vegetables plus 3 minutes for the chops

1 Remove the chops from the refrigerator and then prepare the vegetables.

2 Melt the butter in a saucepan. When it foams, add the onion slices and cook over low heat for 5 minutes. Add a pinch of salt and stir.

3 Bring 1 quart (1 l.) water to a boil with 1 teaspoon coarse salt. Boil the zucchini rounds for 1 minute and then remove them to a colander and run them under cold water. Set aside to drain.

4 Preheat the oven to 400°F/200°C.

5 Slice the tomatoes into rounds ⅛ inch (3 mm.) thick but do not slice all the way through. Leave them attached at the base. (This style of cutting is called *en eventail,* or "fanned.") Slip a zucchini round into each tomato opening.

6 Spread the onions in a baking dish. Set the tomatoes on top of the onions and season with salt and pepper. Drizzle with the olive oil and bake for 15 minutes.

7 Season the chops with salt and pepper on both sides. Heat the neutral oil in a skillet over medium heat. Fry the chops for 1 minute on each side and then 1 minute standing on their fatty edges. Remove them to a plate to rest for 1 minute.

8 Lay the chops on top of the dish of onions and tomatoes and serve.

8 lamb chops, about 1¼ pound (600 g.) total

1 tablespoon butter

1 onion, sliced into thin rounds

Coarse salt

2 medium zucchini, washed and sliced into rounds ⅛ inch (3 mm.) thick

4 medium tomatoes, washed and with their tops removed

Salt

Pepper

3 tablespoons olive oil

1 teaspoon neutral oil

TARRAGON FILET MIGNON OF LAMB WITH CHANTERELLES

Noisettes d'agneau à l'estragon et aux girolles

SERVES 4
PREPARATION 10 minutes
COOKING about 10 minutes

Ask the butcher to bone a rack, slice the resulting fillet into 8 small pieces, and chop up the bones for you to take home with the scraps and trimmings. The lamb medallions and the scraps of meat in the trimmings should be fairly free of fat.

1 Season the lamb medallions with salt on both sides and sprinkle their tops with a few fresh thyme leaves from the sprig.

2 Melt 2 teaspoons butter in a large skillet over low heat. Add the bones and meat trimmings, the sprig of thyme, and the garlic. Cook over low heat for 5 minutes, stirring a bit for even coloring.

3 Add the lamb medallions (without removing the bones and trimmings) and cook them for 2 minutes on each side. While they are still rare in the middle, remove them to a plate and season with pepper. Tent the plate loosely with aluminum foil.

4 Spoon excess fat out of the skillet—it is the yellowish top layer—leaving the brown juices, bones, and trimmings. Return the heat to low and stir in the cream, scraping the bottom and sides of the skillet with a wooden spatula to release any flavorful deposits. Add the tarragon, bring the cream to a boil, and then lower the heat and simmer for 10 minutes.

5 Melt 2 teaspoons butter in another skillet over medium heat. Add the chanterelles and shallot. Cook for 3–4 minutes over medium heat, stirring. Pass the tarragon cream through a strainer (to remove the tarragon leaves, meat trimmings, bones, and garlic) and into the skillet of mushrooms. Stir and taste the creamy mushroom mixture. Season with salt and pepper. Sprinkle half of the parsley over the mushrooms and turn off the heat.

6 Spread the mushroom sauce over the bottom of a deep serving dish and lay the lamb on top of it. Season with fleur de sel and pepper. Garnish with the rest of the parsley.

8 pieces lamb filet mignon (about 1½ pounds/0.75 kg. total) with bones and trimmings
Salt
1 sprig thyme
4 teaspoons butter
1 clove garlic, crushed but not peeled
Pepper
1 cup (25 cl.) heavy cream
2 sprigs tarragon
¼ pound (100 g.) small chanterelle mushrooms, carefully cleaned with a brush and stem ends trimmed
½ shallot, peeled and chopped
Salt
1 teaspoon minced flat-leaf parsley
Fleur de sel

ROAST LEG OF LAMB

Gigot d'agneau rôti

variation

PARSLEYED ROAST LEG OF
LAMB

SERVES   6–8

PREPARATION   5 minutes

COOKING   rare, about 40 minutes; medium rare, about
50 minutes; count on 12–15 minutes per pound
(500 g.)

RESTING   20 minutes

A good-sized bone-in leg of lamb can weigh 2½ pounds (about 1.3 kg.). If you are feeding a crowd, it is better to serve 2 small legs than 1 large one; the smaller legs from younger lambs will taste better. Ask the butcher for a bone-in leg of lamb, trimmed of fat more or less depending on your taste. Ask him to give you the chopped-up trimmings or the chopped bones and trimmings of another cut of lamb. If the scraps of meat are too fatty, remove most of the fat.

In the United States, leg of lamb usually includes the saddle, but it is better for the leg to be separated from the saddle, as is customary in French butchery.

1 lamb leg, 3 pounds (1.5 kg.),
with its trimmings
Salt
Pepper
Neutral oil
4 sprigs fresh thyme
3 cloves garlic, unpeeled and
lightly crushed under your
palm
Fleur de sel

1   Remove the lamb from the refrigerator 30 minutes in advance. Prepare a cooling rack (or a small overturned plate) over a large plate.

2   Preheat the oven to 460°F/240°C at least 10 minutes in advance, making sure that a rack is ready to use in the middle position.

3   If the trimmings are too fatty, remove some of the fat. Season them lightly with salt and pepper. Oil the leg of lamb lightly all over with an oiled pastry brush. Season generously with salt and pepper, and shower with thyme leaves by stripping the leaves from 2 of the sprigs. Discard the branches.

4   Spread the trimmings and garlic cloves evenly in a roasting pan or baking dish large enough to hold the lamb. Put the lamb on top, rounded side up.

5   When the oven has reached 460°F/240°C, put the pan in and cook for 20 minutes. Then remove the pan, turn the lamb with tongs, and put it back in the oven 20 minutes more for a rare finish.

6   During cooking, do not open the oven except the one time to

turn the meat. If you open the door to peek, the oven temperature will fall, and the lamb will not be properly cooked.

7   When the lamb is done, remove it and turn off the oven. Put the leg on the cooling rack and season generously with fleur de sel and pepper. Sprinkle the rest of the thyme leaves all over and tent with aluminum foil.

8   The lamb should rest for 20 minutes. In the meantime, prepare the juice. Spoon excess fat from the surface of the roasting pan. Add 8 tablespoons water to the pan, stirring and scraping with a wooden spatula to loosen all the cooked-on bits. Season with salt and pepper and put the pan back into the oven, no longer on but still hot. Just before serving, put the juices through a fine strainer into a sauceboat. Add any juice that has collected under the resting meat. Ideally, you should have 1 tablespoon juice per diner. The cloves of garlic can be added to the juice or served on the side.

9   Before serving the lamb, snip off any trussing or twine. Carve the lamb by holding the bone. Slice the fleshy part from the top of the bone. (In French this is called the *souris* because its shape resembles a mouse.) Then carve relatively thin slices parallel to the bone. Sprinkle a bit of fleur de sel and pepper on each slice and serve with the roasting juices.

PARSLEYED ROAST LEG OF LAMB

Gigot d'agneau rôti et persillé

PREPARATION   5 minutes

Prepare the *persillade* (chopped parsley and garlic seasoning) while the roast rests.

1   Remove the roasting pan from the oven and turn on the broiler.

2   Put the parsley and garlic in a food processor. Strip the thyme leaves into the processor and discard the branches. Add the bread crumbs and process for 30 seconds, until you have a green powder. It should have about the same consistency as ground coffee. Season with salt and pepper.

3   When the roast has rested for 20 minutes, put it back in the

1 roast leg of lamb, prepared as page 369
½ cup flat-leaf parsley, leaves only
1 clove garlic, peeled, degermed (page 122), and sliced in half lengthwise
1 sprig fresh thyme
½ cup dry bread crumbs
Salt
Pepper

pan, rounded side up, and coat its top and sides with the *per-sillade,* patting it on with your hands to achieve an even finish. The coat should be a little less than ¼ inch (0.5 cm.) thick. Put the roast under the broiler for 3 minutes.

4   When you carve the roast, you can put any parsley that it sheds into the roasting juices.

ROAST SHOULDER OF LAMB

Epaule d'agneau rôtie

variations

PARSLEYED ROAST
SHOULDER OF LAMB
ROAST SHOULDER OF
LAMB WITH A RED BELL
PEPPER CRUST

SERVES   4
PREPARATION   5 minutes
COOKING   30 minutes for a 2-pound/1 kg. shoulder
(45 minutes for a 3-pound/1.5 kg. shoulder)
RESTING   15 minutes

Shoulder of lamb is to be preferred to the leg. The shoulder is not as lean and benefits from the flavor of the shoulder blade, which spreads throughout the meat. Have the butcher leave the bones in even if it will be a little more difficult to carve. The shoulder blades of very young lambs can be sliced right along with the meat. Ask the butcher to give you a handful of chopped-up lamb scraps and bones. The scraps should not be too fatty; if they are, remove some fat.

1 lamb shoulder, 2 pounds
   (1 kg.), with scraps and
   chopped-up bones
Salt
Pepper
Neutral oil
4 sprigs thyme
3 cloves garlic, unpeeled and
   lightly crushed under your
   palm
Fleur de sel

1   Remove the lamb from the refrigerator 20 minutes in advance. Prepare a cooling rack (or a small overturned plate) over a large plate. Preheat the oven to 460°F/240°C at least 10 minutes in advance, with a rack in the middle position.

2   If the trimmings are too fatty, remove some of the fat. Season the trimmings lightly with salt and pepper. Oil the leg of lamb lightly by patting it all over with an oiled pastry brush. Season it generously with salt and pepper and shower with thyme leaves by stripping the leaves from 2 of the thyme sprigs over the lamb. Discard the branches.

3   Spread the trimmings and garlic cloves evenly in a roasting pan or baking dish large enough to hold the lamb. Put the lamb on top, skin side up.

4   When the oven has reached 460°F/240°C, put the pan in and cook for 15 minutes. Then remove the pan, turn the lamb with tongs, and roast 15 minutes more for a rare finish.

5   During cooking, do not open the oven except the one time to turn the meat. If you open the door to peek, the oven temperature will fall, and the lamb will not be properly cooked.

6   When the lamb is done, remove it and turn off the oven. Put the lamb on the cooling rack and season generously with fleur de sel and pepper. Sprinkle the rest of the thyme leaves all over and tent with aluminum foil.

7   Let the lamb rest for 15 minutes. In the meantime, prepare the juice. Spoon excess fat from the surface of the roasting pan. Add 8 tablespoons water to the pan, stirring and scraping with a wooden spatula to loosen all the cooked-on bits, and season with salt and pepper. Put the pan back into the oven, no longer on but still hot. Just before serving, put these juices through a fine strainer into a sauceboat. Add any juices that have collected under the resting meat; ideally, you should have 1 tablespoon of juice per diner. The cloves of garlic can be added to the juice or served on the side.

8   After removing the fleshy part next to the bone (the equivalent of the *souris* on a leg—see page 370), carve the shoulder on the diagonal in relation to the shoulder blade. If the lamb is quite young, you can slice the shoulder blade along with the meat. Season each slice with fleur de sel and pepper.

PARSLEYED ROAST SHOULDER OF LAMB

Epaule d'agneau rôtie et persillée

PREPARATION   5 minutes

Prepare the *persillade* (chopped parsley and garlic seasoning) while the roast rests.

1   Remove the roasting pan from the oven and turn on the broiler.

2   Put the parsley and garlic in a food processor. Strip the thyme leaves into the processor and discard the branches.

1 roast shoulder of lamb, prepared as page 371

½ cup flat-leaf parsley, leaves only

½ clove garlic, peeled, degermed (page 122), and sliced in half lengthwise

Add the bread crumbs and process for 30 seconds, until you have a green powder. It should have about the same consistency as ground coffee. Season with salt and pepper.

3   When the roast has rested for 15 minutes, put it back in the pan, skin side up, and coat it with the *persillade,* patting it on with your hands to achieve an even finish. The coat should be a little less than ¼ inch (0.5 cm.) thick. Put the roast under the broiler for 3 minutes.

4   When you carve the roast, you can put any parsley that it sheds into the roasting juices.

1 sprig fresh thyme
½ cup dry bread crumbs
Salt
Pepper

ROAST SHOULDER OF LAMB WITH A RED BELL PEPPER CRUST

Epaule d'agneau rôtie à la fleur de poivron rouge

PREPARATION   15 minutes

The "dough" for the crust must be prepared at least 30 minutes before the lamb goes into the oven.

1   Heat the olive oil in a skillet over medium heat. Add the bell pepper and cook for 2–3 minutes; it should stay somewhat crisp. Drain well in a colander. Put the bell pepper into a bowl with the butter, garlic, sweet pepper powder, bread crumbs, and a pinch of salt. Mix everything together with a wooden spoon until you have a soft and uniform "dough." Shape it into a ball.

2   On your work surface, cut 2 pieces of parchment paper large enough to cover the lamb shoulder with room to spare. Put the ball of dough between the pieces of paper and use a rolling pin to roll it out until you have a flat piece large enough to cover the shoulder completely. Refrigerate the flattened dough, still between the 2 pieces of parchment paper, for at least 1 hour.

3   Roast the lamb. When the roast is out of the oven and on the cooling rack, turn on the broiler. Take the dough out of the refrigerator and remove the top piece of paper. Invert the dough onto the shoulder so that it covers the top and remove the other piece of paper. Put the lamb back in the oven to broil for 5 minutes, until the crust begins to turn golden.

1 tablespoon olive oil
½ red bell pepper, peeled, seeded (page 130), and chopped into ½-inch (1-cm.) dice
½ cup (130 g.) softened butter (soften in the microwave if necessary)
1 clove garlic, peeled, degermed (page 122), and chopped
1 teaspoon sweet red pepper powder (preferably Espelette pepper)
1¼ cups dry bread crumbs
Salt
1 roast shoulder of lamb, prepared as above

RACK OF LAMB

Carré d'agneau rôti

SERVES   4

PREPARATION   5 minutes

COOKING   20 minutes for a rare finish; 25–30 minutes for medium rare

RESTING   10 minutes

Ask the butcher for a rack of lamb from which the fat has been removed more or less according to your taste and with the vertebrae separated so that the chops will be easier to carve. Ask him for a handful of chopped trimmings, too, for your sauce. If the trimmings are too fatty, remove some of the fat.

1 rack of lamb, 1½ pounds (800 g.), with trimmings
Salt
Pepper
1 clove garlic, unpeeled and lightly crushed under your palm
1 sprig fresh thyme
Fleur de sel

1 Remove the meat from the refrigerator 20 minutes in advance. Put it into the roasting pan or baking dish and prepare a cooling rack (or small overturned plate) over a large plate or platter.

2 Preheat the oven to 440°F/220°C.

3 Season the trimmings lightly with salt and pepper. Cover the ends of the rack's bones with aluminum foil to keep them from burning. Season the meat all over with salt and pepper. Arrange the rack in the roasting pan so that the bones are on the underside and the fatty side is up. Spread the trimmings all around it and add the garlic. Sprinkle the thyme leaves all over the meat and discard the stem.

4 When the oven has reached 440°F/220°C, cook the roast for 20 minutes. (If you prefer medium rare, cook 25–30 minutes.) Remove the lamb to the cooling rack. Season with salt and pepper and tent loosely with aluminum foil.

5 Allow the roast to rest for 10 minutes (or 15 if it is cooked medium rare). In the meantime, prepare the juice. Spoon excess fat from the surface of the roasting pan. Add 8 tablespoons water to the pan, stirring and scraping with a wooden spatula to loosen all the cooked-on bits. Season with salt and pepper. Put the pan back in the oven, no longer on but still hot. Just before serving, put these juices through a fine strainer into a sauceboat. Add any juices that have collected under the resting meat. Ideally, you should have 1 table-

spoon of juice per diner. The clove of garlic can be added to the juice or served on the side.

6   It is easy to carve the roast: Use a large knife to separate the chops. Season each chop on both sides with fleur de sel and pepper.

STEWED SHOULDER OF LAMB WITH SMALL ONIONS ____

Epaule d'agneau en cocotte aux petits oignons

SERVES   4
PREPARATION   10 minutes
COOKING   40 minutes

1   Remove the lamb from the refrigerator 30 minutes in advance.
2   Preheat the oven to 360°F/180°C.
3   Season the lamb with salt and pepper on both sides. Heat 1 teaspoon olive oil in a Dutch oven. Brown the lamb all over in the pot over medium heat for 3–4 minutes total. Put the pot in the oven, uncovered, and cook for 15 minutes.
4   While the lamb is in the oven, put the peeled onions in a saucepan with 6 tablespoons cold water and 2 tablespoons olive oil. Season with salt and pepper, bring to a simmer, and simmer for 5–6 minutes. Stir in the rosemary and cook 1 minute more.
5   After the shoulder has been in the oven for 15 minutes, turn it and add the onions to the pot. Pour the onions' cooking juices over the lamb and cook 25 minutes more, basting from time to time.

1 bone-in lamb shoulder, about
    2 pounds (1 kg.)
Salt
Pepper
2 tablespoons plus 1 teaspoon
    olive oil
10 ounces (300 g.) cipollini or
    pearl onions, peeled
1 teaspoon minced fresh
    rosemary

SPICED STEWED SHOULDER OF LAMB _____

Epaule d'agneau confite aux épices

SERVES   4

PREPARATION   10 minutes

COOKING   3 hours (for 2 shoulders from milk lambs) or
5 hours (for 1 regular lamb shoulder, about
2 pounds/900 g.)

1   Preheat the oven to 250°F/130°C. Season the lamb all over
with salt and pepper.

2   Heat the oil in a large Dutch oven over medium heat. Place
the lamb in the pot skin side down and brown for 5 minutes.
Flip it over and add the potatoes, garlic, shallots, tomatoes,
spices, and ½ cup (10 cl.) water. Cover and bake for 3 hours
(if using milk lamb) or 5 hours (if using regular lamb).

3   Sprinkle the cooked lamb with preserved lemon zest and
cilantro. Serve in the pot.

1 lamb shoulder, 1¾–2 pounds
(800–900 g.)

Salt

Pepper

3 tablespoons olive oil

12 small, firm-fleshed potatoes,
preferably charlottes,
peeled and sliced in half
lengthwise

6 cloves garlic, peeled and
degermed (page 122)

4 shallots, peeled and left
whole

6 dried half-tomatoes (page
588 or store-bought)

1 teaspoon green anise seeds

1 teaspoon cumin seeds

1 teaspoon coriander seeds

10 threads saffron

Zest of 1 preserved lemon,
diced

1 teaspoon cilantro leaves

LAMB TAGINE

Tagine d'agneau

SERVES   4
PREPARATION   10 minutes
COOKING   25 minutes for the rice plus 8–10 minutes for
the lamb

The dried fruit must be soaked an hour in advance.

1   Put the prunes, apricots, and raisins in a small bowl. Pour
1 cup hot water over them and then add the lemon juice. If
the liquid is lower than the top of the fruit, add enough hot
water to cover completely. After 1 hour of soaking, drain the
fruit in a colander.

2   Preheat the oven to 350°F/180°C.

3   Melt 2 teaspoons butter in a Dutch oven. Add half of the
sliced onions, a pinch of salt, and a pinch of pepper. Cook for
3 minutes over low heat, stirring with a wooden spoon. Add
the drained fruit, mix well, and then stir in the honey. Stir in
the rice. Add 1⅔ cups chicken broth along with the bay
leaves and thyme. Bring to a boil, cover, and bake in the preheated oven for 20 minutes.

4   In the meantime, prepare a cooling rack over a large plate (or
a small overturned plate on top of a large one). Melt the
remaining butter in a sauté pan. Brown the cubes of lamb in
the butter, stirring for 3 minutes over medium heat. Add the
remaining onions, the garlic, turmeric, a pinch of salt, and
a pinch of pepper. Cook and stir over medium heat for
5–7 minutes, depending on how well done you like your
lamb. Remove the cooked meat to the cooling rack but leave
the onions and juices in the pan.

5   Heat the onions and juices in the sauté pan over low heat for
1 minute. Add ½ cup water and cook over low heat, scraping
the bottom and sides of the pan with a wooden spatula.

6   Remove the rice from the oven but do not turn off the heat.
Fluff the rice with a fork and remove the bay leaves and
thyme sprig.

7   Spread the slivered almonds on a baking sheet and toast for
a few minutes on a high rack of the oven, long enough to
turn them a little golden but not dark.

8   Heap the rice on a serving dish. Sprinkle it with almonds

---

4 pitted prunes, sliced into
strips ½ inch (1 cm.) thick
6 dried apricots, sliced into
strips ½ inch (1 cm.) thick
2 ounces (60 g.) raisins
Juice of ½ lemon
1 tablespoon butter
2 onions, peeled and sliced into
thin rounds
Salt
Pepper
1 tablespoon honey
1 cup (220 g.) long-grain white
rice
2 cups (45 cl.) chicken broth
(page 77 or made from a
bouillon cube)
2 bay leaves
1 sprig thyme
1¼ pounds (600 g.) of a lamb
leg, chopped into 1½-inch
(3-cm.) cubes
3 cloves garlic, peeled,
degermed (page 122),
and minced
Large pinch of turmeric
2–3 pinches slivered almonds
10 small mint leaves

and arrange the lamb all around it. Spread the onion sauce over the meat and sprinkle mint leaves over the whole.

STEWED LAMB WITH TOMATOES AND OLIVES _____

Agneau en cocotte à la tomate et aux olives

SERVES 4
PREPARATION 15 minutes
COOKING 1½ hours

Ask the butcher to cut the lamb into 12 pieces more or less the same size.

1 Season the lamb all over with salt and pepper. Prepare a cooling rack over a plate (or a small overturned plate on top of a large one).
2 Heat the olive oil over medium heat in a large saucepan or Dutch oven. Add the lamb and brown on all sides, about 3 minutes total. Remove the browned meat to the cooling rack, leaving the juices in the pot.
3 Put the onions and garlic in the pot and cook over very low heat for 5 minutes, stirring. Return the lamb to the pot and sprinkle it with the flour. Stir. Add ½ cup (10 cl.) water and scrape the bottom of the pot with a wooden spatula to loosen any flavorful cooked-on bits. Add the tomatoes, thyme, and olives to the pot along with ½ cup (10 cl.) water. Bring to a simmer and then turn the heat to very low, cover, and simmer for 1 hour, stirring every 15 minutes.
4 Taste for salt and pepper. Sprinkle with basil before serving.

1 boneless lamb shoulder, about 1¼ pounds (600 g.)
Salt
Pepper
1 tablespoon olive oil
4 medium-sized onions, peeled and quartered
5 cloves garlic, peeled
1 tablespoon flour
4 medium tomatoes, peeled, seeded (page 124), and quartered
1 sprig thyme
3 ounces (100 g.) small black olives, preferably Niçoise
2 tablespoons coarsely chopped basil

LAMB STEW

Navarin d'agneau

SERVES 8

PREPARATION 30 minutes

COOKING 1 hour plus 20 minutes for the small onions

The French name for this stew, *navarin,* almost certainly comes from the word for turnip, *navet,* although today it is made with potatoes and not turnips. You can divide the quantities by two to make a stew for four, but this dish is best made in larger quantities. Ask the butcher to cut all the meat into 2-inch (5-cm.) cubes.

1 Heat the olive oil in a large Dutch oven over high heat for 1 minute. Add the cubed meat and brown for 5 minutes, stirring so that all sides are seared. Add the diced carrots and onions. Turn the heat to low and cook for 5 minutes, stirring. You want the vegetables to take on a bit of color.

2 Sprinkle flour over the whole, stir, and cook for 2 minutes, until the vegetables are lightly colored. Add the bouquet garni, garlic, tomato, and just enough water to cover. Raise the heat to high and bring to a boil. Use a skimmer to remove any scummy foam that forms on the surface. Add 2 teaspoons coarse salt and 4 grindings of pepper. Cover, lower the heat so the mixture simmers gently, and cook for 50 minutes, skimming and stirring every 15 minutes.

3 In the meantime, wash and peel the potatoes. Put them in a saucepan, cover them with cold unsalted water, bring the water to a boil, and cook for 1 minute. Remove the potatoes to a colander.

4 When the lamb has cooked for 50 minutes, take the pot off the heat. Remove the meat with a slotted spoon or skimmer and put it in a large bowl. Pour the cooking broth through a fine strainer into the bowl with the lamb and then put the strained broth and lamb back into the pot. Add the potatoes, cover, and put the pot back over low heat for 20–25 minutes.

5 In the meantime, melt the butter in a sauté pan. Add the small onions and cook for 5 minutes over low heat, stirring constantly. Add enough water to cover the onions and season

3 tablespoons olive oil

2 pounds (1 kg.) lamb shoulder, cubed

1 pound (500 g.) lamb neck, cubed

1 pound (500 g.) lamb breast, cubed

3 carrots, peeled and cut into ¼ inch (0.5 cm.) dice

3 medium onions, peeled and cut into ¼ inch (0.5 cm.) dice

¼ cup (30 g.) flour

1 bouquet garni (3 stems flat-leaf parsley, 2 sprigs fresh thyme, and ½ bay leaf, tied together)

4 cloves garlic, peeled and crushed

1 large tomato, unpeeled and chopped into large dice

Coarse salt

Pepper

2½ pounds (1.2 kg.) small, firm-fleshed potatoes such as charlottes

1 tablespoon butter

½ pound (250 g.) small new pearl or cipollini onions, peeled but left whole

Salt

1 teaspoon superfine sugar

2 tablespoons minced flat-leaf parsley

with a pinch of salt and the superfine sugar. Cover and cook for 20 minutes over very low heat, stirring from time to time.

6   After 20–25 minutes, turn off the heat under the pot of meat and potatoes. Prepare a bowl half-filled with cold water. Spoon some of the cold water gently on the surface of the stew and then spoon away the fat that comes to the top. Rinse the spoon in the cold water after each passage. When the small onions are cooked, arrange them on top of the stew and sprinkle with parsley. Serve in the pot.

LAMB STEW WITH YOUNG VEGETABLES

Navarin d'agneau aux primeurs

SERVES   4

PREPARATION   25 minutes

COOKING   1 hour plus 20 minutes for the small onions

1   Heat the olive oil in a large Dutch oven over high heat for 1 minute. Add the cubed meat and brown for 5 minutes, stirring with a wooden spoon that so all sides are seared. Add the diced onion and diced carrot. Turn the heat to low and cook for 5 minutes, stirring. You want the vegetables to take on a bit of color.

2   Sprinkle flour over the whole, stir, and cook for 2 minutes, until the vegetables are lightly colored. Add the bouquet garni, garlic, and tomato, and just enough water to cover. Raise the heat to high and bring to a boil. Use a skimmer to remove any scummy foam that forms on the surface.

3   Add 1 teaspoon coarse salt and 2 grindings of pepper. Cover, lower the heat so the mixture simmers gently, and cook for 50 minutes, skimming and stirring every 15 minutes.

4   In the meantime, remove the peas from their shells. Prepare a bowl half-filled with cold water and 6 ice cubes. Bring 1 quart (1 l.) water to a boil with 2 teaspoons coarse salt. Plunge the shelled peas into the boiling water; when the water begins to bubble again, cook for 3 minutes. Remove the peas to the ice water and leave them for a few minutes, until they have cooled down. Drain the peas and set them aside.

1 tablespoon olive oil

1 boneless lamb shoulder, about 3 pounds (1.2 kg.), cut into 2-inch (5-cm.) cubes

1 medium onion, peeled and cut into ¼-inch (0.5-cm.) dice

1 medium carrot, peeled and cut into ¼-inch (0.5-cm.) dice

2 tablespoons (15 g.) flour

1 bouquet garni (3 stems flat-leaf parsley, 2 sprigs fresh thyme, and ½ bay leaf, tied together)

2 cloves garlic, peeled and crushed

1 medium tomato, unpeeled and chopped into large dice

5   Wash and peel the potatoes. Put them in a saucepan, cover with cold unsalted water, bring the water to a boil, and cook for 1 minute. Remove the potatoes to a colander.

6   When the lamb has cooked for 50 minutes, take the pot off the heat. Remove the meat with a slotted spoon or skimmer and put it in a large bowl. Pour the cooking broth through a fine strainer into the bowl with the lamb and then put the strained broth and lamb back into the pot. Add the potatoes and diced turnips and carrots, cover, and put the pot back over low heat for 20–25 minutes.

7   In the meantime, melt the butter in a sauté pan. Add the small onions and cook for 5 minutes over low heat, stirring constantly. Add enough water to cover the onions and season with a pinch of salt and the superfine sugar. Cover and cook for 20 minutes over very low heat, stirring from time to time.

8   After 20–25 minutes, turn off the heat under the pot of meat and potatoes. Prepare a bowl half-filled with cold water. Spoon some of the cold water gently onto the surface of the stew, then spoon away the fat that comes to the top. Rinse the spoon in the cold water after each passage. Stir in the peas, wait 2 minutes so they heat up, and then arrange the small onions on top of the stew and sprinkle with parsley. Serve in the pot.

Coarse salt
Pepper
$\frac{1}{4}$ pound (100 g.) baby peas in the pod
8 small new potatoes
8 small turnips, peeled and cut into $\frac{1}{4}$-inch (0.5-cm.) dice
8 small carrots, peeled and cut into $\frac{1}{4}$-inch (0.5-cm.) dice
1 tablespoon butter
$\frac{1}{4}$ pound (100 g.) small new or cipollini onions
Salt
1 teaspoon superfine sugar
1 tablespoon chopped parsley

IRISH STEW

Sauté d'agneau à l'irlandaise

SERVES 4–6
PREPARATION 30 minutes
COOKING 2½ hours

This dish's roots lie in the exceptional quality of Ireland's sheep, raised in the green meadows of that island, and potatoes, once its agricultural staple.

1   Lay the meat on a work surface and season lightly with salt and pepper. Put the celery, cabbage, onions, and potatoes in a bowl. Season with 2 teaspoons salt and 1 teaspoon pepper, mixing well.

2   Preheat the oven to 350°F/180°C.

3   Prepare the dough for the pastry seal, called *pâte à luter* in French, see page 383.

4   Spread half of the vegetables evenly in an ovenproof pot or terrine. Lay the pieces of lamb atop the vegetables; they should be snuggled up to one another, not far apart. Cover with the rest of the vegetables and tuck a bouquet garni into each end.

5   Mix the Worcestershire sauce with ½ cup water. Pour it over the contents of the pot or terrine. Add water to the vessel until it is just below the top layer of vegetables.

6   Roll the dough into a tube long enough to circle the pot. Press it onto the rim of the pot or terrine and press the lid down on top of it firmly so that you get a good seal. Bake for 2½ hours.

7   Take the pot out of the oven. Remove the sealing crust and then the cover. Remove the bouquets garnis from the pot and use a paper towel to wipe down its exposed walls. Bring the pot to the table to serve.

1½ pounds (800 g.) mutton shoulder chops

1½ pounds (800 g.) mutton neck

Salt

Pepper

1 stalk celery, washed and sliced into ¼-inch (0.5-cm.) strips and then into ½-inch (1-cm.) pieces

½ pound (200 g.) green cabbage leaves, blanched (page 556) and sliced into ¼-inch (0.5-cm.) strips and then into ½-inch (1-cm.) pieces

½ pound (250 g.) onions, peeled and sliced into thin rounds

3 pounds (1.4 kg.) potatoes, preferably charlotte or Yukon Gold, peeled and sliced into rounds ¼ inch (0.5-cm.) thick

2 bouquets garnis (6 stems parsley, 2 sprigs fresh thyme, and 1 bay leaf in each bundle)

1 teaspoon Worcestershire sauce

PÂTE À LUTER

To prepare a strip of dough to seal a baking pot, put 1⅔ (200 g.) cups flour in a bowl with a pinch of salt and a pinch of sugar. Gradually add ½ cup (15 cl.) cold water to the flour, mixing it in with a wooden spatula. Mix it well. You want to obtain a rather soft dough, yielding enough to conform to the bottom and lid of the pot but firm enough to stick.

Beef

In the Middle Ages, the procession of the fatted calf in the carnival days before Lent celebrated the return of spring—a tradition that may have begun in ancient Egypt. A symbol of abundance and good eating, beef has long been associated with vital force, too. During the years of economic expansion after World War II, it was said in France that a man "earned his steak" rather than "earned his bread," one sacred food replacing another in the old expression. Red meat was strongly recommended as necessary regular nourishment for growing children. Although the consumption of beef declined in the last third of the twentieth century—a tendency encouraged by our recent fear of mad cow disease—it remains one of the choicest of meats and has more pronounced flavors than lamb, veal, or fowl.

CHOOSING BEEF

When purchasing beef, you must know the differences between the cuts meant for boiling or braising and those meant for grilling or roasting. Those that will be cooked with liquid—shank, chuck, ribs, cheeks, tail, pot-au-feu cuts, etc.—must be very fresh. Those that will be dry-grilled or roasted—all kinds of steaks and roasts—need two or three weeks of aging and mellowing after the animal is slaughtered if they are to be enjoyed at their best. (The butcher will take care of this aging for you.) Once carved, however, a steak must be cooked and eaten soon. It is the side of beef that should be aged, not the individual steak. It is especially important that ground beef be freshly cut and ground.

Among the cuts for grilling and roasting, some, such as sirloin steak, are preferred for their extreme tenderness; easy to prepare and eat, they are well suited to modern life. It is the chewier cuts like flank steak and skirt steak, however, that have the best flavor.

Several factors determine the quality of beef: the animal's breed, age, sex, diet, and lifestyle. Free-range, grass-fed cattle are to be preferred.

Pay close attention to how the raw meat looks: It should be bright red, not at all brownish, free of unpleasant odors, and firm. There should be a network of white fat between muscles (the famous "marbling") and many small filaments of fat in the muscles themselves (the veining).

In France, thanks to regulations introduced after the mad cow scare, meat packaging must specify not only the cut and the sell-by date but also information about where the animal was born, raised, and slaughtered. No such regulations exist in the United States, but a reputable butcher should be able to tell you where he got his meat and how it was raised.

There are dozens of breeds of cattle in the United States, but more than 60 percent of the beef consumed here comes from three: the Angus and Hereford cows, first bred in Britain, and Simmental cows, whose origins lie in continental Europe. Other continental breeds, such as the French Charolais and Limousin, have been introduced more recently. They contain less fat and take longer to mature.

The quality of meat in the United States can be uneven. To be sure of constant quality, especially for barbecuing or grilling, you could choose Wagyu beef. This Japanese breed (the name means "Japanese cow") is also called "Kobe-style" because it produces the famous Kobe beef, raised in that city and fed with beer and sake. Its meat shows beautiful marbling: thin white strips of fat that give the meat intese flavor. Wagyu beef is fattier than the British and continental breeds.

Whatever the breed, choose hormone-free beef. Hormones swell the animal's muscles as testosterone does a doped athlete's. The result is the animal produces more meat and therefore sells for a better price, but the consumer is not the winner here. Europeans, maintaining that the hormones might pose risks to human health, have banned them and will accept only hormone-free imports. American authorities and most farmers strongly deny that there is any risk, but the question is still much debated in the scientific community. Lacking definitive answers, hormone-free meat is probably the wisest choice (and it will not shrink as much on the grill or in the frying pan).

Standard cuts of meat are different in France, the United States, and England. The French do not produce T-bones, which are cut in the tenderloin, but they love the standing rib roast on the bone, which is not common in the United States. You can always ask your butcher to cut it the French way, from the rib roast.

PAN FRIED BEEFSTEAK

Beefsteak poêlé

SERVES 1

PREPARATION 2 minutes

COOKING *bleu* (very rare—raw in the middle), 2 minutes; *saignant* (rare), 3 minutes; *à point* (medium rare), 4 minutes

1 Remove the steak from the refrigerator 10 minutes in advance. Prepare a cooling rack over a large plate (or set a small overturned plate on top of the large plate).

2 Season the steak on both sides with salt and pepper. Heat the oil in a heavy skillet over high heat. If you want to add a little flavor, add ½ teaspoon butter. Rotate the skillet to spread the fat around as the butter melts and foams. Lower the heat to medium and lay the steak in the skillet, in a motion away from yourself so as not to splatter yourself with hot fat. For a rare steak, cook for 1½ minutes, occasionally rotating the steak in the skillet and spooning hot fat over it. Then flip the steak with plastic tongs (to avoid puncturing the meat) or 2 spatulas and cook 1½ minutes more, turning and basting as before.

3 Remove the steak to the rack and season with fleur de sel and pepper on both sides. If you like, top with ½ teaspoon butter and parsley to serve.

1 flat iron steak, 4–6 ounces (120 g.)

Salt

Pepper

1 teaspoon neutral oil

1 teaspoon butter (optional)

Fleur de sel

½ teaspoon minced parsley (optional)

MEATBALLS

Boulettes de viande

SERVES 4
PREPARATION 15 minutes
COOKING 5 minutes
The bread crumbs must be soaked 30 minutes in advance.

1   Thirty minutes in advance, spread the bread crumbs in a deep dish and cover with the milk. Mix well, and leave to soak.

2   In a large saucepan or Dutch oven, heat the peanut oil and 1 teaspoon butter. Add the onion and cook for 3 minutes over low heat, stirring with a spatula. With a slotted spoon, remove the onion to a colander.

3   Beat the egg with a fork. Combine the meats, egg, soaked crumbs, and onion in a bowl. Season with salt and pepper and mix well but gently until uniformly combined. Wet your hands and shape the seasoned meat into 30 balls weighing about 1 ounce (25 g.) each.

4   Melt the remaining butter in the onion pot over low heat. When the butter foams, use a slotted spoon to deposit the meatballs in the pot. Cook for 5 minutes over low heat, turning them so they get evenly browned all over. Remove them to a serving platter with a slotted spoon.

5   Pour 4 tablespoons water into the pot and bring to a boil. Let it bubble gently for 15 minutes and then put the meatballs back in the pot. Turn them in the sauce for 2 minutes. Serve with rice or bulgur wheat.

1 cup dry bread crumbs
½ cup (10 cl.) milk
1 teaspoon peanut oil
2 tablespoons butter
1 medium onion, peeled and minced
1 egg
1¼ pounds (600 g.) ground beef
¼ pound (100 g.) ground pork, preferably from the shoulder
Salt
Pepper

PAN FRIED HOMEMADE CHOPPED STEAK

Steak hâché poêlé

variations

PAN FRIED STORE-BOUGHT
CHOPPED STEAK
PAN FRIED CHOPPED
STEAK WITH A FRIED
EGG

SERVES   1
PREPARATION   2 minutes
COOKING   9 minutes for rare; 12 minutes for medium rare
RESTING   3 minutes

1   Remove the ground beef from the refrigerator 10 minutes in advance. Prepare a cooling rack over a large plate (or set a small overturned plate on top of the large plate). Shape the ground beef into a patty 1½ inches (3 cm.) thick and 3 inches (7 cm.) wide, compressing the meat and flattening its broad sides.

2   Season the steak patty on both sides with salt and pepper. Heat the oil in a heavy skillet over high heat. If you want to add a little flavor, add the butter. Rotate the skillet to spread the fat around as the butter melts and foams. Lower the heat to medium and lay the steak in the skillet. For a rare steak, cook for 5 minutes, occasionally rotating the steak in the skillet. Then flip the steak with plastic tongs (to avoid puncturing the meat) or 2 spatulas and cook 4 minutes more, turning as before.

3   Remove the steak to the rack, preferably with the side cooked first facing down, and season with fleur de sel and pepper on both sides. Let the steak rest for 3 minutes. Sprinkle with parsley, if you like, and serve.

6 ounces (180 g.) ground beef
Salt
Pepper
1 teaspoon neutral oil
1 teaspoon butter (optional)
Fleur de sel
½ teaspoon parsley (optional)

PAN FRIED STORE-BOUGHT CHOPPED STEAK

Steak hâché reconstitué poêlé

SERVES   1

PREPARATION   2 minutes

COOKING   4 minutes for rare; 5 or 6 minutes for medium
rare

RESTING   2–3 minutes

This chopped steak is bought already prepared for cooking. Thinner and more compact than the one you would knead yourself at home, it will cook faster, but the homemade one will definitely taste better.

4 ounces (120 g.) chopped
steak

Salt

Pepper

1 teaspoon neutral oil

1 teaspoon butter (optional)

Fleur de sel

½ teaspoon parsley (optional)

1   Remove the steak from the refrigerator 5 minutes in advance. Prepare a cooling rack over a large plate (or set a small overturned plate on top of the large plate).

2   Season the steak on both sides with salt and pepper. Heat the oil in a heavy skillet over high heat. If you want to add a little flavor, add the butter. Rotate the skillet to spread the fat around as the butter melts and foams. Lower the heat to medium and lay the steak in the skillet. For a rare steak, cook for 2 minutes, occasionally rotating the steak in the skillet. Then flip the steak with plastic tongs (to avoid puncturing the meat) or 2 spatulas and cook 2 minutes more, turning as before.

3   Remove the steak to the rack, preferably with the side cooked first facing down, and season with fleur de sel and pepper on both sides. Let the steak rest for 3 minutes. Sprinkle with parsley, if you like, and serve.

PAN FRIED CHOPPED STEAK WITH A FRIED EGG

Steak hâché sauté et oeuf poêlé

SERVES   1

COOKING   2–3 minutes

1   Prepare the steak according to one of the previous 2 recipes. While it rests, put the skillet in which the steak cooked back over medium heat. Rap the egg lightly on your work surface

1 pan fried chopped steak,
as above

1 egg

(not on the edge of a bowl) and open it into a small bowl. Be careful not to break the yolk or drop any shell into the egg. If you do drop shell into the egg, remove it with your fingers. Slide the egg into the skillet.

2 Fry for 2–3 minutes, depending on how well cooked you like your eggs. As the egg cooks, prick the white 2 or 3 times with a spatula and slip the spatula gently under the edge of its border. When it is done, slide the fried egg out of the skillet and onto the steak. Season the white with fleur de sel and pepper.

Fleur de sel
Pepper

PAN FRIED TOURNEDOS

Tournedos poêlé

SERVES   1
PREPARATION   2 minutes
COOKING   6 minutes for very rare; 8 minutes for rare;
10 minutes for medium rare
RESTING   5 minutes

1 Remove the steak from the refrigerator 15 minutes in advance. Prepare a cooling rack over a large plate (or set a small overturned plate on top of the large plate).

2 Season the steak on both sides with salt and pepper. Heat the oil in a heavy skillet over high heat. Add 1 teaspoon butter and rotate the skillet to spread the fat around as the butter melts and foams. Lower the heat to medium and lay the steak in the skillet. For a rare steak, cook for 2 minutes, occasionally rotating the steak in the skillet and spooning the cooking fat over it. Then flip the steak with plastic tongs (to avoid puncturing the meat) or 2 spatulas and cook 2 minutes more, turning and basting as before. Use tongs to set the steak on its side and cook its edges for 2 minutes, turning so it is evenly cooked.

3 Remove the steak to the rack, preferably with the side cooked first facing down, and season with fleur de sel and pepper on both sides. Let the steak rest for 5 minutes. Top with 1 teaspoon butter and sprinkle with parsley, if you like, and serve.

1 tournedos, 6 ounces (180 g.), approximately 1 inch thick, preferably without bacon or other wrapping
Salt
Pepper
1 teaspoon neutral oil
2 teaspoons butter
Fleur de sel
½ teaspoon minced parsley (optional)

PAN FRIED RIB STEAK OR RIB EYE

Entrecôte poêlée

variation

RIB STEAK WITH
VINTNER'S MARROW

SERVES   1
PREPARATION   2 minutes
COOKING   3 minutes for very rare; 4 minutes for rare; 5–6
minutes for medium rare
RESTING   5 minutes

1   Remove the steak from the refrigerator 10 minutes in advance. Use scissors to snip the connective tissues that surround the meat in 2 or 3 places so that the steak will not curl up when it cooks. Prepare a cooling rack over a large plate (or set a small overturned plate on top of the large plate).

2   Season the steak on both sides with salt and pepper. Heat the oil in a heavy skillet over high heat. Add 1 teaspoon butter and rotate the skillet to spread the fat around as the butter melts and foams. Lower the heat to medium and lay the steak in the skillet. For a rare steak, cook for 2 minutes, occasionally rotating the steak in the skillet and spooning the cooking fat over it. Then flip the steak with plastic tongs (to avoid puncturing the meat) or 2 spatulas and cook 2 minutes more, turning and basting as before.

3   Remove the steak to the rack and season with fleur de sel and pepper on both sides. Let the steak rest for 5 minutes. If you like, top with 1 teaspoon butter and sprinkle with parsley before serving.

1 rib steak or rib eye,
   ½ pound (180 g.)
Salt
Pepper
1 teaspoon neutral oil
2 teaspoons butter
Fleur de sel
½ teaspoon minced parsley
   (optional)

RIB STEAK WITH VINTNER'S MARROW

Entrecôte à la moelle vigneronne

SERVES 2

PREPARATION AND COOKING   10 minutes (before the steak
is cooked) plus 10 minutes

The marrow must be soaked at least 1 hour in advance, or, if
possible, the night before.

In Bordeaux, rib steak is traditionally grilled over grapevines
and served with shallot butter.

1   At least 1 hour in advance or the night before, if possible, put
the marrow in a small container. Cover it with 1 quart (1 l.)
cold water and add 3 tablespoons salt. Seal the container and
put it in the refrigerator.

2   When you remove the steak from the refrigerator before
cooking, put the wine in a saucepan and bring it to a boil.
Simmer for 15 minutes while the steak cooks.

3   In the meantime, drain the marrow and slice it into rounds
½ inch (1 cm.) thick. Line a plate with a double thickness of
paper towels. Dice 2 tablespoons butter and put it back in the
refrigerator to stay cold.

4   While the steak rests, remove the grease from the skillet in
which it cooked. Put the skillet back over low heat and melt
the remaining butter. Add the shallots and a pinch of salt and
cook for 3 minutes, stirring with a spatula. Raise the heat to
medium, stir, and add the wine and broth. Simmer over low
heat until the liquid is reduced by half.

5   Bring a small saucepan of water to a boil with 1 teaspoon
salt. When it bubbles, turn off the heat and drop the marrow
into the water. Leave it to rest for 2 minutes.

6   Remove the reduced wine sauce from the heat. Stir in the
cold diced butter and any juices that have collected under the
resting meat.

7   Lay the steak on a warm serving dish and cover it with
rounds of marrow. Pour the sauce over and sprinkle with a
pinch of crushed black pepper and parsley.

Marrow of 3 beef bones; ask
the butcher to empty the
marrow from the bone

Salt

2 rib steaks weighing ½ pound
(180 g.) each or 1 rib
steak weighing ¾ pound
(350 g.), prepared as
described page 390

1 cup (25 cl.) Shiraz or Merlot

4 tablespoons (50 g.) butter,
well chilled

2 shallots, peeled and minced

1 cup (20 cl.) beef broth (from
a pot-au-feu, page 68, or
from a bouillon cube)

Crushed black pepper

1 teaspoon minced parsley

FLAP STEAK WITH SHALLOTS

Bavette à l'échalote

SERVES   4
PREPARATION   5 minutes
COOKING   8 minutes

The unusual cut we call flap steak is called *bavette d'aloyau* in France. It is difficult to find in the United States, so you might try substituting skirt steak. An exceedingly tasty and juicy cut, it must be cooked rare or it becomes tough.

4 slices flap steak, 6 ounces (180 g.) each
1 teaspoon neutral oil
Salt
Pepper
3 teaspoons butter
4 medium or 6 small shallots, preferably gray, peeled and minced
1 tablespoon red wine vinegar
2 tablespoons minced parsley

1   Remove the meat from the refrigerator 15 minutes in advance. Prepare a cooling rack over a large plate or set a small overturned plate on top of a large one.

2   Heat the oil in a large, heavy skillet over medium heat for 1 minute. Season both sides of the steaks with salt and pepper. Put the butter in the skillet. When it foams, lay the steaks in the skillet, in a motion away from you. Sear the steaks over high heat for 2 minutes. Turn them and cook for 2 minutes on the other side. Reduce the heat to very low and remove the meat to the rack. Season with a pinch of salt and a pinch of pepper on both sides.

3   Add the shallots to the skillet and cook over the lowest possible heat for 3 minutes, stirring constantly. It is important that they not turn dark brown. When they are lightly colored, add the vinegar, turn the heat up just a little bit, and cook for 30 seconds. Season with a pinch of salt.

4   Put the steaks on a platter and pour the shallot sauce all over. Sprinkle with parsley and serve.

PAN FRIED BEEF RIB STEAK

Côte de boeuf poêlée

variation

PAN FRIED BEEF RIB STEAK
WITH HERB SAUCE

SERVES 4–6
PREPARATION 5 minutes
COOKING rare, 30 minutes; medium rare, 35–40 minutes
RESTING 15 minutes

1   Remove the meat from the refrigerator 30 minutes in advance. Prepare a cooling rack over a large plate or set a small overturned plate on top of a large one.

2   Heat the oil in a large, heavy skillet over high heat. For a little extra flavor, add 1 or 2 teaspoons butter and rotate the skillet. Lower the heat to medium. When the butter has melted and is beginning to foam, lay the steak in the skillet in a motion away from yourself.

3   Cook the steak for 5 minutes, spooning the cooking fat over it regularly and rotating it in the skillet. Flip the steak and season the exposed, already-browned side with salt and pepper. Cook for 5 minutes and flip again, seasoning the newly exposed side with salt and pepper. Cook 20 minutes more, flipping every 5 minutes. Baste the meat and rotate it in the pan throughout cooking.

4   Use tongs to set the steak on its side; prop it up vertically with the 2 halves of the potato or by balancing a wooden spoon on the edges of the skillet on either side of the meat. Brown the side for 5 minutes, using tongs to rotate the meat so the entire edge is exposed to the heat. Turn the steak on its other edge, bone down and still holding it vertical, and brown that side for 5 minutes.

5   Remove the meat to the cooling rack. Season with fleur de sel and lots of freshly ground pepper. Allow the steak to rest for 15 minutes, turning it every 5 minutes. If you like, top it with 1 teaspoon butter.

6   To carve, hold the bone with a large fork, piercing its exterior membrane. Slice all along the bone to separate the meat from it. Slice the meat $1\frac{1}{2}$ inch (3 cm.) thick on a slight bias toward the bone, beginning with the rounded part. Hold the meat down with the back of the fork so you don't accidentally pierce it. Season each slice with fleur de sel and pepper on both sides. Sprinkle with parsley to serve.

1 whole beef rib steak, with its bone, $2\frac{1}{2}$–3 pounds (1.2–1.5 kg.)
1 teaspoon neutral oil
2 or 3 teaspoons butter (optional)
Salt
Pepper
1 potato, washed and sliced in half lengthwise (optional)
Fleur de sel
1 teaspoon minced parsley

PAN FRIED BEEF RIB STEAK WITH HERB SAUCE

Côte de boeuf, sauce aux herbes

SERVES   4–6
PREPARATION   5 minutes
COOKING   18 minutes

1 pan fried whole beef rib
   steak, prepared as
   described page 393
2 tablespoons butter, well
   chilled
2 shallots, peeled and minced
Salt
⅔ cup (15 cl.) chicken broth
   (page 77 or made from a
   bouillon cube)
1 tablespoon mustard, green
   herbed mustard if possible
1 teaspoon minced chives
1 teaspoon minced flat-leaf
   parsley
1 teaspoon minced tarragon
Pepper

1   Cook the whole rib according to the previous recipe. While the meat rests, spoon the excess fat from the skillet and put the skillet back over low heat. Add 1 tablespoon butter and then the shallots and a pinch of salt. Cook for 3 minutes over very low heat. Add the broth, bring to a boil, and simmer for 15 minutes.

2   In the meantime, dice the remaining butter. When the sauce has simmered for 15 minutes, turn off the heat. With a wooden spoon, stir in the remaining butter, the mustard, any juices that have collected under the meat, and the minced herbs. Taste for salt and pepper, and serve with the meat.

GRILLED BEEF RIB STEAK

Côte de boeuf grillée

SERVES   4–6
PREPARATION   5 minutes
COOKING   rare, 30 minutes; medium rare, 35–40 minutes
RESTING   15 minutes

Rib steak is even better if you grill it outdoors on a barbecue. In Bordeaux it is cooked over the embers of a grapevine fire.

1 whole beef rib steak, with its
   bone, 1½ pounds (1.2 kg.)
Neutral oil
Salt
Pepper
1 potato, washed and sliced in
   half lengthwise
Fleur de sel

1   Remove the rib from the refrigerator 30 minutes in advance. Prepare a cooling rack (or a small overturned plate) over a large plate.

2   Preheat the grill pan over medium heat. Brush the steak all over with oil. When the grill pan is good and hot, lay the rib on it diagonally, using tongs or a spatula and your hand.

Cook for 3 minutes and flip. Season the browned side generously with salt and pepper, and cook for 3 minutes. Flip the rib again and season the exposed side with salt and pepper. Cook 9 minutes more, flipping every 3 minutes and rotating the meat a quarter turn to get crosshatch grill marks.

3   Stand the rib on its boneless edge and prop it up with the two potato halves. Cook for 5 minutes on this edge, using tongs to achieve even cooking. Then turn it to its bone edge, prop it between the potatoes, and cook for 10 minutes.

4   Remove the rib to the rack. Season with fleur de sel and pepper generously. Allow it to rest for 15 minutes, turning it over every 5 minutes.

5   To carve, hold the bone with a large fork, piercing its exterior membrane. Slice all along the bone to separate the meat from it, then carve slices 1½ inches (3 cm.) thick on a bias toward the bone, beginning with the rounded part. Hold the meat down with the back of the fork, so you don't accidentally pierce it. Season each slice with fleur de sel and pepper on both sides.

ROAST BEEF

Rôti de boeuf

SERVES   4
PREPARATION   5 minutes
COOKING   very rare, 25 minutes; rare, 30 minutes; medium rare, 35–40 minutes
RESTING   15 minutes

Preferably, the roast should be without any kind of fatty wrap. A rump steak roast will be tastiest, a sirloin roast will be more tender, and a round roast will also do.

1 beef roast, 1½ pounds (800 g.)
Handful of beef trimmings (scraps of meat and chopped-up bones)

(continued)

1   Remove the roast from the refrigerator 1 hour in advance. Prepare a cooling rack (or a small overturned plate) over a large plate.

2   Twenty minutes in advance, preheat the oven to 460°F/240°C and make sure a rack is in the middle position. Spread the beef trimmings in the bottom of a roasting pan.

Place the roast on top and rub it all over with the oil. Do not salt yet.

3   When the oven is preheated, put the roast in and cook for 10 minutes. It should have some color at this point. Take the pan out of the oven and use tongs to remove the roast to a plate. Season generously all over with salt and pepper. Place the roast back in the pan, with the side that was on top now on the bottom, and return the pan to the oven. Cook for 10 minutes, rotate the roast a quarter turn, and cook 10 minutes more.

4   Turn off the oven and remove the roast to the cooling rack. Season with fleur de sel and pepper and allow it to rest for 15 minutes, giving it a quarter turn every 5 minutes.

5   In the meantime, prepare the juice: Add ⅓ cup (8 cl.) water to the roasting dish with the trimmings. Stir and scrape the bottom of the pan to loosen any cooked-on bits. Return the pan to the oven, which should still be hot even though it is off, and leave it there while you prepare the juice. Before serving, put the contents of the pan through a fine strainer into a sauceboat, adding any juices that have collected under the resting meat. Taste for salt and pepper. Ideally, you will have 1 tablespoon of juice per diner.

6   Before serving, snip the binding twine from the roast. Slice it into relatively thin parallel slices. Season each slice lightly with fleur de sel and pepper on both sides.

1 teaspoon neutral oil
Salt
Pepper
Fleur de sel

ROAST BEEF IN AN HERBED SALT CRUST

Rôti de boeuf en croûte de sel aux herbes

SERVES   6–8

PREPARATION   15 minutes

COOKING   rare, 30 minutes (count on 12 minutes per
pound); medium rare, 35–40 minutes (count on
15–16 minutes per pound)

RESTING   20 minutes

The salt crust must be prepared at least 2 hours in advance
or the night before if possible.

Fillet is a particularly delicate piece of beef and as such must
be served rare; it certainly should not be cooked past medium
rare. More than that and the meat toughens. In this recipe the
meat is seared at a very high temperature and then roasted at
a lower temperature so that it absorbs the aroma of the herbs
and stays tender.

1 pound (500 g.) coarse salt

3 tablespoons plus 1 teaspoon
thyme leaves

1 tablespoon rosemary leaves

2 large eggs, separated
(page 204)

3½ cups (400 g.) flour, plus a
little more for working with
the dough

1 whole fillet of beef,
2½ pounds (1.2 kg.)

1 tablespoon olive oil

1 tablespoon butter

Pepper

1   Put the coarse salt in the bowl of a food processor (fitted with
a dough blade if possible). Add 3 tablespoons thyme leaves
and the rosemary and pulse to mix. With the machine running, add 2 egg whites and ⅔ cup (15 cl.) water. Add the flour
bit by bit until it is combined. Dump the dough out onto a
lightly floured work surface and knead for 2 or 3 minutes,
until it is homogeneous. The dough should be firm, not soft
and sticky, or the beef will steam instead of roasting. If necessary, add a little more flour to make it less sticky. Put the
dough in a lightly oiled bowl, cover it with plastic wrap, and
leave it to rest, refrigerated, for at least 2 hours or up to 24.
This resting time will make the dough less sticky and easier
to work with.

2   Thirty minutes before you plan to begin cooking, remove the
beef from the refrigerator. Remove a rack from the oven. If it
isn't clean, rinse it under hot running water and wipe it clean
with paper towels. Place it over a large plate or platter.

3   Preheat the oven to 370°F/190°C. Prepare a sheet pan or
roasting dish large enough to hold the beef and line it with
parchment paper.

4   Pat the meat dry with paper towels. Do not salt it; this will
draw out its juices, and it will not brown properly.

5   Heat the oil in a pot large enough to hold the meat over medium heat. Add the butter. A minute later, when the butter begins to foam, lay the meat in the pot and sear for 2 minutes. The heat should be quite high. Give the meat a quarter turn, being careful not to pierce it, and sear 2 minutes more. Repeat twice so that all 4 sides are evenly browned. Remove the seared roast to the oven rack over the plate, still careful not to puncture it.

6   Lightly flour a rolling pin and a work surface. Remove the dough from the refrigerator and roll it out into a 10-by-12-inch (26-by-30-cm.) rectangle—large enough to wrap the roast without stretching the dough.

7   Discard one of the egg yolks and beat the other in a bowl with 1½ teaspoons water. Sprinkle the roast with 1 teaspoon thyme leaves and lay it on the rolled-out dough. Wrap it completely in the dough, pressing the seams closed with your fingers. Make sure they are quite well sealed. Place the wrapped roast on the parchment paper–lined sheet pan or baking dish and carefully brush its doughy top with the egg yolk mixture. Be careful not to drip yolk on the parchment paper. If you do drip, wipe it up with a paper towel.

8   Bake the roast on the middle rack of the oven for 30 minutes if you want it to be rare. When you remove the roast from the oven, place it on the prepared oven rack and allow it to rest for at least 20 minutes. The roast will stay hot, so you can wait even longer, but not more than 1 hour.

9   Warm your serving platter in the oven, which should still be hot even though it is off. To serve, make a vertical cut in the salt crust at one end and pull the roast out. Throw the crust away. Season the meat with pepper and slice it thickly on the bias, arranging the slices on the hot serving platter.

BEEF BOURGUIGNON ———————————————

SERVES 6

PREPARATION 20 minutes

COOKING 2¼ hours plus 25 minutes for the onions,
5 minutes for the lardons, and 10 minutes
for the mushrooms

Now we (and the French) say *boeuf bourguignon,* but once upon a time this dish was called *piéce de boeuf à la bourguignonne* (a piece of beef cooked in the style of Burgundy). Then it would have been prepared with a rump roast weighing at least 4 pounds (2 kg.), cooked whole. Now the custom is to chop the meat into cubes so that the dish doesn't have to cook quite so long.

The best red wine sauces include a bit of flour. Classic French cuisine used much too much, and the *nouvelle cuisine* of the 1970s banished it heedlessly. Flour deserves neither this excess of honor nor this complete refusal. Well used, as it is here, it does a fine job of thickening sauces.

1   Put the wine in a saucepan and bring to a boil. Simmer for 20 minutes.

2   In the meantime, heat 1 tablespoon peanut oil in a large saucepan or Dutch oven. Add 3 tablespoons butter; when it foams, add the cubes of meat. Brown them for 5 minutes over medium heat, stirring them with a wooden spoon to make sure they get browned on all sides.

3   Using a skimmer or slotted spoon, remove the meat to a deep dish. Put the carrots and onions into the pot in which the meat was browned and cook for 5 minutes over very low heat, stirring once or twice to keep them from darkening.

4   Sprinkle the meat with the flour and put it back in the pot along with 1 scant teaspoon crushed black pepper. Turn the heat to medium and cook, stirring constantly, for 5 minutes, just long enough to remove the flour's raw taste.

5   Pour half of the broth into the pot and stir. Then pour in the wine and the remaining broth. It should come just high enough to cover the meat. Add the bouquet garni and garlic, and cover. Simmer gently for 2 hours. Every 30 minutes,

1 bottle red Burgundy or Pinot
Noir wine

1 tablespoon plus 1 teaspoon
peanut oil

4 tablespoons (60 g.) butter

2 pounds (900 g.) rump pot
roast, cut into 2-inch
(5-cm.) cubes (ask the
butcher to do this)

2 medium carrots, peeled and
sliced into rounds ¼ inch
(0.5 cm.) thick

2 medium onions, peeled and
sliced into rounds ¼ inch
(0.5 cm.) thick

2 tablespoons flour

Crushed black pepper

3 cups (75 cl.) beef broth (from
pot-au-feu, page 68, or
from a bouillon cube)

1 bouquet garni (1 sprig fresh
thyme, 2 celery stalks,
½ bay leaf, and 3 stems
flat-leaf parsley, wrapped
and tied in a green leek
leaf)

2 cloves garlic, peeled and
degermed (page 122)

(continued)

skim the foam from the surface and then stir the pot to redistribute the meat.

6   While the meat cooks, put the onions into a saucepan with 1 quart (1 l.) water and the coarse salt. Bring the liquid to a boil and simmer the onions for 2 minutes. Drain them in a colander.

7   Melt 1 tablespoon butter in a sauté pan or small saucepan. Add the onions and superfine sugar, season with pepper, cover, and cook over low heat for 20 minutes, rotating the pot every 5 minutes, until the onions are quite tender and pale golden. Keep a close eye on them; they should not turn too dark. Drain them in a colander set on top of a plate.

8   Heat 1 teaspoon peanut oil in a skillet and then add the lardons. Cook them for 5 minutes over medium heat, stirring. When they are browned, use a slotted spoon to put them in the colander with the onions, leaving their fat in the pan. Add the mushrooms to this pan and cook over medium heat for 10 minutes, stirring. Season lightly with salt and pepper. Add the mushrooms to the onions and lardons in the colander.

9   When the stew has been simmering for 2 hours, use a large spoon to remove the grease from its surface. Remove the meat with a slotted spoon and put it in a large, deep serving dish. Put the lardons, onions, and mushrooms into the same dish. Put the meat's sauce through a fine strainer into another saucepan, bring it to a simmer, and simmer for 5 minutes. Taste for salt and pepper. This dish should be quite peppery. Pour the sauce over the meat and vegetables and sprinkle with minced parsley.

16 small white or cipollini onions, peeled
1 teaspoon coarse salt
1 teaspoon superfine sugar
Pepper
½ pound (125 g.) lardons (page 89)
5 ounces (150 g.) small button or cup mushrooms, cleaned and stems trimmed
Salt
1 tablespoon minced parsley

BEEF GOULASH

Boeuf au paprika à la hongroise

SERVES 6–8
PREPARATION 15 minutes
COOKING 2 hours and 10 minutes

Goulash is the national dish of Hungary and a good example of how that country's traditional home cooking exhibits Eastern influences. Goulash takes on different flavors depending on the cook's methods and choice of paprika. Originally, this dish would have been made with horse meat.

Ask the butcher to cut the chuck roast, preferably in the shank, arm clod, or blade, into 2-ounce (60-g.) pieces.

1   Lay the beef pieces on a work surface and sprinkle all over with flour. Melt the lard (or heat the oil) in a Dutch oven. Add the onions and cook for 3 minutes over low heat, stirring. Raise the heat to medium and add the meat. Brown for 5 minutes, stirring so that all sides get browned.

2   Add the tomato paste, tomatoes, and garlic. Sprinkle with the paprika and then pour in the wine and half of the broth. Add the cumin, marjoram, bell peppers, and the rest of the broth. Bring to a simmer, cover, lower the heat, and simmer for 1 hour. Add the potatoes and simmer 1 hour more. Taste for salt and pepper. Add more paprika if you like.

$2\frac{1}{2}$ pounds (1.2 kg.) chuck roast

$\frac{1}{2}$ cup (50 g.) flour

$\frac{1}{4}$ pound (125 g.) lard or 4 tablespoons neutral oil

$1\frac{1}{2}$ pounds (700 g.) onions, peeled and chopped

2 tablespoons tomato paste

1 pound (500 g.) tomatoes, peeled, seeded, and diced (page 124)

2 cloves garlic, peeled and crushed

2 tablespoons paprika

$\frac{1}{2}$ cup (15 cl.) red wine, preferably Pinot Noir or Merlot

2 quarts (2 l.) beef broth (from a pot-au-feu, page 68, or from bouillon cubes)

2 teaspoons cumin

1 teaspoon marjoram

2 green bell peppers, peeled, seeded (page 130), and sliced into strips $\frac{2}{3}$ inch (1.5 cm.) thick and then into pieces $\frac{1}{2}$ inch (1 cm.) long

2 pounds (1 kg.) Yukon Gold potatoes, peeled, quartered, and kept in a bowl of cold water

POACHED BEEF

Boeuf à la ficelle

SERVES   4
PREPARATION   25 minutes
COOKING   1 hour

This method of poaching a nice piece of beef is also used sometimes in pot-au-feu, as described on page 68.

1   Put 2 quarts (2 l.) water in a Dutch oven with the bouillon cubes. Add the bouquet garni and gingerroot, and bring to a boil. When the water bubbles, add all the vegetables except the potatoes. Bring back to a simmer and cook for 20 minutes. Remove the cooked vegetables with a skimmer or slotted spoon and put them in a bowl. Add enough broth to cover them and cover the bowl. Keep the broth simmering.

2   While the vegetables are cooking, cook the potatoes separately. Put them in a saucepan with 1½ quarts (1.5 l.) water (they should be very well covered) and the coarse salt. Bring to a boil and then cook at a low boil for 20 minutes. Add them to the bowl with the other vegetables.

3   Use kitchen twine to tie up each piece of meat, leaving an 8-inch (20-cm.) length of twine at the end of each bundle. Tie the long ends to the middle of a wooden spoon's handle. The pieces of meat should not be too close, and when they are dipped into the pot of broth, none of them should touch the side.

4   Lay the spoon across the pot so that the meat dangles in the simmering broth. Cook for 10–20 minutes, depending on the degree of doneness you prefer.

5   Remove the meat to a platter, remove the twine, and let the meat rest for 5 minutes while you reheat the vegetables in their broth. Season the meat with salt and pepper, surround it with the warm vegetables, and spoon the hot broth all over. Sprinkle with parsley and serve.

4 beef bouillon cubes
1 bouquet garni (3 stems parsley, 1 sprig thyme, and 1 stalk celery, wrapped and tied in a green leek leaf)
1 piece gingerroot, unpeeled
8 medium carrots, peeled and sliced into rounds ½ inch (1 cm.) thick
8 small turnips, peeled
1 celery root, peeled and quartered
1 parsnip, peeled and sliced into rounds ½ inch (1 cm.) thick
8 new or cipollini onions
3 pounds (1.5 kg.) medium leeks, well washed, trimmed, and tied into 2 bundles
8 Yukon Gold potatoes
2 teaspoons coarse salt
1¼ pounds (600 g.) rump pot roast in 4 pieces
Salt
Pepper
1 tablespoon chopped parsley

BEEF CHEEK STEW

Joue de boeuf en civet

SERVES 6

PREPARATION 15 minutes

COOKING 2 hours and 40 minutes

The marinade must be prepared the night before.

1 The night before you plan to cook, put the meat in a bowl with the next 8 ingredients. Cover with plastic wrap and leave in the refrigerator to marinate for 24 hours.

2 The next day, pour the wine from the marinade into a saucepan. Set the beef to drain in a colander. Drain the vegetables in a separate colander and rinse the bowl. Bring the wine to a boil, then turn off the heat. Use a skimmer to remove scum from its surface. Pour the wine through a fine strainer into the rinsed bowl.

3 Preheat the oven to 400°F/200°C.

4 Prepare a cooling rack (or a small overturned plate) over a large plate.

5 Season the meat all over with $\frac{1}{2}$ teaspoon salt and some pepper. Heat 2 tablespoons olive oil in a large Dutch oven over high heat. Add the meat and brown for 5 minutes, stirring with a wooden spoon so all sides brown evenly. With a slotted spoon, remove the meat cubes to the cooling rack but leave the pot over low heat.

6 Pour the remaining tablespoon olive oil into the pot and add the marinated vegetables. Cook for 5 minutes over low heat, stirring. Put the meat back in the pot and sprinkle with the flour. Cook for 1 minute over low heat, stirring. Pour the wine and veal stock into the pot, bring almost to a boil, and then turn off the heat. Cover the pot and put it in the oven for $2\frac{1}{2}$ hours.

7 At the end of the cooking time, take the pot out of the oven and remove the meat with a slotted spoon. Put the meat on a deep serving platter. Pass the sauce through a fine strainer, taste for salt and pepper, and pour it over the meat.

2 pounds (1 kg.) beef cheeks chopped into 2-inch (5-cm.) cubes (ask the butcher to do this)

1 carrot, peeled and cut into pieces $\frac{1}{2}$ inch (1 cm.) thick

1 onion, peeled and cut into $\frac{1}{2}$-inch (1-cm.) dice

$\frac{1}{4}$ celery root, peeled and cut into $\frac{1}{2}$-inch (1-cm.) dice

1 bouquet garni (2 sprigs thyme, 1 bay leaf, and 6 stems parsley, wrapped and tied in a green leek leaf)

1 whole clove

3 juniper berries

2 cloves garlic, peeled and degermed (page 122)

3 cups (75 cl.) Shiraz

Salt

Pepper

3 tablespoons olive oil

1 tablespoon flour

2 cups (50 cl.) brown veal stock (page 37 or made from a bouillon cube)

STEAK TARTARE

SERVES   1

PREPARATION   15 minutes

Originally, steak tartare was made with horse meat. (It was supposed to be the favorite dish of the Tartars.) The meat must not be fatty. The best steak tartare is chopped with a knife. The meat must be eaten very, very soon after it is chopped. You can use more or less mustard and Tabasco here, according to your own tastes.

1 egg yolk (page 204)
½ teaspoon mustard
Salt
1 tablespoon peanut oil
1 tablespoon minced small
   white onion
1 teaspoon chopped capers
1 teaspoon minced parsley
1 tablespoon ketchup
Worcestershire sauce
Tabasco
6 ounces (180 g.) freshly, finely
   chopped meat (fillet,
   sirloin, or eye of rump
   steak)
Pepper

1   Put the egg yolk, mustard, and a pinch of salt in a bowl. Beat with a fork and then slowly incorporate the peanut oil in a very thin stream, as if you were making mayonnaise.

2   Add the onion, capers, and parsley. Mix well to obtain a homogeneous "tartar" sauce. Stir in the ketchup, a thin stream of Worcestershire sauce, and a few drops of Tabasco. Mix well.

3   Lay the meat in the sauce and season with salt and freshly ground pepper. Mix everything together with a fork until the steak is homogeneous and bound together. Shape this mixture so that it is round and eat it immediately.

STEAK AU POIVRE _____

SERVES 4

PREPARATION 5 minutes

COOKING 10 minutes for a rare steak

1 Remove the steaks from the refrigerator 20 minutes in advance. Prepare a cooling rack (or small overturned plate over a large plate).

2 Cover the steaks on both sides with crushed pepper. Pat it on firmly so that it sticks into the flesh. Salt the steaks on both sides. (Be sure to pepper and then salt, or the pepper will not stick to the steaks.)

3 Heat the oil in a sauté pan over high heat. Add 1 teaspoon butter. Rotate the pan as the butter melts, and when it begins to foam, lower the heat to medium. Lay the steaks in the pan and cook for 4 minutes, rotating them in the pan and spooning the cooking juices over them. Flip them with tongs or a spatula and cook 4 minutes on the other side, rotating and basting as before. Stand the steaks on their sides, using tongs to help, and cook them 2 minutes on their edges. Remove the steaks to the cooling rack and tent them loosely with aluminum foil.

4 Put a serving dish and a sauceboat to warm in the oven, turned to 150° F/80° C.

5 Pour the wine into the sauté pan and bring to a boil, stirring and scraping the bottom of the pan with a wooden spatula until the wine is syrupy.

6 Dice the rest of the butter, which should be well chilled. Add the veal stock to the pan and boil for 2 minutes. If you are using the crème fraîche, stir it in. Then stir in the diced butter bit by bit. Put this sauce through a fine strainer into the warmed sauceboat. If you are using the mustard, stir it in now. Taste for salt and pepper.

7 Put the steaks on the warmed serving platter, coat them with sauce, and serve the rest of the sauce on the side.

4 steaks, ½ pound (220 g.) each, from the fillet, rump, or sirloin, and without any kind of fatty wrapping

Crushed pepper—black, gray, or green

Salt

2 tablespoons neutral oil

4 tablespoons (60 g.) cold butter

½ cup (10 cl.) dry white wine

½ cup (10 cl.) brown veal stock (page 37 or from a bouillon cube)

1 tablespoon crème fraîche (optional)

1 tablespoon mustard (optional)

Kid

The kid is a young goat. Between four weeks and four months of age its flesh is much like a milk lamb's and can be prepared as such. The kid must be well flavored before cooking, however, and should be rather more done than not, though not to the point of dryness.

It is usually male kids that are butchered because females are saved for dairying.

Kid was once a popular meat for religious celebrations, but today we rarely eat it. When we do, we'd be well advised to eat it only from March through May.

In its first months, while it is still nursing, a kid has enough baby fat to yield tender, delicate flesh. But if it is slaughtered too young, a kid will produce stringy meat with poorly defined flavor.

Goat farmers sometimes allow kids to graze for a few weeks, since certain devotees of this meat enjoy the stronger taste and deeper color of grass-fed kid. In France most kid comes from Poitou-Charentes, a region that has since the eighteenth century specialized in raising "the poor man's cow." This nickname notwithstanding, kid has at times been so prized that one old recipe (outlandish enough, it is true) calls for kid to be stuffed with sandalwood, camphor, and gold and then basted with rosewater as it roasts.

Look for kid at your farmers' market or in ethnic markets.

QUARTERED KID WITH POTATOES

Quartier de chevreau aux pommes de terre

SERVES 2

PREPARATION 10 minutes (including the *persillade*)

COOKING 40 minutes

1 Preheat the oven to 460°F/240°C. Season the meat on both sides with salt and pepper.

2 Heat the olive oil in a Dutch oven over low heat. Add the butter, and when it foams, brown the shoulder for 2 minutes over low heat. Turn it over and brown 2 minutes on the other side. Surround the shoulder with the potatoes, garlic, and thyme.

3 Add the wine and bring to a boil. Simmer for 15–20 minutes, until the wine has been reduced by half. Add the chicken broth and bring back to a boil.

4 Put the pot in the oven, uncovered, and lower the temperature to 350°F/180°C. Cook for 20 minutes, stirring every 5 minutes and basting the meat with cooking juices.

5 While the kid cooks, prepare the *persillade*. When the pot comes out of the oven, brush the kid with the mustard and spread a generous layer of *persillade* on top of the mustard. Bake 5 minutes more to brown the crust and then serve.

1 baby kid shoulder, about 1½ pounds (800 g.)

Salt

Pepper

1 tablespoon olive oil

3 tablespoons butter

12 very small (bite-sized) new potatoes, washed but not peeled

4 cloves garlic, crushed but not peeled

1 small bunch fresh thyme

½ cup (13 cl.) dry white wine

½ cup (13 cl.) chicken broth (page 77 or made from a bouillon cube)

1 recipe *persillade* (page 370)

2 teaspoons mustard, whole-grain if possible

ROAST KID WITH GREEN GARLIC

Chevreau rôti à l'ail vert

SERVES   4
PREPARATION   10 minutes
COOKING   30 minutes
RESTING   15 minutes

The best time to eat kid coincides with the first appearance of green garlic. In the Charentes region of France, this roast is generously brushed with salted butter instead of oil at the beginning. If you want to try it that way, don't add any salt. Look for green garlic at a farmers' market.

Hindquarters of a kid, about
    3 pounds (1.5 kg.)
2 tablespoons butter
Trimmings from a kid—
    chopped-up bones and
    scraps of meat and fat; ask
    the butcher for 2 handfuls
Salt
Pepper
Neutral oil
3 sprigs fresh thyme
Cloves of ½ head of garlic,
    crushed but not peeled
1 bunch green garlic, rinsed

1   Remove the kid and the butter from the refrigerator at least 30 minutes in advance. Dice the butter and leave it out to soften. Remove a rack from the oven; if it is dirty, rinse it with hot water and wipe it clean with paper towels. Set it over a large platter.

2   Preheat the oven to 440°F/220°C, making sure that one of the racks is in the middle position.

3   Season the trimmings lightly with salt and pepper. Use a pastry brush to oil the entire surface of the kid. Season generously with salt and pepper and, with the back side down, dot with the softened butter. Strip the leaves from the thyme so that they shower down onto the kid. Discard the branches.

4   Spread the trimmings in a roasting pan and dot evenly with the garlic cloves. Lay the kid on top of the trimmings, back side down, and put the pan in the oven. After 10 minutes, turn the kid and baste with roasting juices. Roast 10 minutes more, then add the green garlic to the pan. Roast 10 minutes more, then take the pan out of the oven.

5   Remove the kid to the oven rack over the platter. Season all over with salt and pepper and leave to rest for 15 minutes.

6   While the kid rests, prepare the juice. Spoon excess fat from the pan and discard. Add ½ cup (10 cl.) water to the pan, season with salt and pepper, and stir and scrape the pan with a spatula to loosen any cooked-on bits. Put the pan back in the oven to stay warm.

7   To serve, pass the sauce through a fine strainer into a sauceboat, adding any juices that have collected under the resting

kid. The cloves of garlic can be served on the side, still in their skin, with the green garlic.

Veal

The last decades of the twentieth century saw a precipitous decline in the consumption of veal on account of problems with its industrial production. Long before the panics surrounding avian flu and mad cow disease, there was in France the scandal of calves pumped up with hormones, whose meat would visibly shrink in the skillet. Consumers' appetite for veal was also stunted by revelations about the high doses of antibiotics administered to animals and the way they suffered in industrial pens.

At the same time, conventional taste preferred veal that was white and tender. This milky product was not particularly flavorful, however, so when people did eat veal, it was likely to be a disappointment. Thankfully, some veal producers had an awakening, changed their methods, and now raise animals whose flesh is delicious, succulent, tender, and delicate all at once.

Veal is the meat of an unweaned cow, anywhere up to about one year old. Whether you are shopping at a farmers' market, your butcher's, or a grocery store, ask for veal that has been naturally raised and find out as much as you can about its origins.

CHOOSING VEAL

Good veal is smooth, firm, fine-grained, and almost silken, with fat that is very white and very scarce. In France the best veal comes from Normandy and from the center of the country.

Small pieces of veal, such as scallops and chops, should be pan fried. A *scallop* is not a part of the animal (nor do we mean the shellfish here) but a cut; it is simply a thin slice that is best taken from the round roast or the rib chops. A thick, slightly fatty veal chop should be preferred to two small ones. Medallions, also called *grenadins* in French, are carved like tournedos. Veal *piccata* and *paillard* are very thin scallops.

Rack of veal has a stronger flavor and is good for roasting. The top round, bottom round, and sirloin tip, which are roasted without bones, are drier unless they come from milk-fed veal of very high quality. To feed a crowd you might roast an entire loin, or saddle, of veal, but this is a very large roast.

For sauced dishes and stews, such as a blanquette, use the tenderest morsels—neck, shoulder, breast, shank, rib scraps, or flank. Veal shanks are delicious when poached.

COOKING VEAL

Do not soak veal in cold water before cooking. Some people use this technique to whiten the meat, especially for a blanquette, but it drains the meat of blood and ruins its texture.

Veal calves have not had time to develop much fat. For this reason their meat is quick to dry out and must be cooked slower and at lower temperatures than lamb and beef. Thus, when you fry a thick chop, it is better to use a covered sauté pan or a Dutch oven instead of an uncovered frying pan because the straight sides and cover will keep the air around the meat moist. When you fry scallops, have a paper towel handy for wiping black spots from the meat: These burned bits taste bitter.

Pan fried or grilled, the meat should be pink-tinged and have a bead of blood at its heart. To check whether a large piece is cooked, you can pierce the meat with a skewer, pushing it all the way to the bone. The juices that run out should be nearly clear, barely pink at all. If the juices are reddish, the meat is not yet cooked. If there are no juices, the meat is overcooked.

In short, cook veal with sensitivity and care.

PAN-GRILLED VEAL SCALLOP

Escalope de veau grillée

SERVES 1
PREPARATION   2 minutes
COOKING   4 minutes
RESTING   2 minutes

1 veal scallop, 5 ounces (150 g.)
Salt
Pepper
Neutral oil
Fleur de sel

1   Remove the meat from the refrigerator 10 minutes in advance.

2   Heat a cast-iron grill pan over high heat. Season the veal on both sides with salt and pepper, and brush it with a thin layer of oil. Lay the scallop diagonally on the grill pan and cook for 1 minute. You might need to adjust the heat throughout cooking: The veal should not burn. Flip the scallop with tongs or with the back side of a large fork. Do not use the tines of the fork because they will puncture the meat and release juices.

3   Cook for 1 minute. As the second side cooks, use a paper towel to wipe overly browned bits from the side that has already been seared. Flip the meat over again, rotating it a quarter turn for crosshatch grill marks, and cook for 1 minute. Wipe away brown bits from the newly exposed side. Turn the scallop and cook 1 minute more.

4   Remove the meat to a plate and season on both sides with fleur de sel and pepper. Allow it to rest for 2 minutes before serving.

VEAL PICCATA (*PAILLARD*)

Escalope fine de veau grillée (paillarde)

SERVES 1
PREPARATION   1 minute
COOKING   2 minutes

You can serve this cut with a bit of mustard on a baguette, as it was once served to gamblers at racetracks in France by a cook called Paillard.

1 veal scallop, 5 ounces (150 g.), pounded flat and thin (ask the butcher to do this)

(continued)

1 Remove the meat from the refrigerator 5 minutes in advance. Heat a grill pan over high heat. Season both sides of the veal with salt and pepper. Brush a thin layer of oil on it.

2 When the grill is hot, lay the veal on it on a diagonal. Cook for 30 seconds. You may have to adjust the heat as the meat cooks: It should not burn. Flip the meat with tongs or with the back side of a large fork; do not use the tines of a fork because they will puncture the meat and release juices. Cook for 30 seconds. Flip the meat over again, rotating it a quarter turn for crosshatch grill marks, and cook for 30 seconds. Flip and cook 1 minute more.

3 Remove the meat to a plate and season both sides with fleur de sel and pepper before serving.

Salt
Pepper
Neutral oil
Fleur de sel

PAN FRIED VEAL SCALLOP

Escalope de veau poêlée

variation

PAN FRIED VEAL
SCALLOPS WITH
CREAM SAUCE

SERVES   1
PREPARATION   2 minutes
COOKING   4 minutes
RESTING   2 minutes

1 Remove the meat from the refrigerator 10 minutes in advance.

2 Just before cooking, season the veal on both sides with salt and pepper. Heat the oil in a skillet over high heat. Add the butter. Tilt the skillet as the butter melts. When it begins to foam, lower the heat—neither the butter nor the meat should brown.

3 Lay the meat in the skillet in a motion away from you to avoid splattering yourself with hot fat. Cook for 2 minutes, rotating the meat in the skillet and spooning hot fat over it. Flip it with tongs or a spatula and cook for 2 minutes on the other side, rotating and basting the veal as before.

4 Remove the scallop to a plate. Season both sides with fleur de sel and pepper before serving.

1 veal scallop, 5 ounces (150 g.)
Salt
Pepper
1 teaspoon neutral oil
1 teaspoon butter
Fleur de sel

PAN FRIED VEAL SCALLOPS WITH CREAM SAUCE

Escalope de veau à la crème

SERVES 4
PREPARATION 10 minutes
COOKING 5 minutes

1 Prepare the veal as described above. While the scallops are resting, make the sauce: Add the mushroom slices to the pan used to cook the meat without discarding any of the cooking fat. Cook over rather high heat for 3 minutes, stirring with a wooden spoon. The mushrooms will release some liquid and then that liquid should disappear. Add the port and stir. Add the crème fraîche and stir. Turn the heat to low and cook for 1 minute. You should then have a slightly thick sauce.

2 Off the heat you can, if you like, gently stir in the butter. Add any juices that have collected under the resting meat. Taste the sauce for salt and pepper, and then spread the sauce over the veal.

4 veal scallops, pan fried as described page 412
½ pound (250 g.) white button mushrooms, washed, stem ends trimmed, and sliced vertically into slivers
1½ tablespoons port
1½ tablespoons crème fraîche
1 teaspoon butter (optional)
Salt
Pepper

VEAL SCALLOPS WITH COMTÉ

Escalope de veau au comté

SERVES 4
PREPARATION 20 minutes
COOKING 8 minutes

1 Cut the crusts from the bread and discard. Put the bread in a food processor and pulse to make bread crumbs. Spread the crumbs in a wide, deep dish. Break the eggs into another wide, deep dish and beat them with salt, pepper, and 3 tablespoons oil. Spread the flour in a third dish.

2 Season both sides of each scallop with salt and pepper. Lay 4 of them on your work surface. Top each one with a slice of cheese, a slice of ham, and another scallop. Press down firmly on each pile with a large spatula to make the layers stick together. Trim away any cheese or ham that hangs out past the edge of the scallops.

3 Lightly coat both sides of each scallop bundle with flour and

4 slices stale white bread
3 eggs
Salt
Pepper
6 tablespoons neutral oil
½ cup (60 g.) flour
8 small, very thin veal scallops, approximately 3 ounces (90 g.) each
4 thin slices Comté cheese, about the same size as the scallops

(continued)

then tap to shake off excess flour. Dip them into the eggs and then into the bread crumbs. Lay them on a work surface and tap with a stainless steel spatula to make the bread crumbs stick.

4 Heat the remaining 3 tablespoons oil in a large skillet over low heat. Add 3 tablespoons butter, and when it melts, lay the breaded bundles in the skillet and cook for 4 minutes on each side, still over low heat, until they are nicely browned. Use a large spatula to remove them to a plate.

5 Melt the remaining butter in a small skillet with a pinch of salt. After the butter foams and has turned nut-brown, swirl in the lemon juice. If you like, you can add capers to the browned butter at the same time you add the lemon juice. Pour this sauce over the breaded scallops.

4 slices smoked ham, about the same size as the scallops
6 tablespoons (90 g.) butter
Juice of ½ lemon
1 tablespoon capers (optional)

VEAL AND ENDIVE ROLLS

Paupiettes de veau aux endives

SERVES   4
PREPARATION   20 minutes
COOKING   15 minutes plus 30 minutes for the endives

1 Melt 2 tablespoons butter in a Dutch oven. Add the lardons and cook for 3 minutes over low heat, stirring with a wooden spoon. Add the endives and season lightly with salt. Stir the endives to coat well with fat and leave over low heat for 25 minutes, stirring frequently.

2 Use a skimmer or slotted spoon to remove the endives to a bowl and let them cool completely. Stir in the Gruyère.

3 Lay the scallops on a work surface. Spoon the endive-cheese mixture on the scallops, distributing it evenly. Roll the scallops up and then wrap each one in a slice of bacon. Tie each *paupiette* crosswise with twine.

4 Melt 2 teaspoons butter in the pot you used before. When it has melted, add the *paupiettes* and brown them for 3 minutes over medium heat, rolling them around with a spatula so they get even color on all sides. Sprinkle them with the thyme leaves, lower the heat, cover, and leave over very low

3 tablespoons plus 1 teaspoon butter
3 ounces (90 g.) lardons (page 89)
5 endives, cored and sliced into ½-inch (1-cm.) strips
Salt
3 ounces (100 g.) grated Gruyère cheese
4 veal scallops, about 5 ounces (150 g.) each
4 slices bacon
1 teaspoon fresh thyme leaves

heat for 10 minutes, regularly peeking in to roll them and baste them with cooking juices.

5   Five minutes before the *paupiettes* are done, heat the oil in a skillet and add 2 teaspoons butter. Add the mushrooms and cook over medium heat for 3 to 5 minutes (depending on their size), stirring with a wooden spoon. Season with salt and pepper, stir, and drain.

6   Snip the twine on the *paupiettes*. Serve them on a platter, surrounded by mushrooms and covered in their own cooking juices. Sprinkle with parsley.

1 tablespoon oil
6 ounces (190 g.) white button
    mushrooms, washed and
    stem ends trimmed
Pepper
1 tablespoon minced parsley

PAN FRIED VEAL CHOP

Côte de veau poêlée

SERVES   2
PREPARATION   2 minutes
COOKING   35 minutes
RESTING   15 minutes

variations
VEAL CHOPS WITH
    MELTING BAY-SCENTED
    POTATOES
VEAL CHOPS WITH SWEET
    PEPPERS
VEAL CHOP WITH
    CHANTERELLES

1   Remove the chop from the refrigerator 20 minutes in advance. Prepare a cooling rack (or a small overturned plate) over a plate.

2   Just before cooking, season both sides of the chop with salt and pepper. Put the bones and scraps in a large sauté pan or Dutch oven with the garlic and shallots. Add the oil and turn the heat to medium high. Add the butter and reduce the heat to low. Neither the butter nor the meat should brown. Twirl the pan as the butter melts and begins to foam.

3   Add the chop to the pan. Brown over rather low heat for 5 minutes, rotating it in the pan and spooning cooking fat over it. Flip it over with tongs or a spoon (do not pierce it with a fork to turn). Fry the other side for 5 minutes, rotating and basting as before. Turn again and cook for 5 minutes; turn again and cook 5 minutes more, always over low heat.

4   Stand the chop vertically on its fatty side and cook, still over low heat, for 5 minutes, rocking it back and forth a bit so the whole side gets browned. Stand the chop vertically on its bone side and cook for 10 minutes. (If it is unpleasant for you to do this with tongs or if you don't have tongs, you can

1 veal chop, 14 ounces (440 g.)
    or 2 smaller ones, about
    2½ inches (6 cm.) thick
Salt
Pepper
Small handful of chopped-up
    veal bones and scraps
1 clove garlic, lightly crushed
    but unpeeled
2 shallots, peeled
1 teaspoon neutral oil
1 teaspoon butter
Fleur de sel

prop the chop between 2 pieces of a potato halved lengthwise or between 2 spoons balanced on the rim of the pan on
either side of the chop.)

5   Remove the chop to the rack, being careful not to pierce it.
Season both sides with fleur de sel and pepper. Tent loosely
with aluminum foil and allow to rest for 15 minutes.

6   Prepare the juice: Spoon yellowish fat from the surface of
the sauté pan, leaving behind only brown cooking juices.
Add ½ cup warm water and scrape the caramelized bits with
a wooden spatula until they are all loose and melted into the
juices. Put the liquid through a fine strainer into a small
saucepan and put it over low heat while the meat rests. Serve
this juice on the side.

VEAL CHOPS WITH MELTING BAY-SCENTED POTATOES

Côtes de veau, pommes fondantes au laurier

SERVES   4
PREPARATION   10 minutes
COOKING   1 hour and 35 minutes
Begin preparing the potatoes 1 hour before you plan to cook
the chops.

1   Remove the butter from the refrigerator at least 30 minutes
in advance. Preheat the oven to 400°F/200°C.

2   Before you fry the chops, make 2 incisions in each potato and
slip a fragment of bay leaf into each slit.

3   Heat the oil in a sauté pan or Dutch oven and add 1 teaspoon
butter. When the butter foams, add the potatoes and cook
them over low heat for 5–6 minutes, rolling them around
with a spoon so they get color on all sides. Add the unpeeled
garlic, thyme, and broth. The liquid should reach halfway up
the potatoes; add more broth or water if necessary. Cover
and bake in the oven for 1½ hours.

4   Using a fork, mash 1 tablespoon softened butter with the
parsley, tarragon, lemon juice, and minced garlic. Season
with a pinch of salt and a pinch of pepper. Cover with plastic
wrap and refrigerate.

5   After the potatoes have been in the oven for 45 minutes, prepare the veal chops, following the recipe above but not mak-

1 tablespoon plus 1 teaspoon
   butter
2 large thick veal chops or
   4 small thick veal chops,
   prepared as described
   page 415
8 potatoes, preferably
   charlottes or fingerlings,
   washed and peeled
4 small bay leaves
1 teaspoon oil
2 cloves garlic, one lightly
   crushed but not peeled, the
   other peeled, degermed
   (page 122), and minced
1 sprig fresh thyme

ing the juice at the end. By the time the chops have finished resting, the potatoes should be cooked.

6   Place the chops on a platter surrounded by the potatoes. You can serve the garlic butter on the side, or you can put 2 teaspoons on top of the chop to melt. (Slip the butter-topped chop into the oven, which is off but still hot, for 2 or 3 minutes if the butter is not melting fast enough.) Bring any extra garlic butter to the table.

½ cup (10 cl.) chicken broth (page 77) or made with a bouillon cube
1 teaspoon minced parsley
1 teaspoon snipped tarragon leaves
Juice of ¼ lemon
Salt
Pepper

VEAL CHOPS WITH SWEET PEPPERS
Côtes de veau au poivron doux

SERVES   4
PREPARATION   5 minutes
COOKING   10 minutes

1   About an hour before you plan to cook the chops, roast the peppers in order to remove their skin and seeds easily (see page 130). Slice them lengthwise into strips ½–1 inch (1–2 cm.) long.

2   Cook the veal chops. While they rest, add 8 tablespoons water to the pot they cooked in. Bring it to a boil and simmer for 2 minutes. Taste for salt and pepper, and put this sauce through a fine strainer.

3   Heat the oil in a small saucepan. Cook the onion over low heat about 3 minutes, without allowing it to color. Season lightly with salt, then add the peppers and rosemary. Cook gently for 10 minutes, stirring. Sprinkle with parsley.

4   Spread the peppers on a platter, top with the veal chops, and pour the juice over.

2 large thick veal chops or 4 small thick veal chops, prepared as described page 415
4 green bell peppers
2 red bell peppers
2 yellow bell peppers
Salt
Pepper
2 teaspoons neutral oil
1 medium onion, peeled and sliced into rounds ½ inch (1 cm.) thick
1 small sprig rosemary
1 tablespoon minced parsley

VEAL CHOP WITH CHANTERELLES

Côte de veau poêlée aux girolles

SERVES   2
PREPARATION   5 minutes
COOKING   10 minutes

Clean, drain, and dry the mushrooms in a spinner. If they are large, halve or quarter lengthwise.

1   Spread the mushrooms over 4 sheets of paper towels.
2   Prepare the veal chop. While it rests and after you have made the juice, prepare a colander set over a plate. Heat the oil in a skillet over rather high heat. Add the butter and then the mushrooms. Season with salt and pepper, and cook for 5 minutes, stirring.
3   Put the mushrooms in the colander. Let them drain a little. Put them back in the skillet, still over high heat, for 5 minutes. Stir as they cook. Lower the heat, add the shallot to the skillet, and stir for 30 seconds. Off the heat, stir in the parsley.
4   Serve the chop on a plate surrounded by chanterelle mushrooms and with the sauce on the side.

3 ounces (90 g.) chanterelle mushrooms
1 large thick veal chop or 2 small thick veal chops, prepared as described page 415
1 teaspoon neutral oil
1 teaspoon butter
Salt
Pepper
1 shallot, peeled and minced
1 tablespoon minced parsley

SAUTÉED VEAL CHOP
WITH MUSHROOMS AND POTATOES

Côte de veau sautée aux champignons et pommes de terre

SERVES 2

PREPARATION AND COOKING 1½ hours

1 Melt 2 teaspoons butter in a sauté pan or saucepan over medium heat. Add the onions, sugar, and a pinch of salt. Add enough water to reach halfway up the onions and then cook about 20 minutes over medium heat, rotating the pot every 5 minutes. The water should evaporate almost completely, and the onions should turn light gold. Let them drain in a colander. Rinse the pan or pot with hot water and wipe clean with a paper towel.

2 Remove the chop from the refrigerator.

3 Peel the potatoes and trim them into an elongated football shape. Put them in a saucepan and cover with 1 quart (1 l.) cold water and 1 tablespoon coarse salt. Bring to a boil, boil for 1 minute, and then use a slotted spoon to move them to a colander. Heat the goose fat or butter in a Dutch oven or sauté pan. Sauté the potatoes over medium heat until they are lightly colored on both sides.

4 Season both sides of the chop with salt, pepper, and thyme. Pan fry according to the instructions on page 415 for 15 minutes per side but without adding the shallots or garlic to the pan.

5 After 30 minutes of cooking, remove the chop to a cooling rack, season with fleur de sel and pepper, and tent loosely with aluminum foil. Remove the scraps and bones from the pan and use a spoon to remove the excess fat.

6 Add the 2 peeled but whole shallots, the garlic, and 1 cup (25 cl.) water. Turn the heat on and use a spatula to scrape caramelized bits from the bottom and sides of the pan. Let the liquids simmer until they are reduced by two-thirds. Taste for salt and pepper. Pass the sauce through a fine strainer into a small saucepan and keep it over low heat.

7 Put the horn of plenty mushrooms into the pan used for the onions. Cover and cook over high heat for 3–4 minutes, shaking the pan 2 or 3 times. Place the mushrooms in a colander to cool and drain. Squeeze them to remove excess water.

8 If the shiitakes and chanterelles are big, you can halve or

1 tablespoon butter

10 small white onions, peeled

1 tablespoon confectioners' sugar

Salt

1 veal chop, 1 pound (500 g.), with a small handful of chopped-up bones and scraps

6 ounces (190 g.) firm-fleshed potatoes, preferably Yukon Gold or BF 15

Coarse salt

1 tablespoon goose fat or butter

Pepper

1 teaspoon fresh thyme

Fleur de sel

4 shallots, 2 peeled and left whole, 2 peeled and chopped

1 clove garlic, lightly crushed but unpeeled

2 ounces (70 g.) horn of plenty mushrooms (also called black chanterelles), rinsed

3 ounces (100 g.) Japanese forest or shiitake mushrooms

½ pound (250 g.) chanterelle mushrooms

(continued)

quarter them. Heat 1 teaspoon oil and 1 teaspoon butter in the saucepan over high heat. When the butter foams, add the mushrooms. Season with salt and pepper, and stir with a wooden spoon. Cook over high heat for 3–4 minutes. Add the oyster mushrooms and cook 1 minute more, stirring.

9   Heat ½ teaspoon oil in a large skillet over high heat. Cook the lardons for 2 minutes, stirring, and then remove them with a slotted spoon. Lower the heat as much as possible and add the 2 chopped shallots to the skillet. Season with salt and pepper, and cook for 2 minutes over low heat, stirring. Stir in the mushrooms, lardons, small onions, potatoes, and parsley. Turn off the heat.

10 Turn the heat under the sauce up to high. Put the skillet in which the meat was cooked over medium heat and reheat the chop for 2 minutes per side.

11 Surround the chop with the mushrooms, potatoes, and onions and pour the sauce over the top.

1½ teaspoons neutral oil
2 ounces (60 g.) oyster mushrooms
2 ounces (60 g.) smoked lardons (page 89)
1 teaspoon minced parsley

PAN FRIED VEAL MEDALLIONS

Médaillons de veau poêlés

variation
VEAL MEDALLIONS WITH CARROTS

SERVES   2
PREPARATION   2 minutes
COOKING   10 minutes
RESTING   5 minutes

Ask the butcher to cut the veal from the loin, the top round, or the sirloin tip. Have him tie the medallions up without adding any fatty wrapping.

1   Remove the meat from the refrigerator 10 minutes in advance. Season all over with salt and pepper.

2   Heat the oil in a sauté pan or Dutch oven and then add the butter. When it foams, add the veal and turn the heat to low. Cook for 4 minutes, rotating them in the pan and spooning cooking juices over them. Flip them and cook 4 minutes more, rotating and basting as before. Stand them on their sides and fry their edges for 2 minutes, using tongs to roll them for even cooking.

2 veal medallions, about 5 ounces (150 g.) each and 1 inch thick
Salt
Pepper
1 teaspoon neutral oil
1 teaspoon butter
Fleur de sel

3   Remove the veal to a plate (use tongs—do not pierce the meat with a fork), with the side that was cooked first facing down if possible. Snip the twine with scissors and remove. Season with fleur de sel and freshly ground pepper, and allow to rest for 5 minutes.

VEAL MEDALLIONS WITH CARROTS
Médaillons de veau aux carottes

SERVES   4
PREPARATION   10 minutes
COOKING   10 minutes for the veal plus 35 minutes for the carrots
MAKING THE SAUCE   5 minutes

Ask the butcher to cut the medallions from the loin, the top round, or the sirloin tip. Have him tie them up without adding any wrapping.

1   Fifteen minutes before you plan to sauté the veal, begin to cook the carrots.
2   Preheat the oven to 350°F/180°C.
3   Heat 1 teaspoon oil in a Dutch oven. Add the butter and shallot and cook over low heat for 3 minutes, stirring. Add the carrots and stir so they are thoroughly coated with fat. Sprinkle with 3 pinches of confectioners' sugar, then add the garlic, orange zest, and thyme. Stir. Add the broth. The broth should cover the carrots; if it does not, add more broth or water to cover. Bring to a boil.
4   Cut a circle of parchment paper the same size as the pot. Prick it a few times with a fork or knife. Lay this paper on top of the carrots; this way the liquid will evaporate but the carrots will not burn. Cover the pot and put it in the oven for 30 minutes.
5   Sauté the veal as described in the previous recipe. Leave their cooking juices in the sauté pan when you finish but spoon out the fat. Tent the resting medallions with aluminum foil.
6   Add the wine to the veal pan. Bring to a boil while scraping up caramelized bits from the bottom and sides of the pan with a spatula. Adjust the heat so that the wine simmers.

1 teaspoon neutral oil
2 teaspoons butter
1 shallot, peeled and chopped
1¼ pounds (600 g.) carrots, peeled and sliced into rounds ¾ inch (1.5 cm.) thick
Confectioners' sugar
3 cloves garlic, peeled
Zest of 1 organic orange, in strips, all white pith removed
1 sprig fresh thyme
1 cup (25 cl.) chicken broth (page 77 or made from a bouillon cube)
4 veal medallions, 4 to 6 ounces (150 g.) each and 1 inch thick
½ cup (10 cl.) dry white wine
1 teaspoon minced parsley
Salt
Pepper

7   Remove the carrots from the oven and discard the parch-
    ment paper. Remove the thyme and zest, and add the parsley.
    Taste for salt and pepper. Lay the veal on top of the carrots.
    Pour any juices that gathered under the resting meat into the
    sauce in the sauté pan. Pass the sauce through a fine strainer
    and pour it over the meat. Bring the Dutch oven of carrots
    and veal to the table.

SHOULDER AND BREAST OF VEAL FRICASSÉE

Epaule et tendron de veau en fricassée

SERVES   4–6
PREPARATION   5 minutes
COOKING   about 1 hour

This recipe is made with a piece of middle-cut breast,
which is called *tendron* in French because the meat is
very tender.

1   Put the pieces of veal in a large bowl. Sprinkle with 1 tea-
    spoon salt and 3 pinches of pepper, and toss well.
2   Heat the oil in a Dutch oven. Add the butter. When the butter
    foams, add the veal and cook for 5 minutes over low heat.
    Stir constantly with a wooden spoon since the veal should
    not brown. Add the onions and cook for 1 minute, still over
    low heat. Sprinkle the whole with the flour and stir well. Add
    the bouquet garni and veal stock. Raise the heat to bring to a
    boil. Cover, lower the heat, and simmer over very low heat
    for 1 hour, stirring every 10 minutes. At the end, use a skim-
    mer or slotted spoon to remove the veal to a colander and
    cover it to keep the meat warm.
3   Beat half of the cream and both egg yolks together in a bowl.
4   Spoon the fat from the surface of the pot, leaving behind the
    brown cooking juices. Put the pot back on the burner, bring
    to a simmer, and simmer for 5 minutes. Add the remaining
    cream and simmer 3 minutes more over medium heat. Turn
    off the heat. Vigorously stir the yolk-cream mixture into the
    hot sauce. Whatever you do, do not allow the sauce to boil.
    Taste for salt and pepper.

1¼ pounds (600 g.) boneless
    veal shoulder, cut into
    pieces approximately
    3 ounces (80 g.) each
¾ pound (400 g.) middle-cut
    breast of veal, cut into
    pieces approximately
    3 ounces (80 g.) each
Salt
Pepper
1 tablespoon neutral oil
2 tablespoons butter
2 large onions, peeled and
    sliced into rounds ½ inch
    (1 cm.) thick
1 tablespoon flour
1 bouquet garni (1 stalk celery,
    6 stems parsley, 2 sprigs
    thyme, and ½ bay leaf,
    wrapped and tied in a leek
    leaf)
1 cup (25 cl.) white veal stock
    (page 36 or store-bought)

5   Serve the veal and sauce together. If you like, you can add button mushrooms and small onions (see Veal Stew on page 425).

ROAST VEAL COOKED WITH ITS OWN GARNISH _____
Rôti de veau poêlé dans sa garniture

SERVES   4
PREPARATION   10 minutes
COOKING   40 minutes
RESTING   15 minutes

Ask the butcher to tie the roast but not to wrap it. Ask for a small handful of chopped-up bones and trimmings.

1   Remove the roast from the refrigerator 30 minutes in advance. Season it generously with salt and pepper. Prepare a cooling rack (or small overturned plate) over a large plate. Put a pastry brush in a bowl half-filled with water.
2   Preheat the oven to 350°F/180°C, with a rack in the middle position.
3   Heat the oil in a Dutch oven over medium heat. The cooking vessel should be large enough to hold the roast without the roast coming into contact with its sides. Add the butter, and when it melts, add the veal scraps, all the vegetables, and the bouquet garni. Place the roast on top of them. Throughout cooking, avoid allowing the roast to touch the sides and bottom of the pot.
4   Cook for 10 minutes over medium heat, stirring the vegetables and trimmings regularly and turning the roast with tongs. (Do not turn the roast with a fork, which might puncture it and cause it to lose juices.) The roast should get a bit of color but should not turn brown. Do not add any water or white wine.
5   Cover the pot and put it in the oven. (If you do not have a pot and cover that can go into the oven, you can put the vegetables and trimmings in a baking dish, lay the roast on them, and cover the whole thing tightly with aluminum foil.) Roast for 40 minutes.

⅔ cup (20 cl.) heavy cream
2 egg yolks (page 204)

1 boneless veal roast weighing
   1½ pounds (750 g.) from
   the bottom round, sirloin
   tip, sirloin, loin, or ribs
Salt
Pepper
1 tablespoon neutral oil
1 teaspoon butter
3 new carrots or 2 medium
   carrots, peeled
2 medium onions, peeled and
   chopped into large
   (1-inch/2.5-cm.) dice
1 stalk celery, trimmed and
   chopped into large
   (1-inch/2.5-cm.) dice
1 clove garlic, lightly crushed
   but not peeled
3 tomatoes, quartered
1 bouquet garni (1 bay leaf,
   1 sprig thyme, and
   4–5 stems parsley,
   wrapped and tied
   in a leek leaf)
Fleur de sel

6 Take the pot out of the oven. Remove the meat to the cooling rack and season with fleur de sel and pepper. Leave it to rest for 15 minutes, loosely tented with aluminum foil.

7 In the meantime, prepare the juice. Leave the vegetables and veal scraps in the pot but spoon excess fat from the surface. Add 6 tablespoons water and put the pot over medium heat. Stir and scrape at caramelized bits with a spatula. Brush the interior sides of the pot with a moistened pastry brush.

8 Pass the sauce through a fine strainer and taste for salt and pepper.

9 Remove the roast's twine and cut the roast into slices about ½ inch (1 cm.) thick. The center should be tinged with pink. Season each slice with fleur de sel and pepper on both sides. The roast can be served with noodles, a vegetable purée, other vegetables, or the vegetables in the cooking pot.

VEAL SIRLOIN ROAST WITH BABY POTATOES

Quasi de veau aux pommes de terre nouvelles

SERVES 4
PREPARATION 5 minutes
COOKING 50 minutes

1 Remove the roast and the butter from the refrigerator 30 minutes in advance.

2 Preheat the oven to 340°F/170°C. Prepare a cooling rack (or a small overturned plate) over a large plate.

3 Season the roast all over with 1 teaspoon salt and slightly less pepper. Heat the olive oil in a Dutch oven over low heat. Gently set the veal in the pot and brown for 5 minutes over low heat, turning the roast so it gets colored evenly. (Do not turn the roast with a fork; use tongs or a wooden spoon so as not to puncture the meat.) Regularly spoon cooking juices over the roast.

4 Remove the roast to the cooling rack. Put the lardons and garlic into the pot and cook for 5 minutes over low heat, stirring. Put the veal back in the pot (save the juices that collected under it) along with the potatoes, tomatoes, and

2 pounds (1 kg.) veal sirloin roast, tied by the butcher but not wrapped
2 tablespoons butter
Salt
Pepper
3 tablespoons olive oil
¼ pound (150 g.) smoked lardons (page 89)
8 cloves garlic, lightly crushed under your palm but not peeled
1¼ pounds (600 g.) very small (bite-sized) new

thyme. Put the butter on top of the potatoes and sprinkle with 1 pinch of salt. Pour in the veal stock, cover, and put the pot in the oven. Cook for 40 minutes, basting the roast every 10 minutes.

5   Remove the twine from the roast and slice the roast thickly, seasoning each slice on both sides with salt and pepper. Spread the vegetables on a platter and pour over them the juices that collected under the resting veal. Sprinkle with chervil and lay the sliced veal on top.

potatoes, washed but
    not peeled
½ pound (220 g.) cherry
    tomatoes
4 sprigs thyme
½ cup (10 cl.) white veal stock
    (page 36 or store-bought)
1 tablespoon minced chervil

VEAL STEW _____

Blanquette de veau

variation
    VEAL STEW WITH SPRING
    VEGETABLES

SERVES   4–5
PREPARATION   10 minutes
COOKING   2 hours plus 20 minutes for the small onions,
                5 minutes for the mushrooms, and 30 minutes
                for the sauce

1   Put the meat in a large pot or Dutch oven. Pour in enough water to cover it completely, about 1½ quarts (1.5 l.). Add 1 tablespoon coarse salt. Bring the water to a boil and boil for 2 minutes. With a skimmer or slotted spoon, remove the meat to a colander and rinse it with cold water. Rinse the pot with hot water.

2   Put the veal back in the pot and cover it with water again. Bring to a boil over high heat, skimming away any gray foam or other impurities on the surface. Add 1 tablespoon coarse salt, the white peppercorns, onion, carrot, leek, garlic, celery, and bouquet garni. Lower the heat and simmer for 2 hours.

3   In the meantime, prepare the small onions. See page 426 for directions.

4   Melt 1 tablespoon butter in the pan used for preparing the onions. Add the mushrooms and season with a pinch of salt and a pinch of pepper. Cook over high heat for 5 minutes, stirring well and frequently. Turn off the heat, add the small onions to the mushrooms, and cover.

5   When the veal is out of the oven, use a large skimmer or slotted spoon to remove the meat and vegetables to a platter. Put

1 pound (500 g.) veal shoulder
    or cheek, cut into
    1½–2-inch (4–5-cm.)
    chunks
1 pound (500 g.) veal breast,
    cut into 2–2½-inch
    (4–5-cm.) chunks
Coarse salt
5 white peppercorns
1 medium onion, peeled and
    stuck with 1 whole clove
1 medium carrot, peeled
1 leek, white part only, well
    washed
2 cloves garlic, lightly crushed
    but not peeled
Heart of 1 small bunch of
    celery
1 bouquet garni (6 stems
    parsley, 2 stalks celery, and

(continued)

Melt 1 tablespoon butter in a sauté pan or saucepan. Add the small onions, confectioners' sugar, and a pinch of salt. Add enough water to reach halfway up the onions. Cover and cook over medium heat about 20 minutes, rotating the pot every 5 minutes. The liquid should simmer gently. At the end, the liquid should be almost completely evaporated, and the onions should be tender and light gold. Put them in a colander to drain. Rinse the pan with hot water and wipe it out with a paper towel.

VEAL STEW (cont.)

the cooking liquids through a fine strainer lined with cheese-cloth or a paper towel into a small saucepan. Put the meat and vegetables back into the large pot and add the small onions and mushrooms with their juices. Cover the large pot to keep its contents warm.

6   Put the small saucepan of cooking juices over high heat and bring to a boil. Simmer for 25 minutes.

7   Beat 1 tablespoon crème fraîche with the egg yolks and a pinch of nutmeg in a small bowl.

8   When the juices have simmered for 25 minutes, add the remaining crème fraîche. Stir and simmer 5 minutes more. Turn off the heat. Whisk a ladle of hot sauce into the yolk-cream mixture to warm it up. Whisking constantly, add another ladle of sauce. Then whisk the warmed yolk-cream mixture in the small bowl into the saucepan.

9   Put the large pot of meat and vegetables back over low heat for 5 minutes. Pour the cream sauce into the large pot, stir, and heat until it shivers. Be very careful not to let it bubble and boil. Keep at this temperature for a few minutes, just long enough to reheat the meat and vegetables.

10 Serve with rice and perhaps small, firm vegetables that you have cooked separately.

1 sprig fresh thyme, wrapped and tied in a green leek leaf)

2 tablespoons butter

6 ounces (190 g.) small white flat onions (*grelots*), peeled

2 teaspoons confectioners' sugar

Salt

¾ pound (400 g.) white button mushrooms, cleaned, stem ends trimmed, and quartered lengthwise if large

Pepper

2 cups (45 cl.) crème fraîche

3 large egg yolks (page 204)

Grated nutmeg

VEAL STEW WITH SPRING VEGETABLES

Blanquette de veau aux légumes de printemps

SERVES 4–5
PREPARATION 30 minutes
COOKING 20 minutes

The vegetables listed are just examples of ones you can use. Base your final choice on what looks best at the market. If something isn't available, you needn't use it, and if something special, such as asparagus or chanterelle mushrooms, is in season, put it in.

1   Begin to prepare the veal stew. When the meat is in the oven, carefully wash and trim all the vegetables. Put all the vegetables except the green beans in a large pot and cover them with 1½ quarts (1.5 l.) water. Bring to a boil over high heat. When the water begins to boil, add 2 teaspoons coarse salt. Simmer for 15 minutes and then add the green beans. Simmer 5 minutes more. Prepare a bowl filled two-thirds with cold water and a tray of ice cubes.

2   When the vegetables are cooked but still firm, remove them with a skimmer or slotted spoon to the bowl of ice water. Leave them for 1 minute to cool and then drain them in a colander.

3   Just before serving, melt the butter in a sauté pan or large saucepan over low heat. Add the vegetables and reheat gently for 5 minutes, stirring. Season with salt and pepper and serve on the side.

1 veal stew, prepared as page 425
8 small or 4 medium leeks, white parts only
4 tender stalks celery
12 baby or 4 medium carrots, with 1 inch (2 cm.) of greens attached, peeled if medium
12 baby or 3 small turnips, with 1 inch (2 cm.) of greens attached
1 small bulb fennel, cut into 6 pieces
Coarse salt
¼ pound (100 g.) slender haricots verts (very thin green beans)
1 tablespoon butter
Salt
Pepper

BRAISED VEAL SHANKS WITH SPRING VEGETABLES _____

Jarret de veau à la printanière

SERVES 4
PREPARATION 40 minutes
COOKING 2 hours

1. Preheat the oven to 350°F/180°C.
2. Season the veal with pepper. Melt 3 tablespoons butter in a Dutch oven. When it foams, brown the veal in the butter over medium heat for 3–4 minutes, turning it so it gets evenly colored. Remove the meat to a plate but do not turn off the heat.
3. Add the carrots and onion to the pot with 1 teaspoon butter. Stir and cook over low heat for 10 minutes. In the meantime, pour the wine into a small saucepan. Bring it to a boil, lower the heat, and let it simmer until it has been reduced by two-thirds. Light a long match and touch it to the surface of the wine to set it aflame; this will reduce its acidity. The flame will go out on its own.
4. When the carrots and onion are done, remove them to a colander, but do not turn off the heat. Add the wine to the large pot and raise the heat to high. Use a wooden spatula to scrape the bottom of the pot, loosening any cooked-on bits. Bring the pot to a simmer and hold it there. Sprinkle the veal all over with thyme and put it back in the pot. Add the tomatoes, garlic, and bouquet garni. Pour in the stock or broth, cover, and put back in the oven for 2 hours, basting the meat with cooking juices every 30 minutes.
5. In the meantime, prepare the vegetables. Melt 2 teaspoons butter in a saucepan over low heat. Add the onions, 1 tablespoon sugar, and a pinch of salt. Pour in enough water to reach halfway up the onions. Cut a piece of parchment paper to fit neatly in the saucepan and prick it a few times with a fork or a knife. Place this paper on top of the onions and cook over low heat about 20 minutes, rotating the saucepan twice. By the end of cooking, the water should be almost completely evaporated, and the onions should be tender and lightly golden. Put them in a colander to drain. Rinse the saucepan with hot water and wipe it out with a paper towel.
6. Cook the carrots and then the turnips the same way, but

4 slices of veal shank, about
1½ pounds (750 g.) total,
tied by the butcher
Pepper
6 tablespoons plus 1 teaspoon
(100 g.) butter
2 medium carrots, peeled and
cut into small dice, less
than ½ inch (1 cm.)
1 medium onion, peeled and
minced
1 cup (20 cl.) white wine
2 teaspoons fresh thyme
3 medium tomatoes, quartered
4 cloves garlic, peeled and
degermed (page 122)
1 bouquet garni (2 small stalks
celery, 2 sprigs fresh
thyme, and 5 stems flat-
leaf parsley, wrapped and
tied in 2 leek leaves)
2 cups (50 cl.) white veal stock
(page 36 or store-bought)
or chicken broth (page 77
or made from a bouillon
cube)
24 small white onions,
peeled
Granulated sugar
Salt
8 baby carrots with 1 inch
(2 cm.) greens attached,
scrubbed

without sugar. All these vegetables can be held in the same colander after cooking.

7   Prepare a large bowl half filled with cold water and a tray of ice cubes. In the saucepan you have been using, bring 1 quart (1 l.) water to a boil with 1 teaspoon coarse salt. When it is bubbling, cook the haricots verts for 10 minutes. Remove them to the ice water with a skimmer or slotted spoon, leave them for 1 or 2 minutes, and then put them in a new colander to drain.

8   If necessary, put more ice cubes in the bowl of ice water. Empty the saucepan and fill it with a fresh quart (liter) of water. Bring to a boil with 1 teaspoon coarse salt and cook the leeks the way you cooked the beans. After the leeks cool in the ice water, put them to drain with the beans.

9   Prepare a clean dish towel and, if necessary, put more ice cubes in the bowl of ice water. In a saucepan with tall sides, bring to a boil enough water to cover the asparagus stalks, leaving the tips exposed. Add 1 teaspoon coarse salt. When the water bubbles, lower the asparagus into it, stems down and heads up. Simmer 3 minutes for green asparagus and 5 minutes for young white asparagus. Then use a skimmer to lay the asparagus on its side so that the tips are submerged. Lay a clean towel on top of the water to keep the vegetable submerged. Cook 2 minutes for green asparagus or 4 minutes for white. Remove the asparagus to the ice water and leave for 2 minutes. Be careful not to break the tips. Remove the cooled asparagus to the colander of haricots and leeks.

10 When the veal is cooked, melt 1 tablespoon butter in a large sauté pan or skillet. Add all the vegetables and reheat for 2 or 3 minutes over low heat, spooning butter over them constantly.

11 Remove the veal to a platter and snip off its twine. Put its cooking juices through a fine strainer and pour them all over the veal. Taste for salt and pepper. Lay the vegetables around the veal and sprinkle with fleur de sel. Dust the whole platter with parsley.

8 baby turnips with 1 inch (2 cm.) greens attached, scrubbed

Coarse salt

¼ pound (100 g.) haricots verts (small, slender green beans), trimmed

4 small leeks, well washed and trimmed

8 slender stalks asparagus, tied in a bundle and trimmed to a uniform height

Fleur de sel

1 tablespoon minced flat-leaf parsley

VEAL LOIN AND KIDNEYS

Rognonnade

SERVES   8–10
PREPARATION   20 minutes
COOKING   1¼ hours
RESTING AND SAUCEMAKING   30 minutes

This bountiful dish will make an impression at a full holiday table. Ask the butcher to debone the loin completely and not discard the belly flap. He should also prepare the kidneys, saving a small amount of their fat to give you with some trimmings and chopped-up bones.

1 boneless veal loin, with kidneys and trimmings, as described in the headnote
Salt
Pepper
4 tablespoons (70 g.) clarified butter (page 43)
2 medium carrots, peeled and sliced into rounds ½ inch (1 cm.) thick
2 medium onions, peeled and sliced into rounds ½ inch (1 cm.) thick
3 cloves garlic, lightly crushed but not peeled
1 bouquet garni (2 stalks celery, 3 sprigs thyme, and 6 stems parsley, wrapped and tied in a leek leaf)
Fleur de sel

1   Remove the loin from the refrigerator 30 minutes in advance. Remove the kidneys 15 minutes in advance. Preheat the oven to 410°F/210°C.

2   Melt the kidney fat in a sauté pan or skillet over low heat. This should take about 5 minutes. Just before cooking, season the kidneys generously with salt and pepper. Raise the heat to medium and lay the kidneys in the pan (in a motion away from you so as not to splatter yourself with hot fat). Brown for 2 minutes; use tongs to cook them evenly all over and spoon the cooking fat over them. Remove them to a plate and season lightly with salt and pepper.

3   Flatten the belly flap with the flat side of a cleaver or a chopping board. Season the inside with salt and pepper. Place the kidneys on its center, one behind the other, and roll the whole thing up lengthwise, completely enclosing the kidneys in the belly flap. Secure with twine and season the outside with salt and pepper.

4   Put the meat in a Dutch oven. Use a pastry brush to coat it with the clarified butter. Scatter the trimmings and chopped-up bones around the meat.

5   Rinse the brush under very hot running water and wipe it dry with a paper towel. If the brush is not completely rid of butter, rinse it again. Put the clean brush in a glass of water.

6   Put the pot of meat, uncovered, in the oven for 30 minutes. Turn the meat every 5 minutes so that it gets evenly browned. After 30 minutes, remove the pot from the oven. Use the wet pastry brush to wipe down its interior walls; remove all traces of fat, which might burn if left behind.

7 Add the carrots, onions, garlic, and bouquet garni to the pot. Cover the pot and put it back in the oven for 45 minutes. Flip and baste the veal every 15 minutes, brushing fat from the sides as necessary.

8 Turn off the oven and open its door. Place a platter on the open door and set a cooling rack on top of it. Place the meat on the rack, careful not to drip juices on the oven door. (Sponge them away immediately if you do drip.) Season the roast all over with salt and pepper. Allow the roast to rest for 30 minutes in the warmth of the open oven.

9 In the meantime, prepare the sauce. Spoon yellow liquid fat from the big pot, leaving behind the brown juices. Put the pot on the cooktop. Add 1 quart (1 l.) water and bring to a boil. Use a spatula to scrape up caramelized bits and wipe down the interior walls with the wet pastry brush. Simmer for 20–25 minutes, spooning fat from the surface as necessary.

10 Pour the sauce through a fine strainer into a sauceboat, adding any juices that have collected under the resting roast. Carve the veal into slices and season each slice lightly with fleur de sel and pepper. When morel mushrooms are in season, you might serve them on the side, sautéed at the last minute (see Mushrooms on page 598), with pasta.

VEAL FILET MIGNON WITH TAGLIATELLE, BELL PEPPERS, AND MUSHROOMS

Filets mignons de veau et tagliatelles aux poivrons et champignons

SERVES   4

PREPARATION   10 minutes

COOKING   12 minutes plus 20 minutes for the pasta with peppers

1   Preheat the oven to 400°F/200°C. Season the meat with salt and pepper. Heat 1 tablespoon neutral oil in a Dutch oven over medium heat. Add 2 tablespoons butter, and when it foams, lay the meat in the pot. Brown for 2 minutes, then turn and brown the other side for 2 minutes. Cover and bake in the oven for 8 minutes. Prepare a cooling rack (or a small overturned plate) over a large plate.

2   Turn off the oven and take out the pot. Remove the meat to the rack and season both sides with salt and pepper. Open the door of the oven, set the dish and rack on the open door, and tent loosely with aluminum foil.

3   Spoon excess fat from the pot. Put the pot on a burner and add ½ cup (15 cl.) water. Bring to a boil, stirring and scraping the bottom with a spatula. Boil until the liquid has been reduced by two-thirds; this should take about 15 minutes. Then pass the sauce through a fine strainer into a small saucepan and keep it over very low heat.

4   While the sauce reduces, bring a large pot of water to a boil for the pasta. Include 1 teaspoon coarse salt per quart (liter) of water. Heat 2 tablespoons olive oil in another saucepan. Add the onion and cook for 2 minutes over low heat, stirring. Add the bell peppers and cook for 5 minutes, still stirring. Add the mushrooms and cook and stir 3 minutes more. Season with salt and pepper and stir in the vinegar. Bring to a boil, then turn off the heat and stir.

5   When the water boils, cook the pasta al dente. Drain the pasta and put it in the pot of peppers and onions. Dice 2 tablespoons butter and toss it into the pasta and vegetables.

6   Slice the veal thinly and arrange on a serving plate. Pour the reduced cooking juices over the meat and serve the pasta on the side.

2 small veal filets mignons, about ½ pound (280 g.) each

Salt

Pepper

1 tablespoon neutral oil

4 tablespoons (70 g.) butter

Coarse salt

2 tablespoons olive oil

1 medium onion, peeled and minced

1 red bell pepper, peeled, seeded, and diced (page 130)

1 green bell pepper, peeled, seeded, and diced (page 130)

¼ pound (100 g.) white button mushrooms, cleaned and with stem ends trimmed, halved or quartered if large

2 tablespoons sherry vinegar

6 ounces (190 g.) dried tagliatelle or ½ pound (250 g.) fresh

Pork

For centuries pork was the most commonly consumed meat in rural France. Rare was the small farm without its own pig. Left to range freely, pigs devoured a natural diet that gave their fatty flesh a fine, somewhat wild aroma. The day they were slaughtered was a day of celebration.

Nevertheless, pork has the disadvantages of being difficult to keep fresh and has sometimes been the source of food poisoning and parasites. Fresh pork must be kept cold and cooked soon. Food inspectors keep a close eye on pork now, and over the centuries mankind has developed many ways of preserving it with salt and with smoke.

Are these porcine drawbacks the source of Jewish and Islamic rules against eating pigs? Whether or not this is so, pork remains a forbidden food in these religious communities, so much so that it is simply not served anymore in French school cafeterias.

Pork was neglected in the twentieth century, considered too fatty for contemporary diets. Its quality had also deteriorated, on account of industrial pork farming practices, which surely did little to increase its popularity.

The whole hog, as they say, is edible, from head to tail, including the blood, fat, organs, and skin. Charcuterie was born of this abundance.

The age groups are as follows: suckling pig (*cochon de lait*) is slaughtered at five or six weeks and weighs 18–22 pounds (8–10 kg.); a butcher's pig (*porc charcutier*) is slaughtered at five to six months and weighs 220 pounds (100 kg.); and the sow and the boar, whose flesh is used in charcuterie.

The feet are usually stuffed or served in a salad as they are in Lyon, where pork products are much adored. Knuckle and ham can be salted and are generally poached or roasted, although they can also be dried or smoked to make "raw ham," as they do in Bayonne, the French Alps, and the Ardennes; as the Italians do; and, indeed, as "country ham" is made in America. The loin comprises the loin end; the rib cut, which is sliced into fillets and chops but can be a bit dry; the filet mignon, tender and deliciously fatty but representing a mere 1 pound (500 g.) of this 120–140-pound (60–70-kg.) beast; and the shoulder or blade end, which is heavily veined with fat and yields very rich meat. The loin cuts are usually cooked fresh and are roasted, grilled, or sautéed. The front leg and shoulder yield the Boston butt, picnic shoulder, hock, and spareribs, which are frequently served salted. And let us not forget the belly, smoked or salted, which gives us bacon and lardons.

BEING CHOOSY

Good fresh pork is fine-textured and rosily white with very firm, very white fat. It should also look dry: Pork that is glossy and wet is not to be trusted. It should be firm enough to resist a poking finger.

Dark meat is from an exhausted animal or one that was under stress when it was slaughtered. Meat that is too pale, moist, and soft is from an animal that has gotten too fat, and it will lose a good deal of water during cooking, becoming dry.

SALT PORK

Before refrigerators and freezers, most of a slaughtered pig was salted right away so it would keep as long as possible. Salt effectively removes water, which is full of the things bacteria thrive on. By drying out the meat, salt impeded bacterial growth.

The custom of salting is still with us today because it gives some cuts of pork their own special taste. Pork is usually dry-salted or salted in brine.

Dry, one rubs the meat with coarse sea salt spiked with saltpeter. Then the meat is left to rest on a rack. Any part of the pig can be preserved this way, but it is usually used for small, flat cuts. Larger cuts, such as ham and the rib cut, are usually injected with brine (a combination of water, coarse salt, saltpeter, and a bit of raw sugar). A syringe is used to ensure that the brine makes its way to the heart of the meat. Then the cut is left to soak in a great vat of brine for three or four days. Afterward it is drained. Another method combines the two techniques: the meat is injected with brine and then dry-rubbed with salt.

Today, salt pork is almost always "half-salted." Full salting, which was once used because it preserves the meat longer, requires you to "desalt" the meat before cooking by soaking it in fresh water. But the degree of salting is never consistent. If you must desalt a piece of pork, ask the butcher—or, if you are lucky enough to have one, your *charcutier*—how long it will take. He might answer a few hours, and he might answer more than a day. The soaking water must be changed every once in a while. After it is saturated with salt, it will not be able to draw any more from the meat and must be replaced with fresh water. On the other hand, if you change the water too often, the meat will come to taste waterlogged. It is useless to soak smoked pork, whether it is bacon, butt, or some other piece.

Salt pork can be roasted but is usually poached. Put the morsel of salt pork into a large quantity of cold water. Do not start with hot water, which will cause the meat to disintegrate right away. Add an aromatic dressing of vegetables and spices—carrots, onions, bouquet garni, cloves, or peppercorns—but certainly no salt. Skim the surface regularly and poach gently in barely simmering water for several hours. The water must not boil, as this will make the meat fall apart. The ideal temperature is just below 195°F/90°C. It wouldn't be a terrible idea to use a thermometer here.

There is a very simple way to determine whether a ham is cooked. At the "handle" end of the ham you will find a small bone parallel to the large one. If you can remove it with no tool but your hand, then the meat is cooked.

Once it is cooked, remove the meat from the poaching liquid and, if necessary, remove its rind (the animal's skin) and surface fat. Finish it in the oven on a bed of carrots and sliced onion with a bouquet garni, basting regularly with its own fat. The top of the meat will color in the oven. If you want to accentuate this golden look, once the surface fat has been removed you can carve a crosshatch pattern into the top of the ham and then dust it with confectioners' sugar.

As for half-salted pork, it can be roasted or poached or even simmered in a pot with vegetables, especially cabbage and sauerkraut.

"Fresh" pork is simply raw meat as opposed to meat that has been salted or smoked. Modern methods of preservation by cooling have increased consumption of fresh pork, which now accounts for 30 percent of all pork eaten, at least in France.

Grilling and roasting are good for small pieces: ribs, chops, cutlets, and scallops. Always buy roasts with bones, fat, and, if possible, the rind; they taste much better. Roast them in the oven rather than on a spit; they will be more tender. On the spit, the meat drips away its fat instead of self-basting. Add sage and garlic to pork roasts and perhaps a bit of thyme or rosemary.

Pork should be cooked until it is almost completely white all the way through, with only a faint trace of pink (if any) at the center.

Very thin slices can be seared or, even better, grilled whole on a barbecue. They can also be diced and sautéed with vegetables, herbs, and spices, as they often are in Asia.

IT'S HARD TO TELL PORK FROM WILD BOAR IN A STEW

Like wild boar, pork can be made into a rustic stew thickened with blood. More exotic preparations are also good, with sweet and sour sauces based on sugar or honey, pineapples, bananas, peaches, and so forth, as long as you remember to add a dash of vinegar for that indispensable note of acidity. Finally, an entire pig—whole or split in half—can be roasted on a spit or in the oven. This is usually done with piglets, which are often available during the holidays.

PAN FRIED PORK CHOP

Côte de porc poêlée

variation

PORK CHOPS WITH
CORNICHONS

SERVES 1
PREPARATION 2 minutes
COOKING 12 minutes
RESTING 5 minutes

1   Remove the chop from the refrigerator 20 minutes in advance. Season both sides with salt and pepper.
2   Heat the oil in a sauté pan or frying pan. Add the butter, and when it foams, turn the heat to low and lay the chop in the pan. Cook gently for 6 minutes. Tilt the skillet so that the fat makes its way under the chop. Spoon fat over it, too. Turn the chop with tongs or a spatula and cook the other side for 6 minutes, tilting and basting as before. Let the chop rest on a plate for 5 minutes before eating.

1 bone-in pork chop, 6 ounces (180 g.), approximately ⅔ inch thick
Salt
Pepper
1 teaspoon neutral oil
2 teaspoons butter

PORK CHOPS WITH CORNICHONS

Côtes charcutières

SERVES 4
PREPARATION 5 minutes
COOKING (SAUCE) 6 minutes

1   If you are preparing stock from a store-bought concentrate, make it before you fry the chops.
2   Fry the chops according to the recipe above. While the meat is resting, make the sauce. Spoon excess fat from the surface of the skillet, leaving behind the brown cooking juices. Put the skillet back over low heat. Add the onion and cook for 3 minutes, stirring with a wooden spatula. Add the wine and stir well, scraping up the caramelized bits on the bottom of the pan. Add the stock and cook gently for 2 minutes.
3   Pass the sauce through a fine strainer into a small saucepan. Stir in the mustard and put the saucepan over very low heat. (The sauce should not bubble because this will make the mustard fall apart.) Add the butter and stir until it is completely incorporated. Stir in the cornichons and taste for salt and pepper. Serve the chops coated with sauce.

1 cup (20 cl.) brown veal stock (page 37 or store-bought)
4 pork chops, 6 ounces (190 g.) each, pan fried as described above
1 medium onion, peeled and minced
½ cup (10 cl.) white wine
1 tablespoon mustard
2 teaspoons butter
3 ounces (80 g.) cornichons, sliced lengthwise and then sliced again into matchsticks ⅛ inch (3 mm.) thick
Salt
Pepper

PORK FILET MIGNON STUFFED WITH FRESH HERBS _____

Filet mignon de porc farci aux herbes fraîches

SERVES 4
PREPARATION 20 minutes
COOKING 10 minutes

1 Remove the pork from the refrigerator 15 minutes in advance.

2 Melt 1 teaspoon butter in a skillet over low heat. Add the spinach and herbs and stir well. Cook for 3 minutes, stirring, and then season lightly with salt and pepper. Remove to a plate.

3 Slice the pork medallions almost all the way in half by cutting horizontally through their center (parallel to the surface of the meat), so that they open like butterflies. Open and flatten with your hand. Stuff each one with one-fourth of the wilted greens. Close up the medallions so that they look as they did before (no herbs should stick out from the edges) and tie them up with kitchen twine. Season the packets all over with salt and pepper.

4 Heat the oil and the remaining butter in a large pot. When the butter foams, lay the stuffed meat in the pot and cook 5 minutes per side over low heat, frequently basting with cooking juices. Remove the pork to a plate and snip off the twine.

5 Spoon grease from the surface of the pot and discard. Put the pot back over medium heat and add the wine and mustard. Stir well with a spatula, scraping up the caramelized bits. Bring to a simmer and simmer for 5 minutes. Stir in the cream and cook for 2–3 minutes. Taste for salt and pepper. Pass the sauce through a fine strainer and serve it on the side.

4 slices pork filet mignon, about 3 ounces (90 g.) each and ½ inch (1.5 cm.) thick
2 teaspoons butter
1 ounce (30 g.) baby spinach, washed, well dried, and minced
1 tablespoon minced sage
1 tablespoon minced chervil
1 tablespoon minced flat-leaf parsley
1 tablespoon chives, washed, well dried, and minced
Salt
Pepper
1 teaspoon neutral oil
5 tablespoons dry white wine
1 teaspoon mustard
½ cup (10 cl.) heavy cream

PORK MEDALLIONS WITH SMALL ONIONS _____

Médaillons de porc aux petits oignons

SERVES   2

PREPARATION   15 minutes

COOKING   12 minutes plus 25 minutes for the onions

1   Melt ½ tablespoon butter in a sauté pan. When it foams, add the onions, sugar, and a pinch of salt. Cook over low heat for 3 minutes, stirring with a spatula. Pour in enough water to reach halfway up the onions, cover, and cook over low heat for 20 minutes, rotating the pot every 5 minutes. When the onions are soft and quite glossy, remove the pot from the heat.

2   Season both sides of the pork with salt and pepper. Heat the olive oil in a Dutch oven over low heat, then add 1½ tablespoons butter. Add the rosemary sprigs, garlic, and pork. Cook the meat for 5 minutes on each side, flipping it with tongs or a spoon and basting it with pan juices throughout cooking. Add the onions all around and let them get a bit of color for 2 minutes over very low heat.

3   Remove the pork to a plate and tent loosely with aluminum foil. Spoon fat from the pot and discard. Put the pot back over medium heat. Add the vinegar and stir to coat the onions. Add the pine nuts and 1½ tablespoons water. Simmer for 30 seconds, scraping the pot to loosen flavorful cooked-on bits. Stir in the rosemary leaves and taste for salt and pepper.

4   Put the pork on a platter, scatter the onions all around, and serve.

2 tablespoons butter

12 small new onions, peeled

1 teaspoon granulated sugar

Salt

4 small pork medallions,
    3 ounces (90 g.) each

Pepper

1 teaspoon olive oil

3 sprigs fresh rosemary plus
    1 teaspoon rosemary leaves

1 clove garlic, lightly crushed
    but not peeled

1 tablespoon balsamic vinegar

2 tablespoons pine nuts

PORK BLADE SHOULDER ROAST WITH LEEKS

Echine de porc aux poireaux

SERVES 4

PREPARATION 10 minutes

COOKING 1 hour and 40 minutes

The roast must be seasoned one day in advance.

1 The night before you plan to cook, season the pork. Lay it on a work surface, make small incisions with a knife all over, and stud with garlic. Take half of the sage leaves and crush them in your hand; rub the roast with the crushed sage and coarse salt. Turn the roast so that the bone is facing you and use a sharp knife to make incisions between the bone and the flesh; stuff the crushed sage leaves into these pockets. Rub half of the sprig of thyme over the roast to release its leaves. Wrap the meat in plastic wrap and put it in the refrigerator overnight.

2 The next day, rinse the roast under cold running water. Rinse away all the salt and herbs (leaving the garlic in the pork) and wipe dry with paper towels.

3 Heat the olive oil in a Dutch oven over medium heat. Lay the roast in the pot with any bits of bone you might happen to have. Cook for 10 minutes, turning frequently, until the meat is nicely browned. Add the onions and tomatoes, and cook 5 minutes more.

4 In a small bowl, beat the vinegar and sugar together with a fork. Pour this mixture into the pot. Add the wine and stir. Cook for 5 minutes to reduce the liquid a bit and then tuck the leeks in all around the meat, submerging them in the liquid. Season lightly with salt and pepper and add the rest of the sage, the juniper berries, the remaining ½ sprig thyme, and the butter. Cover, lower the heat, and cook gently for 1½ hours, stirring every half hour. At the end, taste for salt and pepper.

5 With a skimmer or slotted spoon, remove the roast and vegetables to a dish. Discard the thyme. Spoon away the yellow layer of fat at the surface of the pot and discard. Put the pot over medium heat, add ½ cup (10 cl.) water, and bring to a boil while scraping the bottom with a spatula. Simmer for 5 minutes. Pass the sauce through a fine strainer into a sauceboat.

2 pounds (1 kg.) pork blade shoulder roast

4 cloves garlic, peeled and sliced lengthwise into matchsticks ⅛ inch (3 mm.) thick

Handful of fresh sage leaves

2 level teaspoons coarse salt

1 sprig thyme

2 tablespoons olive oil

4 medium onions, peeled and quartered

2 medium tomatoes, peeled, seeded, and diced (page 124)

1 tablespoon white wine vinegar

2 tablespoons superfine sugar

1 cup (25 cl.) dry white wine

6 medium leeks, white parts only, trimmed and well washed

Salt

Pepper

5 juniper berries

1 tablespoon butter

6   Remove the roast's twine and carve the roast into thin slices. Lay the slices on a hot platter and arrange the leeks and onions around them. Serve the sauce on the side.

PORK SKEWERS WITH PRUNES AND BACON

Brochettes de porc aux pruneaux et au bacon

SERVES   2
PREPARATION   30 minutes
COOKING   22 minutes plus 5 minutes for the sauce

1   Make the sauce. Heat 2 tablespoons oil in a saucepan. Add the minced onion, a pinch of salt, and a pinch of pepper. Cook over low heat for 3 minutes, stirring with a spatula. Add the honey, stir well, and add the pineapple juice. Bring to a simmer and then add the ginger and ketchup. Stir well and bring back to a simmer. Stir in the Worcestershire sauce and then turn off the heat.

2   Season the pork lightly with salt and pepper. Heat 1 teaspoon oil in a sauté pan or skillet. Add 1 teaspoon butter. When the butter foams, add the onion rounds and bacon and cook for 3 minutes over low heat, stirring. Remove them to a plate. Put the skillet over very low heat, add the pork cubes, and brown for 5 minutes, stirring so they are evenly colored. Remove them to the plate of onions and bacon. Put the pineapple into the skillet and cook over low heat for 2 minutes, stirring.

3   Roll each prune in a slice of bacon. Prepare the skewers in this order: pork, onion, pineapple, 1 prune wrapped in the smoked bacon, onion, pork, pineapple, 1 prune wrapped in the bacon, pork.

4   Rinse the skillet or sauté pan with hot water and wipe it out with a paper towel. Put it back over low heat and add 1 tablespoon oil and 1 teaspoon butter. When the butter foams, sauté the skewers very gently, 4 minutes per side (12 minutes total). Move the pan about and spoon cooking juices over the skewers. Two minutes before the skewers are finished, turn the heat to low under the saucepan of sauce and stir. Serve the brochettes with the sauce on the side.

3 tablespoons plus 1 teaspoon neutral oil
1 medium onion, peeled and minced
Salt
Pepper
2 tablespoons honey, acacia or chestnut if possible
2 tablespoons pineapple juice
¾ ounce (20 g.) fresh gingerroot, peeled and slivered
2 tablespoons ketchup
1 tablespoon Worcestershire sauce
12 cubes pork loin, about 1 inch (2 cm.) square
2 teaspoons butter
1 medium onion carved into rounds ½ inch (1 cm.) thick
8 chunks smoked slab bacon each about ½ inch thick and 1 inch wide (1 cm. by 2 cm.)
8 cubes pineapple, ½ inch by 1 inch (1 cm. by 2 cm.)
8 pitted prunes

(continued)

5   You can also grill the brochettes on a barbecue. It is very important to precook the diced meat because it will not get cooked where it is stuck on the skewer.

special equipment: 4 long wooden skewers

PORK RIB ROAST

Rôti de porc

SERVES   4
PREPARATION   5 minutes
COOKING   1 hour and 10 minutes

1   Preheat the oven to 400°F/200°C. Place the roast on a work surface. Make small regularly spaced incisions with a knife and stud with garlic. Rub the meat with the coarse salt and 2 pinches of pepper. Do not try to scoop up salt that falls off the meat and put it back on; just leave it on the work surface.

2   Heat the oil in a Dutch oven. Brown the roast for 8 minutes over low heat, turning it with tongs or a spatula so that it gets evenly colored. Place the pot, uncovered, in the oven and bake for 1 hour. Rotate the roast every 15 minutes with tongs or a spoon and baste it with cooking juices.

3   If you would like to serve the cooking juices as sauce, remove the roast to a platter to rest. Spoon as much fat as possible from the surface of the pot, leaving the brown juices. Add ½ cup hot water and scrape at the brown bits with a spatula. Taste for salt and pepper. Put the pot back in the oven for 5 minutes.

4   Serve the sauce on the side.

1 boneless pork rib roast, 2 pounds (1 kg.)
2 cloves garlic, peeled and sliced lengthwise into matchsticks ⅛ inch (3 mm.) thick
1 teaspoon coarse salt
Pepper
1 tablespoon neutral oil
Salt

PORK RIB ROAST WITH TOMATOES, GARLIC, ONIONS, AND CARROTS

Carré de porc aux tomates, ail, oignons, et aux carottes

SERVES   6–8
PREPARATION   15 minutes
COOKING   1¾ hours
RESTING   at least 15 minutes

1 Remove the meat from the oven 30 minutes in advance. Preheat the oven to 400°F/200°C.

2 Heat 1 tablespoon olive oil in a Dutch oven. Cook the onions over low heat for 5 minutes, stirring with a wooden spoon. At the end, season with salt and pepper, and remove them to a colander to drain.

3 Add 2 tablespoons olive oil to the pot and place over medium heat. Add the tomatoes and cook for 10 minutes, shaking the pot from time to time until they are nicely colored. At the end, season lightly with salt and pepper. Remove them to the colander.

4 Add the remaining tablespoon of olive oil to the pot and add the carrots. Season with salt and pepper and cook for 15 minutes over low heat, shaking the pot every 5 minutes, until the carrots are lightly browned and fork-tender. Add the garlic and cook 3 minutes more over very low heat. Remove the carrots to the colander. Discard all oil from the pot and rinse it under hot water.

5 Season the roast lightly with salt and pepper. Slip half of the sage leaves into the twine tying up the roast. Put the onions, carrots, and tomatoes back in the pot, scatter the remaining sage leaves over them, and lay the roast fatty side up on top of this vegetable "rack."

6 Roast uncovered on the middle rack of the oven for 1 hour. Then add ¼ cup water to the pot, cover the roast with a piece of aluminum foil, and roast 15 minutes more. Turn off the oven, set its door ajar, and leave the roast in the half-open oven for 15 minutes (or up to 1 hour). The pork will finish cooking as it rests.

1 pork rib roast, 3 pounds (1½ kg.), boned, rolled, and tied
4 tablespoons olive oil
8 medium onions, peeled and sliced into rounds ½ inch (1 cm.) thick
Salt
Pepper
12 plum tomatoes (if possible; if not, then 6 medium tomatoes), peeled, seeded (page 124), and halved or quartered
8 medium carrots, peeled and sliced into rounds ½ inch (1 cm.) thick
4 cloves garlic, peeled and sliced in half lengthwise
1 small bunch fresh sage, leaves only

PORK FILET MIGNON WITH PRUNES

Filets mignons de porc aux pruneaux

SERVES   4
PREPARATION   30 minutes
COOKING   25 minutes
SAUCE   6 minutes
The prunes must be macerated at least 2 hours in advance.

½ bottle sweet white wine
1 small cinnamon stick
½ bay leaf
6 ounces (190 g.) whole prunes
2 pork filets mignons, about
       14 ounces (400 g.) each
Salt
Pepper
1 teaspoon neutral oil
2 teaspoons butter
1 tablespoon red currant jelly
2 tablespoons crème fraîche

1   Pour the wine into a saucepan and add the cinnamon stick and bay leaf. Bring to a boil and then light a long kitchen match and carefully touch it to the surface of the bubbling wine to set it aflame. This will reduce the wine's acidity. Turn off the heat and submerge the prunes in the hot wine. Leave them to macerate for 2 hours.

2   Remove the pork from the refrigerator 15 minutes before you plan to start cooking. Preheat the oven to 410°F/210°C.

3   Use a slotted spoon to lift the prunes from the wine. Put them in a colander, rinse them, and leave them to drain. Put the saucepan of wine back on the cooktop, bring to a boil, and simmer for 15 minutes.

4   Season the pork with salt and pepper. Heat the oil in a cast-iron Dutch oven and add the butter. When it foams, turn the heat to low and lay the pork in the pot. Brown very gently for 5 minutes on each side. After it has finished browning, cover and bake in the oven for 15 minutes. Baste the pork with cooking juices every 5 minutes. At the end, remove the meat to a serving plate. Open the oven door, set the plate of pork on the open door, and tent it loosely with aluminum foil.

5   Spoon the surface fat from the Dutch oven. Put it back on top of the stove over medium heat and add the wine in which the prunes were soaked. Stir and scrape well with a spatula. Bring to a simmer and simmer for 5 minutes. Pass the sauce through a fine strainer into a small saucepan.

6   Turn the heat under the sauce to low. Stir in the jelly, crème fraîche, and prunes. Bring to a boil and let the pot bubble for 1 minute while you stir with a whisk. Taste for salt and pepper and then turn off the heat.

7   Carve the meat into thin slices and lay them on the warm serving plate. Pour the prunes and sauce over the pork and serve.

PORK FILET MIGNON WITH CABBAGE _____

Filets mignons de porc au chou

SERVES 4

PREPARATION   5 minutes

COOKING   25 minutes plus 15 minutes for the cabbage

The aromatic oil must be prepared at least 30 minutes in advance.

1   Open the cardamom pods, remove the seeds, and crush them. (You can crush them by putting them on a clean dish towel, folding a layer of towel over them, and running over them with a rolling pin.) Put the crushed seeds in a small saucepan and heat over very low heat for 1 or 2 minutes, stirring with a spatula. Add the peanut oil and cook for 2 minutes, still over low heat. Remove the pot from the heat and set it aside for 30 minutes to infuse.

2   Remove the meat from the refrigerator 15 minutes before you plan to cook it.

3   Season both sides of the meat with salt and pepper. In a Dutch oven pretty enough to bring to the table, heat 3 tablespoons infused oil over low heat (include a few cardamom seeds, too). Add the butter, and when it melts, lay the filets mignons in the pot. Cook for 10 minutes on one side, rotating the fillets in the pan and basting them with cooking juices. Turn them over and cook 15 minutes on the second side, rotating and basting as before. Remove them to a plate and tent with aluminum foil.

4   Spoon the fat from the surface of the pot and discard. Put the pot back over low heat and add the cabbage leaves. Stir. Add a few bits of cardamom seed from the infused oil and ½ cup water. Cover and simmer for 10 minutes, stirring once. In the meantime, in a small bowl mix 2 tablespoons infused oil with the vinegar.

5   When the cabbage has simmered for 10 minutes, remove the cover and lay the pork on top of the cabbage. Pour the oil-vinegar mixture over the meat. Cover the pot again and leave for 5 minutes over low heat. Serve in the pot.

5 large pods black cardamom
½ cup (10 cl.) peanut oil
2 pork filets mignons, ¾ pound (400 g.) each
Salt
Pepper
1 teaspoon butter
20 leaves green cabbage, blanched (page 556), chopped in half, and large central ribs removed
1 teaspoon sherry vinegar

PORK BELLY AND POTATOES

Lard aux pommes de terre

SERVES 4–6

PREPARATION 10 minutes

COOKING 1½ hours

1 Put the pork belly in a Dutch oven and cover it generously with cold water. Add the next 9 ingredients, bring to a boil, and then lower the heat so that the pot simmers gently. Cook for 1 hour.

2 After an hour, add the potatoes. Cook 30 minutes more.

3 Put the meat and potatoes in a colander to drain. Carve the pork belly into thick slices. Sprinkle the potatoes with fleur de sel and pepper.

3 pounds (1.5 kg.) pork belly

1 onion, peeled and stuck with 1 whole clove

1 carrot, peeled

2 cloves garlic, peeled and degermed (page 122)

1 bouquet garni (2 sprigs fresh thyme, ½ bay leaf, and 2 stems flat-leaf parsley, wrapped and tied in a leek leaf)

1 ounce (30 g.) fresh ginger, peeled

1 bunch fresh sage

1 teaspoon black peppercorns

1 teaspoon juniper berries

1 teaspoon coriander seeds

8 potatoes (approximately 1 pound/500 g.), preferably charlottes, peeled and washed

Fleur de sel

Freshly ground pepper

SALT PORK WITH LENTILS

Petit salé aux lentilles

variation

HAM HOCK WITH LENTILS

SERVES 4

PREPARATION 15 minutes

COOKING 2 hours plus 45 minutes for the lentils

The salt pork must be soaked 2 hours in advance.

1   Two hours in advance, put the salt pork in a bowl of cold water.

2   When the pork has finished soaking, drain it in a colander. Put it in a Dutch oven, cover it generously with cold water, and bring to a boil. Use a skimmer to remove any foam from the surface of the bubbling liquid. Add 1 whole onion stuck with a clove, 1 bouquet garni, 1 halved carrot, and the peppercorns. Simmer for 2 hours, skimming foam every 30 minutes.

3   When the meat has been simmering for 1¼ hours, put the lentils in a large saucepan. Cover them with cold water; the water should reach 4 times as high as the lentils. Put the saucepan over high heat. As soon as the water begins to boil, lower the heat. Skim. Add the other whole onion stuck with a clove, the other halved carrot, the garlic, and the second bouquet garni. Cover and simmer for 40 minutes.

4   Ten minutes before the lentils are done, add the coarse salt. Five minutes before they are done, cook the unsmoked lardons over low heat in a Dutch oven pretty enough to bring to the table. This should take about 3 minutes. Add the sliced onion and cook for 3 minutes, stirring with a spatula. Add the smoked lardons and brown for 5 minutes, still over low heat and still stirring.

5   The lentils and pork should both be cooked now. Drain the lentils. Remove the bouquet garni, onion, garlic, and carrot. Add the lentils to the pot of lardons.

6   Skim the meat's cooking liquid. Pour 1 cup (20 cl.) of this broth into the lentils. Bring to a simmer and simmer for 5 minutes. Turn off the heat and stir in the butter and parsley. Taste for salt and pepper. Cover the pot to keep it warm.

7   With a skimmer or slotted spoon, remove the pork from its pot. Carve it into slices and serve on top of the lentils.

2 pounds (900 g.) *petit salé*—salt-cured pork belly

3 medium onions, peeled, 2 stuck with 1 whole clove each, the other sliced into thin rounds less than ½ inch (1 cm.) thick

2 bouquets garnis (each one including 2 sprigs fresh thyme, ½ bay leaf, and 2 stems flat-leaf parsley, wrapped and tied in a leek leaf)

2 carrots, peeled and sliced in half lengthwise

5 peppercorns

½ pound (250 g.) lentils, preferably green French variety

3 cloves garlic, peeled; 2 left whole and 1 minced

1 teaspoon coarse salt

1 ounce (30 g.) unsmoked lardons (page 89)

3 ounces (100 g.) smoked lardons (page 89)

2 tablespoons butter

2 tablespoons minced flat-leaf parsley

Salt

Pepper

HAM HOCK WITH LENTILS
Jarret de porc aux lentilles

SERVES 4

COOKING   2½ hours

The pork must be soaked 8 hours in advance.

Follow the recipe page 447, substituting ham hocks for the salt pork and cooking them for 2½ hours instead of 2.

4 small half-salt ham hocks, about ½ pound (250 g.) each

All ingredients for the previous recipe except the salt pork

Charcuterie _____

PAN FRIED BLOOD SAUSAGE _____
Boudin noir poêlé

SERVES 1

PREPARATION   2 minutes

COOKING   10–12 minutes

Boudin noir, a common sausage in France, is prepared with pork meat, fat, and blood. Its taste is not too terribly strong, however. It must be eaten very fresh. You will find it at the butcher's as a very long sausage rolled into a coil, from which your portion will be cut.

1 piece *boudin noir* (blood sausage)

1 teaspoon neutral oil

1   Remove the sausage from the refrigerator 1 hour in advance.
2   Preheat the oven to 325°F/160°C, 15 minutes in advance. Prick the sausage a few times with a fork to prevent it from exploding as it cooks.
3   Heat the oil in a skillet. Tilt and twirl the skillet to spread the oil all over its bottom. Lay the sausage in the skillet and cook for 4 minutes over medium heat, rolling it around with a spatula so it gets evenly colored.
4   Remove the browned sausage to a baking dish and cook in the oven for 6–8 minutes. Serve with mashed potatoes (page 623).

PAN-GRILLED BLOOD SAUSAGE

Boudin noir grillé

SERVES   1
PREPARATION   2 minutes
COOKING   10–12 minutes

1   Remove the sausage from the refrigerator 1 hour in advance.
2   Preheat the oven to 325°F/160°C, 15 minutes in advance. Prick the sausage a few times with a fork to prevent it from exploding as it cooks.
3   Preheat the grill pan for 2 minutes over medium heat. Oil the sausage and put it in the grill pan. Cook over medium heat for 4 minutes, rolling it around with a spatula so that it gets evenly colored.
4   Remove the browned sausage to a baking dish and finish cooking in the oven, 6–8 minutes. Serve with mashed potatoes (page 623).

1 piece *boudin noir* (blood sausage)
Neutral oil

PAN FRIED SMALL CHITTERLINGS

Andouillette poêleé

SERVES   1
PREPARATION   2 minutes
COOKING   14–16 minutes

Andouillette is another typical sausage, made with chitterlings. Veal andouillette was once available, but now it is very hard to find.

1 *andouillette* (small chitterling sausage)
1 teaspoon neutral oil

1   Remove the sausage from the refrigerator 1 hour in advance.
2   Preheat the oven to 400°F/200°C, 15 minutes in advance. Prick the sausage a few times with a fork to prevent it from exploding as it cooks.
3   Heat the oil in a skillet. Tilt and twirl the skillet to spread the oil all over its bottom. Lay the sausage in the skillet and cook for 4 minutes over medium heat, rolling it around with a spatula so that it gets evenly colored.

4   Remove the browned sausage to a baking dish and cook in the oven for 10–12 minutes. Serve with mashed potatoes (page 623).

PAN-GRILLED SMALL CHITTERLINGS _____

Andouillette grillée

SERVES   1
PREPARATION   2 minutes
COOKING   14–16 minutes

1   Remove the sausage from the refrigerator 1 hour in advance.
2   Preheat the oven to 325°F/160°C, 15 minutes in advance. Prick the sausage a few times with a fork to prevent it from exploding as it cooks.
3   Preheat the grill pan for 2 minutes over medium heat. Oil the sausage very lightly and put it in the grill pan. Cook over medium heat for 4 minutes, rolling it around with a spatula so that it gets evenly colored.
4   Remove the browned sausage to a baking dish and finish cooking in the oven, 10–12 minutes. Serve with mashed potatoes (page 623).

1 *andouillette* (small chitterling sausage)
Neutral oil

HAM WITH FRIED PINEAPPLES

Tranches de jambon, poêlées à l'ananas

SERVES 4

PREPARATION AND COOKING 40 minutes for a fresh
pineapple or 20 minutes for canned pineapple

IF YOU ARE USING FRESH PINEAPPLE, cut off its rind and then cut 4 rounds ½ inch (1 cm.) thick. Remove the center of each slice, which is not good to eat, and quarter the remaining flesh. Bring 1½ cups water to a boil with 5 tablespoons superfine sugar. When it is boiling, add the pineapple pieces and simmer for 10 minutes. Remove from the heat and allow the pineapple to cool in the syrup. When they are cool enough to handle, remove them to a plate lined with a paper towel.

IF YOU ARE USING CANNED PINEAPPLE, cut 4 slices into quarters and place them on a plate lined with a paper towel.

1   Preheat the oven to 440°F/220°C.

2   Make caramel sauce: Put 2 tablespoons water in a small saucepan with 3 tablespoons (50 g.) sugar. Warm over low heat and stir with a spatula, constantly scraping the bottom and sides of the pan. When the caramel begins to turn blond, carefully add the vinegar in a very thin stream, stirring constantly. When the mixture begins to foam, add the veal stock, crushed peppercorns, and clove. Bring to a boil and simmer for 3 minutes. If scum forms around the edges, remove it with a skimmer. Put this sauce through a fine strainer and taste for salt and pepper.

3   Melt 1 tablespoon butter in a skillet. Sauté the pineapple pieces 2 minutes per side over medium heat.

4   Butter the serving plate and lay the slices of ham on top of it; they should not touch one another. Cover the plate with aluminum foil and slip it into the oven for 5 minutes. Remove from the oven, top each slice of ham with 4 pieces of pineapple, drizzle the hot caramel sauce over, and serve.

1 pineapple (or one 15-ounce can of pineapple in syrup)

½ cup (135 g.) superfine sugar for fresh pineapple (if you are using canned pineapple you will need only 3 tablespoons/50 g. superfine sugar)

4 tablespoons wine vinegar

1 cup (25 cl.) white veal stock (page 36 or store-bought)

4 black peppercorns, crushed

1 whole clove

Salt

Pepper

1 tablespoon butter plus a little extra for greasing the serving plate

4 thick slices (about ½ inch/ 1 cm.) braised ham

Poultry and Rabbit

Poultry _____

The poultry category includes farmyard birds (for instance, chickens) as well as typically wild birds born and raised in captivity (squab and quail). Chickens and turkeys of all kinds are thought of as white-fleshed, as opposed to dark-fleshed poultry such as ducks, geese, and guinea fowl. French cuisine has traditionally associated rabbit with poultry.

Poultry is a fine food, not only because it tastes so good but because it offers so much protein with relatively little fat. The best poultry is free-range and grain-fed. Check labels or talk to your butcher to find our how a bird was raised.

CHOOSING YOUR BIRD _____

The bird's skin (which will be white or yellow, depending on what it was fed) should be satiny and pearlescent with no bruises from the slaughter. The bird should be clean and dry. To make sure it is not wet, you can slip a finger under the folded wing.

The breast should be large, thick, and rounded. When you press the flesh with your finger, it should be supple but firm. The end of the wishbone should be flexible; this indicates that the fowl is young. You should be able to see the state of the animal's fat through its skin.

White-fleshed poultry is suitable for many kinds of cooking: roasting, spit-roasting, grilling, pan frying, sautéing, fricasseeing, and steaming. Some regional recipes, such as *coq au vin,* use their own particular methods.

Dark-fleshed poultry is best roasted, poached, or braised. Squab can also be grilled.

TRUSSING

Before cooking a whole bird, you should truss it: tie its drumsticks together and its wing tips down so that it will not look sloppy and will be easier to work with. (Sometimes poultry comes pretrussed with elastic string, but it is better to replace this with twine.)

First, season the interior cavity with salt and pepper. Then place the bird on its back. Using a trussing needle and about 20 inches (50 cm.) of kitchen twine, open one leg and stitch through the joint between the drumstick and the thigh. Run the thread through the leg and then through the breast to the other leg; stitch through the joint of the other leg.

Now turn the bird on its belly. Pull the neck skin from the back over the neck hole. Pull the wing tips on top of the back. Stitch through one wing tip, passing the needle between the two small bones, through the chicken under the backbone, and then through the other wing tip. Stitch the neck closed and tie it off. Cut the thread, but not too short.

Place the bird on its back again. With the remaining thread, stitch through the upper joint of one leg (connecting to the breast), then through the breast and through the upper joint of the other leg, and pull. Tie both legs together, going on each side through the breast and then over the legs, and pull. Tie off and tie well. This is called in French cuisine *double bridage*, two-needle trussing.

It isn't as complicated as it looks on paper, but if you'd rather not try, your butcher can truss a bird for you in no time.

FLAVORING AN ENTIRE RAW FOWL

This technique is for use before the animal is trussed. Slip slivers of truffle, fragrant mushrooms, blanched tarragon leaves, or blanched parsley leaves between the skin and the flesh. First slice the truffle or mushrooms into slivers and let them soak in a bit of oil. Blanch tarragon or parsley. Then place the bird on its back. Beginning at the neck and going all the way to the tail if possible, gently work one or two fingers between the skin and flesh, very carefully pulling them apart. Slip the seasoning under the skin, spreading it evenly and being very careful with the breasts and thighs. Pull the neck skin over the neck opening and truss.

When roasting most poultry, you should not preheat the oven. If you turn the oven on just when you put the roasting dish in, the gradual rise in temperature will leave the meat more tender. This is especially true with larger birds (turkey, goose, capon, or even a big chicken). They must cook gently and be basted regularly (every 20–30 minutes) with their cooking juices. A turkey or a large capon is even better when it is poached (about 10 minutes at a simmer) before roasting. By preference, these big fowls should also be stuffed, for the stuffing will moisten and flavor the breast meat during cooking.

Chicken

Roast chicken is an international dinner tradition, easy to make and just the right amount of food for many families. Free-range chickens are the finest, and a good one should make up for any disappointments you may have experienced while dining on factory-raised fowl. There's simply nothing like a farm-fresh chicken that lived in freedom and fed on grains. If it has been a long time for you, seek one out and remind yourself.

To judge whether a chicken is cooked, prick the leg joint: The juices will run clear if it is done. If the juices are still rosy, keep cooking.

HOW TO CARVE A COOKED CHICKEN

To avoid tearing the skin and flesh, always slice neatly through the skin and flesh around the joints before cutting through the joints themselves. If you have powerful poultry shears or an electric knife, first cut the chicken in half lengthwise by cutting all along the backbone and breastbone; this will make carving easier. Cut through the leg joint. Cut through the joint between the thigh and the drumstick: Use a large knife, setting it on the joint and then pressing down forcefully to separate. Carve the breast from the bone, cutting on the bias toward the wings. Cut off the wings, taking a quarter of the breast with each wing.

ROAST CHICKEN

Poulet rôti

variation

ROAST CHICKEN WITH
POTATOES

SERVES   4
PREPARATION   5 minutes
COOKING   1 hour 5 minutes
RESTING   20 minutes

Butter adds a nice flavor to roast chicken, but if you prefer
to avoid butter, you can grease the roasting dish and the
chicken with neutral oil instead. You can also reduce (or even
eliminate) the fat, especially if you are roasting a nice farm
chicken, which should have good natural fat.

1 chicken, about 3 pounds
   (1.5 kg.), with its giblets
6 tablespoons (90 g.) butter or
   neutral oil
Salt
Pepper
Fleur de sel

1   Remove the chicken and the butter from the refrigerator
    20 minutes in advance.
2   Grease the roasting dish with 2 tablespoons softened butter.
    Season the chicken generously and evenly with salt and pep-
    per inside and out. Truss the bird (page 453). Spread soft-
    ened butter all over the chicken's skin using a pastry brush.
    (If you are not using butter, oil the dish and skin instead.)
3   Place the bird in the dish, not on its back or its breast but on
    its side, thigh and wing down. This thick portion will take
    the longest to cook. Chop the giblets and scatter all around
    the chicken (but not under it). Put the dish in the oven.
4   Heat the oven to 410°F/210°C and cook for 25 minutes. Then
    remove the dish from the oven and turn the chicken onto its
    other side, with the other thigh and wing down. (Turn the
    chicken with tongs or by sticking a large fork into the joint
    between the thigh and the drumstick—without piercing the
    flesh itself—and using the fork and a large spoon to move
    the bird. You do not want to lose its juices.) The chicken
    should always rest on the dish, not on the giblets. Pour
    3 tablespoons water over the chicken and put it back in the
    oven for 25 minutes.
5   Remove the dish from the oven again. Put the chicken on its
    back and rotate it a quarter turn. Put it back in the oven and
    cook for 10 minutes. Turn the chicken on its breast and cook
    5 minutes more.

6 Remove the chicken to a platter. Prick the thigh joint to make sure it is cooked. The juices should run clear with no trace of blood.

7 Season with fleur de sel and pepper. Tent loosely with aluminum foil and let the chicken rest for 20 minutes, breast down and with the tail end propped up so that the chicken is almost vertical.

ROAST CHICKEN WITH POTATOES

Poulet rôti aux pommes de terre

SERVES 4
COOKING 1 hour and 5 minutes; the potatoes cook with the chicken
RESTING 20 minutes

1 Remove the chicken and the butter from the refrigerator in advance.

2 Wash the potatoes. You may peel them or not, as you prefer. If they are large, cut them into 6 pieces lengthwise. If they are small, cut them in half. Once they are peeled and cut, put them in a bowl of cold water until you are ready to use them.

3 Toss the potatoes, garlic, onion slices, and shallots with the giblets and season with salt and pepper.

4 After you place the chicken in the roasting dish, scatter the vegetables and giblets around it. Brush the potatoes with some of the butter. If you have chosen to leave the skin on the potatoes, the skin side should be down. Throughout cooking, the chicken should always rest directly on the dish, not on top of the potatoes or giblets.

5 Cook as described page 455. Serve the roast chicken with the potatoes and onions.

1 recipe Roast Chicken (page 455)
8 large or 12 small new potatoes (about 1 pound/500 g.)
4 cloves garlic, unpeeled and crushed under your palm
2 peeled slices from a medium onion, ½ inch (1 cm.) thick
2 shallots, peeled

STEWED CHICKEN

Potée de volaille en cocotte lutée

SERVES   4
PREPARATION   20 minutes
COOKING   2 hours
RESTING   15–20 minutes

6 tablespoons (90 g.) butter

3⅔ cups (450 g.) flour

Salt

2 teaspoons coarse salt

1 green cabbage (outer leaves and core removed and discarded), quartered

1 medium carrot, peeled and sliced into rounds

1 medium onion, peeled and sliced into rounds

¼ celery root, peeled and sliced into rounds

1 medium leek, white part only, carefully washed and sliced into rounds

Crushed black pepper

1 chicken, about 3 pounds (1.5 kg.)

4 cloves garlic, peeled and degermed (page 122)

1 shallot, peeled and thinly sliced

1 bouquet garni (4 sprigs thyme, 6 stems parsley, and 2 small celery stalks, wrapped and tied in a leek leaf)

1 cup (20 cl.) dry white wine

2 cups (45 cl.) chicken broth (page 77 or made from a bouillon cube)

1 egg yolk (page 204) (optional)

1   Remove the butter from the refrigerator and dice it.

2   PREPARE THE SEALING PASTRY (*PÂTE À LUTER*): Mix very well the flour, ½ cup (15 cl.) hot water, and 1½ teaspoons salt. Put the dough in the refrigerator to rest.

3   Preheat the oven to 350°F/180°C. Bring 1 quart (1 l.) water to a boil in a saucepan with 1 teaspoon coarse salt. Prepare a bowl half filled with cold water and half a tray of ice cubes. Boil the cabbage for 3 minutes. Remove it with a slotted spoon to the bowl of ice water. When it has cooled a bit, drain in a colander.

4   Discard the ice water and the hot water in the saucepan. Prepare a new bowl of ice water, using the other half of the tray of ice cubes. Bring 1 quart (1 l.) water to a boil in the saucepan with 1 teaspoon coarse salt. Boil the carrot, onion, celery root, and leek for 2 minutes. Using a slotted spoon, remove them to the ice water and leave for 1 minute. Drain in a colander.

5   Brush with butter the bottom and sides of a Dutch oven large enough to hold the whole chicken. Lay a bed of cabbage and vegetables in the bottom of the pot. Season the bird inside and out with salt and crushed black pepper. Set it on top of the cabbage and tuck the rest of the vegetables in around it, along with the garlic, shallot, and bouquet garni. Add the wine and chicken broth.

6   Put the lid on the pot. Remove the sealing pastry from the refrigerator and roll it into a thin "snake" long enough to reach all the way around the pot. Press it all around the seam between the pot and its lid, making sure that it is sticking. For a more polished presentation, mark a pattern in the dough with the tip of a knife and brush it with beaten egg yolk. (If you drip yolk onto the pot, wipe it off completely.)

8   Bake for 2 hours. Let the pot rest for 15 minutes before serving. Break the sealing pastry open at the table.

CHICKEN WITH BELL PEPPERS AND TOMATOES

Poulet à la basquaise

SERVES   4

COOKING   35 minutes for the chicken plus 3 minutes for
the tomatoes

The Basque region is in southwestern France, at the Spanish
border. *À la basquaise* is a label applied to dishes based on
tomatoes, peppers, bell peppers, garlic, onion, and, often,
Bayonne ham (raw salt-cured ham)—whether the dish is this
sautéed chicken, an omelette, tripe, baby squid, tuna, or
mutton stew. If you like, add to the sauce ¼ pound (150 g.)
ham, chopped into small dice and lightly sautéed, when you
add the chicken to it, 5 minutes before the end of cooking.

1   Heat the olive oil in a Dutch oven over medium heat. Season
each piece of chicken with 2 pinches of salt and a dash of pepper. When the oil is hot, brown the chicken pieces over
medium heat about 10 minutes, turning them from time to
time. Cover the pot, reduce the heat to low, and cook for
20 minutes, turning the chicken pieces every 5 minutes. After
20 minutes, remove the wings and breasts and set them aside.
(Keep them in a 250°F/120°C oven with the door ajar or simply tent loosely with aluminum foil.) Cook the dark meat
about 5 minutes more, still covered, and then remove it to
stay warm with the wings and breasts.

2   Turn the heat under the pot to low and add the onions and a
pinch of salt. Stir constantly for 3 minutes; the onions should
not color. Add the peppers and garlic, and stir for 3 minutes.
Add the tomatoes and stir. Add the bouquet garni, cover, and
cook for 10 minutes over low heat, stirring every 3 minutes.

3   Add the white wine, cover, and simmer for 10 minutes. Put
the chicken back in the pot, cover again, and cook 5 minutes
more. Taste for salt and pepper. Remove the bouquet garni.

4   Serve the chicken coated with sauce.

2 tablespoons olive oil

One 3-pound (1.5 kg.) chicken,
cut into 8 pieces

Salt

Pepper

2 medium onions, peeled and
minced

2 green bell peppers, peeled,
seeded (page 130), and
sliced into thin strips

2 red bell peppers, peeled,
seeded (page 130), and
sliced into thin strips

3 cloves garlic, peeled,
degermed (page 122), and
minced

1½ pounds (750 g.) tomatoes,
peeled, seeded (page 124),
and sliced into thin strips

1 bouquet garni (2 sprigs fresh
thyme, 1 bay leaf, and
4 stems flat-leaf parsley,
wrapped and tied in a
green leek leaf)

1 cup (20 cl.) dry white wine

CHICKEN WITH *VIN JAUNE* AND MORELS

Poulet au vin jaune et aux morilles

SERVES 4
PREPARATION 15 minutes
COOKING 35 minutes

The grapes used to make *vin jaune* (or yellow wine) in the mountainous Jura region of France are harvested late—at the beginning of November—to ensure that they are completely mature. Aged in oak barrels for at least 6 years, this dry wine typically tastes of nuts and prunes. If you cannot find *vin jaune,* you can replace it here with a Chardonnay; you can also replace the morels with chanterelles or even white button mushrooms. You might also try making this dish without the mushrooms and serving it with a basmati rice pilaf simmered in chicken broth (page 654).

¾ pound (400 g.) morel mushrooms (or chanterelles or white button mushrooms), stem ends trimmed, caps rinsed clean, and drained
1 free-range chicken, about 3½ pounds (1.8 kg.), cut into 8 serving pieces
Salt
Pepper
1 tablespoon peanut oil
1 teaspoon butter
1 cup (20 cl.) *vin jaune d'Arbois* or Chardonnay
1⅔ cups (40 cl.) crème fraîche
2 egg yolks (page 204)
1 tablespoon chervil leaves

1   Cook the mushrooms following the recipe on page 602 (or page 599 or page 608), but cook them for only half the time indicated. They will finish cooking with the chicken.

2   Season each piece of chicken with a good-sized pinch of salt and a dash of pepper. Heat the oil in a Dutch oven, then add the butter. When it foams, brown the chicken pieces about 10 minutes over very low heat, turning them regularly.

3   Discard as much of the grease in the pot as possible, leaving behind the brown juices and bits. Add the wine to the pot, boil for 3 minutes (to remove some of its acidity), and then add 1¼ cups (30 cl.) crème fraîche. Cover and cook over low heat for 10 minutes.

4   Remove the wings and breasts, which cook faster than the legs. Put them aside and keep them hot, perhaps in a 250°F/120°C oven with the door ajar. Add the mushrooms to the pot, replace its lid, and cook 15 minutes more. Remove the mushrooms and the chicken remaining in the pot and put them with the breasts and wings.

5   Mix the yolks with the rest of the crème fraîche. To thicken the cooking juices, whisk this mixture into the pot over low heat. Taste for salt and pepper and turn off the heat.

6   Arrange the chicken and mushrooms on a hot serving plate, coat them with sauce, and sprinkle with chervil.

CHICKEN WITH MUSHROOMS AND TARRAGON

Poulet aux champignons et à l'estragon

SERVES   4

PREPARATION   15 minutes

COOKING   35 minutes

1   Put the mushrooms in a saucepan with 3 tablespoons water and 1 scant tablespoon butter. Cover, bring to a boil, and boil for 3 minutes. Remove the mushrooms and save their cooking liquid.

2   Season each piece of chicken with a good pinch of salt and a dash of pepper. In a Dutch oven just large enough to hold the chicken pieces in a single layer, heat 1 tablespoon olive oil and then 1 tablespoon butter. When the butter foams, turn the heat to low and add the pieces of chicken, nestled against each other. Cook over medium heat for 5 minutes to brown, turning to color evenly. Add the wine, bouquet garni, garlic, and shallots. Scatter the diced tomatoes and sprinkle 1 tablespoon tarragon. Add the mushroom cooking juice and bring the liquid to a "shiver" just below the boiling point. Cover and simmer for 30 minutes.

3   At the end of cooking, add the mushrooms to the pot just long enough to warm them. Sprinkle the chicken with the rest of the tarragon and taste for salt and pepper.

¾ pound (350 g.) small white button mushrooms, stem ends trimmed, caps rinsed clean, and drained; quarter them if they are on the large side

2 tablespoons butter

1 free-range chicken, about 3½ pounds (1.8 kg.), cut into 8 pieces

Salt

Pepper

1 tablespoon olive oil

⅓ cup (8 cl.) dry white wine

1 bouquet garni (2 sprigs fresh thyme, 1 bay leaf, and 4 stems parsley, wrapped and tied in a green leek leaf if possible)

2 cloves garlic, peeled, degermed (page 122), and minced

5 shallots, peeled and minced

4 medium tomatoes, peeled, seeded, and diced (page 124)

2 tablespoons minced tarragon

CHICKEN WITH CREAM SAUCE

Poulet à la crème

SERVES   4
PREPARATION   15 minutes
COOKING   35 minutes

1   Melt 1 tablespoon butter in a skillet over medium heat. When it foams, add the mushrooms and stir well to coat with melted butter. Cook for about 3 minutes, stirring for even cooking. Add the garlic, onion, bouquet garni, and wine. Turn the heat to low and cook for 3 minutes. Turn off the heat and put the skillet aside.

2   Season each piece of chicken with 2 pinches of salt and a dash of pepper. Melt the remaining tablespoon butter in a Dutch oven. When it foams, add the chicken pieces, skin side down, and brown over medium heat about 5 minutes, flipping during cooking so that each side turns golden.

3   Add the contents of the skillet to the large pot. Add 3¾ cups crème fraîche or cream and reduce the heat under the pot to low. Cook for 20 minutes uncovered. Remove the pot from the heat, spoon fat from the pot, and discard, leaving behind the brown cooking juices. Put the pot back over low heat and cook for 10 minutes.

4   Remove the chicken pieces with a skimmer or slotted spoon and put them on a hot platter. Keep them warm, perhaps in a 250°F/120°C oven with the door ajar.

5   Spoon fat from the pot again. Put the cooking juices through a fine strainer into a saucepan or bowl and stir in the remaining crème fraîche or cream.

6   Coat the chicken with cream sauce and serve any extra sauce on the side.

2 tablespoons butter

10 white button mushrooms, stem ends trimmed, caps rinsed clean, drained, and quartered

2 cloves garlic, crushed under your palm but not peeled

1 medium onion, peeled and quartered

1 bouquet garni (2 sprigs fresh thyme, 1 bay leaf, and 4 stems flat-leaf parsley, wrapped and tied in a green leek leaf if possible)

1 cup (20 cl.) dry white wine

1 free-range chicken, about 3½ pounds (1.8 kg.), cut into 8 pieces

Salt

Pepper

1 quart (1 l.) crème fraîche or heavy cream

STEAMED POULTRY BREAST

Blanc de volaille à la vapeur

SERVES 1

COOKING 10 minutes

1   Bring 1 quart (1 l.) water to a boil with the bouillon cube and herbs in a covered saucepan fitted with a steamer basket. Remove the breast from the refrigerator.
2   Season both sides of the breast with salt and pepper. When the water boils, lower the heat a bit. Put the breast in the steamer basket, set it in the saucepan, and cover. Cook for 5 minutes, then turn the breast, preferably with tongs or, if not, with a spatula, taking care not to let the steam burn you. Cover and cook 5 minutes more.
3   Remove the breast to a plate and season with fleur de sel and pepper.

1 chicken bouillon cube
2 sprigs thyme
1 sprig rosemary
5 or 6 bay leaves
1 boneless, skinless 6-ounce (180–190-g.) poultry breast (such as chicken or turkey)
Salt
Pepper
Fleur de sel

PAN FRIED POULTRY BREAST

Blanc de volaille poêlé

SERVES 1

COOKING 10 minutes

1   Remove the breast from the refrigerator 10 minutes in advance.
2   Season the meat with salt and pepper on both sides. Heat the oil in a sauté pan. Add the butter and turn the heat to low. When the butter foams, lay the breast in the pan with what was the skin side facing down. Cover the pan and cook for 5 minutes. Turn the meat with plastic tongs or a wooden spatula, then cover and cook 5 minutes more. Remove to a plate and season with fleur de sel and pepper.

1 boneless, skinless 6-ounce (180–190-g.) poultry breast (such as chicken or turkey)
Salt
Pepper
½ teaspoon neutral oil
½ teaspoon butter
Fleur de sel

FLATTENED GRILLED CHICKEN

Poulet à la crapaudine

SERVES 4
PREPARATION 5 minutes
COOKING 1 hour 10 minutes

Flavor this as you see fit: mustard, *herbes de Provence*, saffron, peppers, and curry are all good choices. If you like, marinate the chicken for 2 hours before cooking with one of these additions, a peeled garlic clove, and 3 tablespoons of oil.

One 3-pound (1.5-kg.) chicken, backbone removed (ask the butcher to do this)
Salt
Pepper
Neutral oil
Fleur de sel
Optional flavoring: garlic, mustard, *herbes de Provence*, saffron, hot peppers, curry, etc.

1 Remove the chicken from the refrigerator 20 minutes in advance. Using a sharp knife, on each side of the breast/belly side of the chicken make a small lengthwise slit into which you will slip the ends of its legs.

2 Lay the chicken on its breast and slice the wishbone in half. Break it in order to open the chicken. Pull the neck skin onto the interior side of the chicken to keep it from burning. Flatten the chicken. Season inside and out with salt and pepper. Brush it all over with oil.

3 Heat the grill over high heat. When it is ready, lay the chicken on the grill diagonally skin side down and cook for 2 minutes, still over high heat. Give it a quarter turn and cook 2 minutes more, still with the skin side down.

4 Reduce the heat to low and remove the chicken to a large plate. Season with salt and pepper and wrap it completely in a large piece of aluminum foil, sealing the edges. Remember which side is the skin side and which is the interior. With the skin side down, put it back on the grill, which should still be over low heat. Cook for 30 minutes. Flip the packet carefully and cook 30 minutes more.

5 Cautiously remove the aluminum foil and remove the chicken to a carving board. To avoid tearing, slice through the skin and flesh at the edge of each piece before separating it from the rest of the chicken. Cut the chicken in half, remove the legs, and separate the thighs from the drumsticks. Carve the breast on the bias toward the wing. Remove the wings, taking a quarter of the breast with each wing.

CHICKEN WITH LEMONS

Poulet aux citrons

SERVES 4
PREPARATION 40 minutes
COOKING 40 minutes

1   Spread the onion slices in a baking dish large enough to hold the chicken and drizzle with 3 tablespoons olive oil. Season with salt and pepper.

2   Season the chicken pieces all over with salt and pepper and lay them in the baking dish. Scatter the lemon slices over the chicken and sprinkle with marjoram. Drizzle with the rest of the oil and refrigerate for 30 minutes.

3   Preheat the oven to 410°F/210°C.

4   Remove the dish from the refrigerator. Put the chicken pieces in a Dutch oven and put the baking dish in the hot oven. Brown the chicken over rather high heat for 5 minutes, turning the pieces with a wooden spoon or with tongs. Remove the dish from the oven and lay the chicken on top of the onions and lemons. Bake for 15 minutes, then turn the chicken and baste it with cooking juices. Cook 20 minutes more. Serve in the baking dish.

3 medium onions, peeled and thinly sliced
⅓ cup (10 cl.) olive oil
Salt
Pepper
1 chicken, about 3½ pounds (1.8 kg.), free-range if possible, quartered
2 organic lemons, washed and thinly sliced
1 tablespoon minced fresh sweet marjoram

ROAST FATTED HEN

Poularde rôtie

SERVES   6
PREPARATION   5 minutes
COOKING   1 hour and 40 minutes
RESTING   20 minutes

1 Remove the poultry and butter from the refrigerator 40 minutes in advance.

2 Grease the roasting dish with ½ tablespoon softened butter. Season the chicken generously and evenly with salt and pepper, inside and out, and then truss (page 453). Spread softened butter all over the chicken's skin, using a pastry brush if you like. (Butter will give the roast a nice flavor, but if you don't want to use it, you can instead use neutral oil in the dish and on the skin.)

3 Place the bird in the dish on its side, thigh and wing down. Scatter the chopped giblets all around it, place the crushed garlic in the pan, and put it in the oven.

4 Turn the oven to 250°F/120°C and cook for 30 minutes. Then turn the chicken onto its other side and cook 30 minutes more. (Turn the chicken with tongs or by sticking a large fork into the joint between the thigh and the drumstick—without piercing the flesh itself—and using the fork and a large spoon to move the bird.) Spoon cooking juices over the chicken.

5 Raise the oven temperature to 400°F/200°C. Turn the chicken onto its back, baste, and cook for 20 minutes, basting once halfway. Turn the chicken onto its breast, baste, and cook 20 minutes more, basting once halfway.

6 Remove the chicken to a platter. Prick the thigh joint to make sure it is cooked; the juices should run clear with no trace of blood. If necessary, put the chicken back in the oven on its back for 10 or 15 minutes more.

7 Let the roast rest for 20 minutes, breast down and with the tail end propped up so that the chicken is almost vertical. Tent loosely with aluminum foil.

1 fatted hen or a small capon, about 5–6 pounds (2.4–3 kg.), with giblets (chopped)
1½ tablespoons butter or neutral oil
Salt
Pepper
2 cloves garlic, crushed under your palm but not peeled

ROAST CAPON

Chapon rôti

SERVES 6–8
PREPARATION 5 minutes
COOKING 2 hours
RESTING 30 minutes

A capon (or castrated rooster) leads a less active life than other chickens. It grows more slowly and therefore keeps more of its fat. The ancient Romans raised capons for this reason. The meat is much finer and less dry than a turkey's. A capon, especially if it weighs more than 8 pounds (4 kg.), will roast better if it is poached before it goes in the oven. Just lower it into simmering water and cook for 10 minutes.

1 capon, 7–8 pounds (3.5–4 kg.), with chopped giblets
2 tablespoons butter or neutral oil
Salt
Pepper
2 cloves garlic, crushed under your palm but not peeled

1 Remove the capon and butter from the refrigerator 40 minutes in advance.

2 Grease the roasting dish with ½ tablespoon softened butter. Season the capon generously and evenly with salt and pepper, inside and out, and then truss it (page 453). Spread softened butter all over its skin, preferably using a pastry brush. (Butter will give the roast a nice flavor, but if you don't want to use it, you can instead use neutral oil in the dish and on the skin.)

3 Place the bird in the dish on its side, thigh and wing down. Scatter the chopped giblets all around it, place the crushed garlic in the pan, and put it in the oven.

4 Turn the oven to 250°F/120°C and cook for 20 minutes. Then turn the capon onto its other side, spoon cooking juices over it, raise the heat to 400°F/200°C, and cook 20 minutes more. (Turn the chicken with tongs or by sliding a large fork into the joint between the thigh and the drumstick—without piercing the flesh itself—and using the fork and a large spoon to move the bird.) Spoon cooking juices over the capon every 10 minutes from now until it comes out of the oven.

5 Turn the capon again, onto the first thigh and wing, and cook for 20 minutes. Turn again, onto the second thigh and wing, and cook 20 minutes more.

6 Turn the capon onto its breast, baste, and cook for 20 minutes. Turn it onto its back, baste, and cook 20 minutes more.

7   Remove the capon to a platter. Prick the thigh joint to make sure it is cooked; the juices should run clear with no trace of blood. If necessary, put the bird back in the oven on its back for 10 or 15 minutes more.

8   Let the roast rest for 30 minutes, breast down and with the tail end propped up so that the capon is almost vertical. Tent loosely with aluminum foil.

Guinea Fowl

ROAST GUINEA FOWL

Pintade rôtie

variation
ROAST GUINEA FOWL AND
POTATOES

SERVES 4
PREPARATION   5 minutes
COOKING   1 hour
RESTING   20 minutes

1   Remove the bird and the butter from the refrigerator 20 minutes in advance.

2   Butter the roasting dish generously. Season the guinea fowl generously with salt and pepper, inside and out, distributing the seasoning evenly over the skin. Place the guinea fowl in the baking dish on its side, thigh and wing down. If you are using the giblets, scatter them around (but not under) the bird. Put the dish in the oven, turn it to 410°F/210°C, and cook for 20 minutes.

3   Remove the dish from the oven and turn the guinea fowl onto its other side, the other thigh and wing down. (Turn with tongs or by slipping a large fork into the joint between the thigh and the drumstick—without piercing the flesh itself—and using the fork and a large spoon to move the bird. The bird should always rest right on the roasting dish, not on the giblets.) Pour 4 tablespoons water over the bird and return to the oven for 20 minutes.

4   Remove the roasting dish and put the bird on its back, also rotating it a quarter turn. Cook for 20 minutes.

1 guinea fowl, about 3 pounds (1.5 kg.), with chopped giblets
6 tablespoons (90 g.) butter
Salt
Pepper
Fleur de sel

5   Take the dish out of the oven and remove the guinea fowl to a dish. Prick the thigh joint to make sure it is cooked: The juices should run clear with no trace of blood. Season with fleur de sel and pepper.

6   Let the roast rest for 30 minutes, breast down and with the tail end propped up so that the bird is almost vertical. Tent loosely with aluminum foil.

7   For carving instructions, see below.

ROAST GUINEA FOWL AND POTATOES

Pintade rôtie aux pommes de terre confites

SERVES   4

Just before roasting the guinea fowl, wash and peel the potatoes, quarter them lengthwise, and sprinkle with a pinch of salt. Scatter them in the buttered roasting dish, all around the guinea fowl, along with the thyme, rosemary, and garlic. Add ⅓ cup water and follow the instructions for roasting as page 467.

1 recipe roast guinea fowl, as page 467, using a slightly smaller bird, 2½ pounds (1.2–1.4 kg.)
4 large potatoes, about 4 ounces (120 g.) each
Salt
5 sprigs fresh thyme
4 sprigs fresh rosemary
4 cloves garlic, crushed under your palm but not peeled

HOW TO CARVE A GUINEA FOWL

If available, an electric knife or large kitchen shears should be used to carve a guinea fowl. Snip the trussing off with scissors. Always slice neatly through the skin and flesh around each piece before removing it from the rest of the bird, or the skin and flesh might tear. Remove the legs. Separate the thighs from the drumsticks. Carve the breast on the bias toward the wing. Remove the wings, taking some of the breast with each wing.

GUINEA FOWL WITH CABBAGE _____
Pintade au chou

SERVES   4
PREPARATION   10 minutes
COOKING   50 minutes

1   Remove the guinea fowl from the refrigerator. Preheat the oven to 350°F/180°C.
2   Heat 1 tablespoon goose or duck fat in a Dutch oven. Add the lardons, onions, carrot, and garlic and cook for 5 minutes over low heat, stirring. Add the cabbage, bay leaf, and thyme and cook gently for 3 minutes, stirring.
3   Season the skin of the guinea fowl with salt and pepper. Heat 1 teaspoon goose or duck fat in a skillet. Lay the guinea fowl in the skillet, skin side down, and brown for 3 minutes; then flip and cook the other side for 3 minutes, turning so that the entire surface of each piece gets some color.
4   Lay the poultry pieces on top of the vegetables in the pot. Add the broth, cover, and bake in the oven for 35 minutes.

1 guinea fowl, 3½ pounds (1.8 kg.), quartered (ask the butcher to do this)
1 tablespoon plus 1 teaspoon goose or duck fat
⅓ cup (50 g.) lardons (page 89)
12 new onions, peeled and trimmed of all but 1½ inches (4 cm.) of stem
1 carrot, peeled and sliced into rounds ⅛ inch (3 mm.) thick
2 cloves garlic, crushed under your palm but not peeled
Leaves of ½ Savoy cabbage, blanched (page 556)
1 bay leaf
1 sprig fresh thyme
Salt
Pepper
1 cup (20 cl.) chicken broth (page 77 or made from a bouillon cube)

GUINEA FOWL IN THE POT

Pintade en cocotte

SERVES 4
PREPARATION 5 minutes
COOKING 45 minutes
RESTING 15 minutes

One 3-pound (1.5 kg.) guinea fowl, with its chopped-up giblets
Salt
Pepper
1½ tablespoons neutral oil
2 teaspoons butter
Fleur de sel

1   Remove the guinea fowl from the refrigerator 20 minutes in advance.

2   Season the guinea fowl inside and out with salt and pepper, spreading it as evenly as you can. Put the giblets and oil in a Dutch oven and turn the heat to medium. Stir right away and then add the butter. Lay the guinea fowl in the pot on its side, propped up by the giblets, wing and thigh down. Cook, uncovered, for 15 minutes over low heat. Turn the bird onto its other side, the other wing and thigh down, and cook for 15 minutes. Turn the bird onto its breast and cook 15 minutes more.

3   Remove the guinea fowl to a platter. The breast should still be pinkish inside. To finish cooking the legs, cut them from the body and put them back in the pot over low heat. Cook for 5–7 minutes on each side while the breast rests.

4   While the legs finish cooking, season the rest of the bird with fleur de sel and pepper. Allow it to rest for 15 minutes, breast down, propped up so that it is almost vertical and tented loosely with aluminum foil.

5   For carving instructions, see page 468.

Duck

In the poultry Olympics, duck deserves the gold medal. Among the many French varieties worth mentioning are Nantais duck (from the western port of Nantes, which was once the capital of the duchy of Brittany), which is a little fatty but very fine-fleshed; the Muscovy, called "Barbary duck" in southern France, which is plump and musky-tasting; the Mulard duck from the southwest (known as Moulard in the United States), whose liver and breast are prized; and Normandy's Rouennais duck, with its fine, tender flesh, which is usually killed by smothering, a method of slaughter that leaves the meat very red and somewhat gamy. In the United States you will find for eating mostly Pekin (not to be confused with Peking, which is a way of cooking duck, not a type of duck), Muscovy (the largest of the three), and Moulard (usually a cross between a Pekin and a Muscovy).

CHOOSING THE DUCK

The younger the duck, the more tender its flesh. The duck (technically the female) is usually plumper and tastier than the drake (the male). The wings and skin should both be supple, and you should make sure the breast is nice and meaty. Cook and eat duck as soon as possible after buying it.

REMOVING THE GLANDS

A good butcher will remove from the base of the duck's back the two grease glands that allow the animal to keep its plumage smooth and glossy. If they have not been removed (as is often the case), they will taste bitter. To remove them, place the bird on its breast, legs toward you. With a small knife make a 1-inch (2–3 cm.) incision in the center of the duck, just on top of its rump. Slice gently to the left to extract one gland, which should be about the size of a bean. Turn the duck so that its wings are toward you and make an incision on the other side of the rump to remove the second gland.

Once the glands are removed, you can season the cavity with a mix of spices, which you can grind yourself in a coffee grinder: perhaps ½ cup (125 g.) salt, 1 teaspoon ground ginger, 1 teaspoon ground mace, 1 teaspoon ground coriander seeds, 1 teaspoon cinnamon, 1 teaspoon four-spice powder (a blend of nutmeg, cinnamon, clove, and ginger), and 1 teaspoon pepper. Use what you need to season the duck and then store the spice blend in a sealed box or bottle.

ROAST DUCK

Canette rôtie

variation

ROAST DUCK WITH
SPICED HONEY

SERVES   4

PREPARATION   5 minutes

COOKING   1 hour for rare plus 10 minutes for the legs;
1 hour and 10 minutes for medium rare, plus
10 minutes for the legs

RESTING   15 minutes

Ask the butcher to remove the oil glands and provide you with chopped giblets.

1   Remove the duck from the refrigerator 20 minutes in advance. Remove any bits of feather with tweezers. If the butcher did not, remove the oil glands (page 471), which can adversely affect the taste of the entire bird.

2   Season the vegetables with salt and pepper and shower them with thyme leaves as you strip them from the stem.

3   Season the duck with salt and pepper inside and out, spreading it evenly. Brush with oil.

4   Lightly butter a baking dish. Place the duck on its side (on 1 thigh and 1 wing); prop it up with the giblets, which you should scatter all around. Add the vegetables to the roasting dish, too.

5   Put the dish in the oven with the duck's neck toward the back wall. Turn the heat to 460°F/240°C and cook for 30 minutes.

1 young female duck,
    3½ pounds (1.8 kg.),
    with giblets

4 carrots, peeled

2 medium onions, peeled

Salt

Pepper

1 sprig thyme

Neutral oil

Butter

Fleur de sel

6   Remove the dish from the oven and spoon as much fat as possible out of it. Leave the brown cooking juices, which should be below the fat, in the dish. Turn the duck onto its other side so that it is resting on the other thigh and wing. Put the dish back in the oven for 20 minutes.

7   Remove the dish from the oven and spoon away the fat again. Turn the duck onto its back and rotate it a quarter turn. Cook for 10 minutes if you prefer a rare finish, 20 minutes for medium rare.

8   Remove the dish from the oven but do not turn off the oven. If you plan to eat the vegetables, remove them to a colander to drain. Do not remove the giblets. Spoon fat from the dish again. Remove the duck to a dish or carving board and, using poultry shears if possible, remove the legs from the body. Put the legs back in the roasting dish and put the dish in the oven for 10 minutes; the legs take longer to cook than the rest of the duck.

9   While the legs finish cooking, season the resting part of the duck with fleur de sel and pepper. Allow it to rest for 15 minutes breast down, propped up so that it is almost vertical and tented loosely with aluminum foil.

10 Remove the legs from the oven and season with fleur de sel and pepper. If necessary, spoon any excess fat from the sauce and add ½ cup water to serve as sauce.

ROAST DUCK WITH SPICED HONEY
Canette rôtie au miel épicé

SERVES 4
PREPARATION 20 minutes
COOKING (RARE) 1 hour plus 10 minutes to finish the legs
RESTING 15 minutes
The raisins must be soaked at least 1 hour in advance.

1 At least 1 hour in advance, soak the raisins in a bowl of warm water.

2 Begin to cook the duck according to the previous recipe. Remove it from the oven after 50 minutes. In the meantime, heat the honey in a saucepan over medium heat. When it begins to bubble, add the juniper berries, coriander seeds, coffee beans, peppercorns, cardamom seeds, star anise, and crushed cinnamon stick. Stir with a wooden spoon, turn off the heat and cover.

3 Drain the raisins. Heat 1 teaspoon butter in a skillet over low heat. Add the apple pieces to the skillet in an uncrowded single layer and cook for 10 minutes, turning them regularly with a wooden spoon. Add the remaining butter, confectioners' sugar, cinnamon, a pinch of salt, and a dash of pepper. Sprinkle with the raisins and walnuts. Add 1 tablespoon cider vinegar and simmer for 2 minutes. Turn off the heat.

4 When the duck has been roasting for 50 minutes, remove it but do not turn off the oven. Remove the legs as described in the recipe above. Coat the breast with the spiced honey and put everything back in the oven for 6–8 minutes, drizzling the duck with the spiced honey every 2 minutes. Cook the legs 10 extra minutes.

5 Let the duck rest as described page 473. In the meantime, spoon fat from the juices in the roasting dish. Add 2 teaspoons cider vinegar and the chicken broth or water. Stir and scrape with a spatula. Pour the juices and giblets into a saucepan, thoroughly scraping the bottom to get the best of the cooked juices. Put the saucepan on the stovetop and bring to a boil. Simmer for 2–3 minutes over low heat. Taste for salt and pepper and stir in the remaining teaspoon cider vinegar. Cook no longer than 30 seconds more before putting the sauce through a fine strainer.

6 Arrange the apples, raisins, and nuts all around the roast duck and serve the sauce on the side.

¼ pound (100 g.) golden raisins
1 recipe roast duck as page 472
5 ounces (150 g.) acacia honey
½ tablespoon juniper berries
½ tablespoon coriander seeds
½ tablespoon coffee beans
½ tablespoon black peppercorns
½ tablespoon cardamom seeds (crush the pods to remove the seeds)
1 star anise
1 cinnamon stick, crushed
3 teaspoons butter
2 Golden Delicious apples, peeled, cored, and cut into 6 pieces each
1 large pinch of confectioners' sugar
1 pinch of ground cinnamon
Salt
Pepper
20 walnut halves
2 tablespoons cider vinegar
½ cup (10 cl.) chicken broth (page 77) or water

POT-ROASTED DUCK

Canette en cocotte

SERVES   4
PREPARATION   10 minutes
COOKING   50 minutes for rare; 1 hour for medium rare
RESTING   15 minutes

Ask the butcher to remove the oil glands and give you some giblets.

1   Remove the duck from the refrigerator 20 minutes in advance. Remove any bits of feather with tweezers. If the butcher did not, remove the oil glands (page 471), which can adversely affect the taste of the entire bird.

2   Season the carrots and onions with salt and pepper, and shower them with thyme leaves as you strip them from the stem.

3   Season the duck with salt and pepper inside and out, spreading it evenly.

4   Put the giblets in a Dutch oven with 2 tablespoons oil. Heat for 1 minute over medium heat. Add the butter. Lay the duck in the pot on its side, wing and thigh down, propping it up with the giblets. Brown for 10 minutes, turn onto the other thigh and wing, and brown 10 minutes on the second side. Turn the duck onto its breast and brown 10 minutes more.

5   Once the duck has browned, tuck the vegetables in around it. Add 4 tablespoons water and cover the pot. Simmer over low heat for 20 minutes. Turn the duck onto its side, replace the lid, and cook for 20 minutes, still over low heat. Turn the duck onto its other side, replace the lid, and simmer for 20 minutes.

6   Remove the duck to a deep platter and season with fleur de sel and pepper. Allow it to rest for 20 minutes, breast down and propped up so that it is almost vertical.

1 young female duck
    3½ pounds (1.8 kg.), with giblets
4 carrots, peeled
2 medium onions, peeled
Salt
Pepper
1 sprig thyme
2 tablespoons neutral oil
1 teaspoon butter
Fleur de sel

PAN-GRILLED DUCK BREAST _____

Magret de canard grillé

SERVES   2
PREPARATION   5 minutes
COOKING   15 minutes
RESTING   5 minutes

1   Remove the duck from the refrigerator 10 minutes in advance. Put it on a cutting board, skin side up. With a sharp knife, score the skin diagonally with incisions spaced 2 inches (5 cm.) apart. Then score on the other diagonal so that the breast is marked with a crosshatch pattern of cuts. Season both sides with salt and pepper, sprinkling the skin side more generously. Prepare a rack (or small overturned plate) over a large plate.

2   Fold a piece of aluminum foil the size of the grill pan so that its sides are 1 inch (2.5 cm.) high; or, better yet, put a disposable aluminum pie pan onto the grill pan. Heat the grill over high heat for 5 minutes. Lay the duck breast on the aluminum foil or pie plate, skin side down. Lower the heat to medium low and cook for 10 minutes. Flip the breast with tongs or with a spatula and a hand. Cook the second side for 5 minutes.

3   Remove the duck to the rack or small plate. Season with salt and pepper and allow it to rest for 5 minutes, skin side up.

4   Carve the *magret* on the bias into even slices, following the marks you made before cooking. Season each slice with fleur de sel and pepper.

1 boneless duck breast (also called a *magret*), preferably from a Moulard duck, about ¾ pound (350–400 g.)
Salt
Pepper
Fleur de sel

PAN FRIED DUCK BREAST

Magret de canard poêlé

SERVES   2
PREPARATION   5 minutes
COOKING   14 minutes
RESTING   5 minutes

1   Remove the duck from the refrigerator 10 minutes in advance. Put it on a cutting board, skin side up. With a sharp knife, score the skin diagonally with incisions spaced 2 inches (5 cm.) apart. Then score on the other diagonal so that the breast is marked with a crosshatch pattern of cuts. Sprinkle both sides with salt and pepper, seasoning the skin side more generously. Prepare a rack (or small overturned plate) over a large plate.

2   Heat the oil in a skillet over high heat. Lay the duck in the skillet, skin side down, in a movement away from you so as to avoid splattering oil. Lower the heat to medium and cook for 7 minutes. Flip the duck with plastic tongs or a spatula and your hand. Cook the second side for 7 minutes, frequently twirling the pan and lifting the duck a little bit with your tongs or spatula.

3   If you like, you can add the vinegar to the skillet at this point, stirring it into the duck's cooking juices.

4   Remove the duck to the rack or small overturned plate, skin side up. Season with salt and pepper and allow it to rest for 5 minutes.

5   Carve the breast on the bias into even slices, following the marks you made before cooking. Season each slice with fleur de sel and pepper.

1 boneless duck breast (also called a *magret*), preferably from a Moulard duck, about ¾ pound (350–400 g.)

Salt

Pepper

1 teaspoon neutral oil

1 tablespoon raspberry vinegar (optional)

Fleur de sel

DUCK BREAST IN A SALT CRUST

Magrets de canard en croûte de sel

SERVES   2
PREPARATION   5 minutes
COOKING   16 minutes
RESTING   10 minutes

Do not prepare the duck for cooking too far in advance, or it might become too salty.

1   Mix the coarse salt with the flour and egg whites in a bowl. Preheat the oven to 460°F/240°C.

2   Heat a skillet over high heat. When it is quite hot, lay the duck in the pan, skin side down, and sear for 30 seconds, still over high heat. Turn the duck and sear the other side for 30 seconds. Season both sides with pepper. Remove the duck to a plate, skin side up, and allow it to cool.

3   Lay a bed of the coarse salt mixture in a baking dish. Set the duck on top of the salt, skin side down, and then cover it completely with the remaining salt mixture. Bake for 15 minutes.

4   Let the duck rest for 10 minutes when it comes out of the oven. Then shatter the salt crust, remove the duck, and serve.

6 pounds (3 kg.) coarse gray salt
2 tablespoons flour
2 egg whites (page 204)
2 boneless duck breasts (also called *magrets*), preferably from a Moulard duck, ¾ pound (350–400 g.) each
Pepper

ROASTED DUCK BREAST

Magret de canard au four

SERVES   2
PREPARATION   5 minutes
COOKING   20 minutes
RESTING   5 minutes

1   To avoid sullying your oven, cover a large sheet pan with aluminum foil and pinch the foil up into little walls. Place a large baking dish (at least 11 inches/28 cm.) in the middle of the sheet pan and put both on a rack in the middle of the oven to catch the drippings.

1 boneless duck breast (also called a *magret*), preferably from a Moulard duck, about ¾ pound (350–400 g.)
Salt
Pepper
Neutral oil
Fleur de sel

2   Remove another rack from the oven and set it over a platter. Preheat the oven to 475°F/250°C. Remove the duck from the refrigerator and place it skin side up in the middle of the rack, in the same position as the dish in the oven in relation to the rack it rests on. With a sharp knife, score the skin on the bias with a crosshatch pattern of lines about 2 inches (5 cm.) apart from one another. Sprinkle both sides with salt and pepper, seasoning the skin side more heavily. Brush the flesh (but not the skin) with oil and put the breast back on the rack, skin side up.

3   When the oven is preheated, slip the rack holding the duck into the oven, into the slot just above the rack holding the covered sheet pan and dish. Make sure the duck is right over the baking dish, which is meant to collect the duck's fat as it cooks.

4   Cook for 5 minutes. Pull the lower rack a third of the way out and then pull the duck's rack out so that the duck is over the dish of fat. Turn the breast with tongs. Slide the racks back into position and cook for 5 minutes with the skin side down. Then repeat the turning process so that the skin is facing up.

5   Turn on the broiler and broil the skin for 5 minutes.

6   Turn off the oven. Remove the rack holding the duck and place it over the serving platter. Season on both sides with fleur de sel and pepper and allow to rest for 5 minutes. The skin should still be facing up.

7   Remove the sheet pan and dish from the oven. When they have cooled a bit, carefully pull the aluminum foil into a ball and throw it away. If any fat has gotten onto the sheet pan, pour a little hot water on it; this will make it easier to clean. While the oven is still warm, use a damp sponge to wipe away any spatterings of duck fat, especially on the door.

8   Carve the breast on the bias into even slices, following the marks you made before cooking. Season each slice with fleur de sel and pepper.

Goose

GOOSE WITH CHESTNUT STUFFING

Oie farcie aux marrons

SERVES 8–10
PREPARATION 15 minutes
COOKING 2 hours and 40 minutes

Ask the butcher to grind the pork blade shoulder, neck, chicken livers, and goose liver coarsely.

1 Remove the goose from the refrigerator 40 minutes in advance. Put the bread to soak in a bowl with the milk.

2 Put all the ground meat and livers in a large bowl and mix well. Season with 2 pinches of salt and 1 pinch of pepper. Squeeze as much milk as possible out of the bread and add the bread to the bowl along with the shallots, four-spice powder, and eggs. Mix very well. Incorporate the chestnuts and mix until evenly combined.

3 Season the goose's interior cavity with salt and pepper. Stuff it with the chestnut-meat mixture and then sew it shut with kitchen twine and a trussing needle. Season the outside with salt and pepper and place the goose in a roasting dish, on its side, thigh down.

4 Scatter the onions, carrot, tomato, and giblets all around the goose. Put the dish in the oven and turn the heat to 350°F/180°C. Baste the goose with cooking juices every 10 minutes. Cook on the first side for 40 minutes and then turn it and cook on the other side for 40 minutes. Turn it back to the first side and cook for 30 minutes, then turn again and cook for 30 minutes. Lay the goose on its back and cook for 10 minutes, and then turn it breast side down and cook for 10 minutes.

5 Remove the vegetables with a slotted spoon to serve on the side. Put the cooking juices through a fine strainer into a sauceboat.

1 goose, 8 pounds (4 kg.), with its giblets (chopped or left whole)

6 slices good-quality white sandwich bread, crusts removed

2 cups (50 cl.) milk

½ pound (200 g.) coarsely ground pork blade shoulder

½ pound (200 g.) coarsely ground pork neck

4 chicken livers, ground

1 goose liver, ground

Salt

Pepper

3 shallots, peeled and minced

½ teaspoon four-spice powder (a powdered blend of nutmeg, cinnamon, clove, and ginger)

2 eggs

1½ pounds (750 g.) chestnuts, peeled and ready to cook

2 onions, peeled and cut into ¼-inch (0.5-cm.) dice

1 carrot, peeled and cut into ¼-inch (0.5-cm.) dice

1 tomato, peeled, seeded, and diced (page 124)

GOOSE LEG WITH POTATOES

Cuisse d'oie aux pommes de terre

SERVES 2–3
PREPARATION 15 minutes
COOKING 2¼ hours
The goose must be seasoned the night before.

Ask the butcher to separate the drumstick from the thigh and to cut the thigh in half.

1   The night before, put the 3 pieces of goose into a dish. Rub them with coarse salt, about half of the rosemary, and pepper. Cover with plastic wrap and refrigerate for at least 12 hours.

2   The next day remove the goose from the refrigerator 30 minutes in advance. Use a pastry brush to brush away all traces of salt and rosemary from the meat, then gently wipe the meat clean with a paper towel. Preheat the oven to 250°F/120°C.

3   Heat a Dutch oven over medium heat. When it is hot, add the pieces of goose to the pot, skin side down, and brown for 2 minutes. Then turn the pieces over and brown the remaining surfaces of the goose for 3 minutes. Lower the heat, add the leeks, and cook gently for 2–3 minutes, stirring. The leeks should not color.

4   Add the wine and scrape up any brown bits stuck to the bottom of the pan. Bring the wine to a simmer and then add 1 quart (1 l.) water to the pot. Cover the pot and bake it in the oven for 1¼ hours, turning the goose pieces after 40 minutes.

5   In the meantime, peel the potatoes and slice them into rounds ½ inch (1 cm.) thick. Rinse and dry. Add the potatoes, garlic, and remaining rosemary leaves to the pot after it has been in the oven for 1¼ hours. Season lightly with pepper, cover, and cook 1 hour more.

6   Bring the pot to the table and serve.

1 goose leg, 1¼ pounds (600 g.)
1½ tablespoons (25 g.) coarse salt
2 small sprigs rosemary
Pepper
2 medium leeks, trimmed, carefully cleaned, and sliced into rounds ½ inch (1 cm.) thick
1 cup (20 cl.) dry white wine
4 fingerling potatoes, Belles de Fontenay if possible
2 cloves garlic

Turkey

The Europeans discovered turkey in America—which is why it is called *dinde* in French (*d'Inde,* from the [West] Indies)—but it never became as common in the Old World as it is in the new. Fatted hen, capon, goose, and game are usually preferred for Christmas and New Year's Eve celebrations, and there is, of course, no Thanksgiving outside of the United States and Canada.

Turkey is less fatty than these other birds and therefore tends to dry out during cooking. For this reason it must be regularly basted with its cooking juices. The addition of butter helps, too. A roast turkey will be much better if it is poached (covered with simmering water for 10 minutes) before being put in the oven. Stuffing also improves turkey by moistening the breast during cooking. You can use the simple chestnut stuffing proposed for the goose (see page 480). See also the Truffled Stuffing for Christmas (page 358), and the recipe for Roast Holiday Fowl with Truffled Chestnut Stuffing (page 485).

ROAST TURKEY

Dinde rôtie

SERVES 8–10

PREPARATION 10 minutes

COOKING 2 hours and 10 minutes for the roast plus about 20 minutes for the gravy

1 free-range turkey, 8–10 pounds (4–5 kg.), with its giblets and with its neck chopped in half

4 tablespoons (70 g.) butter

1 onion, peeled and halved

1 carrot, peeled

1 bouquet garni (2 sprigs fresh thyme, ½ bay leaf, 6 stems parsley, and 2 sprigs chervil, wrapped and tied in a leek leaf if possible)

1   Remove the turkey and the butter from the refrigerator 1 hour in advance.

2   Put the onion, carrot, bouquet garni, clove, 2 pieces of neck, wing tips, and giblets into a large Dutch oven (large enough to hold the turkey, too). Put the turkey in the pot and pour in the broth. Cover with aluminum foil, put the lid on the pot, and cook over very low heat for 30–35 minutes.

3   Remove the turkey from the pot of broth and put it on a deep platter. With a skimmer or slotted spoon, remove the vegeta-

bles and giblets to the platter, too. Pour most of the broth into a small saucepan, leaving just a little in the large pot.

4   Brush the turkey with softened butter. Season inside and out with salt and pepper. To keep them from burning, wrap the ends of the drumsticks with aluminum foil. Put the turkey back into the large pot on its side (wing and thigh down), along with the vegetables and giblets. If you have any butter left over, put it into the pot, too. Pour any juices that collected under the turkey into the saucepan of broth.

5   Put the turkey in the oven. Set the oven temperature to 400°F/200°C (the oven should not be preheated) and cook for 1 hour and 40 minutes: 40 minutes on the first side, 40 minutes on the second side, 10 minutes on its back, and finally 10 minutes on its breast. Baste the turkey with its cooking juices at least once every 30 minutes.

6   When the turkey has been in the oven for 1 hour and 15 minutes, begin to prepare the sauce. Bring the small saucepan of broth to a boil and simmer for 20–25 minutes, until the turkey comes out of the oven.

7   When the turkey is cooked, remove it to a platter. Season the skin all over with salt and pepper. Put the vegetables on the serving platter but discard the clove and bouquet garni. You can eat the giblets if you like or save them to make broth.

8   Spoon as much fat out of the turkey pot as possible. Keep the brown cooking juices. Pour the broth from the small saucepan into the large pot and boil for 10 minutes. Put this sauce through a fine strainer and serve it on top of the carved turkey or on the side in a sauceboat.

1 whole clove
1 quart (1 l.) chicken broth (page 77 or made from a bouillon cube) or other poultry broth
Salt
Pepper

ROAST TURKEY BREAST WITH ENDIVES

Blanc de dinde rôti aux endives

SERVES 4

PREPARATION 5 minutes

COOKING 12 minutes plus 30 minutes for the endives

1 Take the turkey out of the refrigerator.

2 Bring 1 quart (1 l.) water to a boil in a saucepan with the coarse salt. Cook the endives at a rapid boil for 30 minutes and then drain them in a colander.

3 Season the turkey breast with salt and pepper. Heat the olive oil in a Dutch oven over medium heat. Add the turkey breast and cook for 1 minute. Turn with a spatula or tongs—do not prick with a fork—and cook for 1 minute on the other side. Tuck the endives in around the turkey and sprinkle the parsley over all. Cover the pot and cook for 5 minutes over low heat. The breast should be just pinkish inside. It may need more time, depending on its thickness, but be careful not to overcook the meat into toughness. Serve in the pot.

1 boneless turkey breast,
  1½ pounds (750 g.)
½ teaspoon coarse salt
8 endives, washed and cored
Salt
Pepper
1 tablespoon olive oil
1 tablespoon minced flat-leaf
  parsley

ROAST HOLIDAY FOWL
WITH TRUFFLED CHESTNUT STUFFING _____

Dinde ou chapon de Noël, farcie à la truffe et au confit de marrons

SERVES   6–8
PREPARATION   45 minutes
COOKING   2 hours 40 minutes

1   Take the bird out of the refrigerator 50 minutes in advance.

2   Heat 1 tablespoon butter in a Dutch oven over low heat. Add the chestnuts and cook for 5 minutes, stirring with a spatula. Add the bouquet garni and chicken broth. The chestnuts should be covered; if they are not, add just enough water to cover them. Cover and bring to a boil, then simmer gently for 25 minutes.

3   Chop the turkey or capon's liver. Heat the oil in a skillet over medium heat. Add 1 teaspoon butter, and when it foams, sauté the liver of the fowl to be roasted for 3 minutes, stirring with a wooden spoon. Season generously with salt and pepper. Add the duck foie gras and just sear it, about 30 seconds. Swirl the pan and season again with salt and pepper. Turn off the heat and remove the liver to a large bowl. Add half of the chestnuts and all the diced truffle, and mix. Set aside the remaining chestnuts.

4   Stuff the fowl. If you have any stuffing left over, set it aside with the remaining chestnuts. Put the fowl in a large roasting dish so that it lies on one side, on its thigh and wing. Scatter its neck and giblets around it. Season the fowl generously all over with salt and pepper, and brush it with the remaining butter.

5   Put the bird in the oven and set the temperature at 350°F/180°C. Cook for 2 hours and 10 minutes, basting with cooking juices every 10 minutes and turning as follows: 30 minutes on the first side, 30 minutes on the second side, 20 minutes on the first side again, 20 minutes on the second side again, 20 minutes on the back, and 10 minutes on the breast.

6   When the fowl has been in the oven for 1½ hours, add the remaining chestnuts to the roasting pan along with any remaining stuffing, the bouquet garni that simmered with the chestnuts, the walnuts, and a generous ladle of broth. Cook 30 minutes more.

1 free-range turkey or capon, 8–10 pounds (4–5 kg.), with giblets and neck cut in 3 pieces

2 tablespoons butter

1 pound (500 g.) chestnuts, peeled and ready to cook

1 bouquet garni (1 sprig fresh thyme, 3 stems parsley, and 1 sprig chervil, tied together)

1 quart (1 l.) chicken broth (page 77 or made from a bouillon cube) or other poultry broth

1 teaspoon neutral oil

Salt

Pepper

2 ounces (100 g.) raw duck foie gras, cut into small pieces

1 ounce (20–30 g.) black truffle, cut into small dice

20 walnut halves

Quail

In Europe most quail is raised on farms; in the United States you will find both farm-raised quail and wild. The wild variety has much tastier meat. Wild quail is less fatty, however, so cook it in a covered pot instead of exposing it to the high, harsh heat of an oven roasting. Unlike larger fowl, quail should be cooked rather briefly at medium heat. For this reason the oven should be preheated when roasting quail.

ROAST QUAIL
Caille rôtie

SERVES   1
PREPARATION   5 minutes
COOKING   20 minutes
RESTING   5 minutes

If you choose this recipe rather than the next one, bear in mind that roast quail is always a little drier than quail cooked in a covered pot.

1 quail, 6 ounces (190–200 g.), with its giblets
Salt
Pepper
1 teaspoon butter, softened
1 sprig fresh thyme, leaves only
1 clove garlic, unpeeled and crushed under your palm
Fleur de sel

1   Remove the quail from the refrigerator 20 minutes in advance. Preheat the oven to 460°F/240°C.
2   Season the quail inside and out with salt and pepper, making sure that you spread the seasoning evenly over its skin. Brush the skin generously with softened butter and sprinkle the thyme leaves over the bird. Season the giblets lightly with salt and pepper. Butter the baking dish and lay the quail in it so that it rests on its side, on its thigh and wing. Add the giblets and garlic. Bake for 5 minutes. Turn the quail onto its other side and cook for 5 minutes. Turn the quail onto its breast, rotate it a quarter turn, and cook for 5 minutes. Turn the quail onto its back and cook for 5 minutes.
3   Remove the quail to a dish and season with fleur de sel and pepper. Allow it to rest for 5 minutes, breast down, propped up on the side of the dish so that it is almost vertical. If the bird was trussed, snip off its trussing and serve.

QUAIL IN A COVERED POT

Caille en cocotte

SERVES   1
PREPARATION   5 minutes
COOKING   15 minutes
RESTING   5 minutes

1   Remove the quail from the refrigerator 10 minutes in advance.

2   Preheat the oven to 350°F/180°C. Season the quail inside and out with salt and pepper, making sure to coat the skin as evenly as possible. Sprinkle the thyme leaves over the quail.

3   Pour the oil into a small Dutch oven and heat over high heat. Add the butter; when it foams, lay the quail in the pot on its side, wing and thigh down. Put the garlic in the pot and lower the heat to medium. Cook for 5 minutes, turning the quail several times so that it gets evenly colored and basting it frequently with cooking juices.

4   Add 1 tablespoon water to the pot. Cover and place in the oven. Bake for 10 minutes. (If you do not have an ovenproof pot with a lid, you can finish cooking the quail on top of the stove, covered, over medium heat for 10 minutes.)

5   Remove the quail from the pot to a plate. Season with fleur de sel and pepper. Allow it to rest for 5 minutes, breast down, propped up on the edge of the plate so that it is almost vertical.

1 quail, 6 ounces (190–200 g.)
Salt
Pepper
1 sprig fresh thyme, leaves only
1 teaspoon neutral oil
1 teaspoon butter
1 clove garlic, unpeeled and crushed under your palm
Fleur de sel

Squab

ROAST SQUAB
Pigeon rôti

SERVES 1
PREPARATION 5 minutes
COOKING 25 minutes
RESTING 5 minutes

Roast squab is always a little drier than squab cooked in a covered pot (page 491).

1 squab, ½ pound (250 g.), gutted and trussed, with its giblets
Salt
Pepper
1 teaspoon butter
1 sprig fresh thyme, leaves only
1 clove garlic, unpeeled and crushed under your palm
Fleur de sel
Slices of bread for frying (optional)

1   Remove the squab from the refrigerator 15 minutes in advance. Preheat the oven to 460°F/240°C.
2   Season the squab inside and out with salt and pepper, making sure you coat the skin as evenly as possible. Brush the skin with some of the butter and sprinkle with thyme leaves. Season the giblets with salt and pepper.
3   Grease the bottom of a roasting dish with the rest of the butter. Lay the squab in the dish on its side, so that it is resting on its thigh and wing, and scatter the giblets all around it. Put the garlic in the dish. Bake for 5 minutes, then turn the squab to its other side and cook for 5 minutes. Rotate the squab a quarter turn and flip it onto its breast for 5 minutes. Turn it onto its back and cook for 10 minutes.
4   Remove the squab to a deep dish and season with fleur de sel and pepper. Allow the squab to rest for 5 minutes, breast down, propped up on the edge of the dish so that it is almost vertical. Snip off the trussing.
5   If you like, spread the liver on slices of bread pan fried in butter and serve beside the squab.

YOUNG SQUAB ROASTED WITH POTATOES

Pigeonneaux rôtis aux pommes de terre

SERVES   4
PREPARATION   20 minutes
COOKING   25 minutes

1   Remove the squab from the refrigerator 10 minutes in advance. Preheat the oven to 350°F/180°C.

2   Melt 1 tablespoon butter in a skillet. When it foams, add the lardons, garlic, potatoes, and thyme, and season with 1 scant teaspoon salt and 1 generous pinch of pepper. Stir so that the potatoes get coated well with fat. Cook for 5 minutes over low heat without allowing them to color. Turn off the heat.

3   Season the squab all over with salt and pepper. Melt 2 tablespoons butter in a Dutch oven. When it foams, lay the squabs in the pot and brown on all sides over medium heat, about 5 minutes, turning them with tongs or a wooden spoon. Scatter the potatoes and lardons around the birds and pour in the broth. Cover and cook in the oven for 20 minutes. Remove from the oven and snip off the trussing.

4 small squabs, about 1 pound (500 g.) total, gutted and trussed but not wrapped in bacon

3 tablespoons butter

1⅓ cups (200 g.) smoked lardons (page 89)

2 cloves garlic, crushed under your palm but not peeled

¾ pound (400 g.) waxy yellow potatoes, preferably BF 15 or charlottes, peeled, sliced into ⅛-inch (3-mm.) rounds, rinsed, and dried completely

4 sprigs thyme

Salt

Pepper

2 cups (45 cl.) chicken broth (page 77 or from a bouillon cube)

ROAST SQUAB WITH LINDEN BLOSSOMS

Pigeon rôti aux feuilles de tilleul

SERVES 4

PREPARATION AND COOKING 25–30 minutes

1. Preheat the oven to 410°F/210°C. Season the squab inside and out with salt and pepper.

2. Melt 1 tablespoon butter in a Dutch oven. Brown the squabs in the butter over low heat, turning them every 5 minutes so that they are evenly colored. Add the garlic and thyme and bake in the oven, uncovered, for 10 minutes, frequently spooning cooking juices over the squabs.

3. In another Dutch oven, melt 1 tablespoon butter. When it foams, turn the heat to low and add the linden leaves, stirring with a wooden spoon to coat them with the hot butter.

4. When the squabs have been baking for 10 minutes, remove the pot from the oven but leave the oven on. Remove the squabs from the pot and nestle them in the pot of linden leaves. Cover and bake for 5 minutes.

5. Put the first Dutch oven with its juices over high heat. Add ½ cup (10 cl.) water and the Cognac. Scrape at the bottom of the pot with a spatula. Bring to a boil over high heat and let this pot bubble away, scraping and stirring frequently, until the liquid has been reduced by half.

6. Serve the squabs in the pot of linden leaves with the reduced juices on the side.

4 small squabs, about 1 pound (500 g.) total, gutted and trussed

Salt

Pepper

3 tablespoons butter

4 cloves garlic, unpeeled and crushed under your palm

2 sprigs thyme

8 small handfuls linden leaves, also called *tilleul* or lime blossom

1 teaspoon Cognac

SQUAB IN THE POT

Pigeon en cocotte

SERVES   1
PREPARATION   5 minutes
COOKING   20 minutes
RESTING   5 minutes

1   Remove the squab from the refrigerator 15 minutes in advance.
2   Preheat the oven to 350°F/180°C. Season the pigeon inside and out with salt and pepper, being careful to coat the skin as evenly as you can. Sprinkle with thyme leaves. Season the giblets with salt and pepper.
3   Put the oil in a Dutch oven and heat it over high heat. Add the butter. When it foams, lay the squab in the pot on its side, wing and thigh down. Scatter the giblets and garlic around it and lower the heat to medium. Brown for 10 minutes, stirring the giblets and turning the squab several times. It should cook at least 2 minutes per side, then 2 minutes on its back and 2 minutes on its belly. Baste the squab with cooking juices throughout.
4   Add 1 tablespoon water to the pot, cover it, and put it in the oven. Cook for 10 minutes. (If your pot is not ovenproof—if it has plastic handles or a plastic knob—you can finish cooking the squab on the cooktop, covered, for 10 minutes over medium heat.)
5   Remove the squab from the pot to a deep plate. Season with fleur de sel and pepper. Allow it to rest for 5 minutes, breast down, propped up on the side of the plate so that it is almost vertical. Snip off its trussing.
6   If you like, fry a piece of bread in butter while the squab rests and then spread it with the liver.

1 squab, ½ pound (250 g.), gutted and trussed but with its giblets and liver
Salt
Pepper
1 sprig fresh thyme, leaves only
1 teaspoon neutral oil
1 teaspoon butter
1 clove garlic, peeled and crushed under your palm
Fleur de sel
Slice of bread to serve with the liver (optional)

Foie Gras and Confit _____

Make sure you start with a fresh liver, which should have a smooth appearance and a subtle, pleasant odor. You can tell whether a raw foie gras is truly top quality by pulling apart its two lobes: If they crack apart immediately, the liver is too fat and will melt when it is cooked. If their connection is too elastic, the liver will be too dry and insufficiently fragrant. The ideal is a liver that stretches a bit and then makes a clean break. Choose a liver that is ecru-colored, tending toward ivory. Do not take the ones that are gray, dingy, mottled with green (on account of excess bile), or brownish red (because of blood).

Autumn is the season to buy foie gras. In November it is cheaper than it will be just before the holidays and celebrations.

GOOSE OR DUCK? _____

Raw, an entire duck foie gras should weigh ¾–1¼ pounds (400–700 g.). A goose's weighs 1¼–1½ pounds (700–750 g.). A whole liver packed into a terrine (page 155) is best made with goose foie gras, which is very delicate. Duck liver, on the

SEASONING BLEND FOR LIVER

Check to see whether the liver has any greenish or red traces. If it does, scrape them away with a small, sharp knife.

Put 2 teaspoons (10 g.) salt and ½ teaspoon (2–3 g.) freshly ground pepper in a bowl. Stir them with a pastry brush before lightly applying the mixture with the brush to both sides of the slice of foie gras or the entire liver to be cooked. You might have some salt and pepper left in the bowl: These measurements are enough for about 1½ pounds (750 g.) of foie gras. You can add ground spices—such as nutmeg or four-spice powder (a blend of powdered nutmeg, cinnamon, ginger, and clove that you can easily mix yourself)—to the salt and pepper; ⅓ teaspoon or even ¼ teaspoon on a whole liver will be sufficient.

other hand, which tastes less subtle and slightly more bitter, is best eaten hot. Foie gras can be eaten baked, steamed, pot-roasted, or pan fried. Here are a few different methods and several sauces that you can modify to suit your own tastes by varying the spices and fruits.

COOK CAREFULLY

For pan frying, liver is cut into "scallops"—thickish slices, about 2 ounces (70 g.) per person. Do not put any fat in the skillet or pot before you begin; the liver will cook in its own fat.

Liver cooks very quickly. As it cooks, it begins to give up its fat right away. If overcooked, it can even melt away completely. The finished piece should be golden blond on the outside and rosy at the center. Serve immediately, piping hot, perhaps with a spiced sauce and some quickly sautéed fruit enlivened by a dash of vinegar. (Hot foie gras calls for a little acidity; if you do decide to serve it with sautéed fruit, prepare this garnish in advance, for the foie gras will not hold while you make it.)

Below you will find some suggestions for sauces (page 496), but you can experiment with other fruits and spices, depending on what you like and what is available.

The fat in the cooking vessel is good for cooking potatoes and mushrooms, among other things. Pour it into a bowl and cover it with plastic wrap. When it solidifies, wrap it tightly in plastic wrap and put it in the refrigerator or freezer.

A fine accompaniment to hot foie gras is a rustic dish such as potatoes or lentils, perhaps warm, in vinaigrette.

STEAMED FOIE GRAS SLICE

Foie gras à la vapeur

SERVES   1
PREPARATION   5 minutes
COOKING   5–7 minutes

1   Put 1 quart (1 l.) water on to boil in a saucepan fitted with a steamer basket. Prepare a dish lined with paper towels.

2   Lightly apply your seasoning blend to both sides of the slice of foie gras. You will have a good deal left over. (It is difficult to prepare a smaller quantity with the correct proportions.)

3   Wrap the seasoned slice completely in plastic wrap. When the water is bubbling vigorously, place the wrapped slice of foie gras in the steamer basket. If you are cooking more than one at a time, they should be in a single layer, not overlapping. Cover and cook for 5–7 minutes. Check to see whether the foie gras is cooked by poking it gently with a finger. If it is lightly firm, it is perfectly cooked. If it is completely firm, it is overcooked.

4   Remove the packet to the paper towel–lined plate and snip off both ends with scissors. Remove the livers. Serve with fleur de sel and freshly ground pepper.

1 recipe seasoning blend for foie gras (page 492)
1 slice raw foie gras, about 2 ounces (70 g.)
Fleur de sel
Pepper

PAN FRIED FOIE GRAS SLICES

Foie gras en tranches, poêlé

SERVES   4
PREPARATION   5 minutes
COOKING   5 minutes

1   Prepare a plate lined with paper towels. Using a brush, lightly apply the seasoning blend to both sides of each slice of foie gras. You will have a good deal left over. (It is difficult to prepare a smaller quantity with the correct proportions.)

2   Heat the skillet for at least 1 minute over medium heat; do not add any fat. When the skillet is quite hot, brown the slices for 15 seconds on each side, turning them with a

1 recipe seasoning blend for foie gras (see page 492)
4 slices foie gras, about 2 ounces (70 g.) each
Fleur de sel
Pepper

wooden spatula. When they are seared, lower the heat and cook gently 2 minutes per side for a rosy center. Remove them to the paper towel–lined plate. Keep the fat and juices in the skillet for a sauce. Serve the foie gras slices with one of the fruit sauces below, fleur de sel, and freshly ground pepper.

HOT FOIE GRAS IN THE POT

Foie gras chaud en cocotte

SERVES   4
PREPARATION   5 minutes
COOKING   20–25 minutes

1 recipe seasoning blend for
    foie gras (see page 492)
1 pound (500 g.) foie gras

1   Using a brush, lightly apply the seasoning blend to the surface of the foie gras, paying special attention to the folded parts. You should use about two-thirds of the seasoning blend. Preheat the oven to 240°F/120°C.

2   Heat a Dutch oven over medium heat. Lay the liver in the hot pot, bulging side up. Sear for 5 minutes, allowing the liver to caramelize. Turn it over, cover the pot, and cook for 5 minutes. Turn the liver again and baste it with its cooking juices. Cook 10 to 15 minutes more, depending on how cooked you would like it to be, basting every 3 or 4 minutes.

3   Remove the foie gras from the pot to a baking dish. Keep it in the preheated oven with the door ajar while you finish the sauce. Keep the cooking juices and fat in the pot to make one of the sauces on page 496.

PORT-PEAR-GRAPE SAUCE FOR HOT FOIE GRAS

Sauce au porto, à la poire, et au raisin

For a hot foie gras serving 4, as page 495
PREPARATION   15 minutes
Sauce preparation should begin 40 minutes in advance.

1   Before you cook the foie gras, pour the port into a saucepan. Bring it to a boil and simmer for 40 minutes.

2   After the liver has been cooked, spoon out the layer of yellow liquid fat from the pot's surface, leaving behind the brown juices at the bottom. Instead of discarding the fat, you can save it for another use or even freeze it as described on page 493.

3   Put the pot or skillet with the brown cooking juices over low heat. Add the reduced port and the pears and season with salt and pepper. Cook gently for 3 minutes, turning them for even coloring. Add the grapes and sprinkle the pot with the sugar. Stir over very low heat for 1 minute. The pears and grapes will caramelize very quickly. Turn off the heat and serve the fruit with the foie gras.

1⅔ cups (40 cl.) red port
2 pears, quartered and seeded but not peeled
Salt
Pepper
10 green grapes
10 purple grapes
2 pinches of superfine sugar

SAUTERNES AND GRAPE SAUCE FOR HOT FOIE GRAS

Sauce au sauternes et au raisin

For a hot foie gras serving 4, as page 495
PREPARATION AND COOKING   20 minutes
Sauce preparation should begin 1 hour in advance.

1   Before you cook the foie gras, pour the Sauternes into a saucepan. Cover partially so that the vapor is able to escape. Bring the wine to a simmer and simmer very gently for 1 hour.

2   After the liver has been cooked, spoon out the layer of yellow liquid fat from the pot's surface, leaving behind the brown juices at the bottom. You can save the fat for another use or even freeze it as described on page 493.

3   Put the pot or skillet over low heat. At this point there should be about ½ cup reduced wine left in the simmering sauce-

½ bottle Sauternes (or Semillon sweet wine)
½ cup (15 cl.) port
¼ teaspoon superfine sugar
Juice of 2 lemons
3 tablespoons chicken broth (page 77 or made from a bouillon cube)
2 green grapes, chasselas if possible
1 pinch of crushed black pepper
Salt

pan. Pour it into the pot in which the liver was cooked, add the port, and bring to a boil, scraping the cooked-on juices at the bottom of the pan with a spatula. Add the sugar, lemon juice, and broth, and bring to a very gentle simmer. Add the grapes and crushed pepper and simmer gently for 10 minutes. Taste for salt and pepper and serve with the hot foie gras.

GOOSE OR DUCK CONFIT

Confit d'oie ou de canard

SERVES 4

PREPARATION 10 minutes

COOKING 1½ to 2 hours (duck); 2 to 3 hours (goose)

RESTING 24 hours

The salting must be done the night before.

This recipe from southwest France was developed in order to preserve meat for long periods. The bird is cooked and then conserved in its own fat. Later the meat is served pan fried or grilled.

1 Line a deep dish with plastic wrap and place the legs in it. Rub them with garlic and then with coarse salt. Rub the thyme sprig between your fingers so that the thyme leaves rain down on the legs; discard the stem. Sprinkle with the cloves and crushed black pepper. Wrap the legs in the plastic wrap and refrigerate for 24 hours.

2 The next day, put the fat to melt in a Dutch oven over the lowest possible heat. Add ½ cup (10 cl.) water so that the fowl will not turn dark brown.

3 Remove the legs from the salt wrap. Discard the cloves and use a pastry brush to wipe away all traces of salt.

4 When the fat is barely shivering—just about to break into a boil—gently add the legs to the pot. Over the lowest possible heat, simmer 1 hour and 40 minutes for duck, 2½ hours for goose. The cooking should be very slow and gentle. You can test whether the legs are cooked by probing them with a skewer: The juices that run out will be completely liquid when the legs are properly cooked.

If using goose: 2 entire goose legs, each about 1¼ pounds (600 g.), and 3 pounds (1.5 kg.) goose fat

If using duck: 2 entire duck legs, each about ½ pound (250 g.), and 2½ pounds (1.2 kg.) duck fat

1 clove garlic, peeled and degermed (see page 122)

2 tablespoons (30 g.) coarse salt

1 sprig fresh thyme

2 whole cloves

1 teaspoon crushed black pepper

Lard

special equipment: 1 earthenware vessel with a glazed interior and a lid, large enough to hold both legs suspended in fat without their touching its sides

5   Prepare a rack over a plate. With a skimmer or slotted spoon, remove the legs to the rack.

6   If you wish to preserve the confit, you can do the following: While the legs rest, clarify the cooking fat. Prepare a fine strainer over a bowl. Ladle the surface fat through the strainer, not taking any of the brown juices below.

7   Ladle 1 inch (2 cm.) of the strained fat into a large earthenware vessel with a glazed interior. Put the vessel in the refrigerator. Do not discard the rest of the strained fat in the bowl.

8   When the fat in the earthenware vessel has hardened (about 10 minutes), lay the cooked legs on top of it, right in the center. They should not touch the edges. Cover them with about three-fourths of the remaining warm fat, never taking any of the brown cooking juices. The legs should be completely covered. Keep the rest of the fat in a different sealed container in the refrigerator.

9   Cover the vessel and refrigerate for 1 or 2 days. Then gently reheat the extra fat and pour it over the legs in the vessel; this will seal any air bubbles.

10 Put the vessel back in the refrigerator for 1 hour. When the fat is solid, heat enough lard to top off the vessel with a layer ½–1 inch (1 or 2 cm.) thick. The lard helps the confit keep better since it is more dense than goose and duck fat.

11 Put the vessel back in the refrigerator. When the lard has hardened, press a piece of parchment paper onto the top of it and cover the pot. Prepared this way, the legs should keep for 5–6 months in the refrigerator.

12 To pan-fry or grill the confit: Preheat the oven 10 minutes in advance to 400°F/200°C. Brown the legs all over in a hot skillet or grill pan or on a hot barbecue pit. This will take about 5 minutes for a duck and 8 minutes for a goose. Remove them to a baking dish in a single layer—they should not overlap or even be too crowded—and bake in the top third of the oven 5 minutes for duck or 7 minutes for goose.

Rabbit

CHOOSING YOUR RABBIT

Take a young rabbit, if possible, 2½ pounds (1.2 kg.) or less. Young rabbits are more tender and easier to carve.

A good rabbit is compact and clean, with a generously sized saddle, a pale, splotch-free liver, rosy flesh, and very white fat around the loin and kidneys, which should be visible. The skin should gleam and feel satiny under your fingers. In France the best rabbits are from Champagne, Gâtinais, and Poitou. In the United States you can find a good hybrid of species from California and New Zealand.

COOKING SLOWLY BUT SURELY

Because it is "white meat," rabbit is associated with poultry in the French culinary tradition. This grouping can cause confusion, since rabbit is not cooked the same way as chicken. Indeed, a rabbit's flesh is much less fatty, and rabbit is not cooked with its skin on. To prevent it from drying out, one must cook rabbit slowly and gently, usually covered.

Rabbit's flavor profile is not as strong as beef's or lamb's. It must therefore be given a boost, perhaps with shallot, thyme, rosemary, parsley, mustard, garlic, or white wine.

CARVING A COOKED RABBIT

With a large knife, chop the rabbit crosswise into three sections: hind legs, trunk of the body (the saddle), and front legs with breast. Slice the front section in half so that you have two separate legs. Slice the saddle crosswise into two or three equal pieces, depending on how large the rabbit is. Slice the hindquarters in half so that you have two separate legs. If the rabbit is rather large, you might chop each hind leg into two pieces.

If you plan to cook pieces rather than a whole rabbit, it's best to ask the butcher to cut it up for you. But if you do find yourself in a situation where you must carve a raw rabbit yourself, do the following: Remove the head. Remove the liver and refrigerate it in a sealed container. With a small, very sharp knife remove the tatters of skin. Use a larger knife to chop off the ends of the front legs and any bones that are peeking out. Keep all these bits to throw into the pot with the cooking rabbit, for they will make the dish more flavorful. Proceed to carve as you would a whole cooked rabbit.

ROASTED RABBIT WITH MUSTARD
Lapin à la moutarde

SERVES 4
PREPARATION 5 minutes
COOKING 50 minutes

1 Preheat the oven to 410°F/210°C. Oil a baking dish. Brush the rabbit all over with at least 2 tablespoons mustard; brush the interior cavity, too. Lay the rabbit in the dish. Dot with butter, sprinkle with thyme leaves, and season with salt and pepper. Add ½ cup (15 cl.) water to the dish.

2 Bake about 50 minutes, rotating the rabbit and spooning cooking juices over it every 10 minutes. When it is cooked, remove the rabbit to a dish to rest.

3 Pour the crème fraîche into the baking dish with the remaining mustard. Use a spatula to stir these additions into the cooking juices and scrape up anything that has cooked onto the dish. Pour the contents of the dish into a small saucepan and simmer for 2–3 minutes, whisking constantly. Taste for salt and pepper.

4 Carve the rabbit and coat with sauce to serve.

Neutral oil

1 whole rabbit, 2½ pounds (1.2–1.4 kg.)

4 tablespoons strong mustard, preferably Dijon

2 tablespoons butter

1 sprig fresh thyme, leaves only

Salt

Pepper

1 cup (25 cl.) crème fraîche

RABBIT STEW

Civet de lapin

SERVES   4

PREPARATION   15 minutes (for the marinade)

COOKING $2\frac{1}{4}$ hours

The rabbit must be marinated the night before.

1   The night before, stick wooden toothpicks in the rabbit to secure what is left of the skin. Lay the pieces of rabbit in a deep dish or terrine so that they are not overlapping and add the next 9 ingredients; cover everything with the wine. Cover with plastic wrap and refrigerate overnight, turning once, after about 6 hours.

2   The next day, use a skimmer or slotted spoon to remove the rabbit pieces to a colander to drain. Save the marinade.

3   Heat 1 tablespoon neutral oil in a Dutch oven over medium heat. Add the rabbit pieces and brown for 5 minutes, still over medium heat, stirring with a wooden spoon so that they get lightly browned all over. Add a pinch of salt and a pinch of pepper.

4   Use a skimmer or slotted spoon to lift the vegetables, garlic, bay leaf, and thyme from the marinade and put them into the pot. Turn the heat to low and cook for 5 minutes, stirring. Hold a sifter or fine strainer over the pot, dump the flour into it, and sift the flour into the pot. Stir well, cover, and cook for 10 minutes over low heat. Stir, cover again, and cook 10 minutes more.

5   Put the marinade through a fine strainer into the pot of rabbit. Cover and cook over low heat for $1\frac{1}{2}$ hours, stirring every half hour.

6   Turn off the heat. Prepare a fine strainer over a saucepan next to the pot of rabbit. Pour 4 large ladles of cooking broth into the saucepan through the strainer. Bring to a boil and let the broth bubble gently and reduce for 15 minutes. Taste for salt and pepper.

7   With a skimmer or slotted spoon, remove the rabbit to a deep dish. Coat with the reduced cooking juices and serve.

---

1 rabbit, $3\frac{1}{2}$ pounds (1.7 kg.), cut into 8 pieces by the butcher

2 small stalks celery, coarsely chopped into $\frac{1}{2}$-inch (1-cm.) pieces

1 onion, peeled and coarsely chopped into $\frac{1}{2}$-inch (1-cm.) pieces

$\frac{1}{2}$ leek, carefully washed and coarsely chopped into $\frac{1}{2}$-inch (1-cm.) pieces

1 carrot, peeled and coarsely chopped into $\frac{1}{2}$-inch (1-cm.) pieces

2 cloves garlic, peeled and degermed (page 122)

1 sprig thyme

1 small bay leaf

3 juniper berries

1 whole clove

1 bottle Shiraz

1 tablespoon neutral oil

Salt

Pepper

$1\frac{1}{2}$ tablespoons flour

MUSTARDY RABBIT POT

Lapin en cocotte à la moutarde

SERVES 4
PREPARATION 5 minutes
COOKING 1 hour

1   Preheat the oven to 460°F/240°C. Mix the mustard with 1 tablespoon olive oil, 2 pinches of salt, and 1 pinch of pepper. Brush both sides of each piece of rabbit with this mixture.

2   Heat 1 teaspoon olive oil in a Dutch oven. Lay the pieces of rabbit in the pot (they need not be in a single layer) and immediately put the pot in the oven, uncovered. Bake for 10 minutes, stirring after 5 minutes.

3   After 10 minutes, add the broth and thyme to the pot. Cover and cook for 50 minutes, stirring and basting every 10 minutes.

4   Remove the pot from the oven. Remove the rabbit to a dish and discard the thyme. Put the pot over high heat, add the wine, and scrape up the cooked-on juices with a spatula. Turn the heat to medium and cook for at least 15 minutes, stirring regularly. The sauce should become thick and smooth but should not stick to the pot. Stir in the crème fraîche and simmer for 5 minutes. Taste for salt and pepper. If you like, you can also stir in another tablespoon mustard. Serve the rabbit with the sauce.

¼ cup (110 g.) mustard
1 tablespoon plus 1 teaspoon olive oil
Salt
Pepper
1 rabbit, 2½ pounds (1.3 kg.), cut into 8 pieces by the butcher
1 cup (25 cl.) chicken broth (page 77 or made from a bouillon cube)
4 sprigs fresh thyme
½ cup (10 cl.) dry white wine, preferably sauvignon
1 cup (25 cl.) crème fraîche

RABBIT HINDQUARTERS WITH MUSCADET

Derrière de lapin au muscadet

SERVES 4–6

PREPARATION 10 minutes for the marinade

COOKING 55 minutes for the rabbit plus 20 minutes for the sauce

The marinade must be prepared the night before.

1 The night before, lay the rabbit pieces in a deep dish or other container with the 10 ingredients of the marinade. Cover and refrigerate about 12 hours, turning the rabbit pieces 3 times during this period.

2 The next day, remove the rabbit and shallots from the marinade with a slotted spoon and put them in a colander to drain. Do not discard the marinade.

3 Preheat the oven to 325°F/160°C.

4 Melt half of the butter in a Dutch oven over low heat. Add the rabbit pieces, season with salt and pepper, stir, and adjust the heat to medium low. Brown lightly for 5 minutes, turning the pieces for even coloring.

5 Add the shallots and lardons to the pot, cover, and bake in the oven for 50 minutes. Every 15 minutes, spoon the cooking juices over the rabbit.

6 In the meantime, strain the marinade into a saucepan and bring to a boil. Boil gently, with small bubbles, for 20 minutes.

7 When the rabbit is done, remove the rabbit, shallots, and lardons from the pot and pour in the reduced marinade. Raise the heat to high and use a spatula to scrape up the bits cooked onto the bottom of the pot.

8 When the browned bits are scraped up and stirred in, put this sauce through a fine strainer and then return it to the pot. Add the rabbit, shallots, and lardons, turn the heat to low, and stir. Dice the rest of the butter and stir it in bit by bit. Taste for salt and pepper.

9 Carve the rabbit and serve it coated with sauce.

Rear saddles of 2 young rabbits, hind legs still attached (about 1¼ pounds/600 g. each, from a 2½-pound/1.2-kg. whole rabbit)

FOR THE MARINADE

1 carrot, peeled and chopped into ½-inch (1-cm.) pieces

¼ celery stalk

2 cloves garlic, peeled

16 shallots, peeled

½ bottle Muscadet or sauvignon

½ cup (10 cl.) Madeira

1 teaspoon crushed black pepper

1 clove

1 sprig rosemary

1 bouquet garni (3 stems flat-leaf parsley, 1 sprig fresh thyme, and ½ bay leaf, wrapped and tied in a leek leaf if possible)

5 tablespoons (80 g.) butter

Salt

Pepper

1 cup (5 ounces/150 g.) lardons (page 89)

RABBIT SHOULDER WITH PRUNES

Epaules de lapin aux pruneaux

SERVES   4
PREPARATION   10 minutes
COOKING   50 minutes

1   Heat 1 teaspoon oil in a large pot. Cook the shallots over very low heat for 3 minutes, stirring. Remove them to a bowl and set aside.

2   Season the rabbit all over with salt and pepper, then sprinkle it with flour. Spread the flour as evenly as possible, using your hands if necessary.

3   Heat 2 tablespoons oil in the pot over medium heat. When it is hot, brown the rabbit for 5 minutes, moving it around to color evenly. Reduce the heat to low and add the shallots, bouquet garni, and Armagnac. Stir over low heat for 5 minutes, then add the wine. Leave over low heat for 15 minutes, then add the broth. Leave over low heat 20 minutes more, then add the prunes and cook a final 5 minutes, still over low heat.

2 tablespoons plus 1 teaspoon neutral oil

4 shallots, peeled and sliced into rounds ⅛ inch (3 mm.) thick

8 rabbit shoulders (the front legs with a piece of the saddle attached), about ¼ pound (120 g.) each

Salt

Pepper

1½ tablespoons flour

1 bouquet garni (3 stems flat-leaf parsley, 1 sprig fresh thyme, and ½ bay leaf, tied together)

¼ cup (5 cl.) Armagnac

½ cup (15 cl.) dry white wine (such as sauvignon)

1 cup (25 cl.) chicken broth (page 77 or made from a bouillon cube)

10 ounces (300 g.) large, soft, pitted prunes

RABBIT STEWED WITH PEPPERS

Lapin compoté aux poivrons

SERVES 4

PREPARATION 10 minutes

COOKING 1 hour and 40 minutes

RESTING 1 hour

This Provençal rabbit can be served with its liver on the side, fried in butter at the very last minute.

1 Preheat the oven to 350°F/180°C. Season the rabbit with salt and pepper. Heat the olive oil in a Dutch oven. Brown the rabbit for 5 minutes over medium heat, turning the pieces with a wooden spoon for even coloring. Add the onions and lardons, cover, turn the heat to low, and cook for 5 minutes. Add the wine, cover again, and cook for 3 minutes. Add the pepper strips, garlic, rosemary, and 1 cup (20 cl.) water. Season with salt and pepper, cover, and bake for 1½ hours.

2 At the end of cooking, remove the pot from the oven but let it rest, covered, for 1 hour. Just before serving, reheat on the stovetop. Sprinkle with parsley and serve.

1 rabbit, about 3 pounds (1.6 kg.), cut into 8 pieces by the butcher

Salt

Pepper

2 tablespoons olive oil

12 small new onions, peeled

⅔ cup (100 g.) smoked lardons (page 89)

½ cup (15 cl.) white wine (such as sauvignon)

3 red bell peppers, peeled, seeded (page 130), and sliced lengthwise into strips ½ inch (1.5 cm.) thick

4 cloves garlic, unpeeled

1 sprig rosemary

2 tablespoons minced flat-leaf parsley

SAUTÉED RABBIT WITH CHANTERELLES, BABY ONIONS, AND FAVA BEANS

Lapin sauté aux girolles, petits oignons, et fèves

SERVES 4–6

PREPARATION 15 minutes

COOKING 30 minutes for the rabbit plus 20 minutes for the onions, plus 3 minutes for the chanterelles, plus 5 minutes for the fava beans, plus 3 minutes for the liver

All components of this recipe are cooked separately and then combined at the end.

1 Preheat the oven to 210°F/100°C. Sprinkle the rabbit pieces with thyme, salt, and pepper. Brush them generously with the mustard.

2 Heat 1½ tablespoons olive oil in a Dutch oven. Add 1 tablespoon butter. When the butter foams, add the rabbit to the pot. Stir, cover, and cook over low heat for 15 minutes. Turn the rabbit pieces, cover, and cook 15 minutes more over low heat. With a skimmer or slotted spoon, remove the rabbit to a smaller Dutch oven. Season evenly with salt and pepper and cover. Save the pot of cooking juices. Keep the smaller pot of rabbit in the warm oven, covered, while you prepare the rest of the dish.

3 Spoon fat from the top of the pot in which the rabbit cooked and discard. Be careful not to remove any brown cooking juices. Put the pot over high heat, add the broth, and stir and scrape the flavorful bits from the bottom of the pot with a spatula. Bring to a boil, lower the heat, and simmer for 30 minutes.

4 In the meantime, put the onions in a saucepan with the sugar and 1 tablespoon butter. Place over low heat and add a dash of salt and pepper. Cover and cook over very low heat for 20 minutes. Rotate the saucepan every 5 minutes to keep the onions from browning and sticking.

5 Heat ½ tablespoon olive oil in a sauté pan or small Dutch oven over medium heat. Add the mushrooms, sprinkle with salt and pepper, and cook for 3 minutes, stirring with a

1 large or 2 small rabbits, 3½ pounds (1.8 kg.) total, cut into pieces by the butcher, with liver(s)

½ tablespoon fresh thyme leaves

Salt

White pepper

2 tablespoons strong mustard

2 tablespoons olive oil

3 tablespoons plus 1 teaspoon butter

2 cups (45 cl.) chicken broth (page 77 or from a bouillon cube)

6 ounces (200 g.) small white onions, peeled

½ tablespoon confectioners' sugar

½ pound (250 g.) chanterelle mushrooms, stem ends removed, rinsed, drained, and dried with paper towels

1 scant cup (4 ounces/120 g.) smoked lardons (page 89)

½ pound (250 g.) shelled and peeled fava beans (from about 1 pound/500 g. whole pods)

½ tablespoon red wine vinegar

1 tablespoon snipped flat-leaf parsley

1 teaspoon chopped fresh sage or thyme

wooden spoon. Remove the mushrooms to the colander with the onions.

6   When the onions and mushrooms are cooked, cook the fava beans in the mushroom pan. Heat 1 tablespoon butter in the pan. When it foams, add the mushrooms, onions, and lardons. Stir and cook over low heat for 2 minutes, then add the fava beans. Stir, cover, and cook over very low heat while you cook the liver. The onions, mushrooms, and fava beans should cook very slowly into a thick, tender blend.

7   Season the rabbit's liver generously with salt and pepper. Melt 1 teaspoon butter in a small skillet over medium heat. When it foams, add the liver. Cook for 2–3 minutes, rotating it in the skillet and turning it over. It should stay tender and pink inside. Remove the cooked liver to a plate. Turn off the heat, swirl the vinegar into the skillet, and put the liver back in, turning it to coat it in vinegary cooking juices.

8   Put the hot broth through a fine strainer. Take the pot out of the oven, remove the rabbit with a slotted spoon, and arrange it on a deep dish. Surround it with the onions, mushrooms, favas, and lardons. Drizzle the rabbit with strained sauce and sprinkle with parsley. Quarter the liver and serve it on the side, sprinkled with sage or thyme.

SAUTÉED RABBIT WITH MUSHROOMS ⎯⎯⎯⎯⎯⎯⎯⎯⎯⎯⎯⎯

Lapin sauté aux champignons

SERVES 4

PREPARATION 15 minutes

COOKING 40 minutes for the rabbit plus 10 minutes for
the lardons and mushrooms

1   Preheat the oven to 210°F/100°C. Sprinkle the rabbit pieces with thyme, salt, and pepper. Brush them generously with the mustard.

2   Heat 1½ tablespoons olive oil in a Dutch oven. Add the butter. When the butter foams, add the rabbit to the pot. Stir, cover, and cook over low heat for 20 minutes. Turn the rabbit pieces, cover, and cook 20 minutes more over low heat. With a skimmer or slotted spoon, remove the rabbit to a smaller Dutch oven. Season evenly with salt and pepper, and cover. Save the pot of cooking juices. Keep the smaller pot of rabbit in the warm oven, covered, while you prepare the rest of the dish.

3   Spoon fat from the top of the pot in which the rabbit cooked and discard. Be careful not to remove any brown cooking juices. Put the pot over high heat, add the broth, and stir and scrape the flavorful bits from the bottom of the pot with a spatula. Bring to a boil and leave to simmer, uncovered, while you cook the mushrooms.

4   Heat 1 teaspoon olive oil in a skillet over medium heat. Add the lardons and brown for 5 minutes, stirring with a wooden spoon. Add the mushrooms and sauté for 5 minutes, stirring. Drain the lardons and mushrooms in a colander.

5   Put the simmered broth through a fine strainer. Remove the rabbit from the oven and arrange it on a platter. Coat it with sauce, surround it with mushrooms and lardons, sprinkle with parsley, and serve.

1 rabbit, about 2½ pounds (1.2 kg.), cut into pieces by the butcher

1 tablespoon fresh thyme

Salt

Pepper

2 tablespoons mustard

1½ tablespoons plus 1 teaspoon olive oil

1 tablespoon butter

1 cup (25 cl.) chicken broth (page 77 or made from a bouillon cube)

⅔ cup (3 ounces/100 g.) smoked lardons (page 89)

½ pound (250 g.) white button mushrooms, cleaned, stems removed (save them for soup), and quartered

1 tablespoon minced parsley

Game

Furred Game

In France all large game with fur is called venison: deer of every stripe, wild boar, and baby wild boar. Hare, or wild rabbit, is small furred game, which in French is sometimes called "lesser venison."

Hunting is very popular in France. Other than a few small migratory birds that are endangered, hunted game can legally be sold by French butchers and eaten in French restaurants during the locally determined season. Hunted game is far better than farmed game, which is all nonhunters can find in the United States and Canada, where butchers are not allowed to sell the spoils of the hunt. Farmed game, most of which comes from New Zealand, must do for North Americans who are not familiar with a shotgun. Sometimes (from mid-August to February) one can find on the Internet and in some shops wild game imported from Scotland, beginning with grouse—mostly feathered game and hare, but sometimes deer, too.

A SHORT HANGING

If you must keep an animal for a few days before cooking it, it is best to leave it in its skin at the bottom of your refrigerator. Definitely do not keep it in a plastic bag or any other wrapping that will hold in moisture. Game must be kept in a well-ventilated place.

Game meat must be aged a bit to give it a chance to mellow; this aging must be carried out very carefully. Small game—rabbits—can be aged for three days. Large game needs more time but should not be aged longer than eight days, after which point they will taste off. For this reason you must know when your game was killed; often a few days pass between the hunt and the sale, in which case the carcass has already been aged a short and probably sufficient time.

Sometimes it's a good idea to put game to soak in a marinade—a spiced bath of oil and wine that holds raw meat for a limited time before cooking. This soaking tenderizes the flesh and gives it some flavor. Wine and vinegar work against time to keep the meat edible a little bit longer. The marinade can be used later as a cooking medium or as the aromatic base for a sauce. On the other hand, marinating makes meat softer and darker, and therefore a less lovely roast.

It is imperative that marinade be made and kept in a glass or stainless steel container. Do not marinate in a plastic container: The marinade could pick up bad flavors from the plastic, and the plastic might be damaged by the acids.

Wine will not preserve raw wild meat forever. Do not keep meat in a marinade for more than a few days, for it will become acidic and begin to decompose. You will find more precise instructions below.

Despite what many people think, the marinade itself—that is, the aromatized wine—is also good for only a few days. After that it will become acidic and begin to ferment. There are two kinds of marinade, however, and they keep for different durations: raw marinade and cooked marinade.

Raw marinade is a blend of wine, garlic, spices, aromatic vegetables, and so forth. This is the simplest of marinades. The meat is not completely submerged and must be turned a few times over the course of marinating. It must be made the night before you plan to eat but should not be kept for more than thirty-six hours.

A cooked marinade has a few advantages. It can be kept for nine or ten days, and it offers more protection to the meat. It also has a stronger flavor. If you have time to prepare it, it is to be preferred. The ingredients and proportions are the same as those given in these recipes, but the process is different. A cooked marinade must cover the marinating meat completely, so be sure you make enough.

This base recipe can be altered (and is, in the other recipes in this chapter).

MARINADE FOR GAME

Check each recipe to find out whether you should be making this marinade with red wine and red wine vinegar, or white wine and white wine vinegar, and with peanut or olive oil.

FOR A RAW MARINADE Combine all ingredients in a glass or stainless steel container with the meat to be marinated. This marinade is for meat to be cooked the next day. Refrigerate the container for 24 hours (or no longer than 36 hours). Make sure your refrigerator maintains a safe temperature: 37–40°F (3–4°C). The meat need not be completely covered by the wine; turn the meat three or four times while it is marinating so that all parts of it get a good soak.

FOR A COOKED MARINADE The ingredients and proportions are the same except that you must use an extra ½ cup (10 cl.) oil to brown the vegetables and you must make enough to cover the meat completely since the meat will sit in the cooked marinade for up to three days.

1 Bring the wine to a boil in a saucepan. Touch a long kitchen match to its surface to set it aflame. In a Dutch oven, heat ½ cup (10 cl.) oil over medium heat. Add the vegetables and cook over low heat for 3–4 minutes, stirring with a wooden spoon. They should get lightly colored but should not really darken. Add all the other ingredients to the pot including the boiled wine. Turn the heat to high, bring to a boil, and boil quietly (with small bubbles) for 30 minutes. Allow the marinade to cool and then pour it into a glass or stainless steel container with the meat. You might need to top the container with a thin layer of oil, which should protect the contents from oxidation.

2 Refrigerate the meat in the cooked marinade at 37–40°F (3–4°C). Do not leave it for more than three days. If you cannot cook the meat after three days, remove it with a slotted spoon. Do not pierce the meat with a fork, use very clean utensils, and do not touch the raw meat with your hands. Pour all the marinade into a saucepan and boil it for 30 minutes. Add ½ cup (10 cl.) vinegar and allow the marinade to cool, then put the meat back in to soak. You can repeat this one more time, keeping the meat for a total of almost ten days, but it isn't really a good idea: The taste and texture of the meat will be strongly affected.

1 bottle Shiraz or dry white wine (such as sauvignon or Chardonnay)

½ cup (10 cl.) oil (peanut or olive, depending on the recipe)

1 medium carrot, about 3 ounces (100 g.)

1 large onion, about 3 ounces (100 g.)

1 stalk celery

1 leek leaf

3 shallots

2 cloves garlic, peeled and degermed (page 122)

1 cup (25 cl.) wine vinegar (red or white, depending on the recipe)

½ cup (10 cl.) Cognac

5 parsley branches

3 sprigs thyme

½ bay leaf

2 whole cloves

10 juniper berries, crushed

2 teaspoons (12 g.) salt

6 black peppercorns

Chopped-up bones and scraps from the type of animal you plan to cook (optional; for cooked marinade only)

3   If you like, enrich a cooked marinade by adding chopped bones and scraps of meat and fat to the pot before you cook the vegetables. Brown the trimmings in the hot oil for 5 minutes and then add the vegetables. It's best to use the bones and scraps of the type of animal you are cooking, but pork or lamb scraps can work nicely for venison, too.

WILD RABBIT STEW

Civet de lapin de garenne

SERVES   6–8

PREPARATION   50 minutes

COOKING   3 hours

The caul wrapper must be put to soak an hour in advance.

A *civet* is distinguished from a regular stew (*ragoût*) by the inclusion of blood, usually from the animal being stewed. Blood must be very fresh, bought the same day you serve the dish and kept in the refrigerator until the last minute.

Ask the butcher to cut each rabbit into 8 pieces (the hind legs, the forelegs with a piece of the saddle, and the fillets of the saddle, each cut in two) and to give you the bones, livers, lungs, and hearts. Ask him for 1⅓ cups (30 cl.) of blood, too—a rabbit's, if possible, but otherwise pig's blood. Keep it very cold until you use it.

1   One hour in advance, pour 1 quart (1 l.) water into a bowl with the vinegar. Put the pieces of caul in the bowl and soak for 1 hour. In the meantime, prepare all the vegetables.

2   After an hour, carefully rinse the caul pieces, drain them, and put them on a plate lined with 3 pieces of paper towel. Lay 3 pieces of paper towel on top of them, too.

3   Bring the Shiraz to a boil in a large saucepan. Light a long kitchen match and touch it to the surface of the Shiraz to set it aflame, removing some acidity. (Do not light the pot if it is under a low-hanging cabinet or hood; the flames can leap quite high.) Let the fire burn out and allow the wine to cool.

2 tablespoons distilled white vinegar

3 pieces pork caul

2 bottles Shiraz

2 wild rabbits, each cut into 8 pieces as described in the headnote

16 thin slices smoked bacon

32 juniper berries

½ tablespoon fresh thyme leaves

2 tablespoons olive oil

4 tablespoons (70 g.) butter

2 small carrots, peeled and diced

2 shallots, peeled and diced

1 large onion, peeled and diced

Salt

1 leek, white part only, diced

2 large pinches of flour

2 cloves garlic, peeled and degermed (page 122)

1 bouquet garni (6 sprigs fresh thyme, 4 small celery

4   Wrap each piece of rabbit in a slice of bacon, keeping the organs apart. Put 2 juniper berries on each piece and sprinkle with thyme leaves. Wrap each piece in caul fat and secure with a wooden skewer.

5   Heat the olive oil in a large stew pot or Dutch oven over high heat. Add 3 tablespoons butter. When it foams, lay the rabbit bundles in the pot and brown all over, still over high heat. Remove them with a skimmer to a dish to rest. If the pot is not large enough to accommodate all the rabbit at once, you can do this in batches.

6   Add the carcasses to the pot and brown them over high heat. When they have a good color, use a skimmer to remove them to another dish.

7   Preheat the oven to 530°F/275°C. Add the carrots, shallots, and diced large onion to the stew pot. Season lightly with salt and cook over medium heat, stirring with a spatula, for 4–5 minutes, until the vegetables have developed a nice color. Add the leek, lower the heat as much as possible, and cook 3 minutes more, stirring; the leek should not color.

8   Put the rabbit bundles back in the pot, along with any juices that collected under them. Sprinkle with the flour but do not stir. Add the garlic and bouquet garni. Season generously with salt and pepper. Put the uncovered pot into the oven for 3 minutes, just long enough to cook the flour.

9   Remove the pot and lower the heat to 400°F/200°C. Pour the Shiraz into the pot; it should cover the meat. Add the Cognac. Turn the heat to high and stir and scrape the bottom of the pot with a spatula to loosen any flavorful cooked-on bits. Add the carcasses and their juices. Bring to a boil. Cut a piece of parchment paper the size of the pot. Prick it a few times with a fork or a knife. When the liquid begins to bubble, turn off the heat, lay the parchment paper on the surface of the liquid, and cover the pot. Bake it in the oven for 2 hours. Throughout cooking, the liquid should be just shivering—neither bubbling nor standing stock still. Check on it every once in a while and adjust the heat if necessary.

10   In the meantime, cook the small white onions and mushrooms. Over low heat, melt 2 teaspoons butter in a sauté pan or small saucepan. Add the onions and sprinkle them with the sugar and a pinch of salt. Cut a circle of parchment paper the size of the pan and prick it a few times with a fork or a knife. Add enough water to the pan to reach halfway up the

stalks, and 8 parsley stems, wrapped and tied in 2 white leek leaves)

Pepper

1½ tablespoons Cognac

30 small white onions, peeled

1 tablespoon sugar

1 pound (500 g.) small white button mushrooms, stem ends trimmed, rinsed, and drained

1⅓ cups (30 cl.) rabbit's blood (or, if rabbit is not available, pig's blood)

2 tablespoons minced flat-leaf parsley

onions, then lay the paper on top of them. Cook over low heat about 20 minutes, rotating the pot twice for even heating. At the end, the water should be almost completely evaporated and the onions should be tender and lightly golden. Put them in a colander to drain. Rinse the sauté pan with hot water and wipe it out with a paper towel.

11 Melt the remaining teaspoon butter in a skillet. When it foams, add the mushrooms and season with salt and pepper. Cook for 2 minutes over low heat, stirring with a wooden spoon. Put the mushrooms to drain in a separate colander. Rinse the skillet with hot water and wipe it out with a paper towel.

12 When the stew has been cooking for 2 hours, check to see whether it is done: Prick a piece of meat with a trussing needle. If it does not encounter any resistance, the meat is cooked. If it is, remove it to a dish and tent loosely with aluminum foil.

13 Put the sauce remaining in the stew pot through a fine strainer into a saucepan. Discard the vegetables and the bouquet garni. Bring the stewing sauce to a boil and then adjust the heat so that it simmers very gently for 30 minutes. From time to time use a skimmer to remove scum from the surface of the liquid, rinsing the skimmer after each pass through the pot. Remove grease, too, by gently ladling a small amount of cold water onto the surface of the liquid and then spooning away the grease and foam that rise to the top.

14 While the pot simmers, mince or grind the rabbits' liver, lungs, and heart. In a small bowl, combine them with the blood so that you end up with 2 cups (50 cl.) of thick liquid for 1 quart (1 l.) of stew.

15 When the pot has simmered for 30 minutes, degrease it a final time. Pour a ladle of the hot liquid into the bowl of blood, stirring as you pour. Stir 1 or 2 more ladles into the bowl, and then stir the contents of the small bowl into the pot. Reheat as gently as possible, stirring over very low heat about 15 minutes, just long enough to thicken it a bit. Do not allow the liquids to boil or even to begin to simmer: The blood will coagulate, and the stew will fall apart. Taste for salt and season generously with pepper.

16 Put the stewing pot back over low heat and add the meat. Strain the simmered stew sauce into the pot and reheat gently, never allowing it to simmer.

17 Reheat the onions for 3–4 minutes in their sauté pan. Reheat the mushrooms in their skillet for 1 minute.

18 Serve the rabbit stew in a deep dish, surrounded with the mushrooms and onions and sprinkled with parsley.

VENISON STEW

Civet de chevreuil

SERVES 12

PREPARATION 10 minutes for the marinade plus 40 minutes

COOKING 1 hour and 40 minutes

The marinade must be prepared at least 2 hours in advance.

Because deer's blood cannot be preserved long enough to cook, this civet is made with pig's blood.

1 Put all the venison pieces in a large terrine or bowl with the onion, carrot, bouquet garni, garlic, cloves, juniper berries, and grapeseed oil. Leave it to marinate for 2 to 3 hours, giving the meat a stir every now and then.

2 Near the end of the marinating, heat the peanut oil in a Dutch oven large enough to hold the whole stew. Add the butter, and when it foams, cook the lardons about 2 minutes over low heat so that they turn a little golden but do not darken. Remove them with a skimmer or slotted spoon to a plate. Add the mushrooms to the pot. Season with salt and pepper and cook for 5 minutes, stirring, still over low heat. Remove them to the plate of lardons. Do not discard the fat in the pot.

3 Remove the venison from its marinade with a slotted spoon and drain it in a colander set over a dish. Heat the pot you used to cook the lardons and mushrooms over medium heat. Working in batches if necessary, evenly brown the venison pieces; this will take about 5 minutes per batch. When all the meat is browned, put it all in the pot and stir in $1\frac{1}{2}$ teaspoons salt and $\frac{1}{2}$ teaspoon pepper. Sprinkle with the flour and stir for 1–2 minutes over medium heat so that the flour is evenly distributed and cooked.

4 Add the wine and broth to the pot. Add all the marinade, including the vegetables and bouquet garni, along with any

One 4-pound (2-kg.) boneless venison shoulder, cut by the butcher into $\frac{1}{4}$-pound (80-g.) pieces

One 4-pound (2-kg.) boneless venison neck, cut by the butcher into $\frac{1}{4}$-pound (80-g.) pieces

1 medium onion, peeled and sliced into rounds $\frac{1}{2}$ inch (1 cm.) thick

1 carrot, peeled and sliced into rounds $\frac{1}{2}$ inch (1 cm.) thick

1 bouquet garni (2 sprigs fresh thyme, 1 sprig rosemary, 1 bay leaf, and 5 stems flat-leaf parsley, wrapped and tied in a green leek leaf)

4 cloves garlic, peeled and degermed (page 122)

2 whole cloves

1 tablespoon juniper berries

$\frac{1}{2}$ cup grapeseed oil

$\frac{1}{4}$ cup peanut oil

2 tablespoons butter

(continued)

marinade that collected underneath the draining venison. Cover and cook gently about 1 hour; the cooking time will depend on the age of the deer. When a paring knife slips into the meat without meeting resistance, it is done.

5   Use a skimmer or slotted spoon to remove the meat to another pot along with the mushrooms and lardons. Cover and put over very low heat; you just want to keep everything warm.

6   Turn the heat under the large pot of liquid to high. Let it simmer for 25 minutes; at the end it should be reduced by two-thirds for a total of about 2½ cups (60 cl.). Stir in the crème de cassis.

7   Combine the blood and vinegar in a small bowl. Over the lowest heat possible, whisk the blood-vinegar mixture into the reduced stewing liquid. The combination should thicken but must not be allowed to boil. Taste for salt and be generous with the pepper.

8   Spread the mushrooms and lardons on a deep serving dish. Arrange the venison on top. Pass the sauce through a fine strainer and ladle it over the stewed meat.

3 cups (¾ pound/400 g.) lardons (page 89)
2 pounds (1 kg.) small white button mushrooms, stem ends trimmed, rinsed, and drained
Salt
Pepper
1½ tablespoons flour
1 bottle Shiraz
3 cups (70 cl.) chicken broth (page 77 or made from a bouillon cube)
⅓ cup crème de cassis
½ cup (15 cl.) pig's blood
1½ teaspoons red wine vinegar

WILD BOAR STEW

Civet de sanglier

SERVES   4–6
PREPARATION   10 minutes for the marinade
COOKING   2 hours and 40 minutes
The meat should marinate two days in advance.

The unsweetened chocolate in this sauce lends it richness and a hint of bitterness and balances the acidity of the wine and vinegar.

1   Two days in advance, put all the marinade ingredients in a large terrine or bowl with the meat. Cover with plastic wrap, and refrigerate for 2 days.

2   Two days later, remove the bowl from the refrigerator. Lift the meat, vegetables, and aromatics from the marinade with

FOR THE MARINADE
1 medium carrot, peeled and cut into ½-inch (1-cm.) rounds
1 medium onion, peeled and cut into ½-inch (1-cm.) rounds
4 cloves garlic, peeled and cut in half lengthwise

a slotted spoon. Save the marinade liquid for later. Do not discard the vegetables and aromatics.

3   Heat the peanut oil for 1 or 2 minutes in a large skillet over medium heat. When it is quite hot, brown the meat all over, 3–4 minutes, still over medium heat. Season with 2 teaspoons salt and 1 small teaspoon pepper. Remove the browned meat to the stew pot and add the thyme from the marinade.

4   In the same skillet, cook the carrot, onion, and garlic from the marinade for 2–3 minutes over low heat; they should not color. Remove them with a slotted spoon to the pot of meat.

5   Turn the heat under the stew pot to medium. Sprinkle its contents with flour and cook and stir for 1–2 minutes so that the flour gets evenly distributed and cooked.

6   Add the tomato pieces and the reserved marinade, and bring to a boil. When the pot bubbles, use a skimmer to lift foam from its surface, rinsing the skimmer in a bowl of cold water after each pass. Lower the heat so that the pot barely simmers, cover, and cook gently for 2½ hours. Every half hour, skim and stir the pot.

7   At the end of cooking, combine the blood and vinegar in a small bowl. Remove the meat from the stew and put it in another pot. Discard the vegetables and aromatic garnish. Put the stewing juices through a fine strainer into a saucepan and bring to a simmer. Skim the surface and then whisk in the blood-vinegar mixture. Whisk constantly as the sauce thickens and do not allow it to boil. Whisk in the chocolate. Taste. It should be quite peppery. Add salt and pepper if necessary.

8   Pour the thickened sauce into the pot of meat and reheat without allowing a bubble.

5 sprigs thyme
1 teaspoon juniper berries
1 whole clove
2 generous pinches of crushed black pepper
2 bottles Shiraz

FOR THE STEW
1 boneless shoulder of wild boar, about 3 pounds (1.5 kg.), chopped into ¼-pound (80-g.) pieces
2 tablespoons peanut oil
Salt
Pepper
2 tablespoons flour
1 tomato, quartered
1⅓ cups (30 cl.) pig's blood
3 tablespoons wine vinegar or sherry vinegar
2 ounces (60 g.) unsweetened chocolate (chopped or powdered)

ROAST HAUNCH OF YOUNG BOAR

Cuissot de marcassin rôti

SERVES   6–8
PREPARATION   10 minutes for the marinade plus 15 minutes
COOKING   40 minutes
FINISHING   15 minutes
The marinade must be prepared the night before.

1   The night before you plan to cook, put the marinade ingredients in a large bowl with the meat and the bones. Cover and
refrigerate for at least 12 hours, turning the haunch once
after about 6 hours.

2   The next day, preheat the oven to 400°F/200°C. Grease a
large baking dish, earthenware if possible, with 3 tablespoons olive oil. Prepare a fine strainer over a saucepan and
put the contents of the marinating bowl through the strainer.
Put the solids caught in the strainer into the baking dish
along with the carrot, onion, celery, juniper berries, and bouquet garni. Reserve the marinade.

3   Massage each side of the haunch with 2 teaspoons salt and
½ teaspoon pepper. Lay the haunch on the baking dish and
dot it with half of the butter. Bake for 40 minutes, basting
with cooking juices every 10 minutes and turning it over
halfway through. Dice the remaining butter and put it back
in the refrigerator.

4   While the meat is in the oven, bring the marinade to a boil
and then remove foam from the surface with a skimmer,
rinsing the skimmer in a bowl of cold water after each pass
through the hot liquid. Pass the sauce through a fine strainer
again and then simmer for 20–25 minutes. It should reduce
by half. Keep it warm over very low heat.

5   After 40 minutes, turn off the oven and remove the boar
from the oven. Place it on an ovenproof platter. Season all
over with salt and pepper. Put the boar in the oven to stay
warm, leaving the door ajar.

6   Pour the contents of the roasting dish (including the vegetables) into the pot of reduced marinade. Cook over medium
heat for 4–5 minutes, approaching but not reaching a boil.
Turn off the heat and leave the pot to infuse for 5 minutes.
Carefully pass the sauce through a fine strainer into another

FOR THE MARINADE
1 bottle Shiraz
1 leek, white part only,
    carefully washed and cut
    into rounds ½ inch (1 cm.)
    thick
3 sprigs thyme
2 sprigs rosemary
2 cloves garlic, peeled and
    degermed (page 122)
1 bay leaf
4 whole cloves
1 teaspoon pepper
1 teaspoon coriander seeds

FOR THE ROAST
1 boar haunch, 5 pounds
    (2½ kg.), trimmed of fat
    and veins; ask the butcher
    to dress the haunch
1 pound (500 g.) chopped
    bones, from a boar if
    possible (if not, then from a
    pig)
3–4 tablespoons olive oil
½ carrot, peeled and sliced
    into rounds ¼ inch
    (0.5 cm.) thick
½ onion, peeled and sliced into
    rounds ¼ inch (0.5 cm.)
    thick

saucepan. Bring to a boil, turn off the heat, and spoon fat from the surface.

7   Dilute the cornstarch with ⅓ cup water in a small bowl. Stir this mixture into the sauce, then stir in the chilled butter, piece by piece. Put the sauce back over low heat, stir for a couple of minutes, taste, and correct the salt and pepper.

8   Ladle a small amount of sauce onto the warm boar and serve the rest in a sauceboat on the side.

1 stalk celery, cut into ½-inch (1-cm.) pieces
1 teaspoon juniper berries, crushed
1 bouquet garni (2 sprigs thyme, 1 bay leaf, and 5 stems parsley, wrapped and tied in a green leek leaf)
Salt
Pepper
10 tablespoons (150 g.) butter
1 tablespoon cornstarch

BLACK PEPPER–CRUSTED VENISON CHOPS

Côtelettes de chevreuil panées au poivre noir

SERVES   2
PREPARATION   20 minutes
COOKING   10 minutes

1   Season both sides of each chop with a generous pinch of crushed black pepper. Pat it on to make it stick.

2   Heat the olive oil in a skillet over medium heat for 1 minute. When it is very hot, lay the chops in the pan and sear each side for 1 minute. Turn them with tongs or a wooden spatula—do not spear them with a fork. Remove them to a plate and season all over with thyme.

3   Spoon excess fat from the skillet, leaving behind the brown juices. Put the skillet over low heat. Add ½ teaspoon butter, and when it melts, add the shallot and cook over low heat for 3 minutes, stirring. Add the vinegar and cook, stirring regularly, until the liquid has almost completely disappeared, at least 3 minutes. Stir in the wine and reduce by half (about 2 minutes). Turn off the heat. Stir in the cream and then the red currant jelly. The sauce should be rich and creamy. Stir in the ginger and a generous pinch of salt.

4   Pass the sauce through a fine strainer into another skillet. Lay the seared chops in the sauce, cover the skillet, and turn the heat to very low, just to keep warm.

5   Clean the first skillet and put the remaining butter into it. Melt over medium heat and then grill the gingerbread for

4 bone-in venison chops, ¼ pound (80 g.) each
Crushed black pepper
1 tablespoon olive oil
4 sprigs thyme, leaves only
1 tablespoon butter
1 shallot, peeled and minced
1 tablespoon wine vinegar
3 tablespoons white wine (such as Chardonnay)
3 tablespoons heavy cream
1 tablespoon red currant jelly
1 teaspoon minced fresh ginger
Salt
4 slices gingerbread
⅓ cup cranberry preserves
2 tablespoons lemon juice
Pepper

2 minutes per side so that it gets nicely colored. Arrange them on a platter and slip them into a 250°F/120°C oven to keep warm.

6   Heat the cranberry preserves in a saucepan with the lemon juice and 3 or 4 grindings of pepper.

7   To serve, put the chops on a platter with the cranberry preserves and drizzle the sauce all around them. Serve the grilled gingerbread on the side. This goes well with noodles, chestnut purée, or mashed celery root.

PAN FRIED VENISON
WITH TRUFFLES AND PEPPER SAUCE

Chevreuil poêlé à la truffe et sauce poivrade

SERVES   4

PREPARATION   10 minutes

COOKING   3 minutes

The marinade for the sauce must be prepared two days in advance.

1   Two days in advance, make the marinade for the sauce poivrade, making only one-fourth of the recipe.

2   Two days later, make the sauce poivrade.

3   Beat the yolk in a deep dish with ½ teaspoon water and a small pinch of salt. Beat until the mixture is homogeneous. Spread the parsley in a second dish and the minced truffle in a third. Prepare a platter to receive the coated scallops. Dip each scallop in the egg, then dip one side of the scallop in the parsley and the other side in the truffles. Line them up on the waiting platter.

4   Melt 1 tablespoon butter in a skillet. When it foams, fry the pear slices for 2 minutes per side over low heat.

5   Reheat the sauce poivrade over the lowest heat possible. Season the dipped scallops with salt and pepper. In a large skillet, heat the oil and the remaining 1 tablespoon butter. Raise the heat to medium and sauté the scallops for 2 minutes. Turn with a spatula (do not pierce them with a fork or metal tongs) and sauté the second side for 1 minute.

¼ recipe sauce poivrade (page 53)

1 egg yolk (page 204)

Salt

1 tablespoon minced parsley

⅓ cup (½ ounce/15 g.) minced truffle

1¼ pounds (600 g.) venison fillet, sliced into 12 scallops and pounded flat by the butcher

2 tablespoons butter

2 pears, peeled and sliced into rounds ½ inch (1 cm.) thick

Pepper

1 tablespoon neutral oil

Cranberry sauce or preserves for garnish

6   Serve the scallops drizzled with warm sauce and surrounded by pear slices, with a dab of cranberry sauce on top of each slice of pear.

Hare

The ancient Greeks ate hare because it was believed to enhance physical beauty. Legend has it that the Roman emperor Alexander Severus ate hare every day.

A male hare is called a buck, and the female a doe. Babies (four months or younger) are called leverets and should weigh about 3⅓ pounds (1.5 kg.). A nine-month-old hare is called a three-quarters (*trois-quarts*) and weighs 5 pounds (2.5 kg.). One-year-olds, weighing 8 to 12 pounds (4–6 kg.), are called *capucins* in France. For roasting and stewing, you want the three-quarters. The older animals are tough and fibrous, best saved for pâtés, terrines, stuffed rolls, or mousse.

CHOOSING A GOOD HARE

How can you tell whether a hare is young? By the daintiness of its paws (claws should be well concealed by hair), its pointed ears, and the luster of its coat. Avoid buying older hares, which have longer teeth, white fur around the nose, and prominent claws.

A hare shot in the belly soon loses all its blood. It is better to take one hit in the head or shoulder and to check the eyes for freshness; they should still be shiny. The best hares in France come from Brie, Beauce, Champagne, Gascogne, Normandy, and Poitou. Mountain-dwelling hares are particularly fine, since their flesh takes on the aromas of their local fodder.

HARE: EAT IT FRESH

Hanging does not suit hare, which should be eaten very fresh, *au bout du fusil,* as the French say—at gunpoint. But if you do not plan to eat it right away, leave it in its skin and do not dress it until you are ready to cook. If, however, a hunter presents you with a poorly killed hare that is not intact, skin and gut it immediately. Rinse it with cold running water, wipe it dry with paper towels, and rub it with olive oil. It should not be marinated unless you plan to preserve it, for its delicate taste will be obscured by marinating it. If you plan to make a stew or sauté, you will use most of the animal, including the legs, thighs, and shoulders. For a stew you must have the blood. The heart, liver, and lungs will be ground up and blended with the blood and a bit of Cognac or vinegar.

HARE ROYALE

Lièvre à la royale du sénateur Couteaux à la façon poitevine

SERVES   4–5
PREPARATION   45 minutes
COOKING   6 hours
SAUCE AND FINISHING   1¾ hours

This distinguished dish is the subject of a long-standing culinary feud between two regions, Poitou and Perigord. At the end of the nineteenth century, the Viennese senator Aristide Couteaux developed an especially fine variation of "hare royale" in Paris, and it has carried his name ever since. It is alleged that the savory smell of hare would waft through the neighborhood surrounding Paris's Opera-Comique, attracting throngs of passersby. A newspaper called *Le Temps* published the senator's recipe, which led to his being summoned to the Luxembourg Palace to explain the finer points of the dish to the senate. In the end, a parliamentary group was established for senators partial to the pleasures of the table.

This is holiday food, the kind that takes you almost all day to make. Ask the butcher to cut the hare into pieces that aren't too large—front legs into two pieces, back legs into three. Use the saddle for another recipe (such as the following one); in this one it would be overcooked and stringy.

1 pound (500 g.) pork caul fat
3 bottles Shiraz
One 6-pound (3-kg.) hare, minus the saddle, chopped into pieces as described in the headnote, with its liver, lungs, heart, and kidneys
20 shallots, peeled
10 cloves garlic, peeled and degermed (page 122)
½ cup (10 cl.) hare's blood (or pig's blood if hare's is not available)
½ cup (10 cl.) wine vinegar
4 small pinches of fresh thyme leaves
4 juniper berries, crushed
Salt
Pepper

Based on the version from Poitou, this recipe does not use any foie gras. The other recipe, from Perigord, calls for an entire foie gras, but the flesh of the hare, which has a rather high taste, hardly needs that added richness. Some people, however, like a little foie gras in the sauce. If you do, that option is given at the end.

1. Put the caul fat to soak in cold water. Pour all the red wine into a large saucepan and bring to a boil. Light a long kitchen match and touch it to the surface of the bubbling wine to set it aflame and remove some of its acidity. Turn off the heat and put the pan aside.

2. Inspect the hare's liver. If the bile sac (which is green) is broken, discard the liver. Grind the liver, lungs, heart, and kidneys very fine. Put 5 of the whole shallots and 3 of the garlic cloves through the grinder with the organs. Cover and refrigerate.

3. Mix the blood and vinegar until completely combined. Put the mixture in a sealed glass or stainless steel container in the refrigerator.

4. Preheat the oven to 250°F/120°C. Mix the thyme leaves and crushed juniper berries with 1 tablespoon salt and 1 teaspoon pepper. Season the pieces of hare with this mixture. Wrap each piece in a slice of bacon.

5. Gently wring out the caul, carefully unfold it, and lay it on a cutting board. Chop it into enough pieces to wrap each piece of hare. Wrap the hare and secure each bundle with a toothpick.

6. Put the carrot, onion, bouquet garni, and the remaining shallots and garlic in a large Dutch oven. Lay the hare bundles on top of the vegetables and season them with 1 teaspoon salt and 2 pinches of pepper. Add the red wine, bring it to a boil, and set it aflame again. Cover and stew in the oven for 6 hours. Check on the pot frequently, especially at the beginning. The wine should not boil but should "shiver" or barely simmer. You want to see quivering columns of small bubbles, not rambunctious rolling. If you do catch the wine boiling, leave the door of the oven open to cool it off a bit. Perhaps you should lower the oven temperature a bit, too.

7. After 6 hours, carefully lift the shallots, garlic, and hare from the pot with a skimmer or slotted spoon. Put them in another

½ pound (200 g.) bacon slices or 1 for each piece of hare
1 carrot, chopped into rounds
1 large onion, peeled and coarsely chopped
1 bouquet garni (2 sprigs fresh thyme, 1 stalk celery, 5 stems flat-leaf parsley, and 1 small leek cut into half or in thirds, all tied together)
1 teaspoon Cognac
2 tablespoons (30 g.) leftover foie gras terrine (optional)

special equipment: toothpicks

pot, cover them with a damp but well-wrung-out dish towel, and cover the pot. Set this pot aside.

8   Put the stewing liquid through a fine strainer (or, preferably, a chinois) into a saucepan. Press down on the solids in the strainer to extract as much liquid as possible. Allow the sauce to cool completely and then remove the layer of greasy fat from its surface.

9   Remove the ground organs, shallots, and garlic from the refrigerator. Whisk a ladle of the strained cooking liquid into the ground mix until it is evenly incorporated. Whisk in another ladle, then whisk the ground mix and sauce mixture into the big pot of sauce. Simmer very gently for 1 hour over very low heat.

10 Prepare a very fine strainer or chinois over another saucepan and put the simmered sauce through it, pressing on the solids to extract their juices. Simmer for 15 minutes over low heat to reduce the sauce a little more. Skim impurities from the surface.

11 Whisk $1\frac{1}{3}$ cups (30 cl.) sauce into the blood-vinegar mixture you prepared before. Pour this into the large pot of sauce, whisking gently the whole time. Pour the sauce into the pot of rabbit. Reheat gently, covered, without allowing the liquids to bubble. Finish by stirring in the Cognac. Taste for salt and pepper.

12 Arrange the rabbit bundles on a warmed platter and brush them with sauce. Freeze any leftover sauce. You can use it for something else, perhaps a stew.

13 If you happen to have any leftover foie gras terrine and want to try an enriched sauce, grind 2 or 3 tablespoons foie gras by rubbing it through a sieve. Do not pack it down but keep it ready in the refrigerator in a sealed container. Whisk it into the sauce just before you pour it back over the pot of hare.

SADDLE OF HARE WITH SMALL ONIONS

Râble de lièvre aux petits oignons

SERVES 2

PREPARATION AND COOKING 1 hour

1 Season the hare with ⅔ teaspoon salt and 2 pinches of pepper. Heat the olive oil in a Dutch oven. When the oil is quite hot, brown the rabbit over low heat without letting it burn, 3–4 minutes per side. Turn the meat with a wooden spoon; do not pierce it with a fork to turn it. Turn off the heat and remove the hare to a dish to rest. Sprinkle with the leaves of 3 thyme sprigs. Tent loosely with aluminum foil.

2 Discard the fat in the pot. Rinse the pot with hot water and wipe it out with a paper towel. Melt 3 tablespoons butter over low heat. Add the lardons, garlic, and leaves of 1 thyme sprig and stir well. Add the onions and season with ⅓ teaspoon salt and 2 pinches of pepper. Stir, cover, and cook very gently for 3 minutes. Remove the lardons but continue to cook the onions, covered and over very low heat, for 10 minutes. Shake the pot regularly to keep the onions from sticking. With a slotted spoon, remove the onions and garlic from the pot and set them aside with the lardons.

3 Spoon the cooking fat from the pot and discard it, leaving behind the brown juices. Put the pot back over high heat and add the vinegar. Stir and scrape well to loosen any juices cooked on the bottom of the pot. Cook for 3 minutes. Add the white wine and simmer for 15–20 minutes; the wine should reduce by half. Turn off the heat and stir in the cream.

4 Pass the sauce through a fine strainer into another pot. Put the hare in the sauce (still careful not to pierce it) along with any juices that have collected under it during resting. Add the onions, garlic, and lardons and simmer over low heat for 3 minutes. Taste for salt and pepper.

5 Remove the hare, onions, and lardons with a skimmer or slotted spoon. Arrange them on a hot serving dish. Sprinkle with the remaining thyme sprigs and the crushed black pepper.

6 Whisk the remaining butter into the pot to thicken the sauce. Stir in the Chartreuse and taste for salt and pepper.

1 hare saddle, 13–14 ounces (400–450 g.)
Salt
Pepper
1 tablespoon olive oil
6 sprigs thyme, leaves only
6 tablespoons (100 g.) butter
¼ cup (1 ounce/30 g.) smoked lardons (page 89)
1 clove garlic, crushed but unpeeled
12 small white onions, peeled
1 tablespoon wine vinegar
½ cup (10 cl.) dry white wine
½ cup (10 cl.) heavy cream
2 pinches of crushed black pepper
1 tablespoon Chartreuse

7   Saddle of hare is carved lengthwise into slices. Spoon some
sauce onto the hare and serve the rest on the side in a warm
sauceboat.

SADDLE OF HARE WITH FAIRY RING MUSHROOMS _____

Râble de lièvre aux mousserons

SERVES   4

PREPARATION   15–20 minutes for the marinade plus
25 minutes

COOKING   20–25 minutes

The marinade must be prepared a day in advance.

1   The day before, put the saddles of hare in a deep dish or large
bowl and rub them with the olive oil. Add to the bowl the
onions, carrots, celery, parsley, thyme, and white wine. Cover
loosely with aluminum foil and refrigerate overnight (no
longer than 24 hours), turning the meat 3 or 4 times over the
course of marinating.

2   The next day, preheat the oven to 480°F/260°C. Remove the
hare from the refrigerator and from the marinade and pat it
dry with paper towels. Put the marinade through a fine
strainer into a bowl and keep the vegetables in the strainer.

3   Melt 1½ tablespoons butter in a Dutch oven over low heat.
When it foams, brown the hare all over, turning it with a
wooden spoon, still over low heat. Season with salt and pepper. When the hare is evenly, nicely browned, add the vegetables in the strainer. Stir and then put the uncovered pot in
the oven for 5 minutes. Turn the hare and cook 5 minutes
more for a relatively rare finish. If you prefer the meat more
thoroughly cooked, leave it in the oven 2 minutes more.

4   Remove the pot from the oven but do not turn the oven off.
Place a rack or small overturned plate over a larger plate and
set the hare on top of it. Season all over with salt and pepper
and tent loosely with aluminum foil. Remove the vegetables
to a colander.

5   Melt 1½ tablespoons butter in a saucepan or skillet over low
heat. Add the shallots, season with a pinch of salt, and cook

2 saddles of hare,
13–14 ounces (400–450 g.)
each, skinned by the
butcher

3 tablespoons olive oil

2 medium onions, peeled and
cut into small dice

2 medium carrots, peeled and
cut into small dice

3 stalks celery, cut into small
dice

6 stems parsley, plus
1 tablespoon minced
parsley for garnish

3 sprigs fresh thyme

½ cup (10 cl.) white wine (such
as Muscadet or sauvignon)

4 tablespoons (60 g.) butter

Salt

Pepper

4 shallots, peeled and sliced
into rounds ¼ inch
(0.5 cm.) thick

for 5 minutes over very low heat, stirring with a wooden spatula.

6   In the meantime, melt 1 tablespoon butter in a skillet. When it foams, add the mushrooms and cook about 30 seconds without stirring. Stir and cook 30 seconds more. Season with 2 pinches of salt and 1 pinch of pepper and turn off the heat. When the mushrooms finish cooking, add them to the shallots.

7   Spoon fat from the hare cooking pot and discard. Put the pot back over high heat and add the strained marinade. With a wooden spatula, scrape up the cooked-on brown bits from the bottom of the pot. Add the crème fraîche, stirring constantly. Bring to a boil and simmer until the liquid has been reduced by half, by which time it should be rich and smooth. Season generously with pepper and lightly with salt. Stir in the lemon juice. Pass the sauce through a fine strainer into a sauceboat.

8   Rinse the pot and wipe it out with paper towels. Put the hare back in the pot and put the pot in the still-hot oven for 1 or 2 minutes to reheat. Add the juices that collected under the resting meat to the sauceboat.

9   Saddle of hare is carved lengthwise into slices. Arrange the hare on a platter and coat it with sauce. Surround with mushrooms and sprinkle with parsley to serve.

¾ pound (400 g.) fairy ring mushrooms (*mousserons*), stems removed, cleaned, and with larger caps cut into halves or quarters
2 cups (45 cl.) crème fraîche
Juice of 1 lemon

MEDALLIONS OF HARE WITH BACON

Médaillons de lièvre au lard fumé

SERVES 4

PREPARATION 50 minutes

COOKING 2 minutes and 30 seconds

The caul must be soaked 1 hour in advance.

1   One hour in advance, soak the caul in 1 quart (1 l.) cold water and 2 tablespoons white vinegar.

2   Wash the bones and trimmings and put them in a colander to drain. Heat 2 tablespoons oil in a Dutch oven over high heat for 2 minutes. When the oil is about to smoke, use a skimmer or slotted spoon to put the bones and trimmings into the pot. Brown for 5 minutes, stirring with a wooden spoon for even coloring, still over high heat. Add the shallots, carrot, and onion. Lower the heat to medium and cook for 3 minutes, stirring. Add the wine vinegar, 1 cup (25 cl.) water, the garlic, and 2 juniper berries. Scrape up bits cooked on the bottom of the pot. Lower the heat and cook gently for 30 minutes.

3   In the meantime, slice the rind and connective tissue from the hare. Season lightly with salt and generously with pepper. Sprinkle with thyme. Crush the 4 remaining juniper berries and sprinkle them on the meat. Lay 2 slices of bacon under and 2 slices of bacon over each piece of hare.

4   Wring out the caul and wrap the pieces of hare in the caul. With a string, tie them up like roasts: Tie once around the middle, once lengthwise to the two ends, and then tie at $\frac{1}{2}$-inch (1-cm.) intervals along the length.

5   When the sauce has bubbled for 30 minutes, season with salt and pepper and simmer 5 minutes more. Taste again for seasoning.

6   Slice the bundles of hare into medallions $1\frac{1}{2}$ inches (3 cm.) thick. Season with salt and pepper. Heat 1 tablespoon oil and then 1 tablespoon butter in a large skillet over medium heat. When the butter foams, add the medallions and sauté for 1 minute and 30 seconds. Turn them with tongs or a spatula and cook the second side for 1 minute. Set them on their sides and cook their edges until they are nicely colored.

7   Remove to a plate and serve coated with hot sauce.

$\frac{1}{2}$ pound (200 g.) pork caul fat

2 tablespoons distilled white vinegar

2 saddles of hare (1 pound/ 450 g. each), filleted and skinned by the butcher, with a handful of chopped bones and trimmings

3 tablespoons neutral oil

2 shallots, peeled and chopped

1 medium carrot, peeled and chopped

1 medium onion, peeled and chopped

1 tablespoon wine vinegar

2 cloves garlic, peeled and chopped

6 juniper berries

Salt

Pepper

2 teaspoons thyme leaves

16 slices smoked bacon

1 tablespoon butter

Feathered Game

Whether or not you are a hunter, autumn brings with it a whiff of game. It must be enjoyed while it lasts since the season is short.

Pheasant, partridge, wild duck, wood pigeon, woodcock, thrush, lark, and quail—there are so many kinds of feathered game. In France, unhappily for connoisseurs but luckily for the preservation of species, some of the best wild winged delights can no longer be sold legally. The only way to taste them is to eat them in other countries, such as Spain or Switzerland, make friends with hunters, or take up hunting oneself.

It must be admitted that these birds no longer taste the way they once did. Some of them are now raised in captivity and then set free for the hunt. These birds do not develop the heightened flavors characteristic of animals who have spent their lives struggling to survive in nature. Even wild birds' diets have changed, especially in regions that produce a lot of corn, where the meat of pheasants, for example, is yellower, fattier, and more tender. Finally, several species of small migratory birds that in the nineteenth and twentieth centuries were among the glories of regional cookery—the plover, for instance—have all but disappeared.

CHOOSING GAME BIRDS

Don't be seduced by flamboyant plumage. A striking appearance is not necessarily a sign of quality. The best game birds are usually the females. Their plumage is more drab and their tails are not as impressive, but their flesh is more delicate.

When you buy small game birds, make sure they are young by checking to see whether their beaks are still supple.

If a hunter gives you a bird, make sure that its flesh is not in tatters and that its plumage is dry. If the feathers are wet, the animal has been stored chilled and in poor conditions.

If the bird was very recently killed, if its flesh is not bruised, and if it is not damp, wait two or three days before plucking it. Keep it in the refrigerator—this will improve the flesh and make plucking easier—but be sure to keep it dry and wrapped in a clean dish towel. The bird should certainly not be wrapped in plastic or plopped into a plastic bag, which will retain moisture.

Pluck the bird with care, beginning always with the head and doing your best not to tear the skin. It is best to go feather by feather if you have the patience, especially for the larger feathers. When you have finished plucking, you must quickly burn off any remaining feathers: Hold the bird by its feet so that its body dangles down and pass it through a flame for a mere instant. The skin should not get cooked at all. You just want to burn off the down and the small feathers under the wings.

Lovers of game do not gut woodcock and other small birds. It is always necessary, however, carefully to remove their digestive tracts, crops, and gizzards. Make a ½-inch (1-cm.) incision at the top of the belly, just below the rib cage. Slip a trussing needle into the incision and pull out what you are looking for.

NO HANGING AROUND

Once upon a time, game birds required a period of hanging; people waited quite a while before eating the hunted bird. It was thought that only flesh that had begun to decay was sufficiently tender and flavorful. Today, this method is recognized as an error of taste that also has the potential to make its practitioners quite sick. Nothing is better than a small bird eaten at gunpoint—that is, the very same day it is shot. Large birds can be aged (but not submitted to hanging) for two or three days but no more.

PREPARING FEATHERED GAME

For maximum enjoyment the dark meat must be well trimmed of veins and connective tissue. Ask your butcher to do it for you. If you must do it yourself, before cooking make an incision at the base of the drumstick where there is no more flesh. Use a small knife to lift out a bit of the tubes you find, then pierce them with a trussing needle or grip them with tweezers and pull them out. Do this until you have removed all the tubes.

These birds can be cooked any number of ways, some of them quite complicated. The essential thing is not to distort each bird's special taste. Roasting is a fine way of preserving the animal's essence, especially spit roasting, in which rotation keeps juices circulating and spreading throughout the cooking flesh. You can protect the breast with a fig leaf or a slice of lard, which will prevent it from drying out; but avoid smoked bacon, which will interfere with the taste of the game, especially in a young animal.

To roast on a spit or in the oven, season the bird inside and out with salt and pepper. Rub it with 1 tablespoon of butter. Begin cooking in a very hot oven, 460°F/240°C. Baste frequently with cooking juices. When cooking is three-fourths done, remove the lard wrapper so that the breast can brown. Season again with salt and pepper. Allow the bird to rest for 8 or 10 minutes before serving; the meat is too hot to eat. Make a little sauce by adding 1 or 2 tablespoons of cold water to the pan. Do not use broth or wine, which will overpower the bird's taste.

Pheasant

The fine flesh of pheasants has long been a favorite of gourmets, but it has lost some of its nobility as farm-raised varieties have become more common and food sources have become more rich, thanks to the great plains of grain. Pheasant probably comes from China. Its name is from the Latin *phasianus,* from the Greek *phasianos,* meaning "from Phasis," a city on the Black Sea in what is now Georgia. Legend has it that Jason and the Argonauts brought it back to the Mediterranean with the Golden Fleece. After conquering the Greeks, the Romans spread pheasant throughout their empire. The outrageous emperor Elagabalus fed pheasant to his lions. Vitellus required one of his provinces to regularly provide him with the brains of five hundred pheasants, an anecdote that bolsters the myth of Roman decadence, which was, for the most part, a nineteenth-century invention.

The male is called a cock and the female a hen. The cock is distinguished by his splendid outfit; the hen is not as fancily dressed. She is more slender, has a shorter tail, and lacks spurs on her heels. Her plumage may not be as enticing, but the flesh she offers is more savory and more tender.

A young pheasant usually has gray legs and feet. The most trusted sign of a pheasant's youth is the tip of the last large wing feather, which should be pointed; in an older pheasant it is rounded.

It is advisable to leave a pheasant in its feathers for two or three days, wrapped in a towel in the cellar or the refrigerator, an appropriate period of "hanging." But if a dead animal has obvious wounds or is damp, it must be plucked right away. If you buy a pheasant or any other game bird from a store, it has probably already been dead for a day or two, possibly more; ask the person who sells it to you.

The Gypsies have their own traditional way of preparing pheasant: They pack it in clay and bake it in this hermetically sealed wrapper. When the package is cracked open, the feathers are stuck in the clay. Hedgehogs are also sometimes cooked *à la gitane* (Gypsy style). In all other recipes, however, pheasant must be plucked before it is cooked. If it isn't, put it in the refrigerator for a few hours before you pluck it. This will make the job easier. Do not hesitate to pass the plucked bird through a flame to get rid of down and other small feathers, and be sure to remove the veins and connective tissue from the legs, as described on page 530. Gut the bird carefully and truss it with twine. When you buy a pheasant, the butcher should do all this for you.

Tradition gives us many pheasant dishes, and they are often very complicated. These convoluted preparations mask the animal's flavor. One of the best ways to prepare pheasant is also the simplest: roasted in the oven or on a spit. Following the general instructions on page 531, it will take a pheasant about 20 minutes per pound to roast.

PHEASANT WITH TRUFFLES AND MUSHROOMS, A STEW

Faisan à la truffe et aux champignons (salmis)

SERVES 4

PREPARATION 15 minutes

COOKING 16–18 minutes for the pheasant plus 30 minutes for the mushroom sauce

Ask the butcher to gut, dress, and thoroughly pluck the bird.

1 pheasant, about 2–2½ pounds (1–1.2 kg.) for a female

About 6 tablespoons (90 g.) butter

Salt

Pepper

3 tablespoons game stock (page 38) or white chicken stock (page 36)

1½ tablespoons Cognac

2 shallots, peeled and minced

½ cup (10 cl.) dry white wine (such as sauvignon)

10 whole peppercorns, crushed

½ pound (250 g.) small white button mushrooms, stem ends trimmed, rinsed, and drained; if you have large mushrooms, cut into quarters

1 small truffle, minced

1. Remove the pheasant and the butter from the refrigerator 30 minutes in advance. Check the pheasant for down, especially under the wings. If necessary, pass feathery parts of the bird through a flame to burn off any small feathers that remain.

2. Preheat the oven to 460°F/240°C. Season the pheasant inside and out with salt and pepper, making sure you spread the seasoning as evenly as possible over the skin. Brush the skin thickly with butter, using about 2 tablespoons. (If it isn't soft enough for brushing, you can soften it in the microwave.) Put the bird in a Dutch oven, laying it on its side so it is resting on its thigh. Put the pot over high heat for 2 minutes to brown the pheasant, then turn it onto its other thigh for 2 minutes. To turn the bird, use a wooden spoon or anything that does not pierce its skin and flesh. Spoon cooking juices over the pheasant. Lay it on its back for 2 minutes, then put it into the oven for 10–12 minutes, uncovered.

3. Remove the pot, turn off the oven, and keep the oven door shut. Put the pheasant on a cutting board to cool for 10 minutes. Do not discard the cooking juices in the pot.

4. With a large knife and poultry shears, if you have them, cut the pheasant into 4 pieces—cut first lengthwise and then across its "waist." Remove the flesh from the bone and the skin from the flesh. Keep the skin and bones for later.

5. Prepare the stock. Then melt 2 tablespoons butter in an ovenproof sauté pan over low heat. Add the flesh of the pheasant and the Cognac. Light a long kitchen match and touch it to the surface to set the Cognac aflame. When the flames die, stir in the stock. Cover the pan and put it in the oven, which should still be hot even though it is off. Slip a serving platter into the oven to warm, too.

6   With a cleaver or large knife, chop the bones, skin, and any scraps of flesh. Put them in the large pot and warm them over low heat, stirring and scraping with a wooden spatula. Add the shallots, white wine, and crushed peppercorns. Cook over low heat for 10 minutes. Put this broth through a fine strainer (or, even better, a chinois) into a saucepan, pressing on the solids to extract as much juice as possible. Discard what is left in the strainer and rinse it under hot water until it is clean.

7   Bring the saucepan of juice to a boil, then lower the heat so it bubbles very gently.

8   In the meantime, melt 1 tablespoon butter in a sauté pan or skillet. When it foams, add the mushrooms and cook over low heat for 10 minutes, stirring. Turn off the heat.

9   Put the simmering broth through the fine strainer again. Return to the saucepan over low heat. Add the mushrooms and stir in 1 tablespoon diced chilled butter.

10   Lay the pheasant's flesh on the warmed serving platter and pour the mushroom sauce over it. Sprinkle with minced truffle and serve.

PHEASANT PATTIES WITH FOIE GRAS

Tourtes de faisan au foie gras

SERVES 4

PREPARATION   25 minutes for the stuffing plus 45 minutes

COOKING   20 minutes

The stuffing is best prepared the day before.

Ask the butcher to debone the pheasant and to grind ¼ pound (100 g.) of its breast with the chicken liver and pork neck. The grind should be quite coarse, more like a dice. Cut the rest of the pheasant meat into ½-inch (1-cm.) dice.

1 boneless pheasant, prepared as described in the headnote

¼ pound (100 g.) ground chicken liver, minced

¼ pound (100 g.) ground pork neck, minced

2 tablespoons butter

Salt

Pepper

2 pinches of thyme leaves

1 scant teaspoon superfine sugar

2 egg yolks (page 204)

Flour for dusting

1½ pounds (800 g.) store-bought puff pastry

4 slices raw duck foie gras, 1 ounce (30 g.) each

1   The night before: If the butcher did not do it, remove ¼ pound (100 g.) of the pheasant's breast and grind it coarsely with the chicken livers and pork neck. Chop the rest of the pheasant into ½-inch (1-cm.) dice. Discard any bits of bone or tendon that you encounter.

2   Heat the butter in a skillet over low heat. When it foams, add the diced pheasant and cook over medium heat for a minute or two. Season with ½ teaspoon salt and a generous pinch of pepper. Remove the pheasant with a slotted spoon to a large bowl to cool.

3   Add the thyme and sugar to the ground meats. Season with 2 generous pinches of salt and a small pinch of pepper. Mix well, cover, and refrigerate, overnight if possible.

4   The next day, beat the egg yolks with a pinch of salt and a few drops of water. Lightly flour a work surface and roll out the puff pastry to a thickness of ⅛ inch (3 mm.). Cut 8 disks with 6-inch (15-cm.) diameters. Line a sheet pan with parchment paper and lay the disks on it. Lay another piece of parchment paper over the pastry disks and top it with another sheet pan. Put the whole thing in the refrigerator.

5   Remove the ground meat stuffing from the refrigerator and give it a quick stir. Turn it out onto a cutting board and divide it into 4 equal parts. Put a slice of foie gras in the center of each mound. Using your hands, roll each mound of stuffing and foie gras into a ball and flatten a bit.

6   Remove the pastry dough and sheet pans from the refrigerator. Brush the center of 4 of the disks with the beaten egg yolk; be careful not to get any yolk on the parchment paper.

Place a flattened stuffing ball on top of each yolk-brushed disk and cover with a clean disk. Pinch the disks together all the way around, sealing them shut. For a clean look, you can trim the edges with a knife to make the packets very round. You can also make designs in the pastry by pressing but not piercing them with a knife. Brush the top of each patty with beaten yolk, careful again not to drip yolk on the parchment paper. (If you do, wipe it up completely with a paper towel.) Refrigerate for 30 minutes.

7   Preheat the oven to 440°F/220°C. When it is hot, bake the patties for 20 minutes.

FOIE GRAS–STUFFED PHEASANT WITH ENDIVE

Faisan farci de foie gras aux endives

SERVES   4

PREPARATION   1 hour

COOKING   40 minutes for the breasts; 45 minutes for the legs

Ask the butcher for a pheasant that is ready to cook— skinned and deveined. Ask for the wing tips, feet, and neck.

1   Put 1 quart (1 l.) water in a saucepan with 1 teaspoon coarse salt and the lemon juice and bring to a boil. When it bubbles, add the endives and simmer for 30 minutes. Remove them to a colander to drain. When they are cool enough, squeeze them to remove as much water as possible.

2   Season the interior cavity of the pheasant with salt and pepper. Season the foie gras with salt and pepper and stuff it into the pheasant. Truss the bird and season its skin.

3   Melt 1 tablespoon butter in a Dutch oven over medium heat. Brown the pheasant all over, turning it with a wooden spoon, about 4 minutes. Add the neck, wing tips, and feet and stir. Lower the heat and add the carrot, onion, garlic, and thyme. Cook for 1 minute, stirring. Lay the bird on its side so that it rests on its thigh and wing, and put the uncovered pot in the oven for 3 minutes. Turn the bird onto the other side and

Coarse salt

Juice of 1 lemon

8 small endives, outer leaves removed, cored

1 ready-to-cook pheasant, preferably female, prepared as described in the headnote

Salt

Pepper

3 ounces (100 g.) raw foie gras

2 tablespoons butter

¼ medium carrot, peeled and cut into small dice

¼ medium onion, peeled and cut into small dice

1 clove garlic, unpeeled

1 sprig fresh thyme

bake for 3 minutes. Lay the bird on its back and bake for 4 minutes. Remove the pheasant to a deep dish and let it rest breast down, propped up so that it is almost vertical. Tent loosely with aluminum foil.

4   Turn the heat under the pot to low and cook the carrot, onion, and garlic for 3 minutes, stirring. Add ½ cup (20 cl.) water, turn the heat to high, and use a spatula to scrape up anything stuck to the bottom of the pot. Bring to a boil and simmer for 10 minutes.

5   Preheat the oven to 450°F/230°C. Melt 1 tablespoon butter in a skillet over low heat. Add the drained endives, sprinkle them with the sugar, and brown for 5 minutes, rolling them around with a wooden spatula to achieve even coloring. Set them aside.

6   Cut a band of puff pastry 4 inches (10 cm.) wide and long enough to encircle the big pot. Beat the yolk with ⅓ teaspoon water and a pinch of salt. Paint the yolk onto one side of the pastry.

7   Put the pheasant back in the pot, adding any juice that collected under it as it rested. Cover the pot and seal it with the pastry: Flour your fingers lightly and press the yolk-painted side of the pastry to the seam between the pot and its lid, working your way around to seal it completely. If you like, you can use the tip of a knife to impress a decorative pattern on the pastry. (You can use the sealing dough on page 383 instead of puff pastry, if you like, but the result will not be as beautiful.)

8   Paint the exposed side of the pastry seal with yolk. If any drips onto the pot, wipe it away with a damp paper towel. Put the sealed pot in the oven, lower the heat to 400°F/200°C, and cook for 15 minutes. Remove the pot from the oven and allow it to rest for 10 minutes, closed; do not turn off the oven.

9   Open the pot in front of your guests. Snip off the bird's trussing. Carve the breasts and serve them with endive and cooking juices. Remove the legs, but put them back in the pot along with the carcass. Cover and bake 5 minutes more so that the legs will be properly cooked when you serve them.

1 teaspoon confectioners' sugar
1 long roll store-bought puff
   pastry or 1 recipe sealing
   pastry (*pâte à luter*,
   page 383)
1 egg yolk (page 204)
Flour

TRUFFLED PHEASANT

Faisan truffé

SERVES   4
PREPARATION   30 minutes
COOKING   20 minutes
RESTING   10 minutes

Ask the butcher for a pheasant that is ready to cook—skinned and deveined. Ask him to give you the liver, wing tips, feet, and neck.

1   Melt the goose fat in a skillet over high heat. When it is melted and hot, sauté the diced pheasant liver for 15 seconds, stirring with a wooden spoon. Season with 2 pinches of salt, 1 pinch of pepper, and a pinch of thyme leaves. Put the sautéed liver in a bowl with the diced foie gras terrine. Put the skillet with its fat back on the burner over low heat. Add the minced onion, season with a pinch of salt, and cook for 3 minutes, stirring. Add the sautéed onion to the bowl of liver.

2   Peel the truffle and add the peelings to the bowl of liver and onions, stirring them in well. Taste for salt and pepper. Chop the truffle into 10 slivers and season the slivers all over with salt and pepper. Pour the oil into a saucer and rub the truffles briefly in the oil; then slip them under the pheasant's skin, between the skin and the flesh. Use your fingers gently to create pockets between the skin and the flesh, and then put 1 bit of truffle on each drumstick, 2 on each thigh, and 2 on each side of the breast.

3   Preheat the oven to 440°F/220°C. Season the bird's cavity with salt and pepper and stuff with the liver-onion mixture. Truss. Season the outside with salt and pepper and brush with the butter. Lay the bird in a baking dish on its side, so that it is resting on a thigh and wing. Put the neck, wing tips, and feet in the dish. Bake for 8 minutes. Turn the bird onto its other side and cook for 8 minutes. Lay it on its back and bake for 4 minutes. Add the garlic, the remaining thyme, carrot, and diced onion to the dish and bake 4 minutes more.

4   Remove the dish from the oven but do not turn the oven off. Remove the pheasant to a deep dish; prop it up on the side so

1 tablespoon (20 g.) goose fat
Liver of the pheasant, cut into ¼-inch (0.5-cm.) dice
Salt
Pepper
1 large sprig fresh thyme
2 ounces (60 g.) duck foie gras terrine (page 153 or store-bought) cut into ¼-inch (0.5-cm.) dice
1 medium onion, peeled, and ½ minced, ¼ cut into large dice, ¼ discarded
1 truffle (⅔ ounce/20 g.), brushed clean with a paper towel
1 teaspoon neutral oil
1 ready-to-cook pheasant, preferably a female, prepared as described in the headnote
1 tablespoon butter, softened
1 clove garlic, unpeeled
¼ medium carrot, peeled and cut into large dice

that it is resting on its breast and almost vertical. Tent loosely with aluminum foil.

5   Dump the contents of the roasting dish into a small saucepan, scraping up and adding as much of the cooked-on brown juice as possible. Add ½ cup (10 cl.) water and turn the heat to high. Simmer for 10 minutes, then put these juices through a fine strainer into a sauceboat. Taste for salt and pepper.

6   Snip off the bird's trussing. Carve the breast and serve with a spoonful of sauce from the sauceboat. Remove the legs and put them back in the oven, with the carcass, for 5 minutes to finish cooking.

Partridge

We speak here of young partridge or, in French, *perdreau,* a highly sought-after bird with delectable flesh. Along with woodcock, it is tops in the world of feathered game. Like many other fowl, however, it is now subject to farming procedures and somewhat less tasty.

The gray partridge is generally called the English partridge, and the red-legged partridge, which is more common in France, is, of course, the French partridge. The gray partridge is more common in the United States, but the term *partridge* is sometimes used for quail and grouse in North America. In France there is also the rock partridge, which is sometimes confused with the red-legged partridge. The rock partridge is larger and very rare, however, and is most often found in the Alps and in southern France. The chukar looks somewhat similar and was introduced as a replacement bird when rock partridges were overhunted.

From a distance it is hard to tell the difference between a gray partridge and a red-legged one. Side by side, even, they have the same shape, but the fully grown red-legged bird is slightly larger than the gray. Their plumage is differently colored, too: The red-legged partridge (*Alectoris rufa*), more common in middle and southwest France, has a red back and belly; its white throat is ringed by a thick black band, and its beak and legs are red. The gray partridge (*Perdix perdix*), which is to be found in the north and around the Loire, has a grayish red back and an ash-gray belly with a dark horseshoe shape on its chest. Its beak and legs are gray-blue.

ROASTING PARTRIDGE

An excellent way to enjoy young partridge is simply roasted. The young bird's flesh is still meltingly tender; an older partridge has tougher muscles and must be prepared differently. Spit-roasting is ideal for young partridge. However you cook it, a partridge should be removed from the heat before its juices run clear if you want to preserve its special taste. Prick the thickest part of the breast of a properly cooked partridge with a skewer, and the juices should run clear and then slightly rosy.

Preheat the oven to 460°F/240°C at least 10 minutes in advance. Season the partridge generously with salt and pepper. Rub it with butter. Roast for 12–18 minutes, depending on its size, turning it once or twice during cooking. When it comes out of the oven, snip off its trussing (the butcher will generally truss it) and remove any self-basting wrap (such as bacon) from its breast. Season again: With the tip of a knife, make a shallow incision between the thigh and the body on each side and insert a dash of salt, a dash of pepper, and perhaps a drop of lemon juice. Lay the bird on its back and allow it to rest about 6 minutes, during which time it will finish cooking.

While the bird rests, pour 1 tablespoon water and 1 tablespoon Cognac into the roasting dish. Scrape the bottom of the dish with a wooden spatula to loosen any browned bits. Put the dish back in the oven, which is not on but should still be hot, and leave it there until the meat has finished resting.

BREAST OF YOUNG PARTRIDGE WITH KALE AND FOIE GRAS

Suprême de perdreau au chou et au foie gras

SERVES 2
PREPARATION 45 minutes

The partridges should be completely plucked and gutted, breasts removed, and legs deveined. Ask the butcher to prepare the birds this way.

1   Bring 1 quart (1 l.) water to a boil with 2 teaspoons salt. Boil the kale for 1 minute and then rinse it under cold water. Lay it on a dish towel or paper towel to drain and trim off the end of the thick stem. Flatten the leaves of the kale on a cutting board or other work surface.

2   Season both sides of each partridge breast with a generous pinch of salt and a small pinch of pepper, and then lay the 4 breasts on the 4 leaves. Lay a slice of foie gras on top of each breast. Fold the leaves up and over the meat to form a closed bundle. Wrap each bundle with bacon and then in plastic wrap. Be sure to keep the foie gras at the top of the bundles.

3   Bring 1 quart (1 l.) water to a boil in a saucepan fitted with a steamer basket. When it bubbles, lay the wrapped bundles in the steamer basket, cover the pot, and steam for 14 minutes.

4   Remove the packets and discard their plastic wrapping. Lay the cabbage bundles on warmed plates and sprinkle with chives, 1 teaspoon fleur de sel, and the crushed white pepper.

5   The partridge legs can be seasoned with salt and pepper, pan fried for 18 minutes in the butter, and served on top of a little salad on the side.

Salt
4 whole leaves kale
2 young partridges
Pepper
4 thin slices uncooked duck foie gras, about ⅔ ounce (20 g.) each
4 slices bacon
10 chives, minced
Fleur de sel
Pinch of crushed white pepper
2 teaspoons butter

ROAST YOUNG PARTRIDGE WITH LINDEN BLOSSOMS

Perdreaux rôtis au tilleul

SERVES 2

PREPARATION 45 minutes

COOKING 20 minutes

RESTING 10 minutes

1. Preheat the oven to 400°F/200°C. Season the inside of each partridge with 2 pinches of salt and 1 pinch of pepper. Truss them and season the outside, too.

2. Melt half of the butter in a cast-iron Dutch oven. When the foam subsides, lay the partridges in the pot on their sides and brown for 1–2 minutes over low heat. Turn them onto their other side and cook 1–2 minutes more. Try not to brown the part of the breast attached to the back, for it will dry out. Regularly spoon the pot juices over the partridges. Lay them on their backs for 1–2 minutes to finish. Toss the giblets into the pot and stir for 2–3 minutes to sear all over.

3. Put the rosemary in the pot and bake uncovered for 10 minutes, basting regularly with cooking juices.

4. In the meantime, melt the remaining butter in a sauté pan. Add the linden leaves and toss to coat well with the butter.

5. Remove the pot from the oven and put the birds in a baking dish, preferably made of glass. Cover the partridges with the buttery linden leaves and cover the dish. Put the partridges in the oven and cook for 3–5 minutes. When the dish comes out of the oven, remove the birds to a plate to rest, breast down, while you prepare the sauce.

6. Add the Armagnac to the cast-iron pot in which the partridges were seared. Add 3 tablespoons water and bring to a boil, scraping the bottom of the pot with a wooden spatula to loosen any baked-on juices. Stir in a dash of crushed black pepper. Simmer for a few minutes, just until the sauce is thickened. Put it through a fine strainer into a warm sauceboat.

7. Cover a serving platter with half of the linden leaves. Remove the birds' trussing, season them with salt and pepper, and lay them on the bed of leaves. Drizzle with sauce and top with the rest of the leaves. Serve immediately with the rest of the sauce on the side.

2 young partridges with their giblets

Salt

Pepper

4 tablespoons (60 g.) butter

2 sprigs rosemary

2 cups linden leaves, also called *tilleul* or lime blossom

1½ tablespoons Armagnac

Crushed black pepper

STUFFED YOUNG PARTRIDGES

Perdreaux farcis

variation

YOUNG PARTRIDGE WITH
TRUFFLES AND
MUSHROOMS,
A STEW

SERVES 2

PREPARATION 15 minutes for stuffing plus 30 minutes

COOKING 20 minutes for the onions plus 16–18 minutes
for the partridges

Each partridge should be about ¾ pound (400 g.), plucked, gutted, legs' veins removed, and trussed by the butcher. Ask him for the livers, necks, and wing tips, too.

1 stick (¼ pound/110 g.) butter

14 small new onions, peeled

Pinch of superfine sugar

Salt

4 sprigs thyme

1 ounce (30 g.) lard, minced

3 ounces (80 g.) partridge or
chicken livers

Pepper

2 sprigs fresh rosemary

3 tablespoons Cognac

4 slices good-quality white
sandwich bread, crusts
removed

3 cloves garlic, peeled and
degermed (page 122),
1 minced and 2 left whole

½ teaspoon mustard

Dash of nutmeg

2 young partridges

Juice of 1 lemon

1   Melt 5 tablespoons (75 g.) butter in a Dutch oven over medium heat. Let the butter foam, but do not let it brown; lower the heat if necessary. Add the new onions, 1 tablespoon water, the superfine sugar, a pinch of salt, and a sprig of thyme. Lower the heat, stir, cover, and cook for 15–20 minutes, until the onions are golden and meltingly soft. Give the pot a good shake every 5 minutes to keep the onions from sticking or scorching. When they are finished, put them aside.

2   Melt the lard in a skillet. When it is quite hot, add the livers. Season with 2 generous pinches of salt and a small pinch of pepper. Sprinkle with the leaves of 1 sprig of thyme and 1 sprig of rosemary. Stir and sauté over high heat for 3 minutes. The livers should remain rosy. Add 1 tablespoon Cognac to the skillet and set it on fire by lighting a long kitchen match and touching it to its surface.

3   Put the livers through a fine grinder or a sieve. Mix them with the crustless bread, minced garlic, mustard, and nutmeg until thoroughly combined.

4   Preheat the oven to 440°F/220°C. Season the insides of the partridges with 2 generous pinches of salt and 1 pinch of pepper. Season their skin, too. Stuff with the liver mixture, sew up the neck hole, and truss.

5   Melt 2 tablespoons butter in a Dutch oven over low heat. It should not begin to color. When it foams, lay the partridges in the pot on their sides. Brown for 2 minutes and then turn with a wooden spoon (do not spear with a fork) to cook the other side for 2 minutes. Try not to brown the breast, for this will dry it out. Turn the birds onto their backs and cook for 2 minutes, basting with cooking juices frequently.

6 Remove the pot from the heat and scatter the giblets, whole garlic, and remaining thyme and rosemary around the birds. Bake in the oven for 10–12 minutes, basting 3 or 4 times.

7 Turn off the oven and take out the pot. Remove the partridges to an ovenproof dish to rest. Snip off their trussing and season each bird with 2 pinches of salt and 1 pinch of pepper, spreading the seasoning around evenly. Put them back in the oven but leave its door open.

8 Pour the remaining 2 tablespoons Cognac and 4 tablespoons water into the pot, scraping its bottom with a wooden spatula. Put it over medium heat and simmer and stir for 3 minutes. Put the cooking juices through a fine strainer, season with a pinch of pepper, and keep in a covered saucepan over very low heat to stay warm.

9 Gently reheat the onions. Just before serving, spritz the partridges' legs with lemon juice.

10 Lay the partridges in a deep serving dish. Surround them with onions and serve the sauce on the side.

YOUNG PARTRIDGE WITH TRUFFLES AND MUSHROOMS, A STEW

Perdreau à la truffe aux champignons (salmis)

SERVES 4

Follow the recipe for Pheasant with Truffles and Mushrooms on page 533, replacing the pheasant with two young partridges.

Vegetables

Fresh Vegetables _____

There are fresh vegetables (many of which we associate with spring), starchy vegetables, and dry vegetables (beans). The French call fresh shell beans half-dry vegetables.

Most fresh vegetables can be eaten raw or barely cooked (see the chapter on hors d'oeuvres, page 121). The vitamins, minerals, and fiber they offer are essential to our well-being.

Some raw vegetables, such as potatoes and artichokes, must be kept in cold water after they have been peeled or else the air will turn them brown. You will find this information here.

Not long ago it was standard practice to cook vegetables for a very long time, until they were quite soft. Today, however, we tend to eat them firm, even crunchy, in order to appreciate each vegetable's particular tastes and qualities. To preserve texture, taste, and color, a cook must rapidly chill (or "shock") vegetables after cooking if they are not to be used or eaten right away. This can be done in a bowl of ice water or, for smaller vegetables, under cold running water. Without this speed cooling, the vegetables will continue to cook slowly for quite a long time, turning mushy and dull-colored. Chilled vegetables should be reheated very briefly so that they do not start to cook again.

If you plan to eat vegetables immediately after they've been cooked, there is no need to cool and reheat them; their textures and colors will be at their finest. If you do shock vegetables in a bowl of cold water, do not leave them long to soak, or they will become waterlogged. As soon as they are cool (but not chilled), put them in a colander to dry. It is certainly not a good idea simply to turn off the heat under a pot of simmering vegetables, leaving them to sit in the hot cooking water. They will continue to cook and will be quite mushy and unappealing by the time you remove them.

Potatoes and mushrooms merit their own sections in this chapter.

"Dry vegetables"—beans and lentils—are always eaten

cooked. Do not soak them in advance, as is commonly advised, since they might begin to sprout and ferment. A rapid boil before the long cooking, which is sometimes mentioned as a time-saving trick, should also be avoided. Just cook them long and gently; it's the best way.

Artichokes

Catherine de Médicis brought this Sicilian vegetable to France. For a long time artichokes were thought to ameliorate melancholy and fuel amorousness. A member of the thistle family, the artichoke is actually a flower bud with a tender heart.

Green or purple, small or large, round or oval, artichokes can be quite diverse. The most famous is the large round green globe artichoke of Brittany, but also beloved are the macau from the southwest of France and the smaller, pointed violet artichoke of Provence, also called *poivrade* and sold in bouquets of four or five heads. A young violet artichoke, available between April and July, is simply the best. It is tender and so can be eaten raw with a sprinkle of salt. Simply quarter, perhaps sprinkle with a few drops of lemon juice and olive oil, season with fleur de sel, and enjoy. The large artichokes of Brittany, cooked with their leaves, must be eaten with some dispatch.

Choose artichokes whose leaves are unblemished, tight, and brittle. One must not cut off the stem; it should be pulled out so as to remove as many fibers as possible. (For instructions on preparing an artichoke and separating the heart while it is raw, see page 179.) A cut artichoke discolors quickly; protect it in water with lemon juice or olive oil.

To keep raw artichokes fresh for a few days after purchase, put their stems in water as you would flowers. To keep cooked artichoke hearts for one or two days, keep them in their cooking water in the refrigerator.

BARIGOULE ARTICHOKES

Artichauts à la barigoule

SERVES 4
PREPARATION 30 minutes
COOKING 1 hour 30 minutes

Barigoule is not, as some French wits have teased, the name of a chef "known throughout Provence" but, rather, the Provençal name for a kind of fairy ring mushroom (or *mousseron*) with which you can stuff the artichoke. In that region, people were traditionally content to trim small violet artichokes at the stem and grill them with a bit of olive oil. The idea of stuffing them came later.

1 Trim the artichokes and prepare the hearts. Keep them in a bowl of water spritzed with lemon juice.

2 Bring a small saucepan of water to a boil and boil the zest for 30 seconds. Juice the orange.

3 Heat 1 teaspoon olive oil in a saucepan over low heat. Add the butter, and when it foams, add the shallots and cook for 3 minutes, stirring with a wooden spatula. Add the mushrooms and cook 3 for minutes, stirring. Strip the leaves from 1 sprig of thyme and sprinkle them into the pot; discard the stem. Season with 2 pinches of salt and 1 pinch of pepper and stir well.

4 Preheat the oven to 325°F/160°C. Line the bottom of an ovenproof casserole dish with the ham and add the remaining thyme, the bay leaves, blanched orange zest, and artichoke hearts. Season with salt and pepper and then spoon the mushrooms and shallots over the artichokes. Add 2 teaspoons olive oil, the wine, and orange juice. If necessary, add just enough water to cover the artichokes. Cover and bake in the oven for 1½ hours.

20 small violet artichokes
Lemon juice
Juice and zest of 1 organic orange, zest free of bitter white pith and cut into ½-inch-by-¼-inch (1-cm.-by-½-cm.) pieces
1 tablespoon olive oil
1 teaspoon butter
3 ounces (80 g.) shallots, peeled and minced
½ pound (250 g.) white button mushrooms, stem ends trimmed, cleaned, and sliced into ⅛-inch (3-mm.) slivers
2 sprigs fresh thyme
Salt
Pepper
2 thin slices country ham
2 bay leaves
½ bottle dry white wine (such as sauvignon)

Asparagus

Asparagus doesn't wait around; as soon as it is gathered, it begins to become more and more fibrous. To really enjoy asparagus, you should eat it the day it is picked.

One of the quintessential vegetables of spring, asparagus comes to the market in March. There is sweet white asparagus, the more or less bitter violet variety, the delicious green stalks with their more pronounced taste, and then the incomparable wild version.

The best asparagus have firm, smooth stalks without too many scales, and their buds are tight. Their color should be bright and clear. Their freshness can be judged by their fragility and by the moisture that appears when they are broken. They should break easily and neatly, with a clean snap. To keep them—which you can do for two or three days at most—do not expose them to air or light. Wrap them in a damp cloth and store them in the vegetable bin of the refrigerator.

PREPARING ASPARAGUS

Begin by using a little knife to remove the scales at the base of the head and all around the stem. Sometimes they harbor dirt or sand that neither washing nor cooking can budge. Then peel the stalk with a vegetable peeler, working from top to bottom. Plunge each stalk into a bowl of cold water as you peel your way through the bunch. Wash them well and drain in a colander.

COOKING ASPARAGUS UPRIGHT

The best part of asparagus—the tip—is also the most fragile and the fastest-cooking. To protect the tip while the stalk cooks, asparagus should be cooked upright so that the head is not submerged.

Choose asparagus that have a fairly consistent thickness so that they will cook in the same amount of time. If you must cook asparagus of different sizes, sort them by thickness and cook one batch at a time.

Asparagus can be steamed, but it tends to dull their color, which is too bad, especially for the green variety. It's best to cook them in simmering salted water.

Serve asparagus warm; they are much better that way. If you don't plan to eat them immediately after cooking, shock them in ice water to stop their cooking. Do not discard the cooking water. Remove the asparagus from the ice water, wrap them in a damp towel, and keep them in a warm place. When it's time to eat, bring the cooking water back to a very low simmer (but not a boil) and lower them in for a few seconds.

Hot asparagus are lovely with Mousseline Sauce (page 52) or Hollandaise Sauce (page 52). Eat cold asparagus with mayonnaise (page 55). Mayonnaise is less wonderful with hot asparagus because it cannot coat the hot stalks.

You can pair asparagus with eggs—scrambled, in an omelette, or baked (see the Eggs chapter, page 203). Green asparagus are the best match for eggs. White asparagus goes well with fish and meat—veal sweetbreads, for example. The tips make a nice addition to a salad or hors d'oeuvre.

Due to its reputation as an aphrodisiac, asparagus was never served at girls' convent schools in nineteenth-century France.

BASIC ASPARAGUS

Cuisson des asperges

variations

ASPARAGUS WITH HOLLANDAISE OR MOUSSELINE SAUCE
ASPARAGUS WITH MAYONNAISE
ASPARAGUS WITH HERBED VINAIGRETTE
ASPARAGUS WITH CRÈME FRAÎCHE AND CHERVIL

SERVES 2
PREPARATION 10 minutes
COOKING 5 minutes for green to 12 minutes for white

1 Wash the asparagus. Use a little knife to remove the scales around the tip and down each stalk. Peel the stalk with a vegetable peeler. As you finish each stalk, drop it in a container of cold water.

2 Tie the asparagus into bundles of 10 or 12. Tie them in 2 places: 2 inches (5 cm.) below the tips and 3 inches (8 cm.) lower than that—not too tight. Arrange each bundle so that all the tips are at the same level and then trim the bottoms of the stalks so that they are even. The stalks should now be no longer than 7 inches (18 cm.).

20 white or 30 green asparagus
1 teaspoon coarse salt

3   Fill a high-sided pot with enough water to reach the base of the asparagus tips (if the bunches are standing upright). Do not add the asparagus yet, but add the coarse salt and bring the water to a simmer.

4   Lower the asparagus bundles vertically into the pot; their heads should stay above the water. Cook green asparagus this way for 3 minutes, white asparagus for 7 minutes. Then use a skimmer to topple the bunches into the water, submerging the heads. Since the bundles will float, you should cover the surface of the water with a clean dish towel to keep them down for uniform cooking. Simmer green asparagus this way for 2 minutes, white for 5 minutes. The time may vary a little based on the size and freshness of the vegetables (the fresher they are, the shorter the cooking time). They are done when the tip of a knife pierces them without meeting any resistance. Do not overcook asparagus or they will become waterlogged.

ASPARAGUS WITH HOLLANDAISE OR MOUSSELINE SAUCE

White asparagus cooked this way is wonderful with hollandaise sauce or mousseline sauce. Follow the recipes on page 52, making only one-fourth the quantity indicated by quartering all ingredients. Serve the asparagus warm with the sauce.

ASPARAGUS WITH MAYONNAISE
Asperges à la mayonnaise

After cooking, shock the asparagus in ice water for 30 seconds and then drain it in a colander. Serve cooled with mayonnaise, again quartering the recipe on page 55.

ASPARAGUS WITH HERBED VINAIGRETTE

Asperges, sauce vinaigrette aux herbes

SERVES 4

PREPARATION AND COOKING 15 minutes

1 Prepare the asparagus as indicated in the recipe for basic asparagus (page 549). Prepare the vinaigrette and add the minced herbs to it.

2 Serve the asparagus hot or cooled but not refrigerated, preferably on a special asparagus dish or on a dish covered with a clean dish towel (to absorb excess moisture). Serve the vinaigrette on the side.

4 pounds (2 kg.) large asparagus

Coarse salt

1 cup (25 cl.) vinaigrette for green salads (page 59)

½ tablespoon minced chervil

½ tablespoon minced tarragon

½ tablespoon minced flat-leaf parsley

ASPARAGUS WITH CRÈME FRAÎCHE AND CHERVIL

Asperges à la crème fraîche et cerfeuil

SERVES 4

1 Put an empty bowl in the freezer. Prepare the asparagus as indicated in the recipe for basic asparagus (page 549). After cooking, shock the asparagus in a bowl of ice water for 30 seconds, then drain it in a colander.

2 Remove the bowl from the freezer and add the crème fraîche to it. Season with 3 pinches of salt and a dash of cayenne pepper. Beat with a whisk for about 1 minute, long enough to obtain a light but rich cream. Stir in the chervil and lemon juice.

3 Serve the asparagus cooled but not refrigerated, preferably on a special asparagus dish or on a dish covered with a clean dish towel (to absorb excess moisture). Serve the cream sauce on the side.

4 pounds (2 kg.) large white asparagus

Coarse salt

1 cup (25 cl.) well-chilled crème fraîche

Salt

Cayenne pepper

½ bunch chervil, chopped

Juice of ¼ lemon

WHITE ASPARAGUS WITH ORANGE SAUCE

Asperges blanches sauce à l'orange

SERVES 2

PREPARATION AND COOKING 15 minutes

The sauce should be prepared after the asparagus is cooked.

1 Prepare the asparagus as indicated in the recipe for Basic Asparagus (page 549). Prepare a bowl filled with cold water and ice cubes. When the asparagus is cooked, remove it from the pot with a skimmer and plunge it into the ice water. Leave it for 30 seconds and then drain.

2 Preheat the broiler. Prepare the clarified butter.

3 Put a kettle on to boil. Put a bowl in a large pot. When the water boils, pour it into the pot so that it reaches halfway up the outside of the bowl. Put the orange juice and yolks into the bowl and whisk. Turn on the heat, very low, and continue to whisk without stopping: The sauce should be thickening. Trace an *s* with your whisk. When you can see the bottom of the bowl in its wake, start whisking in the clarified butter little by little. Then whisk in the olive oil. Season with salt and pepper, whisk well, and remove from the heat.

4 Lay the asparagus side by side in a baking dish. Cover the stalks with orange sauce but leave the tips clean. Broil for 2–3 minutes about 5–7 inches from the heat source. Remove the dish as soon as the sauce begins to color. Serve.

16 large white asparagus

7 tablespoons (100 g.) clarified butter (page 43)

Juice of 1 orange

3 egg yolks (page 204)

½ cup (10 cl.) olive oil

Salt

Pepper

GREEN ASPARAGUS WITH PARMESAN

Asperges vertes au parmesan

SERVES 2

PREPARATION AND COOKING 15 minutes

1 Peel, wash, and drain the asparagus. Heat the oil in a pot for 1 minute over medium heat. Add the asparagus in a single layer, side by side. Roll them around in the oil with a wooden spoon and sprinkle with a pinch of salt. Cook for 6 minutes, constantly rolling the asparagus around. Use the tip of a

12 green asparagus

1 tablespoon olive oil

Salt

knife to check whether they are cooked; they should be lightly firm.

2 Put the asparagus on a dish and shower them with Parmesan shavings. Sprinkle with cooking juices and season with a pinch of pepper. If you have on hand the cooking juices left over from a chicken or veal roast, those would be good here, too.

½ ounce (15 g.) Parmesan cheese, shaved into flakes or ribbons with a vegetable peeler

Pepper

GREEN ASPARAGUS TIPS WITH MIXED HERBS _____

Asperges vertes aux fines herbes

SERVES   2 as a side dish
PREPARATION   10 minutes
COOKING   6 minutes

This makes a fine side dish for scrambled eggs, omelettes, duck breast, and rib steak (*côte de boeuf*), among other foods.

1 Peel and carefully wash the asparagus tips. Warm 2½ table-spoons oil in a pot over low heat. When it is hot, add the asparagus and stir well to coat with oil. Add the chicken broth, cover, and cook for 3 minutes over low heat.

2 Check to see whether the stock has evaporated. If it has, add a little water. Cover and cook 3 minutes more.

3 Turn off the heat. Sprinkle with a few drops of lemon juice and shower with the herbs. Taste for salt and pepper. Remove to a plate, drizzle with 1 teaspoon olive oil, and serve.

½ pound (250 g.) green asparagus tips

2½ tablespoons plus 1 teaspoon olive oil

½ cup (10 cl.) chicken broth (page 77 or made with a bouillon cube)

Lemon juice

1 tablespoon minced chervil

1 tablespoon minced chives

1 tablespoon minced flat-leaf parsley

Salt

Pepper

GREEN ASPARAGUS WITH COMTÉ AND OYSTER MUSHROOMS

Asperges vertes au comté et aux pleurotes jaunes

SERVES 4
PREPARATION 15 minutes
COOKING 20 minutes

1   Wash and trim the asparagus. Prepare a dish lined with 4 layers of paper towels. Bring 2 quarts (2 l.) water seasoned with 1 tablespoon coarse salt to a boil in a large pot. Plunge the asparagus into the simmering water and cook for 2 minutes, turning them with a skimmer. Remove with a skimmer or slotted spoon to the paper towel–lined dish to dry, patting it with the paper towels as necessary.

2   Melt 2 tablespoons butter in a skillet. When it foams, lay the asparagus in the skillet and turn the heat to low. Use a wooden spoon to turn them and baste with the butter. Sprinkle with the cheese and chives, continuing to cook and toss for 10 minutes.

3   Heat the roast chicken juices over low heat. Melt 1 tablespoon butter in another skillet. When it foams, add the mushrooms and sauté quickly over rather high heat. Turn them in the butter for a few seconds and then turn off the heat: Oyster mushrooms cook very quickly. Season lightly with salt and pepper.

4   Lay the asparagus on a dish and scatter the mushrooms over them. Drizzle with the warmed chicken juices and serve.

16 large green asparagus
Coarse salt
4 tablespoons (60 g.) butter
1 cup (4 ounces/110 g.) grated
    Comté cheese
2 bunches chives, minced
2 tablespoons juice from a
    roast chicken
40 yellow oyster mushroom
    caps, cleaned with a brush
Salt
Pepper

Beets

Beets have been familiar since antiquity to vegetable gardeners and the people they feed. In France beets are most often eaten in salad, but they can be eaten hot just as well.

Roasting in the oven is the best way to cook beets (see page 162). Their skin turns wrinkly and almost black. Boiled or steamed beets might be prettier, but they lose some flavor to the cooking water. Small beets are tastier than large ones, which are often quite fibrous.

BEET PURÉE

Purée de betteraves rouges

SERVES   4
PREPARATION   10 minutes
COOKING   40 minutes

This side dish goes especially well with game.

1   Heat the oil in a saucepan or pot over low heat. Add the onion and cook gently for 3 minutes, stirring with a wooden spoon. Add the vinegar and simmer for 15 minutes. Add the tomatoes, stir, and cook for 4 minutes, still over low heat. Add the beets, garlic, thyme, a pinch of salt, and a pinch of pepper. Stir well, cover, and cook gently for 15 minutes.

2   To make sure the beets are cooked, pierce one with the tip of a knife. It should slide in easily. At this point, blend the contents of the pot in a blender or food processor.

3   Pour the purée back into the saucepan and cook gently over very low heat for 2 or 3 minutes, just long enough to dry it out a bit. Stir constantly and scrape the bottom and sides of the pan to keep the purée from sticking. Turn off the heat, whisk in the crème fraîche, and serve.

2 tablespoons rapeseed oil if possible; if not, then peanut oil
1 onion, peeled and minced
2 tablespoons wine vinegar
2 tomatoes, peeled, seeded, and diced (page 124)
½ pound (250 g.) raw red beets, washed, peeled, and cut into ½-inch (1-cm.) dice
1 clove garlic, peeled, degermed (page 122), and minced
½ teaspoon thyme leaves
Salt
Pepper
2 tablespoons heavy cream or crème fraîche

Cabbage

The Greeks and Romans ate cabbage at banquets to mitigate the effects of drinking alcohol; philosophers recommended it. Diogenes in his barrel ate only cabbage and drank only water (the original cabbage soup diet, perhaps). He lived to be ninety.

The most familiar varieties of cabbage are the round, tight heads that can be white, green, or red. The French consider all types of kale part of the cabbage family, and they are indeed related.

A freshly picked cabbage should be heavy; its leaves should be firm and bright and should squeak under your fingers. The stem stump should be cut cleanly and should not seem to be turning brown.

Like many vegetables, cabbage does not keep particularly well and is best eaten as soon as possible after you bring it home. It cooks down quite a lot and will end up about half of its original volume. Cabbage that has been blanched before its final cooking is easier to digest; it just needs a quick dip in some boiling water. For instructions on washing, trimming, and blanching cabbage, see below.

BLANCHING CABBAGE

In a large saucepan, bring 1–2 quarts (1–2 l.) water (depending on the amount of cabbage) to a boil with 1–1½ tablespoons coarse salt. Remove the large outer leaves from the cabbage and cut out its core. Separate it into leaves and wash them in vinegar water—6 tablespoons distilled white vinegar per quart/liter water. Rinse well under cold water.

Plunge the cabbage leaves into the boiling water and cook for 2 minutes (4 minutes if you are blanching the heart of the cabbage without separating its leaves). Use a skimmer or slotted spoon to remove the cabbage from the water to a colander and rinse it under cold running water. Drain. Spread the leaves on a large plate, top with another plate, and press down to extract as much liquid as possible.

BUTTERED CABBAGE

Embeurrée de chou

SERVES 4 as a side dish
PREPARATION AND COOKING 20 minutes

This is good with fish, meat, or game.

Coarse salt
Leaves of 1 green cabbage, about 2 pounds (1 kg.), blanched (see above)
1 stick (¼ pound/120 g.) well-chilled butter, diced
Pepper
1 small cleaned truffle or 1 small can grated truffle (optional)

1   Bring 1½ quarts (1.5 l.) water to a boil with 2 teaspoons coarse salt. When the water is bubbling, add the already blanched cabbage leaves. Cook for 15 minutes. Use a slotted spoon or skimmer to remove the cabbage to a colander. Drain well, pressing down on the cabbage to extract as much water as possible.

2   Put the still-hot cabbage into a pot over medium heat. Add the cold, diced butter bit by bit, stirring it in with a wooden

spoon. Add 2 pinches of pepper and crush and stir the cabbage with a fork. Taste for salt and pepper.

3   For a special meal, you could grate some truffle over the cabbage just before serving.

RED CABBAGE WITH APPLES AND CHESTNUTS ——————

Chou rouge aux pommes et aux marrons

SERVES   5–6 as a side dish
PREPARATION   20 minutes
COOKING   1 hour and 10 minutes
The marinade must be prepared the night before.

This is good with game.

1   The night before, put the cabbage in a bowl with the sugar, vinegar, and a pinch of salt. Toss well, cover, and leave at room temperature overnight.

2   The next day, preheat the oven to 350°F/180°C. Melt the goose fat in a Dutch oven. When it has melted, add the onions and cook over low heat for 3 minutes, stirring with a wooden spoon. Add the cabbage and red wine and stir well.

3   Cut a piece of parchment paper the size of the pot; cut a little circle from its center, which will act as a chimney for cooking vapors. Lay the paper on the cabbage, cover the pot, and bake it in the oven for 30 minutes.

4   Remove the pot from the oven and stir in the chestnuts. Replace the parchment paper, cover, and bake 20 minutes more.

5   In the meantime, peel the apples and cut them into ½-inch (1-cm.) dice. Remove the seeds.

6   After 20 minutes, add the apples to the pot. Replace the parchment paper, cover, and bake 10 minutes more.

7   Remove the pot, discard the paper, season with salt and pepper to taste, and serve hot.

1 red cabbage, outer leaves and core removed, quartered, and then cut into shreds ¼ inch (0.5 cm.) thick
Pinch of sugar
1 teaspoon wine vinegar
Salt
3 tablespoons (45 g.) goose fat
1 large onion, peeled and sliced into rounds ⅛ inch (3 mm.) thick
1 cup (25 cl.) light red wine such as Pinot
½ pound (250 g.) peeled chestnuts
4 lady apples
Pepper

GREEN CABBAGE WITH BACON

Chou vert au lard

SERVES   4 as a side dish
PREPARATION   10 minutes
COOKING   1½ hours

This is good with pork or feathered game.

1   Preheat the oven to 400°F/200°C. Melt the goose fat in a pot. Add the onions and carrots, season with a dash of salt, and cook for 5 minutes over low heat, stirring with a wooden spoon. Add the blanched cabbage leaves, juniper berries, nutmeg, and a pinch of pepper. Tuck the pork belly and bouquet garni into the cabbage.
2   Add the chicken broth and bring to a boil. Cut a piece of parchment paper the size of the pot and pierce it a few times with a fork or the tip of a knife. Lay it on top of the cabbage, cover the pot, and bake in the oven for 1½ hours.
3   Remove the pork belly and bouquet garni after cooking. Slice the pork belly and lay it over the cabbage. Season with salt and pepper to taste.

2 tablespoons goose fat
2 medium onions, peeled and sliced into very thin rounds (less than ¼ inch/0.5 cm.)
2 medium carrots, peeled and sliced into very thin rounds (less than ¼ inch/0.5 cm.)
Salt
1 green cabbage, separated into leaves and blanched (page 556)
5 juniper berries
Pinch of grated nutmeg
Pepper
½ pound (250 g.) half-salt pork belly
1 bouquet garni (1 sprig fresh thyme, 5 stems parsley, and 1 sprig chervil, tied together)
2 cups (50 cl.) chicken broth (page 77 or made from a bouillon cube)

CABBAGE WITH MELTED TOMATOES AND SAFFRON _____

Chou à la fondue de tomates et au safran

SERVES   4
PREPARATION   10 minutes
COOKING   25 minutes

1   Preheat the oven to 400°F/200°C. Heat the olive oil in a pot over low heat and cook the shallot for 3 minutes, stirring with a wooden spoon. Add a pinch of salt, the tomatoes, one-fourth of the minced garlic, the bouquet garni, and the saffron. Cook for 10 minutes over low heat, stirring regularly.
2   Mix the parsley, the remaining garlic, and a pinch of pepper in a bowl. Lay the cabbage leaves in a baking dish. Top them with the tomato sauce and sprinkle with the parsley-garlic combination. Bake about 10 minutes.

1 tablespoon olive oil
1 shallot, peeled and minced
Salt
4 tomatoes, peeled, seeded, and diced (page 124)
4 cloves garlic, peeled, degermed (page 122), and minced
1 bouquet garni (1 sprig fresh thyme, 5 stems parsley, and 1 sprig chervil, tied together)
6 saffron threads
1 tablespoon minced parsley
Pepper
Leaves of ½ green cabbage, blanched (page 556), and sliced lengthwise into strips ½ inch (1 cm.) wide

BRUSSELS SPROUTS SAUTÉED IN BUTTER _____

Chou de Bruxelles sautés au beurre

SERVES   4 as a side dish
PREPARATION   10 minutes
COOKING   25 minutes

1   Put 1 quart (1 l.) water on to boil with 1 teaspoon coarse salt. Pick over the Brussels sprouts, removing any damaged or tired-looking leaves. Soak them for 2 minutes in a bowl of vinegary cold water (2 tablespoons vinegar per quart/liter of water). Rinse and drain.
2   Prepare a salad bowl half filled with cold water and a tray of

Coarse salt
1 pound (500 g.) Brussels sprouts
Malt vinegar

(continued)

ice cubes. When the pot of water is boiling, boil the Brussels sprouts for 1 minute. Remove them with a skimmer or slotted spoon to the bowl of ice water, leave them for 1 minute, and then put them in a colander to drain.

1 tablespoon butter
Salt
Pepper

3   Discard the ice water and boiling water. Bring 1 quart (1 l.) fresh water to a boil with 1 teaspoon coarse salt. When it bubbles, add the Brussels sprouts and simmer for 20 minutes. Do not let the water bubble vigorously, because this might break the sprouts apart. You want them to stay quite firm.

4   Fill the bowl with ice water again. When the sprouts are done, use a skimmer to remove them to the ice water. Drain them in a colander and then lay them on a plate lined with a clean cloth or paper towels.

5   Melt the butter in a skillet. Add the dried sprouts, turn the heat to low, and season with 2 pinches of salt and 1 pinch of pepper. Cook for 5 minutes, turning them in the butter with a wooden spoon.

Carrots

Up until the Renaissance, the carrot was nothing more than a root, and a pallid, tough, fibrous one at that. No wonder it didn't have many fans. Cross-breeding, however, made the carrot into the delicious orange specimen we know today.

Hippocrates attributed to the carrot several virtues that have been confirmed by modern medicine. Its high levels of carotene help children grow and give a boost to eyesight. It restores the blood and firms up the skin. It is also said in France that eating carrots makes us nicer.

The tender baby carrots of springtime are the best. The beds of carrots raised in Créances, France, on the English Channel, benefit from a blanket of hay, heather, rushes, and seaweed.

CHOOSING CARROTS

The younger and more orange a carrot, the more sugary it is. It should be tender and have skin that is thin, smooth, even, and unblemished; its green top should be firmly attached. A cracked carrot is one that was pulled from the earth later than it should have been.

Raw and grated, a sugary carrot gets along well with an acidic mixture of lemon, olive oil, and a bit of garlic. Try raw grated carrot with walnuts and hazelnuts, too (or with their oil) or almonds, pine nuts, raisins puffed by a short steaming, and, of course, parsley.

Cooked carrots are complemented by anything that supports a sugary note, most notably cumin and cilantro.

PEELING CARROTS

Small new carrots don't really need to be peeled; a good scrubbing will do. Larger carrots should be peeled lengthwise with a vegetable peeler for the nicest presentation.

GLAZED CARROTS

Carottes "glacées"

SERVES   4 as a side dish
PREPARATION   15 minutes
COOKING   about 30 minutes

1   Put the carrots in a large pot with 2 cups (50 cl.) water. The water should just cover them; if it doesn't, add more. Add a pinch of salt and the rest of the ingredients. (If you had to add much more water, add proportionally more sugar, too.)

2   To make sure the carrots cook gently and without coloring, cut a circle of parchment paper the size of the pot, prick it a few times with a fork or knife, and lay it on top of the carrots. Bring to a simmer and cook about 25 minutes over medium heat.

3   Remove the parchment paper and cook for 5 minutes uncovered. Rotate the pot on the burner and keep an eye on the heat. The carrots are cooked when all the water has disappeared, at which point they should be meltingly tender, glossy with butter and sugar, and perhaps slightly blonded by the heat.

1¼ pounds (600 g.) carrots, peeled and cut into rounds ⅛ inch (3 mm.) thick
Salt
4 tablespoons (60 g.) butter
2 tablespoons (30 g.) sugar

MELTING CARROTS WITH CUMIN

Carottes fondantes au cumin

SERVES 4
PREPARATION 15 minutes
COOKING about 30 minutes

2½ pounds (800 g.) young, tender carrots, peeled or scrubbed and cut into rounds ⅛ inch (3 mm.) thick
1 clove garlic, peeled and minced
½ teaspoon superfine sugar
½ teaspoon cumin
2 tablespoons olive oil
Salt
1 bouquet garni (2 stems parsley, 1 stalk celery, 1 sprig fresh thyme, and 1 stem cilantro, tied together)
Juice of 3 oranges

1 Put the carrots in a large pot. Add the garlic, sugar, cumin, olive oil, and a pinch of salt. Stir with a wooden spoon and add enough water to reach halfway up the carrots. Add the bouquet garni.
2 Cut a circle of parchment paper the size of the pot, prick it a few times with a fork or knife, and lay it on top of the carrots. Bring the pot to a boil and simmer for 25 minutes over medium heat.
3 Remove the parchment paper and the bouquet garni. Add the orange juice and cook 5 minutes more over low heat, until all the cooking juices have evaporated. Twirl the pot so the oil and sugar coat the carrots evenly, leaving them brilliantly, uniformly glazed.

NEW CARROTS FOR ROAST CHICKEN

Carottes nouvelles en cocotte pour un poulet rôti

SERVES 4 as a side dish
PREPARATION 10 minutes
COOKING 8 minutes

3 tablespoons plus 1 teaspoon olive oil
24 new carrots, with 2 inches (5 cm.) of their tops, scrubbed
4 cloves garlic, crushed but not peeled
4 small new onions, peeled
½ teaspoon superfine sugar
1 cup (20 cl.) chicken broth (page 77 or made from a bouillon cube)
Juices from a roast chicken, 10–15 tablespoons if possible
1 teaspoon minced parsley
Fleur de sel
Pepper

1 Heat 3 tablespoons olive oil in a large pot. Add the carrots, garlic, and onions. Sprinkle with sugar and add 3 tablespoons chicken broth. Cover and cook over low heat for 4 minutes. Add the rest of the broth and cook for 2 minutes, still covered. Add the roast chicken juices and cook, covered, 1 minute more.
2 Add the parsley, fleur de sel, a teaspoon olive oil, and a grinding of pepper. Taste for salt and pepper and serve.

Cauliflower

Choose cauliflower with no discoloration, and don't store them for too long before eating. If blotches appear on the florets while the vegetable is waiting for you to cook it, scrape the blemishes off with a sharp knife. Remove the green leaves and the stem. Pull or cut the florets apart.

Before cooking, cauliflower must always be blanched in a good deal of salted water to render it more digestible. For 1 pound (500 g.) cauliflower, blanch in $2\frac{1}{2}$ quarts (2.5 l.) water seasoned with 2 teaspoons coarse salt. Boil the florets for 2 minutes and then remove them with a slotted spoon. Discard the cooking water, bring a pot of fresh water to a boil, add the florets, and cook for 30 minutes at a fairly vigorous bubble to prevent the vegetable from becoming waterlogged. Drain and then cool in a bowl of ice water for 2 minutes.

Now the florets are ready to be served in a salad or cooked to finish, perhaps sautéed in butter. They can be baked in a gratin or puréed. For a purée, bundle the cauliflower in a clean dish towel and wring it out to remove as much water from the florets as possible. Blend them in a blender or food processor and then put them through a food mill into a saucepan. Cook over low heat with some crème fraîche, stirring with a spatula. Off the heat, stir in some butter before serving.

CAULIFLOWER WITH HARD-BOILED EGGS

Chou-fleur aux oeufs durs

SERVES   4 as a side dish
PREPARATION   25 minutes
COOKING   15 minutes

1   Preheat the oven to 400°F/200°C. Soak the cauliflower for 10 minutes in vinegar water—use 1 tablespoon vinegar per quart (liter) of water—and then rinse under cold running water.

2   Bring 1 quart (1 l.) water to a boil with 1 teaspoon coarse salt.

½ head cauliflower, separated into florets and rinsed
Distilled white vinegar
Coarse salt

(continued)

Prepare a large bowl half filled with cold water and a tray of ice cubes. When the pot bubbles, cook the cauliflower at a simmer for 10 minutes. Use a slotted spoon to remove it to the ice water. Leave it there to cool for 1 minute, then drain. Place the cauliflower on a dish lined with paper towels.

3 Grease the inside of a gratin dish with butter. Spread the cauliflower florets in the dish and dot with a little more butter. Bake for 15 minutes in the preheated oven.

4 Sprinkle the dish of cauliflower with the minced eggs, parsley, and bread crumbs. Drizzle with melted foamy butter.

Butter

3 hard-boiled eggs, peeled, white and yolks separated, and minced (page 208)

3 tablespoons minced parsley

½ cup dry bread crumbs

Celery and Celery Root

There are two kinds of celery: the stalky variety, which has been bred for maximum stalk growth above ground, and the round celery root, which is cultivated for abundant subterranean flesh.

Choosing a good celery root is easy. Simply make sure it is firm and heavy but not too big: The larger balls are often hollow. A celery root left whole can be kept in the refrigerator for several days before eating, but once the root is cut, it must be used as soon as possible. If you must keep a cut celery root for a while before cooking, rub it with lemon juice to reduce darkening and wrap it in plastic wrap to prevent its strong odor from perfuming the entire refrigerator.

Celery root is a fine choice of side dish with roast or sauced meat and game. Many Americans don't know that you can cook celery stalks, too—but you can.

HEART OF CELERY WITH BUTTER OR COOKING JUICES _____

Coeur de céleri-branche au beurre ou au jus

SERVES 4 as a side dish
PREPARATION AND COOKING   10 minutes using canned
celery or 40 minutes using
raw celery

This is good with a roast or grilled meat.

1   Drain the celery. If the hearts are large, cut them in half.
2   Heat the butter in a skillet. When it foams, add the celery
hearts and brown for 5 minutes over low heat, turning them
with a wooden spoon for even coloring. Sprinkle with
2 pinches of salt and 1 pinch of pepper. While the celery
cooks, use butter from the skillet to baste it. Cook canned
celery this way for 10 minutes total; cook raw celery for
40 minutes.
3   If you have juices left over from a roast, add them to the hot
skillet with the celery and spoon them over.

2 cans heart of celery (or poach
2 celery hearts in
simmering water until
crisp-tender)
2 teaspoons butter
Salt
Pepper
Juices from a roast if available
(optional)

CELERY ROOT PURÉE _____

Purée de céleri-rave

SERVES 4 as a side dish with pork, poultry, or game
PREPARATION   10 minutes
COOKING   20 minutes

1   Put ½ cup (10 cl.) water in a pot. Put the celery root and
potato chunks into the pot with the rosemary, some coarse
salt, and the milk. Pour in just enough water to cover everything. (The little bit of water at the beginning was just to
keep the milk from coating the pot.) Bring to a boil, cover,
and simmer for 20 minutes.
2   Drain the vegetables and discard the rosemary. Purée in a
blender or food processor and then blend in the crème
fraîche. Gently blend in the chilled butter.
3   Taste for salt and pepper and serve.

1 celery root, about 1 pound
(500 g.), peeled and
chopped into 1-inch (2-cm.)
chunks
2 medium potatoes, peeled and
cut into 1-inch (2-cm.)
chunks
1 small sprig rosemary
Coarse salt
1 cup (25 cl.) milk
2 tablespoons crème fraîche
1 tablespoon butter, diced and
well chilled
Salt
Pepper

CELERY ROOT WITH RAISINS AND CILANTRO ─────────

Céleri aux raisins secs et à la coriandre

SERVES 4
PREPARATION 15 minutes
COOKING 15 minutes
Raisins must soak at least 1 hour in advance.

1   At least 1 hour in advance, put the raisins to soak in a bowl of warm water.
2   Peel the celery root, rinse it with cold water, and cut it into ½-inch (1-cm.) dice. Sprinkle and toss the pieces with the lemon juice to keep them from turning too dark.
3   Drain the raisins. Heat the olive oil in a large saucepan. Add the celery root, onions, bouquet garni, coriander seeds, and raisins. Stir with a wooden spoon. Sprinkle with the cumin and add the broth. Stir, bring to a boil, and lower the heat.
4   Bring the wine to a boil in a small saucepan and then add it to the pot of celery root. Cover and cook for 12 minutes over low heat. At the end of cooking, add the tomatoes and vinegar. Taste for salt and pepper. Put the celery root in a serving dish and sprinkle it with cilantro to serve.

1 small handful (1 ounce/30 g.) raisins, Corinthian if possible
1 celery root, about 1 pound (500 g.)
Juice of 1 lemon
1 cup (15 cl.) olive oil
16 small white onions, peeled
1 bouquet garni (1 stalk celery, 2 sprigs fresh thyme, and 5 stems flat-leaf parsley, tied together)
1 tablespoon coriander seeds
½ teaspoon powdered cumin
1⅓ cups (20 cl.) chicken broth (page 77 or made from a bouillon cube)
1 cup (15 cl.) dry white wine
2 tomatoes, peeled, seeded, and diced (page 124)
5 tablespoons sherry vinegar
Salt
Pepper
1 tablespoon minced cilantro

Chestnuts

The first chill of autumn coincides with the return of chestnuts. The French call chestnuts that have more than one meat in the same husk *chataignes* and ones that have a single meat *marrons*. Today, most of the chestnuts we buy have already been husked and preserved, frozen, or vacuum-packed.

CHOOSING CHESTNUTS

If you buy whole chestnuts in the husk, the skin should be shiny and of a fine clear brown. The inside should be as crisp and cool as a freshly cut potato. Don't take dull or swollen chestnuts.

ROASTING CHESTNUTS

To roast chestnuts the way street vendors do, you need to choose specimens that are round on one side and flat on the other. The success of this cooking method depends entirely on the way you cut the chestnut: A poorly sliced chestnut will explode or cook badly. Take the chestnut in your left hand. With a sharp, pointy knife, make a lengthwise incision in its skin on the round side without slicing into the flesh. Leaving the flesh uncut is key. As it cooks, the chestnut gives off steam and puffs up a little. If it isn't well cut beforehand, the steam cannot escape fast enough, and the meat of the nut will cook too quickly and crumble. If the incision is made from the pointy tip to the bottom, it won't be large enough, and the chestnut will be crushed. A properly cooked chestnut should be easy to peel.

Put a skillet over medium heat. Lay the chestnuts in it cut side down; the chestnuts should not be touching. Cover and stir from time to time. At the beginning, a good deal of steam will escape from the skillet. After 15 or 20 minutes, a little smokiness will indicate that the chestnuts are cooked. Then it is time to remove the skin: Turn the heat to high. When the chestnuts have taken on a deep color, turn them onto the flat side to scorch them lightly. The skins should fall away of their own accord.

Preheat the oven to 400°F/200°C. Slice the husks on their rounded sides and bake for 7–8 minutes on a sheet pan with a little water. Remove the husks while they are still hot.

Another way: Make the incisions and then put the chestnuts, a few at a time, into very hot frying oil. Leave them for 2–3 minutes, drain, and remove the husks as soon as you can handle them, while they are still hot.

CHESTNUT PURÉE

Purée de marrons

SERVES   4

COOKING   about 1 hour

MAKING THE PURÉE   20 minutes

Chestnut purée is usually served with game, but it is also delicious with turkey, goose, and capon.

1 pound (500 g.) peeled chestnuts

1½ quarts (1.5 l.) milk

1 bouquet garni (2 sprigs thyme, 1 bay leaf, and 5 stems parsley, wrapped and tied, if possible, in a leek leaf)

1 stalk celery

Salt

Pepper

1 cup (30 cl.) heavy cream

2 tablespoons butter

1   Put the chestnuts in a saucepan with the milk, bouquet garni, celery, and 2 cups (50 cl.) water. Cook very gently for 40 minutes. Add 2 pinches of salt and 1 pinch of pepper. Simmer 20 minutes more, until the chestnuts are so soft you can crush them between your fingers.

2   Heat the cream gently. Drain the chestnuts and put them in small batches through a food mill fitted with its finest disk. Put the puréed chestnuts in a saucepan.

3   Use a spatula to fold the butter into the purée, stirring until it is completely incorporated. Stir in the hot cream in small ladles, continuing until you have a smooth purée. You may not need to use all the cream. The quantity you need will depend on the quality of the chestnuts you use.

4   Taste for salt and pepper and reheat gently for 5 minutes, stirring all the while and making sure you do not allow the purée to boil.

CHESTNUTS WITH ONIONS AND WALNUTS

Marrons confits aux petits oignons et aux noix

SERVES 4

PREPARATION 10 minutes

COOKING 55 minutes

1   Melt the butter in a Dutch oven large enough to hold all the chestnuts and vegetables in a single layer. When it foams, add the chestnuts, fennel, onions, and shallots and brown for 5 minutes over low heat, stirring with a wooden spoon. Add the chicken broth; the liquid should cover the vegetables. If it does not, add water to cover.

2   Cover the pot and simmer for 40 minutes without stirring. At the end of cooking, remove the cover and turn the heat to high for 4–5 minutes. Stir a little with a wooden spoon, very gently so as not to break up the chestnuts. Spoon cooking juices over the chestnuts, add the walnuts, and cook 5 minutes more without stirring.

3   Taste for salt and pepper. Serve very hot with all the cooking juices.

3 tablespoons butter

1¼ pounds (600 g.) peeled, ready-to-cook chestnuts

Heart of 1 small fennel bulb, trimmed and thinly sliced lengthwise

3 ounces (80 g.) small white onions, peeled

6 shallots, peeled

2 cups (50 cl.) chicken broth (page 77 or made from a bouillon cube)

2 ounces (60 g.) shelled fresh walnuts

Salt

Pepper

Eggplant

This beautiful foreigner of Indian origin was cultivated in China before the Middle Ages. The Arabs brought it to Europe. Like the tomato, a member of the solanaceous family of flowering plants, the eggplant, also like the tomato, was once reputed to be poisonous. For a long time eggplants were considered merely ornamental; only at the end of the eighteenth century did France discover their culinary potential.

Whether round or oblong, deep purple or white, every type of eggplant is good to eat. When you buy an eggplant, make sure it is fresh and not overripe, for an older eggplant will develop grains that spoil its flesh. Small, firm, somewhat chubby eggplants are preferable to large ones, for they have sweeter flesh with fewer grains. The skin should be taut, smooth, glossy, and without blemish.

It is all but impossible to ponder the way eggplant tastes without also thinking of typically Mediterranean flavors, especially olive oil and tomato. Eggplant can be eaten puréed, in custard, baked, fried, stuffed, or pan fried. There is also, of course, the eggplant purée we call "eggplant caviar," a sort of poor man's version of the piscine delicacy (see page 128). Fried slices of eggplant make a fine accompaniment for grilled lamb or rib steak.

EGGPLANT CONFIT

Aubergines confites

SERVES 8
PREPARATION 15 minutes
COOKING 25 minutes
This dish should be prepared half a day before you plan to eat it.

1 Wash the eggplants and remove their caps and bottoms. Slice them in half lengthwise and then quarter each piece horizontally.

2 Bring a small saucepan of water to a boil. Boil the lemon slices for 30 seconds. Drain them in a colander and rinse under cold water. Leave them in the colander to drain.

3 Heat the olive oil in a saucepan or other pot. Add the shallots, coriander seeds, sugar, and a dash of salt. Cook over low heat for 3 minutes, stirring with a wooden spoon. Add the wine, lemon juice, bay leaf, and savory. Stir well and add the eggplant pieces, tomatoes, carrots, and blanched lemon slices. Cover and simmer over low heat for 20 minutes.

4 Sprinkle with cilantro and refrigerate for half a day. Serve chilled.

2 pounds (1 kg.) eggplants, preferably baby ones
1 organic lemon, washed and sliced into rounds ⅛ inch (3 mm.) thick, plus juice of ½ lemon
½ cup (10 cl.) olive oil
2 shallots, peeled and minced
2 tablespoons crushed coriander seeds
½ tablespoon (10 g.) sugar
Salt
½ cup (10 cl.) dry white wine
1 bay leaf
2 sprigs savory
2 tomatoes, peeled, seeded, and diced (page 124)
3 ounces (100 g.) carrots, peeled and sliced into rounds ⅛ inch (3 mm.) thick
1 tablespoon minced cilantro

FRIED EGGPLANT

Aubergines frites

SERVES   4 to 6 as a side dish for grilled meat
PREPARATION AND COOKING   20 minutes

1   Prepare 3 deep dishes for breading, all in a row. Put the flour in the first. Beat the egg in the second with 1 pinch of salt and 1 pinch of pepper. Put the bread crumbs in the third.

2   Trim the eggplants of their caps and bottoms, and slice on a slight diagonal into rounds ¼ inch (0.5 cm.) thick. Dip each slice (coating it on both sides) into the flour, then the egg, and then the crumbs.

3   Prepare a dish lined with paper towels to drain the eggplant after frying. Fill a deep pot or Dutch oven with olive oil; the oil should reach to within 1 inch (2 cm.) of the top of the pot. Heat to 350°F/180°C. Pinch together a bit of flour and egg; when you drop this into oil that is the right temperature, it will bubble and sizzle right away.

4   When the oil is hot enough, fry the breaded eggplant slices. You will have to do this in several batches; they should not be crowded or on top of one another. If necessary, add oil and turn up the heat for proper sizzly cooking. Brown the first side for 2 minutes, then turn the slices with a skimmer or Chinese spoon. Cook the other side for 1–2 minutes, until it is golden, too. Adjust the heat as necessary.

5   Use the skimmer or Chinese spoon to remove the slices to the paper towel–lined plate. Turn them over and season with fleur de sel. They should be golden and very crunchy. Bring the oil back to the proper temperature and fry the next batch.

3 tablespoons flour
1 egg
Salt
Pepper
¾ cup dry bread crumbs
2 medium eggplants, about
    1½ pounds (750 g.) total
Olive oil for frying
Fleur de sel

STEWED EGGPLANTS WITH TOMATO

Compotée d'aubergines à la tomate

SERVES   6
PREPARATION   10 minutes
COOKING   30 minutes

1   Remove the caps and bottoms of the eggplants. Wash, dry, and peel them, leaving a band of skin on 2 of them. Slice them into rounds ½ inch (1 cm.) thick. Prepare a dish lined with 4 layers of paper towel.

2   Heat ½ cup (10 cl.) olive oil in a large skillet over rather high heat. Lay the eggplant rounds in the skillet in a single layer; work in batches if necessary. Cook for 2–3 minutes over medium heat, then flip and cook the other side for 2 minutes. Use a slotted spoon or skimmer to remove them to the paper towel–lined dish. Sauté the remaining slices if you are working in batches.

3   Heat 4 tablespoons olive oil in a Dutch oven. Add the tomatoes, tomato sauce, garlic, hot pepper, and cumin. Stir with a wooden spoon over low heat and season with salt and pepper. Simmer over low heat until the liquids have evaporated. Add the eggplants and 1 tablespoon each of cilantro and parsley. Mash everything together with a fork and cook over low heat for 20 minutes, stirring regularly.

4   At the end of cooking, mash again with a fork. Taste for salt and pepper and stir in the vinegar. Just before serving, stir in the diced preserved lemon and sprinkle with the remaining cilantro and parsley.

3 medium eggplants, about
    2 pounds (1 kg.) total
¾ cup olive oil
1¼ pounds (600 g.) very ripe
    tomatoes, peeled, seeded,
    and diced (page 124)
½ pound (250 g.) tomato sauce
1 clove garlic, peeled,
    degermed (page 122), and
    minced
1 small red hot pepper, fresh or
    dried
1 teaspoon ground cumin
Salt
Pepper
2 tablespoons minced cilantro
2 tablespoons minced flat-leaf
    parsley
1 tablespoon distilled white
    vinegar
1 salt-preserved lemon,
    chopped into small dice

BAKED EGGPLANT WITH PEPPERS AND SAVORY

Gratin d'aubergines et de poivrons à la sarriette

SERVES 4

PREPARATION 10 minutes

COOKING 45 minutes

1 Preheat the oven to 400°F/200°C. Trim the caps and bottoms of the eggplants. Wash, dry, and peel them. Slice into rounds ¼ inch (0.5 cm.) thick. Quarter the peppers.

2 In a small baking dish, layer the pepper and eggplant slices, alternating the vegetables and propping up the eggplant slices diagonally so that they are almost vertical. Season lightly with salt and pepper, add the olive oil, and bake for 30 minutes.

3 Remove the dish but leave the oven on. Scatter the olives over the vegetables and top with garlic, savory, and Gruyère. Bake 15 minutes more and then serve.

3 small eggplants, about ¾ pound (350 g.) total

4 red bell peppers, cooked, peeled, and seeded (page 130)

Salt

Pepper

½ cup (10 cl.) olive oil

50 pitted small black olives, Niçoise if possible

2 cloves garlic, peeled, degermed (page 122), and minced

1 tablespoon savory sprigs

1 cup (4 ounces/100 g.) grated Gruyère cheese

SAUTÉED EGGPLANT WITH MIXED HERBS

Aubergines sautées aux fines herbes

SERVES 4

PREPARATION 10 minutes

COOKING 7–8 minutes

The eggplant must be salted 1 hour in advance.

1 One hour before you plan to cook, trim the caps and bottoms of the eggplants. Wash them but do not peel. Slice them into rounds ½ inch (1 cm.) thick. Spread the slices on a dish and sprinkle with coarse salt. Leave them for 1 hour to drain.

2 After an hour, discard the water and salt in the dish. Dry the eggplants between layers of paper towel. If traces of salt remain, wipe them off with the paper towels along with the water.

4 small elongated eggplants, very firm, glossy, without blemish, taut-skinned, and of a deep purple color, about 1 pound (500 g.) total

Coarse salt

(continued)

3   Season the dried eggplants with pepper. Spread the flour in a dish and coat the eggplant slices in flour. Tap them to shake off any excess and set aside.

4   Prepare a dish lined with 4 layers of paper towel. Heat the olive oil in a large skillet over high heat for 1 minute, then lay the eggplant slices in the skillet in a single layer. If they won't all fit without crowding or overlapping, work in batches. Cook 3–4 minutes over medium heat, until they are pale gold; turn with a spatula and cook the other side for 3 minutes, too. Remove the eggplants to the paper towel–lined dish to drain a bit and then arrange them on a serving platter. Mix together the parsley, chervil, and basil, sprinkle over the eggplants, and serve hot.

Pepper

3–4 tablespoons flour

1 cup (20 cl.) olive oil

1 tablespoon minced parsley

1 tablespoon minced chervil

1 tablespoon minced basil

EGGPLANT TOWERS WITH MOZZARELLA AND TOMATO

Mille-feuilles à l'aubergine confite

SERVES   4

PREPARATION   15 minutes

COOKING   15 minutes

Use the best fresh mozzarella you can find for this dish, preferably mozzarella di bufala instead of a tasteless imitation.

1   Put 10 tablespoons olive oil into the freezer. Heat the remaining 6 tablespoons in a skillet over low heat. Cook the eggplant slices 4–5 minutes on one side and then 4–5 minutes on the other side, all over low heat. Season lightly with salt and pepper. Remove the eggplant and set aside. Cook the zucchini slices in the same skillet for 3 minutes per side, still over low heat. Sprinkle with salt and thyme.

2   Remove the oil from the freezer. Put half of it in a blender along with all but a few leaves of the basil. Blend until smooth. Give the mixture 2 pinches of salt and then add the rest of the oil in a thin stream while running the blender.

3   Season the mozzarella slices with salt and pepper.

4   Build 4 little stacks on a serving dish or individual plates: Begin with a slice of eggplant, then a tomato, a slice of moz-

1 cup (25 cl.) olive oil

2 medium eggplants, 1¼ pounds (600 g.) total, washed and cut into 8 slices ½ inch (1 cm.) thick

Salt

Pepper

2 medium zucchini, chopped on the diagonal into slices ¼ inch (0.5 cm.) thick

1 teaspoon thyme leaves

2 fistfuls basil leaves, washed and dried

1 ball mozzarella di bufala (about ¼ pound), cut into 8 slices

zarella, a slice of zucchini, and then repeat the layers. Season with a little fleur de sel and pepper. Drizzle each stack with a tablespoon of basil oil and drizzle a ring of the green oil around the vegetables. Garnish with basil leaves and serve at room temperature.

8 dried (or semidried) tomatoes, (page 588 or store-bought)
Fleur de sel

EGGPLANT WAFFLES WITH PORCINI MUSHROOMS

Gaufre d'aubergine aux cèpes

SERVES 4
PREPARATION   10 minutes
COOKING   6–7 minutes

1   Heat a waffle iron. Wash the eggplants and cut 4 slices from them, each one 4 inches by 2 inches, and ½ inch thick (10 by 5 by 1.5 cm.). Season the slices with salt and pepper and coat with 2 tablespoons olive oil. Cook in the waffle iron for 6–7 minutes.

2   In the meantime, beat the lemon juice with some salt and pepper. Whisk in 5 tablespoons olive oil. Lightly brush the quartered mushrooms with some of this lemon sauce.

3   Lay the eggplant "waffles" on a serving platter or individual plates and top with mushrooms and then arugula. Sprinkle lightly with fleur de sel and pepper and use a vegetable peeler to shave some Parmesan over each waffle. Top with a few drops of balsamic vinegar and serve.

2 round eggplants, about ½ pound (250 g.) each
Salt
Pepper
7 tablespoons olive oil
Juice of ½ lemon
4 small porcini mushrooms, cleaned and quartered lengthwise
Handful of arugula leaves, cleaned
Fleur de sel
Parmesan cheese
Balsamic vinegar

Endive

Endives are generally eaten raw, in a little salad with walnuts and walnut oil or neutral oil seasoned with a pinch of curry powder. In northern France and in Belgium, however, there is a strong tradition of cooking endive and bitter frisée.

Wash endives carefully, but do not leave them to soak, in a basin of cold water. Remove the cone-shaped core to tone down the vegetable's bitterness. In terms of trimming, all you need to do is remove any bruised leaves from the outside of the endive and chop off a bit of the green tip.

CREAMED ENDIVES

Endives à la crème

SERVES   4 as a side dish
PREPARATION   5 minutes
COOKING   5 minutes

1   Slice the endives lengthwise into strips less than ¼ inch (0.5 cm.) wide. Cut these strips into ¼-inch (0.5-cm.) pieces. Melt the butter in a skillet. When it foams, add the endives and cook for 2 minutes over low heat, stirring with a wooden spoon to coat evenly with butter. Season with 2 pinches of salt and 1 pinch of pepper. Stir in the cream and cook 2 minutes more.

2   If you like, you can add paprika to the cream before you pour it into the skillet.

16 small endives, cleaned and trimmed
2 teaspoons butter
Salt
Pepper
½ cup (10 cl.) heavy cream
⅓ teaspoon paprika (optional)

SAUTÉED ENDIVES

Endives poêlées

SERVES   4 as a side dish
PREPARATION   5 minutes
COOKING   35 minutes

This is good with duck or pheasant.

1   Bring 1 quart (1 l.) water to a boil in a saucepan with 1 teaspoon coarse salt. Add the lemon juice and 1 tablespoon sugar.

2   When the water bubbles, add the endives and boil somewhat vigorously for 30 minutes. When they are quite tender, remove the endives to a colander to dry, pressing on them with a ladle to remove as much water as possible.

3   Melt the butter in a Dutch oven (large enough to hold the endives in a single layer) over medium heat. When it foams, add the endives in a single layer. Sprinkle with the remaining sugar, 2 pinches of salt, and 1 pinch of pepper. Cook for 3 minutes over medium heat, then turn them with a wooden spoon and cook the other side for 3 minutes. Drain them in a colander and serve.

Coarse salt
2 tablespoons lemon juice
1½ tablespoons superfine sugar
8 endives, cleaned, dried, and trimmed
2 teaspoons butter
Salt
Pepper

ENDIVE LEAVES WITH HONEY

Effeuillée d'endives au miel

SERVES 4
PREPARATION 5 minutes
COOKING 5 minutes

1   Slice the endives lengthwise into strips less than ¼ inch (0.5 cm.) wide. Cut these strips into pieces ¼ inch (0.5 cm.) long.

2   Heat the olive oil in a Dutch oven over medium heat. Add the endives and cook for 3 minutes, stirring with a wooden spoon. Add 2 pinches of salt, 1 pinch of pepper, and 1 tablespoon water. Cover and cook for 5 minutes over low heat.

3   Remove the cover but leave the heat on. Sprinkle with four-spice powder and honey. Stir and cook over high heat for 2 minutes.

4   Remove to a dish, sprinkle with chives, and serve.

8 medium endives, washed, dried, and trimmed
1 tablespoon olive oil
Salt
Pepper
Pinch of four-spice powder (a blend of powdered nutmeg, cinnamon, clove, and ginger; you can mix it yourself)
1 teaspoon honey
1 teaspoon snipped chives

Fava Beans

An ancestral vegetable originally from Asia, fava beans have been cultivated since antiquity.

Fava beans must be very fresh. Just feel the pods to make sure they are well filled. They should feel rather firm, but it is a bad sign if they are swollen.

Very young fava beans can be eaten raw with nothing but salt. Slightly older beans must be removed not only from their pods but also from their individual shells to be enjoyed.

The larger a fava bean gets, the thicker and more indigestible its individual coat. To peel, give the beans a quick dip in boiling salted water (see page 168). Poached in simmering water for 5–6 minutes and seasoned with butter or olive oil, fava beans can be made into a purée or a soup and are often paired with savory, a favorite complement.

SMOTHERED FAVA BEANS WITH ONIONS AND SMALL LARDONS

Etuvée de fèves aux oignons et aux petits lardons

SERVES   2–4 as a side dish
PREPARATION   10 minutes
COOKING   30 minutes

This is good with rabbit and veal liver.

1   Melt the butter in a small pot. Add the onions, sugar, and salt and stir with a wooden spoon. Cook for 3 minutes over low heat, stirring, and then cover and cook over low heat for 20 minutes or until the onions are easily pierced with a fork. Stir every 2 or 3 minutes.

2   Heat 1 teaspoon olive oil in another pot. Add the lardons and brown over medium heat for 4 minutes, stirring. Spoon away and discard as much fat as possible but do not remove the lardons. Put the pot over low heat and add the onions and fava beans. Reheat gently and sprinkle with thyme, pepper, and the remaining tablespoon olive oil. Season with fleur de sel and serve.

1 teaspoon butter
16 small white onions, peeled
1 teaspoon superfine sugar
Salt
1 teaspoon plus 1 tablespoon olive oil
1 cup (120 g.) smoked lardons (page 89)
½ pound (250 g.) fava beans from about 2 pounds (1 kg.) whole pods shelled, peeled, and poached (page 577; see page 168 for peeling instructions)
Generous pinch of thyme leaves
Pepper
Fleur de sel

Green Beans

Green beans—and especially the young, slender green beans called by their French name, *haricots verts*—must be very fresh. If you try to bend a green bean, a good one will snap cleanly instead of folding in half. Green beans become more fibrous very soon after they are harvested. They have strings that must be removed. Choose the thinnest green beans you can find, all the same size. If they seem a little shriveled, you can soak them in very cold water for an hour; they'll firm up a bit.

Trim them with care, snipping off both ends. Unless they are truly just-picked, remove the string from each bean by snapping it in half and simply pulling the string away.

Trimmed green beans should be cooked uncovered in a good deal of salted boiling water (2 teaspoons of coarse salt per quart/liter). Unless you plan to eat them right away, put them in ice water to cool immediately after removing them from the cooking water.

GREEN BEANS AND PEAS WITH TOMATOES AND HAM ————

Haricots verts et petits pois aux tomates et jambon cru

SERVES   4 as a side dish
PREPARATION AND COOKING   35 minutes

This is good with lamb and veal.

1   Put 1 quart (1 l.) water in a saucepan with 1 teaspoon coarse salt. Bring to a bubble and boil the peas for 3–4 minutes. With a skimmer, remove them to a colander and rinse with cold water for 1 minute. Drain.

2   Bring 2 quarts (2 l.) fresh water to a boil in a saucepan with 1 tablespoon coarse salt. When the pot bubbles, boil the green beans for 10–15 minutes, depending on their size and freshness. They should still be firm when you finish. With a skimmer, remove them to a colander and rinse under cold running water for 1 minute. Leave them in the colander to drain.

3   Heat 2 tablespoons olive oil in a pot over medium heat. When it is quite hot, add the diced ham and cook for 3 minutes without allowing it to dry out; adjust the heat if necessary. Add the green beans, fava beans, and peas and stir. Then add the tomatoes and chicken broth (or water) and cook gently for 7–8 minutes.

Coarse salt

¼ pound (100 g.) green peas, shelled

½ pound (250 g.) green beans, French-style *haricots verts* if possible, trimmed and with the strings removed

2 tablespoons olive oil

3 ounces (100 g.) cured, uncooked ham, cut into dice ½ inch by ½ inch (1 cm. by 1 cm.)

¼ pound (100 g.) fava beans, shelled and peeled (page 168)

2 tomatoes, peeled, seeded, and diced (page 124)

4 tablespoons chicken broth (page 77) or use water

Leeks

In France, leeks are called poor man's asparagus, but the truth is that they are not a vegetable to turn up your nose at. Long before it landed in European pots, the leek had a special place in Egyptian and Hebrew cookery. The Romans enjoyed leeks, too, and Nero would eat them to soothe his voice after declaiming his poems. For centuries in France, leeks have been an important vegetable.

Leeks are available all year round. In autumn and especially in winter they are large and have a stronger taste. In spring the first slender leeks of the new crop arrive with their own tender, exquisite flavor. They can be simply grilled over coals, without any precooking, and eaten with some fleur de sel and a drizzle of olive oil. Their wild cousins, ramps, are the stars of American farmers' markets for a brief period every spring.

When buying leeks, look for fresh specimens with brilliant green leaves that squeak when rubbed between your fingers. The white part should be firm, and the little root end should be firmly attached.

Leeks must be washed several times in warm water as you pull their leaves apart a bit. When you have the time, it's best to soak them for 10 minutes in warm water (page 126). If you cook leeks and don't plan to use them right away, put them straight into a bowl of ice water when they come out of the cooking water. This will keep them firm.

Leeks are finished in much the same way asparagus are, but for the most part it is only the white part that is eaten. The green part can be delicious, too, if the leek in question is very young.

Leeks are quite versatile and go well with chicken, beef, veal, pork, fish, and shellfish.

LEEKS AND LARDONS

Poireaux à la poitrine fumée

SERVES 4
PREPARATION 10 minutes
COOKING 40 minutes

Heat the oil in a saucepan or Dutch oven. Add the lardons and cook about 3 minutes over low heat, until they are just barely turning blond. Add the leeks, ½ teaspoon salt, and a pinch of pepper. Toss to mix with a wooden spoon, cover, and cook over very low heat about 35 minutes, stirring from time to time until the leeks are stewed and melted. Taste for salt and pepper.

1 teaspoon neutral oil

2 cups (200 g.) smoked lardons (page 89) or chopped bacon

6 leeks, white parts only, well washed, dried with a clean cloth or paper towel, and chopped into 1-inch (2-cm.) pieces

Salt

Pepper

Peas

In the spring, when they are fresh, peas are delicious. During the rest of the year you can buy frozen or canned peas.

Fresh peas can be smothered (*à la française*, with very little water) or cooked in boiling salted water. Canned peas should not be boiled; they will turn tough. Frozen peas need not be thawed before they are cooked.

Add a little sugar to cooking peas; they can use it.

SMOTHERED PEAS WITH ONIONS *À LA FRANÇAISE* _____

Petits pois aux petits oignons (à la française)

SERVES   4
PREPARATION   10 minutes
COOKING   20–30 minutes

Put all the vegetables and herbs in a saucepan with the sugar, half of the butter, and 2 pinches of salt. Mix well. Add ½ cup water, cover, and bring to a boil. Cook gently for 20–30 minutes, depending on the type of pea and the season. At the end of cooking, remove the bouquet garni and gently stir in the rest of the butter. Taste for salt and add a little more sugar if you think the peas need it.

2¼ pounds (1.2 kg.) pea pods, shelled and washed
1 small head lettuce, washed and quartered
12 small new onions, peeled
1 bouquet garni (3 stems parsley, 2 sprigs chervil, and 1 small sprig savory, tied together)
½ teaspoon superfine sugar
4 tablespoons (65 g.) butter
Salt

BUTTERED PEAS _____

Petits pois au beurre

SERVES   4
PREPARATION   10 minutes for fresh peas
COOKING   8–10 minutes

1   Bring 1 quart (1 l.) water to a boil with 1 teaspoon coarse salt. Add the peas and the mint to the boiling water. When it returns to a boil, cook for 8–10 minutes, depending on the type of pea and the season.

2   Drain the peas. Spread them on a dish and sprinkle with sugar. Dot with butter and stir gently but well to coat the peas with butter. Serve very hot.

Coarse salt
2¼ pounds (1.2 kg.) pea pods, shelled and washed
1 small sprig fresh mint
½ teaspoon superfine sugar
4 tablespoons (65 g.) butter

Salsify

Salsify and its cousin called *crosne* in French (and Chinese artichoke in English) are two of those old-fashioned, knobby winter vegetables that have been somewhat forgotten. They are marvelous accompaniments, however, to roast meat, whether beef, pork, veal, or poultry. True, it takes some time to prepare them for cooking. You might be able to find good frozen salsify, which is already peeled, cleaned, and ready to go.

But if what you have to deal with is fresh salsify: Wash it carefully and peel it with a vegetable peeler, putting each piece into a bowl of lemon water as soon as it is finished. (Salsify is quick to darken.) Cut it into even-sized pieces 2 inches (4 or 5 cm.) long.

Prepare a mixture that will allow you to keep and cook salsify and some other white vegetables: Pour a bowl of cold water into a large bowl. Add 1½ tablespoons flour, 1½ tablespoons coarse salt, 2 tablespoons lemon juice, and 3 tablespoons oil. Mix well and then pour the bowl's contents into 2 quarts (2 l.) water waiting in a large pot or Dutch oven. Stir with a whisk and bring to a boil, whisking constantly to prevent the flour from sticking to the pot and burning. When the water boils, add the salsify and cover the pot, leaving the lid ajar to discourage boiling over. Boil for 30–40 minutes. To make sure the vegetable is cooked, prick it with the tip of a knife, which should slide in easily. Salsify should be eaten right away with a little butter, or it should be kept in the refrigerator.

SALSIFY WITH ROAST JUICES

Salsifis au jus

SERVES   4 as a side dish for a roast
PREPARATION   15 minutes
COOKING   40 minutes

Prepare the salsify as indicated page 583. When it has finished cooking, drain. Melt the butter in a casserole. When it foams, add the drained salsify and cook for a few minutes over low heat, stirring. Add the juices from the roast and simmer about 10 minutes. Taste for salt and pepper and serve sprinkled with chervil.

2½ pounds (800 g.) salsify
1½ tablespoons flour
1½ tablespoons coarse salt
2 tablespoons lemon juice
3 tablespoons oil
4 tablespoons (65 g.) butter
Juice from a meat or poultry
   roast
Salt
Pepper
1 tablespoon minced chervil

CHINESE ARTICHOKES SAUTÉED IN BUTTER

Crosnes sautés au beurre

SERVES   4
PREPARATION   10 minutes
COOKING   20 minutes

Wash and peel the tubers as indicated on page 583 for salsify. Bring 2 quarts (2 l.) water to a boil in a pot with the coarse salt. Boil the Chinese artichokes for 12–15 minutes. This is a vegetable that should remain slightly crunchy, or it will have an unpleasantly floury mouthfeel. Drain. Melt the butter in a skillet. When it foams, add the drained vegetable and cook for 5 minutes, stirring. Taste for salt and pepper and sprinkle with chervil to serve.

1 pound (500 g.) Chinese
   artichokes
1½ tablespoons coarse salt
3 tablespoons butter
Salt
Pepper
1 tablespoon minced chervil

Spinach

Despite the reputation it gained from the cartoon character Popeye, spinach does not contain huge amounts of iron, but it is full of vitamins A and C and various minerals. Its leaves should be glossy and bright green, and its stems should be cleanly cut.

Sautéed, steamed, or boiled, spinach cooks down dramatically. You should begin with about ½ pound (250 g.) raw spinach per person. Raw or cooked, spinach is a delicate vegetable and does not keep well. It soon begins to disintegrate into black mush.

BASIC SPINACH

Cuisson des épinards

SERVES 4 as a side dish
PREPARATION 10 minutes
COOKING 3–4 minutes

This is good with eggs, haddock, roasts, and more.

Wash the spinach in 2 changes of water, using a good deal of water each time. Remove the stems (this is not necessary if the spinach is quite young). Melt the butter in a sauté pan or skillet. Add the spinach and turn the heat to medium. Season with a pinch of pepper and a pinch of nutmeg, and salt lightly, just a pinch—spinach is naturally salty. Stick the clove of garlic on a fork and rub it over the spinach just to perfume its surface. Cook for 3–4 minutes, stirring with a large wooden spoon. This encourages evaporation and helps the spinach maintain its lovely green.

2 pounds (1 kg.) spinach
1 tablespoon butter
Pepper
Pinch of grated nutmeg
Salt
1 clove garlic, peeled

CHOPPED SPINACH AND SOFT-BOILED EGGS WITH CRUNCHY HAM

Epinards hâchés, oeufs mollets, et croustilles de jambon cru

SERVES 4

PREPARATION AND COOKING 45 minutes

1 Preheat the oven to 180°F/80°C. Line a sheet pan with parchment paper and lay the ham on top of it. Bake in the oven for 35 minutes.

2 Cook the spinach as indicated in the previous recipe. Drain the spinach and squeeze it even drier. Shape it into 4 balls and put them through a chopper. (If you don't have a chopper, chop the balls on a cutting board with a large, very sharp knife.)

3 Melt 2 teaspoons butter in a pot. When it foams, add the spinach and season with 2 pinches of salt, 1 pinch of pepper, and 1 pinch of grated nutmeg. Stir. When the spinach is hot again, divide it among 4 small ovenproof plates. Lay a shelled soft-boiled egg in the middle of each bed of spinach.

4 When the ham is quite dry, slice each piece in half lengthwise. Put 2 pieces of ham on each plate. At the last minute, slash each egg in half. Serve.

4 small slices cured, uncooked ham
2 pounds (1 kg.) fresh spinach
1 tablespoon plus 2 teaspoons butter
Pepper
Grated nutmeg
Salt
1 clove garlic, peeled
4 soft-boiled eggs (page 205)

Tomatoes

Although it is indigenous to the Americas, the tomato has become essential to many European cuisines, including that of France. The tomato is at once a condiment, a vegetable, and a fruit.

Of all fresh vegetables, the tomato is the most widely cultivated in France, even more than the potato. Few vegetables lend themselves to such an astonishing variety of uses. Its slightly sour, somewhat acidic, and even sweet taste allows it to enter into culinary wedlock with all kinds of crustaceans, shellfish, fish, meat, other vegetables, eggs, and pasta. Tomatoes also make good soup, cold or hot (pages 114 and 84) and can even be used as a base for sweets and refreshing sorbets or as a garnish for fish and meat.

In general, tomatoes are red, but there do exist yellow, purplish, green, and even white and black varieties, such as the delectable black Crimean tomato. As for shape, tomatoes fall into three categories: round, which includes cherry tomatoes; oblong; and ribbed, which bulge irregularly from cap to base.

_____

A tomato should feel firm to the touch but also juicy. Its skin should be shiny, smooth, unmarked, and uniformly colored. Besides the way it looks, the way it smells should be considered. Snap off a bit of the stem, if you can, and take a good whiff. The odor should be that of a tomato and certainly not that of a lime.

Tomatoes keep well enough, but they are sun fruits at heart and are not fond of a chill. It is best to store them in a cool room, 53–57°F (12–14°C).

The entire tomato is edible, but for many recipes you will discard the skin and seeds. Actually, it is always best to peel tomatoes before eating (for instructions, see page 124). The best way to skin a tomato, when possible, is to stick it on a fork and turn it in an open flame until its skin cracks away.

DICED COOKED TOMATO _____

Tomate concassée

Heat the olive oil in a saucepan or Dutch oven. Add the butter. When it foams, add the tomatoes and all the other ingredients. Season to taste with salt and pepper. Stir and bring to a boil over medium heat, stirring occasionally. Cook for 30 minutes, stirring regularly and scraping the sides and bottom of the pot with a spatula.

1 tablespoon olive oil

1 tablespoon butter

1 pound (500 g.) very ripe tomatoes, peeled, seeded, and chopped (page 124)

1 medium onion, peeled and minced

1 clove garlic, crushed

1 bouquet garni (½ bay leaf, 3 sprigs fresh thyme, and 5 stems parsley, tied together)

½ teaspoon confectioners' sugar

Salt

Pepper

PROVENÇAL TOMATOES

Tomates à la provençale

SERVES   8
PREPARATION   10 minutes
COOKING   20 minutes

1 Preheat the oven to 400°F/200°C. Mix the bread crumbs with the parsley, garlic, a pinch of salt, and a dash of pepper.

2 Heat the olive oil in a skillet large enough to hold the tomatoes in a single layer set over medium heat. When the oil is hot, lay the tomatoes in the skillet cut side down. Brown without stirring until they are almost caramelized, about 5 minutes.

3 Lay the tomatoes side by side in a single layer in a baking dish, cooked side up. Pour their cooking juices all over them and season with 3 pinches of salt. Spread the crumb-parsley-garlic mixture over the tomatoes and sprinkle the thyme over all.

4 Bake in the middle of the oven, uncovered, until the crumbs are nicely toasted, about 15 minutes.

¼ cup dry bread crumbs
2 tablespoons minced flat-leaf parsley
4 cloves garlic, peeled, degermed (page 122), and minced
Salt
Pepper
2 tablespoons olive oil
8 medium tomatoes, halved through their equators
1½ teaspoons thyme leaves

OVEN-DRIED TOMATOES

Tomates confites

PREPARATION   10 minutes
COOKING   3 hours

1 Preheat the oven to 170°F/80°C. Bring 1 quart (1 l.) water to a boil. When it bubbles, boil the tomatoes for 1 minute. Remove them with a skimmer and put them in a colander to drain.

2 Peel and quarter the tomatoes. Scoop out their seeds with a spoon.

3 Lay all the tomato quarters side by side in a sheet pan or baking dish. Season with a bare trace of fleur de sel and pepper, but hold yourself back: Long cooking will concentrate the salt and pepper a good deal. Pour 1 tablespoon olive oil over each tomato and top with the garlic and thyme.

PER TOMATO YOU WILL NEED
Fleur de sel
Pepper
1 tablespoon olive oil
1 clove garlic, crushed but not peeled
1 sprig fresh thyme

4   Bake for 1½ hours. Flip the tomatoes and bake 1½ hours more.

5   The tomatoes will keep for a few days. To keep them longer—for a few weeks—put them in a jar, cover them with olive oil, and seal.

6   To make half-dried tomatoes, follow this recipe but bake the tomatoes 30 minutes per side (1 hour total).

Turnips

There is no disputing that turnips are best when they are very small, in the spring. Peel them carefully, for they have a double skin. Rinse them clean but do not put them in water to soak; they are spongy and will become waterlogged.

Take turnips that are as close in size as possible for even cooking.

BUTTERED TURNIPS

Navets au beurre

SERVES   4
COOKING   12–15 minutes

1   Put the turnips in a saucepan large enough to hold them all in a single layer. Add enough cold water to reach halfway up the turnips, the sugar, butter, and coarse salt. Cut a round of parchment paper to fit inside the pot; pierce it a few times with a fork or sharp knife. Place it on top of the turnips.

2   Bring to a boil and then adjust the heat so that the liquid simmers. Swirl the pot and gently turn the turnips every once in a while. The turnips should be cooked when all the water has disappeared, at which point they will be a very pale gold and glossy with butter and sugar.

1½ pounds (800 g.) small new turnips, peeled
1 tablespoon sugar
4 tablespoons (65 g.) butter
Scant teaspoon coarse salt

SMOTHERED BABY TURNIPS WITH CHICKEN JUICES _____

Petits navets nouveaux étuvés au jus de volaille

SERVES 4
PREPARATION 10 minutes
COOKING 15 minutes

1   At least 15 minutes in advance, peel and wash the turnips. Put them in a bowl and sprinkle with the confectioners' sugar and 2 pinches of salt. Toss and leave to rest.

2   Fifteen minutes later, melt the butter in a sauté pan or other pot large enough to hold the turnips in a single layer without crowding. Add the turnips and cook for 5 minutes over medium heat, turning them with a wooden spoon.

3   Add to the pot 5 tablespoons chicken broth and 5 table-spoons juices from the roast. Cover and simmer for 5 minutes, still over medium heat.

4   Add the remaining broth and juices. Turn the turnips, replace the cover, and cook 5 minutes more. Serve sprinkled with parsley.

1½ pounds (800 g.) small new turnips, peeled
2 teaspoons (10 g.) confectioners' sugar
Salt
2 tablespoons butter
½ cup (10 cl.) chicken broth (page 77 or made from a bouillon cube)
½ cup (10 cl.) juices from a roast chicken
1 tablespoon minced parsley

Zucchini _____

For a long time the only place in France you could find zucchini was in a Provençal market. This vegetable hails from South America, like its cousin the squash, but now it is grown everywhere.

There are several varieties of zucchini: round or oblong, solid green or striped or marbled, yellow or a green so pale as to be almost white.

Small zucchini are the best. They should be firm to the touch with glossy skin free of blemishes and scratches, and the cap should be firmly attached. If the skin feels slightly rough when you stroke it, you can be sure the zucchini was recently harvested. Zucchini don't keep very well in the refrigerator; after a few days they become mushy and begin to grow mold.

Zucchini blossoms are also good to eat, stuffed or fried. When they are in season, they are very sought after in the Midi region of France. They are quite fragile. Choose the "male" flowers if you can; they are larger. The smaller females are more easily used as an addition to a salad. Male or female, blossoms are too delicate to wash. Simply pat them very gently with paper towels to lift away any traces of dirt, being careful all the while not to do any damage.

It is nice to peel strips of skin lengthwise from zucchini to achieve a striped effect. Then slice them into rounds ¼ inch (0.5 cm.) thick to pan fry in 1½ tablespoons of hot oil, sautéing each side for 2 minutes. Or steam the rounds for 10 minutes. Zucchini also make a fine soup (page 85) or gratin (page 666).

FRIED ZUCCHINI

Courgettes frites

SERVES   4
PREPARATION   15 minutes
COOKING   10 minutes

1   Prepare 3 deep dishes in a row. Spread the flour in the first one, beat the egg with salt and pepper in the second, and spread the crumbs in the third. Dip each zucchini slice in the flour, tapping off any excess, and then in the egg and in the bread crumbs. Set each breaded slice on a dish as you go.

2   Bring the oil to 350°F/180°C. Prepare a dish lined with 3 layers of paper towels. If you do not have a thermometer, you can check the oil's temperature by dropping in a sliver of breaded zucchini; this should set the oil bubbling.

3   Working in batches of 10, fry the zucchini slices for 2 minutes. Turn them with a skimmer or Chinese spoon and cook the other side for 1 minute. They should become golden and quite crunchy. The oil should not smoke; if it threatens to (or does), lower the heat, even if it means you have to turn the heat back up to prepare the oil for the next batch of slices.

4   With a skimmer or slotted spoon, remove the zucchini to the paper towel–lined plate. Sprinkle with fleur de sel and serve immediately.

⅓ cup (50 g.) flour
1 egg
Salt
Pepper
1 heaping cup dry bread crumbs
¾ pound (350 g.) zucchini, washed and sliced into rounds ¼ inch (6 mm.) thick
1 quart (1 l.) neutral oil for frying
Fleur de sel

SUMMER SQUASH AND BLOSSOMS WITH MINT AND FRESH ALMONDS

Courgettes et fleurs à la menthe et aux amandes fraîches

SERVES   4

PREPARATION AND COOKING   45 minutes

2 young zucchini

4 ounces (100 g.) fresh
    almonds, peeled

1 tablespoon curry powder

Salt

Pepper

4 zucchini blossoms, "male" if
    possible

6 small white onions, peeled

Flour

Olive oil for frying

Fleur de sel

1 tablespoon butter

⅔ cup (2½ ounces/75 g.)
    lardons (page 89)

2 teaspoons minced mint
    leaves

1   Wash the zucchini and dry them with a paper towel. Cut strips of flesh with the skin still attached, about ¼ inch (6 mm.) wide and deep. (You will not use the zucchini cores in this recipe and can save them for another use, such as soup.) Cut the strips into ¼-inch (6-mm.) dice and put them in a plastic bag. Add the almonds and curry to the bag along with some salt and pepper; shake vigorously to combine and set the bag aside to rest.

2   Gently clean the blossoms (page 591) and slice them into thirds lengthwise; be careful not to bruise or tear the delicate petals. Sprinkle the onions and blossoms with flour, tapping them to remove any excess.

3   In a small pot for frying, heat 1 quart (1 l.) olive oil to 300°F/150°C. Prepare a plate lined with 3 layers of paper towel. When the oil is hot, fry the onions for 2 minutes. Turn them with a skimmer and fry 1 minute more. If the oil smokes or threatens to smoke, lower the heat; if the oil is too hot, the onions will burn. With a skimmer or Chinese spoon, remove the onions from the oil, letting as much oil as possible drip back into the pot. Lay them on the paper towel–lined dish to drain. Sprinkle with fleur de sel. Fish out of the oil any stray bits of breading or onion.

4   Put 1 tablespoon flour in a bowl with ⅔ cup cold water and beat together. Bring the frying oil back to 300°F/150°C. With your fingers, carefully dip the zucchini blossoms in the bowl of batter and then fry them for 1 minute. Turn and fry 1 minute more. Remove them with the skimmer or Chinese spoon to the paper towel–lined plate. Season with fleur de sel.

5   Melt the butter in a skillet. Brown the lardons over medium heat for 3 minutes, stirring and tossing with a wooden spoon. Remove the lardons, rinse the skillet with hot water, and wipe it out with a paper towel. Heat 6 tablespoons olive oil in the skillet over high heat. Add the diced zucchini and almonds and stir. Cook over high heat for 3–4 minutes, stir-

ring occasionally. The zucchini should still be crisp. Turn off the heat. Taste for salt, pepper, and curry, adding more if necessary. Sprinkle with the mint leaves and toss to mix.

6 Lay the zucchini and almonds in the middle of a dish, topped with lardons and surrounded by fried onions and blossoms.

STUFFED ZUCCHINI

Courgette farcie

SERVES 4
PREPARATION 30 minutes
COOKING 10 minutes

1 Wash the zucchini and dry them with paper towels. Cut 4 lengthwise ribbons of zucchini skin and flesh, rather wide and ¼ inch (6 mm.) thick. Season these ribbons on both sides with salt and pepper. Cut the rest of the zucchini into small dice.

2 Heat 3 tablespoons olive oil in a skillet over high heat. Add the zucchini ribbons and cook for 3 minutes. Turn them with a wooden spatula and cook 2 minutes more, still over high heat. Set them aside.

3 Add the remaining 2 tablespoons olive oil to the skillet and warm over low heat. Add the onions and cook for 1 minute, stirring and seasoning with 2 pinches of salt. Add the diced zucchini, raise the heat to high, and stir and cook 2 minutes more. Put the skillet aside and allow the zucchini to cool.

4 Preheat the oven to 400°F/200°C.

5 When the sautéed zucchini is warm but not hot, add the egg, two-thirds of the grated Parmesan, and the basil. Mix well and add salt and pepper to taste. Put a tablespoon of this stuffing in the middle of each zucchini ribbon and fold the ends over the middle. Brush a baking dish with olive oil, lay the zucchini bundles in it, and sprinkle with the rest of the Parmesan. Bake for 10 minutes and serve hot from the oven.

4 zucchini, about ½ pound (200 g.) each
Salt
Pepper
5 tablespoons olive oil
8 small white onions, peeled and finely sliced
1 egg yolk (page 204)
½ cup (2 ounces/50 g.) grated Parmesan cheese
1 tablespoon minced basil

ZUCCHINI STUFFED WITH TOMATOES

Courgettes farcies à la tomate

SERVES 4
PREPARATION 1 hour
COOKING 20 minutes

1 Preheat the oven to 440°F/220°C. Make small incisions in the eggplant and insert the garlic matchsticks. Wrap the eggplant in aluminum foil and bake for 1 hour.

2 In the meantime, cut the zucchini in half lengthwise. Use a spoon to scoop out their flesh, leaving just ⅛ inch or so (a few millimeters) of it attached to the skin. Season the cavities with salt and pepper, and turn the zucchinis cut side down on a rack placed over a plate (they will lose some water). Cut the scooped-out flesh into ¼-inch (0.5-cm.) dice and put it in a bowl.

3 Heat 1 tablespoon olive oil in a skillet. Add the tomatoes, season lightly with salt and pepper, and cook over low heat for 15 minutes, stirring with a wooden spoon. Remove the tomatoes to a bowl.

4 Add 1 more tablespoon olive oil to the skillet and warm over low heat. Add the onions, season with a pinch of salt, and cook, stirring, for 1 minute over low heat. Add the zucchini dice, return the heat to high, and cook and stir for 3 minutes. Season with salt and a pinch of curry powder and stir. Remove the contents of the skillet to the bowl in which the diced zucchini rested before.

5 Add the minced almonds to the bowl of zucchini and onion, along with the mint and cream cheese. Stir well to combine.

6 After 1 hour, remove the eggplant from the oven and lower the heat to 350°F/180°C. Cut the eggplant in half and scoop out its flesh with a spoon. Chop the pulp and add it to the bowl. Season with salt, pepper, and curry and stir.

7 Oil a baking dish. Lay the scooped-out zucchini boats side by side in the dish and stuff them with the mixture in the bowl. Pour the chicken broth into the dish and bake in the oven for 20 minutes.

1 eggplant
1 clove garlic, peeled and chopped into matchsticks
4 zucchini, washed and dried
Salt
3 tablespoons olive oil
1 pound (500 g.) tomatoes, peeled, seeded, and diced (page 124)
Pepper
2 small white onions, peeled and thinly sliced
Pinch of curry powder
1 tablespoon peeled and minced fresh almonds
1 tablespoon minced mint leaves
1 tablespoon *fromage blanc* or cream cheese
½ cup (20 cl.) chicken broth (page 77 or made from a bouillon cube)

Mixed Vegetable Dishes

SPRING VEGETABLES
Printanière de légumes

SERVES 4

PREPARATION 1 hour

COOKING at least 30 minutes: 3 minutes for the peas, 5 minutes each for the fava beans and mushrooms, 5 to 10 minutes for the green beans, 25 minutes each for the onions, turnips, carrots, and celery plus 5 minutes all together at the end

To preserve their characteristic flavors, all the vegetables must be cooked separately and then combined and warmed with butter at the end. For this spring dish use as many of the vegetables as you like and can find. If one or two are unavailable or not to your liking, just add a little more of some of the others or something else.

6 tablespoons (80 g.) butter

¼ pound (100 g.) small new white onions, peeled

2 tablespoons sugar

Salt

Pepper

12 small baby turnips, trimmed and peeled

1 heart of celery, stalks cut into ½-inch (1-cm.) pieces

12 small new carrots with 1 inch (2.5 cm.) greens attached, scrubbed or peeled as necessary

(continued)

1   Heat 1 tablespoon butter in a saucepan for 1 minute. When it foams, add the onions and cook for 3 minutes over low heat, stirring. Add 1 tablespoon sugar, 2 pinches of salt, and 1 pinch of pepper. Cover and cook over low heat for 25 minutes, rotating the saucepan 3 times in the last 5 minutes.

2   In the meantime, if you have enough saucepans, you can begin to cook the other vegetables. Cook the turnips and celery in separate pots the same way you cooked the onions but without the sugar. If you must cook 1 vegetable at a time, rinse out the saucepan when the onions are finished and move on to the turnips. Do the same for the celery.

3   To cook the carrots, cut out a circle of parchment paper the size of the saucepan you will use for them. Prick it a few times with a fork or knife. Heat 1 tablespoon butter over low heat for 1 minute, then add the carrots and stir for 3 minutes with a wooden spoon. Add 2 pinches of salt, 1 pinch of pepper, and 1 tablespoon sugar. Just barely cover the carrots with water and lay the piece of parchment paper on top. Cook over low heat, uncovered, for 20 minutes. In the last 5 minutes, rotate the saucepan on the burner and peek to

make sure the carrots are not sticking to the bottom. If necessary, add ½ cup water.

4   Bring 2 cups water to a boil with ⅓ teaspoon coarse salt. Add the peas and let simmer for 3 minutes. Put them in a colander and cool them under running water, about 1–2 minutes. Drain. Change the water and do the same with the fava beans for 5 minutes and the green beans for 5 minutes if they are slender or 10 minutes if they are larger. Cool them all the same way. Once they have drained, you can combine all the vegetables in one salad bowl.

5   Heat 1 tablespoon butter in a sauté pan or skillet. Add the mushrooms and cook over medium heat for 5 minutes, stirring with a wooden spoon. Sprinkle with a pinch of salt and a pinch of pepper.

6   When it is time to serve the vegetables, melt 1 tablespoon butter in a large pot. When it foams, add all the vegetables except the asparagus tips. Stir, taste, and season with fleur de sel and pepper if necessary. Warm over low heat for 5 minutes, stirring twice. Add the asparagus tips and cover the dish to keep warm until the minute it is served.

Coarse salt

Peas (as many as are in 10 pods), shelled

Small fava beans (as many as are in 10 pods), shelled and peeled (see page 168)

20 *haricots verts* or the slenderest green beans you can find, ends trimmed

3 ounces (100 g.) chanterelle or white button mushrooms, ends trimmed and caps cleaned

12 green asparagus stalks, already cooked (page 549), tips only

Fleur de sel

RATATOUILLE

SERVES 8
PREPARATION 45 minutes
COOKING 40 minutes

The secret of a good ratatouille is to cook the vegetables separately so each will taste truly of itself.

1 Heat 4 tablespoons olive oil in a large pot. Add the onions and cook over low heat for 3 minutes, stirring with a wooden spoon. Add the bell peppers and garlic and stir. Sprinkle with 2 pinches of salt and 1 pinch of pepper and stir. Cover and cook over low heat for 5 minutes. Add the tomatoes and another pinch of salt and pepper. Leave to cook, covered, over low heat.

2 In the meantime, heat 4 tablespoons olive oil in a skillet or sauté pan over medium heat for 2 minutes. Sauté the zucchini for 4 minutes, stirring with a wooden spoon. Remove with a skimmer or slotted spoon to a plate. Cook the eggplant for 4 minutes over medium heat in the same skillet, then remove it to the plate with the zucchini. Sprinkle the zucchini and eggplant with thyme, 2 pinches of salt, and 1 pinch of pepper. Put them in the pot with the onions, bell peppers, and tomatoes. Add a dash of saffron if you like. Add the bouquet garni, cover, and cook over low heat for 25 minutes.

3 At the end of cooking, remove the bouquet garni, taste for salt and pepper, and stir in 2 tablespoons olive oil.

10 tablespoons (15 cl.) olive oil
2 medium onions, thinly sliced
1 green bell pepper, peeled, seeded (page 130), and sliced into pieces 1 inch by ½ inch (2 cm. by 1 cm.)
1 red bell pepper, peeled, seeded (page 130), and sliced into pieces 1 inch by ½ inch (2 cm. by 1 cm.)
4 cloves garlic, peeled, degermed (page 122), and minced
Salt
Pepper
2 pounds (1 kg.) tomatoes, peeled, seeded, and diced (page 124)
3 small zucchini, washed but unpeeled, chopped into pieces 1 inch by ½ inch (2 cm. by 1 cm.)
2 small eggplants, washed but unpeeled, chopped into pieces 1 inch by ½ inch (2 cm. by 1 cm.)
½ teaspoon fresh thyme leaves
Dash of saffron threads (optional)
1 bouquet garni (2 sprigs thyme, 1 bay leaf, and 6 stems parsley, tied together)

Mushrooms

Most mushrooms grow only in the wild. Only a few varieties, such as button and oyster, have been successfully cultivated.

Wild mushrooms must be gathered by knowledgeable hunters, since eating certain species can cause serious illness and even death.

They should be as fresh as possible and have firm skin. Mushrooms gathered in the morning and cooked that same day have a taste that simply cannot be compared to that of mushrooms cooked the next day. Don't buy mushrooms that show traces of mold, look drably matte or wrinkled, or feel spongy; they are probably rotten or worm-infested. When cooked, they will give off a lot of water.

If you must store mushrooms for a few hours before cooking, wrap them in a barely dampened cloth and put them at the bottom of the refrigerator.

The smaller the mushroom, the better. Large mushrooms are old and more likely to be hiding spoiled sections.

CLEANING MUSHROOMS

In general, you should avoid washing mushrooms and should certainly not try to clean them by soaking them in water. It is generally best to separate the cap from the stem and then sweep the cap gently with a pastry brush. If the mushrooms are quite dirty, wipe them clean with a paper towel.

No matter what kind of mushroom you're dealing with, you should trim away the earth end of the stem. Whittle it away with a small knife as you would sharpen a pencil. Use a small knife to scrape away the stem's surface layer. Afterward, lay them on a paper towel.

White button mushrooms and morels are not so very fragile and can be rinsed in water. Button mushrooms especially should be rinsed several times (but still not soaked). Then wipe them clean and dry with paper towels.

Chanterelles

Chanterelles appear in late spring and are the most common wild mushroom (though they are still quite precious). The early ones are better than those you will find in autumn.

This mushroom's color ranges from pale yellow to a deep gold. It is shaped like a funnel with rippled sides; the ripples of young mushrooms fold under, and the ripples on an older mushroom fold up. Its underside is creased down into a thick stem that thins out toward the bottom.

CHANTERELLES

Girolles

variation

CREAMED CHANTERELLES

SERVES 4
PREPARATION 15 minutes
COOKING about 5 minutes

1 Cut the larger mushrooms into halves or thirds so that all the mushrooms and mushroom pieces are about the same size.

2 In a large saucepan or pot, bring 3 quarts (3 l.) water to a boil with 1 tablespoon coarse salt. When it bubbles, lower the mushrooms in and then remove them immediately. Drain well and place on paper towels to dry.

3 Melt ½ tablespoon butter (or heat 1 teaspoon olive oil) in a skillet. When it foams, cook the shallots with a dash of salt about 3 minutes over low heat, stirring, until they are translucent. Remove them with a slotted spoon.

4 Melt the remaining butter in the same skillet. When it foams, add the chanterelles and turn the heat to medium. Cook and stir about 5 minutes. The best way to tell whether they are done is to taste: They should still be tender and should be lightly golden but certainly not burnt and dried out.

5 When the mushrooms are done, turn off the heat. Put the shallots back in the skillet, season to taste with salt and pepper, and, if you like, sprinkle with herbs. Stir and serve.

Garlic is not recommended for chanterelles, since its pungent flavor will obliterate the mushroom's delicate one. If, however, you are a die-hard garlic lover, you might rub the skillet with a peeled clove before adding the butter for a subtle touch of flavor.

1¼ pounds (600 g.) chanterelle mushrooms, cleaned with paper towels
Coarse salt
1½ tablespoons butter or olive oil
2 shallots, peeled and minced
Salt
Pepper
1 tablespoon minced flat-leaf parsley or chervil (optional)

CREAMED CHANTERELLES

Fricassée de girolles à la crème

SERVES 4

Prepare the chanterelles according to the previous recipe. When the mushrooms have finished cooking, add the crème fraîche to the skillet and boil rapidly for 1 minute, stirring so that the chanterelles are evenly, perfectly coated with cream. Taste for salt and pepper and serve.

1¼ pounds (600 g.) chanterelle mushrooms cooked as page 599

2 tablespoons crème fraîche

STEWED CHANTERELLES WITH ZUCCHINI AND FAVA BEANS

Ragoût de girolles, de courgettes, et de fèves

SERVES 4
PREPARATION 5 minutes
COOKING 7 minutes

1   Heat 2 tablespoons olive oil in a saucepan or Dutch oven large enough to hold all the zucchini in a single layer. When it is hot, lay the zucchini rounds in the pot over low heat. Add the garlic, drizzle with the remaining olive oil, season with ½ teaspoon salt and a pinch of pepper, and cook for 3 minutes. The zucchini should not color in this time. Turn them over and raise the heat to medium. Add the mushrooms and cook for 30 seconds, stirring, and then cover and cook 2 minutes over medium heat. Add the fava beans, cover, and cook 2 minutes more.

2   Taste for salt and pepper. Garnish with chives, toss, and serve.

3 tablespoons olive oil

2 zucchini (about ½ pound/ 250 g.), washed but unpeeled and sliced into ¼-inch (0.5-cm.) rounds

2 cloves garlic, peeled, degermed (page 122), and cut in half

Salt

Pepper

½ pound (250 g.) chanterelle mushrooms, brushed and wiped with paper towels

3 ounces (100 g.) fava beans, shucked and peeled

1 tablespoon minced chives

CHANTERELLES WITH DRIED APRICOTS AND FRESH ALMONDS

Girolles aux abricots secs et aux amandes fraîches

SERVES 4
PREPARATION 30 minutes
COOKING 6 minutes

1 Bring 3 quarts (3 l.) water to a boil with 1 tablespoon coarse salt. When it bubbles, submerge the chanterelles for a few seconds and then remove them with a slotted spoon or skimmer. Drain them well.

2 Melt the butter in a big pot or saucepan. When it foams, add the onion and a pinch of salt. Cook and stir for about 3 minutes over low heat; do not allow the onion to color. Stir in the apricots. Pour in the kirsch and let it reduce for 1 minute, stirring constantly.

3 Add the mushrooms and chicken broth and cook over low heat for 6 minutes. Stir in the almonds, chervil, lemon juice, and, if you are using it, curry powder to finish. Taste for salt and pepper.

Coarse salt
¾ pound (400 g.) chanterelle mushrooms, wiped clean with paper towels
1 teaspoon butter
1 medium onion, peeled and finely chopped
8 dried apricots, finely chopped
3 tablespoons kirsch
½ cup (15 cl.) chicken broth (page 77 or made from a bouillon cube)
20 fresh almonds, peeled and slivered
1 tablespoon minced chervil
Juice of ½ lemon
Dash of curry powder (optional)
Salt
Pepper

Morels

Morels are a special case on account of what is lodged in their honeycomb texturing: dirt, sand, and even little beasties. You must cut morels in half, remove any live creatures, and rinse the mushrooms quickly under barely warm running water. If you soak them in water, their flavor will be carried away along with their dirt.

These mushrooms are available only from the end of March through May. They are characterized by their conical caps, which are imprinted with a spongy network. Blond, black, gray, sometimes white, purple, or even greenish, morels exist in at least twenty different forms. Certain members of the morel family are toxic when eaten raw; therefore, morels must always be cooked.

MORELS

Morilles

SERVES 4 as a side dish
PREPARATION 15 minutes
COOKING about 5 minutes

These are good with asparagus, veal roast, scrambled eggs, or in an omelette.

1 If some of the morels are especially large, remove their stems so that you end up with mushrooms and pieces that are all about the same size.

2 Melt ½ tablespoon butter in a skillet. When it foams, turn the heat to low and add the shallots and a dash of salt. Cook and stir about 3 minutes, until the shallots are translucent. Remove them with a skimmer.

3 Melt the remaining butter in the same skillet. When it foams, add the mushrooms and stir so that the butter coats them well. Turn the heat to low and cook for 3 minutes. Put the shallots back in the skillet with 1–2 tablespoons crème fraîche, according to your taste, and cook 2 minutes more. The mushrooms should still be tender when you finish. Season to taste with salt and pepper.

1¼ pounds (600 g.) morel mushrooms, cleaned as indicated page 601
1½ tablespoons butter
2 small shallots, peeled and minced
Salt
1–2 tablespoons crème fraîche, according to taste
Pepper

MORELS AND ASPARAGUS WITH CHERVIL ──────────────

Etuvée de morilles et d'asperges au cerfeuil

SERVES   4
PREPARATION   15 minutes
COOKING   about 5 minutes

1   Wash the mushrooms according to the directions on page 601. Trim away the least attractive parts of the mushrooms so that you end up with about 3 ounces (100 g.) of scraps. Bring the broth to a boil in a saucepan. Submerge the scraps in the broth, turn down the heat, cover the saucepan, and leave to infuse over very low heat for 20 minutes.

2   Set a food mill fitted with its finest screen over another saucepan. Put the contents of the infusing saucepan, including the broth, through the food mill into the saucepan. Bring to a boil and let the pot bubble for 10 minutes, then lower the heat and stir in the cream with a wooden spoon. Cook for 1 minute without allowing the liquids to bubble. Remove the butter from the refrigerator and dice 3 tablespoons. Stir it in bit by bit. Add 3 drops Tabasco and taste for salt and pepper.

3   Melt ½ tablespoon butter in a skillet. When it foams, turn the heat to low and cook the shallot with a dash of salt until it is translucent, about 3 minutes. Remove the shallot with a slotted spoon.

4   Melt 1 tablespoon butter in the same skillet. When it foams, add the mushrooms over low heat and stir to coat with butter. Add the asparagus and cook and stir for 3 minutes. Put the shallot back in the skillet, along with the chervil, and cook 2 minutes more. Season to taste with salt and pepper.

5   Spread some of the morel cream on a serving dish and lay the whole morels and asparagus on top of it.

1¼ pounds (600 g.) morel mushrooms
2 cups (50 cl.) chicken broth (page 77 or made from a bouillon cube)
½ cup (15 cl.) heavy cream
4½ tablespoons (65 g.) butter, well chilled
Tabasco sauce
Salt
Pepper
1 shallot, peeled and minced
20 large green asparagus, cooked according to the recipe on page 549
1 tablespoon minced chervil

Oyster Mushrooms

The oyster mushroom, when cultivated, is one of the most affordable, along with the white button mushroom. Held in high esteem in culinary circles, the oyster mushroom lends dishes a subtle flavor.

There are two main types of oyster mushroom. The rarer is called *oreille de chardon* in French. It appears only in the spring and fall, and is very hard to find, which is a shame because its musky taste is finer than that of the more common oyster mushroom. The *oreille de chardon* is generally eaten fresh when available but can also be preserved in oil or dried.

The shell-shaped oyster mushroom sometimes occurs naturally but for the most part is a product of cultivation. Its flesh is elastic but firm.

Cultivated mushrooms can be gray or yellow. The yellow ones are to be preferred, as are the small ones.

OYSTER MUSHROOMS

Pleurotes

SERVES 4

PREPARATION AND COOKING 15 minutes

1   Melt the butter or heat the olive oil in a skillet. When it foams, turn the heat to low and cook the shallot with a pinch of salt for about 3 minutes, stirring. Remove the shallot with a skimmer or slotted spoon.

2   Turn the heat to high. Add the mushrooms and garlic. Be prepared for them to cook very quickly. Leave them just a few seconds on the first side, turn them over, and remove them with a skimmer after a few seconds on the other side. In a bowl, combine the mushrooms and shallot. Season with ½ teaspoon salt and a pinch of pepper. Stir in the parsley and correct the seasoning if necessary.

1 tablespoon butter or olive oil
1 shallot, peeled and minced
Salt
1¼ pounds (600 g.) oyster mushrooms, swept clean with a pastry brush and stems and caps separated
1 clove garlic, peeled, degermed (page 122), and very finely minced (optional)
Pepper
1 tablespoon minced flat-leaf parsley

Porcini

This is the king of mushrooms, "the flesh of the gods," as Nero said. There are four groups in the porcini family, listed here in descending order of desirability: the Bordeaux porcini, with its more or less brownish ochre–colored cap; the bronzed porcini or *tête de negre,* with its musky odor; the pine porcini, which is mahogany colored; and the summer porcini, a seasonal treat that is pale in color and has a decorative web around its food. They come for the most part from southwest France, Auvergne, Sologne, and Alsace. Fresh porcini mushrooms are very hard to find in the United States, and even dried porcinis are quite expensive.

PORCINI MUSHROOMS

Cèpes

SERVES 4
PREPARATION 15 minutes
COOKING about 5 minutes

1¼ pounds (600 g.) porcini mushrooms, stem ends trimmed and cleaned with paper towels

2 tablespoons olive oil

2 cloves garlic, peeled, degermed (page 122), and minced

Salt

Pepper

1 tablespoon flat-leaf parsley

Slice the caps and stems of the mushrooms into slivers ⅛ inch (3 mm.) thick. Heat the oil in a skillet. When it is hot, sauté the strips for 3 minutes over low heat, stirring regularly to prevent them from sticking. Stir in the garlic and cook 2 minutes more. After about 5 minutes total, the mushrooms should be done, but the best way to make sure is to taste. They should still be tender and lightly golden but not burned, which would leave them dry. Season to taste with salt and pepper, and sprinkle with parsley.

PORCINI SALAD

Salade de cèpes

SERVES 4
PREPARATION 20 minutes

You must have particularly fresh mushrooms to make this salad. It won't have quite the same effect, but you can also make this salad with white button mushrooms instead of porcinis.

1   Prepare the vinaigrette: Whisk the lemon juice with a pinch of salt and a dash of pepper. Whisk in the oil.
2   Put the mushroom slivers in a bowl, pour the vinaigrette over them, sprinkle with nuts, and toss well.

2 tablespoons lemon juice
Salt
Pepper
4 tablespoons olive oil
1¼ pounds (600 g.) porcini mushrooms, stem ends trimmed, cleaned with paper towels, and sliced into slivers
2 tablespoons chopped walnuts or slivered fresh almonds

BORDEAUX-STYLE PORCINIS

Cèpes à la bordelaise

SERVES 4
PREPARATION 15 minutes
COOKING 7 minutes for the caps plus 5 minutes for the stems

1   Mince the mushroom stems but leave the caps whole. Heat 1 tablespoon olive oil in a skillet and cook the shallots for 3 minutes over low heat, stirring.
2   Heat 2 tablespoons olive oil in a large skillet over high heat. When it is hot, add the porcini caps. Cook over low heat for about 7 minutes, turning them over in the middle of cooking. Do not allow them to burn; adjust the heat if necessary. Season with ½ teaspoon salt and a pinch of pepper. Remove them to a warm plate with their rounded sides down.
3   At the same time, heat 2 tablespoons olive oil in another skillet. When it is hot, sauté the minced stems for 3 minutes over low heat, stirring constantly. Season with ½ teaspoon salt and a pinch of pepper. Stir in the garlic and cook 2 minutes

1¼ pounds (600 g.) porcini mushrooms, stem ends trimmed and cleaned with paper towels
5 tablespoons olive oil
2 shallots, peeled and minced
Salt
Pepper
2 garlic cloves, peeled, degermed (page 122), and minced
1 tablespoon chopped flat-leaf parsley

more. Taste to make sure the mushrooms are cooked and add salt or pepper as necessary. Stir in the parsley.

4   Garnish the porcini caps with the minced stems and serve.

PORCINIS WITH CURED, UNCOOKED HAM

Cèpes au jambon cru

SERVES   4
PREPARATION   5 minutes
COOKING   9 minutes

1   Slice the mushroom stems from the caps so that the caps are left level. Cut the stems into small dice, less than ¼ inch (0.5 cm.). Heat the oil in a skillet and brown the caps for 5 minutes over low heat. Season with salt and pepper and remove them to a baking dish, rounded side down.

2   Preheat the oven to 420°F/220°C.

3   In the same skillet, melt the butter. When it foams, add the diced stems and cook for 3 minutes over low heat, stirring. Add the ham, shallot, and a pinch of pepper. Cook 3 minutes more. Stir in the parsley.

4   Garnish the caps with the parsley-stem mixture. Sprinkle each mushroom with some bread crumbs and put the dish in the oven for 3 minutes.

4 medium-sized porcini mushrooms, stem ends trimmed and cleaned with paper towels

1 tablespoon walnut oil

Salt

Pepper

2 teaspoons butter

3 ounces (80 g.) cured, uncooked ham cut into small dice (less than ¼ inch/0.5 cm.)

1 shallot, peeled and minced

1 tablespoon minced flat-leaf parsley

¼ cup dry bread crumbs

White Button Mushrooms

This cultivated mushroom is also the most commonly eaten. The best button mushrooms are the smallest. You can find frozen and canned button mushrooms, too.

WHITE BUTTON MUSHROOMS

Champignons de Paris

SERVES 4

PREPARATION 25 minutes

1. Cut the larger mushrooms into halves or quarters so that you end up with mushrooms and mushroom pieces that are all about the same size.

2. Melt the butter or heat the olive oil in a skillet. When it foams, add the shallot and a pinch of salt. Cook over low heat for about 3 minutes. The shallot should not color. Raise the heat to medium, add the mushrooms, and cook for 3–5 minutes, depending on their size. Stir well so that they get evenly colored. Season with ½ teaspoon salt and a pinch of pepper as you cook and stir.

3. Remove the mushrooms and shallots from the skillet with a slotted spoon so that some of the butter drips off. Lay the mushrooms in a dish, stir in the parsley, and season with salt and pepper to taste.

1¼ pounds (600 g.) white button mushrooms, stem ends trimmed, rinsed, and wiped clean with paper towels

1 tablespoon butter or olive oil

1 shallot, peeled and minced

Salt

Pepper

1 tablespoon minced flat-leaf parsley

Potatoes

Steak with French fries—*steak frites*—is one of the great national dishes of France. It is astonishing, then, to think that in the eighteenth century it took a good deal of one man's determination and planning to convince the king that the country had to start eating the American tuber, which was at the time considered fit only for pigs. The agronomist Antoine-Augustin Parmentier did not introduce potatoes to France, as is often said, but he did champion them as a possible staple food for the country, which was overly dependent on fickle grain crops and therefore dangerously vulnerable to famine. Potatoes were held in such low esteem that Parmentier had to be quite sneaky. He arranged for guards to watch over the king's potato fields during the day but left them unguarded at night, at which time the neighboring peasants would make haste to steal and replant in their own fields this crop that must be so terribly valuable. Why else would the king give it such protection? Louis XV himself helped make potatoes fashionable at court by wearing a potato flower in his buttonhole. More seriously, Parmentier wrote and distributed texts and took other actions to popularize the cultivation and consumption of potatoes.

In the early twentieth century, one of Parmentier's intellectual heirs—M. de Vries, a teacher by trade and a devotee of vegetable hybrids—set his heart on developing a new, more hardy variety of potato. Thus was born in 1905 the bintje, now the most frequently consumed potato in the world. It is much like the Yukon Gold but is less mealy. He named it after one of his pupils, having blessed his previous creations with the names of his nine daughters.

Called *solanum tuberosum Linneaus* in learned circles, the potato encompasses about three thousand species. As a member of the solanaceous family, it counts as cousins such formidable herbs as bittersweet, belladonna, mandrake, stinkweed, henbane, and tobacco, as well as more civilized plants, among them tomatoes, hot peppers, eggplants, and even the pretty petunia.

COMMERCIAL VARIETIES

There are hundreds of potato varieties, but the Russet Burbank (named after Luther Burbank, a farmer who developed the hybrid in Lunenburg, Massachusetts, in the 1870s) accounts for almost 40 percent of production in the United States. Its dry matter is medium-high, which means it is best for mashed or baked potatoes, soups, gratins, and French fries. It will not hold up as well when steamed, boiled, or sautéed.

The round or long white potatoes called bintjes have more or less the same characteristics as russets.

Yukon Gold potatoes have even more dry matter, so they are good for fries, mash, or soups, but not for boiling or steaming.

If you intend to boil, steam, or sauté your potatoes, to include them in a salad, or to cook them in a stew, look for the BF 15, nicola, charlotte, or ratte varieties. Or, even better, use new potatoes, harvested early, which are firm, sweet, and delicious.

Red potatoes have a firm texture and can generally be used the same way. Round red potatoes are sometimes incorrectly called "new potatoes."

TERROIR

The notion of *terroir,* which originated in France and was first applied mostly to wine, is that the special qualities of the land and climate in any given location affect and distinguish the taste and quality of the food grown on it. Potatoes can be spoken of in terms of *terroir,* too. A specific variety will not taste or cook up the same if it is grown in Lyon instead of the island of Noirmoutier. The island's sandy soil and muck impart a special flavor. The ratte from Touquet has its devoted disciples, as does the ratte of Lyon, which is also called a "quenelle."

CHOOSING POTATOES

Whatever variety you need for your cooking, choose a firm potato with smooth skin and no nubby "eyes." Cooking time will vary greatly according to size, so try to use potatoes that are all about the same size.

Never keep potatoes in a damp place, in a plastic bag, or in the light. They will turn green.

Do not keep potatoes near anything pungent, for they are apt to take on bad flavors.

After you have peeled and cut potatoes, you must keep them in cold water if you do not plan to cook them right away, for they can turn dark very quickly. When it is time to remove them, do so by lifting them out with your hands. The starch will have fallen to the bottom of the container, and you don't want to spread it back over the potatoes by dumping the whole thing into a colander.

Usually a potato is cooked until the tip of a knife can penetrate it with ease. If the knife slips out again without taking any bits of potato with it, then the tuber is cooked just right. If the knife does pull out some crumbs of the potato, then it is already a little overcooked.

SMOTHERED POTATOES

Pommes de terre à l'étouffée

SERVES   4

PREPARATION   20 minutes

COOKING   5 minutes plus 1 hour

1   Preheat the oven to 340°F/170°C.

2   Put all the vegetables and the bouquet garni in a Dutch oven. Top with the lard and season with 1 teaspoon salt and 1 teaspoon pepper. Stir. Cook over low heat for 5 minutes.

3   In the meantime, use a wooden spoon to stir 1 teaspoon salt and the flour bit by bit into ¼ cup water, adding just enough flour to make a supple dough. Roll it between your hands to make a long, skinny "snake" of dough.

4   When the pot has been cooking for 5 minutes, cover it and then press the dough all around the seam to seal the lid to the base. Bake in the oven for 1 hour.

5   Remove the bouquet garni and sprinkle with parsley to serve.

2 pounds (1 kg.) potatoes, Yukon Gold, BF 15, or eerstelings, peeled and sliced into rounds ¼ inch (0.5 cm.) thick

4 leeks, white parts only, carefully washed and cut into 1-inch (2-cm.) pieces

4 turnips, peeled and quartered

1 bouquet garni (5 stems parsley, 2 sprigs thyme, 1 bay leaf, and 1 sprig rosemary, wrapped and tied in a green leek leaf if possible)

4 ounces (125 g.) lard

Salt

Pepper

1½ cups (7½ ounces/200 g.) flour

1 tablespoon minced parsley

POTATOES ROASTED WITH GARLIC AND ONIONS

Pommes de terre boulangère

SERVES 6

PREPARATION 15 minutes

COOKING 10 minutes plus 1¼ hours

1   Preheat the oven to 410°F/210°C. Melt ½ tablespoon butter in a sauté pan or pot. Add the onions and stir with a wooden spoon. Cook, stirring frequently, for 3 minutes and then add the garlic and potatoes. Season with 1 teaspoon salt and 2 pinches of pepper. Stir well and cook over low heat for 2 minutes.

2   In the meantime, reheat the chicken broth or dissolve half a bouillon cube in 2 cups (50 cl.) water.

3   Grease a baking dish with 1 teaspoon softened butter. Put the potato-onion mixture in the dish and use a spatula to pat it down evenly. Lay a bouquet garni on each side of the dish and pour the hot broth over the potatoes. Dot with the remaining butter and bake for 1¼ hours.

4   Discard the bouquets garnis and serve in the dish.

1 tablespoon butter

5 medium onions, peeled and thinly sliced

1 clove garlic, peeled and crushed under your palm

2 pounds (1 kg.) potatoes, preferably Yukon Gold or BF 15, peeled, sliced into rounds ⅛ inch (3 mm.) thick, rinsed, and drained

Salt

Pepper

2 cups (50 cl.) chicken broth (page 77 or made from a bouillon cube)

2 bouquets garnis (in each one 5 stems parsley, 2 sprigs thyme, and 1 bay leaf, preferably wrapped and tied in green leek leaves)

COMTÉ POTATOES

Pommes de terre au comté

SERVES 4

PREPARATION 25 minutes

COOKING 2 hours

Peel and slice the potatoes into rounds 1 inch (2 cm.) thick. A mandoline will make this operation considerably easier. Rinse and dry the potatoes with a clean cloth.

Preheat the oven to 300°F/150°C. Melt 2 teaspoons butter in a Dutch oven over low heat. Put down a layer of potatoes and then a layer of cheese. Season with 1 pinch of salt and 1 dash of pepper, and repeat 3 times. Pour the beef broth over and dot with the remaining butter. Cover and bake in the oven for 2 hours. Garnish with parsley before serving.

1 tablespoon butter

2 pounds (1 kg.) potatoes, preferably Yukon Gold, BF 15, or charlottes

½ pound (250 g.) Comté cheese, cut into slices ⅛ inch (3 mm.) thick

Salt

Pepper

½ cup (10 cl.) beef broth from a pot-au-feu (page 68) or made from a bouillon cube

1 teaspoon minced flat-leaf parsley

BACON POTATOES

Pommes de terre au lard

SERVES 4

PREPARATION 15 minutes

COOKING 5 minutes plus 15 minutes

1 Melt the lard in a sauté pan over medium heat. Add the lardons and potato slices and season with 2 teaspoons salt and 2 pinches of pepper. Add the rosemary. Turn the heat to high and cook the potatoes and lardons until they have taken on some nice color, about 5 minutes. Cover the pot, lower the heat, and cook for 15 minutes, stirring regularly.

2 Taste and correct the seasoning if necessary. Sprinkle with parsley to serve.

3 ounces (100 g.) lard

2 cups (½ pound/250 g.) lardons (page 89)

3 pounds (1.5 kg.) potatoes, preferably Yukon Gold, BF 15, or charlottes, peeled and sliced into rounds less than ¼ inch (0.5 cm.) thick, then rinsed and dried with a clean cloth

Salt

Pepper

1 sprig rosemary

1 tablespoon minced flat-leaf parsley

POTATOES AND LEEKS

Pommes de terre aux poireaux

SERVES 4
PREPARATION 20 minutes
COOKING 45 minutes

Use charlottes or BF 15 potatoes if possible, otherwise Yukon Gold.

1   Heat 2 teaspoons butter in a Dutch oven. When it foams, add the leeks and onion and cook over low heat for 3 minutes, stirring; do not allow them to color. Sprinkle with the flour and stir it in with a wooden spoon, still over the lowest possible heat. Cook for 5 minutes, stirring, without allowing the mixture to brown.

2   Add the milk all at once and stir well. Season with 1 teaspoon salt, 2 pinches of pepper, and a dash of nutmeg. Add the potatoes and bouquet garni and cook uncovered over low heat for 35 minutes. Preheat the broiler.

3   After 35 minutes, taste for salt and pepper and discard the bouquet garni. Brush a baking dish with the remaining butter, softened, and pour the potato mixture into the dish. Bake about 10 minutes, until the top of the potatoes turns lightly golden.

1 tablespoon butter
3 leeks, white parts only, carefully washed and sliced into rounds ⅛ inch (3 mm.) thick
1 medium onion, peeled and sliced into rounds ⅛ inch (3 mm.) thick
1 heaping teaspoon flour
3 cups (75 cl.) milk
Salt
Pepper
Grated nutmeg
2 pounds (1 kg.) potatoes, peeled, sliced into rounds ⅛ inch (3 mm.) thick and rinsed
1 bouquet garni (2 sprigs thyme, 1 bay leaf, and 5 stems parsley, wrapped and tied in a leek leaf)

POTATOES WITH CHIVES

Pommes de terre à la ciboulette

SERVES 4
PREPARATION 35 minutes
COOKING 25 minutes

1 Scrub the potatoes but do not peel. Put them in a saucepan with 2 quarts (2 l.) water and 1 tablespoon coarse salt. Bring to a boil and adjust the heat so that the pot simmers for 25 minutes.

2 Mix 2 pinches of fleur de sel and 2 pinches of pepper with the minced chives in a bowl.

3 Put a kettle on to boil. Put the lemon juice and 3 tablespoons water in a small saucepan with a pinch of salt. Bring to a boil. With a wooden spoon, stir in 1 tablespoon chilled butter. The mixture should not boil; adjust the heat to prevent it from bubbling if necessary. When the butter has almost completely melted, stir in another tablespoon. Repeat until only 3 tablespoons butter remain. Remove the pot from the heat and stir in the remaining butter.

4 Put the saucepan with the butter in a larger pot or saucepan and pour hot water from the kettle into the larger pot so that it reaches halfway up the small saucepan. Turn the heat under the pot to very low to keep the butter sauce warm.

5 When the potatoes are cooked, drain, peel, and slice them into rounds ½ inch (1 cm.) thick. Spread the potatoes in a deep serving dish and drench them in butter. Sprinkle with the salt, pepper, and chive mixture and serve.

8 potatoes, preferably roseval (a firm, waxy-fleshed red potato) (3 pounds/1.5 kg. total)
Coarse salt
Fleur de sel
Pepper
1 tablespoon minced chives
Juice of ½ lemon
Salt
2 sticks (½ pound/200 g.) butter, well chilled and diced

CINDERELLA POTATOES

Pommes de terre sous la cendre

SERVES 4
PREPARATION 5 minutes
COOKING 1 hour

1 Build a fire in a fireplace in advance; you need a good layer of ashes. Scrub the potatoes but do not remove their peels. If you like to eat the skin, wrap them very well in aluminum foil. Otherwise, the skin is protection enough.

2 Tuck the potatoes into the ashes. Cover them with plenty of ashes and then lay some glowing coals on top. Do not put the potatoes in direct contact, top or bottom, with the hot coals or they will burn. Leave to cook about 1 hour, until the tip of a knife easily pierces the potato.

3 Remove the potatoes from the ashes and serve with butter (salted or unsalted), coarse salt, and pepper. You can also add crème fraîche into which you have stirred some snipped herbs, perhaps chives.

4 pounds (2 kg.) large potatoes, preferably BF 15 or bintje
Butter
Coarse salt
Pepper
Crème fraîche and minced chives (optional)

LYON POTATOES

Pommes de terre à la lyonnaise

SERVES 4
PREPARATION 15 minutes
COOKING 45 minutes

1 Scrub the potatoes but do not peel. Put them in a saucepan with 2 quarts (2 l.) water and 1 tablespoon coarse salt. Bring to a simmer and cook with gentle bubbles for about 20 minutes; the potatoes should still be firm at the end. Drain and peel the potatoes and slice them into rounds less than ¼ inch (0.5 cm.) thick.

2 Melt 1½ teaspoons butter in a rather large skillet. Add the potatoes and sauté for 15 minutes over low heat, stirring every 5 minutes with a wooden spoon.

3 In the meantime, melt ½ teaspoon butter in another skillet. Cook the onions over low heat for 5 minutes.

4 Stir the onions into the potatoes. Cover and cook for 5 min-

2 pounds (1 kg.) potatoes, rattes or belles de Fontenay if possible
Coarse salt
2 teaspoons butter
3 red onions, peeled and sliced into rounds less than ¼ inch (0.5 cm.) thick
Fleur de sel
Pepper
1 tablespoon minced flat-leaf parsley

utes, still over low heat. Season with 1 teaspoon fleur de sel and a pinch of pepper. Sprinkle with parsley.

POTATOES IN BÉCHAMEL SAUCE

Pommes de terre en béchamel

SERVES 6
PREPARATION 25 minutes
COOKING 25 minutes

1 Scrub the potatoes but do not peel. Put them in a saucepan with 2 quarts (2 l.) water and 1 tablespoon coarse salt and bring to a boil. Simmer for about 25 minutes, until a knife slips easily and cleanly in and out of the potato.
2 While the potatoes cook, prepare the béchamel sauce. Stir in the lemon juice, paprika, 10 drops of Worcestershire sauce, the chives, fennel or dill, and nutmeg. Stir until well and evenly combined. Taste for salt and pepper.
3 When the potatoes are cooked, drain, peel, and cut into thick rounds. Spread them on a dish and coat them with the béchamel.

3 pounds (1.5 kg.) firm-fleshed potatoes such as BF 15 or rattes
Coarse salt
1 quart (1 l.) béchamel sauce (page 51)
Juice of ½ lemon
1 teaspoon paprika
Worcestershire sauce
1 tablespoon minced chives
1 tablespoon minced fennel greens or dill
Dash of grated nutmeg
Salt
Pepper

POTATOES AND ARTICHOKES SAUTÉED WITH ALMONDS

Pommes de terre et artichauts sautés aux amandes

SERVES 6
PREPARATION 15 minutes
COOKING 5 minutes plus 25 minutes plus 5 minutes

1 Heat 1 tablespoon olive oil in a sauté pan over high heat. When it is hot, add the potatoes and artichokes and sauté, stirring frequently, for 5 minutes. While cooking, season with 1 teaspoon salt and a generous pinch of pepper. Lower the heat, cover, and cook for 25 minutes, giving the pan a

1 tablespoon plus 1 teaspoon olive oil
1 pound (500 g.) potatoes, preferably rattes or BF 15,
(continued)

good shake from time to time to prevent the vegetables from sticking.

2   Heat 1 teaspoon olive oil in a small skillet. Sauté the almonds over low heat until they turn a nut-brown color, about 5 minutes. Season with a pinch of salt.

3   Toss the almonds with the cooked potatoes and artichokes and pour into a serving dish. Garnish with celery sticks and taste for salt and pepper.

peeled and cut into small ⅛-inch (3-mm.) dice
4 uncooked artichoke hearts (page 179), slivered and kept in a bowl of lemony water
Salt
Pepper
6 ounces (190 g.) slivered almonds
4 celery stalks, cut into matchsticks

POTATOES IN A SALT CRUST

Pommes de terre en croûte de sel

SERVES   4
PREPARATION   15 minutes
COOKING   50 minutes

1   Preheat the oven to 350°F/180°C. Combine the coarse salt, flour, egg white, and herbs in a bowl. Spread a layer of this mixture in the bottom of a large pot or terrine. Lay the potatoes on top of it and cover completely with the rest of the salt mixture, packing it down firmly. Cook over high heat for 3 minutes. Bake in the oven uncovered for 45 minutes.

2   Unmold the block of salt on a dish towel. With a hammer, crack the crust to liberate the cooked herb-scented potatoes.

2 pounds (1 kg.) coarse salt
2 tablespoons flour
1 egg white (page 204)
4 tablespoons minced mixed herbs; choose among savory, thyme, fennel, dill, sage, rosemary, mint, and basil
2 pounds (1 kg.) potatoes, preferably charlottes or rattes, scrubbed, peeled, and held in a bowl of cold water

CREAMY POTATOES

Pommes de terre à la crème

SERVES   4
PREPARATION   10 minutes
COOKING   25 minutes plus 10 minutes

1   Put the potatoes in a saucepan with 2 quarts (2 l.) water and 1 tablespoon coarse salt. Bring to a brisk simmer and cook for 25 minutes, until the tip of a knife slides easily and cleanly in and out of a potato. When they are cooked, peel the potatoes and slice them into rounds ¼ inch (0.5 cm.) thick. Lay the potatoes in a sauté pan over very low heat.

2   Set aside 4 tablespoons cream to finish the dish. Pour the rest into a saucepan and bring to a boil. When it bubbles, pour it over the potatoes. Season with a pinch of salt and a dash of pepper.

3   Cook over medium heat, stirring, until the cream is quite thick and rich, about 10 minutes. At the end of cooking, stir in the remaining cream and, if you like, the minced dill or fennel.

2 pounds (1 kg.) firm-fleshed potatoes such as rattes or BF 15, scrubbed but not peeled
Coarse salt
1 quart (1 l.) heavy cream
Salt
Pepper
1 tablespoon minced dill or fennel greens (optional)

POTATOES WITH *FROMAGE BLANC*

Pommes de terre au fromage blanc

SERVES   4
PREPARATION   20 minutes
COOKING   50 minutes plus 20 minutes

1   Preheat the oven to 410°F/210°C. Prick each potato a few times with a fork to prevent it from bursting in the oven and to make sure it dries out as it cooks. Bake for 50 minutes, then remove the potatoes but do not turn off the oven.

2   Peel the potatoes and put their flesh through the fine disk of a food mill or a ricer. Use a spatula to fold in the *fromage blanc,* eggs, flour, and heavy cream. Season with 2 teaspoons salt, 1 teaspoon pepper, and a dash of grated nutmeg.

3   Grease a baking dish with 1 teaspoon softened butter and

2 pounds (1 kg.) potatoes, preferably BF 15 or eerstelings, scrubbed but not peeled
½ pound (190 g.) *fromage blanc*
2 eggs
1½ tablespoons flour
4 tablespoons heavy cream
Salt
Pepper
Grated nutmeg
2 teaspoons softened butter

spread the potato mixture in the dish. Smooth the surface with a spatula and dot with about 1 teaspoon butter. Bake for 20 minutes.

TWICE-BAKED POTATO SURPRISE ⎯⎯⎯⎯⎯⎯⎯⎯⎯

Pommes de terre à l'oeuf en surprise

SERVES 6

PREPARATION   40 minutes

COOKING   38 minutes

1   Preheat the oven to 350°F/180°C. Prick the potatoes with a fork to prevent them from bursting in the oven. With the tip of a knife, trace a circle in the skin at one end of each potato; this is a "cap" that you will later remove, as with a stuffed tomato.

2   Bake the potatoes about 30 minutes, turning them every 10 minutes. Prepare the poached eggs if you have not already.

3   When the potatoes are cooked, remove them but do not turn off the oven. Cut away the caps you traced before. Scoop out the flesh with a small spoon, leaving a thin layer of flesh behind and being very careful not to tear or break the skins. Put the flesh in a bowl and add to it the butter and crème fraîche. Season with 2 pinches of salt and 1 pinch of pepper. Sprinkle with chives and stir well to combine.

4   Season the insides of the empty potato shells with a dash of salt each. Fill each one halfway with the seasoned flesh, add an egg, and then top off with more potato. Put the caps back in place, lay the potatoes in a baking dish, and bake for 8 minutes to finish.

6 good-sized potatoes, preferably Yukon Gold or BF 15, about 3 pounds (1.5 kg.) total, scrubbed but not peeled

6 poached eggs (page 210)

10 tablespoons (150 g.) butter

3 tablespoons crème fraîche

Salt

Pepper

1 tablespoon minced chives

TWICE-BAKED POTATOES
WITH HAM AND MUSHROOMS

Pommes de terre au jambon et aux champignons

SERVES   6

PREPARATION   30 minutes

COOKING   1 hour and 10 minutes

1   Preheat the oven to 410°F/210°C.

2   Lay the potatoes on a baking sheet and roast for 25 minutes. Flip them over and roast 25 minutes more. Remove them but do not turn off the oven.

3   Slice the potatoes in half lengthwise. Carefully scoop out the flesh, leaving the skin intact. Put the flesh in a bowl and mash it with a fork. Mash in the butter and egg yolks, then add the mushrooms, ham, Parmesan, 1 tablespoon salt, 1 teaspoon pepper, and a dash of nutmeg. Mix in the minced chervil and parsley and stir well to make sure the mixture is evenly combined.

4   Lower the oven temperature to 350°F/180°C. Fill the hollow potato skins with the seasoned flesh, smoothing the top of each one well with the back of a spoon. Arrange the stuffed potato halves in a baking dish and sprinkle with the Gruyère.

5   Bake for 20 minutes, until the cheese has melted and is prettily browned.

$2\frac{1}{2}$ pounds (750 g.) medium-sized potatoes, preferably BF 15 or eestelings, scrubbed but not peeled

10 tablespoons (150 g.) butter

4 egg yolks (page 204)

6 ounces (190 g.) white button mushrooms, stem ends trimmed, washed, and cut into $\frac{1}{8}$-inch (2-mm.) slivers

$\frac{1}{2}$ pound (250 g.) ham, cut into $\frac{1}{4}$-inch (0.5-cm.) dice

$\frac{1}{2}$ cup ($2\frac{1}{2}$ ounces/50 g.) grated Parmesan cheese

Salt

Pepper

Grated nutmeg

1 tablespoon minced chervil

1 tablespoon minced parsley

1 cup (3 ounces/100 g.) freshly grated Gruyère cheese

GRAPE PICKER'S POTATOES

Pommes de terre des vendangeurs

SERVES 6
PREPARATION 15 minutes
COOKING 1 hour 45 minutes

1   Preheat the oven to 410°F/210°C. Grease the inside of a Dutch oven with butter. Line the bottom and sides of the pot with bacon, allowing some to hang over the edge. Add one-third of the potatoes in a layer, then one-third of the Gruyère and one-third of the pork belly. Season with a pinch of pepper and repeat the layers twice. Fold the overhanging bacon on top of the layers and dot with ⅔ teaspoon butter. Cover with aluminum foil and then with the pot's cover. Bake in the oven for 1½ hours.

2   After the pot comes out of the oven, allow it to rest for 15 minutes. Then slide a knife all around the inside edge of the pot to make sure the bacon is not stuck. Unmold onto a dish.

1 teaspoon butter
6 ounces (190 g.) smoked striped bacon slices
4 pounds (2 kg.) potatoes, preferably BF 15, peeled and sliced into rounds ⅛ inch (3 mm.) thick, rinsed and dried with a clean cloth
1 cup (3 ounces/100 g.) freshly grated Gruyère cheese
5 ounces (150 g.) salted pork belly, thinly sliced
Pepper

Mashed Potatoes

For successful mashed potatoes, salt the cooking water when it is still cold and salt the finished purée carefully. If you can, use a food mill or potato ricer instead of a blender or food processor. When the potatoes have gone through the ricer, put them in a saucepan over medium heat and turn them vigorously with a wooden spatula to dry them out a bit. Stir in the butter first and the whole milk later. Finish mixing with a whisk for lighter texture.

MASHED POTATOES

Purée de pommes de terre

SERVES 6
PREPARATION 15 minutes
COOKING 35 minutes

1 Put the potatoes in a saucepan with 2 quarts (2 l.) cold water and 1 tablespoon coarse salt. Bring to a simmer, cover, and cook until a knife slips in and out of the potatoes easily and cleanly, about 25 minutes.
2 Drain the potatoes and peel them. Put them through a potato ricer (or a food mill fitted with its finest disk) into a large saucepan. Turn the heat under the saucepan to medium and dry the potato flesh out a bit by turning it vigorously with a spatula for about 5 minutes.
3 In the meantime, rinse a small saucepan, pour out the excess water, but do not wipe it dry. Add the milk and bring to a boil.
4 Turn the heat under the potatoes to low and incorporate the well-chilled butter bit by bit, stirring it in energetically for a smooth, creamy finish. Pour in the very hot milk in a thin stream, still over low heat and still stirring briskly. Keep stirring until all the milk has been absorbed. Turn off the heat and taste for salt and pepper.
5 For even lighter, finer potatoes, put them through a very fine sieve before serving.

2 pounds (1 kg.) potatoes, preferably Yukon Gold, Yellow Finn, rattes, or BF 15, scrubbed but unpeeled
Coarse salt
2 cups (50 cl.) whole milk
2 sticks (½ pound/250 g.) butter, diced and kept well chilled until used
Salt
Pepper

MASHED POTATOES WITH OLIVE OIL

Purée à l'huile d'olive

SERVES 6
PREPARATION 10 minutes
COOKING 35 minutes

1 Put the potatoes in a saucepan with 2 quarts (2 l.) cold water and 1 tablespoon coarse salt. Bring to a simmer, cover, and cook until a knife slips in and out of the potatoes easily and cleanly, about 25 minutes.

2 pounds (1 kg.) medium potatoes, preferably Yukon Gold, Yellow Finn, or BF 15, all about the same size, peeled
Coarse salt

(continued)

2   Drain the potatoes and discard the cooking water. Put them through a potato ricer (or a food mill fitted with its finest disk) back into the hot saucepan.

3   Turn the heat under the saucepan to low and stir the purée with a wooden spatula as you incorporate, very gradually, the olive oil. Do not rush this; it should take about 10 minutes.

4   Season with 2 teaspoons salt and ½ teaspoon pepper. Whisk for a smooth, rich finish. Taste and correct salt and pepper if necessary. Serve in a warm dish.

2 cups (50 cl.) olive oil
Salt
Pepper

GARLIC MASHED POTATOES WITH PARSLEY SAUCE

Purée aillée au jus de persil

SERVES 4
PREPARATION 35 minutes
COOKING 25 minutes

1   Put the potatoes in a saucepan with 2 quarts (2 l.) cold water and 1 tablespoon coarse salt. Bring to a simmer, cover, and cook until a knife slips in and out of the potatoes easily and cleanly, about 25 minutes.

2   In the meantime, put the unpeeled garlic in another saucepan with 2 quarts (2 l.) water and bring to a boil. As soon as the water bubbles, turn off the heat. Repeat 3 times, changing the water each time. Then peel the garlic, remove its green germ, and mash it into a purée.

3   Put the parsley in a saucepan with 1 quart (1 l.) cold water and 2 teaspoons salt and bring to a boil. As soon as it bubbles, turn off the heat. Remove the parsley to a colander and rinse with cold running water.

4   Rinse the saucepan used for the parsley but do not dry it. Pour in the milk, add the butter, and heat until the liquid is shuddering (just about to boil). Turn off the heat.

5   Drain the cooked potatoes and discard their cooking water. Put them through a potato ricer (or a food mill fitted with its finest disk) back into the hot saucepan. Incorporate the hot milk and butter mixture and the garlic purée. Season with salt and pepper. Keep warm over very low heat.

1½ pounds (800 g.) potatoes, preferably bintjes or Yellow Finn, scrubbed but not peeled
Coarse salt
1 pound (650 g.) young garlic
1 tablespoon chopped flat-leaf parsley
Salt
1 cup (20 cl.) milk
4 tablespoons (60 g.) butter
Pepper

6   Purée the parsley in a blender or cut it so fine that it is like a purée. Put it in a small saucepan with ½ cup (10 cl.) water and heat for 5 minutes over low heat. Season with 2 pinches of salt and a dash of pepper.

7   Heap the mashed potatoes into a dome on a serving platter and pour the parsley sauce all around.

GOLDEN MASHED POTATO DUMPLINGS

Quenelles de pommes de terre gratinées

SERVES   4

PREPARATION   35 minutes

COOKING   1 hour

The mashed potatoes should be prepared at least 4 hours in advance but preferably the day before.

1   At least 4 hours in advance or the day before, put the potatoes in a saucepan with 2 quarts (2 l.) cold water, 1 tablespoon coarse salt, the bouquet garni, and the garlic. Bring to a simmer, cover, and cook until a knife slips in and out of the potatoes easily and cleanly, about 25 minutes.

2   Drain the potatoes and peel them. Put them through a potato ricer (or a food mill fitted with its finest disk).

3   Prepare the clarified butter.

4   Rinse a small saucepan but do not dry it. Pour in the milk and add 1 tablespoon butter. Heat until the liquid shivers and is just about to boil. Remove from the heat and whisk in the flour. Put the saucepan back over low heat and stir vigorously with a wooden spatula to dry the mixture out a bit, about 1 minute.

5   Fold the puréed potato flesh into the milk-butter-flour mixture. Season generously with salt and add a pinch of pepper and a dash of nutmeg. Whisk in the clarified butter and then the eggs and egg whites. Mix very well, until the substance is homogeneous. Put it in a bowl, cover with plastic wrap, and refrigerate for at least 4 hours. If you can leave the potatoes in the refrigerator overnight, even better.

6   Four hours later (or the next day), preheat the broiler. Use 2 spoons to make 4 football-shaped dumplings out of the

1 pound (500 g.) potatoes, preferably charlottes, bintjes, or Yellow Finn, scrubbed but not peeled

Coarse salt

1 bouquet garni (2 sprigs thyme, 1 bay leaf, and 5 stems parsley, wrapped and tied in a green leek leaf if possible)

1 clove garlic

½ cup (10 cl.) clarified butter (page 43)

1 cup (20 cl.) milk

1 tablespoon butter, plus a little extra for greasing the dish

½ cup (90 g.) flour

Salt

Pepper

Grated nutmeg

3 whole eggs plus 2 egg whites (page 204)

1 cup (3 ounces/100 g.) grated Comté cheese

cold potato mixture. Bring 2 quarts (2 l.) water and 2 tea-spoons coarse salt to a simmer in a saucepan. Simmer the dumplings for 20 minutes and then remove them to a clean dish towel. Pat them dry.

7   Butter a baking dish and lay the dumplings in it. Sprinkle with the grated cheese and bake for 5 minutes, until they are golden. Serve piping hot.

DUCHESS POTATOES
Pommes duchesse

SERVES   4
PREPARATION   25 minutes
COOKING   35 minutes

This classic dish is also the base for other preparations such as potato cakes (croquettes).

1   Preheat the oven to 410°F/210°C.
2   Peel the potatoes and put them in a saucepan with 2 quarts (2 l.) cold water and 1 tablespoon coarse salt. Bring to a sim-mer, cover, and cook until a knife slips in and out of the pota-toes easily and cleanly, about 25 minutes.
3   Drain the potatoes and discard the cooking water. Lay the potatoes on a sheet pan and put it the oven for 10 minutes with the door open; this will rid them of steam. Remove the potatoes, close the oven door, and raise the heat to 430°F/220°C. Put the potatoes through a ricer (or a food mill fitted with its finest disk) back into the saucepan they cooked in.
4   Turn the heat under the saucepan to medium and cook for 2 minutes, stirring vigorously to dry the potato purée fur-ther. Add all the cold butter but 1 teaspoon bit by bit, stirring with energy until each bit melts and is completely incor-porated. Fold in 1 whole egg and the 5 yolks. Mix until the potatoes are smooth and homogeneous. Season with 1½ tea-spoons salt, ½ teaspoon pepper, and a pinch of nutmeg. Taste and correct the salt and pepper if necessary.
5   Grease a sheet pan with the remaining teaspoon butter.

2 pounds (1 kg.) medium-sized
   potatoes, preferably BF 15,
   eestelings, charlottes, or
   sieglindes
Coarse salt
10 tablespoons (160 g.) butter,
   well chilled
2 whole eggs and 5 yolks
   (page 204)
Salt
Pepper
Grated nutmeg

Deposit the potatoes on it like cookies, either scooping them free-form into little dollops or using a pastry bag to pipe them into a more clearly defined shape of your choice. Beat the remaining egg with a few drops of water and brush this mixture onto the potatoes with a pastry brush.

6   Bake in the oven for about 6 minutes, until they have colored prettily.

THIN POTATO CAKE

Pommes darphin

SERVES   4
PREPARATION   15 minutes
COOKING   about 13 minutes

The potatoes should be peeled, sliced into thin rounds with a mandoline, and patted dry without rinsing.

2 pounds (1 kg.) potatoes, charlottes or BF 15
Salt
Pepper
1 stick (¼ pound/100 g.) butter

1   Preheat the oven to 350°F/180°C. Toss the potato slices with 1 teaspoon salt and ½ teaspoon pepper. Melt the butter over low heat in a small saucepan. Pour the melted butter over the potatoes and stir so that all the slices are well and evenly coated.

2   Put the buttered potatoes in an ovenproof skillet over high heat for 2 minutes. Flip the whole thing over (with a spatula or by tossing it into the air like a crêpe) and cook the other side for 2 minutes. Wiggle it around in the skillet with a spatula so that the potatoes do not stick.

3   Put the skillet in the oven. After 8 minutes, squeeze out excess butter by taking a pot lid a little smaller than the skillet, pressing it down on the potato cake, and pouring out the butter. Flip the cake and bake again until the potatoes are tender inside and crispy outside, about 5 minutes.

POMMES DAUPHINE _____

SERVES 8
PREPARATION 50 minutes
COOKING about 20 minutes

1 MAKE A *PÂTE À CHOUX* Rinse out a saucepan but do not dry it off. Add the milk, butter, 1 teaspoon salt, 4 gratings of nutmeg, and a dash of cayenne pepper. Heat over medium heat, stirring with a wooden spoon, until the milk boils. Add the flour all at once and stir well. Simmer for 8–12 minutes, stirring, to dry out the dough. You want it eventually to form a ball that does not stick to the saucepan or to the spoon.

2 Turn off the heat, dump the dough in a bowl, and mix the eggs into it one by one with a wooden spoon. You should end up with a soft yielding dough.

3 Using 2 pounds (1 kg.) potatoes, prepare Duchess Potatoes according to page 626 but skipping the 2 last steps. Instead of shaping and cooking, fold them into the *pâte à choux* you have just made. Mix well until uniform.

4 Heat the frying oil to 350°F/180°C in a fryer or heavy-bottomed Dutch oven. Choose 1 of 2 ways to make the potato dough into little dumplings:

5 You can put the dough in a pastry bag fitted with a large unribbed tip and squeeze it out directly into the oil, snipping the tube of dough every inch (2 cm.). Or you can use 2 spoons to shape little bullets, dropping each one into the oil as you go. Either way, the dumplings will sink when they first hit the oil. When they float back up, turn them over with a skimmer or Chinese spoon so that they get colored evenly.

6 Cook about 4 minutes total. Lift them from the oil and drain on paper towels. Sprinkle with salt.

2 cups (50 cl.) milk
1 stick (¼ pound/125 g.) butter
Salt
Nutmeg to grate
Cayenne pepper or other hot
 chili powder
2 cups (250 g.) flour
8 eggs
2 pounds (1 kg.) Duchess
 Potatoes (page 626) before
 the final shaping and
 baking
3 quarts (3 l.) neutral oil for
 frying

POTATO CROQUETTES

Croquettes de pomme de terre

SERVES   4
PREPARATION   40 minutes
COOKING   about 3 minutes

1. Using 2 pounds (1 kg.) potatoes, prepare Duchess Potatoes (page 626) but do not complete the final shaping and cooking. Oil a small sheet pan and spread the potatoes smoothly on it. Cut out a piece of parchment paper the size of the sheet pan, oil it, and put it oiled side down on top of the potatoes. Refrigerate the sheet pan for at least 10 minutes, until the potato mixture is chilled.

2. When the sheet pan comes out of the refrigerator, invert it so that the potato sheet is on top of its piece of parchment paper. Cut the potatoes into regularly shaped tiles weighing about 2–2½ ounces (40–50 g.) each.

3. Spread a little flour in a dish. Dredge the potato tiles in the flour and tap to remove the excess.

4. Use a fork to beat the eggs with 2 pinches of salt and a dash of pepper. Beat them as you would for an omelette and then beat in 2 tablespoons oil.

5. Spread the bread crumbs in another dish. Begin to heat the frying oil to 350°F/180°C in a fryer or large, heavy-bottomed Dutch oven.

6. Dunk the floured potato slices in the egg mixture and then coat them with the crumbs, patting so that the breading sticks well but any excess falls off. Keep the breaded potato cakes in the refrigerator until ready to fry.

7. When the oil is hot, and no more than 5 minutes before you plan to serve them, fry the potato cakes. Work in batches if necessary. They should not be crowded in the oil. Lift them from the oil with a Chinese spoon or skimmer when they are beautifully golden, about 3 minutes. Drain on paper towels, season with a pinch of salt, and serve immediately.

2 pounds (1 kg.) Duchess Potatoes (page 626)
2 tablespoons neutral oil plus 3 quarts (3 l.) neutral oil for frying
Flour
3 eggs
Salt
Pepper
2 cups dry bread crumbs

ALMOND-CRUSTED POTATO CAKES

Croquettes amandines

SERVES 4

PREPARATION 40 minutes in addition to the preparation of Duchess Potatoes

COOKING 3 minutes

1 Using 2 pounds (1 kg.) potatoes, prepare Duchess Potatoes (page 626) but do not complete the final shaping and cooking. Oil a small sheet pan and spread the potatoes smoothly on it. Cut out a piece of parchment paper the size of the sheet pan, oil it, and put it oiled side down on top of the potatoes. Refrigerate the sheet pan for at least 10 minutes, until the potato mixture is chilled.

2 When the sheet pan comes out of the refrigerator, invert it so that the potato sheet is on top of its piece of parchment paper. Cut the potatoes into regularly shaped tiles weighing about 2–2½ ounces (40–50 g.) each.

3 Spread a little flour in a dish. Dredge the potato tiles in the flour and tap to remove the excess.

4 Beat the eggs with 2 pinches of salt and 1 dash of pepper. Then beat in 2 tablespoons oil.

5 Combine the slivered almonds and bread crumbs in another dish. Dunk the floured potato slices in the egg mixture, holding them down with a fork. Then coat them with the almond-crumb mixture, patting so that it sticks well. Keep the breaded potato cakes in the refrigerator until ready to fry.

6 Heat the frying oil to 350°F/180°C in a fryer or large, heavy-bottomed Dutch oven. When the oil is hot, and no more than 5 minutes before you plan to serve them, fry the potato cakes. Work in batches if necessary. They should not be crowded in the oil. Fry them for 2 minutes, flip them with a Chinese spoon or a skimmer, and fry them 1 minute more. Lift them from the oil with a Chinese spoon or skimmer when they are beautifully golden. Drain on paper towels, season with a pinch of salt, and serve immediately.

2 pounds (1 kg.) Duchess Potatoes (page 626) that have not undergone the final shaping and baking

Flour

3 eggs

Salt

Pepper

2 tablespoons neutral oil plus 3 quarts (3 l.) neutral oil for frying

½ pound (250 g.) slivered almonds

1¼ cups dry bread crumbs

GOLDEN POTATO CAKE

Galette dorée de pommes de terre

SERVES 4
PREPARATION   55 minutes
COOKING   8 minutes

Be sure to butter the cake pan well and then sprinkle it lightly with flour. Otherwise, the potato cake will stick to the pan and will not unmold prettily.

1   Preheat the oven to 410°F/210°C. Steam the potatoes for about 40 minutes (in a saucepan fitted with a steamer basket or in a couscoussier). When they are cooked, drain and peel the potatoes. Put them through a ricer (or a food mill fitted with its finest disk) into a bowl.

2   Add to the potatoes the flour, 1 egg, the cream, 2 teaspoons salt, 1 teaspoon pepper, and a dash of grated nutmeg. Stir to combine and then shape this mixture into a ball. Flour a work surface and pat the ball out so that it is about the same size as your cake pan (an 8- or 9-inch cake pan should do). Grease the bottom and sides of the pan with ½ teaspoon butter and sprinkle with ½ teaspoon flour, then tap and shift it so that the flour is spread around evenly. Tap out any excess flour. Pat the potato mixture into the greased and floured pan.

3   Beat the remaining egg with a pinch of salt. Use a pastry brush to coat the cake with beaten egg and then mark a pattern in it with the tines of a fork dipped in water. Dot with 1 teaspoon butter.

4   Bake for 8 minutes. Unmold before serving.

2 pounds (1 kg.) potatoes, preferably eerstelings, scrubbed but not peeled

⅔ cup (80 g.) flour, plus a little extra for flouring the work surface and cake pan

2 eggs

2 tablespoons heavy cream

Salt

Pepper

Grated nutmeg

1½ teaspoons butter

Fries

It is something of a paradox that the potato owes much of its reputation to fries, for it contains a lot of water and therefore should not be a particularly strong candidate for frying: When the potato hits the hot oil, it expels water, which makes the oil's temperature fall. One must therefore take certain precautions when frying potatoes. Before frying, dry the potatoes very well with a clean dish towel or several paper towels. Do not fry too many at once; work in small batches. Use at least 2 quarts (2 l.) of oil for frying.

Use neutral oil, preferably peanut. Do not use this oil for frying other foods—for instance, do not fry fish and chips in the same oil—for used oil can impart bad flavors. If you want to reuse the oil for another batch of the same food (please don't even think of trying to use it in a salad dressing), put it through a fine strainer to remove little carbonized bits, seal it in a bottle, and keep it in a cool, dark place. Don't reuse oil more than a few times, and don't keep it longer than a few months. If the oil darkens, throw it away. Finally, follow the general instructions for frying (page 16): Put the frying pot on a back burner, not at the front of the cooktop, and never, ever leave it unattended.

The secret of great French fries is that they must be fried twice. First, precook in 340°F/170°C oil. If you don't have a thermometer, test the oil's temperature by dropping in a tiny scrap of potato: As soon as it hits the oil, tiny bubbles should spew all around it. If it takes a few seconds for this to happen, the oil is not hot enough yet. If the bit of potato quickly darkens, the oil is too hot. The oil should not smoke. Whatever the oil's temperature, remove the test potato before adding the first batch of fries; otherwise, it will burn and smell bad.

When fries are submerged in hot oil for their precooking, they will at first set off a vigorous bubbling. This will calm when the potatoes have expelled most of their water. After about 10 minutes, the potatoes will begin to turn blond. At this point they should be removed and drained. Turn up the heat under the oil so that it reaches 350°F/180°C. The potatoes will be fried again for a few minutes, which will make them golden and crisp (see the following recipe for more detailed instructions). Remove them before they begin to darken; drain and spread on a dish lined with paper towels. Sprinkle with fleur de sel and serve very hot.

The classic recipe calls for fries to be sliced into regular, square-sided sticks 2½ inches (6–7 cm.) long and ½ inch (1 cm.) thick. But poorly hewn fries of irregular shape, length, and thickness are more satisfying to bite into because they offer a range of textures. The pointy ends are the crunchiest.

FRENCH FRIES

Frites (pommes Pont-Neuf)

variations

SHOESTRING POTATOES

FRIED DICED POTATOES

SERVES 4

PREPARATION 10 minutes

COOKING 10 minutes plus 3 minutes

2 pounds (1 kg.) potatoes,
preferably BF 15,
eestelings, charlottes, or
belles de Fontenay

3 quarts (3 l.) neutral oil for
frying

Fleur de sel

1   Peel the potatoes and chop them into irregular sticks. The largest ones should be 1–1½ inches (5–7 cm.) long and ½ inch (1 cm.) thick. Do not square off the ends. Wash them well with water, drain, and dry as completely as possible with a clean towel.

2   Heat the oil to 340°F/170°C in a large, heavy-bottomed pot or deep fryer. Drop in a little piece of potato to test the oil's temperature: It should set off a stream of small bubbles immediately. Remove the test potato. When the oil is the correct temperature, begin frying the potatoes, one small batch at a time. Cook until they are seared but not browned, about 10 minutes. Remove them with a Chinese spoon or skimmer and drain.

3   Raise the temperature of the oil to 350°F/180°C. Prepare a dish lined with 4 layers of paper towels. When the oil is the correct temperature, submerge the potatoes a second time, still working in small batches. Cook about 3 minutes, until they are golden and crisp. Remove them with a Chinese spoon, shaking gently to drain off as much oil as possible. Lay them on the paper towel–lined dish.

4   Sprinkle with 2 teaspoons fleur de sel and toss gently to spread it evenly. Serve hot.

SHOESTRING POTATOES

Pommes allumettes

Follow the instructions for French Fries above but cut the raw, peeled potatoes into ¼-inch-thick (4-mm.) matchsticks instead. They will take slightly less time to cook, but the color and crunchiness cues remain the same.

FRIED DICED POTATOES
Pommes bataille

Follow the instructions for French fries page 633 but cut the raw, peeled potatoes into ½-inch (1-cm.) dice instead. They will take slightly less time to cook, but the color and crunchiness cues remain the same.

POTATO CHIPS
Chips

SERVES 4
PREPARATION 15 minutes
COOKING 4 minutes

1   Heat the oil to 350°F/180°C in a large, heavy-bottomed pot or deep fryer.

2   Peel the potatoes and slice them with a mandoline into very thin rounds, about ¹⁄₁₆ inch (1 mm.). Soak them in 2 quarts (2 l.) water to rid them of as much starch as possible. Set aside for about 10 minutes. Drain and dry with a clean cloth.

3   When the oil is the proper temperature, lower the potato slices into it, working in batches if necessary so that they are not too crowded. Fry about 4 minutes, stirring constantly with a wooden spatula or a skimmer to keep them from sticking to each other.

4   As soon as they are golden, lift them from the oil with a Chinese spoon or skimmer and drain them on a cloth or on paper towels. Season with a pinch of salt.

2 pounds (1 kg.) potatoes, preferably BF 15, eestelings, charlottes, or belles de Fontenay

3 quarts (3 l.) neutral oil for frying

Salt

Sautéed Potatoes

Potatoes can be sautéed in oil, a blend of oil and butter, or, even better, clarified butter (page 43). Most delicious of all is to sauté them in goose or duck fat. Like fries, potatoes sautéed raw (without parboiling) must be served right away. If they sit around, they will soon turn mushy.

SAUTÉED POTATOES

Pommes sautées à cru

SERVES 4
PREPARATION 10 minutes
COOKING 15 minutes

1 Melt the butter or goose fat in a skillet. Sauté the potato slices over medium heat about 15 minutes, until they are lightly golden all over. Shake the skillet frequently to prevent them from sticking.
2 Spread the potatoes on paper towels to allow the excess fat to drain. Heap them on a dish and season with salt.

6 tablespoons (90 g.) butter or goose fat
2 pounds (1 kg.) evenly sized medium potatoes, preferably charlottes, peeled and sliced into rounds ⅛ inch (3 mm.) thick and then rinsed and patted dry
Salt

POTATOES SAUTÉED IN GOOSE FAT

Pommes sarladaises

SERVES 4
PREPARATION 15 minutes
COOKING 15 minutes

Sarlat, a city in the Dordogne that was home to the French judge and writer Etienne de La Boétie in the sixteenth century, is the land of foie gras and truffles. For this reason some people slip truffles into *pommes sarladaises*. But in truth the dish belongs to that region's popular cookery, a cookery perfected by peasants and housewives, and should derive its richness from goose fat alone. These potatoes go nicely with duck or goose confit or grilled duck breast.

1 Melt the goose or duck fat in a skillet. Sauté the potato slices over medium heat for 10 minutes, frequently giving the skillet a rough shake to prevent them from sticking. Add the garlic and cook 5 minutes more. The potatoes should have turned lightly golden all over.
2 Spread the potatoes on paper towels to drain away excess fat. Heap them on a dish, season with salt, and sprinkle with parsley.

3 ounces (90 g.) goose or duck fat
2 pounds (1 kg.) evenly sized medium potatoes, preferably charlottes, peeled and sliced into rounds ⅛ inch (3 mm.) thick and then rinsed and patted dry
2 cloves garlic, peeled, degermed (page 122), and minced
Salt
1 tablespoon minced parsley

SLAPPED POTATOES

Pommes "tapées"

SERVES 4
PREPARATION 15 minutes
COOKING 55 minutes

This dish gets its name from the way you whack the potatoes with the palm of the hand to burst and flatten them.

1   Put 1 quart (1 l.) water in a saucepan fitted with a steamer basket or 2 cups (50 cl.) water in a pressure cooker. Add the garlic, herb, and fennel fronds and bring to a boil. Put the potatoes in the steamer basket in a single layer and cook about 40 minutes (about 15 minutes in a pressure cooker—until it begins to whistle).

2   Lay a dish towel on a work surface, cover it with plastic wrap, and set the cooked potatoes on top of it. Spread another piece of plastic wrap over the potatoes. Whack each potato with the palm of your hand to burst it open slightly.

3   Heat the butter in a skillet. Sauté the crushed potatoes over medium heat for 7 minutes per side. Season with fleur de sel and pepper.

5 cloves garlic, peeled and
    degermed (page 122)
$\frac{1}{2}$ bunch savory or thyme
2 sprigs fennel fronds
2 pounds (1 kg.) small
    potatoes, rattes or BF 15,
    peeled unless very young
$1\frac{1}{2}$ tablespoons butter
Fleur de sel
Pepper

BAKED POTATO CAKES

Pommes macaire

SERVES 4
PREPARATION 25 minutes
COOKING 1$\frac{3}{4}$ hours

1   Preheat the oven to 410°F/210°C. Wrap the potatoes in aluminum foil and place them on a sheet pan. When the oven is hot, cook them for 1$\frac{1}{2}$ hours.

2   Discard the aluminum foil. Slice the potatoes in half lengthwise and scoop out the flesh. Season the flesh with 1 teaspoon salt, $\frac{1}{3}$ teaspoon pepper, and a dash of grated nutmeg. Mash the flesh with a fork as you incorporate the butter and crème fraîche.

4 pounds (2 kg.) large potatoes,
    BF 15 or bintjes, scrubbed
    but not peeled
Salt
Pepper
Grated nutmeg
13 tablespoons (190 g.) butter,
    diced and kept well chilled
2 tablespoons crème fraîche

3   Melt the clarified butter or goose fat in a skillet. Divide the potato mixture into quarters and pat each quarter into a cake ½ inch (1 cm.) thick. Cook for 6 minutes per side over medium heat.

5 tablespoons (3 ounces/80 g.) clarified butter (page 43) or goose fat

SMOOTH POTATO PANCAKES
WITH CRÈME FRAÎCHE AND CHIVES

Galette à la crème et à la ciboulette

SERVES   4
PREPARATION   20 minutes
COOKING   25 minutes

1   Begin to prepare the potato cake but do not go through with the final cooking in the skillet.

2   Break the eggs into the potato purée. Add the crème fraîche and chives and mix carefully until evenly combined.

3   Melt a generous tablespoon butter in a skillet. When it foams, put one-fourth of the potato mixture in the skillet and immediately flatten it into a pancake. Cook about 3 minutes per side over medium heat.

4   Repeat 3 times with the remaining potatoes. Add more butter to the skillet if necessary. Taste and correct seasoning if necessary.

4 pounds (2 kg.) Baked Potato Cakes (page 636)
6 eggs
2 tablespoons crème fraîche
2 tablespoons minced chives
Butter
Salt
Pepper

POTATO CAKES WITH ONIONS

Galettes aux oignons

SERVES 4
PREPARATION 40 minutes
COOKING 15 minutes

1 Put the 2 halved onions in a saucepan with 1 quart (1 l.) cold water and 1 teaspoon coarse salt. Bring to a simmer and cook at a low bubble for 30 minutes.

2 Prepare a bowl of water large enough to hold the potatoes. Scrub and peel the potatoes and slice them into rounds ⅛ inch (3 mm.) thick, dropping the slices into the bowl of water as you go. When you finish, drain the potatoes. Season with 1 teaspoon salt and ½ teaspoon pepper.

3 Preheat the oven to 350°F/180°C. On your work surface, divide the potato slices into 4 piles. Use each one to build a rosette-shaped cake, laying the slices half on top of one another in a spiraling single layer. Brush each one with clarified butter.

4 Heat the remaining clarified butter in an ovenproof skillet. Use a large, flat spatula to lift the potato rosettes into the skillet without breaking them apart. Cook over high heat until each cake is browned on both sides, about 5 minutes total. Then slip the skillet into the oven and cook for 10 minutes.

5 Melt the butter in a skillet over low heat. When it foams, add the 3 sliced-up onions and cook for 3 minutes, stirring with a wooden spoon, always over low heat.

6 Drain the simmering onions and purée them in a blender. Heat the chicken broth and stir in the puréed onions. Season with 2 pinches of salt and 1 pinch of pepper.

7 Coat a serving dish with the warm onion sauce. Lay the sautéed onion rounds over the sauce and top with the crispy potato cakes, sliced in half.

5 medium onions, 2 of them peeled and halved, the other 3 sliced into rounds ⅛ inch (3 mm.) thick

Coarse salt

5 large potatoes (2½ pounds/1.2 kg.), preferably charlottes

Salt

Pepper

3 tablespoons (45 g.) clarified butter (page 43)

1 tablespoon butter

1 cup (20 cl.) chicken broth (page 77 or made from a bouillon cube)

POTATO CAKES WITH PORCINIS

Galettes aux cèpes

SERVES   4
PREPARATION   30 minutes
COOKING   10 minutes plus 5 minutes

1   Wash the potatoes but do not peel them. Slice them into rounds ⅛ inch (3 mm.) thick and divide the slices into 4 equal piles.

2   Cut out 4 parchment paper circles with the diameter of a bowl. Use a pastry brush to coat them with softened butter. (Soften some butter in the microwave if necessary.) Build a rosette out of potato slices on each circle of paper, leaving a ½-inch (1-cm.) border bare. Refrigerate the rosettes about 10 minutes.

3   Separate the mushrooms' caps and stems. Slice each stem lengthwise into 3 slivers. Season the caps and stems with 1 teaspoon salt and a pinch of pepper.

4   Heat the walnut oil in a skillet. Cook the mushrooms for 5 minutes over medium heat, stirring with a wooden spoon. Drain and remove the mushrooms to a plate.

5   Preheat the oven to 250°F/120°C. In the still-hot skillet, melt 1 tablespoon butter. When it foams, flip the potato rosettes into the skillet so that the parchment paper ends up on top. When the first side is colored (about 5 minutes over low heat), remove the paper, flip the cake, and brown the other side (about 5 minutes). Season with 1 teaspoon salt and 1 pinch of pepper. Remove the potato cakes to an ovenproof dish and put them in the oven to keep warm. Turn off the oven.

6   Wipe out the skillet and then cook the pork belly for 30 seconds on each side. Remove the pork belly to a plate. In the same skillet, without discarding the pork belly cooking juices, reheat the mushrooms over low heat, stirring for about 5 minutes. Stir in the chives at the last minute.

7   Top the potato cakes with mushrooms and sprinkle with parsley.

4 large potatoes (3 pounds/ 1.5 kg.), preferably charlottes
1 tablespoon butter plus a little extra for greasing
8 porcini mushrooms, each about 5 ounces (150 g.), brushed clean and stems scraped
Salt
Pepper
1 tablespoon walnut oil
12 slices salted and dried pork belly, each about ⅛ inch (2 mm.) thick
1 tablespoon minced chives
1 teaspoon minced parsley

POTATO CAKES WITH CHERVIL

Galettes au cerfeuil

SERVES 4

PREPARATION 15 minutes

COOKING 20 minutes

1   Mix half of the chervil with the egg, beating the 2 together. Peel the potatoes but do not wash them. Grate them with a mandoline, a food processor, or even the large holes on a box grater. Pat them dry with a clean cloth or paper towels and then combine them with the chervil-egg mixture. Season with 2 pinches of salt and 1 pinch of pepper.

2   Preheat the oven to 400°F/200°C. Use your hands to shape the potatoes into 4 cakes. Heat the peanut oil in a skillet and then add the butter. When it foams, turn the heat to medium and cook the potato cakes until they are pale golden all over, about 8 minutes per side. Remove them to a sheet pan and finish with about 5 minutes in the oven.

3   Drain the cakes on paper towels. Serve them on warm plates, sprinkled with the rest of the chervil.

2 tablespoons chopped chervil

1 egg

4 potatoes, about 3 pounds (1.5 kg.), preferably BF 15 or belles de Fontenay

Salt

Pepper

1 teaspoon peanut oil

1 tablespoon butter

Beans and Lentils

Dried legumes are inexpensive, easy to prepare, and a perfect side dish during the winter months. When you buy them, try to find out how recently they were harvested. Unfortunately, this information is not usually easy to come by.

Since they can be quite dirty, dried beans and lentils must always be washed before cooking. Lentils and split peas should not be soaked in water before cooking; they might begin to sprout and ferment. Just rinse them under running water before blanching them in cold salted water—1 teaspoon of coarse salt per quart (liter)—that you have brought just up to a boil. Remove them after less than a minute with a skimmer or slotted spoon and then cook them in fresh water.

Chickpeas and dried beans, on the other hand, can be

soaked before cooking to soften their skins and reduce boiling time. Soak for 2 hours in warm water at room temperature or for 12 hours in cold water in the refrigerator.

BUTTERED WHITE BEANS

Haricots blancs au beurre

SERVES 4
PREPARATION 10 minutes
COOKING 1 hour

White beans are much better fresh from the pod. They can be found in the summertime at farmers' markets. They should not be cooked in an overwhelming amount of water— the water level should be 1¼ inches (3 cm.) above the beans at the beginning—and the water should simmer or shudder very gently, not boil. Dried white beans should be soaked for 2 hours in warm water before cooking according to package instructions.

1   Put the beans, carrot, onion, garlic, and bouquet garni in a large pot with water to cover by 1¼ inches (3 cm.). Bring to a boil, remove foam from the surface of the liquid with a skimmer, and lower the heat so that the liquid simmers gently and consistently. Cover and cook for 30 minutes.

2   After 30 minutes, add the coarse salt. Simmer, covered, 30 minutes more; the cooking time will vary depending on the type and age of the beans. Peek every once in a while to make sure the beans remain immersed in liquid; if they are not, add enough hot water to cover them.

3   When the beans are cooked—plumped up and yielding readily when pressed between two fingers—remove the other vegetables and the bouquet garni with a skimmer. The liquid should be mostly gone by now; if it is not, drain the beans.

4   Stir in the butter. Taste and season with salt and pepper as necessary. Stir gently so as not to break the beans open. Sprinkle with parsley to serve.

variations

NAVY BEANS WITH LEEKS
AND CELERY
CREAMED NAVY BEANS
MOTLEY BEANS

2 pounds (1 kg.) fresh white
    beans in the pod, shelled
    and rinsed
1 medium carrot, peeled
1 medium onion, peeled and
    stuck with 1 whole clove
3 cloves garlic, peeled and
    degermed (page 122)
1 bouquet garni (1 sprig fresh
    thyme, 2 sprigs chervil, and
    4 stems parsley, tied
    together)
1 teaspoon coarse salt
3 tablespoons butter
Salt
Pepper
½ tablespoon minced parsley

NAVY BEANS WITH LEEKS AND CELERY
Haricots cocos à la paimpolaise

SERVES 4
PREPARATION 15 minutes
COOKING 30 minutes

1 Begin to cook the beans according to the recipe for Buttered White Beans page 641. (Do not add the butter at the end, but do drain the beans if necessary.) While they cook, put the butter, leek, celery, and onion in another pot. Cook gently for 10 minutes, stirring, without allowing the vegetables to color. Season with 2 pinches of salt and 1 pinch of pepper.

2 Add the tomatoes, garlic, and bouquet garni. Cook 15 minutes over low heat. Remove the bouquet garni.

3 When the beans have finished cooking, drain them and add them to the pot of vegetables. Taste for salt and pepper, season if necessary, and cook 2–3 minutes more over low heat.

4 Just before serving, drizzle the walnut oil over the beans and sprinkle with parsley.

White beans cooked as page 641 from 2 pounds (1 kg.) fresh beans in the pod; no butter added at the end
4 tablespoons (60 g.) butter
1 leek, white part only, carefully washed and cut into rounds less than ¼ inch (0.5 cm.) thick and then into ⅛-inch (3-mm.) slivers
1 stalk celery, washed and cut like the leek
1 medium onion, peeled and cut like the leek
Salt
Pepper
2 large tomatoes, peeled, seeded, and diced (page 124)
1 clove garlic, peeled, degermed (page 122), and crushed
1 bouquet garni (1 sprig fresh thyme, 2 sprigs chervil, and 5 sprigs parsley, tied together)
½ tablespoon walnut oil
½ tablespoon minced parsley

CREAMED NAVY BEANS
Haricots cocos à la crème

SERVES 4

Cook the white beans as indicated on page 641 with no but-ter added at the end. When they are cooked, drain any excess liquid and then stir in the crème fraîche. Bring to a boil and simmer for 3 minutes.

2 pounds (1 kg.) white beans in the pod
4 tablespoons crème fraîche

MOTLEY BEANS
Haricots panachés

SERVES 4

1 Cook the white beans according to the recipe on page 641, but with more water to start. It should cover the beans by 2 inches (5 cm.). Cook for 1½ hours. If you are using frozen beans, however, 1 hour should be enough.

2 When the beans are cooked, remove the cooking vegetables and aromatics. Drain most of the water from the beans but leave a little in the pot. Add the green beans and butter and mix well. Taste for salt and pepper and sprinkle with parsley.

½ pound (250 g.) shelled small white beans (*flageolets*)
¾ pound (400 g.) cooked green beans (page 579), cooled and cut into 2-inch (4–5-cm.) sections
4 tablespoons (60 g.) butter
Salt
Pepper
1 tablespoon minced parsley

WHITE KIDNEY BEANS

Mojettes

SERVES 4
PREPARATION 15 minutes
COOKING about 25 minutes

The white kidney bean hails from the Atlantic coast of France, where it is called *mojette, mogette,* or *mojhette.* Although it has a fine and very special taste, not many people grow it now. In Poitou, only about 125 acres (50 hectares) around the village of Arcais are devoted to its cultivation.

In Poitou, some people prefer to finish the dish with walnut oil instead of butter; others just add a few leaves of flat-leaf parsley, minced.

1   Melt the goose fat or butter in a pot over low heat. Add the onions, season with a pinch of salt, and cook about 3 minutes. Stir with a wooden spoon and do not allow them to color. Add the beans and cook for 2 minutes, stirring. Cover with water by 1¼ inches (3 cm.). Add the garlic, carrots, bacon, and bouquet garni. Cover and simmer for 10 minutes. Make sure the beans stay covered with water. If you peek in and the beans are no longer submerged, add hot water to cover.

2   Remove the cover and season with 2 pinches of salt and 1 pinch of pepper. Cook about 15 minutes more.

3   Remove the bouquet garni, carrots, garlic, and bacon. Stir in 1½ teaspoons butter and correct the seasoning.

2 teaspoons goose fat or butter plus 1½ teaspoons butter

6 small new onions, peeled and minced

Salt

2 pounds (1 kg.) fresh white kidney beans, removed from their pods and rinsed

2 cloves garlic, peeled, degermed (page 122), and minced

2 carrots, peeled

2½ ounces (50 g.) smoked bacon cut into 4 pieces

1 bouquet garni (2 stems flat-leaf parsley, 1 sprig thyme, ½ bay leaf, 1 small stalk celery, and 1 whole clove, wrapped and tied in a leek leaf if possible)

Pepper

Lentils

For a long time lentils were the food of the poor. Today they have earned a nobler rank by proving themselves central members of many a national cuisine and many a regional cuisine of France.

There are numerous kinds of lentils. The best is famously the small green lentil from Puy, which is more tender than larger yellowish lentils from the north of France. Fresh lentils are a rarity.

Lentils go very well with pork, duck, game, and anything fatty, such as foie gras. They can be served hot or cold, in a salad, in a purée, or in a soup.

It used to be necessary to pick over lentils with some care before cooking, as most batches also included some small stones. This is no longer the case for the most part, but lentils can be quite dirty and must be rinsed well before cooking. They should definitely not, however, be soaked in water in advance. Some people say this makes them plumper, more tender, and more digestible, but the truth is the opposite: Soaking lentils can make them start to germinate and ferment, which actually makes them less tasty and harder on your stomach.

Simply cook them in a lot of water—four times their volume. This is easily measured by pouring water into the pot so that it reaches four times higher than the lentils. Salt 15 or 20 minutes after you begin so as not to end up with too much.

LENTILS

Lentilles

SERVES 4
PREPARATION 5 minutes
COOKING about 1 hour

½ pound (250 g.) lentils, green Puy variety if possible, well rinsed with cold water

1 onion, peeled and stuck with 1 whole clove

2 cloves garlic, peeled and degermed (page 122)

2 carrots, peeled and cut into rounds 1 inch (2 cm.) thick

1 bouquet garni (2 sprigs thyme, 1 bay leaf, 5 stems parsley, wrapped and tied in a green leek leaf if possible)

3 ounces (100 g.) smoked bacon, cut into 4 pieces (optional)

Salt

Pepper

1 tablespoon butter

1 Put the lentils in a pot with 2 quarts (2 l.) cold water. Bring to a boil without covering. Use a skimmer to remove foam from the surface regularly, rinsing the skimmer in a bowl of cold water after each passage through the pot. When there is no more foam (after about 10 or 15 minutes), add the onion, garlic, carrots, and bouquet garni. Cover and cook at a low simmer according to package instructions, which will vary depending on the kind of lentil you are using. If you are using bacon, add it 10–15 minutes before the end of cooking; otherwise, add 1 teaspoon salt and 1 pinch of pepper at this point.

2 Taste at the end of cooking. The lentils should be soft. If they aren't, cook a little longer. Correct seasoning with salt and pepper as necessary. Drain the lentils, remove the aromatics and vegetables, and stir in the butter to finish.

Pasta, Rice, Grains, and Gratins

Pasta

Pasta is the bread of the Italians. It sets off the tastes of everything it accompanies.

Dried pasta is made with hard semolina flour and water. Sometimes eggs are used, too. Good-quality industrial pasta is smooth and regular; its color is ivory tending toward yellow, and it should snap cleanly when you break it.

Pasta comes in innumerable shapes, of which long, thin spaghetti and tagliatelle are probably the best known to most of the world's eaters. Pasta is also the base for such preparations as lasagna and ravioli.

Once pasta is cooked, it must be bound with some sort of fat: butter, cream, or olive oil. It takes well to saffron, curry, all the herbs including parsley and basil, and all kinds of tomatoes, onions, and hot peppers. Let us not forget seafood, such as mussels, clams, and prawns, and even meat—such as bacon. The Italians tend to sprinkle their pasta with grated Parmesan unless the topping is particularly delicately flavored, as is the case with shrimp and sea scallops.

COOKING PASTA

If you are cooking fresh pasta, count on cooking 3–4 ounces (100 g.) per person. For dry pasta you will need 2–3 ounces (60–80 g.) per person depending on whether it is intended as an appetizer, a side dish, or the center of the meal.

Use 1 quart of water with 2 teaspoons of coarse salt for 4 ounces (100 g.) of pasta. (In grams it is much easier to remember: 1/10/100—1 liter of water, 10 g. coarse salt, and 100 g. pasta.) To keep pasta from sticking together, you must boil a generous amount of water over very high heat. To keep the pot from boiling over, you can lower the heat after you've added the pasta and the water has come back to a boil.

Add 2 or 3 tablespoons of olive oil to the water to keep the noodles from sticking together as they cook. Some say this doesn't work because the oil floats on the water's surface; this is true, but frequent stirring will coat the pasta with the oil from the surface, and the pasta will get slicked with oil when you drain it. Olive oil is especially useful when cooking gnocchi, which float on the surface.

Bring the water to a boil. When it bubbles vigorously, add the salt and drop in the pasta without breaking it, even if it is spaghetti or another long shape. As the ends in the water soften, the exposed ends will slip into the pot. Only then should you stir with a large fork to prevent sticking. Do not cover the pot. It is said that in the courts of Naples, cooking the family pasta with a cover on the pot is recognized as reasonable and sufficient grounds for divorce!

Each region of Italy has its own traditions, but for the most part pasta today is cooked *al dente:* It is no longer raw but still offers a little resistance to the teeth. The best way to tell whether pasta is cooked is to taste it. If possible, lift cooked pasta from the pot with a skimmer or tongs instead of dumping it into a colander, since pouring the cooking water all over it will coat it with starch.

To prevent sticking, you must toss drained pasta immediately with the butter, oil, or cream you are using.

PENNE WITH ANCHOVIES

Penne rigate alla Paolina

SERVES 4
PREPARATION 15 minutes
COOKING 10 minutes

1. Rinse the anchovies under running water for 10 minutes. Chop them coarsely.

2. Heat 1½ tablespoons olive oil in a large pot over low heat. Sprinkle the bread crumbs into the hot oil. Stir well with a wooden spatula. Add the onions, garlic, tomatoes, pine nuts, whole cloves, and anchovies. Stir well and keep over low heat.

3. Wash the cauliflower and broccoli florets in 1 quart (1 l.) water to which you have added the vinegar. Rinse.

4. Bring 2 quarts (2 l.) water to a boil in a large pot with 1 tablespoon coarse salt. Add the cauliflower and cook for 5 minutes. Add the broccoli and cook 4 minutes more. Using a skimmer, lift the vegetables from the pot and put them in a colander to drain; cover the colander with a dish towel to keep warm.

5. Bring the vegetable cooking water back to a boil and boil the pasta for 8 minutes or until *al dente*. Lift the pasta from the water.

6. Pour the anchovy-tomato sauce into a deep pasta bowl. Add the pasta and drizzle with 1 tablespoon olive oil. Toss well. Add the cauliflower, broccoli, basil, 2 pinches of salt, and 1 pinch of pepper. Toss again. Taste and correct the seasoning if necessary.

12 salt-packed anchovy fillets
2½ tablespoons olive oil
½ cup dry bread crumbs
2 medium onions, peeled and minced
2 cloves garlic, peeled, degermed (page 122), and minced
4 tomatoes, peeled, seeded, and diced (page 124)
2 tablespoons pine nuts
2 whole cloves
10 ounces (300 g.) very small cauliflower florets
10 ounces (300 g.) very small broccoli florets
2 tablespoons distilled white vinegar
1 tablespoon coarse salt
¾ pound (320 g.) penne
1 tablespoon chopped basil
Salt
Pepper

TAGLIATELLE WITH PESTO

Tagliatelles au pistou

SERVES 4
PREPARATION 15 minutes
COOKING 6 minutes

You can reduce the amount of garlic, if you wish, to one or even half a clove.

1 Toast the pine nuts about 2 minutes in a skillet without any fat, over very low heat. In a blender or food processor, purée the basil, garlic, and olive oil with 2 pinches of salt and 1 pinch of pepper. Combine the basil purée and pine nuts in a saucepan and heat over low heat. Taste for salt and pepper. When the sauce is hot (about 5 minutes), remove the saucepan from the heat.

2 Bring 4 quarts (4 l.) water to a boil with the coarse salt. Cook the tagliatelle *al dente:* about 1 minute if fresh or about 8 minutes if dried. Remove the pasta from the cooking water with a skimmer and toss it into the pot of warm pesto.

3 Reheat the pesto and pasta for about 2 minutes over low heat, adding 2 tablespoons pasta cooking water. Toss well and correct the seasoning.

3 tablespoons pine nuts
2 bunches basil, leaves only, washed
2 cloves garlic, peeled, degermed (page 122), and minced
7 tablespoons olive oil
Salt
Pepper
1½ tablespoons coarse salt
14 ounces (400 g.) fresh tagliatelle or 12 ounces (320 g.) dried tagliatelle

SPAGHETTI WITH CLAMS

Spaghettis con vongole

SERVES 4
PREPARATION 15 minutes
COOKING 10 minutes

You can replace the clams with cockles if you like. (See page 227 to wash them thoroughly.)

1 Heat the olive oil in a large pot over medium heat. Add the clams and ginger, stir, and pour in the white wine. Add the butter and garlic. Season with 3 pinches of salt and 2 pinches

2 tablespoons olive oil
40 clams, washed in several changes of water
Two ½-inch (1-cm.) slices of fresh, peeled ginger

(continued)

of pepper. Cover and cook for 2 minutes and then add the parsley. Stir, turn off the heat, replace the cover, and let the pot rest for 2 minutes.

2   Bring 4 quarts (4 l.) water to a boil with ½ tablespoon coarse salt in a large pot. Cook the spaghetti until *al dente,* about 8 minutes.

3   Lift the spaghetti out of the cooking water, drop it in the pot of clams, and toss. Reheat for 2 minutes over low heat with a ladle of the pasta cooking water. Mix well and taste for salt and pepper.

½ cup (10 cl.) dry white wine
1 tablespoon butter
2 cloves garlic, peeled, degermed (page 122), and minced
Salt
Pepper
4 tablespoons chopped flat-leaf parsley
½ tablespoon coarse salt
¾ pound (320 g.) spaghetti

TAGLIATELLE WITH COCKLES

Tagliatelles aux coques

SERVES   4
PREPARATION   5 minutes
COOKING   30 minutes (1 to 8 minutes for the pasta)
The cockles must soak in water overnight (see page 227).

1   Put the cockles in a large pot with 1 tablespoon butter. (Put the rest of the butter back in the refrigerator so that it stays well chilled.) Season with pepper, cover, and cook over high heat for 1–2 minutes, shaking the pot. When the cockles have opened, turn off the heat. Use a skimmer or slotted spoon to remove the cockles to a bowl and then take them out of their shells. Put the cockles in another bowl and cover with plastic wrap. Line a fine strainer with a clean dish towel and put the cooking juices through it into a saucepan. Bring to a boil and simmer for 10 minutes.

2   In the meantime, bring 3 quarts (3 l.) water and 1 tablespoon coarse salt to a boil. When the pot is bubbling vigorously, add the pasta and cook until *al dente*—about 8 minutes for dried pasta, about 1 minute for fresh. Taste to make sure the pasta is properly done. Drain in a colander and then put the pasta back in the pot but do not put it over a burner.

3   Add the crème fraîche to the saucepan of simmering cockle juices. Bring to a boil and simmer for 4 minutes, stirring with

2 pounds (1 kg.) cockles, carefully washed
2 tablespoons butter
Pepper
Coarse salt
14 ounces (400 g.) fresh tagliatelle or 10 ounces (300 g.) dried tagliatelle
1 cup (20 cl.) crème fraîche
Salt
2 sprigs fresh thyme, leaves only

a wooden spatula. Dice the remaining cold butter and stir it into the sauce piece by piece. Taste for salt and pepper.

4   Turn the heat under the pasta to low, pour the sauce all over it, and toss. Add the cockles and toss again. Sprinkle with thyme leaves.

PASTA WITH SHERRY VINEGAR

Tagliatelles au vinaigre de xérès

SERVES   2
PREPARATION   15 minutes
COOKING   15 minutes

1   Heat the olive oil in a skillet. Add the onion and a small pinch of salt and cook for about 3 minutes over medium heat, stirring, without allowing the onion to color. Add the bell peppers and cook and stir for 3 minutes. Add the mushrooms, 2 teaspoons salt, and ½ teaspoon pepper. Cook, stirring, over medium heat for 2 minutes. Turn off the heat and stir in the vinegar.

2   Bring 1½ quarts (1.5 l.) water to a boil with 2 teaspoons coarse salt. When it bubbles vigorously, add the pasta and cook *al dente,* about 8 minutes for dried pasta and 1 minute for fresh. Drain the pasta and spread it on a hot dish or pasta bowl.

3   Pour the vegetable-vinegar sauce over the pasta. Add the butter, toss, and taste for salt and pepper.

2 tablespoons olive oil
1 onion, peeled and minced
Salt
1 green bell pepper, peeled, seeded (page 130), and cut into pieces ½ inch by 1 inch (1 cm. by 2 cm.)
1 red bell pepper, peeled, seeded (page 130), and cut into pieces ½ inch by 1 inch (1 cm. by 2 cm.)
4 large white button mushrooms, cleaned and sliced from top to bottom into slivers ⅛ inch (3 mm.) thick
Pepper
2 tablespoons sherry vinegar
Coarse salt
6 ounces (160 g.) tagliatelle (½ pound/210 g. if the pasta is fresh)
½ tablespoon butter

TAGLIARINI WITH LANGOUSTINES

Tallerines aux langoustines

SERVES 4

PREPARATION 10 minutes

COOKING 15 minutes

1   Combine the diced tomatoes and 1 tablespoon olive oil in a bowl. Cut the langoustines in half lengthwise, shell and all.

2   Heat 1 tablespoon olive oil in a sauté pan or large skillet over medium heat. Add the garlic, turn the heat to low, and cook about 2 minutes, until it is lightly colored. Add the langoustines, flesh side down, cover, and cook for 1 minute. Flip them over and add the tomatoes, parsley, hot pepper, and 3 pinches of salt. Cover and cook over low heat for 2 minutes. Remove from the heat.

3   Bring 4 quarts (4 l.) water to a boil with 1½ tablespoons coarse salt. When the water bubbles vigorously, add the pasta and cook, stirring often, until *al dente,* about 8 minutes. When they are cooked, remove them from the water and drain.

4   Add the pasta to the skillet with the langoustines and mix gently. Taste for salt and pepper and reheat over low heat for 2 minutes.

4 tomatoes, peeled, seeded, and diced (page 124)

2 tablespoons olive oil

12 langoustines

4 cloves garlic, peeled, degermed (page 122), and minced

1 tablespoon minced flat-leaf parsley

1 small hot pepper, cut in half

Salt

Coarse salt

¾ pound (320 g.) tagliarini (very thin tagliatelle) or flat spaghetti

Pepper

Rice

Rice comes in eight thousand varieties and forms a significant part of the diet of three-fourths of humanity. There are two main categories of rice. Long-grain rice is less starchy, more flavorful, and less sticky. Basmati and Thai rice are long grain; this kind of rice is usually served as a side dish or used to make salads. Short- or round-grain rice is starchy and sticky; this is what the Italians use to make risotto and the Japanese use to make sushi. It is also used to make rice desserts.

Rice is never eaten raw. There are many ways to cook it: the "creole" way, which is to drop it into boiling salted water;

steaming, which takes 20–40 minutes for rice that has been rinsed in cold water; over very low heat in milk, which makes it plump up and is a good method for desserts; and the Asian way, which is to cook the rice slowly in an equivalent volume of water.

Count on 4 tablespoons (2 ounces/60 g.) rice per person as a side dish, ⅓ cup (2½ ounces/75 g.) per person for a main dish.

PLAIN RICE

Riz nature

SERVES   4 as a side dish
PREPARATION   3 minutes
COOKING   10–20 minutes

The classic way to cook rice: simply drop it into boiling water.

1 tablespoon coarse salt
1¼ cups (½ pound/250 g.)
   long-grain rice
Butter
Salt
Pepper

1   Pour 3 quarts (3 l.) water into a saucepan. Like pasta, rice should cook in a good deal of water. Add the coarse salt and bring to a boil. Rinse the rice well under cold water. When the water is boiling, add the rice all at once and stir until the pot boils again.

2   Simmer gently for 10–20 minutes depending on the rice (check the instructions on its package). Keep an eye on the pot as it cooks. Taste and add salt if you need to.

3   Drain the rice in a large colander. Add butter, salt, and pepper to taste.

PILAF

Riz pilaf

SERVES 4
PREPARATION 10 minutes
COOKING about 15 minutes plus 3 minutes of resting

1   Preheat the oven to 400°F/200°C. Melt 3 tablespoons butter
    in a saucepan. When it foams, add the onion and cook gently
    for about 3 minutes without allowing it to color. Add the rice
    and stir for 2–3 minutes so that the grains are all evenly
    coated with butter and do not stick together. Pour in enough
    water to reach 1½ times the rice's height. Stir, add the bou-
    quet garni and 1 teaspoon salt, and bring to a boil.

2   Cut out a circle of parchment paper the size of the rice pot and
    pierce it a few times with a fork or knife. When the pot boils,
    lay the parchment paper on top of it and cover the pot. Bake
    in the oven for 15 minutes, then taste to see whether the rice
    is cooked. Cooking time will vary depending on the qualities
    of the specific rice you are working with.

3   When the rice is cooked, remove the pot from the oven and
    leave it to rest, covered, about 5 minutes.

4   Remove the cover, the parchment paper, and the bouquet
    garni. Add ½ tablespoon butter sliced into slivers. Fluff with
    a fork to spread the butter evenly and separate the grains of
    rice from one another.

3½ tablespoons butter
1 medium onion, peeled and
    minced
1¼ cups (½ pound/240 g.)
    rice, preferably basmati or
    Thai jasmine
1 bouquet garni (1 sprig thyme,
    1 bay leaf, and 5 stems
    parsley, wrapped and tied
    in a green leek leaf if
    possible)
Salt

PARMESAN RISOTTO

Risotto au parmesan

variation

ASPARAGUS RISOTTO

RISOTTO WITH MUSSELS

SERVES   4

PREPARATION   5 minutes

COOKING   about 25 minutes

1   Bring the broth to a boil and keep it over low heat. It does not
need to stay bubbly, but it does need to stay quite hot.

2   Heat the olive oil in a heavy-bottomed saucepan. When it is
hot, add the onion and cook over low heat for 5 minutes, stirring with a wooden spoon. The onion should not color. Add
the rice and stir well to coat the grains with oil. Cook, stirring, for about 3 minutes, until the rice is pearly. The grains
should not stick together and should become translucent.
They should not color, however.

3   When the rice is pearly, add the wine, stir well, and cook
3 minutes more over low heat.

4   Start adding the hot broth to the pot of rice 1 ladle at a time.
When added to the rice, the liquid should shiver just below
the boiling point. Wait until the liquid is almost entirely
evaporated before you add the next ladle. You don't have to
stir the entire time. Little by little the rice will take on the
consistency of a purée. The risotto is cooked when each grain
is tender all the way through. It's possible that you won't
need to use all the broth, but it should take about 20 minutes
to finish.

5   Stir in the grated cheese off the heat. Check the seasoning
and add a little salt and some pepper as you like.

1½ quarts (1.5 l.) chicken broth
(page 77 or made from
bouillon cubes)

3 tablespoons olive oil

1 onion, peeled and minced

1¼ cups (½ pound/240 g.)
round Italian rice,
preferably arborio

½ cup (10 cl.) dry white wine

⅔ cup (2½ ounces/75 g.)
grated Parmesan cheese

Salt

Pepper

ASPARAGUS RISOTTO

Risotto aux asperges

SERVES 4
PREPARATION 15 minutes
COOKING about 25 minutes

1. Begin to prepare the Parmesan risotto. Heat 2 cups (50 cl.) water in a small saucepan. When the risotto is all but done, mix in the asparagus stems. Stir the cold diced butter into the risotto and cook 2 minutes more. Stir in the Parmesan and taste for salt and pepper.
2. Boil the asparagus tips for 1 minute in the small saucepan, just long enough to heat them up. Scatter them over the risotto and serve.

1 recipe Parmesan Risotto (page 655)
20 medium-sized green asparagus, cooked according to the recipe on page 549, stems and tips separated
1 tablespoon butter, diced and well chilled
Salt
Pepper

RISOTTO WITH MUSSELS

Risotto aux moules

SERVES 4
PREPARATION 20 minutes
COOKING about 25 minutes

1. Heat the olive oil in a large pot over low heat. Add the garlic over very low heat and cook gently for 2 minutes, stirring regularly with a wooden spoon. The garlic should not color. Stir in a pinch of cayenne pepper and add the mussels and wine. Raise the heat to high, cover, and cook until the mussels open, about 4 minutes. Shake the pot frequently as the mussels cook.
2. Put the cooking juices through a fine strainer into a bowl. Remove the mussels from their shells.
3. Make the Parmesan risotto but use the mussels' cooking liquid instead of chicken broth. When the rice has cooked, add the shelled mussels and diced chilled butter over low heat. Stir well to incorporate and add 1 last ladle of the mussels' cooking liquid and the parsley.

2 tablespoons olive oil
2 cloves garlic, peeled, degermed (page 122), and minced
Cayenne or other hot chili pepper
3 pounds (1.5 kg.) mussels, cleaned and scrubbed (page 228), and washed in several changes of water
1 cup (25 cl.) dry white wine
1 recipe Parmesan Risotto (page 655) minus the chicken broth
1 tablespoon butter, diced and well chilled
1 tablespoon parsley

VEGETABLE PAELLA

Paella de légumes

SERVES 4
PREPARATION   30 minutes
COOKING   30 minutes

1   Separate the cauliflower into small florets and soak them for 10 minutes in 1 quart (1 l.) water and the vinegar. In the meantime, blend the tomatoes, garlic, parsley, and a pinch of salt into a homogeneous purée in a blender or food processor. Cut the artichoke hearts into ½-inch (1-cm.) dice and drop them immediately into a bowl of lemony water.

2   Drain and rinse the cauliflower florets. Soak the spinach in the vinegar water for 2 or 3 minutes, then rinse and wash in 2 changes of water. Drain the spinach, squeezing it to remove as much water as possible. Drain the artichoke hearts.

3   Heat the olive oil in a large skillet—a paella pan or wok if possible—over medium heat. Add the spinach and stir with a wooden spoon. Add the fava beans, green beans, diced artichoke, and cauliflower. Season with 2 pinches of salt and stir. Cook for 5 minutes, stirring, and then add the tomato purée and saffron. Stir. Add 1½ quarts (1.5 l.) water, bring to a boil, and simmer for 5 minutes. Add 2 cups (50 cl.) more water, bring back to a boil, and simmer for 5 minutes. Add the rice and cook over high heat for 10 minutes and then over low heat for 5 minutes. The rice should absorb all the cooking juices. Taste and add salt if necessary. Allow the paella to rest for a few minutes before serving.

¼ pound (80 g.) cauliflower
1 tablespoon distilled white vinegar
4 tomatoes, peeled, seeded, and diced (page 124)
4 cloves garlic, peeled, degermed (page 122), and minced
1 tablespoon minced flat-leaf parsley
Salt
Hearts of 4 small artichokes (page 179)
Juice of 1 lemon
½ pound (200 g.) fresh spinach
1 cup (20 cl.) olive oil
¼ pound (100 g.) shelled and peeled fava beans (page 168)
¼ pound (100 g.) *haricots verts* or slender green beans, ends trimmed, strings removed, and cut into ½-inch (1-cm.) pieces
2 generous pinches of saffron threads
10 ounces (300 g.) paella rice (short grain)

Grains

P olenta is a traditional dish in northern Italy and there-fore is also to be found in the region of Savoy, which was controlled by Italian counts and dukes and finally the kings of Sardinia for almost one thousand years before it became part of France in 1860. Polenta is made of corn flour, which comes in three different grain sizes: fine, medium, and large. Savoyards swear by large-grained polenta, as do most devotees of the dish. Polenta goes very well with sauced meats and with game.

POLENTA

SERVES   6–8 as a side dish
PREPARATION AND COOKING   25 minutes
Polenta should be prepared two hours in advance.

1   Rinse a saucepan under running water but do not dry it off. Add the milk, butter, garlic, ⅔ teaspoon salt, 5 pinches of grated nutmeg, and a generous pinch of pepper. Bring to a boil over high heat. When the butter has completely melted, lower the heat and gradually shower the polenta into the liquid as you stir with a wooden spoon. Cook for 8 minutes over medium-low heat, stirring almost constantly.

2   In the meantime, mix the eggs and yolks together in a bowl. After 8 minutes, take the saucepan off the heat, add the eggs slowly to the polenta, stirring vigorously, and cook 3–4 minutes more over lower heat, depending on the kind of polenta you are using.

3   Remove the pot from the heat and stir in the Parmesan and Gruyère. Taste for salt and pepper. Remove the garlic cloves.

4   Grease a rimmed sheet pan with oil using a pastry brush and pour the hot polenta into it. Smooth it with the spoon; you should make an even layer about 1 inch (2 cm.) thick. Refrigerate for at least 2 hours.

5   After refrigeration, cut the polenta into squares with a knife or into any shape you like with a cookie cutter. You can either

1 quart (1 l.) milk
6 tablespoons (100 g.) cold butter
2 cloves garlic, peeled
Salt
Grated nutmeg
Pepper
1⅓ cups (½ pound/240 g.) medium-grained polenta
2 eggs plus 3 egg yolks (page 204)
½ cup (50 g.) grated Parmesan cheese
½ cup (50 g.) grated Gruyère cheese
Neutral oil for greasing the sheet pan

sauté the polenta in butter in a skillet or bake it in the oven with some Parmesan on top.

6   To finish on the stovetop: Melt 1 tablespoon butter in a skillet over high heat. When it foams, add the polenta and brown both sides of each piece, about 2 minutes per side. Spoon melted butter over the polenta as it cooks. Remove to a hot dish and serve right away.

7   To finish in the oven: Preheat the oven 10 minutes in advance to 400°F/200°C. Grease a baking dish, preferably ceramic, with ½ tablespoon butter. Lay the polenta in the dish in a single layer and sprinkle with Parmesan. Bake about 8–10 minutes without turning the pieces. Remove from the oven and serve.

Either 1 tablespoon butter or ½ tablespoon butter and a little more grated Parmesan cheese to finish

BULGUR AND VEGETABLES
Boulghour

SERVES   4–6
PREPARATION   10 minutes
COOKING   15 minutes

Bulgur is wheat that has been parboiled, dried, and crushed. It is frequently used in Middle Eastern cuisines. In the West it is most frequently used as a healthy replacement for rice. It should be cooked in three times its own volume of salted water.

1   Preheat the oven to 400°F/200°C.

2   Heat the olive oil in a pot pretty enough to bring to the table. When it is hot, add the bulgur. Stir to coat well with the oil and heat up a bit, about 2 minutes over low heat. When the wheat has gotten a little hot, add the carrots, turnips, and peppers. Mix well and cook for 2 minutes. Season with ⅓ teaspoon salt and a dash of pepper.

3   Pour the chicken broth into the pot and bring to a boil. Cover, lower the heat, and cook for 12 minutes just below the boiling point (the water should shiver but not bubble) without stirring.

2 tablespoons olive oil
1⅔ cups (10 ounces/300 g.) bulgur wheat
2 carrots, peeled and diced small, yielding ⅔ cup
2 turnips, peeled and diced small, yielding ⅔ cup
½ red bell pepper, peeled, seeded (page 130), and diced small, yielding ⅔ cup
½ green bell pepper, peeled, seeded (page 130), and diced small, yielding ⅔ cup
Salt
Pepper
1½ cups (70 cl.) chicken broth (page 77 or made from a bouillon cube)

(continued)

4   In the meantime, spread the pine nuts on a sheet pan and toast in the oven for 1–2 minutes, until they get a little color.

5   When the bulgur is done, remove the pot's lid and fluff its contents with a fork.

6   Taste for salt and pepper. Serve in the pot, sprinkled with the pine nuts and parsley.

2 tablespoons pine nuts

1 tablespoon minced flat-leaf parsley

COUSCOUS

SERVES   6–8

PREPARATION   30 minutes

COOKING   about 15 minutes

Thanks to its former colonies in Northern Africa, France is quite familiar with couscous. There was a time when France counted almost as many "couscous" restaurants as pizzerias. Make sure you buy couscous and not semolina. The secret to success is to cook the couscous three times. Couscous is good with stewed or grilled lamb, *merguez* (a spicy lamb sausage), chickpeas, and all kinds of vegetables—peas, carrots, turnips, corn, and fava beans, for example. There is also Jewish couscous from Tunisia, which is served with fish. There is a special vessel for cooking couscous, the *couscoussier,* a big steamer pot that is found in every French kitchen. You can, of course, make couscous with a regular steamer instead. Cooking time will change with its size and shape.

3⅓ cups (1 pound/500 g.) small or medium couscous

3 tablespoons olive oil

Salt

4 tablespoons (70 g.) butter, cut into small pieces

1   Fill the bottom part of a couscoussier with 2 quarts (2 l.) water. (If you use a steamer basket, you will probably need less water.) Bring to a boil over high heat.

2   In a bowl, toss the couscous and oil together very well. Pour the couscous into the top part of the couscoussier or steamer and place it on top of the bottom part when the water bubbles. Do not cover. Cook uncovered just until the steam makes its way up and out of the couscous, which should take 3–4 minutes.

3   Remove the couscous to a large bowl. Sprinkle it with 3 tablespoons water and mix well with a large fork, lifting

the grains up to separate them. Put the couscous back in the top part of the couscoussier or steamer and cook again until the steam emerges from its surface.

4   Pour the couscous into the bowl again. Sprinkle with 3 table-spoons water and 1 teaspoon salt and lift and separate as before. If clumps form, crush them gently with the back of a fork.

5   Put the couscous back in the couscoussier or steamer. When the steam emerges for the third time, spread the couscous in the bowl for the third time. Fold in the bits of butter and taste for salt.

Gratins

POTATO GRATIN

Gratin de pommes de terre

SERVES   6
PREPARATION   35 minutes
COOKING   1 hour

A mandoline will make slicing the potatoes easier, but you can also do it by hand.

2 cups (50 cl.) milk
⅓ cup (180 g.) crème fraîche
Salt
Pepper
Grated nutmeg
2 pounds (1 kg.) potatoes, preferably charlottes or belles de Fontenay, peeled, washed, and sliced into rounds ⅛ inch (3 mm.) thick
1 clove garlic
1 tablespoon butter

1   Preheat the oven to 350°F/180°C.

2   Rinse a saucepan under running water and shake it out but do not wipe it dry. Add the milk and bring to a boil. When it bubbles, add the crème fraîche and season with ⅔ teaspoon salt, 1 pinch of pepper, and 1 dash of grated nutmeg. Stir.

3   Add the potatoes to the milk and stir with a wooden spoon. Cook over low heat for 20 minutes, stirring gently from time to time to keep the milk and potatoes from sticking to the bottom of the saucepan. Taste for salt and pepper.

4   Peel the garlic and rub it all over the inside of a baking dish large enough to hold the potatoes and milk. Add the potatoes and milk and pat them down evenly with the back of a spoon. Dot with the butter and bake for 1½ hours.

5   If the potatoes seem to be getting too much color as they cook, cover the dish with aluminum foil or even lower the

heat near the end of cooking if necessary. Serve in the baking dish.

POTATO AND LEEK GRATIN

Gratin de pommes de terre et de poireaux

SERVES 4
PREPARATION 20 minutes
COOKING 55 minutes

A mandoline will make slicing the potatoes easier, but you can also do it by hand.

1. Preheat the oven to 250°F/120°C and place a rack in the bottom third of the oven.
2. Melt 2 teaspoons butter in a saucepan. When it foams, add the leek and season with 1 pinch of salt and 1 dash of pepper. Cover and cook over low heat for 10 minutes. The leek should not color.
3. In a bowl, combine the crème fraîche, 1 pinch of salt, 2 pinches of five-spice powder, and 1 dash of pepper.
4. Butter a baking dish. Put down one-third of the potatoes in a layer. Top with one-third of the leeks and one-third of the seasoned crème fraîche. Repeat twice.
5. Pour 1 quart (1 l.) water into a deep sheet pan or dish large enough to accommodate the dish of potatoes and leeks. Put the gratin dish in the water and put both in the oven for 45 minutes.

2 teaspoons butter, plus extra for greasing the dish
3 ounces (100 g.) leek, white part only, carefully washed and cut into rounds ⅛ inch (3 mm.) thick
Salt
Pepper
¾ cup (180 g.) crème fraîche
Five-spice powder
8 medium potatoes, about 1½ pounds (750 g.) total, preferably charlottes or belles de Fontenay, peeled, washed, and sliced into rounds ⅛ inch (3 mm.) thick

POTATO GRATIN WITH ROQUEFORT

Gratin de pommes de terre au roquefort

SERVES   4

PREPARATION   30 minutes

COOKING   1¼ hours

A mandoline will make slicing the potatoes easier, but you can also do it by hand.

1   Preheat the oven to 350°F/180°C. In a large bowl, whisk together 4 egg yolks and ½ cup (10 cl.) crème fraîche or heavy cream. Add the potatoes and season with 2 teaspoons salt and ½ teaspoon pepper. Crumble in almost all the Roquefort and add the onion, garlic, and thyme. Mix very well.

2   Grease a baking dish with 1 teaspoon butter and spread in it the potato mixture. Dot with 2 teaspoons butter and cover with aluminum foil. Bake for 1 hour.

3   After 50 minutes of cooking, heat the remaining crème fraîche or heavy cream with 1 teaspoon butter and the rest of the cheese in a small saucepan, whisking frequently, until it bubbles very gently. Remove from the heat, allow it to cool a bit, and then whisk in the remaining egg yolk.

4   When the gratin has been baking for 1 hour, remove the aluminum foil and coat the gratin with the cream-butter-egg mixture in the small saucepan. Bake 15 minutes more, until the gratin is beautifully golden.

5 egg yolks (page 204)

1 cup (20 cl.) crème fraîche or heavy cream

2 pounds (1 kg.) medium potatoes, preferably BF 15, charlottes, or rattes, peeled, washed, and cut into rounds ⅛ inch (3 mm.) thick

Salt

Pepper

5 ounces (160 g.) Roquefort or other blue cheese

1 medium onion, peeled and finely minced

1 clove garlic, peeled, degermed (page 122), and minced

2 sprigs fresh thyme

4 teaspoons butter

GILDED POTATOES

Pommes de terre gratinées

SERVES 4
PREPARATION 25 minutes
COOKING 1 hour and 40 minutes

1 Preheat the oven to 410°F/210°C. Wash the potatoes but do not peel. Prick them with a fork so that they don't explode during cooking. Wrap each one in aluminum foil and place them on a sheet pan. When the oven is hot enough, bake 1½ hours. Remove the potatoes when they're done, but do not turn off the oven.

2 Discard the aluminum wrappers and slice the potatoes in half. Carefully remove the flesh, leaving the skins intact. Crush the flesh by putting it through a potato ricer or a food mill fitted with its finest disk. Fold in almost all the diced butter, keeping about 1 teaspoon, and the crème fraîche or cream. Mix very well. Season with 1½ teaspoons salt, ½ teaspoon pepper, and a pinch of nutmeg. Taste and add more salt, pepper, or nutmeg as necessary.

3 Lay the empty potato skins in a baking dish. Fill them with the enriched and seasoned potato purée. Top with Gruyère and bread crumbs and finish each skin with a little piece of the remaining butter. Bake until the tops are golden, about 8 minutes.

2 pounds (1 kg.) firm-fleshed potatoes such as BF 15 or charlottes
13 tablespoons (200 g.) butter, diced
1 cup (20 cl.) crème fraîche or heavy cream
Salt
Pepper
Grated nutmeg
½ cup (2 ounces/60 g.) grated Gruyère cheese
¾ cup dry bread crumbs

CAULIFLOWER GRATIN

Chou-fleur en gratin

SERVES 4–6
PREPARATION AND COOKING 30 minutes

1 Remove the butter from the refrigerator. Preheat the oven to 400°F/200°C and place a rack two-thirds of the way up. Soak the cauliflower florets for 10 minutes in a bowl of water and vinegar, using 1 tablespoon vinegar per quart (liter) of water. Rinse with fresh water.

1½ teaspoons butter
1 cauliflower, broken into florets and rinsed
Distilled white vinegar

2   Bring 1 quart (1 l.) water to a boil with 1 teaspoon coarse salt. Boil the florets for 10 minutes and then remove them with a skimmer or slotted spoon to a colander. Rinse under cold running water for 2 minutes. Drain.

3   Prepare the Mornay sauce. Grease a baking dish with 1 teaspoon softened butter. Spread the cauliflower in the dish and pour the sauce over it. Sprinkle evenly with 2 pinches of pepper and the Gruyère, and dot with ½ teaspoon butter. Bake for 15 minutes.

Coarse salt
3 cups (75 cl.) Mornay sauce
   (page 51)
Pepper
1 cup (110 g.) grated Gruyère
   cheese

LEEK GRATIN

Poireaux en gratin

SERVES   4
PREPARATION   10 minutes
COOKING   40 minutes

1   Preheat the broiler and set an oven rack in the top position. Prepare a bowl containing 1½ quarts (1.5 l.) cold water and a tray of ice cubes. Bring 3 quarts (3 l.) water to a boil with 1 teaspoon coarse salt. When the water bubbles, boil the leeks for 4 minutes. Use a skimmer or slotted spoon to remove them to the ice water. Leave in the ice water for 2 minutes and then drain.

2   Melt 1½ tablespoons butter in a large pot. Add the leek pieces in a single layer and roll them around in the butter with a wooden spatula. Season with 2 pinches of salt and 1 pinch of pepper. Cover and cook over very low heat for 30 minutes, stirring regularly. The leeks should not color.

3   In the meantime, grease a baking dish with 1 teaspoon butter. When the leeks are cooked, lay them in the dish in a single layer. Sprinkle with Gruyère and broil until the cheese is golden, about 5 minutes.

Coarse salt
8 leeks, white parts only,
   washed and cut into 3-inch
   (6-cm.) chunks
2 tablespoons butter
Salt
Pepper
½ cup (2½ ounces/50 g.)
   grated Gruyère cheese

ZUCCHINI GRATIN WITH FRESH CHEESE

Gratin de courgettes au fromage frais

SERVES 4

PREPARATION AND COOKING 45 minutes

1   Remove the butter from the refrigerator. Preheat the oven to 300°F/150°C and place a rack in the lower third.

2   Line a dish with several layers of paper towels. Heat the olive oil in a skillet over medium-high heat. One minute later, when the oil is quite hot, sauté the zucchini slices, still over rather high heat. Season with salt, pepper, a pinch of cumin, and a pinch of nutmeg. Flip and stir with a wooden spoon for about 4 minutes of total cooking. Lift out with a slotted spoon and lay the zucchini slices on the paper towel–lined dish.

3   In a bowl, whisk together the cheese and crème fraîche. Whisk in the eggs one by one and then the sage. Add a pinch of salt and a pinch of pepper.

4   Pour 1 quart (1 l.) water into a deep baking sheet or dish large enough to hold the gratin dish. Place it on the oven rack. Put the zucchini slices in the bowl of cheese, eggs, and cream and stir with a wooden spoon.

5   Brush the gratin dish with the softened butter. Pour the zucchini-cheese mixture into the dish evenly. Place the gratin dish in the pan of water and cook for 30 minutes. Serve hot.

Butter

2 tablespoons olive oil

1 pound (500 g.) small zucchini, washed and sliced into rounds ⅛ inch (3 mm.) thick

Salt

Pepper

Powdered cumin

Grated nutmeg

½ pound (200 g.) fresh sheep's or goats' milk cheese or *fromage blanc*

2 tablespoons crème fraîche or heavy cream

5 eggs

1 tablespoon small sage leaves sliced into thin strips

GOLDEN HAM AND ENDIVE ROLL

Roulade de jambon et endives gratinée

SERVES 4

PREPARATION AND COOKING   20 minutes

1   Preheat the oven to 350°F/180°C. Put the endives in a skillet with 1 teaspoon butter and cook for 3 minutes, rolling them around with a wooden spoon over low heat. Wrap each endive in a piece of ham. Butter a gratin dish and lay the ham-endive rolls in it.

2   Put the béchamel sauce in a saucepan if it is not already in one and add the crème fraîche or heavy cream. Bring to a boil while stirring. When the mixture bubbles, turn off the heat. Taste for salt and pepper and coat the rolls with the sauce. Sprinkle the grated Gruyère over all and bake for 10–12 minutes.

4 large endives, cooked
   according to the
   instructions on page 576
   but without addition of
   cream at the end
1 tablespoon butter
4 slices ham
2 cups (50 cl.) béchamel sauce,
   (half of the recipe on
   page 51)
1½ tablespoons crème fraîche
   or heavy cream
Salt
Pepper
½ cup (2½ ounces/50 g.)
   grated Gruyère cheese

BEEF AND POTATO HASH

Hachis Parmentier

SERVES   4–6

PREPARATION AND COOKING   40 minutes

This main dish, which bears the name of the scientist who fought widespread prejudice to popularize the potato in the eighteenth century, is traditionally made with leftover boiled meat. It is excellent with a green salad.

1   Make the mashed potatoes or grate them. Melt 2 teaspoons butter in a large pot over low heat. Add the onion and cook for 3 minutes over low heat, stirring with a wooden spoon. When it is translucent, add the meat, turn up the heat a bit, and cook and stir. Add the broth. Cover and simmer for 20–30 minutes.

2   Preheat the oven to 460°F/240°C. Taste the beef for salt and pepper and sprinkle with chervil. Grease a baking dish with butter and pour the meat and onions in evenly. Cover the meat with the mashed potatoes and smooth them with the back of a spoon.

3   Combine the Gruyère and bread crumbs in a dish. Sprinkle the top of the gratin dish heavily with the cheese-crumb mixture. Bake for 5 minutes.

2 pounds (1 kg.) potatoes, preferably bintjes, mashed as on page 623 or simply grated

3 teaspoons butter

1 large onion, peeled and minced

1 pound (500–600 g.) boiled beef (perhaps the leftovers from a pot-au-feu), ground or finely chopped

2 cups (50 cl.) beef broth (from a pot-au-feu, page 68, or made from a bouillon cube)

Salt

Pepper

1 tablespoon minced chervil

1 cup (3 ounces/100 g.) grated Gruyère cheese

½ cup dry bread crumbs

One-Dish Meals and Regional Specialties

There are countless regional specialties in France. What you will find in this chapter are just a few of the best-known ones. These local favorites tend to be one-dish meals, old recipes that include a variety of ingredients and can make a satisfying supper with no starter or side dishes. They are rarely technically challenging, but many of them do take some time.

Each of these recipes varies a little from place to place and season to season, giving rise to endless controversies about which variation is the authentic one. The truth is that dishes like these have always been changed to suit the moment, and many were invented quite simply to use up leftovers, without any thought of authenticity.

AÏOLI

SERVES 4
PREPARATION 20 minutes
COOKING 15 minutes for the carrot and cauliflower;
20 minutes for the turnips and potatoes;
25 minutes for the leeks; 4 minutes for the
mussels; 5 minutes for the cod
The cod must be soaked 24 hours in advance.

This dish of fish and vegetables from southern France is served with a garlic mayonnaise.

1   The day before: Put the salt cod skin side up in a basin of fresh water and soak for 24 hours. Change the water every 8 hours.
2   The next day, cook the vegetables: Begin by putting 4 saucepans on to boil, each containing 1 quart (1 l.) water and 1 teaspoon coarse salt. Prepare a large bowl two-thirds full of cold water and a tray of ice cubes. Put 1 quart (1 l.) water in a bowl with the distilled vinegar and soak the cauliflower florets for 10 minutes.

4 salt cod fillets, ½ pound
(200 g.) each
Coarse salt
3 tablespoons distilled white
vinegar
1 small cauliflower, rinsed and
broken into florets
4 young leeks, white parts only,
carefully cleaned
4 baby turnips, peeled

(continued)

AÏOLI (cont.)

3 When the saucepans are boiling, put a different vegetable into each one: leeks, turnips, potatoes, and carrots. After 15 minutes, remove the carrots with a slotted spoon, put them in the ice water for 1 minute, and then drain them in a colander. Discard their cooking water and put a fresh quart (liter) water on to boil with 1 teaspoon coarse salt.

4 Five minutes after removing the carrots, use a slotted spoon to remove the potatoes and turnips and put them in the ice water for 1 minute. Drain in a colander. Five minutes later, remove the leeks, chill them for 1 minute, and drain.

5 Cook the mussels. Save their cooking liquid and remove them from their shells.

6 Put the cod fillets skin side up in a large pot and cover them with water. Do not salt. Bring almost to a boil and then keep at a shivering preboil for 5 minutes.

7 Put the vegetables and mussels in a large pot. Put the mussels' cooking juices through a fine strainer into this pot. Cover, bring to a boil, and simmer over low heat for 2–3 minutes, just long enough to reheat the vegetables and mussels. Taste for salt and pepper.

8 Remove the cod's skin and put the cod in the center of a serving dish. Arrange the vegetables and mussels around it and serve the garlic mayonnaise on the side for dipping.

4 medium potatoes, such as BF 15, peeled and kept in a bowl of cold water
4 young carrots, peeled or scrubbed
1 recipe Mariner's Mussels (page 229) using 1½ pounds (750 g.) mussels, with their cooking juices
Salt
Pepper
1 cup (25 cl.) garlic mayonnaise (page 56)

ALIGOT

SERVES 4
PREPARATION 25 minutes
COOKING 35 minutes

This dish from the Massif Central (France's central mountain range) is often served with grilled pork or sausages. Traditionally, it is a summertime food, prepared in the mountain cabins where shepherds go to make their cheese.

1 Put the potatoes in a saucepan with 2 quarts (2 l.) water and 2 teaspoons salt. Bring to a boil and cook at a simmer for

1 pound (500 g.) firm-fleshed potatoes, such as rattes, scrubbed but not peeled
Salt
3 tablespoons (45 cl.) heavy cream or crème fraîche
3 gratings of nutmeg

about 25 minutes, until a knife slides easily and cleanly in and out of the potatoes. When they are finished, lift them from the cooking water with a skimmer or slotted spoon and put them in a colander to drain. Do not discard the cooking water.

2   Heat the cream in a small saucepan. When it begins to bubble, stir in the nutmeg and turn off the heat.

3   Peel the potatoes and put them through a ricer into a bowl. Discard about half of the potato cooking water. You should leave enough in the pot so that when the bowl of potatoes is placed in the pot, the water will reach halfway up the outside of the bowl. Put the pot over low heat and carefully lower the bowl of potatoes into the pot.

4   Stir the potato purée with a wooden spoon for 2 or 3 minutes. Stir in the diced chilled butter until it is completely melted and incorporated. Add half the hot cream, the garlic, and half of the cheese. Stir for 2 or 3 minutes, until the cheese has melted and is well mixed into the potatoes. Add half of the remaining cream and the rest of the cheese and stir 2 minutes more.

5   Finish by stirring in the rest of the cream. Taste for salt and pepper.

5 tablespoons (80 g.) butter, diced and kept very cold
2 cloves garlic, peeled, degermed (page 122), and minced
10 ounces (300 g.) fresh tomme (fresh sheep's milk cheese) cut into ¼-inch (0.5-cm.) dice
Pepper

FRENCH ONION SOUP

Soupe à l'oignon

SERVES   8
PREPARATION   20 minutes
COOKING   50 minutes

Onion soup *gratinée* (what an American would call "French onion soup") originated in Lyon, a city in the southeast of France once renowned as a center of textile manufacturing. But somewhere along the line this rich soup became a popular late-night supper in Les Halles, the old central food market in the heart of Paris. Now Lyonnais and Parisians argue about its real origins. Some people add a level tablespoon of flour to the cooked onions to thicken the broth a bit. Comté is the best cheese here.

2 pounds (1 kg.) onions
10 tablespoons (150 g.) butter
2 quarts (2 l.) chicken broth (page 77) or the broth from a pot-au-feu (page 68 or broth made from bouillon cubes)

(continued)

1   Peel the onions and slice them into thin rounds. Melt the butter in a soup pot and add the onions, stirring them to coat well with the butter. Cook over low heat about 30 minutes, until they are slightly golden.

2   Add the broth. Stir and bring to a simmer. Cover and simmer about 15 minutes over low heat, stirring from time to time.

3   Preheat the broiler. When it is hot, lightly toast the bread on both sides. Remove the toasted slices of bread but leave the broiler on.

4   Blend the soup to get the onions well broken up. Season to taste with salt and pepper. Fill ovenproof bowls with soup.

5   Top each bowl of soup with a slice of toast and cover the toast with grated cheese. Give each bowl a twist of pepper and put under the broiler for 3–4 minutes, long enough for the cheese to melt and crisp a bit but not to burn.

½ pound (200 g.) country bread cut in 8 thin slices
Salt
Pepper
3 cups (10 ounces/300 g.) freshly grated cheese (Comté, Gruyère, or Emmentaler)

MONKFISH SOUP FROM SÈTE

Bourride de lotte à la sétoise

SERVES   4
PREPARATION   15 minutes
COOKING   30–35 minutes, including 3 minutes for the fish

Sète is a port city in the south of France that takes special pride in its own version of fish soup. Unlike the famous *bouillabaisse* of Marseille, which is made with coastal fish (rock-dwelling fish, *poissons de roche*), this soup is made with deep-sea fish, *poissons de mer*. The sauce is spiced with garlic, saffron, and chili.

1   Pour the fish stock into a large pot with the saffron, garlic, and tomatoes. Bring to a gentle boil. Use a skimmer to remove any foam from the surface, rinsing the skimmer in cold water after each passage through the hot stock.

2   Add the leeks and cook for 3 minutes at a bare simmer. Remove the leeks and tomatoes with the skimmer.

3   Bring the stock back to a boil, add the potatoes, and simmer for 10 minutes. Remove the potatoes with the skimmer and keep them with the leeks and tomatoes.

3 cups (75 cl.) fish stock (page 40 or store-bought)
2 pinches of saffron threads
4 cloves garlic, peeled and degermed (page 122)
4 tomatoes, peeled, seeded, and diced (page 124)
4 leeks, carefully washed and sliced on the bias into rounds 1 inch (2 cm.) thick
4 large firm-fleshed potatoes, such as charlottes or BF 15, peeled, washed, and sliced into rounds 1 inch (2 cm.) thick

4   Keep the stock at a simmer. Add the fish and simmer for 3 minutes. It is cooked when it is opaque and white all the way through. Use the skimmer to remove the fish to the plate of vegetables. Keep the fish and vegetables hot, perhaps by stashing them in a 250°F/120°C oven with the door ajar.

5   Raise the heat under the stock to high and boil for 15–20 minutes. Add a pinch of pepper and a pinch of cayenne. Put the stock in a blender with the olive oil and blend at high speed to obtain an emulsion. Taste for salt and pepper.

6   Coat the warm vegetables and fish with the sauce.

1¼ pounds (600 g.) monkfish cut into 8 pieces as equal in size as possible
Pepper
Cayenne or other powdered hot chili pepper
3 tablespoons olive oil
Salt

BOUILLABAISSE

SERVES   10
PREPARATION   30 minutes
COOKING   1 hour for the stock plus 25 minutes for the soup and fish

Every coastal village in the south of France claims to guard the recipe for the *true* bouillabaisse. One thing is certain: This fish soup takes its Provençal name (*bouiabaisso*) from two verbs, *bouillir* (to boil) and *abaisser* (to reduce), for its cooking alternates between the highest heat and the most gentle.

Originally, fishermen made bouillabaisse for themselves with whatever portion of their catch they could not sell. Later, sea bass came into use, as did rock lobsters. J.-B. Reboul, the author of *La Cuisinière Provençale* (The Provençal Cook), cited no fewer than forty fish appropriate for use in bouillabaisse. Well . . .

You need at least seven or eight guests to make a good bouillabaisse so that you can use a large variety of coastal rockfish, each of which will have its own particular taste and aroma. The success of the recipe depends entirely on the combination of all these different flavors.

Ask the fishmonger to scale and gut the fish and to remove their heads. The larger ones should be cut into 2-inch (5-cm.) sections, and the fishmonger should give you the

One 2-pound (1-kg.) scorpion fish (*rascasse*)
1½ pounds (800 g.) John Dory
¾ pound (400 g.) conger eels
4 weever fish
¾ pound (400 g.) monkfish
1 tub gurnard (*galinette,* a kind of mullet)
¾ pound (400 g.) red gurnard (*grondin,* another kind of mullet)
5 small "sea cicadas" (*cigales de mer,* a kind of small rock lobster), if possible
4 velvet swimming crabs, if possible

(continued)

heads and other trimmings (gills and bones) to take home. The small fish can be left whole.

1   Rinse all the fish with cold water and carefully pat them dry with paper towels. Wash the sea cicadas and the velvet swimming crabs in cold water. Refrigerate all the fish until ready to use.

2   Make the fish stock. Heat 6 tablespoons olive oil in a large pot. Add the onion, shallots, leek, and fennel. Cook for 5 minutes over low heat, stirring with a wooden spoon. Add the fish heads, bones, and trimmings and the velvet swimming crabs, if using. Cook for 5 minutes over medium heat. Add the bouquet garni, garlic, orange zest, and tomato. Cook over high heat for 10 minutes, stirring constantly. Add 4 quarts (4 l.) cold water, 1½ tablespoons coarse salt, and the peppercorns. Bring to a boil, then lower the heat and simmer for 40 minutes.

3   Use a skimmer to remove the bouquet garni, orange zest, crabs, fish heads, and bones and discard. Put everything remaining in the pot through a food mill fitted with a medium disk and then through a fine strainer. Press down on the solids to remove as much liquid as possible.

4   Wash out the large pot and pour the stock back in. Bring to a boil and skim any foam from the surface with a skimmer.

5   Cook the fish. Preheat the oven to 320°F/160°C. Add the sea cicadas (if using) to the pot of stock. When it comes back to a boil, add the fish with the firmest flesh: the monkfish, gurnards, and scorpion fish. When the liquid comes back to a boil, add the remaining fish, 1 tablespoon coarse salt, 1 small teaspoon pepper, and the saffron. Simmer for 10 minutes over medium heat.

6   Place the baguette slices on a sheet pan and toast in the oven for 5–10 minutes. You just want to dry them out a bit. Peel the remaining 4 cloves garlic and rub the dry bread with the garlic. Put the bread on a dish or in a basket to serve on the side.

7   Taste the soup for salt and pepper. Remove the sea cicadas and slice them in half. Remove all the fish with a skimmer and arrange them on a large, warm serving platter. Lay the sea cicadas on top of the fish and sprinkle the whole with parsley. Keep the platter in the oven, turned off but still hot, with the door ajar.

FOR THE FISH STOCK
6 tablespoons olive oil
1 medium onion, peeled and sliced into rounds ⅛ inch (3 mm.) thick
6 shallots, peeled and sliced into rounds ⅛ inch (3 mm.) thick
1 small leek, white part only, well washed and thinly sliced
½ small fennel bulb, trimmed and thinly sliced
Heads, bones, and trimmings of all the fish and crabs
1 bouquet garni (2 bay leaves, 4 sprigs thyme, and 10 stems flat-leaf parsley, wrapped and tied in a green leek leaf)
4 cloves garlic, peeled and sliced into rounds ⅛ inch (3 mm.) thick
Zest of 1 organic orange, free of bitter white pith and cut into 1 inch by ½ inch (2 cm. by 1 cm.) slivers
1 large ripe tomato, stem end removed and coarsely chopped
Coarse salt
1 teaspoon peppercorns

Pepper
⅓ teaspoon saffron threads
2 stale baguettes, cut into thin slices
4 cloves garlic
Salt
2 tablespoons minced flat-leaf parsley
3 tablespoons olive oil
Rouille (page 57)

8   Bring the stock to a boil over high heat. Vigorously whisk in
     3 tablespoons olive oil. Drizzle the platter of fish with several
     ladles of the hot soup and serve the rest on the side in a
     tureen. Serve with the *rouille* and the garlic-rubbed bread.

PROVENÇAL BEEF STEW
Daube provençale

SERVES   6

PREPARATION   30 minutes (for the marinade) plus
                      30 minutes

COOKING   4 hours

The marinade should be prepared at least 4 hours in
advance, the day before if possible.

At one time this traditional beef stew would have simmered
for hours in the corner of a Provençal hearth or stove. This
version uses cubed beef for braising; the cheek is the best
part for this purpose.

In Provence they also make a daube from the Camargue
bull, using the same proportions, and from lamb shoulder or
neck chopped into 2-ounce (50-g.) morsels. The recipe is very
much the same, but with lamb one uses dry white wine
instead of red, and lemon zest instead of orange. The meat is
not larded, and the pork rind and dried orange zest are not
used. Lamb daube spends less time in the oven, about
3 hours.

Like most stews, this daube improves with time and is
better reheated or even cold. If you plan to serve it cold, you
might add a chopped veal foot to the pot when you add the
stew meat; this will encourage a jelly-like consistency.

20 stems flat-leaf parsley,
    leaves only, minced
7 cloves garlic, one peeled,
    degermed (page 122), and
    minced, and the other
    6 peeled
⅔ cup (3 ounces/100 g.)
    lardons (page 89)
3 pounds (1.5 kg.) beef stew
    meat (cheeks, if possible,
    or shoulder or chuck), cut
    into 2-inch (5-cm.) cubes
1 bottle Shiraz
1 teaspoon (5 cl.) Cognac
3 whole cloves
9 tablespoons olive oil
1 bouquet garni (5 stems
    parsley, 2 sprigs fresh
    thyme, 1 bay leaf, 2 small
    celery branches, 2 pieces
    dried orange rind, and
    1 sprig fresh sage, wrapped
    and tied in a green leek
    leaf)

(continued)

1   The night before, mix the minced parsley and minced garlic.
     Roll the lardons in this mixture. Use the tip of a knife to
     make an incision in each cube of stew meat and slip the lar-
     dons into these little pockets. Put the stuffed cubes into a ter-
     rine or large bowl with the wine, Cognac, cloves, and
     2 tablespoons olive oil. Add the bouquet garni, peppercorns,
     and the remaining garlic. Mix, cover, and marinate in the

refrigerator for at least 4 hours but preferably overnight, stirring 2 or 3 times.

2   The next day, put the pork rind in a saucepan with 1 quart (1 l.) water. Bring to a boil and let the water bubble for 2 minutes. Use a skimmer or slotted spoon to remove the pork to a colander and rinse it under cold water. Let it drain in the colander. Line the bottom of your stew pot with the blanched pork rind. (The pot should be large enough to hold all the rest of the ingredients, too; a *daubiere* or clay cocotte would be ideal, but lacking those you could use a cast-iron Dutch oven or other heavy pot.)

3   Drain the beef cubes in a colander set over a bowl; do not discard the marinade. Carefully pat the cubes dry with paper towels. Heat the remaining 7 tablespoons olive oil in a large pot over high heat. When the oil is hot, add the stew meat and brown all over, about 5 minutes. Remove the meat to a dish with the skimmer.

4   In the same pot, sauté the carrots and celery over medium heat for 5 minutes, stirring frequently. Season with 1½ teaspoons salt and ½ teaspoon pepper and stir in 2 pinches of grated nutmeg.

5   Preheat the oven to 250°F/130°C. Build the daube layer by layer in the pot lined with pork rind. First put down a layer of meat, then tomato, then carrots, celery, onions, orange zest, and olives. Pour the reserved marinade and beef broth over the whole thing. If the vegetables are not completely covered, top off with water. Taste the liquid and season if necessary, but be careful: The dish will cook for 4 hours, the salt will concentrate, and you will not be able to add water while the pot is sealed.

6   Prepare the sealing pastry (*pâte à luter*). Combine the flour with 1 cup (22 cl.) water in a small bowl and mix until it forms a dough. Roll it out with your hands into a long "snake" of dough. Put the cover on the pot of stew and seal the lid to the pot by pressing the dough all around the seam and joining it at the ends.

7   Bake for 4 hours. Take the pot out of the oven, remove the sealing pastry in front of your guests, and then take the pot back to the kitchen to degrease the surface of the broth. Remove the bouquet garni and, if you can find them, the whole cloves. Serve very hot.

2 teaspoons black peppercorns

½ pound (250 g.) fresh pork rind

1½ pounds (800 g.) new carrots, peeled and sliced into thin rounds less than ¼ inch (0.5 cm.) thick

1 heart of celery, washed and sliced into thin rounds less than ¼ inch (0.5 cm.)

Salt

Pepper

Grated nutmeg

1 pound (500 g.) small tomatoes, peeled, seeded, and diced (page 124)

½ pound (200 g.) small new onions, peeled

Zest of 1 organic orange, free of bitter white pith, cut into 1 inch by ½ inch (2 cm. by 1 cm.) slivers

3 ounces (100 g.) black olives, Niçoise if possible, pitted

1 cup (20 cl.) beef broth from a pot-au-feu (page 68 or made from a bouillon cube)

1 pound (500 g.) flour

POTATO BALLS FROM LIMOUSIN

Farcidure de pommes de terre

SERVES 4
PREPARATION 15 minutes
COOKING 1 hour

1 Grate the potatoes and toss them with 1½ teaspoons salt. Put them in a colander to drain for 5 minutes.

2 Beat the eggs with the flour.

3 Combine the potatoes, egg mixture, garlic, leek, sorrel, and parsley in a bowl and season with 1 teaspoon salt and a pinch of pepper. Shape this mixture into balls the size of a small apple. Push 3 lardons into each potato ball.

4 Bring 3 quarts (3 l.) water to a boil in a saucepan with ½ tablespoon salt. Poach the potato balls in simmering water for 1 hour. Drain before serving.

2 pounds (1 kg.) potatoes, preferably BF 15 or eerstelings, peeled

Salt

2 eggs

3 level tablespoons flour

1 clove garlic, peeled and put through a garlic press or pounded or chopped into a purée

1 leek, white part only, carefully washed and sliced into rounds less than ¼ inch (0.5 cm.) thick

3 sorrel leaves, chopped into thin strips

2 tablespoons minced flat-leaf parsley

Pepper

⅔ cup (3 ounces/100 g.) lardons (page 89)

VEGETABLE SOUP WITH *PISTOU*

Soupe au pistou

SERVES   4

PREPARATION   30 minutes

COOKING   20 minutes

1   Heat 2 tablespoons olive oil in a soup pot. Cook the leek and onion for 3 minutes over low heat, stirring with a spatula. Add the celery, carrot, tomato, potato, and navy beans. Stir well and cook for 2 minutes over low heat. Add 1 quart (1 l.) water and 1 teaspoon coarse salt. Bring almost to a boil and use a skimmer to remove foam from the surface of the liquid. Simmer very gently for 10 minutes.

2   In the meantime, break up the spaghetti: Wrap it completely in a clean dish towel, hold the ends tightly, and crack the spaghetti against the side of a table. Dump the contents of the towel into a bowl.

3   When the soup has been simmering for 10 minutes, add the green beans, zucchini, and spaghetti. Simmer 10 minutes more.

4   In the meantime, make the *pistou:* Using a blender or food processor, blend the garlic, basil, 2 tablespoons grated Parmesan, and ⅔ cup (15 cl.) olive oil into a purée. Blend in the rest of the Parmesan.

5   When the soup has been simmering for 20 minutes total, gently stir in half of the *pistou* sauce. Season with pepper. Drizzle each bowl of soup with a tablespoon olive oil. Spread the rest of the *pistou* on the croutons and serve them on the side.

1 cup (24 cl.) olive oil

1 leek, white part and a small part of the green, carefully washed and cut into rounds ¼ inch (0.5 cm.) thick

1 medium onion, peeled and sliced into rounds ¼ inch (0.5 cm.) thick

1 stalk celery, coarse fibers peeled away, cut into ½-inch (1.5-cm.) pieces

1 carrot, peeled and cut into ½-inch (1-cm.) dice

1 tomato, peeled, seeded, and diced (page 124)

1 potato, peeled and cut into ½-inch (1-cm.) dice and then rinsed well and kept in a bowl of cold water

½ pound (200 g.) fresh navy beans or *haricots cocos*

Coarse salt

2 ounces (50 g.) spaghetti

½ pound (200 g.) slender green beans (*haricots verts*), ends trimmed, strings removed, and cut into ½-inch (1-cm.) pieces

1 small zucchini, washed and chopped into large pieces

4 cloves garlic, peeled and degermed (page 122)

20 basil leaves

1 cup (3 ounces/100 g.) grated Parmesan cheese

Pepper

Croutons, preferably made from slices of sourdough bread pan fried in olive oil

CASSOULET _____

SERVES   10

PREPARATION   30 minutes

COOKING   1¾ hours plus 4 hours in the oven

"Cassoulet," the great cook Prosper Montagne said, "is the god of southwestern food [in France], a god in three persons (*according to the cities*). The Father, which is Castelnaudary's cassoulet (ham, loin, sausage, fresh bacon, and, perhaps, goose confit); the Son, which is that of Carcassonne (there, one adds leg of mutton and, in season, partridge); and, of course, the Holy Ghost, which is that of Toulouse, of mutton and bacon and pork belly."

In the beginning, one cooked cassoulet in a glazed earthen dish called a *cassole,* which is how it got its name. At that time it was made with fava beans, until white beans came to France from Spain in the sixteenth century. Once the *cassole* was filled, it would be placed on the coals in the hearth where it would cook slowly for several hours.

1   Cook the beans. Put them in a large pot with the carrot, the 2 onions stuck with cloves, 6 cloves garlic, the pork rind, and bouquet garni. Cover generously with cold water and put the pot over high heat. Lower the heat before the pot starts to bubble and cook at a bare simmer for 1 hour. Add the garlic sausage and uncooked pork sausage, and simmer 15 minutes more. Remove the pot from the heat and taste for salt and pepper.

2   Prepare the meat. Put the pork belly in a large pot, cover it with cold water, bring to a boil, and cook at a bubble for 5 minutes. Use a skimmer to remove the pork to a colander; rinse with cold water and leave to drain.

3   In another pot, melt 4 tablespoons fat from the confit. When the fat is hot, brown the lamb chunks all over for about 3 minutes over high heat; if necessary, work in batches so the chunks are not crowded and so that all end up beautifully golden. Remove them to a plate. Cook the sliced onions in the same pot for 3 minutes over low heat, stirring with a wooden spatula. Add the tomatoes, the remaining 4 cloves

2 pounds (1 kg.) dry white beans, preferably tarbais or lingot (large white beans or navy-type beans)

1 carrot, peeled

4 onions, peeled, 2 stuck with 1 whole clove each and 2 sliced into rounds ⅛ inch (3 mm.) thick

10 cloves garlic, peeled and crushed

½ pound (250 g.) fresh pork rind

1 bouquet garni (4 sprigs fresh thyme, 3 bay leaves, and 10 stems parsley, wrapped and tied in a green leek leaf if possible)

1 uncooked garlic sausage, about ½ pound (250 g.)

¾ pound (300 g.) uncooked pork sausage (*saucisses de Toulouse*)

Salt

Pepper

½ pound (250 g.) lean pork belly

1½ pounds (800 g.) duck confit, with its fat

1½ pounds (800 g.) boneless lamb shoulder, chopped into 2-inch (5-cm.) chunks

1 pound (500 g.) lamb neck, chopped into 2-inch (5-cm.) chunks

(continued)

garlic, and 10 tablespoons bean cooking liquid. Let the pot bubble for 10 minutes over low heat.

4   Fish the bouquet garni, onions, pork rind, and sausages from the bean-cooking pot. Discard the bouquet garni and leave everything else on a plate. Drain the beans over a bowl so that you keep their cooking liquid. Add the drained beans to the pot of onions and tomatoes, the pot in which you browned the meat.

5   Preheat the oven to 250°F/120°C. Slice the garlic sausage into rounds ½ inch (1 cm.) thick. Line a large terrine with the pork rind. Fill the terrine with alternating layers of meat, small sausages (*saucisses*), sliced garlic sausage, and the bean-onion-tomato mixture. Finish with a layer of the beans and top them with 2 tablespoons confit fat spread evenly over their surface. The liquid in the terrine should reach the top layer of beans and just barely cover them; if it does not, add some bean cooking liquid.

6   Bake for 3 hours. If necessary, add bean cooking liquid to the cassoulet as it bakes to maintain a high level of liquid.

7   Mix the bread crumbs with the minced parsley. When the cassoulet has baked for 3 hours, sprinkle it with the parslied crumbs and put it back in the oven for 1 hour to brown.

3 fine, very ripe tomatoes, peeled, seeded, and diced (page 124)
1¼ cup dry bread crumbs
1 small bunch flat-leaf parsley, leaves only, minced

STUFFED CABBAGE FROM THE AUVERGNE

Chou farci auvergnat

SERVES 6

PREPARATION   1 hour

COOKING $1\frac{1}{2}$ hours

1   If you are beginning with raw chicken thighs instead of left-overs, poach the thighs for 30 minutes in 1 quart (1 l.) simmering water with 1 bouillon cube. Drain the chicken, saving 1 cup (25 cl.) poaching broth to use later.

2   Melt 2 ounces (50 g.) lard in a Dutch oven over low heat. Let the pot cool down so that it is just warm and then line its bottom and sides with cabbage leaves in several layers if necessary, letting them hang over the top edges.

3   Bring the milk to a boil in a small saucepan, scraping the bottom and sides with a wooden spatula. As soon as the milk bubbles, add the bread, remove the saucepan from the heat, stir to form a doughy substance, and then allow the pot to cool.

4   Preheat the oven to 400°F/200°C. Remove the bones from the chicken thighs. Put the boned chicken, garlic, onion, parsley, bread and milk, and the remaining lard in a food processor. Chop it quite fine. Dump the chopped stuffing into a large bowl. Add the eggs and yolks, four-spice powder, 2 scant teaspoons salt, and 1 scant teaspoon pepper. Stir well with a large spoon until you have a homogeneous stuffing.

5   Put the stuffing in the cabbage-lined pot. Fold the overhanging cabbage leaves over the top so that the stuffing is wrapped up. Top with a layer of bacon, covering the top of the cabbage completely. Pour the chicken broth over, cover, and bake in the oven for $1\frac{1}{2}$ hours, basting with cooking juices every half hour.

6   Discard the bacon and slice the stuffed cabbage like a cake. Serve very hot in the pot.

2 cooked, boned chicken thighs—leftovers from Stewed Chicken (page 76)—or 2 uncooked, bone-in chicken thighs plus 1 bouillon cube

$\frac{1}{2}$ pound (250 g.) lard

Leaves of 1 large cabbage, blanched (page 556)

6 tablespoons milk

$\frac{1}{2}$ pound (200 g.) good quality white sandwich bread, crusts removed

1 clove garlic, peeled

1 medium onion, peeled and quartered

1 tablespoon flat-leaf parsley leaves

4 whole eggs plus 3 yolks (page 204)

$\frac{1}{2}$ teaspoon four-spice powder (a blend of powdered nutmeg, cinnamon, ginger, and cloves that you can make yourself)

Salt

Pepper

12 strips bacon

1 cup (25 cl.) chicken broth (page 77), if you begin with cooked chicken thighs instead of uncooked

POTATO TART FROM PICARDY

Clafoutis de pommes de terre de Picardie

SERVES 6
PREPARATION   20 minutes
COOKING   about 1 hour

1   Preheat the oven to 300°F/150°C. Combine the apples, potatoes, and gingerbread in a bowl. Season with ⅔ teaspoon
salt, 2 pinches of pepper, 3 pinches of grated nutmeg, and a
pinch of cinnamon and mix again.

2   Grease a baking dish with ½ teaspoon softened butter.
Spread the potato-apple-gingerbread mixture in the dish.
Beat the eggs and crème fraîche together and pour them all
over the contents of the baking dish.

3   Mash together the crustless white bread and the remaining
teaspoon softened butter. Spread this mixture evenly over
the baking dish and bake for 1 hour.

2 apples, peeled, cored, and
    sliced into rounds no more
    than ⅛ inch (3 mm.) thick
1 pound (500 g.) potatoes
    (BF 15 if possible,
    otherwise fingerlings or
    Yukon Gold), peeled and
    sliced into rounds no more
    than ⅛ inch (3 mm.) thick
2 slices gingerbread, cut into
    1-inch (2-cm.) dice
Salt
Pepper
Nutmeg
Cinnamon
1½ teaspoons softened butter
3 eggs
3 tablespoons crème fraîche
2 slices good quality white
    sandwich bread, crusts
    removed

PORK SHOULDER STEW

Potée Lorraine

SERVES 8

PREPARATION   30 minutes

COOKING   2½ hours

The meat must be soaked 2 hours in advance.

In the east of France, next to Alsace (both regions were long disputed between France and Germany), Lorraine is home to most of the vineyards that produce Champagne. This is a dish for autumn and winter, which can be quite cold in this region.

1 half-salt upper pork shoulder

1 pound (500 g.) smoked pork belly

2 bunches kale, blanched 1 minute and cooled under the tap

1 pound (500 g.) medium turnips, peeled and rinsed

8 carrots, peeled and rinsed

2 large onions, peeled and stuck with 2 whole cloves each

1 bouquet garni (2 sprigs fresh thyme, 1 bay leaf, and 3 stems flat-leaf parsley, wrapped and tied in a green leek leaf)

6 ounces (20 g.) crushed black pepper, tied in a gauze or muslin sack

4 small smoked sausages

2 pounds (1 kg.) firm-fleshed potatoes (charlottes, BF 15, or other fingerling varieties), peeled and kept in a bowl of cold water

1 pound (500 g.) country bread in thin slices

Salt

Pepper

1   Two hours in advance, put the pork shoulder and belly in a basin and cover generously with cold water. Leave to soak about 2 hours to remove the salt.

2   Rinse the pork shoulder and belly and blanch them 2 minutes in simmering unsalted water. Put the blanched meat in a colander and rinse in cold running water.

3   Put the pork shoulder and belly into a large Dutch oven. Add all the vegetables (except the potatoes) and the bouquet garni. Cover with cold water but do not salt. Bring to a boil and boil for 3 minutes. Use a skimmer to remove any foam that forms on the surface. Add the crushed black pepper. Lower the heat and simmer for 30 minutes.

4   Add the sausages and simmer 1½ hours more. Add the potatoes and simmer very gently for 30 minutes. In the meantime, grill or toast the country bread.

5   At the end of cooking, ensure that the potatoes are cooked by piercing one with the end of a knife; it should slide in easily. Taste the broth for salt and pepper. Use a skimmer gently to remove the meat and then the vegetables from the broth. Remove the cloves from the onions and discard the bouquet garni and sack of pepper. Arrange all the vegetables, including the kale, in a deep serving dish.

6   Put the cooking broth through a very fine strainer into a saucepan. Bring it to a boil. As soon as it bubbles, put it into a tureen.

7   Serve the soup with the grilled bread, meat, and vegetables on the side.

CABBAGE STEW WITH GARLIC SAUSAGE

Potée au chou et au saucisson à l'ail (potée auvergnate)

SERVES 6
PREPARATION 40 minutes
COOKING 3 hours

The pork and cabbage stew from the central mountains of Auvergne is distinguished by the addition of a ham bone and garlic sausage.

1 Two hours in advance, put the half-salt pork belly in a basin and cover generously with cold water. Leave to soak about 2 hours to remove the salt.

2 Rinse the pork belly and blanch all the meat (except the sausage) in simmering unsalted water (page 693). Put the meat in a large pot and cover generously with cold water. Bring to a boil and let the pot bubble for 5 minutes. Use a skimmer to remove any foam from the surface. Add the bouquet garni, onion, garlic, and peppercorns. Do not add salt. Cover and simmer but do not boil, skimming foam every 30 minutes, for 1 hour.

3 Add the cabbage, carrots, turnips, and leeks. Simmer very gently, covered, for 1½ hours. Add the potatoes. Prick the sausage with a fork to prevent it from bursting and add it, too. Taste for salt and pepper. Simmer 30 minutes more.

4 Use a skimmer to lift the meat and vegetables from the broth. Bring the stew to the table in a large, deep serving dish, vegetables on the bottom, sliced meat on the top. The custom in Auvergne is to soak bread in the cooking broth, but this may not be to your taste.

1 pound (500 g.) half-salt pork belly
1 pig's tail
2 pig's feet
20 ounces (600 g.) salt-cured lean pork belly (*petit salé*)
2 ham bones (optional)
1 bouquet garni (2 sprigs fresh thyme, 2 bay leaves, 5 stems flat-leaf parsley, wrapped and tied in a green leek leaf)
1 medium onion, peeled and stuck with 2 whole cloves
2 cloves garlic, peeled
1 scant teaspoon black peppercorns
Leaves of 1 large round green cabbage, blanched (page 556)
¾ pound (300 g.) carrots, peeled
¾ pound (300 g.) turnips, peeled
6 small leeks, trimmed, well washed, and tied in a bundle
6 medium firm-fleshed potatoes (BF 15, fingerling, or Yukon Gold), scrubbed
1 garlic sausage
Salt
Pepper
Bread (optional)

ROUEN DUCK

Canard au sang à la rouennaise

SERVES 4

PREPARATION AND COOKING 1½ hours

Duck from Rouen (Normandy) is larger than duck from Nantes (Brittany) and is traditionally raised at Yvetot. It gets its particularly gamy taste from the way it is slaughtered: It is smothered and therefore retains all its blood, unlike most other ducks, which are slaughtered and then bled. At the beginning of the nineteenth century a Pere Mechenet in Rouen popularized his own recipe for "pressed" duck: The carcass was pressed to remove its juices at the table for all to watch, a practice that caught on quickly in Paris.

Ask the butcher for a duck that has been gutted and "flamed" to remove all bits of feathers.

1 smothered duck (Rouen if possible), 3½ pounds (1.8 kg.), with its liver
Salt
Pepper
4 tablespoons (60 g.) butter
3 shallots, peeled and minced
½ cup (10 cl.) hard cider
Juice of ½ lemon
½ cup (10 cl.) Calvados

special equipment: spit for roasting and duck press, if possible

1   Chop and then crush the duck's liver. Preheat the oven to maximum temperature: 530°F/280°C, if possible. Season the exterior and the interior cavity of the duck with salt and pepper. Spit-roast it in the oven for 20 minutes without adding any fat.

2   After 20 minutes, lower the oven temperature to 450°F/230°C. Season the duck again with salt and pepper. Remove it from the spit and use a very sharp knife to remove its legs. Put them in a Dutch oven with 1 tablespoon butter. Put the pot in the oven uncovered for 5–6 minutes to finish cooking the legs.

3   Lay the duck on its back. Carve the flesh from the breast, slicing all along the wishbone and then detaching it.

4   Add the breast pieces to the pot with the thighs. Tent with aluminum foil and keep warm by setting the pot on the open oven door. (The oven should no longer be on.)

5   Prepare the sauce: Press the duck's carcass in a duck press if possible. If not possible, chop up the carcass, crush it coarsely, and then put it in between 2 plates and press to extract as much blood and juice as possible.

6   Put the shallots in a saucepan with the cider and a dash of salt. Bring to a boil and bubble for 10 minutes. Turn the heat to low and add the duck's juices and blood along with the

crushed liver, the remaining 3 tablespoons butter, a few drops of lemon juice, and the Calvados. Season heavily with pepper. Bring the sauce to a simmer but do not let it boil. Taste and add salt if necessary.

7   Pour the sauce into the pot with the duck meat and simmer for 5–10 minutes over low heat, never allowing the sauce to bubble. This would cause it to fall apart.

BRESSE POTATO CAKE

Farçon de Bresse

SERVES   6
PREPARATION   50 minutes
COOKING   15 minutes

Bresse, in Burgundy, is well known for its poultry. This rather rich potato cake is delicious with a roasted chicken or a poached hen.

1   Put the potatoes in a large saucepan with 2 quarts (2 l.) cold water and 2 teaspoons coarse salt. Add the leeks, onion, and garlic, bring to a simmer, and simmer for 20–25 minutes. The potatoes are cooked when the tip of a knife slides in and out of them easily and cleanly.

2   Drain all the vegetables and blend them coarsely in a blender or food processor. Whisk in the butter, ½ cup (10 cl.) crème fraîche, and the eggs and yolks; do not do this in the blender or food processor. Mix well and then whisk in two-thirds of the cheese and all the parsley. Taste for salt and pepper.

3   Pour the potato mixture into a baking dish. Pour the remaining crème fraîche over the top and sprinkle with the rest of the cheese. Bake for 15 minutes.

2 pounds (1 kg.) firm-fleshed potatoes (charlottes, belles de Fontenay, or fingerlings), peeled
Coarse salt
2 leeks, white parts only, sliced into rounds
1 medium onion, peeled and sliced into rounds
2 cloves garlic, peeled and degermed (page 122)
1 stick (¼ pound/135 g.) butter, diced and well chilled
1 cup (20 cl.) crème fraîche
2 eggs plus 3 yolks (page 204)
1½ cups (5 ounces/150 g.) grated Gruyère cheese
1 bunch flat-leaf parsley, finely chopped
Salt
Pepper

SAUERKRAUT WITH SAUSAGES AND PORK

Choucroute

SERVES 8

PREPARATION 1 hour

COOKING 3 hours

Choucroute is the name of the sauerkraut made from white cabbage cultivated in Alsace (far eastern France, next to Germany). It is thinly sliced, salted, and preserved in wooden barrels or large stoneware crocks. Choucroutes differ from one another depending on the kind of cabbage used, the place of production, the harvest conditions, and the preparation methods used. There are many different recipes for choucroute. This one is typically Alsatian and differs from the versions one finds in Germany.

Traditionally, choucroute cabbage should be white (the variety called *quintal d'Alsace*), but Grimod de la Reynière— a famous epicure and the author of a gourmand's almanac— tells us that red cabbage is sometimes used in Germany (and sometimes even in Alsace).

It is not advisable to salt choucroute as it cooks since the salty meats should provide enough. You can taste at the end and add salt if necessary.

The best choucroute is very white, and the best time to cook it is September to February. After that it must be washed more and more carefully before it is dressed and sometimes even cooked in hot water.

Never pour Champagne into a choucroute. This trick is sometimes used in restaurants to increase the bill, but the truth is that after it has been cooked, there is no difference between expensive Champagne and another white wine.

4 pounds (2 kg.) shredded raw cabbage, as white as possible

1 smoked pork shoulder, 1½ pounds (750 g.)

1 cured ham shank

1 pound (500 g.) lean half-salt slab bacon

2 pounds (1 kg.) salted pork ribs

½ cup (120 g.) goose fat

2 medium onions, peeled and sliced into rounds ⅛ inch (3 mm.) thick

1 bottle Riesling or sylvaner wine

1 cup (50 cl.) chicken broth (page 77 or made from a bouillon cube)

1 bag of spices (1 tablespoon juniper berries, 3 whole cloves, 1 teaspoon peppercorns, 1 bay leaf, and 2 peeled cloves garlic, securely tied in a small muslin or cheesecloth sack)

2 carrots, peeled

1 uncooked smoked sausage

8 *saucisses de Strasbourg* (hot dogs)

8 medium firm-fleshed potatoes (BF 15, fingerlings, or Yukon Gold), well scrubbed

Salt

Pepper

1. Wash the cabbage very carefully in cold water. Keep changing the water until it stays quite clear even when the cabbage is submerged in it. Drain in a colander and squeeze it out with your hands, fistful by fistful, to extract as much water as possible.

2. Put all the meat except the sausages in a large saucepan and cover with 4 quarts (4 l.) cold water. Bring to a boil over high heat and boil for 5 minutes. Remove the saucepan from the

heat and remove foam from its surface with a skimmer. Lift the meat from the water into a colander and rinse under cold running water. Drain in the colander.

3   Melt the goose fat in a large cast-iron Dutch oven or tall, thick-bottomed saucepan. Add the onions and cook for 3 minutes over low heat, stirring constantly with a spatula. Add the cabbage and fluff it up with a fork, coating it with fat. Pour in the wine and chicken broth and stir.

4   Nestle the bag of spices in the center of the cabbage. Add the carrots. Tuck the pork shoulder and ham shank into the cabbage.

5   Cut a piece of parchment paper a little larger than the pot. Rub it with goose fat and lay it on top of the pot, goose fat side down. Cover the pot with its lid; you want it sealed shut as completely as possible. Cook for 30 minutes over very low heat.

6   Remove the cover and tuck the bacon and ribs into the middle of the pot. Cook 1½ hours more, keeping an eye on the pot to make sure it always has some liquid at the bottom. Add water if necessary.

7   In the meantime, prick the smoked sausage with a fork to keep it from bursting as it cooks. Heat 1 quart (1 l.) water in a saucepan. When it barely simmers, lower the heat, add the *saucisses de Strasbourg,* and simmer for 2 minutes. Remove them.

8   When the choucroute has been cooking for 2 hours total, nestle the smoked sausage in the cabbage. Lay the potatoes on top of the cabbage to cook them in its steam. Cover and cook 50 minutes more at a simmer. Then lay the drained *saucisses de Strasbourg* next to the potatoes on top of the cabbage to warm it. Cook 10 minutes more.

9   Remove the meats and discard the spice bag. Taste for salt and pepper, keeping in mind that the choucroute may already be quite salty. Drain the choucroute as much as possible. Even after cooking, it should be white, somewhat sour, and lightly crunchy.

STUFFED CABBAGE

Farci poitevin

SERVES   8–10
PREPARATION   1 hour
COOKING   3½ hours

These stuffed cabbage balls from Poitou in the west are traditionally cooked in a pot-au-feu, but you can cook them in broth just as well.

1   Save the largest cabbage leaves to be stuffed later. Chop the heart finely. Chop all the greens and herbs finely.

2   Put the chopped greens and all the herbs except the thyme in a large terrine. Add the pork, onions, and garlic.

3   Put the flour in another bowl and whisk in the eggs, blending until you have a lumpless dough. Mix this dough into the contents of the terrine. Add the bread crumbs, season with 1 tablespoon salt and ½ teaspoon pepper, and mix very well.

4   Line a large bowl with a clean dish towel or, even better, a special net for stuffing. You could also use a big piece of muslin. Line whatever cloth or net you use with large cabbage leaves; they should overlap slightly so that there are no gaps. Fill this cloth and cabbage hammock with the stuffing from the terrine, packing it in lightly. Fold the cabbage leaves over the top and then the cloth or net. Pull the whole thing into a round bundle, tying it up if necessary.

5   Bring 3 quarts (3 l.) water to a boil in a large pot. Add the thyme, 1 tablespoon salt, and ½ teaspoon pepper, and then lower the stuffed ball into the liquid. Keep it submerged, holding it down with a wooden spatula if necessary, for 5 minutes. Cover and simmer for 3 hours.

6   Pull the ball from the water but do not turn off the heat. Set a colander or steamer basket on top of the pot of still-simmering broth. Lay the ball in the steamer basket and let it sit over the simmering liquid for 30 minutes.

7   Turn off the heat under the pot, remove the stuffed ball, and allow it to cool a bit before removing the cloth or net. To serve, slice it as you would a melon.

Heart and leaves of 1 large round green cabbage, blanched (page 556)

Greens from 4 bunches of beets or chard, carefully washed, large central ribs removed, if necessary

1 pound (500 g.) spinach, well washed, large or tough stems removed

1 pound (500 g.) sorrel, well washed, large or tough stems removed

2 heads lettuce, washed

1 bunch flat-leaf parsley, leaves only

1 small bunch chives

1 small bunch scallions

1 small bunch chervil, leaves only

1 sprig tarragon

2 pounds (1 kg.) pork throat, rind removed, cut into small dice or very coarsely ground

2 large onions, peeled and minced

4 cloves garlic, peeled and minced

1 cup (130 g.) sifted flour

8 eggs

2 cups dry bread crumbs

Salt

Pepper

5 sprigs fresh thyme

POTATO PANCAKE WITH BACON AND CHEESE

Truffade

SERVES   4–5
PREPARATION   15 minutes
COOKING   25 minutes

This potato dish is popular in rural Auvergne and Limousin, two mountainous regions in France's center well known for their cattle, and is associated with fresh sheep's cheese (*tomme fraîche de cantal*). It is made with lard, which is seldom seen in French cuisine now but was the most common fat in the old days. It makes a nice side dish for meat but is also good as a main dish with a green salad on the side.

1   Melt 1 tablespoon lard in a skillet. Add the lardons and brown for 5 minutes, stirring. Remove them with a slotted spoon.

2   Melt 6 tablespoons (100 g.) lard in a skillet. Add the potatoes, garlic, and lardons. Cook over low heat for 20 minutes, until the potatoes are cooked and lightly colored. Taste for salt and pepper.

3   Add the remaining lard and the diced cheese to the skillet. Stir gently to spread as evenly as possible so that the cheese melts from the heat of the potatoes. Leave the bottom untouched for a while so that the lowest layer of potatoes colors lightly and sticks together a bit. You want to unmold the contents of the skillet as a cake, either by slipping it out onto a plate or holding an inverted plate on top of the skillet and then turning the whole thing over onto the plate.

10 tablespoons (150 g.) lard
1 cup (5 ounces/150 g.) lardons (page 89)
2 pounds (1 kg.) firm-fleshed potatoes (BF 15, charlottes, fingerlings, or Yukon Gold), peeled, sliced into rounds ⅛ inch (3 mm.) thick, rinsed, and patted dry with a cloth
1 clove garlic, peeled and crushed
Salt
Pepper
½ pound (250 g.) tomme (fresh sheep's milk cheese), cut into small dice

EEL STEW

Matelote d'anguille au vin

SERVES 4

PREPARATION AND COOKING 1½ hours

1. Wash the skinned eels and put them in a basin of cold water with a trayful of ice cubes. Leave them for 30 minutes to drain out the rest of their blood.

2. In the meantime, heat 2 teaspoons butter in a saucepan. Add the minced shallot and cook for 3 minutes over low heat, stirring with a wooden spatula. Add the Pinot Noir, 1 clove garlic, bouquet garni, whole clove, and some pepper. Bring to a boil and simmer gently for 10 minutes.

3. Prepare a *beurre manié:* Mash 1 teaspoon well-softened butter into 1 tablespoon flour until they are homogeneously incorporated.

4. Put the onions in a saucepan. Add just enough water to cover them along with 1 teaspoon butter, 1 teaspoon sugar, and a pinch of salt. Cover with parchment paper trimmed to fit and pierced with a fork and cook gently for 20–25 minutes. Shake the saucepan in a circle from time to time to move the onions about for brilliant, even, blond coloring.

5. Heat ½ teaspoon butter in a skillet. When it foams, add the mushrooms and cook for 10 minutes over medium heat, stirring. Season with salt and pepper and remove with a slotted spoon to a plate. Cook the lardons in the same skillet for 5 minutes, stirring with a wooden spoon.

6. Toast the white sandwich bread and rub it with the remaining clove of garlic to make garlic croutons.

7. Drain the eels and pat them dry with paper towels. Season with salt and pepper and sprinkle evenly with flour. Heat the peanut oil and 1 teaspoon butter in a stew pot. When the butter is quite foamy, add the eel sections and brown them evenly for 4 minutes. Sprinkle with marc, light a kitchen match, and set the marc aflame. Add the wine, bring to a boil, cover, and simmer for 6 minutes. Remove the eel to a plate and tent with aluminum foil.

8. Bring the liquid contents of the eel-cooking pot to a boil and cook for 15 minutes. Add the flour-butter mixture bit by bit, stirring it in with a wooden spoon. Bring back to a boil and

2 small eels, about 1¼ pounds (600 g.) each; ask the fishmonger to remove their skin

2 tablespoons butter

1 shallot, peeled and minced

1 bottle Pinot Noir

2 cloves garlic

1 bouquet garni (1 small stalk celery, 5 stems flat-leaf parsley, 1 sprig thyme, and ½ bay leaf, wrapped and tied in a leek leaf)

1 whole clove

Pepper

1 tablespoon flour plus a little extra for flouring the eel

12 small white onions, peeled

1 teaspoon sugar

Salt

½ pound (200 g.) white button mushrooms, washed, stem ends removed, and quartered

Pepper

½ cup (3 ounces/100 g.) lardons (page 89)

8 slices good quality white sandwich bread

2 tablespoons peanut oil

Dash of marc

1 tablespoon minced parsley

let the pot bubble for 1 or 2 minutes. Turn off the heat. Put this sauce through a fine strainer into a bowl. Stir in 2 teaspoons butter, the mushrooms, lardons, and onions. Taste for salt and pepper.

9 Lay the eel pieces in a deep serving dish and cover them with the sauce. Garnish with the garlic croutons and sprinkle with minced parsley.

BUCKWHEAT PORRIDGE WITH BACON

Soupe au sarrasin et au lard

SERVES 8
PREPARATION 5 minutes
COOKING 25 minutes

Buckwheat flour came to France from the East at the end of the fourteenth century and had spread as far as Brittany just a hundred years later. This new cereal was not good for making bread but soon became a staple food in Brittany in the form of porridge and crêpes. Then, this peasant soup, a specialty of the Cornouaille region, would have been a whole meal in itself, maybe with some small golden croutons fried in lard.

3 ounces (50 g.) lard

3 shallots, peeled and minced

¾ pound (400 g.) smoked lardons (page 89)

1 bouquet garni (2 stems flat-leaf parsley, 1 sprig fresh thyme, ½ bay leaf, 1 small stalk celery, and 5 peppermint leaves, tied together)

Nutmeg

2 quarts (2 l.) chicken broth (page 77, or made from a bouillon cube)

1⅔ cups (200 g.) buckwheat flour

Salt

Pepper

1 Melt the lard in a saucepan. Add the shallots and lardons and cook over low heat for 5 minutes, stirring with a wooden spoon. Add the bouquet garni, a pinch of nutmeg, and 1 quart (1 l.) chicken broth. Simmer for 10 minutes and then remove the bouquet garni.

2 Put the buckwheat flour in a bowl and whisk in the second quart (liter) chicken broth. Whisk very well until you have a uniform and lumpless substance. Pour this mixture into the pot of chicken broth; stir right away with a wooden spoon and bring to a bare simmer. Stirring constantly, hold at a bare simmer for 10 minutes. Use a skimmer to remove the grayish foam from the surface.

3 If the porridge is too thick, stir in a glass of water, but it should be quite substantial and rich. Taste and add salt and pepper if necessary.

Potées

A *potée* is a kind of stew, a thick mixture of meats (mostly pork) and vegetables (especially cabbage). It is one of the most popular dishes throughout France where, depending on the region, you will find it called *garbure, oille, hochepot,* and other ancient names. It is often cooked in an earthenware vessel but sometimes in a cauldron, cocotte, or cast-iron stew pot. Cabbages meant for this kind of stew must be blanched to be more digestible (page 556).

BLANCHING THE MEAT

You should also blanch the meats to get rid of their impurities. Here is how to do it.

Prepare a bowl of cold water. Put the meats in a large saucepan and cover generously with cold water; do not add any salt. Bring to a boil and let the pot bubble for 5 minutes. If necessary, use a skimmer to remove any foam from the surface of the pot. Rinse the skimmer in the bowl of cold water after each passage through the hot liquid. Use a skimmer or slotted spoon to remove the meat to a colander. (Do not dump the meat into a colander—you will just coat it with its own impurities and gelatin.) Rinse the meat under cold running water and let it drain. Discard the blanching water and wash the saucepan.

ALSATIAN MEAT STEW
Baeckeofe

SERVES   6–8

PREPARING THE MARINADE   45 minutes

PREPARATION AND COOKING   4 hours

The marinade must be prepared 24 hours in advance.

The ultimate dish of Alsace and Lorraine. Traditionally, it was cooked in an earthenware terrine in the village baker's oven. You can replace the lamb with pieces of goose; if you do, add 5 small carrots to the marinade.

1 pig's foot, cut in half

1 oxtail

1 pound (500 g.) boneless pork loin blade end

1 pound (500 g.) bone-in lamb shoulder

1 pound (500 g.) beef shank or brisket

(continued)

1   The day before, put the pig's foot and oxtail in a large pot and cover them with 1½ quarts (1.5 l.) water. (The water should cover them generously.) Bring quickly to a boil and boil for 5 minutes. Turn off the heat. Use a skimmer to remove any foam that has formed on the surface of the liquid. Lift the meat from the water with the skimmer and put it in a colander. (Do not just dump the contents of the pot into the colander.) Rinse under cold running water for 30 seconds.

2   Put all the meat in a basin or other large container with the onions, garlic, leeks, cloves, bouquet garni, wine, peppercorns, and 1 tablespoon coarse salt. Stir well and refrigerate. After 12 hours, stir well again. Refrigerate for 12 more hours.

3   The next day preheat the oven to 350°F/160°C. Remove the marinating meat from the refrigerator. Put a large colander or strainer over a bowl to catch the marinade liquid and put the contents of the basin through the colander or strainer.

4   Spread half of the potato slices in a large ovenproof terrine with a lid. Add everything caught in the colander or strainer to the terrine and top with the rest of the potatoes. Pour in the marinade liquid, which should reach up to 1 inch (2 cm.) below the top layer of potatoes. If it does not reach high enough, add some water. Cover the terrine with its lid.

5   Make the sealing pastry. Pour ⅔ cup (15 cl.) cold water into a bowl. With a wooden spatula, gradually incorporate the flour, stirring until you have a dough supple enough to stop up the crack between the terrine and its lid and firm enough to stick to the terrine. Roll it between your hands into a dough "snake" as long as the perimeter of the terrine. Press it into the seam between the terrine and lid all the way around.

6   Bake for 3 hours. To serve, break the sealing pastry and remove the lid. Degrease the broth by pouring a spoonful of cold water onto its surface. The fat will rise to the top, and you can remove it with a small ladle or large spoon. Rinse the ladle or spoon in cold water after each passage through the hot liquid.

2 medium onions, peeled and sliced into rounds ⅛ inch (3 mm.) thick

2 cloves garlic, peeled and sliced into rounds ⅛ inch (3 mm.) thick

2 leeks, white parts only, carefully washed and sliced into rounds ⅛ inch (3 mm.) thick

2 whole cloves, crushed

1 bouquet garni (2 sprigs thyme, 2 bay leaves, 1 stalk celery, and 10 stems parsley, wrapped and tied in a green leek leaf, if possible)

1 bottle Riesling or sylvaner wine

1 heaping teaspoon peppercorns

Coarse salt

3 pounds (1.5 kg.) firm-fleshed potatoes (BF 15, charlottes, or belles de Fontentay; otherwise fingerlings or Yukon Gold), peeled and sliced into rounds ⅛ inch (3 mm.) thick

2½ cups (300 g.) flour

VEGETABLE AND GOOSE CONFIT SOUP

Garbure béarnaise

SERVES 6

PREPARATION 30 minutes

COOKING 2 hours and 40 minutes

This stew comes from Gascony, the grand duchy on the Spanish border south of Bordeaux and Toulouse, which included, not far from the Atlantic coast, Béarn, birthplace of the well-known béarnaise sauce. *Garbure* takes its name from *gerbe,* for "sheaf," which suggests the "bouquet" of vegetables it offers. There are many versions of *garbure.* Depending on the season, one might add fava beans, peas, red chard, or grilled chestnuts, for example.

One tradition: Thirty minutes before the end of cooking, add a morsel of goose, duck, turkey, or pork confit and serve it on the side.

Another tradition: Not long ago it was the custom, after finishing *garbure* (or other peasant soup) to pour the dregs from one's wineglass (a few tablespoons) into one's dish, mix it with what was left of the soup, and drink it straight from the plate. This was called *faire chabrot* (or *goulade, trébuc,* or *tromblon,* depending on the local idiom) and is worth trying.

This soup, like many of these traditional recipes, was commonly made with leftovers. The heart of this one was the bone of a salt-cured ham, another specialty of the southwest (known today as "Bayonne" ham, after the French port), with whatever bits of meat were still attached to it. If you can find such a bone, it will make the soup even better.

1   Put the ham, pork belly, and bouquet garni in a Dutch oven. Cover with 2½ quarts (2.5 l.) cold water. Add the peppercorns but do not salt. Bring to a boil. With a skimmer, remove any foam that forms on the surface. Cover and cook over low heat for 1½ hours.

2   After 1½ hours, add the beans, leeks, carrots, turnips, potatoes, onions, and garlic. Cover the pot and cook over low heat for 40 minutes. Taste for salt and pepper.

3   Add the cabbage and the goose confit along with any fat that clings to it. Cook 30 minutes more.

½ pound (200 g.) Bayonne ham (salt-cured ham)

¾ pound (400 g.) salt-cured lean pork belly (*petit salé*)

1 bouquet garni (4 stems flat-leaf parsley, 1 sprig fresh thyme, and 1 small bay leaf, wrapped and tied in a green leek leaf)

7 peppercorns

3 ounces (100 g.) fresh white shell beans, shelled

2 leeks, trimmed, well washed in warm water, and sliced into rounds 1 inch (2 cm.) thick

¾ pound (400 g.) carrots, peeled and sliced into rounds 1 inch (2 cm.) thick

6 ounces (200 g.) turnips, peeled and sliced into rounds 1 inch (2 cm.) thick

¾ pound (400 g.) potatoes, peeled, washed, sliced into rounds 1 inch (2 cm.) thick, and kept in a bowl of cold water

10 ounces (300 g.) onions, peeled and sliced into rounds 1 inch (2 cm.) thick

2 cloves garlic, peeled and minced

Salt

(continued)

4   To serve, remove the meats, slice them, and arrange on a serving platter. Serve very hot.

Pepper

1 green cabbage, separated into leaves and blanched (page 556)

2 thighs of goose confit, with their fat

POTATOES FROM BERRY

Pommes de terre berrichonnes

SERVES   **6**

PREPARATION   **25 minutes**

COOKING   **30 minutes**

1   Melt the butter in a pot. When it foams, add the lardons, onions, and garlic and cook over medium heat for 3 minutes, stirring. Do not allow the vegetables to color. Add the potatoes, bouquet garni, and chicken broth. Season with 1 teaspoon pepper and 10 drops Worcestershire sauce. Cover and cook just below a bubble for 30 minutes.

2   Remove the bouquet garni. Taste and adjust the seasoning if necessary. Sprinkle with minced parsley to serve.

7 tablespoons (100 g.) butter

½ pound (250 g.) lardons (page 89)

2 medium onions, peeled and minced

1 clove garlic, peeled, degermed (page 122), and minced

2 pounds (1 kg.) medium oblong-shaped potatoes (charlottes, rattes, or other fingerlings), peeled and sliced in half lengthwise

1 bouquet garni (5 stems parsley, 2 sprigs thyme, and 2 bay leaves, wrapped and tied in a green leek leaf if possible)

1 quart (1 l.) chicken broth (page 77 or made from a bouillon cube)

Pepper

Worcestershire sauce

Salt

1 tablespoon minced flat-leaf parsley

REBLOCHON POTATOES

Tartiflette de Savoie

SERVES 4

PREPARATION AND COOKING 1 hour

1   Put the potatoes in a saucepan and cover them with 1 quart (1 l.) water and 1 level tablespoon salt. Bring to a boil and simmer for 20–40 minutes, depending on the size of the potatoes. When they are finished, the tip of a knife will slide easily and cleanly in and out of them. Drain.

2   While the potatoes cook, melt the butter in another saucepan. When it foams, add the onion and cook over low heat for 3 minutes; the onion should not brown. Add the wine and simmer for 20 minutes.

3   When the potatoes are cool enough to handle, peel them and chop them into large chunks.

4   Preheat the oven to 480°F/240°C.

5   In a large bowl, gently mix the potato chunks with the lardons and reduced wine. Pour the combination into a baking dish. Whip the chilled heavy cream.

6   Remove the crust from the Reblochon and chop it into pieces. Put them in a baking dish and bake for 18 minutes; they should get warm but not too hot. Put the warmed cheese in a blender or food processor and blend briskly as you add the broth (or 3 tablespoons water if you have no broth). Add the whipped cream to the blended cheese. Taste for salt and pepper. Spread this creamy cheese over the top of the potatoes.

7   Sprinkle the dish on the diagonal with the grated Beaufort cheese. Bake for 8–12 minutes. You want the *tartiflette* to get a little color. Serve very hot.

6 medium potatoes, scrubbed

Salt

1 tablespoon butter

1 onion, peeled and minced

¼ cup dry white wine such as sauvignon

½ cup (2 ounces/60 g.) small smoked lardons (page 89)

2 cups (50 cl.) cold heavy cream

½ lb (200 g.) Reblochon cheese

3 tablespoons chicken broth (page 77), vegetable broth (page 35), or water

Pepper

A generous ½ cup (2 ounces/ 60 g.) grated Beaufort cheese (similar to Gruyère)

Dessert

Intimately associated with childhood memories, dessert ends a meal on a convivial note. In France, dessert used to be preceded by the *entremets* ("in between"), a sort of first dessert appetizer course, but today desserts are simpler and such lines are no longer drawn.

Sugar is the indispensable base ingredient of dessert. Nevertheless, in classic French cooking it was (and to a certain extent still is) overused. If sugar, like salt, brings out and exalts flavors, it can also obliterate them when used too generously. So sugar plays a somewhat diminished role in these recipes. Naturally, you can sweeten them to suit your taste.

Granulated sugar is the most frequently used since it doesn't form lumps. Confectioners' sugar is used to decorate desserts before serving, to make sorbet, and to firm up whipped egg whites and give them a smooth look.

Brown sugar and raw, unrefined sugar (*cassonade*) lend a dish an agreeable caramel flavor.

Vanilla is often called upon to contribute to desserts. You must extract the tiny seeds from the inside of the bean. The beans themselves should be glossy and not too dry. The best and rarest vanilla beans come from Tahiti. When you need to flavor an ingredient or dish with vanilla beans, do it the night before if you can.

You can easily make your own vanilla-scented sugar. Keep vanilla pods (empty vanilla beans) after you have scraped out the seeds and tuck them into a canister of

CITRUS ZESTS

Sometimes desserts incorporate citrus zests, which add not only a fine taste but also a very special texture. Use organic fruit and wash it beforehand. Zest is peeled from the skin of a lemon or an orange. Slicing from top to bottom with a paring knife or perhaps even a vegetable peeler, cut away the colored top layer of skin without taking any of the white pith beneath, which is bitter. The zest is then chopped into tiny matchsticks about 1 inch by $\frac{1}{8}$ inch (3 cm. by 3 mm.) and blanched—passed briefly through boiling water to remove any lingering traces of bitterness. At this point zests are often preserved in sugar syrup.

superfine sugar. Seal it well and wait several weeks for the vanilla flavor to infuse the sugar. You'll need at least four pods for 4 cups (900 g.) sugar.

Traditionally, people whipping egg whites into stiff peaks (*blancs en neige*) are advised to add a pinch of salt at the beginning. But this little addition changes the flavor of the whites, and it's better to use a pinch of superfine sugar instead.

Sometimes you will need melted chocolate or butter. Don't hesitate to use the microwave, but never heat butter or chocolate too long at once. It is better to keep putting butter or chocolate in for a few more seconds than to find that you've microwaved it too long and spoiled it.

Base Recipes

RICH CRUST FOR PIES AND TARTS

Pâte sablée

MAKES   crusts for two 9-inch (20-cm.) tarts serving 6 each
PREPARATION   20 minutes
The dough must be prepared at least 30 minutes in advance.

You can find store-bought doughs that are quite good, and you should not hesitate to buy them when you are running short of time. Nevertheless, buttery, sweet pie and tart crust is so much better when it is homemade. It is relatively easy to make, a matter of learning to handle the dough properly.

For starters, all the ingredients should be at the same temperature. Don't try, for instance, to blend egg yolks straight out of the refrigerator with room-temperature butter. And whatever you do, don't overwork the dough. Although it will look fairly uniform, you want its elements to retain their integrity at a very small level; otherwise, the dough will become rubbery. With a delicate hand and a little practice, you can make it in the food processor, too, always using a dough blade.

Confectioners' sugar produces a finer crust that holds its

10 tablespoons (155 g.) butter
1 vanilla bean
1½ cups (210 g.) sifted flour
¼ cup (40 g.) fine almond flour
1 cup (120 g.) confectioners' sugar
Salt
2 egg yolks (page 204)

shape better as it cooks. You must make enough dough for at least two crusts at once, even if you need only one; you can save the other in the freezer until you are ready to use it. This dough keeps for 2 days in the refrigerator and at least 3 months in the freezer.

1   Remove the butter from the refrigerator 30 minutes in advance. Cut it into pieces and leave it out at room temperature.

2   Slice the vanilla bean in half lengthwise, scrape out the tiny seeds with a spoon, and put them in a cup. (You can store the emptied pod in a sealed canister of superfine sugar to make vanilla-scented sugar for another use.)

3   Put the sifted flour in a bowl with all the almond flour and 4 tablespoons (40 g.) sugar. Mix well with a whisk or a fork to combine.

4   Put the flour mixture on a work surface and shape it into a little mountain with a crater at its peak (the "well"). Put the butter, a pinch of salt, the remaining sugar, and vanilla seeds in the well. Add 3 or 4 tablespoons water. Mix these ingredients together within the well without incorporating the flour just yet. Incorporate the egg yolks into this mixture but don't overwork them. Sprinkle flour over the top, mix the contents of the well with this bit of flour, and then incorporate the rest of the flour. (You should no longer see white traces when you finish.)

5   Mix the dough by pressing small handfuls quickly from one palm to the other, letting it fall to the work surface in little heaps. Do this 2 or 3 times at most and then pull the lumps together into a ball.

6   Divide the ball in half. Wrap in plastic wrap and put in the lower part of your refrigerator for at least 30 minutes to give the dough a chance to firm up before you roll it out.

7   When you roll out the dough with a rolling pin, be sure to flour your work surface well to keep bits of dough from sticking to the pin and tearing up the dough.

BASIC SWEET CRUST FOR PIES AND TARTS

Pâte brisée sucrée

MAKES   crusts for two 9-inch (20-cm.) tarts serving 6 each
PREPARATION   10 minutes
The dough must be prepared at least 1 hour in advance.

Although this crust is less sugary and more firm than Rich Crust (*Pâte sablée*), it is made almost the same way. The only differences are that in this crust the vanilla is optional and the confectioners' sugar is replaced by a smaller quantity of granulated sugar. This crust is recommended for tarts topped with rather wet fruits, such as plums, since it is firmer when cooked and less likely to become soaked through with juices.

10 tablespoons (155 g.) butter
1 vanilla bean (optional)
1½ cups (210 g.) sifted flour
¼ cup (40 g.) fine almond flour
1 tablespoon (15 g.) granulated sugar
1 pinch of salt
2 egg yolks (page 204)

1   Remove the butter from the refrigerator 30 minutes in advance. Cut it into pieces and leave it out at room temperature.

2   If you use the vanilla bean, slice it in half lengthwise and scrape out the tiny seeds with a spoon. Put them in a cup. (Keep the emptied pod in a sealed canister of superfine sugar to make it taste like vanilla for another use.)

3   Put the sifted flour on a work surface or in a large bowl. Mix the almond flour and vanilla seeds in with a whisk or a fork. Shape the flour into a little mountain with a crater at its peak (the "well"). Put the sugar, salt, butter, and egg yolks in the well. With the tips of your fingers, mix everything together well and knead a bit, working from the center and incorporating more and more flour from the edge as you go. Add 4 tablespoons warm water gradually as you incorporate more flour; this must be done very quickly, or you will end up with a rubbery, tough dough. (You can do this mixing in a food processor, too: Just put the flour in first, pulse it with the almond flour and vanilla seeds, and then pulse in the rest of the ingredients, including the water.)

4   When all the flour is incorporated (with no white traces visible), separate the dough into 4 small balls. Crush each one lightly by giving it one good whack with the palm of your hand. Then gather the 4 balls together without kneading them. Wrap in plastic wrap and refrigerate for at least 1 hour to give the dough a chance to firm up before you roll it out.

5   When you roll out the dough with a rolling pin, be sure to

flour the work surface well to keep bits of dough from sticking to the pin and tearing up the dough.

BLIND-BAKING RICH OR BASIC CRUST

For a single crust that serves 6
PREPARATION   20 minutes plus 30 minutes in the refrigerator
COOKING   about 20 minutes

Crust is usually "blind-baked"; that is, it is baked before the
filling is added. This way it will end up crisper and will not
get soggy when it is filled and baked again. (Some tarts are
baked to completion before filling and then filled and eaten
without further baking.)

½ recipe Rich Crust (page 699)
    or Basic Sweet Crust for
    Pies and Tarts (page 701)
Flour for dusting
Softened butter for greasing

*special equipment: tart mold,
    approximately 9 inches
    (20 cm.), and a rolling pin*

1   Preheat the oven to 350°F/180°C.
2   When the dough has rested in the refrigerator long enough,
     remove it and flatten it with the palm of your hand. Lightly
     but evenly and completely flour the work surface and rolling
     pin. Roll the dough out into a circle as perfect as you can
     make it. Its diameter should be at least equal to the diameter
     of the tart mold or pie dish plus 2 times the height of its side.
     THE SIMPLE WAY   Use a pastry brush to grease your tart
     mold or pie dish lightly with softened butter. Sprinkle it with
     flour and twirl and tap the pan to spread the flour evenly all
     over. Pat out any excess flour. Prick the rolled-out dough all
     over with a fork about 20 times. Carefully roll the dough up
     around the rolling pin and then unroll it over the tart mold.
     Gently press the dough into the mold so that it is completely
     and closely lined. Gently fold and press any overhanging
     dough over the outside edge and slice it off with a small
     knife or by passing the rolling pin over the top edges of the
     mold. (This will detach the extra crust.) Refrigerate for at
     least 30 minutes.
     THE SOPHISTICATED WAY   Use a pastry brush to grease
     your tart mold or pie dish lightly with softened butter. Sprin-
     kle it with flour and twirl and tap the pan to spread the flour
     evenly all over. Pat out any excess flour. Lay the base of the

tart mold on the pastry and cut out a round of dough exactly this shape. (Do not discard the edge bits left over when you cut out the circle.) Prick this round all over with a fork about 20 times. Roll the dough up around your rolling pin and unroll it into the tart mold. Use your hand to roll the leftover edge bits of dough into a small ball and then roll it out into a dough "snake" about 1 inch (2 cm.) thick and as long as the tart's circumference. Dip a pastry brush in water and use it to moisten the edges of the bottom circle of tart dough already in the mold. Lay the dough snake all around the moistened edge and pinch it up into an even border. Hold the dough roll steady with your left index finger as you pinch with your right thumb and index finger. Refrigerate the dough-filled tart mold for at least 30 minutes.

3   After chilling, bake for 20 minutes. Set the crust on a cooling rack to cool. Now it is ready to be filled, and in some cases it will be filled and baked again.

QUICK "PUFF PASTRY"

Pâte feuilletée rapide

MAKES   20 ounces/600 g. dough for two 9-inch/20-cm. tarts serving 6 to 8 each

PREPARATION $1\frac{1}{3}$ hours

True puff pastry is hard to make and takes a long time. This recipe is faster but still yields excellent results. If this quick version is still more trouble than you'd like to go to, you can find completely acceptable ready-made puff pastry at the grocery store.

Why so much work? Because the flakiness of the cooked pastry is the result of the way butter that is trapped between layers of dough expands and puffs up as it cooks. It is therefore necessary to stack many thin layers of dough on top of one another to trap the butter and puff as it inflates.

If you make this recipe in the summer, chill your mixing bowl and rolling pin in the refrigerator before you start. It is best to prepare puff pastry 24 hours in advance and to keep it in the refrigerator, where it will stay fresh for 2 or 3 days. It can also be kept in the freezer for 3 months.

2 sticks plus 1 tablespoon ($8\frac{1}{2}$ ounces/250 g.) butter

$\frac{1}{2}$ teaspoon (3 g.) salt

1 teaspoon distilled white vinegar

$1\frac{1}{2}$ cups (200 g.) very fine flour, plus extra for dusting

QUICK "PUFF PASTRY" (cont.)

1   Put the butter in a bowl and melt it in the microwave.

2   Combine ½ cup (13 cl.) cold water, the salt, and the vinegar in a bowl.

3   Sift the flour into a large bowl. Make a well in its center and add the water-salt-vinegar mixture. Using the tips of your fingers, begin to pull the flour into the liquid. Mix gently and knead just until all the liquid has been absorbed; be careful not to overwork the dough. Add the butter and mix briefly, just long enough to incorporate it evenly. Pull the dough into a ball.

4   Flour a work surface and lightly flour the ball of dough, too. Lay the dough on the work surface. Begin to roll it out into a 6-inch (15-cm.) square. Give it a quarter turn and roll again. (You will make a lot of "turns" in this recipe. They should always be made in the same direction; for instance, you might always turn your dough clockwise.)

5   Flip the dough over onto its other side and repeat. Use your hands to shape the dough into a square if necessary. Roll the square into a rectangle, 24 inches by 8 inches (60 cm. by 20 cm.) and of an even thickness throughout.

6   Now you have a rectangle before you, running the long way from left to right. Fold the left third onto the center and the right third onto the center over the left third. Give it a light roll with the rolling pin, always from left to right or right to left but in any case parallel to the folds. You have just completed the first "turn."

7   Throughout the rest of the recipe, if the dough seems to be sticking, lift it from the work surface and flour lightly beneath it.

8   Give the dough a quarter turn and roll it into a rectangle 24 inches by 8 inches (60 cm. by 20 cm.) as before, always rolling from left to right or right to left. Fold this rectangle into thirds as before, the second "turn."

9   Wrap the dough in plastic wrap or in a moistened dish towel and refrigerate for 20 minutes. Then perform two more turns to complete this "4-turn" puff pastry.

PUFF PASTRY

Pâte feuilletée

MAKES   enough for 2 tarts serving 6 each
PREPARATION   1 hour
RESTING   1½ hours

1   Dice 5 tablespoons (70 g.) butter and microwave just long enough to melt it. Gently mix in the salt and 6 tablespoons water.

2   Pour the flour into a large bowl and make a crater (a "well") in its peak. Pour the butter and water into the well and stir just until everything comes together into a ball. (You can also mix the dough by pulsing the ingredients in a food processor fitted with a dough blade.)

3   As soon as the dough forms a ball, remove it from the bowl or food processor. Knead it a little bit but not too much. This dough is called the *détrempe.* Use a knife to mark a cross-shaped incision in the top of the ball of dough. Wrap it in a clean dish towel and refrigerate for at least 30 minutes.

4   Cut out a piece of parchment paper and lay it on your work surface. Lay the well-chilled butter on the parchment paper and roll it out with a rolling pin into a square about ½ inch (1 cm.) thick.

5   Remove the dough from the refrigerator. Spread it out on your work surface by opening up the cross you marked, so that you end up with a central square surrounded by 4 triangular "petals," like a square envelope. The central square should be about the same size as the square of butter, maybe a little larger, and about ½ inch (1.5 cm.) thick. The 4 "petals" should be a little less thick, perhaps ¼ inch (75 mm.) thick. Lay the butter on top of the central square of dough. Fold the dough edges over the square of butter, like an envelope. Make sure the dough encloses the butter completely. Use the rolling pin on the 2 edges of the packet, which will keep the pastry from losing its shape.

6   Dust the work surface and rolling pin with flour. Roll the dough and butter envelope lengthwise so that its surface area is tripled. Pat it with a paper towel to remove any excess flour. Fold the dough into thirds by folding each edge over the middle. You have just completed the first turn.

2 sticks (½ pound/220 g.) butter: 5 tablespoons (70 g.) to melt plus 11 tablespoons (150 g.) well chilled

½ teaspoon salt

1½ cups (210 g.) sifted flour

7   Give the dough a quarter turn clockwise. Roll it out as before. Fold it in thirds to complete the second turn. Gently press 2 fingers into the middle of the dough to mark the fact that you have completed two turns. Wrap the dough in a clean dish towel and refrigerate for at least 30 minutes to give the butter a chance to chill and harden again.

8   When the dough has chilled, perform the third and fourth turns, always rotating the dough clockwise. Press 4 fingers into the dough, wrap the dough in the dish towel again, and refrigerate for 30 minutes.

9   When the dough has chilled a second time, perform the fifth and sixth turns, still rotating the dough clockwise. After the sixth turn, wrap the dough in the dish towel again and refrigerate for a final 30 minutes. Now the pastry is ready to bake.

VANILLA CUSTARD CREAM

Crème anglaise à la vanille

MAKES   almost 2 cups (15 ounces/40 cl.)
PREPARATION   15 minutes
COOKING   about 10 minutes

1   Fill a medium-sized saucepan with cold water, dump it out, but do not wipe the saucepan dry; this will keep the milk from sticking as it cooks. Add the milk to the saucepan.

2   Slice the vanilla bean in half lengthwise and scrape out the tiny seeds into the milk. Add a coffee bean if you have one; it will bring out the taste of the vanilla. Stir. Bring the milk to a boil, stirring well. As soon as it begins to bubble, lower the heat to very gentle, cover, and leave the pot to infuse for 10 minutes.

3   In the meantime, beat together the yolks and sugar, using either a whisk or a handheld electric beater. Beat until the mixture is smooth, pale, and doubled in volume. The electric beater will make this easier; it should take about 5 minutes.

4   Fill a sink with cold water, enough to reach halfway up the saucepan in which you're cooking the milk.

5   When the milk has infused, remove the coffee bean, whisk lightly, and bring back to a boil. Once it is bubbling, whisk

1¼ cups (30 cl.) milk
1 vanilla bean
1 coffee bean (optional)
4 egg yolks (page 204)
¼ cup (60 g.) granulated sugar

2 ladles of hot milk into the yolks and then turn the heat under the milk to low. Work quickly as the egg-milk mixture becomes liquid. Whisk this liquid egg-milk mixture into the saucepan of hot milk. Cook for at least 5 minutes, still over low heat, as the custard thickens. Stir with a spatula and scrape the bottom of the saucepan to keep it from sticking. Do not allow the mixture to bubble; it should stay at about 170°F/80°C. If it goes higher, turn off the heat. Remove the spatula you've been stirring with and run a finger across its back: If the track remains (instead of being immediately covered by cream), the custard is finished. If the track disappears, the custard has not finished cooking. If you have overcooked the custard, it will contain little bits of coagulated yolk about the size of crushed pepper. Past this point there's no saving the custard: You just have to start over.

6   As soon as the custard is finished, halt its cooking right away by lowering the saucepan into the sink of cold water. Stir with the spatula 5 minutes more as the custard cools, to encourage it to cool evenly.

7   Pour the cooled custard cream into a bowl, cover with plastic wrap, and refrigerate. The custard should be eaten cold in the following hours. Do not try to store it for later use.

FLOATING ISLAND WITH SUNBURNED CASTAWAYS _____

Ile flottante aux pralines roses

SERVES   6
PREPARATION   10 minutes
COOKING   20 minutes

1   Grease the mold with softened butter. Sprinkle with sugar and shake the mold so that it is completely lined with sugar. Refrigerate.

2   With a handheld electric mixer, beat the egg whites with a pinch of sugar until they are stiff and glossy. Add the remaining sugar and whisk 2 or 3 times. Very gently fold in the crushed candied almonds. Remove the mold from the refrigerator and fill it quickly, doing your best not to leave any air pockets.

Softened butter for greasing
the pan
10 tablespoons (150 g.)
granulated sugar, plus a
little extra for the pan
7 egg whites (page 204)
5 pink sugar–coated almonds,
crushed

(continued)

3   Preheat the oven to 260°F/130°C. Place the mold in a deep sheet pan or dish and pour 1 quart (1 l.) water all around it in the sheet pan or dish. Bake about 20 minutes. When the surface begins to crack, the whipped egg whites are cooked. Remove from the oven and allow the mold to cool before refrigerating it.

4   Spread the slivered almonds on a sheet pan and toast in the oven for 2 minutes.

5   When the mold has been refrigerated for a while, unmold the "island" into a deep dish. Sprinkle with the toasted slivered almonds. Just before serving, pour the custard cream all around the island.

3 ounces (100 g.) slivered almonds

1 quart (1 l.) vanilla custard cream (page 706; triple the recipe)

special equipment: a 2-cup (50-cl.) mold

FRUIT SAUCE

Coulis de fruits

MAKES   about 1 cup (25 cl.)
PREPARATION   10 minutes

For the fruit you can choose among strawberries, raspberries, apricots, cherries, blackberries, and red currants. You should end up with ½ pound (250 g.) after all the trimming and pitting.

1   Put the fruit in a blender or food processor. Blend into a purée. Taste. Add sugar and lemon juice if you like. The amounts will depend on your taste, the season, and especially on the acidity of the fruit: Apricots and currants need more sugar and less lemon juice than raspberries, for instance. So taste and add sugar and lemon juice bit by bit until you are pleased with the results. Blend again very briefly.

2   Put the purée through a sieve, fine strainer, or chinois. Store the sauce in a closed container; it will keep in the refrigerator for 2 or 3 days.

½ pound (250 g.) fruit, washed, trimmed, peeled, and pitted as necessary

1 tablespoon confectioners' sugar, or as much as necessary

½ tablespoon lemon juice, or to taste

CARAMEL

MAKES   3 ounces (90 g.)
COOKING TIME   about 10 minutes

1   Put the sugar in a saucepan with the vinegar and 3 tablespoons water. Next to the stovetop, prepare a glass containing 3 tablespoons cold water, a bowl of cold water, and a pastry brush.

2   Put the saucepan over high heat and bring to a boil, stirring occasionally with a wooden or other heat-proof spatula. Let the mixture simmer over medium heat as you constantly wipe the interior sides of the saucepan with the dampened pastry brush to keep sugar from burning on the pan. Beware of spitting: The sugar is very hot, and if a bit of it splatters and lands on your skin, it can burn you badly. If necessary, lower the heat: The sugar should not get too dark.

3   When the mixture has taken on a pale golden caramel color, remove the saucepan from the heat and carefully pour in the glass of water. The caramel may spit and hiss when water touches it. Put the saucepan back over medium heat, bring just to a bubble, and turn the heat off right away.

½ cup (90 g.) granulated sugar
⅔ teaspoon distilled white vinegar

CHOCOLATE SAUCE

Sauce au chocolat

MAKES   about ½ pound (250 g.)
PREPARATION   5 minutes
COOKING   2–3 minutes

1   Put the chopped chocolate in a bowl with 1 tablespoon water. Melt it in the microwave on medium. Check on it frequently, stirring well each time you check. Remove the chocolate as soon as it has melted.

2   Put the sugar in a saucepan with 1 cup (20 cl.) water. Bring to a boil and then turn the heat to low. Stir in the melted choco-

8 ounces (220 g.) dark chocolate (66 percent cocoa), chopped
3 tablespoons (45 g.) granulated sugar
4 tablespoons heavy cream

late and then the cream. Stir well, bring back to a bubble over
low heat, and simmer for 2 minutes.

3 Serve with vanilla ice cream or chocolate cake.

Fruit-Based Desserts

MELON SOUP WITH RASPBERRIES

Soupe de melon aux framboises

SERVES 4

PREPARATION 10 minutes

This dish should be made at least 2 hours in advance.

1 Cut the melons in half and remove their seeds. Peel one half
and chop the flesh into small dice less than ¼ inch (0.5 cm.)
or scoop it into pieces with a melon baller.

2 Use a large spoon to scoop the flesh from the remaining
3 melon halves. Purée in a blender with 4 mint leaves and
the sugar. Refrigerate the purée and the diced or balled
melon separately for at least 2 hours before serving.

3 To serve, put the diced or balled melon into 1 large or 4 individual soup dishes. Pour the melon purée over and decorate
with raspberries and mint leaves.

2 ripe melons
1 small bunch of mint, washed
1 tablespoon (15 g.)
    confectioners' sugar
½ pound (250 g.) raspberries,
    washed

STRAWBERRIES AND BASIL

Fraises au basilic

SERVES 6

PREPARATION 5 minutes

1 In a blender or food processor, purée half of the strawberries
with the rest of the ingredients. Coat the remaining strawberries with this sauce.

2 This dessert goes nicely with basil sorbet (page 761).

2 pounds (1 kg.) strawberries,
    hulled
3 tablespoons (45 g.)
    granulated sugar
12 basil leaves
1 cup (20 cl.) robust red wine
    such as Shiraz

ROASTED STRAWBERRIES WITH GREEN PEPPER, PEPPER COOKIES, AND HERBED ICE CREAM

Fraises rôties au poivre vert, tuiles au poivre, et glace aux herbes

SERVES   4

PREPARATION AND COOKING   45 minutes

1   If you are using fresh herbs, rinse them, discard the stems, and freeze the leaves at least 30 minutes in advance. Crush the herbs into a powder.

2   Whisk together the yolks and 1 cup sugar. Heat the milk and cream in a small saucepan. When it is hot but not boiling, stir it into the bowl of yolks and sugar with a wooden spoon. Stir in the herbs. Allow the mixture to cool and then cover and refrigerate for at least 30 minutes before churning it in an ice cream maker (according to the maker's instructions).

3   Preheat the oven to 400°F/200°C. Make the cookies by combining the melted butter, ¼ cup (45 g.) sugar, the flour, and 2 egg whites in a bowl with a wooden spoon. Line a sheet pan with parchment paper and dot it with spoonfuls of dough. Flatten each spoonful and sprinkle them evenly with the crushed peppercorns. When the oven is hot enough, bake the cookies for 3 minutes.

4   Melt the remaining butter in a skillet over low heat. When it foams, add the strawberries, the remaining sugar, and the green peppercorns. Cook for 2 minutes, stirring gently with a wooden spoon. Turn off the heat and add lemon juice to taste.

5   Serve the strawberries topped by scoops of ice cream. Use 2 tablespoons to shape the ice cream into a football-shaped quenelle for a sophisticated presentation. Top each scoop of ice cream with a pepper cookie.

3 tablespoons (45 g.) mixed fresh or frozen herbs (basil, chervil, and dill)

12 egg yolks and 2 egg whites (page 204)

1⅓ cups (340 g.) granulated sugar

3 cups (75 cl.) milk

1 cup (25 cl.) heavy cream

8 tablespoons (90 g.) butter, half melted

¼ cup (35 g.) flour

2 black peppercorns, crushed

1 pound (500 g.) strawberries, hulled and sliced in half lengthwise

1 ounce (30 g.) pickled green peppercorns

Juice of 1 lemon

STRAWBERRY MARASCHINO SOUP

Soupe de fraises au marasquin

SERVES 4
PREPARATION 1 hour

1 Put the sugar in a small saucepan, add 1 cup (25 cl.) water, and bring to a boil. Add the rhubarb and simmer for 3 minutes and then remove the saucepan from the heat. Cover with plastic wrap and allow it to infuse.

2 Blend one-third of the strawberries into a purée in a food processor or blender. Slice the remaining strawberries in half lengthwise. In a large bowl, combine the puréed strawberries and maraschino liqueur. Add the halved strawberries and stir gently. Cover with plastic wrap and refrigerate for 30 minutes.

3 Put the mint leaves in a bowl and sprinkle them with 2 tablespoons lemon juice. Add the olive oil and a dusting of powdered sugar and stir.

4 Dot the strawberry soup with caramelized rhubarb pieces, shower with mint leaves, and dust with confectioners' sugar to serve.

⅓ cup (60 g.) granulated sugar
1 stalk rhubarb, trimmed and chopped into 4-inch (10-cm.) pieces
1¾ pounds (900 g.) strawberries, hulled
10 ounces (30 cl.) maraschino liqueur (a relatively dry cherry liqueur, not the juice from maraschino cherries)
1 tablespoon mint leaves
Juice of 1 lemon
1 teaspoon olive oil
Confectioners' sugar for final sprinkling

STRAWBERRY SOUP WITH ORANGE FLOWER WATER

Soupe de fraises à la fleur d'oranger

SERVES 4
PREPARATION AND COOKING 30 minutes
MACERATION 1 hour

1 Combine the strawberries, vinegar, and half of the sugar in a bowl. Stir and leave in the refrigerator for 1 hour to macerate.

2 Put the zest in a saucepan, cover it with water, and bring to a boil. As soon as the water boils, drain and rinse the zest under cold running water.

3 Put the zest back in the saucepan with the remaining sugar and 1 tablespoon water. Cook gently about 20 minutes to "candy" the lemon zest. Then let it rest for 1 hour.

1 pound (500 g.) very ripe strawberries, hulled and quartered
1 teaspoon balsamic vinegar
⅓ cup (80 g.) granulated sugar
Zest of 1 washed organic lemon, cut into matchsticks (page 698)
1 cup (20 cl.) orange juice
1 teaspoon (5 cl.) orange flower water

4 Just before serving, combine the orange juice and orange flower water in a bowl. Pour it over the strawberries and sprinkle with the candied zest. Serve well chilled.

CITRUS GELATIN WITH TINY FRAGRANT STRAWBERRIES ___
Gelée de citron aux fraises des bois

SERVES 6
PREPARATION 15 minutes
RESTING 1 hour

3 gelatin leaves ($\frac{2}{3}$ ounce/2 g. each)
3 tablespoons (45 g.) granulated sugar
1 teaspoon washed organic lemon zest, chopped into tiny matchsticks (page 698)
1 vanilla bean, sliced in half
2 cups (45 cl.) orange juice
Lemon sorbet
$1\frac{1}{2}$ pounds (700 g.) tiny strawberries

1 Put the gelatin leaves in a bowl of cold water. Put the sugar in a saucepan with $\frac{1}{2}$ cup (10 cl.) water, the zest, and the halved vanilla bean and bring to a boil. When the saucepan bubbles, turn off the heat. Stir in the orange juice. Put the mixture through a fine strainer into a bowl and then add the gelatin.
2 Refrigerate at least 1 hour. Serve with scoops of lemon sorbet and top with tiny fragrant strawberries.

CHERRY SOUP WITH MINT _____
Soupe de cerises à la menthe

SERVES 6–8
PREPARATION AND MACERATION $1\frac{1}{3}$ hours

3 cups (75 cl.) Shiraz
$1\frac{1}{2}$ teaspoons cornstarch
2 pounds (1 kg.) bing or black cherries, washed and pitted
32 mint leaves, 24 with their stems tied together into a small bouquet and 8 of them minced

1 Pour the wine into a saucepan and bring to a boil over high heat. Simmer for 15 minutes.
2 Mix together the cornstarch and 1 tablespoon water in a small bowl. Slip the mixture into the saucepan and simmer 30 seconds more, stirring constantly as the liquid thickens. Add the cherries and bring back to a boil. Remove from the heat.

3   Pour the cherry mixture into a tureen, add the bouquet of mint leaves, cover with plastic wrap, and leave the tureen to infuse for 30 minutes.

4   Remove the mint bouquet and refrigerate the soup for 30 minutes. Sprinkle with minced mint just before serving.

CHERRY BAKE

Gratin de cerises

SERVES   4

PREPARATION AND COOKING   30 minutes

1   Put a large bowl for whipping the cream into the refrigerator to chill. Put the butter, 3 tablespoons (45 g.) sugar, and the cherries and their juices in a small saucepan. Cover and boil for 3 minutes. Remove the saucepan from the heat, pour in the kirsch, cover, and let cool.

2   Put a kettle on to boil. Put a heat-proof bowl in a large saucepan and fill the bowl with the egg yolks, wine, and remaining tablespoon sugar. Pour the almost-boiling water from the kettle into the large saucepan so that it comes halfway up the outside of the bowl of yolks. Turn the heat under the saucepan to low.

3   Preheat the broiler. Use a handheld electric mixer to beat the yolks-wine-sugar mixture until it has doubled in volume. Remove this sabayon from the heat and allow it to cool.

4   Whip the cream in the bowl you chilled in the refrigerator. Gently fold the whipped cream into the sabayon.

5   Drain the cherries and spread them in a baking dish; they need not be in a single layer. Spread the sabayon on top of them and broil for 3 minutes, just long enough to color the surface.

2 tablespoons butter
4 tablespoons (60 g.) granulated sugar
1½ pounds (750 g.) cherries, washed and pitted
½ tablespoon kirsch
3 egg yolks (page 204)
½ cup (10 cl.) white wine
½ cup (10 cl.) heavy cream, well chilled

MORELLO CHERRY–RASPBERRY COMPOTE WITH KIRSCH __

Compote de griottes et de framboises au kirsch

SERVES 6

PREPARATION   10 minutes

COOKING   8 minutes

1   Put ½ cup (10 cl.) water in a saucepan with the sugar and pectin and bring to a boil. Add the cherries to this bubbling syrup and poach over low heat for 8 minutes. Stir in the kirsch and raspberries and then remove the saucepan from the heat.

2   Pour the cherries into a compote or other serving dish. Allow to cool and then refrigerate until serving. Serve well chilled.

1⅔ cups (400 g.) granulated sugar

½ ounce (15 g.) pectin

2 pounds (1 kg.) fresh morello cherries, washed and pitted

2–3 tablespoons kirsch

½ pound (250 g.) raspberries

SPICED ROASTED PEARS _____

Poires rôties aux épices

SERVES   4

PREPARATION AND COOKING   45 minutes

You can serve this dessert with vanilla ice cream (page 757) or pear sorbet (see Fruit Sorbet, page 759)

1   Pour 1 quart (1 l.) water into a saucepan large enough to hold the water and, eventually, the pears. Add the sugar, 1 ounce (30 g.) honey, the vanilla bean, cinnamon stick, star anise, peppercorns, ginger, and lemon zest. Cover and bring to a boil.

2   In the meantime, peel the pears without removing their stems. From the bottom, cut out the core of each pear with a paring knife. Rub them well with the halved lemon.

3   When the spiced syrup is boiling, add the pears and cook, covered, for 15–20 minutes at a low bubble. Pierce one of the pears to verify that they are cooked; they should be very tender. Allow them to cool in the syrup. When they are no longer hot, drain the pears and set aside 1 ladle of their cooking juice.

¾ cup (180 g.) granulated sugar

2 ounces (60 g.) honey (linden, if possible)

1 vanilla bean, sliced in half

1 cinnamon stick

1 star anise

6 peppercorns

2 teaspoons fresh ginger, peeled and cut into tiny matchsticks ¼ inch by ⅛ inch (5 mm. by 2 mm.)

1 organic lemon, 3 strips of zest removed and sliced in half

4 Bartlett pears

(continued)

SPICED ROASTED PEARS (cont.)

4   Whip the cream. Don't whip it too stiff: It should thicken up a little but stay creamy and pourable.

5   Heat the remaining honey gently in a skillet. Add the reserved pear cooking liquid and the pears and let them color in the skillet, 6–7 minutes (depending on how ripe they are). Roll them in the juice and honey.

6   Remove the pears to a platter or to individual serving cups. Add the whipped cream and ground cinnamon to the honey and pear syrup and cook for 2–3 minutes over low heat, until the sauce is thick and smooth. Stir in the eau-de-vie.

7   Coat the pears with the warm sauce and serve.

½ cup (12 cl.) heavy cream, well chilled
Pinch of ground cinnamon
½ tablespoon pear eau-de-vie (Poire William)

PEARS POACHED IN RED WINE WITH CASSIS

Poires pochées au vin rouge et au cassis

SERVES   4

PREPARATION AND COOKING   35 minutes
This dessert should be prepared a day in advance.

1   Pour 2 cups (50 cl.) water into a saucepan. Add the sugar, cinnamon sticks, and halved vanilla bean. Cover and bring to a boil.

2   Peel the pears and submerge them in the bubbling syrup. Add the wine, cover, and cook at a gentle bubble for 15 minutes. Pierce one of the pears to verify that they are cooked. They should still be firm at this point.

3   Put the black currant pulp into a bowl and stir the hot pear cooking syrup into it. Then pour the pulp and syrup into the saucepan of pears. Add the orange slices, cover, and bring back to a boil. Remove the saucepan from the heat and allow it to cool, still covered.

4   When the pears have cooled, refrigerate them for 24 hours. To serve, drizzle with crème de cassis. This is nice with vanilla ice cream (page 757).

3 tablespoons (45 g.) granulated sugar
3 cinnamon sticks
1 vanilla bean, sliced in half
4 Comice pears, peeled
½ bottle Pinot
2 ounces (60 g.) black currant pulp, store-bought
1 organic orange, washed and sliced into rounds
1 tablespoon crème de cassis (black currant liqueur)

PEARS POACHED IN WHITE WINE AND SPICES

Poires pochées au vin blanc et épices

SERVES 4

PREPARATION AND COOKING 55 minutes

This dessert should be prepared a day in advance.

1 Put the Lillet in a saucepan and bring it to a boil. Light a long kitchen match, touch it to the surface of the liquid to set it aflame, and let the flames die out. Simmer for 10 minutes.

2 Bring a small saucepan of water to a boil with the juice of ½ lime. When it bubbles, add the three zests. When the water returns to a boil, drain immediately into a colander and rinse the strips of zest under cold water.

3 Peel and quarter the pears. Remove their seeds and fibrous centers. Plunge them into the simmering wine, cover the saucepan, and cook at a gentle bubble for about 15 minutes, depending on how ripe the pears are. Slip the tip of a knife into a pear to see whether it is cooked. It should still be barely firm. At that point, add the zests, ginger, sugar, cinnamon stick, halved vanilla bean, and peppercorns. Bring back to a simmer and then remove the pears, but do not discard the cooking syrup.

4 Allow the pears and syrup to cool a bit before refrigerating them separately. The next day, coat the pears with cooking syrup and serve cold, perhaps with a pear sorbet (see Fruit Sorbet, page 759).

½ bottle white Lillet wine

1 organic lime, 1 strip of its zest cut as on page 698, and its juice

1 organic lemon, 1 strip of its zest cut as on page 698

1 organic orange, 1 strip of its zest cut as on page 698

8 Bartlett or conference pears

1 teaspoon fresh ginger, peeled and cut into slivers ¼ inch by ⅛ inch (5 mm. by 3 mm.)

2 tablespoons (30 g.) granulated sugar

1 cinnamon stick

1 vanilla bean, sliced in half

½ teaspoon peppercorns

BAKED APPLES

Pommes au four

SERVES 4

PREPARATION 10 minutes

COOKING 40 minutes

1 Preheat the oven to 350°F/180°C. Wash and dry the apples. Cut out the core from the bottom or top of each apple and remove all the seeds. Use a skewer to pierce each apple in

4 firm, sweet apples

(continued)

6 different places, evenly spaced. Stick the pieces of vanilla bean into these holes.

2 Place each apple on its own square of aluminum foil. Soak the sugar cubes one by one in the Calvados and drop a brandied cube into each apple. If you like, sprinkle with a little cinnamon before sealing each apple up tightly in its square of aluminum foil.

3 Set the apple packets on a sheet pan lined with parchment paper. Bake for about 40 minutes.

4 Serve with *fromage blanc* seasoned with a dash of cinnamon.

2 vanilla beans, sliced in half lengthwise and each half chopped into 6 pieces
4 sugar cubes
1 small glass Calvados
Ground cinnamon (optional)
7 ounces (200 g.) *fromage blanc*

CARAMELIZED PINEAPPLE

Ananas caramélisé

SERVES 6

PREPARATION AND COOKING 45 minutes

1 Remove the butter from the refrigerator 30 minutes in advance. Cut it into pieces and put it in a bowl. Slice the vanilla beans in half lengthwise and scoop out the tiny seeds; place them on top of the butter. When the butter is soft enough, mash the vanilla seeds into it with a fork.

2 In the meantime, prepare the pineapple. Slice off the top and bottom. Use a large sharp knife to slice away the rind. Cut the flesh horizontally into 12 even slices. Use a small knife to remove the tough heart of each slice and discard these pieces of core, leaving behind rings of sweet, tender pineapple.

3 When the butter has softened and has been seasoned with vanilla, heat it in a large sauté pan or skillet over low heat. When it foams, lay the pineapples in the skillet in a single layer. You will probably have to work in several batches. Cook for 2–3 minutes on each side, until the slices are quite golden.

4 Remove the pineapple slices to a plate. Add to the skillet 2 tablespoons vinegar, the sugar, and the rum. Cook over medium heat for 2 minutes, stirring with a spatula.

5 Coat the pineapple rings with the sauce and sprinkle with crushed pistachios if you like. You can serve the pineapples, still warm, with coconut ice cream, too.

3 tablespoons butter
3 vanilla beans
1 fresh, very ripe pineapple
2 or 3 tablespoons cider vinegar
6 tablespoons (90 g.) granulated sugar
2 tablespoons dark rum
2 tablespoons crushed pistachio (optional)

Sweets to Start _____

Traditionally in France, a small sweet or *entremets* is served before the dessert proper.

ORANGE MOUSSE _____
Crème mousseuse à l'orange

SERVES   4
PREPARATION   25 minutes
The mousse must be prepared at least 2 hours in advance.

You can make this recipe many different ways by varying the flavoring; try lemon, strawberry, raspberry, mint, coffee, verbena, etc. Just replace the orange and lemon juice with an equivalent amount (approximately 2 cups/45 cl.) of the other fruits, crushed and strained. In the case of coffee, just use cold coffee or even instant coffee.

2 well-chilled eggs, separated (page 204)
Salt
1 tablespoon confectioners' sugar
2 tablespoons superfine sugar
1 level teaspoon cornstarch
Juice of 4 oranges, filtered through a fine strainer
Juice of 1 lemon, filtered through a fine strainer

1   Put the well-chilled egg whites in a bowl with a dash of salt. Beat them slowly with a whisk or a handheld electric mixer, picking up speed as you go. The whites are ready when the whisk leaves a clear trail in them and they do not stick to the sides of the bowl. Add the confectioners' sugar and beat gently for 1 minute.

2   Put the egg yolks, superfine sugar, and cornstarch in another bowl. Whisk together until they are homogeneously combined. Beat in the orange and lemon juice bit by bit, whisking constantly. Pour the mixture into a saucepan and warm over low heat for 12 minutes, still whisking. Pour the warmed yolks into the whipped whites and fold them in with a wooden spatula.

3   Pour into a serving bowl and refrigerate for at least 2 hours. Serve well chilled.

CREAM CUSTARD CARAMELIZED WITH BROWN SUGAR ____

Crème froide caramélisée à la cassonade

SERVES **6**

PREPARATION   10 minutes

COOKING   45 minutes

This dessert should be prepared the day before.

1 Put the egg yolks in a bowl. Scoop the tiny seeds from the vanilla beans into the bowl with the yolks. Add the sugar and whisk the contents of the bowl until they have paled and thickened. Whisk in the cold milk and then the heavy cream. Cover with plastic wrap and refrigerate for 12 hours.

2 Preheat the oven to 200°F/90°C. Pour the vanilla cream into 6 small ramekins or crème brûlée dishes, filling them three-fourths full. Be sure not to leave any vanilla seeds in the bowl; scoop them into the dishes using a spatula. Bake for 45 minutes.

3 When the custards are cooked, allow them to cool to room temperature. When they have cooled, refrigerate for at least 2 hours or, preferably, overnight.

4 When the custards are quite cold, preheat the oven's broiler. Sift the brown sugar onto the custards. When the broiler is quite hot, slip the custards under it for just a few moments, just long enough for the brown sugar to melt and caramelize. Serve right away.

9 egg yolks (page 204)
4 vanilla beans, sliced in half lengthwise
10 tablespoons (150 g.) granulated sugar
1 cup (25 cl.) milk, well chilled
3 cups (75 cl.) heavy cream
¼ cup (45 g.) brown sugar

UPSIDE-DOWN CARAMEL CREAM ____

Crème renversée au caramel

SERVES   **4**

PREPARATION   20 minutes

COOKING   about 30 minutes

1 Rinse a saucepan under cold running water and empty it out without wiping it dry. Pour the milk into the saucepan and scrape the tiny seeds from the halved vanilla bean into the milk. Bring to a boil and then turn off the heat.

2 cups (50 cl.) milk
1 vanilla bean, sliced in half
1 recipe caramel (page 709)
3 eggs
¼ cup (60 g.) granulated sugar

2   Prepare the caramel. Pour it into an 8-inch cake pan while it is still warm, turning the cake pan all about so the caramel coats its bottom and sides.

3   Preheat the oven to 400°F/200°C. Break the eggs into a bowl. Whisk them together, add the sugar, and whisk again. Pour the warm milk gently into the eggs, whisking briskly and constantly.

4   Put a kettle on to boil. Line a baking dish (not much shallower than your cake pan) with parchment paper and pierce it 4 or 5 times with a fork or a knife. Set the pan on top of the parchment paper–lined baking dish. Put the warm egg-milk mixture through a fine strainer into the cake pan and cover with aluminum foil. Pour the boiling water into the baking dish all around the cake pan.

5   Bake in the oven about 30 minutes. To check on its progress, pierce the cream with a metal skewer or trussing needle. When it comes out clean, the cream is cooked.

6   Allow the cooked cream to cool to room temperature and then refrigerate. Just before serving, slip a small knife all around the inside edge of the pan. Place an upside-down plate over the pan, grip it tightly on both sides, and invert the pan onto the plate. Before lifting the pan away, give it a little shake to help the caramel cream come out whole.

LITTLE CHOCOLATE CUSTARDS

Petits pots de crème au chocolat

SERVES   6
PREPARATION   15 minutes plus 1 hour of resting
COOKING   30–35 minutes
The pots de crème must be made at least 3 hours in advance.

You can serve these pots de crème with Lemon Madeleines or Chocolate Madeleines (pages 742).

½ cup (13 cl.) milk
3 ounces (90 g.) dark chocolate
    (66 percent cocoa),
    chopped into small pieces
1 cup (20 cl.) heavy cream
3 large egg yolks (page 204)
¼ cup (60 g.) granulated sugar

*special equipment: handheld
    electric mixer and 6 small
    (4-ounce/12-cl.) ramekins*

1   Rinse a saucepan under cold running water and empty it out without wiping it dry. (The water clinging to the pot's sides will keep the milk from sticking.) Pour the milk into the saucepan and heat the milk. When it is hot, add the chocolate

and stir with a wooden or other heat-proof spatula until completely melted. Remove the saucepan from the heat and stir in the cream. Stir well. Allow the mixture to cool a bit.

2   Put the egg yolks in a bowl with the sugar and beat with a handheld electric mixer on low (or use a whisk if necessary). Don't beat so hard that the mixture is frothing; you just want to break up the yolks and mix in the sugar. Beating constantly, gently pour the chocolate milk mixture into the bowl of yolks. Put the mixture through a fine strainer and allow it to rest for 1 hour.

3   Before the chocolate mixture finishes resting, preheat the oven to 340°F/170°C. Put a kettle on to boil. Line a baking dish (not much shallower than your ramekins) with parchment paper and prick the paper several times with a fork or a knife. Put the ramekins in the parchment paper–lined dish.

4   When the chocolate mixture has rested for 1 hour, pour it into the ramekins. Pour boiling water into the baking dish so that it reaches halfway up the outsides of the ramekins. Cover the baking dish with plastic wrap to prevent the formation of a skin on top of the pots de crème. (The plastic wrap is safe to put in the oven; it will not melt.) Bake for 30–35 minutes. When done, the creams should be firm around the edges but still jiggly in the center.

5   Remove the baking dish from the oven and carefully lift the ramekins from the water. Allow to cool for 2 hours at room temperature before covering with plastic wrap and refrigerating. Serve very well chilled.

SIMPLE CHOCOLATE MOUSSE

Crème au chocolat

SERVES   4–6
PREPARATION AND COOKING   20 minutes
RESTING   30 minutes

1¼ cups (30 cl.) heavy cream, well chilled
5 ounces (150 g.) dark chocolate (66 percent cocoa)
1 tablespoon (15 g.) granulated sugar

1   Put a bowl for the whipping cream in the refrigerator to chill. Rinse a small saucepan under cold running water and empty it out without wiping it dry. (The water clinging to the

pot's sides will keep the cream from sticking.) Pour in ½ cup plus 2 tablespoons cream and grate the chocolate into it. Bring to a boil while stirring with a spatula. When the cream bubbles, remove it from the heat right away. Pour it into a bowl and refrigerate for at least 30 minutes.

2   When the chocolate cream is well chilled, remove the chilled empty bowl from the refrigerator and add the remaining heavy cream, also well chilled. Add the sugar and beat gently with a handheld electric mixer or a whisk. Beat slowly at first and then, as the cream begins to thicken, accelerate. Beat until the cream is white, smooth, and doubled in volume.

3   Remove the chilled chocolate from the refrigerator and gently fold in the whipped cream with a spatula, lifting the chocolate up and over the cream until completely combined. Refrigerate again to serve well chilled. You might garnish this with cherries soaked in kirsch and serve with vanilla custard cream (page 706). You'll need 1 cup (20 cl.).

LITTLE VANILLA CUSTARDS

Petits pots de crème à la vanille

SERVES   6
PREPARATION   15 minutes
COOKING   30–35 minutes
The pots de crème must be made at least 3 hours in advance.

1   Rinse a saucepan under cold running water and empty it without wiping it dry. (The water clinging to the pot's sides will keep the milk from sticking.) Put the milk and cream in the saucepan. Scoop the vanilla seeds out of the beans and into the milk. Add the empty beans to the milk, too. Heat until the liquid is just about to boil and then remove it from the heat, cover with plastic wrap, and leave to infuse for 15 minutes.

2   Remove the vanilla beans from the liquid and follow the recipe for Little Chocolate Custards (page 721), using the egg yolks and sugar but replacing the chocolate milk mixture with this vanilla-infused milk.

½ cup (13 cl.) milk
1 cup (20 cl.) heavy cream
1 vanilla bean, sliced in half
3 large egg yolks (page 204)
⅓ cup (60 g.) granulated sugar

special equipment: handheld electric mixer and 6 small ramekins

CHESTNUT CREAM

Crème aux marrons

MAKES   almost ½ pound (200 g.)
PREPARATION   5 minutes

1   Thirty minutes in advance, put a bowl in the refrigerator.
2   When the bowl is chilled, pour the chilled cream into it and whisk in the instant coffee. Gently fold in the chestnut purée. Keep in the refrigerator.

½ cup (10 cl.) heavy cream, well chilled
1 teaspoon instant coffee
3 ounces (100 g.) chestnut purée (page 568)

CHERRY CUSTARD TART

Clafoutis aux cerises

SERVES   8
PREPARATION   10 minutes
COOKING   45 minutes

The word *clafoutis* comes from a word in the dialect of the central region of France, *clafir,* which means "to fill." The cherries are not pitted for this tart. In principle, a clafoutis can only be made with cherries, but in practice, many similar desserts made with other fruits style themselves as such.

1   Remove the butter from the refrigerator 30 minutes in advance to soften. Preheat the oven to 350°F/180°C.
2   Break the eggs into a bowl and add the yolks and granulated sugar. Whisk for 2 minutes to obtain a paler, homogeneous mixture. Stir in the flour, cream, and, if you are using it, the kirsch. Whisk to mix well.
3   Grease the bottom and sides of a gratin dish with the softened butter. Sprinkle it with the superfine sugar and shake it about to coat evenly. Spread the cherries in the dish and then pour in the batter.
4   Bake in the top half of the oven for 45 minutes. Allow to cool before serving.

1 tablespoon butter
5 eggs plus 2 egg yolks (page 204)
½ cup (120 g.) granulated sugar
½ cup (70 g.) sifted flour
1 cup (25 cl.) heavy cream
2 tablespoons kirsch (optional)
3 tablespoons superfine sugar
1 pound (500 g.) bing or black cherries, washed, stems removed, and pits intact

PEAR CUSTARD TART

"Clafoutis" aux poires

SERVES   6
PREPARATION   30 minutes
COOKING   45 minutes

An apple *"clafoutis"* can be made in the same way as this tart but with 1½ pounds (750 g.) firm, sweet apples instead of the pears, regular sugar instead of the vanilla sugar, and Calvados instead of the pear eau-de-vie.

1 tablespoon butter
2 large eggs
½ cup (120 g.) vanilla sugar, store-bought or homemade (page 698)
1 vanilla bean, sliced in half
⅓ cup (45 g.) sifted flour
½ cup (10 cl.) heavy cream
½ cup (10 cl.) whole milk
2 tablespoons pear eau-de-vie (Poire William) (optional)
3–4 Bartlett pears (about 1½ pounds/750 g. total)
Confectioners' sugar

1   Remove the butter from the refrigerator 30 minutes in advance to soften. Preheat the oven to 350°F/180°C.

2   Break the eggs into a bowl and add 6 tablespoons vanilla sugar. Scoop the tiny seeds out of the split vanilla bean and into the bowl. (Keep the empty beans in a canister with sugar to make your own vanilla sugar.) Whisk for 2 minutes to obtain a pale homogeneous mixture. Stir in the flour, cream, milk, and, if you are using it, the eau-de-vie. Whisk to mix well.

3   Grease the bottom and sides of a gratin dish with the softened butter. Sprinkle it with 2 tablespoons vanilla sugar and shake it about to coat evenly.

4   Peel and quarter the pears. Slice away their seeds and tough spots at their cores. Cut each quarter lengthwise into 4 evenly thin slices.

5   Arrange the pear slices in a spiral in the prepared gratin dish. Pour the batter over the pears and bake for 45 minutes in the top half of the oven. Allow to cool before serving. Garnish with a sprinkling of confectioners' sugar.

CRÊPES

SERVES 6

PREPARATION 15 minutes

The batter should be prepared 1 hour in advance.

These crêpes can be topped or filled with sugar and butter, jam, chocolate chips, or Chestnut Cream (page 724).

2 tablespoons butter, plus
    some for the skillet
3 eggs plus 1 yolk (page 204)
1 vanilla bean, split in half
2 cups (50 cl.) milk
1½ cups (200 g.) flour
¼ cup (45 g.) granulated sugar

1   Put the butter in a small bowl and microwave on medium just long enough to melt it. Put the eggs and yolk in a separate bowl and whisk together. Scrape the vanilla seeds from the halved bean into a small saucepan. Add the emptied vanilla pod and milk to the saucepan. Put over low heat, stir with a wooden spoon just until heated through, and then turn off the heat.

2   Put the flour in a heap in a bowl and make a little crater or "well" in its peak. Pour the beaten eggs and sugar into the well and stir together with a wooden spoon. Whisk in the warm milk and melted butter, beating briskly so that you end up with a lumpless batter. Let this batter rest for 1 hour.

3   To cook the crêpes, bring 1 quart (1 l.) water to a boil in a saucepan and then turn off the heat. Cover the saucepan with a plate.

4   Heat ½ teaspoon butter in a 10-inch skillet. Twirl the skillet so the melted butter spreads evenly. Pour about ⅓ ladle of batter into the skillet and immediately tilt and twirl the skillet to spread the batter evenly over the bottom of the pan. Cook for about a minute over medium heat, until the bottom of the crêpe is beautifully golden. Flip with a spatula—or, if you dare, by tossing the crêpe into the air and catching it in the skillet with the uncooked side down. Cook the second side about a minute. The crêpe should have brown patches but should not be burned anywhere. One by one, stack the crêpes on the dish on top of the saucepan of hot water, which will keep them warm.

WAFFLES I

Gaufres

MAKES 15 waffles
PREPARATION 20 minutes
RESTING 1½ hours
COOKING 4 minutes per waffle

1 Sift the flour into a large bowl and make a well in its peak. Crack the eggs and yolk into a bowl and beat together. Scoop the tiny seeds from the ½ vanilla bean into the beaten eggs. (Save the empty vanilla bean half to make vanilla sugar for other recipes.) Beat the granulated sugar and the salt into the eggs.

2 Melt the butter in the microwave. Warm the milk in a saucepan and dissolve the yeast in it. Pour the yeasty milk into the flour well. Add the egg mixture and the cream and stir with a wooden spoon. Add the melted butter and stir until you have a very smooth batter. Cover the bowl with a clean dish towel and leave it for at least 1½ hours at room temperature. (You can also refrigerate the batter overnight and make waffles in the morning.)

3 Heat the waffle maker. Use a pastry brush to coat it lightly with oil.

4 Pour a small amount of batter on one side of the waffle maker and cook according to your maker's instructions, probably about 4 minutes total. Remove the waffle and repeat until the batter is gone.

5 When all the waffles are cooked and warmed, dust with confectioners' sugar and serve.

1½ cups (210 g.) flour
2 eggs plus 1 yolk (page 204)
½ vanilla bean, sliced in half
2 tablespoons (30 g.) granulated sugar
Pinch of salt
5 tablespoons (70 g.) diced butter
⅔ cup (18 cl.) milk
½ ounce (15 g.) active dry yeast
½ cup (12 cl.) heavy cream
Neutral oil for greasing the waffle maker
Confectioners' sugar for serving

special equipment: waffle maker

WAFFLES II

Gaufres

MAKES   10 waffles
PREPARATION   15 minutes
RESTING   30 minutes
COOKING   4 minutes per waffle

Here is another waffle recipe, this one richer in butter and cream and made with a whipped egg white instead of yeast. It does not need to rest quite as long as the yeasted waffles.

⅓ cup (75 g.) butter plus 1 teaspoon for cooking the waffles
3 eggs, separated (page 204)
2 tablespoons (30 g.) granulated sugar
1 cup (150 g.) sifted flour
Pinch of salt
5 tablespoons (8 cl.) milk
1 cup (25 cl.) heavy cream

1   Dice the butter and melt it in the microwave. Put the egg whites in a bowl with 1 teaspoon granulated sugar and begin to whisk slowly. As the mixture thickens, speed up the whisking. The whites are well whipped when the whisk leaves a visible trace and they no longer stick to the sides of the bowl. You can do this with a handheld electric mixer, too.

2   Pour the flour into another bowl and make a well at its peak. Put 1 tablespoon sugar and the salt in the well with the yolks, milk, cream, and melted butter. Stir everything together with a wooden spoon until you have a homogeneous mixture. (You can also complete this step in a food processor fitted with a dough blade; just pulse slowly until evenly incorporated.)

3   Fold one-third of the whipped whites into the batter. When it is evenly incorporated, fold in the remaining whipped whites. Refrigerate for 30 minutes.

4   Cook the waffles as indicated in the previous recipe.

APPLE CHARLOTTE

Charlotte aux pommes

SERVES 6
PREPARATION 40 minutes
COOKING about 35 minutes
RESTING 30 minutes

With this dessert one might serve thick crème fraîche or an apricot sauce (see Fruit Sauce, page 708).

6 tablespoons (90 g.) butter
10 ounces (300 g.) brioche-type bread
1 vanilla bean, sliced in half
2 pounds (1 kg.) firm sweet apples, peeled, cored, and cut into 8 slices each
1 teaspoon ground cinnamon
½ tablespoon dark rum
½ cup (120 g.) superfine sugar

special equipment: 1 small ovenproof charlotte or soufflé mold

1   Line the bottom of the mold with parchment paper. Melt 5 tablespoons (75 g.) butter in a saucepan over very low heat. Preheat the oven to 300°F/150°C.

2   Trim 12 slices of bread into triangles and use a pastry brush to coat them on one side with melted butter. Line the bottom of the mold with these triangles of bread, placing them buttered side down and making them overlap just a bit at their edges.

3   Trim more slices of bread into rectangles as tall as your mold and about 1½ inches (4 cm.) wide. Brush them on one side with melted butter and stand them all around the edges of the mold, with the buttered side up against the mold and the unbuttered side facing in. They should overlap a little bit. Make sure you are not leaving any gaps in the bread lining.

4   Scoop the tiny seeds out of the vanilla bean and keep them in the spoon. Melt 1 tablespoon butter in a skillet. When it foams, add the apples and stir in the vanilla seeds, empty vanilla pods, cinnamon, and rum. Cook for 5 minutes over low heat. Sprinkle with the sugar and turn off the heat. Remove the empty vanilla bean halves.

5   Pour the apple mixture into the bread-lined mold, spreading it evenly and patting it down a bit with a fork. Trim the remaining bread slices to cover, brush them with butter, and lay them on top of the apples, buttered side up.

6   Place the filled mold on a sheet pan to deflect some heat from the charlotte. Without the sheet, the bread on the bottom may cook too quickly. Bake for 35 minutes. Test to see whether the apples are cooked by piercing 1 or 2 with the tip of a knife. They should be meltingly tender. The slices of bread should be golden and cooked stiff and dry enough to hold their shape when the charlotte is unmolded.

7   Slip the blade of a knife all around the edges of the mold. Since you lined the bottom of the mold with parchment paper, it should be quite easy for you to invert the charlotte onto a plate. Serve warm or cold.

POUND CAKE I

Quatre-quarts

SERVES   6
PREPARATION   10 minutes
COOKING   35 minutes

Pound cake is called *quatre-quarts* (four quarters) in French because it was traditionally made with equal parts flour, sugar, butter, and eggs. (They also call it *tôt fait* or "soon made" because it is a very simple cake to bake.) Here the amounts of sugar and butter have been reduced and 2 egg yolks have been added. If you want to make a traditional (and richer) French pound cake, increase the butter and sugar to 10 tablespoons (5 ounces/160 g.) each.

When you mix the batter, you can flavor it by adding a tablespoon or two of orange flower water or rum. In this case you will need to bake the cake 5 minutes longer. (Check to make sure it is cooked by slipping in a knife, which should emerge clean and dry.) You can also add raisins (about 2 ounces/60 g.) soaked in rum or the grated zest of an organic lemon (which you would add to the butter and sugar before creaming).

1 stick (¼ pound/110 g.) butter
½ cup (120 g.) granulated sugar
3 eggs plus 2 yolks (page 204)
1⅓ cups (160 g.) flour
1 tablespoon (9 g.) baking powder

1   Remove the butter from the refrigerator 30 minutes in advance and cut it into pieces. (If you are in a hurry, you can soften just-from-the-refrigerator butter in the microwave.)
2   Preheat the oven to 370°F/190°C. Line the bottom and sides of a 9 by 5 inch loaf pan with parchment paper.
3   Put the softened butter and the sugar in a bowl and beat with a fork for 1 minute. Beat in the eggs and yolks and then the flour and baking powder. Stir carefully with a spatula to make sure all the ingredients are evenly incorporated.
4   Pour the batter into the pan and bake for 35 minutes.

POUND CAKE II

Quatre-quarts

SERVES   6
PREPARATION   15 minutes
COOKING   35 minutes

This cake takes slightly longer than the previous version. Its batter is airier since the egg whites are whipped. You can vary the flavoring as described in the previous version.

1 stick (¼ pound/110 g.) butter
3 eggs, separated (page 204), plus 1 yolk
½ cup (120 g.) granulated sugar
1⅓ cups (160 g.) flour
1 tablespoon (9 g.) baking powder

1 Remove the butter from the refrigerator 30 minutes in advance and cut it into pieces. If you are in a hurry, you can soften just-from-the-refrigerator butter in the microwave.
2 Preheat the oven to 370°F/190°C. Line a 9 by 5 inch loaf pan with parchment paper.
3 Put the egg whites in a bowl with 1 tablespoon sugar and begin to beat slowly with an electric mixer. As the mixture thickens, speed up the mixer. The whites are well whipped when the beaters leave a visible trace and the whites no longer stick to the sides of the bowl.
4 In another bowl, beat the softened butter and the remaining sugar. Beat for 1 minute. Add the egg yolks and then the flour and baking powder. Stir carefully with a spatula until all is evenly incorporated. Fold in one-third of the whipped whites to lighten the batter and then gently fold in the rest of the whites.
5 Pour the batter into the cake pan and bake for 35 minutes.

APPLE POUND CAKE

Quatre-quarts aux pommes

SERVES 6
PREPARATION   15 minutes
COOKING   35 minutes

1	Thirty minutes in advance, remove the butter from the refrigerator and cut it into pieces. (If you are in a hurry, you can soften just-from-the-refrigerator butter in the microwave.)
2	Preheat the oven to 370°F/190°C.
3	Make the caramel and pour it into a 9 by 5 inch loaf pan, tilting the pan to coat evenly.
4	Wash the apples and quarter them. Peel them if you like. Remove the seeds and lay the apples in the caramel in the cake pan.
5	In a mixing bowl, beat together the softened butter and sugar. Stir in the eggs, yolks, flour, and baking powder. Mix carefully until all ingredients are homogeneously incorporated.
6	Pour the batter over the apples and bake for 35 minutes. Allow the cake to cool before unmolding.

10 tablespoons (155 g.) butter
1 recipe caramel (page 709)
4 fine acidic apples, such as Granny Smith
½ cup (120 g.) granulated sugar
3 whole eggs plus 2 yolks (page 204)
1⅓ cups (160 g.) flour
1 tablespoon (9 g.) baking powder

YOGURT CAKE

Gâteau au yaourt

SERVES 6
PREPARATION   20 minutes
COOKING   35 minutes

1	Thirty minutes in advance, remove the butter from the refrigerator and cut it into pieces. (If you are in a hurry, you can soften just-from-the-refrigerator butter in the microwave.)
2	Preheat the oven to 370°F/190°C.
3	Grease a 9-inch-long loaf pan and coat it with flour, tapping out the excess. In a food processor, combine the softened butter, yogurt, eggs, yolk, and sugar. Sift the flour and baking powder together, add to the wet ingredients, and mix again.

1 stick (¼ pound/125 g.) butter, plus a little extra for greasing the pan
2½ cups (300 g.) flour, plus a little extra for flouring the pan
5 ounces (150 g.) plain yogurt
3 eggs plus 1 yolk (page 204)
¾ cup (180 g.) granulated sugar
1 tablespoon (9 g.) baking powder
1½ tablespoons white rum

Mix in the rum, running the machine until you have a smooth batter.

4   Pour the batter into the prepared pan and bake for 35–40 minutes. The cake is properly cooked when the blade of a knife comes out of it clean. Unmold the cake while it is still hot.

PARISIAN CUSTARD TART

Flan parisien

SERVES 8
PREPARATION   30 minutes
COOKING   35–40 minutes

1   Roll the tart dough out to a thickness of ⅛ inch (3 mm.) and spread it into the tart pan. Refrigerate the dough-lined pan while you make the custard filling.

2   Heat the milk in a small saucepan over low heat. Do not boil it. Break the eggs into a bowl and add the sugar, cornstarch, and vanilla extract. Whisk briskly but not with so much energy that the mixture turns pale. Whisk in the warm milk, and when it is incorporated, whisk in 2½ cups (70 cl.) water.

3   Pour this mixture into the saucepan and cook over medium heat about 5 minutes, whisking the whole time. When the custard begins to thicken, remove it from the heat. Whatever you do, don't let it boil.

4   Pour the cream into the dough-lined tart pan. Smooth its surface with a spatula and allow it to cool for a few minutes.

5   Bake for 35–40 minutes. Allow to cool before serving.

1 recipe Basic Sweet Crust for Pies and Tarts (page 701), uncooked
3 cups (75 cl.) milk
6 eggs
1⅔ cups (400 g.) superfine sugar
4 ounces (135 g.) cornstarch
2 teaspoons vanilla extract

special equipment: tart pan 8 by 6 inches (20 cm. by 18 cm.) and about 2 inches (5 cm.) high

CARAMEL CREAM MOUSSE

Bavarois au caramel

SERVES 4

PREPARATION 35 minutes

This dessert should be prepared at least half a day in advance.

1 Put the gelatin leaves to soak in a small bowl of cold water. Put a bowl in the refrigerator to chill; later you will use it for whipping the cream.

2 Prepare the caramel and leave it in its saucepan.

3 Put the egg yolks and 2 tablespoons (30 g.) sugar in a bowl. Whisk until the mixture is foamy and pale.

4 Pour ½ cup (10 cl.) heavy cream into the caramel. (Put the remaining cream back in the refrigerator to stay cold.) Bring to a boil while stirring with a spatula. Whisk the hot cream and caramel into the egg yolk mixture, beating constantly, and then pour everything back into the saucepan. Turn the heat to low and stir until the custard has a thick, creamy consistency. Do not allow it to boil. The temperature should stay around 160°F/70–75°C.

5 Whisk in the gelatin leaves, beating briskly to make them dissolve. Pour this mixture through a fine strainer into a bowl and refrigerate, stirring every 5 minutes to keep the gelatin from gelling.

6 Remove the chilled bowl from the refrigerator and pour into it the remaining cream and sugar. Beat slowly with a whisk, holding the bowl at an angle. When the cream begins to thicken, speed up your beating and whip it into a thick cream. It should be white, smooth, and doubled in volume when you finish.

7 Remove the bowl of gelatin-custard from the refrigerator, stir well with a wooden spoon, and gently fold in the whipped cream. Line a mold or large bowl with plastic wrap, letting it hang over on either side, and pour in the cream custard. Refrigerate for at least half a day. To serve, invert the mold onto a plate; it should come out quite easily and cleanly, thanks to the plastic wrap.

8 Serve with vanilla custard cream (page 706); you will need 1 cup (20 cl.), which you might want to flavor with rum or Grand Marnier. You can also coat the unmolded cream cus-

3 gelatin leaves

1 recipe caramel (page 709)

3 egg yolks (page 204)

¼ cup (60 g.) granulated sugar

2½ cups (60 cl.) heavy cream, well chilled

tard with orange or apricot marmalade that you have puréed
and heated in a saucepan just before serving.

STRAWBERRY OR RASPBERRY CREAM MOUSSE _____
Bavarois aux fraises (ou aux framboises)

SERVES 6

PREPARATION   30 minutes

The mousse must be prepared 2 hours in advance.

This simplified recipe, which significantly reduces the classic
version's dose of eggs and cream, can be made with any fruit.
Just replace the strawberries with 1 pound (500 g.) of puréed
and strained fruit. Do not use dried fruit or fruit preserved in
syrup; they have too much sugar for this recipe.

1 pound (500 g.) strawberries
    or raspberries, fresh or
    frozen, hulled if fresh
6 gelatin leaves
1 pound (500 g.) *fromage blanc*
½ cup (10 cl.) heavy cream
1 egg white (page 204), very
    well chilled
2 tablespoons (30 g.)
    granulated sugar

*special equipment: a brioche
    mold or soufflé dish,
    blender, and handheld
    electric mixer*

1   Put a mixing bowl and the mold in the refrigerator. Purée the
    fruit in a blender or food processor and put the purée
    through a fine strainer into a heat-proof bowl.
2   Soak the gelatin leaves in a small bowl of water. Put a kettle
    on to boil.
3   Using a handheld electric mixer or just a whisk, vigorously
    beat together the *fromage blanc* and cream. Put the egg
    white in the refrigerated mixing bowl with a dash of granu-
    lated sugar. Begin to beat it slowly and speed up only as it
    thickens. It is sufficiently whipped when the beaters leave
    visible traces and the white does not stick to the sides of the
    bowl. Gently fold the whipped white into the whipped
    cheese and cream. Add the remaining sugar and stir.
4   Drain the gelatin leaves. Add 3 leaves to the strawberry purée
    and put the bowl in a saucepan. Pour boiling water from the
    kettle into the saucepan so that it reaches halfway up the out-
    side of the bowl of purée. (If necessary, add hot water from
    the tap to bring the water level this high.) Turn the heat
    under the saucepan to low. Whisk the purée by hand just
    until it is warm and the gelatin has melted. Remove the
    bowl, add the remaining gelatin leaves, and stir.
5   Stir the fruit-gelatin mixture into the cream mixture until
    evenly incorporated. Taste and add more sugar if you think it
    necessary.

6   Remove the mold from the refrigerator and line it with a sheet of plastic wrap, allowing the plastic wrap to hang over the top edges. Pour the cream into the mold and freeze for 2 hours. To unmold, place a plate upside down on top of the mold, grasp the edges tightly, and flip the whole thing over. Remove the plastic wrap.

7   Make a sauce if you like (see Fruit Sauce, page 708) with 1 pound (500 g.) strawberries or raspberries, the juice of 1 lemon, and perhaps ½ teaspoon kirsch.

BITTERSWEET CHOCOLATE MOUSSE
Mousse au chocolat amer

SERVES   6–8
PREPARATION   30 minutes
RESTING   1 hour

You can add a pinch or more of ground cinnamon if you like.

2 tablespoons butter

5 ounces (150 g.) bittersweet chocolate (66 percent cocoa), chopped, plus extra to shave for garnish

4 large eggs, separated (page 204) and well chilled

1 tablespoon (15 g.) vanilla sugar (page 698)

4 tablespoons (6 cl.) heavy cream, well chilled

1   Remove the butter from the refrigerator at least 30 minutes in advance and cut it into pieces. Put a mixing bowl in the refrigerator to chill.

2   Melt the chocolate in the microwave. Proceed carefully in stages, stirring frequently, so as not to burn the chocolate. When it has melted almost completely, stir in the butter until the 2 ingredients are seamlessly married. Pour into a bowl to chill.

3   Put the yolks in a bowl with the vanilla sugar. With a whisk or a handheld electric mixer, beat for 2 minutes, until the mixture foams and turns a pale yellow. Stir in the melted chocolate until homogeneously incorporated.

4   Remove the mixing bowl from the refrigerator and add the heavy cream. With a whisk or preferably a handheld electric mixer, beat slowly; as the cream begins to swell and thicken, beat more vigorously. The cream is properly whipped when it clings to the whisk or beaters. Use a rubber spatula to fold it into the chocolate mixture.

5   Put the chilled egg whites in the same bowl with a dash of sugar. Begin to beat slowly and then pick up speed as the

white thickens. It is properly whipped when the whisk or beaters leave a visible path and when it no longer sticks to the edges of the bowl.

6   Gently, by hand, whisk one-third of the whipped whites into the chocolate mixture. Then use the rubber spatula to fold in the rest of the whites. Work slowly and patiently, folding gently until no traces of white remain. Pour the mousse into a serving vessel or vessels, cover, and refrigerate for at least 1 hour before serving.

7   Use a vegetable peeler to shower the mousse with chocolate shavings before serving.

MIRABELLE PLUM SOUFFLÉ

Soufflé aux mirabelles

SERVES   4
PREPARATION   45 minutes
COOKING   about 25 minutes

The mirabelle plum of Lorraine—which Crusaders brought back to France from the Middle East—has golden skin with red freckles and sugary flesh. These plums are harvested in high August and are used to make, among other things, an eponymous eau-de-vie. They can be found in the United States, too.

1   Melt 5 tablespoons (75 g.) butter in a skillet and leave the rest out to soften. When it foams, add the plums and 1 tablespoon superfine sugar and cook over high heat for 3 minutes. Remove 2 tablespoons plum flesh and put it in a bowl with 2 tablespoons eau-de-vie to macerate; leave the rest of the plums in the skillet. Turn the heat to low and cook 12–14 minutes more, depending on the size of the plums, stirring with a spatula.

2   Brush the insides of the molds with softened butter; brush vertically, from bottom to top. Pour ½ tablespoon superfine sugar into each mold and shake it around to coat evenly and completely.

3   Preheat the oven to 350°F/180°C.

1 stick (¼ pound/120 g.) butter
¾ pound (400 g.) mirabelle plums, washed, pitted, and halved
¼ cup (95 g.) granulated sugar
4 tablespoons mirabelle eau-de-vie
3 tablespoons (60 g.) superfine sugar
5 eggs, separated (page 204), one of the whites discarded
2 tablespoons (30 g.) flour
1 cup (20 cl.) milk

special equipment: 4 soufflé molds, 3 inches (8 cm.) in diameter, and a fine strainer or food mill

4   Whisk together the 5 egg yolks, flour, and ¼ cup granulated sugar. Whisk until the yolks have paled.

5   Rinse a saucepan with cold water and empty it out without wiping it dry. Add the milk and heat. When the milk is hot but not boiling, remove it from the heat. Whisk into it the egg-flour-sugar mixture, put it back over the heat, and bring to a boil. Let simmer over very low heat for 4–5 minutes, whisking as the mixture thickens. Whisk in the marinated plums and the remaining eau-de-vie.

6   Put the 4 egg whites in a bowl with a dash of granulated sugar. Begin to beat slowly with a whisk to make them more fluid, and then pick up speed as they begin to thicken. When they are half whipped, add the remaining granulated sugar. Don't make the egg whites too stiff. You want them to remain homogeneous and smooth.

7   Gently whisk one-third of the whipped whites into the batter. When they have been incorporated, pour the batter into the bowl of whites and gently fold them together.

8   Pour the soufflé mixture into the molds so that they are one-third full. Put a dab of macerated plums in each mold and cover to the top with more soufflé mixture. Smooth the top of each one with a spatula. Bake the soufflés in the bottom of the oven for 7–8 minutes. Do not open the oven to check on them as they cook!

DENSE CHOCOLATE CAKE

Gâteau au chocolat

SERVES   4
PREPARATION   30 minutes
COOKING   about 20 minutes

You can replace the almond flour with 1 ounce (30 g.) chopped fresh nuts. This cake is meltingly tender in the center and will improve overnight.

4 tablespoons (65 g.) butter
3 ounces (100 g.) dark
    chocolate, chopped

1   Take the butter out of the refrigerator, cut it into little pieces, and leave it out to soften. Prepare the rest of the ingredients (chopping, sifting, separating, measuring) while it sits out.

2   Put a kettle of water on to boil. Put the chopped chocolate and 2 tablespoons water (not boiling) in a heat-proof bowl that you have set inside a saucepan. When the kettle boils, pour the water into the saucepan so that it reaches halfway up the outside of the bowl of chocolate. Turn the heat under the saucepan to low and stir the chocolate as it melts. When it has almost completely melted, energetically stir in all but 1 tablespoon softened butter, using a spatula. Stir in the 3 egg yolks and then the confectioners' sugar. Stir in the almond flour and flour until completely incorporated. Remove the bowl from the saucepan and allow it to cool.

3   Preheat the oven to 350°F/180°C.

4   Pour the egg whites into a mixing bowl and add the superfine sugar. Begin to whisk slowly and then pick up speed. The whites are properly whipped when the whisk leaves traces in the whites and they no longer stick to the sides of the bowl.

5   Energetically stir one-fourth of the whipped whites into the chocolate mixture. When they are incorporated, gently fold in the rest of the whites, lifting the chocolate up and over them and turning the bowl as you go. Continue slowly until all traces of white have disappeared.

6   Grease the cake pan or mold with the remaining softened butter and sprinkle it with flour. Shake the flour all around to coat evenly and tap out any excess. Fill the pan with batter, smooth the surface with a spatula or the back of a spoon, and bake about 20 minutes in the lower part of the oven.

7   Check to see whether the cake has finished cooking by slipping in the blade of a knife. It should emerge from the edges dry, but from the center it will carry a little of the hot batter.

8   When the cake comes out of the oven, unmold it onto a large plate and then invert it onto a cooling rack. Eat warm or cold. It will be even better the next day.

3 eggs, separated (page 204)
½ cup (60 g.) confectioners' sugar, sifted
¾ cup (60 g.) fine almond flour
1 level tablespoon flour, sifted, plus a little extra for flouring the cake pan
Dash of superfine sugar

special equipment: an 8-inch round cake pan or any small round or rectangular mold

Tarts and Small Cakes

BRIOCHE

MAKES   one 1-pound (500-g.) brioche
PREPARATION   10 minutes
RESTING   1 hour
COOKING   30 minutes

The classic brioche preparations (especially the kind with a billowy, mushrooming head) are time-consuming, complicated, and best realized with professional ovens. Here is a simplified version for home cooks. You can use a plain loaf pan.

1 stick (¼ pound/110 g.) butter
½ cup (10 cl.) milk
2 cups (250 g.) flour
⅔ ounce (20 g.) active dry yeast
3 eggs
2 tablespoons (30 g.) granulated sugar
Pinch of salt

1   Dice the butter and microwave it just until it is melted. Warm the milk in a small saucepan over low heat.

2   Whisk together the flour and yeast in a bowl. Heap it into a hill and make a well in its peak. Pour into the well the warm milk, melted butter, eggs, sugar, and salt. Stir to mix but don't overwork the dough.

3   You can also mix all these ingredients in a food processor fitted with a dough blade. Pulse slowly just until completely combined and be careful not to overwork the dough.

4   Cover the bowl of dough with a clean dish towel and let it rest for 1 hour.

5   Preheat the oven to 350°F/180°C and line the mold with parchment paper.

6   When the dough has rested for an hour, tip it into the mold gently, trying not to take the air out of it, and bake for 30 minutes.

MADELEINES

variations

PISTACHIO MADELEINES

LEMON MADELEINES

CHOCOLATE MADELEINES

CHOCOLATE HAZELNUT
MADELEINES

MAKES   24

PREPARATION   20 minutes plus 1 hour in the refrigerator

COOKING   12–15 minutes

If you are baking for someone with a nut allergy, the almond flour in this recipe (and any other) can be replaced with regular flour. If you want to use almond flour but have only whole almonds on hand, try grinding them yourself in a food processor or coffee grinder, taking care to stop before they turn into a sort of creamy nut butter.

1   Use a pastry brush to coat the hollows of the madeleine mold with softened butter. Sprinkle with flour, tap the pan and shake the flour around to spread evenly, and pat out any excess.

2   Melt the butter in a saucepan and then pour it into a bowl to cool.

3   Sift together the flour and confectioners' sugar. Stir in the almond flour with a whisk.

4   Beat the egg whites just until they become fluid. Whisk in the flour-sugar mixture until fully combined. Stir in the melted butter and honey, whisking until you have a homogeneous batter.

5   Fill the madeleine mold: Spoon batter into the hollows so that they are filled almost to the top. Refrigerate for 1 hour to firm up before baking.

6   Thirty minutes in advance, preheat the oven to 400°F/200°C.

7   After an hour's refrigerated rest, bake for 12–15 minutes, until the madeleines are lightly golden and firm to the touch but still somewhat tender. Remove the mold from the oven and rap them on a flat surface (such as your counter) to detach the little cakes from the mold. Tip them onto a cooling rack; if necessary, use a knife to help reluctant madeleines detach.

8   Serve warm or at room temperature. When the madeleines have cooled completely, you can keep them in a sealed container for several days.

2 sticks (½ pound/220 g.) butter, plus softened butter for greasing the mold

⅔ cup (90 g.) sifted flour, plus a little extra for dusting the greased mold

1¾ cups (220 g.) confectioners' sugar, sifted

½ cup (80 g.) very fine almond flour

6 large egg whites (page 204)

1 tablespoon honey, preferably a strong variety such as chestnut

special equipment: sheet madeleine mold or molds to hold twenty-eight 3-inch (8-cm.) madeleines

PISTACHIO MADELEINES
Madeleines aux pistaches

Replace the almond flour with unsalted pistachio flour, and replace the heavily scented honey with something milder, such as lavender. Just before filling the molds, you can stir 1 teaspoon pistachio extract into the batter.

LEMON MADELEINES
Madeleines au citron

Just before filling the molds, stir into the batter the grated zest of 2 organic lemons and 5 tablespoons lemon juice. Incorporate evenly and completely.

CHOCOLATE MADELEINES
Madeleines au chocolat

Replace the heavily scented honey with something milder, such as lavender. Just before filling the molds, stir into the batter 5 ounces (150 g.) melted dark bittersweet chocolate. Incorporate evenly and completely.

CHOCOLATE HAZELNUT MADELEINES
Madeleines au chocolat et aux noisettes

Replace the almond flour with hazelnut flour, and replace the heavily scented honey with something milder, such as lavender. Just before filling the molds, melt 7 ounces (200 g.) hazelnut-flavored milk chocolate and stir it completely into the batter.

SPONGE CAKE

Génoise

variation

CHOCOLATE SPONGE CAKE

MAKES   one 8-inch (20-cm.) round cake
PREPARATION   20 minutes
COOKING   20 minutes

1   Preheat the oven to 370°F/190°C. Use a pastry brush to grease the bottom and sides of the cake pan generously with butter. Sprinkle it with flour and shake to distribute the flour evenly. Tap out any excess flour.

2   Take a saucepan large enough to hold a heat-proof mixing bowl. Fill the saucepan with water to reach one-third of the way up its side and bring to a boil. Lower the heat and allow the water to simmer.

3   Put the eggs in a heat-proof mixing bowl and whisk until they are foamy. Whisking constantly, add the sugar in a thin, slow, continuous stream. Whisk for 2 or 3 minutes, until the sugar has been completely dissolved in the eggs.

4   Put the bowl of eggs and sugar into the saucepan of simmering water. Whisk by hand for 1 minute and then remove the bowl from the saucepan. With a handheld electric mixer, beat the mixture until it doubles in volume. It should be thick and lemon yellow, and it should form a ribbon when drizzled onto itself: If you lift up the beaters and let the batter clinging to them fall back onto the surface of the batter in the bowl, it will sit on the surface, visible, for a moment or two before collapsing into the whole. This will take several minutes or more.

5   Stir in the melted butter. Whisk in the flour in several batches. Be sure the whisk reaches the bottom of the bowl so that you don't have any floury lumps or patches. You must mix until the batter is homogeneous, but you don't want to overwork it, either.

6   Pour the batter into the prepared cake pan and smooth its surface with a spatula. Bake in the middle of the oven for 18–20 minutes. When the cake is finished, the tip of a knife should emerge from it dry and clean. Remove the pan from the oven and unmold right away. Allow to cool before serving.

1 tablespoon melted butter, plus a little extra softened butter for greasing the cake pan

1 cup sifted flour (135 g.), plus a little extra for dusting the greased cake pan

4 large eggs

⅓ cup (80 g.) granulated sugar

special equipment: handheld electric mixer, 8-inch (20-cm.) round cake pan

CHOCOLATE SPONGE CAKE
Génoise au chocolat

Replace 2 tablespoons of the flour with 1 tablespoon sifted cocoa powder.

BRIOCHE BREAD PUDDING
Diplomate

SERVES 6
PREPARATION 20 minutes
COOKING 1 hour

1 Preheat the oven to 350°F/180°C.

2 Put the eggs, yolks, and granulated sugar in a bowl. Whisk together without going so far that the mixture begins to turn pale. Whisk in the milk and dark rum.

3 Slice the brioche into 1-inch (2-cm.) dice. Butter the baking dish and refrigerate it long enough to firm up the butter. When it comes out of the refrigerator, sprinkle the baking dish with superfine sugar and shake it to coat evenly. Tap out any excess sugar.

4 Fill the baking dish with brioche and raisins and pour the egg mixture over them. Wait a few minutes while the brioche soaks up the egg. While you wait, put a kettle on to boil and set the baking dish in a larger baking dish. When the water boils, pour it into the outer baking dish so that it reaches halfway up the outside of the smaller baking dish.

5 Bake for at least 1 hour. To see whether the pudding is done, slip a knife into its middle and press down next to it with your hand. If it oozes liquid, it is not done, but if no liquid comes out, then you should remove it from the oven.

6 Allow the pudding to cool to room temperature. Serve with vanilla custard cream (page 706).

3 eggs plus 3 egg yolks
  (page 204)
¾ cup plus 2 tablespoons
  (215 g.) granulated sugar
3 cups (75 cl.) whole milk
3 tablespoons dark rum
5 ounces (150 g.) brioche-type
  bread, crusts removed
Butter for greasing the baking
  dish
Superfine sugar for dusting the
  baking dish
2 ounces (60 g.) raisins

*special equipment: one 8-inch
(20-cm.) square baking dish*

FINANCIERS

variation

CHOCOLATE FINANCIERS

MAKES   6 small cakes

PREPARATION   15 minutes

COOKING   20–30 minutes

½ cup (55 g.) confectioners'
   sugar

⅓ cup (45 g.) flour, plus a little
   extra for flouring the
   greased molds

1   Preheat the oven to 350°F/180°C.

2   Combine the confectioners' sugar, flour, and almond flour in
    a bowl and whisk to combine completely.

¼ cup (40 g.) almond flour

4 tablespoons (60 g.) butter,
   plus a little extra for
   greasing the molds

3   Melt the butter in a saucepan over low heat and then pour it
    into a separate bowl to cool.

4   Whisk the egg whites without whipping them into a foam.
    You want them to become rather liquid and flowing. Gently
    stir them into the flour and sugar mixture. Still stirring quite
    gently, incorporate the cooled melted butter.

4 large egg whites or 5 small
   egg whites (page 204)

5   Butter the molds and sprinkle them evenly with flour, shak-
    ing out any excess. Pour the batter into the molds and bake
    for 20 minutes, until the cakes are beautifully golden and the
    edges are beginning to turn brown. Remove the financiers
    from the oven and let them rest for 10 minutes before
    unmolding.

*special equipment: 6 small
rectangular "financier"
molds 4-inches (10-cm.) long*

CHOCOLATE FINANCIERS

5 ounces (150 g.) dark,
   bittersweet chocolate, cut
   into small pieces

MAKES   6 small cakes

PREPARATION   20 minutes

COOKING   20–30 minutes

½ cup (15 cl.) heavy cream

¼ cup (30 g.) confectioners'
   sugar

⅓ cup (45 g.) flour, plus a little
   extra for flouring the
   greased molds

1   Put the chopped chocolate in a bowl. Pour the cream into a
    small saucepan and bring to a boil while stirring constantly
    with a spatula. When it begins to bubble, pour the cream
    over the chocolate and stir carefully until you have a smooth,
    glossy substance.

¼ cup (40 g.) almond flour

4 tablespoons (60 g.) butter,
   plus a little extra for
   greasing the molds

2   Proceed to make the financiers as above. After stirring in the
    melted butter, carefully and completely stir in the melted
    chocolate and cream. Grease and flour the molds and bake as
    above.

4 large egg whites or 5 small
   egg whites (page 204)

*special equipment: 6 small
rectangular "financier"
molds, 4-inches (10-cm.)
long*

CHOCOLATE CHOCOLATE CHUNK COOKIES

Cookies chocolat

MAKES   15 cookies
PREPARATION   15 minutes
COOKING   10 minutes

1   Remove the butter from the refrigerator at least 30 minutes in advance. Preheat the oven to 350°F/180°C. Line a sheet pan with parchment paper.

2   Combine the butter, brown sugar, granulated sugar, fleur de sel, and vanilla extract in a bowl. Stir in the flour, baking powder, cocoa, and chopped chocolate.

3   Scoop 15 balls of the dough onto the sheet pan and flatten each one to a thickness of ½ inch (1 cm.). Cook about 8 minutes. Remove and cool on a cooling rack.

1½ sticks (6 ounces/170 g.) butter
½ cup (120 g.) brown sugar
¼ cup (60 g.) granulated sugar
1 pinch of fleur de sel
⅓ teaspoon vanilla extract
1½ cups (180 g.) flour
1 teaspoon baking powder
3 tablespoons (35 g.) cocoa powder
6 ounces (180 g.) dark chocolate, chopped into pieces about the size of chocolate chips

CAKE

variation
LEMON CAKE

SERVES   6–8
PREPARATION   15 minutes
COOKING   50 minutes

This cake is excellent sliced and toasted. A homemade cake keeps for several days. Just wrap it in plastic wrap when it has cooled and keep it at room temperature. Cake should not be kept in the refrigerator, but you can freeze it. It will be good for several weeks.

1   Put the milk in a small saucepan and scoop the tiny seeds from the vanilla beans into the milk. Bring the milk just up to a boil, turn off the heat, and set the saucepan aside for the milk to infuse.

½ cup (10 cl.) milk
1 vanilla bean, sliced in half
10 tablespoons (150 g.) butter, plus a little extra for greasing the pan
2½ cups (300 g.) flour, plus a little extra for flouring the greased pan
2 cups (250 g.) confectioners' sugar

2   Dice the butter and melt it in the microwave at low power.

3   Use a pastry brush to grease the bottom and sides of the cake pan with butter. Sprinkle the pan with flour, turn it all around to spread the flour evenly, and tap out any excess.

4   Preheat the oven to 350°F/180°C.

5   Sift the sugar into a bowl. Whisk in the eggs. When the eggs and sugar are thoroughly combined, whisk in the melted butter and warm milk. Add the flour and baking powder, whisking constantly throughout.

6   Pour the batter into the prepared cake pan and bake for 8 minutes. Lower the heat to 300°F/150°C and cook about 40 minutes more. The cake is finished when the blade of a knife inserted in its center comes out dry.

7   Remove the finished cake from the oven, unmold it onto a cooling rack, and let cool.

8   Just after cooking you can, if you like, use a pastry brush to coat the cake with syrup. Just boil 4 tablespoons water with 1 heaping tablespoon (20 g.) confectioners' sugar for a couple of minutes. Allow it to cool before brushing it on the still-warm cake.

3 large eggs
1 teaspoon baking powder

special equipment: round cake pan, about 10 inches (26 cm.)

LEMON CAKE

Cake au citron

1   Eliminate the vanilla bean and prepare the grated zest of 1 organic lemon (see page 698). Begin to make the cake as above. When the confectioners' sugar has been sifted into the mixing bowl, add the lemon zest before adding the eggs. Mix the sugar and zest well with your fingers and then proceed as above.

2   If you choose to coat the still-warm cake with syrup, make the same confectioners' sugar syrup and stir in 1 tablespoon lemon juice when it has cooled.

DOUBLE CHOCOLATE CAKE

Cake aux deux chocolats

SERVES 6–8
PREPARATION 20 minutes
COOKING 55 minutes

1 Remove the butter from the refrigerator at least 30 minutes in advance to soften. Preheat the oven to 350°F/180°C.

2 Heat the milk in a small saucepan over low heat. Put the eggs, butter, sugar, salt, and warm milk together in a bowl or, if possible, a food processor. Scoop the tiny seeds from the vanilla beans into the bowl. Stir or process very well. Add the flour, cocoa powder, and baking powder and mix well again. Stir in the white chocolate chips.

3 Grease 1 large or 2 small cake pans with butter. Pour in the batter and bake for 8 minutes. Lower the heat to 300°F (150°C) and bake about 45 minutes more.

3 sticks (¾ pound/320 g.) butter, plus a little extra for greasing the cake pan

½ cup (15 cl.) milk

6 medium eggs

2 cups (480 g.) confectioners' sugar

Pinch of salt

2 vanilla beans, sliced in half

3 cups (420 g.) flour

½ cup (60 g.) unsweetened cocoa powder

2 teaspoons (10 g.) baking powder

4 ounces (120 g.) white chocolate chips (or chopped white chocolate)

special equipment: round cake pan, about 10 inches (26 cm.)

BANANA CAKE

Cake à la banane

SERVES 6
PREPARATION 15 minutes
COOKING 45 minutes

1 Remove the butter, milk, and eggs from the refrigerator 1 hour in advance. Dice the butter while it is still cold.

2 In a blender or food processor, purée the bananas with the hazelnut oil and milk.

3 Preheat the oven to 340°F/170°C.

4 Combine the softened butter and the confectioners' sugar, stirring well. Stir in the eggs and then, one by one, the flour, hazelnut flour, baking powder, chocolate chips, and banana purée. Grease the cake pan with butter and pour in the batter.

5 Bake for 40–45 minutes. Allow the cake to cool in the pan for 10–15 minutes before unmolding.

6 Serve in slices, perhaps with chocolate sauce (page 709).

10 tablespoons (150 g.) butter, plus a little extra for greasing the cake pan

4 tablespoons milk

3 eggs

3 bananas, peeled and cut into pieces

3 tablespoons hazelnut oil

1⅓ cups (150 g.) confectioners' sugar

1 cup (150 g.) sifted flour

⅓ cup (45 g.) hazelnut flour

1 teaspoon (5 g.) baking powder

2 ounces (60 g.) chocolate chips

special equipment: one 11-inch (26-cm.) cake pan

CUSTARD CAKE FROM BRITTANY

Far breton

SERVES 6
PREPARATION   10 minutes
COOKING   30 minutes

1   Remove the butter from the refrigerator 30 minutes in advance.
2   Preheat the oven to 350°F/180°C. Generously butter the baking dish, using all of the butter.
3   Combine the flour and sugar in a bowl by stirring with a whisk. Add the eggs (but *not* the yolk) and whisk briskly to obtain a smooth, uniform mixture.
4   Add the milk little by little, whisking the whole time, and then the dark rum. Pour the batter into the buttered dish and scatter the prunes over it.
5   Put the yolk in a bowl and beat it. Brush it onto the cake before putting it in the oven.
6   Bake about 25–30 minutes. The top should be golden. Serve warm if possible.

4 tablespoons (50 g.) softened half-salt butter
1 cup (140 g.) flour
½ cup (120 g.) confectioners' sugar
4 eggs plus 1 yolk (page 204)
2 cups (50 cl.) milk
1 tablespoon dark rum
6 ounces (190 g.) pitted soft prunes

special equipment:
  1 rectangular baking dish 8 inches by 10 inches (20 cm. by 24 cm.)

BITTERSWEET CHOCOLATE TART

Tarte au chocolat amer

SERVES 6
PREPARATION   15 minutes
COOKING   15–20 minutes

1   Preheat the oven to 300°F/150°C.
2   Rinse a saucepan out with water; shake out the excess water but do not wipe the pan dry. Add the cream and milk to the saucepan. Stir and bring to a boil over medium heat. Remove the saucepan from the heat, add the chocolate pieces, and stir until the chocolate has completely melted and the mixture is dark and homogeneous. Allow to cool.
3   Beat the egg in a bowl. When the chocolate mixture has cooled, whisk in the beaten egg until it is completely absorbed.

1 cup (20 cl.) heavy cream
4 tablespoons whole milk
6½ ounces (200 g.) dark bittersweet chocolate (60 percent cocoa), cut into small pieces
1 extra-large egg

4 Pour this chocolate filling into the precooked crust and smooth it with a spatula. Cook in the top third of the oven for 15–20 minutes.

5 Allow the tart to cool and eat warm or at room temperature. To serve, sprinkle with cocoa powder to taste. Do not refrigerate the tart.

1 Rich Crust for Pies and Tarts (page 699), precooked for 25 minutes at 350°F/180°C in a mold about 10 inches (25 cm.) in diameter and cooled completely

Unsweetened cocoa powder for dusting the tart (optional)

LEMON TART

Tarte au citron

SERVES 6
PREPARATION AND COOKING   30 minutes

1 Bring a kettle full of water to a boil. Put a small mixing bowl in a saucepan and put the eggs, yolk, and sugar in the small bowl. Whisk energetically to combine and then whisk in the lemon zest and juice. Pour the boiling water into the saucepan so that it reaches halfway up the outside of the mixing bowl. (If you don't have enough boiling water to reach this level, just add some hot water from the tap.)

2 Put the saucepan over low heat and cook for 25 minutes, whisking fairly constantly until you have obtained a smooth, thick cream. Turn up the heat and whisk in the cold diced butter. Continue to whisk on this livelier heat. Pour the mixture into a bowl and allow it to cool. If you need to cool it quickly, put the bowl in a basin or larger bowl filled with cold water that reaches halfway up the side of the bowl.

3 Pour the lemon cream into the precooked crust and smooth its top with a spatula. The tart is ready to serve.

3 eggs plus 1 yolk (page 204)

⅓ cup (80 g.) granulated sugar

Grated zest of 1 organic lemon (see page 698)

¾ cup (20 cl.) lemon juice from 3 or 4 organic lemons

1 stick (¼ pound/120 g.) butter, diced and well chilled

1 Rich Crust for Pies and Tarts (page 699), precooked for 25 minutes at 350°F/180°C in a mold about 10 inches (25 cm.) in diameter and cooled completely

ORANGE TART

Tarte à l'orange

SERVES **8**

PREPARATION **45 minutes**

1   Mix the cornstarch with 1 tablespoon water in a small bowl. Combine the eggs, yolks, and sugar in a mixing bowl or terrine. With a whisk or a handheld electric mixer, beat until the mixture turns pale, 2 or 3 minutes. Beat in the orange zest and cornstarch mixture. Put a kettle on to boil.

2   Pour 4 tablespoons orange juice into a small saucepan and add the butter. Bring to a boil while stirring with a large spoon. Allow the mixture to boil for 30 seconds and then whisk it into the beaten eggs.

3   Put a mixing bowl in a saucepan. Pour the eggs-orange juice-butter mixture in the bowl and pour boiling water from the kettle into the saucepan so that it reaches halfway up the outside of the bowl. Turn the heat under the saucepan to low. Whisk as the orange cream thickens, until the whisk leaves a distinct trail in it when you trace an *S*—about 10 minutes. Remove the bowl from the saucepan of water and continue to whisk for 3 minutes to make the orange cream thick and glossy. Refrigerate.

4   If you decide to garnish the tart with oranges, purée the apricot jam in a blender or food processor and pour it into a small saucepan.

5   Use a small, sharp knife to slice the peel from 8 oranges; the flesh of the oranges should be completely exposed, and there should be no white pith left. Remove the membranes from the orange sections. (Slip a knife between the flesh and membrane of one section and remove it. Continue gently to pull or slice sections one by one from the membranes that separate them. The sections should be intact at the end of this process.) Put the orange sections in a colander to drain.

6   Heat the puréed apricot jam over low heat for 3 minutes, stirring with a spatula.

7   Use a spatula to spread the chilled orange cream in the precooked crust. Arrange the orange sections in a rosette on top of the cream. With a pastry brush, lightly coat the oranges with hot apricot jam.

8   Keep in a cool place until serving but do not refrigerate.

1 teaspoon cornstarch

2 whole eggs plus 2 yolks (page 204)

3 tablespoons (45 g.) granulated sugar

Grated zest of 2 organic oranges (see page 698)

Juice of ½ orange

4 tablespoons (70 g.) butter

3 ounces (100 g.) apricot jam (optional)

8 oranges (optional)

1 Rich Crust for Pies and Tarts (page 699), precooked for 25 minutes at 350°F/180°C in a mold about 10 inches (25 cm.) in diameter and cooled completely

FRUIT TART

Tarte aux fruits

SERVES 8
PREPARATION 15 minutes
COOKING about 30 minutes

1 Preheat the oven to 350°F/180°C. Wash all the fruit, slice each piece in half, and remove pits and seeds.

2 You can sprinkle the bottom of the precooked crust with granulated sugar and semolina to keep the fruits' juices from soaking the crust. Arrange the halved fruit skin side up and very snug in the crust; begin with the edge and work your way in. The pieces of fruit should be right up against one another.

3 Bake for 30 minutes in the top half of the oven. The tart is finished when the edges of the crust are deeply golden (almost brown) and the fruit is clearly cooked. Remove the tart from the oven and set it on a rack to cool. Dust with confectioners' sugar to serve, if you like.

4 If you like, fill the precooked crust with Almond Cream before filling it with fruit. Arrange the fruit on top of the almond cream and bake as above.

About 2 pounds (1 kg.) fruit—apples, peaches, nectarines, or pears, but not berries
1 precooked Basic Sweet Crust for Pies and Tarts (page 701), blind-baked (page 702) in an appropriate tart pan
3 tablespoons (45 g.) granulated sugar
3 ounces (50 g.) fine semolina
Confectioners' sugar to serve
Almond cream (below) (optional)

ALMOND CREAM

Crème d'amandes

PREPARATION 10 minutes

1 Remove the butter and eggs from the refrigerator 1 hour in advance. If you are starting with whole almonds instead of almond flour, grind them to a powdery "flour" in the food processor. Don't blend too long, or they will turn into almond butter.

2 Stir the butter and sugar into the almond flour until you have a homogeneous mixture. Stir in the eggs and the zest if you are using it. Stir until completely combined.

3 Pour this almond cream into a precooked tart shell and follow the rest of the recipe for a fruit tart.

5 tablespoons (75 g.) butter
2 eggs
3 ounces (90 g.) whole blanched almonds or almond flour
⅓ cup (80 g.) granulated sugar
Grated zest of 1 organic lime (page 698) (optional)

APPLE OR PEAR CRUMBLE

Crumble aux pommes ou poires

SERVES 4
PREPARATION 20 minutes
COOKING 15 minutes

1 Cut the butter into small dice. Use the tips of your fingers to rub and crush it into the brown sugar, half of the vanilla sugar, all the almond flour, flour, and 1 pinch of cinnamon. Don't mix too much; it doesn't need to become a homogeneous dough. Put the bowl in the freezer for 30 minutes.

2 Preheat the oven to 370°F/190°C. Peel the apples (or pears), remove any seeds or other tough parts of the core, and cut into ½-inch (1-cm.) dice. Put the diced fruit in a bowl with 1 tablespoon superfine sugar (add sugar to taste depending on how sweet and ripe the fruit is naturally) and the remaining vanilla sugar and toss. Add the lemon juice and eau-de-vie if you are using it. Mix well.

3 Remove the crumble topping from the freezer and break it up. You can do this by pulsing it in a food processor about 15 seconds or by crushing it with a large spoon and your hands. You want to end up with something about the form and size of couscous.

4 Fill the ramekins with fruit and top with crumble. Dust with a little confectioners' sugar and bake for 15 minutes in the top half of the oven, until the topping begins to take on a nice color.

5 Remove the ramekins from the oven and wait 15 minutes before eating. Dust again with confectioners' sugar and serve warm.

2 tablespoons butter
2 tablespoons (30 g.) brown sugar
1 tablespoon (15 g.) vanilla sugar (see page 698)
¼ cup (40 g.) fine almond flour
⅓ cup (40 g.) sifted flour
Ground cinnamon
4 ripe apples or Bartlett pears
3 tablespoons (45 g.) superfine sugar
1 tablespoon confectoners' sugar, plus a little extra for dusting
Juice of 1 lemon
1 tablespoon pear or apple eau-de-vie (optional)

special equipment: 4 ovenproof ramekins

APPLE TART

Tarte fine aux pommes

SERVES 8
PREPARATION 25 minutes
COOKING 45 minutes

1 Combine the brown sugar, almond flour, and cinnamon. Spread three-fourths of this mixture on the bottom of the uncooked puff pastry.

2 Preheat the oven to 370°F/190°C. Melt the butter in a bowl in the microwave.

3 The easy way: Peel, quarter, and core the apples. Slice the quarters into slivers and arrange them on top of the puff pastry, beginning around the edge. They should be nestled up against one another. Use a pastry brush to coat the apples with melted butter.

4 The elegant way: Peel and core the apples with an apple corer (or use a knife to carve out the core). Slice the apples horizontally into thin rounds so that each piece has a hole in its center. Lay them atop the puff pastry, beginning by circling the outer edge and placing them so that their edges overlap. Leave an empty spot with no apples in the center of the pastry. Brush with melted butter. Lay another layer of apples within the circle created by the first, lining up their holes. Brush with melted butter. Arrange the remaining rounds in the center and brush with butter.

5 Sprinkle with the remaining brown sugar–almond flour mixture. Bake in the top half of the oven for 45 minutes. When you remove the tart from the oven, dust it generously with confectioners' sugar while it is still warm. Preheat the broiler. When it is hot, put the tart under it for a minute or 2 to caramelize. Keep a very close eye on it or it will burn. Serve hot.

3 tablespoons (45 g.) brown sugar

5 tablespoons (50 g.) fine almond flour

⅓ teaspoon ground cinnamon

1 puff pastry tart crust, about 10 inches (25 cm.) in diameter without a border

2 tablespoons butter

5 baking apples, firm and sweet (Granny Smith, Mutsu, Crispin, etc.)

Confectioners' sugar for dusting

STRAWBERRY TART

Tarte sablée aux fraises

SERVES   8

PREPARATION   10 minutes

This tart is not cooked.

You can also make this tart with *fraises des bois,* a special variety of tiny, fragrant strawberries.

1 Rich Crust for Pies and Tarts (page 699)
2 ounces (60 g.) strawberry preserves
1 pound (500 g.) strawberries, washed and hulled
Confectioners' sugar

1   Precook the crust for 25 minutes at 350°F/180°C in a mold about 10 inches (25 cm.) in diameter. Cool completely.

2   Put the strawberry preserves in a small saucepan and heat until warmed through. Put through a strainer into a bowl.

3   Use a pastry brush to coat the bottom of the crust with some of this jam. Save the rest for glazing the strawberries.

4   Place the strawberries in the crust one by one, pointed end up. Start by making a ring around the perimeter and work your way in. They should cover the surface of the crust. Brush them with the remaining strained preserves.

5   If you like, dust the edge of the crust with confectioners' sugar, but do not dust the strawberries. Shield them with a round of parchment paper.

6   Serve right away: This tart can't wait and certainly must not be refrigerated. It is lovely with vanilla ice cream (page 757) or a sorbet (page 759).

Ice Cream and Sorbet

A word of advice: If you want to be quite sure your ice cream or sorbet will churn well, don't fill your maker's bowl past more than half its announced capacity. For instance, if it says it holds 1 quart (1 l.), don't churn more than ½ quart of it at a time. It is also best to make sure your custard or sorbet base is thoroughly chilled before churning; eagerness will not be rewarded here.

Homemade ice cream is far better than store-bought, but it does not keep well for more than two days.

VANILLA ICE CREAM

Glace à la vanille

MAKES   about 1 quart (1 l.)

PREPARATION   25 minutes

CHILLING BEFORE CHURNING   at least 1 hour

1 Scoop the tiny seeds from the vanilla beans and keep them in the spoon or in a small bowl.

2 Rinse out a saucepan with water but do not wipe it dry. (Rinsing it out helps keep the milk from sticking.) Pour the milk into the saucepan and turn the heat under it to high. Add the empty vanilla beans and coffee bean. Bring to a boil and then remove the saucepan from the heat. Cover and let infuse for 15 minutes.

3 Put the yolks in a bowl with the sugar and vanilla seeds. Beat with a handheld electric mixer until the sugary yolks are thick and creamy yellow. Put the saucepan of milk back over high heat and bring to a boil again. Whisk a ladle of boiling milk into the beaten yolks. Continuing to whisk, pour the bowl of yolks into the saucepan of hot milk. Turn the heat to low and cook, stirring constantly with a wooden spoon, until the mixture thickens and takes on a creamy consistency. Do not allow it to boil. The custard is ready when it "coats the spoon," when a finger drawn through the custard left on the back of the stirring spoon leaves a clear trail instead of instantly being covered with liquid. Another way to tell that the custard is done is to take its temperature, which should be 185°F/85°C but not higher. This cooking should take about 5 minutes.

4 Remove the saucepan from the heat and stir in the heavy cream. Put the custard through a fine strainer into a bowl. Allow it to cool to room temperature and then chill for at least 1 hour (and preferably overnight) before churning.

5 For faster cooling, put a mixing bowl into the freezer when you begin. When the custard is cooked, remove the chilled bowl from the freezer, pour the custard into it, and put the bowl of custard in a larger bowl that you have filled with ice cubes and water. Stir the custard from time to time using a spatula. Dip in a finger: The custard must be cold to the touch to be cooked. This will take about 30 minutes.

4 vanilla beans, sliced in half lengthwise

2 cups (50 cl.) whole milk

1 coffee bean

8 egg yolks (page 204)

½ cup (120 g.) granulated sugar

1 cup (25 cl.) heavy cream

special equipment: ice cream maker

6   When the cream is completely chilled, churn it in your ice cream maker following the manufacturer's instructions.

FROZEN YOGURT WITH BLACKBERRY SAUCE AND GENOA BREAD

Crème glacée au yaourt, coulis de mûres, et pain de Gênes

SERVES   4

PREPARATION   45 minutes

COOKING (GENOA BREAD)   15 minutes

1   Use a wooden spoon to combine the almond paste and eggs. Stir in the orange flower water. Incorporate the flour and then 3 tablespoons melted butter. Use a pastry brush to coat the molds with the remaining melted butter. Divide the dough among the molds and refrigerate.

2   In a blender or food processor, purée the blackberries with the lemon juice and confectioners' sugar. Put the purée through a fine strainer and refrigerate.

3   Energetically beat together the yogurt, cream, glucose, and granulated sugar. Refrigerate for 20 minutes and then put through a fine strainer.

4   Preheat the oven to 350°F/180°C. Churn the yogurt mixture in an ice cream maker according to the manufacturer's instructions.

5   When the oven is hot, bake the molds of "Genoa bread" for about 15 minutes.

6   Put 2 scoops of frozen yogurt on each plate. Pour the blackberry sauce around the frozen yogurt and top each scoop with a verbena leaf. Serve the Genoa bread, still warm, on the side.

7 ounces (200 g.) almond paste

3 eggs

1 teaspoon orange flower water

2 tablespoons (15 g.) sifted flour

4 tablespoons (60 g.) melted butter

10 ounces (300 g.) fresh blackberries

Juice of ½ lemon

2 tablespoons (30 g.) confectioners' sugar

16 ounces (450 g.) plain whole-milk yogurt

2½ tablespoons (80 g.) heavy cream

3 tablespoons glucose syrup

⅓ cup (80 g.) granulated sugar

8 small verbena leaves

special equipment: 4 circular molds or ramekins, 3 inches (8 cm.) in diameter; ice cream maker

LIGHT RASPBERRY ICE CREAM

Glace allégée aux framboises

SERVES 4–5
PREPARATION 5 minutes

10 ounces (300 g.) frozen raspberries
5 ounces (150 g.) fat-free *fromage blanc,* well chilled
7 ounces (200 g.) unsweetened reduced-fat condensed milk
4 tablespoons NutraSweet (aspartame sweetener)

Put all the ingredients in a blender or food processor and blend for 1 minute. Serve immediately.

FRUIT SORBET

Sorbet au fruit

PREPARATION 5 minutes

This recipe works for any fruit but citrus (no grapefruit, orange, or lemon). You can change the quantities as long as you keep the proportions.

2 cups (50 cl.) fruit pulp, prepared as described
¾ cup (90 g.) confectioners' sugar
Juice of ½ lemon

special equipment: ice cream maker

1   Peel and trim the fruit. Put its flesh through a fine strainer by mashing it through with a large spoon, or purée the fruit first and then put it through a strainer.
2   Measure 2 cups (50 cl.) of the strained fruit pulp and mix it with the sugar and lemon juice. Chill thoroughly before churning it in an ice cream maker according to the manufacturer's instructions.

GRAPEFRUIT GRANITA

Granité de pamplemousse

PREPARATION 5 minutes

Combine all the ingredients in a saucepan over low heat and melt the sugar in the juices. Pour the mixture into a tub or basin (a container shallower than it is wide, such as a 9-by-13 Pyrex baking dish). Put it in the freezer until it begins to

1 quart (90 cl.) grapefruit juice
½ cup (10 cl.) lemon juice
6 tablespoons (90 g.) granulated sugar

crystallize and then scrape it with a fork. Repeat 3 times, once every 15 minutes, until you have an icy slush.

MINT GRANITA

Granité à la menthe

SERVES 6–8
PREPARATION 10 minutes

1 Put the sugar in a saucepan with 2 cups (40 cl.) water. Bring to a boil and then turn off the heat. Add the mint. Remove from the burner, cover, and let infuse for 30 minutes. Then put the liquid through a fine strainer.
2 Put the mint syrup in a shallow dish in the freezer until it begins to crystallize and then scrape it with a fork. Repeat 3 times, once every 15 minutes, until you have an icy slush.

⅔ cup (120 g.) granulated sugar
1 small bunch fresh mint

CITRUS SORBET

Sorbet citron

PREPARATION 5 minutes

1 Put the lemon juice through a fine strainer. Combine all the ingredients in a bowl with 1 cup (25 cl.) water and whisk to dissolve the sugar.
2 Chill and churn in an ice cream maker according to the manufacturer's instructions.
3 If you don't have an ice cream maker, you can make this mixture into a granita by pouring it into a shallow container, freezing it, and scraping with a fork every 15 minutes for 1¼ hours, until it is an icy slush.

½ cup (15 cl.) lemon juice
⅓ cup (8 cl.) lime juice
¾ cup (180 g.) granulated sugar

special equipment: ice cream maker

BASIL SORBET

Sorbet au basilic

PREPARATION   5 minutes
COOLING   1 hour

The glucose syrup will give your sorbet a velvety texture.

1   Put the sugar and glucose syrup in a saucepan with 1 cup (25 cl.) water. Bring to a boil, stirring gently with a spatula. When the mixture bubbles, turn off the heat and pour it into a bowl. Leave for 30 minutes to cool.

2   Put the orange juice and lemon juice through a fine strainer and stir them into the bowl of sugar syrup. Refrigerate for 30 minutes. Add the basil leaves and purée in a blender or food processor until completely smooth and homogeneous.

3   Churn in an ice cream maker according to the manufacturer's instructions.

½ cup (120 g.) granulated sugar
3 tablespoons glucose syrup
⅔ cup (15 cl.) orange juice
⅔ cup (15 cl.) lemon juice
15 medium basil leaves, washed

special equipment: ice cream maker

FROMAGE BLANC SORBET

Sorbet au fromage blanc

PREPARATION   5 minutes

Combine both ingredients thoroughly and churn in an ice cream maker according to the manufacturer's instructions.

½ lb (250 g.) whipped reduced fat (20%) *fromage blanc*
½ cup (10 cl.) sugar syrup (or 10 level tablespoons superfine sugar)

special equipment: ice cream maker

Jams and Preserves

J am should be cooked in a copper pot if possible. If you don't have copper cooking vessels, use a heavy thick-bottomed saucepan or perhaps a Dutch oven.

To jell the jams and preserve them, you must add sugar (granulated or confectioners'). The less you add the better. You can reduce sugar by using pectin (a natural thickening agent extracted from apples, citrus skin, or beets). It must be mixed with sugar before it is added to the jam. Stir together 2 parts sugar and 1 part pectin, and that is your sugar-pectin mixture. If you need only 2 tablespoons sugar-pectin mixture, stir together 4 teaspoons sugar and 2 teaspoons pectin, or make a large batch (it keeps well) and use only what the recipe calls for. Sugar and pectin are often sold premixed, and you might also find special "sugar for jam," which is enriched with pectin.

But all you really need to make jam is fruit and sugar. The fruit should be ripe, fragrant, and definitely not spoiled. Jam can always be enlivened with spices or aromatics; peaches go well with whole cloves, rhubarb with ginger, figs with cardamom, and orange marmalade with cinnamon.

Jam is a preserve, which means that the equipment you use (pots, spatulas, ladles) must be impeccably clean. And the jars must be sterilized in boiling water for 10 minutes, removed directly from the pot with tongs, and drained just before being filled. You'll also find that a cooking thermometer comes in handy for checking temperatures.

Pour the jam into jars as soon as you finish cooking it. If you plan to store it for a long time, fill sterilized jars almost to the brim. Carefully wipe the edges and sides of the jar with paper towels, seal the jars with their lids, and turn them upside down until completely cool. You can use half-pint, pint, or quart jars—whatever you like.

POTATO PRESERVES

Confiture de pomme de terre

MAKES   about 2 quarts/4 pints
PREPARATION   10 minutes
COOKING   30 minutes

1   Wash the potatoes but do not peel. Put them in a saucepan of cold water with a generous pinch of salt. Bring to a boil, then lower the heat and simmer about 25 minutes.

2   While the potatoes cook, scoop the tiny seeds from the vanilla beans into a bowl. Add the sugar-pectin mixture, cinnamon, and 1 cup (20 cl.) cold water. Mix well with a whisk. Pour the contents of the bowl into a saucepan and bring to a boil to obtain a syrup. Skim and turn off the heat. Stir in the empty vanilla pods.

3   When the potatoes are cooked, peel, drain, and put them through a vegetable mill or potato ricer. Stir the purée into the sugar syrup with a whisk. Bring to a boil, stirring with a wooden spoon. Cook for 5 minutes at a simmer. The temperature of the mixture should be 220°F/105°C. Divide the vanilla beans among the jars, fill with jam, and seal.

2 pounds (1 kg.) potatoes, charlottes or fingerlings
Salt
2 vanilla beans, sliced in half lengthwise
3 cups (750 g.) granulated sugar
2 tablespoons sugar-pectin mixture (⅓ pectin)
½ teaspoon ground cinnamon

RED FRUIT JAM

Confiture aux fruits rouges

MAKES   about 1½ quarts/3 pints
PREPARATION   20 minutes
COOKING   25 minutes

1   Pick over the raspberries and wash all the other fruit. Hull the strawberries and slice them in half lengthwise. Remove the stems and pits from the cherries.

2   Pour ½ cup (15 cl.) water into a copper pot and add the sugar. Bring to a boil (230°F/110°C), add the cherries and lemon juice, and cook for 10 minutes. Add the strawberries and cook for 5 minutes. Add the raspberries and red currants and cook 10 minutes more. The temperature of the mixture should be 220°F/105°C.

½ pound (250 g.) each fruit: raspberries, strawberries, red currants, and cherries
2½ cups (600 g.) granulated sugar
Juice of 1 lemon

RED FRUIT JAM (cont.)

3   As soon as the fruit has finished cooking, fill the jars almost
    to the brim. Carefully wipe the edges and sides of the jars
    with paper towels, seal the jars with their lids, and turn them
    upside down until completely cool.

BLACK CURRANT–RASPBERRY JAM

Confiture de cassis et framboises

MAKES   about 1½ quarts/3 pints
PREPARATION   5 minutes
COOKING   10 minutes
The fruit must macerate overnight.

1   One day in advance, carefully wash the black currants and
    pull them from the stem. In a copper pot, if possible, stir
    together the black currants, sugar-pectin mixture, sugar, and
    strained lemon juice. Bring to a boil. As soon as it bubbles,
    pour the contents of the saucepan into a bowl, cover with
    plastic wrap, and refrigerate for 12 hours.

2   The next day, put the chilled sugared currants through a veg-
    etable mill. Pour the resulting pulp into a copper saucepan,
    bring to a boil, and remove any foam with a skimmer. Add
    the raspberries and cook over high heat for 10 minutes, stir-
    ring constantly with a wooden spatula and skimming regu-
    larly. The temperature of the fruit mixture should reach
    220°F/105°C. Remove the saucepan from the heat and pour
    into jars as indicated on page 762.

7 ounces (200 g.) black
    currants
2 tablespoons sugar-pectin
    mixture (page 762)
2½ cups (570 g.) granulated
    sugar
Juice of 1 lemon, strained
1½ pounds (750 g.) raspberries

CHERRY JAM

Confiture de cerises

MAKES   about 1½ quarts/3 pints
PREPARATION   10 minutes
COOKING   15 minutes

1   Rinse the cherries with cold water and remove their stems.
    Slice them in half and remove their pits.

2 pounds (1 kg.) cherries

2 Put the sugar-pectin mixture, sugar, and 1 cup (25 cl.) water in a copper pot. Bring to a boil (230°F/110°C) and then add the halved cherries and lemon juice. Cook about 15 minutes, stirring with a wooden spatula and removing foam from the surface with a skimmer. The fruit should become translucent, and the temperature should be 220°F/105°C. Immediately pour into jars and seal.

3 tablespoons sugar-pectin mixture (page 762)
2½ cups (570 g.) granulated sugar
Juice of 1 lemon

FIG AND HONEY JAM

Confiture de figues au miel

MAKES   about 1½ quarts/3 pints
PREPARATION   10 minutes
COOKING   10 minutes
The fruit must be macerated the day before.

1 The day before, rinse the figs and cut each fig into sixths. Put them in a bowl with the sugar and lemon juice and let macerate overnight.
2 The next day, pour everything into a copper pot with the honey and sugar-pectin mixture. Stir with a wooden spoon and bring to a boil. Cook about 10 minutes, stirring and skimming foam from the surface from time to time. The temperature should be steady at about 220°F/105°C. Turn off the heat and immediately pour the jam into jars.

2 pounds (1 kg.) fresh figs
1⅔ cups (400 g.) granulated sugar
Juice of 1 lemon
6 ounces (170 g.) honey
2 tablespoons sugar-pectin mixture (page 762)

STRAWBERRY JAM

Confiture de fraises

MAKES   about 1½ quarts/3 pints
PREPARATION AND COOKING   10 minutes
The fruit must be macerated the day before.

1 The day before, rinse and hull the strawberries. Put them in a bowl with the sugar. Put the lemon juice through a fine strainer into the bowl. Stir and leave to macerate overnight.
2 The next day, pour the macerated strawberries and their liquid into a copper pot, if possible. Bring to a boil as you stir

2 pounds (1 kg.) strawberries
2½ cups (570 g.) granulated sugar
Juice of 1 lemon

with a wooden spatula and remove foam from the liquid's surface with a skimmer. As soon as the pot begins to bubble, lift the strawberries out with a slotted spoon or skimmer. Continue to cook the lemony sugar syrup until it reaches a temperature of 220°F/105°C. Then put the strawberries back in the pot. As soon as it comes back to a boil, turn off the heat and pour the jam into jars.

STRAWBERRY CINNAMON JAM

Confiture de fraises à la cannelle

MAKES   about 1 scant quart/1½ pints
PREPARATION AND COOKING   20 minutes

Quickly rinse the strawberries and hull them. Put them in a copper pot, if possible, with the sugar and bring to a boil over low heat. Stir with a wooden spatula and remove foam from the surface with a skimmer. As soon as the liquid begins to bubble, remove the pot from the heat and allow it to cool. Put its contents through a fine strainer into a bowl; keep the fruit in the strainer. Put the juice back in the pot, add the sugar-pectin mixture and boil, stirring, until it has been reduced by half. Put the strawberries back in the pot, add the cinnamon sticks, and cook 8–10 minutes more over high heat, stirring and skimming regularly. Turn off the heat. Remove the cinnamon sticks and add the lime juice. Stir vigorously and then pour the jam into jars.

1 pound (500 g.) very ripe strawberries
1¼ cups (300 g.) raw sugar
1½ tablespoons sugar-pectin mixture (page 762)
2 cinnamon sticks
Juice of ½ lime

RASPBERRY JAM

Confiture de framboises

MAKES   about 1½ quarts/3 pints
PREPARATION   5 minutes
COOKING   10 minutes

Pick over the raspberries and remove any that are spoiled. Put them in a copper jam pot, if possible, with the sugar. Strain the lemon juice into the pot. Stir gently with a wooden

2 pounds (1 kg.) raspberries
2½ cups (600 g.) granulated sugar
Juice of 1 lemon

spatula and bring to a boil. Regularly remove foam from the surface with a skimmer. Cook over high heat, stirring constantly, about 10 minutes. The temperature of the cooking jam should be steady at 220°F/105°C. Turn off the heat and pour the jam into jars.

CHERRY AND RED CURRANT JAM
Confiture de griottes et groseilles

MAKES   about 1 generous quart/2½ pints
PREPARATION   15 minutes
COOKING   10 minutes

1   Rinse the cherries and remove their stems and pits. Rinse the red currants and remove them from the stem.
2   Put the red currants in a saucepan with ½ cup (10 cl.) water. Bring to a boil as you lightly crush the fruit with a wooden spatula. When the mixture boils, put it through a fine strainer (a chinois if possible), pressing on the fruit to extract as much juice as possible. You should end up with about 1 cup (25 cl.) red currant juice.
3   Put the sugar in a copper pot with ½ cup (15 cl.) water and cook into a boiling syrup (240°F/115°C). Add the cherries, bring back to a boil, and cook about 5 minutes, until the cherries are translucent. Stir in the currant juice and lemon juice, and bring back to a boil. Use a skimmer to remove foam from the surface and boil for 5 minutes.
4   Pour into jars immediately.

1 pound (500 g.) morello
   cherries
⅔ pound (300 g.) red currants
1 pound (500 g.) sugar
Juice of 1 lemon, put through a
   fine strainer

DULCE DE LECHE
Confiture de lait vanillé

MAKES   about 1½ quarts/3¼ pints
COOKING   2 hours

This dairy sweet is a specialty of Argentina, but now it is popular all over the world. It is good on a sliced banana, on ice cream, or even all by itself.

Rinse a copper pot under cold running water and empty out the water but do not wipe the pot dry. Add the milk and sugars to the pot. Scrape the tiny seeds from the vanilla bean halves into the pot and then add the empty halves. Bring to a boil, lower the heat, and simmer over low heat for 2 hours, stirring frequently with a wooden spatula. When the mixture has thickened and turned pale brown, turn off the heat. Remove the empty vanilla beans and pour the *dulce de leche* into jars.

1 quart (1 l.) whole milk
1 pound (500 g.) pectin-enriched sugar
1 pound (500 g.) granulated sugar
1 vanilla bean, sliced in half

BLUEBERRY JAM

Confiture de myrtilles

MAKES   about 2 quarts/4 pints
PREPARATION   10 minutes
COOKING   5 minutes
The fruit must be macerated overnight.

1   The day before, remove the blueberries from their stems, if necessary, and rinse quickly. Put the blueberries in a copper pot with 1 cup (25 cl.) water and the sugar, lemon juice, and sugar-pectin mixture. Bring to a boil, cook 2 minutes, and pour the mixture into a bowl. Cover with plastic wrap and refrigerate overnight.

2   The next day, put the macerated fruit through a fine strainer, keeping the blueberries whole in the strainer. Pour the juice into a copper pot and bring to a boil (230°F/110°C). Use a skimmer to remove foam that forms on the surface. Add the fruit, bring back to a boil, and cook for 5 minutes, stirring with a wooden spatula and skimming foam regularly. Turn off the heat and pour into jars immediately.

2 pounds (1 kg.) blueberries
3 cups (750 g.) granulated sugar
Juice of 1 lemon, strained
2 tablespoons sugar-pectin mixture (page 762)

PEACH JAM

Confiture de pêches

MAKES   about 1½ quarts/3 pints
PREPARATION   10 minutes
COOKING   5 minutes

1   Peel and quarter the peaches, removing their pits. Toss them with the lemon juice.
2   Put the peaches, sugar-pectin mixture, sugar, and ½ cup (15 cl.) water in a copper pot. Bring to a boil (230°F/110°C). Cook for 5 minutes over high heat, regularly skimming foam from the surface and stirring the fruit with a wooden spatula until the fruit is translucent. Remove the peaches and divide them among the jam jars. Cook the syrup 2 minutes more to thicken it up a bit and then pour it into the jam jars with the peaches.

2½ pounds (1.3 kg.) white peaches
Juice of 1 lemon
2 tablespoons sugar-pectin mixture (page 762)
2½ cups (500 g.) granulated sugar

PEACH JAM WITH VERBENA

Confiture de pêches blanches parfumée à la verveine et à l'orange

MAKES   1 scant quart/1½ pints
PREPARATION AND COOKING   10 minutes
MACERATING TIME   3 hours

1   Bring 1½ quarts (1.5 l.) water to a boil in a saucepan. Prepare a bowl half filled with cold water and a tray of ice cubes. Wash the peaches. When the water boils, submerge the peaches for 1 minute. Use a slotted spoon to remove them to the bowl of ice water. When they have cooled a bit, remove their skin with a small knife. Quarter them, remove their pits, and toss the quarters with the lemon juice. Sprinkle with all the sugar, stir, and macerate for 3 hours in the refrigerator.
2   Pour the macerating liquid into a copper pot and bring to a boil. Simmer until the liquid has been reduced by half. Add the peaches and verbena leaves. Cook for 5 minutes, stirring with a wooden spatula and removing foam with a skimmer. The temperature should hold steady at 220°F/105°C. Pour the jam into jars immediately.

1 pound (500 g.) white peaches
Juice of 1 lemon
1¼ cups (300 g.) granulated sugar
10 verbena leaves

RED TOMATO PRESERVES

Confiture de tomates rouges

MAKES   about 2 quarts/4 pints
PREPARATION   10 minutes
COOKING   15 minutes

Put the sugar in a copper pot with 1 cup (20 cl.) water. Bring gently to a boil, removing foam with a skimmer. The liquid should reach 230°F/110°C. Scrape the tiny seeds from the vanilla bean into the pot and then add the emptied bean to the pot as well. Add the tomatoes and lemon juice and bring to a boil. Skim and cook over high heat for 15 minutes, stirring frequently with a wooden spatula, until the tomatoes are translucent. The jam should reach 220°F/105°C. Remove the empty vanilla bean halves and pour the jam into jars immediately.

3 cups (720 g.) granulated sugar
½ vanilla bean, sliced in half
2 pounds (1 kg.) small, very ripe tomatoes, peeled, seeded, and diced (page 124)
Juice of 1 lemon, strained

APRICOT AND VANILLA JAM

Confiture d'abricots à la vanille

MAKES   about 1½ quarts/3 pints
PREPARATION   10 minutes
COOKING   20 minutes
The fruit must macerate overnight.

1   The day before, rinse the apricots, remove their pits, and put them in a bowl with the sugar. Scrape the tiny seeds from the vanilla beans into the bowl and add the emptied beans to the bowl, too. Add the lemon juice, stir, and macerate overnight.

2   The next day, pour everything into a copper pot. Bring to a boil over low heat and cook over low heat for 20 minutes, stirring with a wooden spatula and regularly removing foam from the surface of the liquid with a skimmer. The temperature should reach 220°F/105°C.

3   Turn off the heat and pour the jam into jars immediately.

2 pounds (1 kg.) ripe apricots
2¼ cups (500 g.) granulated sugar
2 vanilla beans, sliced in half lengthwise
Juice of 1 lemon

INDEX

clafoutis:

    Cherry Custard Tart, 724

    Pear Custard Tart, 725

Clafoutis aux cerises, 724

"Clafoutis" aux poires, 725

Clafoutis de pommes de terre de Picardie, 682

clams, 225–7

    choosing, 225

    eating raw, 225

    in Green Sauce, 225–6

    Spaghetti with, 649–50

    Stuffed, 226–7

    washing, 225

Clarified Butter, 43–4

cockles, 225, 227–8

    Cold, with Chorizo, 135

    Curried Mussels and, 231

    with Saffron and Thyme, 228

    Sea Bream Stuffed with Shellfish, 308–9

    Spaghetti with, 649–50

    Tagliatelle with, 650–1

    washing, 227

en cocotte: covered roasting, 11

cod, 266–70

    black (black pollack), 285

    choosing, 266–7

    Fillets, Pan Fried, with Zucchini, 268

    fishermen's traditions and, 266

    Fried, with Aromatic Herbs, 269

    Fried, with Cabbage, 267–8

cod, salt, 266

    Aïoli, 669–70

    "instant," 267

    poaching, 267

    Purée, 270–1

    soaking, 267

Coeur de céleri-branche au beurre ou au jus, 565

coffee, 7

Colbert Fried Whiting, 334

colin (yellow pollack), 285

    with Cabbage, 286

Collinet, 48

composed salads, 182–7

    Arugula and Parmesan, 182

    Brussels Sprouts and Chicken Livers, 185

    Frisée with Lardons, 183

    Mussel, 187

    Pasta, 183

    Potato and Smoked Fish, Scandinavian-Style, 184

    Scallops and Chanterelles, 186

Compote, Morello Cherry–Raspberry, with Kirsch, 715

Compote de griottes et de framboises au kirsch, 715

Compotée d'aubergines à la tomate, 572

Comté (cheese):

    Green Asparagus with Oyster Mushrooms and, 554

    Ham and Cheese Matchsticks, 123

    Potatoes, 613

    Veal Scallops with, 413–14

    Vegetable Cake, 141

Concombre au fromage de chèvre, 133

Concombre aux oeufs de saumon, 132

confit(s):

    Eggplant, 570

    Goose, and Vegetable Soup, 695–6

    Goose or Duck, 497–8

Confit d'oie ou de canard, 497–8

Confiture aux fruits rouges, 763–4

Confiture d'abricots à la vanille, 770

Confiture de cassis et framboises, 764

Confiture de cerises, 764–5

Confiture de figues au miel, 765

Confiture de fraises, 765–6

Confiture de fraises à la cannelle, 766

Confiture de framboises, 766–7

Confiture de griottes et groseilles, 767

Confiture de lait vanillé, 767–8

Confiture de myrtilles, 768

Confiture de pêches, 769

Confiture de pêches blanches parfumée à la verveine et à l'orange, 769

Confiture de pomme de terre, 763

Confiture de tomates rouges, 770

Consommé de boeuf, 79–80

Consommé de volaille, 80–1

consommés, 63, 78–81

    Beef, 79–80

    Chicken, 80–1

    clarification of, 78

conversions of metric measures, 25–7

    note about, 25

    for specific ingredients, 25–7

cookies:

    Chocolate Chocolate Chunk, 746

    Pepper, Roasted Strawberries with Green Pepper, Herbed Ice Cream and, 711

Cookies chocolat, 746

cooking methods, 8–21

    braising, 9–10

    en cocotte: covered roasting, 11

    deep frying, 16–17

    grilling, 8–9

A NOTE ABOUT THE AUTHOR

Joël Robuchon was born in Poitiers, France, in 1945 and began his apprenticeship at a hotel restaurant when he was fifteen years old. In 1981, he opened his own restaurant in Paris, Jamin, which had earned three Michelin stars by 1984, and enjoyed the fastest rise in the guidebook's history. Named "Chef of the Century" in 1984 by the *Gault Millau,* he now works as a consultant and runs L'Atelier restaurants around the world.

A NOTE ON THE TYPE

This book was set in Celeste, a typeface created in 1994 by the
designer Chris Burke. He describes it as a modern, humanistic face
having less contrast between thick and thin strokes than other
modern types such as Bodoni, Didot, and Walbaum. Tempered by
some old-style traits and with a contemporary, slightly modular let-
terspacing, Celeste is highly readable and especially adapted for
current digital printing processes which render an increasingly
exacting letterform.

Composed by North Market Street Graphics,
Lancaster, Pennsylvania

Printed and bound by R.R. Donnelley,
Crawfordsville, Indiana

Designed by Soonyoung Kwon